HOLT SCIENCE & TECHNOLOGY

Life
Science

HOLT, RINEHART AND WINSTON

A Harcourt Classroom Education Company

Austin • New York • Orlando • Atlanta • San Francisco • Boston • Dallas • Toronto • London

Staff Credits

Editorial

Robert W. Todd, Executive Editor

David F. Bowman, Managing Editor

Laura Zapanta, Editor

Bill Burnside, Charlotte Luongo, Kelly Rizk, Robin Goodman (Feature Articles)

ANNOTATED TEACHER'S EDITION

David Westerberg

ANCILLARIES

Jennifer Childers, Senior Editor

Chris Colby, Kristen Falk, Molly Frohlich, Robin Goodman, Shari Husain, Monique Mayer, Kristen McCardel, Sabelyn Pussman, Erin Roberson

COPYEDITORS

Dawn Spinozza, Copyediting Supervisor

Brooke Fugitt, Kathryn O'Shields, Cindy Foreman

EDITORIAL SUPPORT STAFF

Jeanne Graham, Rose Segrest, Tanu'e White

EDITORIAL PERMISSIONS

Cathy Paré, Permissions Manager

Jan Harrington, Permissions Editor

Art, Design, and Photo

BOOK DESIGN

Richard Metzger, Design Director

Marc Cooper, Senior Designer

Sonya Mendeke, Designer

Alicia Sullivan, Designer (ATE), **Cristina Bowerman**, Design Associate (ATE), **Eric Rupprath**, Designer (Ancillaries), **Holly Whittaker**, Traffic Coordinator

IMAGE ACQUISITIONS

Joe London, Director

Elaine Tate, Art Buyer Supervisor

Julie Kelly, Art Buyer

Tim Taylor, Photo Research Supervisor

Stephanie Friedman, Assistant Photo Researcher

PHOTO STUDIO

Sam Dudgeon, Senior Staff Photographer

Victoria Smith, Photo Specialist

Lauren Eischen, Photo Coordinator

DESIGN NEW MEDIA

Susan Michael, Design Director

DESIGN MEDIA

Joe Melomo, Design Director

Production

Mimi Stockdell, Senior Production Manager

Beth Sample, Production Coordinator

Suzanne Brooks, Sara Carroll-Downs

Media Production

Kim A. Scott, Senior Production Manager

Nancy Hargis, Production Supervisor

Adriana Bardin, Production Coordinator

New Media

Jim Bruno, Senior Project Manager

Lydia Doty, Senior Project Manager

Jessica Bega, Project Manager

Armin Gutzmer, Manager Training and Technical Support

Cathy Kuhles, Nina Degollado, Technical Assistants

Design Implementation and Production

Umlaut LLC

Printed in the United States of America

ISBN 0-03-051949-7

2 3 4 5 6 7 048 05 04 03 02 01 00

Acknowledgments

Chapter Writers

Katy Z. Allen
*Science Writer and Former
Biology Teacher*
Wayland, Massachusetts

Linda Ruth Berg, Ph.D.
*Adjunct Professor–Natural
Sciences*
St. Petersburg Junior College
St. Petersburg, Florida

Jennie Dusheck
Science Writer
Santa Cruz, California

Mark F. Taylor, Ph.D.
Associate Professor of Biology
Baylor University
Waco, Texas

Lab Writers

Diana Scheidle Bartos
Science Consultant and Educator
Diana Scheidle Bartos, L.L.C.
Lakewood, Colorado

Carl Benson
General Science Teacher
Plains High School
Plains, Montana

Charlotte Blassingame
Technology Coordinator
White Station Middle School
Memphis, Tennessee

Marsha Carver
Science Teacher and Dept. Chair
McLean County High School
Calhoun, Kentucky

Kenneth E. Creese
Science Teacher
White Mountain Junior High
School
Rock Springs, Wyoming

Linda Culp
Science Teacher and Dept. Chair
Thorndale High School
Thorndale, Texas

James Deaver
Science Teacher and Dept. Chair
West Point High School
West Point, Nebraska

Frank McKinney, Ph.D.
Professor of Geology
Appalachian State University
Boone, North Carolina

Alyson Mike
Science Teacher
East Valley Middle School
East Helena, Montana

C. Ford Morishita
Biology Teacher
Clackamas High School
Milwaukie, Oregon

Patricia D. Morrell, Ph.D.
*Assistant Professor, School of
Education*
University of Portland
Portland, Oregon

Hilary C. Olson, Ph.D.
Research Associate
Institute for Geophysics
The University of Texas
Austin, Texas

James B. Pulley
*Science Editor and Former
Science Teacher*
Liberty High School
Liberty, Missouri

Denice Lee Sandefur
Science Chairperson
Nucla High School
Nucla, Colorado

Patti Soderberg
Science Writer
The BioQUEST Curriculum
Consortium
Beloit College
Beloit, Wisconsin

Phillip Vavala
Science Teacher and Dept. Chair
Salesianum School
Wilmington, Delaware

Albert C. Wartski
Biology Teacher
Chapel Hill High School
Chapel Hill, North Carolina

Lynn Marie Wartski
*Science Writer and Former
Science Teacher*
Hillsborough, North Carolina

Ivora D. Washington
Science Teacher and Dept. Chair
Hyattsville Middle School
Washington, D.C.

Academic Reviewers

Renato J. Aguilera, Ph.D.
Associate Professor
Department of Molecular, Cell,
and Developmental Biology
University of California
Los Angeles, California

David M. Armstrong, Ph.D.
Professor of Biology
Department of E.P.O. Biology
University of Colorado
Boulder, Colorado

Alissa Arp, Ph.D.
*Director and Professor of
Environmental Studies*
Romberg Tiburon Center
San Francisco State University
Tiburon, California

Russell M. Brengelman
Professor of Physics
Morehead State University
Morehead, Kentucky

John A. Brockhaus, Ph.D.
*Director of Mapping, Charting,
and Geodesy Program*
Department of Geography and
Environmental Engineering
United States Military Academy
West Point, New York

Linda K. Butler, Ph.D.
Lecturer of Biological Sciences
The University of Texas
Austin, Texas

Barry Chernoff, Ph.D.
Associate Curator
Division of Fishes
The Field Museum of Natural
History
Chicago, Illinois

**Donna Greenwood
Crenshaw, Ph.D.**
Instuctor
Department of Biology
Duke University
Durham, North Carolina

Hugh Crenshaw, Ph.D.
Assistant Professor of Zoology
Duke University
Durham, North Carolina

Joe W. Crim, Ph.D.
Professor of Biology
University of Georgia
Athens, Georgia

Peter Demmin, Ed.D.
*Former Science Teacher and
Chair*
Amherst Central High School
Amherst, New York

Joseph L. Graves, Jr., Ph.D.
*Associate Professor of
Evolutionary Biology*
Arizona State University West
Phoenix, Arizona

William B. Guggino, Ph.D.
*Professor of Physiology and
Pediatrics*
The Johns Hopkins University
School of Medicine
Baltimore, Maryland

David Haig, Ph.D.
Assistant Professor of Biology
Department of Organismic
and Evolutionary Biology
Harvard University
Cambridge, Massachusetts

Roy W. Hann, Jr., Ph.D.
Professor of Civil Engineering
Texas A&M University
College Station, Texas

John E. Hoover, Ph.D.
Associate Professor of Biology
Millersville University
Millersville, Pennsylvania

Joan E. N. Hudson, Ph.D.
*Associate Professor of Biological
Sciences*
Sam Houston State University
Huntsville, Texas

**Laurie Jackson-Grusby,
Ph.D.**
*Research Scientist and Doctoral
Associate*
Whitehead Institute for
Biomedical Research
Massachusetts Institute of
Technology
Cambridge, Massachusetts

George M. Langford, Ph.D.
Professor of Biological Sciences
Dartmouth College
Hanover, New Hampshire

Melanie C. Lewis, Ph.D.
Professor of Biology, Retired
Southwest Texas State
University
San Marcos, Texas

V. Patteson Lombardi, Ph.D.
*Research Assistant Professor of
Biology*
Department of Biology
University of Oregon
Eugene, Oregon

Glen Longley, Ph.D.
*Professor of Biology and Director
of the Edwards Aquifer
Research Center*
Southwest Texas State
University
San Marcos, Texas

William F. McComas, Ph.D.
*Director of the Center to
Advance Science Education*
University of Southern
California
Los Angeles, California

LaMoine L. Motz, Ph.D.
Coordinator of Science Education
Oakland County Schools
Waterford, Michigan

Acknowledgments (cont.)

Nancy Parker, Ph.D.
Associate Professor of Biology
Southern Illinois University
Edwardsville, Illinois

Barron S. Rector, Ph.D.
*Associate Professor and
    Extension Range Specialist*
Texas Agricultural Extension
    Service
Texas A&M University
College Station, Texas

Peter Sheridan, Ph.D.
Professor of Chemistry
Colgate University
Hamilton, New York

Miles R. Silman, Ph.D.
Assistant Professor of Biology
Wake Forest University
Winston-Salem, North
    Carolina

Neil Simister, Ph.D.
Associate Professor of Biology
Department of Life Sciences
Brandeis University
Waltham, Massachusetts

Lee Smith, Ph.D.
Curriculum Writer
MDL Information Systems, Inc.
San Leandro, California

Robert G. Steen, Ph.D.
Manager, Rat Genome Project
Whitehead Institute—Center
    for Genome Research
Massachusetts Institute of
    Technology
Cambridge, Massachusetts

Martin VanDyke, Ph.D.
*Professor of Chemistry
    Emeritus*
Front Range Community
    College
Westminister, Colorado

E. Peter Volpe, Ph.D.
Professor of Medical Genetics
Mercer University School of
    Medicine
Macon, Georgia

Harold K. Voris, Ph.D.
Curator and Head
Division of Amphibians and
    Reptiles
The Field Museum of
    Natural History
Chicago, Illinois

Mollie Walton
Biology Instructor
El Paso Community College
El Paso, Texas

Peter Wetherwax, Ph.D.
Professor of Biology
University of Oregon
Eugene, Oregon

Mary K. Wicksten, Ph.D.
Professor of Biology
Texas A&M University
College Station, Texas

**R. Stimson Wilcox,
Ph.D.**
Associate Professor of Biology
Department of Biological
    Sciences
Binghamton University
Binghamton, New York

**Conrad M. Zapanta,
Ph.D.**
Research Engineer
Sulzer Carbomedics, Inc.
Austin, Texas

Safety Reviewer

Jack Gerlovich, Ph.D.
Associate Professor
School of Education
Drake University
Des Moines, Iowa

Teacher Reviewers

Barry L. Bishop
Science Teacher and Dept. Chair
San Rafael Junior High
    School
Ferron, Utah

Carol A. Bornhorst
Science Teacher and Dept. Chair
Bonita Vista Middle School
Chula Vista, California

Paul Boyle
Science Teacher
Perry Heights Middle School
Evansville, Indiana

Yvonne Brannum
Science Teacher and Dept. Chair
Hine Junior High School
Washington, D.C.

Gladys Cherniak
Science Teacher
St. Paul's Episcopal School
Mobile, Alabama

James Chin
Science Teacher
Frank A. Day Middle School
Newtonville, Massachusetts

Kenneth Creese
Science Teacher
White Mountain Junior High
    School
Rock Springs, Wyoming

Linda A. Culp
Science Teacher and Dept. Chair
Thorndale High School
Thorndale, Texas

Georgiann Delgadillo
Science Teacher
East Valley Continuous
    Curriculum School
Spokane, Washington

Alonda Droege
Biology Teacher
Evergreen High School
Seattle, Washington

Michael J. DuPré
Curriculum Specialist
Rush Henrietta Junior-Senior
    High School
Henrietta, New York

Rebecca Ferguson
Science Teacher
North Ridge Middle School
North Richland Hills, Texas

Susan Gorman
Science Teacher
North Ridge Middle School
North Richland Hills, Texas

Gary Habeeb
Science Mentor
Sierra-Plumas Joint Unified
    School District
Downieville, California

Karma Houston-Hughes
Science Mentor
Kyrene Middle School
Tempe, Arizona

Roberta Jacobowitz
Science Teacher
C. W. Otto Middle School
Lansing, Michigan

Kerry A. Johnson
Science Teacher
Isbell Middle School
Santa Paula, California

M. R. Penny Kisiah
*Science Teacher and Dept.
    Chair*
Fairview Middle School
Tallahassee, Florida

Kathy LaRoe
Science Teacher
East Valley Middle School
East Helena, Montana

Jane M. Lemons
Science Teacher
Western Rockingham Middle
    School
Madison, North Carolina

Scott Mandel, Ph.D.
*Director and Educational
    Consultant*
Teachers Helping Teachers
Los Angeles, California

Thomas Manerchia
*Former Biology and Life
    Science Teacher*
Archmere Academy
Claymont, Delaware

Maurine O. Marchani
Science Teacher and Dept. Chair
Raymond Park Middle
    School
Indianapolis, Indiana

Jason P. Marsh
Biology Teacher
Montevideo High School
    and Montevideo Country
    School
Montevideo, Minnesota

Edith C. McAlanis
Science Teacher and Dept. Chair
Socorro Middle School
El Paso, Texas

Kevin McCurdy, Ph.D.
Science Teacher
Elmwood Junior High School
Rogers, Arkansas

Kathy McKee
Science Teacher
Hoyt Middle School
Des Moines, Iowa

Alyson Mike
Science Teacher
East Valley Middle School
East Helena, Montana

Donna Norwood
*Science Teacher and Dept.
    Chair*
Monroe Middle School
Charlotte, North Carolina

James B. Pulley
Former Science Teacher
Liberty High School
Liberty, Missouri

**Acknowledgments
continue on page 838.**

Contents in Brief

Contents

Unit 7 ··· **Human Body Systems**
⋮ **Timeline** 518

Investigate!

Now is the time to Investigate!

Science is a process in which investigation leads to information and understanding. The **Investigate!** at the beginning of each chapter helps you gain scientific understanding of the topic through hands-on experience.

QuickLab

Not all laboratory investigations have to be long and involved.

The **QuickLabs** found throughout the chapters of this textbook require only a small amount of time and limited equipment. But just because they are quick, don't skimp on the safety.

MATH BREAK

Science and math go hand in hand.

The **MathBreaks** in the margins of the chapters show you many ways that math applies directly to science and vice versa.

APPLY

Science can be very useful in the real world.

It is interesting to learn how scientific information is being used in the real world. You can see for yourself in the **Apply** features. You will also be asked to apply your own knowledge. This is a good way to learn!

Connections

One science leads to another.
You may not realize it at first, but different areas of science are related to each other in many ways. Each **Connection** explores a topic from the viewpoint of another science discipline. In this way, areas of science merge to improve your understanding of the world around you.

Oceanography
CONNECTION

Chemistry
CONNECTION

Environment
CONNECTION

Meteorology
CONNECTION

Physics
CONNECTION

Geology
CONNECTION

Astronomy
CONNECTION

Feature Articles

Feature articles for any appetite!

Science and technology affect us all in many ways. The following articles will give you an idea of just how interesting, strange, helpful, and action-packed science and technology are. At the end of each chapter, you will find two feature articles. Read them and you will be surprised at what you learn.

The Study of Living Things

Life science is the study of living things—from the tiniest bacterium to the largest tree! In this unit, you will discover the similarities of all living things. You will learn about the tools life scientists use, and you'll learn to ask your own questions about the living world around you.

People have always searched for answers about life. This time-line includes a few of the many people who have studied living things through the centuries. And there's always more to be learned, so keep your eyes open.

2640 B.C.

Si Ling-Chi, Empress of China, observes silkworms in her garden and develops a process to cultivate them and make silk.

1944

Oswald T. Avery proposes that DNA is the material that carries genetic properties in living organisms.

1946

ENIAC, the first entirely electronic computer, is built. It weighs 30 tons and takes up 450 m².

1967

The first successful human heart transplant is performed by Dr. Christiaan Barnard.

1970

Floppy disks for computer data storage are introduced.

1010

Arab physicist Ibn al Haytham discovers that vision is caused by the reflection of light from objects into the eye.

1590

Zacharius Jansen constructs the first microscope. It contains two lenses and a tube.

1685

Improvements to microscopes allow the first observation of red blood cells.

1914

George Washington Carver's studies on agriculture and soil conservation lead to research on peanuts.

1934

Dorothy Crowfoot Hodgkin uses X-ray techniques to determine protein structure.

1931

The first electron microscope is developed.

1983

Dian Fossey writes *Gorillas in the Mist,* a book about her research on mountain gorillas in Africa and her efforts to save them from poachers.

1984

A process known as DNA fingerprinting is developed by Alec Jeffries.

1998

In China, scientists discover a fossil of a dinosaur with feathers.

1 The World of Life Science

Imagine . . .

You are walking through a field with some classmates. Suddenly you notice that there are frogs hopping around all over the place! You and your classmates start catching the frogs with a net. As you lift the first frog from the net, you notice something. Its legs seem to be broken. You look at your friend's frog. It seems to be injured, too. You look at another. A frog with no eyes? Wait a minute! These frogs aren't injured. They're deformed! What are these, aliens from outer space?

Believe it or not, this really happened to a group of students from Le Sueur, Minnesota, during a visit to a wildlife refuge. About half of the frogs they collected were deformed. The students and their teacher were stunned by what they found. What could have caused these deformities? Was

it just some weird natural phenomenon, or were the frogs exposed to some sort of chemical? The students gathered more information on the frogs and alerted local scientists. Students and scientists from all over the country are now working together to solve the mystery of the freaky frogs.

The students, like almost all scientists, began their research by noticing something about the natural world and then asking questions about what they observed. In this chapter, you will learn how questions fuel the study of science and how scientists go about finding answers to these questions.

What Do You Think?

In your ScienceLog, try to answer the following questions based on what you already know:

1. What tools do life scientists use?

2. What methods do scientists use to study life science?

2. Study the picture of the fish below. Try to imagine how your five small shapes can be arranged to create the fish. Then test your idea. If necessary, make several tries. **Hint:** You may need to turn one or more shapes over. Record your solution in your ScienceLog.

TRY at HOME

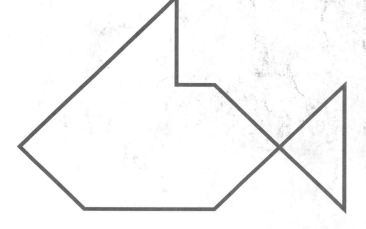

Figure It Out

In this activity you will test your ability to do some of the things scientists do—make observations and use them to solve a puzzle.

Procedure

1. Fold a **square piece of paper** along the lines shown in the figure below. First fold the square in half. Fold it in half again. Then fold down the corners from A to B and from A to C. Unfold the paper. Using **scissors,** cut along the folds, indicated by dark lines in the figure below, to form five shapes.

Analysis

3. Did you figure out how to correctly arrange the small shapes just by making observations? What observations provided clues?

4. How did testing your ideas help you solve the puzzle?

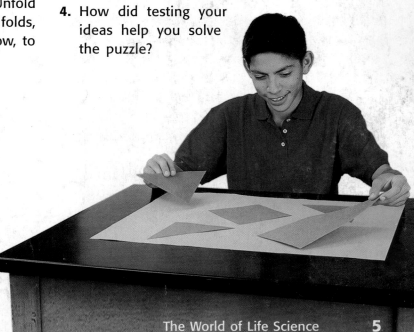

Asking About Life

Terms to Learn

life science

What You'll Do

◆ Explain the importance of asking questions in life science.
◆ Give three reasons why life science is beneficial to living things.

It's summer. You are lying in the grass at the park, casually observing your surroundings. Three dogs are playing on your left. A few bumblebees are visiting nearby flowers. An ant makes off with a crumb from your sandwich. Suddenly a question pops into your head. "Why don't ants grow as big as people?" Then you think of another question. "Why do the bumblebees visit the purple flowers but not the white ones?"

Congratulations! You have just taken the first steps toward becoming a life scientist. How did you do it? You observed the living world around you. You were curious, and you asked questions about your observations. After all, that's what science is all about. **Life science** is the study of living things.

How do birds know where to go when they migrate?

Why do leaves change color in the fall?

How do fireflies make light?

Why did the dinosaurs die out?

It All Starts with a Question

The world around you is full of an amazing diversity of life. Single-celled algae float unseen in ponds. Giant redwood trees seem to touch the sky. Forty-ton whales swim through the oceans. For every living thing, or *organism,* that has ever lived, you could ask many questions, such as "How does it obtain food?" "Where does it live?" and "Why does it behave in a particular way?"

In Your Own Backyard Questions are easy to find. Take a look around your room, around your home, and around your neighborhood. What questions about life science come to mind? The student at left didn't have to look far to realize that he had questions about some very familiar organisms. Do you know the answer to any of his questions?

Touring the World Your neighborhood gives you just a taste of the questions that the world holds. The world is made up of many different places to live, such as deserts, forests, coral reefs, and tide pools. Just about anywhere you go, you will find some kind of living organism.

Looking for Answers

Close your eyes for a moment, and imagine a life scientist. What do you see? Is it someone in a laboratory, peering into a microscope? Which of the people in **Figure 1** do you think are scientists?

Figure 1 *Life scientists are people who ask many different kinds of questions.*

Irene Duhart Long asks, "How does the human body respond to space travel?"

Geerat Vermeij asks, "How have shells changed over time?"

Irene Pepperberg asks, "Are parrots smart enough to learn a language?"

Who? If you guessed that all of the people in Figure 1 are scientists, then you are right. Anyone can investigate the world around us. Women and men from any cultural or ethnic background can become life scientists.

Where? Doing investigations in a laboratory is an important part of life science, but life science can be studied in many other places too. Life scientists carry out investigations on farms, in forests, on the ocean floor—even in space. They work for businesses, hospitals, government agencies, and universities. Many are also teachers.

What? What a life scientist studies is determined by one thing— his or her curiosity. Life scientists specialize in many different areas of life science. They study how organisms function and behave and how organisms interact with each other and with their environment. Life scientists explore how organisms reproduce and how organisms pass traits from one generation to the next. Some life scientists investigate the origins of organisms and how organisms change over time.

Would you like to make a career out of learning about lizards? Turn to page 32 to read about someone who has.

Why Ask Why?

What is the point of asking all these questions? Life scientists might find some interesting answers, but do any of the answers really matter? Will the answers affect *your* life? Absolutely! As you study life science, you will see how it affects you and all the living things around you.

Combating Disease Polio is a disease that affects the brain and nerves, causing paralysis. Do you know anyone who has had polio? Probably not. The polio virus has been eliminated from most of the world. But at one time it was much more common. Before life scientists discovered ways to prevent the spread of the polio virus, it infected 1 in every 3,000 Americans.

Today scientists continue to search for ways to fight diseases such as tuberculosis and acquired immune deficiency syndrome (AIDS). The scientist in **Figure 2** is trying to learn more about AIDS, which now kills thousands of people every year. Life scientists have discovered how the virus that causes AIDS is carried from one person to another and how it affects the body. By learning more about the virus, scientists may find a cure for this deadly disease.

Inherited Diseases Some diseases, such as cystic fibrosis, are inherited. They are passed from parents to children. Susumu Tonegawa, shown in **Figure 3,** is one of the many scientists worldwide who are studying the human genome. An organism's genome is inherited from its parents. The genome is the information in an organism's cells that controls the cells' activities. Changes in small parts of an organism's genome may cause the organism to be born with or to develop certain diseases. By learning about the human genome, scientists hope to find ways to cure or prevent inherited diseases.

How do certain chemicals affect the virus that causes AIDS?

Figure 2 *Abdul Lakhani studies AIDS to find a cure for the disease.*

Which part of a person's genome is responsible for certain inherited diseases?

Figure 3 *Susumu Tonegawa's work may help in the battle to fight inherited diseases.*

Protecting the Environment If you were to make a list of environmental problems, it would probably be long. Many environmental problems are caused by people's misuse and improper disposal of natural resources. Understanding how we affect the world around us is the first step in finding solutions to problems such as pollution and the extinction of wildlife.

Why should we try to decrease air and water pollution? Pollution can harm our health and the health of other organisms. Water pollution may be a cause of the frog deformities seen in Minnesota and other states. Pollution in oceans kills marine mammals, birds, and fish. By finding ways to produce less pollution, we can help make the world a healthier place.

When we cut down trees to clear land for crops or to get lumber to build houses, we alter and sometimes destroy habitats. Dale Miquelle, shown in **Figure 4,** is part of a team of Russian and American scientists studying the Siberian tiger. Hunting and deforestation have almost caused the tigers to become extinct. By learning about the tigers' food and habitat needs, the scientists hope to develop a conservation plan that will ensure their survival.

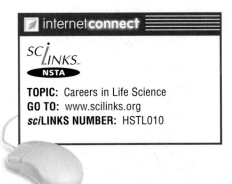

How much space does a tiger need in order to survive?

Figure 4 *To learn how much territory a Siberian tiger covers, Dale Miquelle tracks a tiger that is wearing a radio-transmitting collar.*

REVIEW

1. Define life science.

2. What benefits can life science provide?

3. Where do life scientists work? What do life scientists study?

4. Do you agree with the following statement? *The information learned by life scientists isn't very important.* Explain your answer.

5. **Applying Concepts** Look at the scene below, and list five questions about the organisms. See if any of your classmates have the answers.

🏁 internet**connect**

SC*i*LINKS.
NSTA

TOPIC: Careers in Life Science
GO TO: www.scilinks.org
*sci*LINKS NUMBER: HSTL010

Section 2

Thinking Like a Life Scientist

Terms to Learn

scientific method   variable
hypothesis   theory
controlled   technology
  experiment

What You'll Do

◆ Describe the scientific method.
◆ Evaluate the designs of experiments.
◆ Interpret the information in tables and graphs.
◆ Explain how scientific knowledge can change.

No matter where life scientists work or what questions they try to answer, all life scientists have two things in common. They are curious about the natural world, and they use similar methods to investigate it. Imagine that you are one of the students who discovered the deformed frogs discussed at the beginning of this chapter. If you wanted to investigate the cause of the frogs' deformities, where would you begin? Actually, you've already taken the first steps in the scientific process. You've made observations, and you've asked questions. What's next?

The Scientific Method

Most life scientists use the scientific method as the basis of their investigations. The **scientific method** is often described as a series of steps that is used to answer a question or solve a problem. **Figure 5** outlines the six steps of the scientific method. Take a moment to read each step.

● **Ask a question** based on observations.

● **Form a hypothesis,** which is a possible explanation for what you have observed.

● **Test the hypothesis** by conducting experiments.

● **Analyze the results** collected from experiments.

● **Draw conclusions** from the results of your experiment.

● **Communicate results** to other scientists.

Figure 5 *Life scientists often use the scientific method to solve problems and answer questions.*

Science Is a Creative Process You may think that following each step in order will automatically produce the correct answer to your question or problem. But many questions cannot be answered that easily. Life scientists must use their imaginations to explain what they have observed. They must also be creative when designing experiments to test their explanations. Scientists may have to repeat steps of the scientific method or do them in a different order. In addition, every question doesn't necessarily require an experiment. Sometimes only observations are needed to find an answer. And sometimes an answer cannot be found.

In the next few pages, you will see how the six steps of the scientific method were used in a real-life investigation.

Ask a Question

Have you ever observed something out of the ordinary or difficult to explain? The observation usually raises questions. Looking for answers often involves making more observations.

A Real-World Question Once the students from Le Sueur realized there was something wrong with the frogs, they decided to continue their observations by collecting some data, as shown in **Figure 6.** They counted the number of deformed and normal frogs they caught. The students also photographed the frogs, took measurements, and wrote a thorough description of each frog.

In addition, the students collected data on other organisms living in the pond. They also conducted many tests on the pond water, measuring things such as the level of acidity. The students carefully recorded their data and observations.

Figure 6 *Collecting data was the first step in the students' investigation.*

Make Accurate Observations Observations can take many forms. They may be measurements of length, volume, time, or speed. They may describe how loud or soft a sound is or indicate the color or shape of an organism. Observations may reveal the number of organisms in an area or patterns of their behavior. The range of observations a scientist can make is endless. But no matter what observations reveal, they are useful only if they are accurately made and recorded. A few of the tools that scientists use to make observations are shown in **Figure 7.**

Figure 7 *Microscopes, rulers, and thermometers are some of the many tools scientists use to collect information.*

Why did the chicken cross the highway? See page 33 to find out about "The Homesick Chicken," a science-fiction mystery.

Form a Hypothesis

After making observations, scientists form one or more hypotheses. A **hypothesis** is a possible explanation or answer to a question. When scientists form hypotheses, they think logically and creatively and consider what they already know.

A hypothesis must be testable by experimentation. A hypothesis is not testable if no observations or information can be gathered or no experiment can be designed to test the hypothesis. Just because a hypothesis is not testable does not mean that it is wrong. It just means that there is no way to support or disprove the hypothesis.

Different scientists may have different hypotheses for the same problem. In the case of the frogs, the hypotheses shown below were formed. Which, if any, of these explanations was correct? To find out, each hypothesis would have to be tested.

Hypothesis 1: The deformities were caused by one or more chemical pollutants in the water.

Hypothesis 2: The deformities were caused by attacks from parasites or other frogs.

Hypothesis 3: The deformities were caused by an increase in exposure to ultraviolet light from the sun.

✓ Self-Check

Which of the following statements is a hypothesis?

1. Deformed frogs have been found in the United States and Canada.
2. Insecticides caused the frog deformities.
3. The frogs in Le Sueur were deformed.

(See page 782 to check your answers.)

Predictions

Before scientists can test a hypothesis, they must first make predictions. A prediction is a statement of cause and effect that can be used to set up a test for a hypothesis. Predictions are usually stated in an "If . . ., then . . ." format.

More than one prediction may be made for each hypothesis. For each of the hypotheses on the previous page, the following predictions were made:

Hypothesis 2
Prediction: If a parasite is causing the deformities, then this parasite will be found more often in frogs that have deformities.

Hypothesis 1
Prediction: If a substance in the pond water is causing the deformities, then the water from ponds with deformed frogs will be different from the water from ponds in which no abnormal frogs have been found.

Prediction: If a substance in the pond water is causing the deformities, then some tadpoles will develop deformities when they are raised in pond water collected from ponds with deformed frogs.

Hypothesis 3
Prediction: If an increase in exposure to ultraviolet light is causing the deformities, then some frog eggs exposed to ultraviolet light in a laboratory will develop into deformed frogs.

Once predictions are made, scientists can conduct experiments to see which predictions, if any, prove to be true and support the hypotheses.

Have Aliens Landed?

You and a friend are walking through a heavily wooded park. Suddenly, you come upon a small area where all of the trees are lying on the ground. What knocked them down or caused them to fall over? Your friend thinks that extraterrestrials caused the trees to fall. Is your friend's hypothesis testable? In your ScienceLog, explain your answer. What other hypothesis can you come up with?

Test the Hypothesis

After scientists make a prediction, they test the hypothesis. Scientists try to design experiments that will clearly show whether a particular factor caused an observed outcome. A *factor* is anything in an experiment that can influence the experiment's outcome. Factors can be anything from temperature to the type of organism being studied.

Under Control Scientists strive to perform controlled experiments. A **controlled experiment** tests only one factor at a time. There is a control group and one or more experimental groups. All of the factors for the control group and the experimental groups are the same except for one. The one factor that differs is called the **variable.** Because the variable differs between the control group and the experimental groups, scientists can be more certain that differences in the variable are causing any differences observed in the outcome of the experiment.

Designing an Experiment Designing a good experiment requires a lot of planning. Let's examine the prediction for Hypothesis 3: *If an increase in exposure to ultraviolet light is causing the deformities, **then** some frog eggs exposed to ultraviolet light in a laboratory will develop into deformed frogs.*

To test a hypothesis, a scientist must first identify the variable. In this case, the variable is the amount of ultraviolet (UV) light exposure. This is shown in the table at left. All other factors, such as the kind of frog, the number of frog eggs in each aquarium, and the temperature of the water, should be the same in the control group and the experimental groups.

Design of Experiment to Test the Effect of UV Light on Frogs				
Group	Factors			
	Kind of frog	Number of eggs	Temperature of water	Variable: UV light exposure
#1 Control	leopard frog	100	25°C	0 days
#2 Experimental	leopard frog	100	25°C	15 days
#3 Experimental	leopard frog	100	25°C	24 days

Collect Data As you can see from the table on the previous page, each group in the experiment contains 100 eggs. Scientists always try to test many individuals. The more organisms tested, the more certain scientists can be that differences in the outcome of an experiment are actually caused by differences in the variable and not by natural differences between individuals. Scientists also support their conclusions by repeating their experiments. If an experiment produces the same results again and again, scientists can be more certain about the effect the variable has on the outcome of the experiment. The experimental setup to test Hypothesis 3 is illustrated in **Figure 8.**

Figure 8 *This controlled experiment was designed to test whether UV light can cause frog deformities.*

Control Group

#1
No UV light exposure

Experimental Groups

#2
UV light exposure for 15 days

#3
UV light exposure for 24 days

✔ Self-Check

Henry is testing the effects of different antibacterial soaps on the growth of bacteria. His experiment contains several jars of the same strain of bacteria. Which of the jars described below is the control group?

1. To Jar A, Henry adds two drops of Supersoap.
2. To Jar B, Henry adds two drops of Anti-B Suds.
3. To Jar C, Henry adds no soap.

(See page 782 to check your answer.)

Group	Length of UV light exposure	Number of deformed frogs
#1	0 days	0
#2	15 days	0
#3	24 days	47

Figure 9 *The table and the bar graph show that some frog eggs exposed to UV light for 24 days developed into frogs with deformities.*

Analyze the Results

A scientist's work does not end when an experiment is finished. Scientists must organize the data so that they can be analyzed. For example, they may put the data into a table or a graph. The data collected from the UV light experiment are shown in **Figure 9.**

Draw Conclusions

After scientists have analyzed the data from several experiments, they can draw conclusions. They decide whether the results of the experiments support a hypothesis.

When scientists find that a hypothesis is not supported by the tests, they must try to find another explanation for what they have observed. Proving that a hypothesis is wrong is just as helpful as supporting it. Why? Either way, the scientist has learned something, which is the purpose of using the scientific method to investigate or answer a question.

Is It the Answer? The UV light experiment supports the hypothesis that the frog deformities can be caused by exposure to UV light. Does this mean that UV light definitely caused the frogs living in the Minnesota wetland to be deformed? No, the only thing this experiment shows is that UV light may be a cause of the deformities. Tests performed in a laboratory may have different results than tests performed in the wild. In addition, the experiment did not investigate the effects of parasites or some other substance on the frogs. In fact, many scientists think that more than one factor could be involved.

÷ 5 ÷ Ω ∞ + Ω ∨ 9 ∞ ≤ Σ 2

MATH BREAK

Averages

Finding the average of a group of numbers is one way to analyze data. Three seeds kept at 25°C sprouted in 8, 8, and 5 days. To find the average number of days that it took the seeds to sprout, add 8, 8, and 5 and divide the sum by 3, the number of subjects (seeds).

$$\frac{(8 + 8 + 5)}{3} = \frac{21}{3} = 7 \text{ days}$$

Three seeds kept at 30°C sprouted in 6, 5, and 4 days. What's the average number of days that it took these seeds to sprout?

Puzzles as complex as the deformed-frog mystery are rarely solved with a single experiment. The quest for a solution may continue for years. Finding an answer doesn't always end an investigation. Often that answer begins another investigation.

Communicate Results

Scientists form a global community. After scientists complete their investigations, they communicate their results to other scientists, as the student in **Figure 10** is doing. Other scientists may repeat the experiments to see if they get the same results. The information can also help scientists discover new questions and answers. New answers may strengthen scientific hypotheses or show that the hypotheses need to be altered. The paths from observations and questions to communicating results are shown in **Figure 11.**

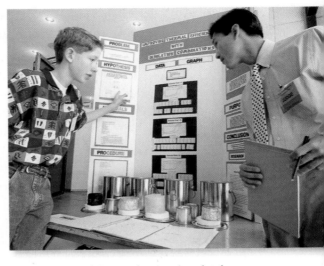

Figure 10 *This student scientist is communicating the results of his investigation at a science fair.*

Figure 11 *Scientific investigations do not always proceed from one step to the next. Sometimes steps can be skipped, and sometimes they must be repeated.*

Scientific Knowledge Changes

As you read earlier, there can be more than one prediction for a hypothesis. Each time a prediction is proven true, the hypothesis gains more support. A unifying explanation for a broad range of hypotheses and observations that have been supported by testing is a **theory.**

However, when scientists reexamine data or experimental results, they may draw different conclusions. Other times, new observations show that the old conclusions are wrong. Or, new observations just show that more research is needed.

Life scientists are always asking new questions or looking at old questions from a different angle. As they find new answers, scientific knowledge continues to grow and change.

New Tools New technology allows scientists to get information that wasn't available previously. **Technology** is the use of knowledge, tools, and materials to solve problems and accomplish tasks. For example, scientists have long wondered whether Neanderthals are the ancestors of humans. Neither Neanderthal fossils, which show what they looked like, nor dating techniques, which reveal when Neanderthals lived, provided enough data to answer the question. The technology for comparing genetic information was developed recently. The scientist shown in **Figure 12** is using this technology to look for the answer.

Figure 12 *Dr. Mark Stoneking is using modern techniques to find out if Neanderthals are our ancestors.*

Temperature (°C)	Time to double (minutes)
10	130
20	60
25	40
30	29
37	17
40	19
45	32
50	no growth

REVIEW

1. What are the six basic steps of the scientific method?

2. What causes scientific knowledge to change and grow?

3. **Graphing Data** The table at left shows how long it takes for one bacterium to divide and become two bacteria. Plot this information on a graph, with temperature on the *x*-axis and the time to double on the *y*-axis. What temperature allows the bacteria to multiply most quickly?

What You'll Do

◆ Describe the tools life scientists use for seeing.
◆ Explain how life scientists use computers.
◆ Explain the importance of the International System of Units.

Tools of Life Scientists

Life scientists use various tools to aid them in their work. These tools are used to make observations and to gather, store, and analyze information.

Tools for Seeing

If you look at a jar of pond water, you may see some scum and a few creatures swimming around. But examine that same water under a microscope or with a magnifying lens, and presto!—a complex community of organisms suddenly appears.

To make accurate observations of organisms and parts of organisms that are too small to be seen with the naked eye, life scientists use tools that can magnify. People have used glass as a magnifier for almost 3,000 years. Today life scientists use magnifying lenses and microscopes.

Compound Light Microscope One type of microscope commonly used today is the compound microscope, shown in **Figure 13.** The **compound light microscope** is made up of three main parts—a tube with lenses, a stage, and a light. Specimens viewed through a compound microscope are sometimes stained with special dyes, which enable the specimens to be seen more clearly.

Specimens are placed on the stage so that the light passes through them. The lenses at each end of the tube magnify the image, making it appear larger than it actually is.

Ocular lens

Objective lens

Stage

Light

Figure 13 *A compound light microscope can produce an image that is 1,000 times (1,000×) larger than the actual specimen. The paramecium shown here has been magnified 200×.*

A hidden world all around you? See what it means on page 689 of your LabBook.

Electron Microscope In **electron microscopes,** tiny particles of matter called electrons are used to produce magnified images. Living specimens cannot be examined with an electron microscope because the process that prepares specimens for viewing kills them. There are two kinds of electron microscopes used in life science—the transmission electron microscope and the scanning electron microscope.

Transmission electron microscopes can magnify specimens up to 200,000 times (200,000×) their actual size. The scanning electron microscope can produce images that are up to 100,000 times their actual size. The images that electron microscopes produce are clearer and more detailed than those made by compound microscopes. **Figure 14** shows each kind of electron microscope, with a description of its specialized purpose and an example of the image that it can produce.

Figure 14 *The transmission electron microscope produces a greatly magnified image. The scanning electron microscope provides a clear view of surface features.*

Transmission Electron Microscope

- Electrons pass through the specimen.
- A flat image is produced.

Paramecium (15,000×)

Scanning Electron Microscope

- Electrons bounce off the surface of the specimen.
- A three-dimensional (3-D) image is produced.

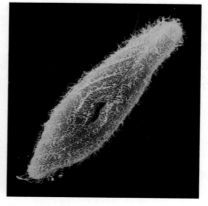

Paramecium (1,500×)

QuickLab

See for Yourself

Take a look at one of your fingernails. In your ScienceLog, draw and describe what you see. Then, look at your nail with a **magnifying lens.** How does this affect what you can see? Draw and describe how your nail looks when it is magnified.

X Rays Life scientists also use several tools to help them see internal structures of organisms. For almost a century, X rays have provided pictures of internal body structures such as the bones, heart, and lungs. If you have ever broken a bone, you have had an X ray, such as the one shown in **Figure 15.** X rays have also been used to help life scientists learn about the structures of proteins, which are important to the life processes of every organism.

Figure 15 *This X ray shows a broken arm.*

CT Scans and MRI CT (computed tomography) scans and MRI (magnetic resonance imaging) usually provide clearer, more detailed images of internal tissues than do X rays. In a CT scan, such as the one shown in **Figure 16,** low-dosage X-ray beams are passed through the body at different angles. Often a dye is injected to help highlight the tissues. MRI uses short bursts of a magnetic field and produces images like the one shown in **Figure 17.** With CT scans and MRI, data are transferred to a computer that creates an image that an expert can interpret. Both of these techniques are especially useful for studying the brain and spinal tissue.

Figure 16 *The internal tissues of the brain are shown in this CT scan.*

Computers

Since the first electronic computer was built in 1946, improvements in technology have made computers more powerful and easier to use. The amount of information that a computer can collect, store, organize, and analyze is enormous. Modern computers can complete billions of calculations in the same amount of time that it took early computers to do thousands. With the help of computers, life scientists are able to solve problems that they were not able to solve in the past.

Computers can be used to create graphs, solve complex mathematical problems, and analyze data. Computers also help scientists share data and ideas with each other and prepare reports and articles about their research.

Figure 17 *This image, showing blood circulation through the lungs, was produced with MRI.*

Systems of Measurement

The ability to make accurate and reliable measurements is an important tool in science. There are many different systems of measurement used throughout the world. At one time in England, the standard for 1 inch was three grains of barley arranged end to end. Even modern standardized units were once based on parts of the body, as shown in **Figure 18.** Such systems were not very reliable because they were based on objects that varied in size.

In the late 1700s, the French Academy of Sciences began to develop a global measurement system now known as the International System of Units, or SI. Today most scientists and almost all countries use this system. Using SI measurements helps scientists share and compare their observations and results.

The table below contains commonly used SI units for length, volume, mass, and temperature. Prefixes are used with these units to change them to larger or smaller units. For example, *kilo* means 1,000 times and *milli* indicates 1/1,000 times. All units are based on the number 10, which makes conversions from one unit to another easier.

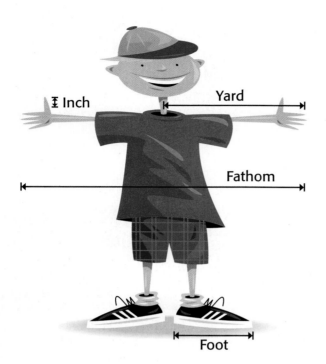

Figure 18 *The modern English system is widely used in the United States. The units were once based on parts of the human body.*

Common SI Units		
Length	**meter (m)**	
	kilometer (km)	1 km = 1,000 m
	decimeter (dm)	1 dm = 0.1 m
	centimeter (cm)	1 cm = 0.01 m
	millimeter (mm)	1 mm = 0.001 m
	micrometer (μm)	1 μm = 0.000 001 m
	nanometer (nm)	1 nm = 0.000 000 001 m
Volume	**cubic meter (m³)**	
	cubic centimeter (cm³)	1 cm³ = 0.000 001 m³
	liter (L)	1 L = 1 dm³ = 0.001 m³
	milliliter (mL)	1 mL = 0.001 L = 1 cm³
Mass	**kilogram (kg)**	
	gram (g)	1 g = 0.001 kg
	milligram (mg)	1 mg = 0.000 001 kg
Temperature	**Kelvin (K)**	
	Celsius (°C)	0°C = 273 K
		100°C = 373 K

The Long and the Short of It How long is a lizard? A life scientist, like the one in **Figure 19,** would probably use millimeters (mm) to describe a small lizard's length. If you divide 1 m into 1,000 parts, each part equals 1 mm. This means that 1 mm is one-thousandth of a meter. Although that seems pretty small, some organisms and structures are so tiny that even smaller units must be used. To describe the length of microscopic objects, scientists use micrometers (μm) or nanometers (nm). The scale in **Figure 20** compares the sizes of different organisms.

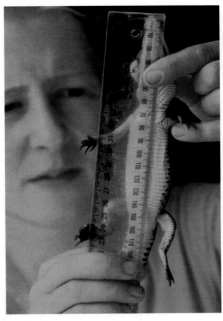

Figure 19 *This scientist is measuring a lizard's length using a metric ruler.*

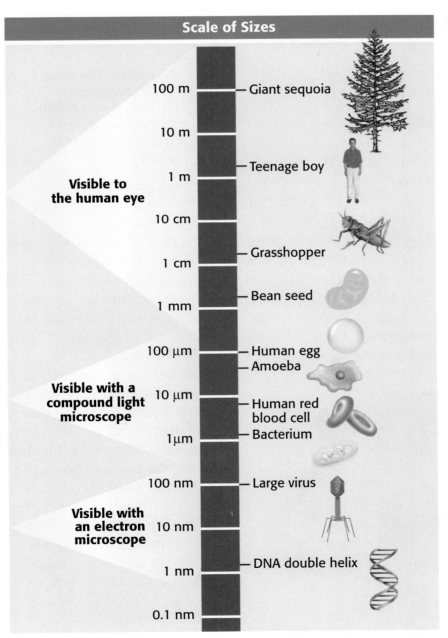

Scale of Sizes

Visible to the human eye

100 m	Giant sequoia
10 m	
1 m	Teenage boy
10 cm	
1 cm	Grasshopper
1 mm	Bean seed

Visible with a compound light microscope

100 μm	Human egg / Amoeba
10 μm	Human red blood cell
1μm	Bacterium

Visible with an electron microscope

100 nm	Large virus
10 nm	
1 nm	DNA double helix
0.1 nm	

Figure 20 *This scale compares organisms that can be seen with the naked eye with organisms and structures that are microscopic.*

Activity

Measure the width of your desk, but do not use a ruler. Pick an object to use as your unit of measurement. It could be a pencil, your hand, or anything else. Use that unit to determine how wide your desk is, and compare your measurement with those of your classmates. Explain why it is important to use standard units of measurement.

TRY at HOME

MATH BREAK

Finding Area

You can use the equation at right to find the area of any rectangular surface.

1. What is the area of a square with sides measuring 5 m?

2. What is the area of the top of your desk?

3. A rectangle has an area of 36 cm² and a length of 9 cm. What does its width measure?

Area How much carpet would it take to cover the floor of your classroom? Answering this question involves finding the area of the floor. **Area** is a measure of how much surface an object has.

Some quantities, such as area, can't be expressed with one measurement. That is, they are formed from combinations of two or more measurements. To calculate area, first measure the length and width, and then use the following equation:

$$\text{Area} = \text{length} \times \text{width}$$

The units for area are called square units, such as m², cm², and km². **Figure 21** will help you understand square units.

Figure 21 *The area of this rectangle is 20 cm². If you count the smaller squares within the rectangle, you'll count 20 squares that each measure 1 cm².*

Is the Glass Half Full or Half Empty? Suppose that some hippos born in a zoo are being relocated to their native habitat in Africa. How many hippos will fit into a moving crate? That depends on the volume of the crate and the volume of the hippos. **Volume** is the amount of space that something occupies or, as in the case of the crate, the amount of space that something contains.

The volume of a liquid is most often described using liters (L). One liter takes up the same amount of space as a cube whose sides are each 1 dm long. Just like the meter, the liter can be divided into smaller units. A milliliter (mL) is one-thousandth of a liter. A microliter (μL) is one-millionth of a liter. Graduated cylinders or graduated beakers are used to measure the volume of liquids.

The volume of a solid object, such as a crate, is described using cubic meters (m^3). Smaller objects can be measured in cubic centimeters (cm^3) or cubic millimeters (mm^3). One cm^3 is equal to one mL. To calculate the volume of a cube (or any other rectangular shape), multiply the length by the width by the height. Find the volume of the aquarium in **Figure 22.**

An object like a hippo or a rock has an irregular shape. If you multiplied its length, width, and height, you would not get a very accurate measure of its volume. One way to figure out the volume of an irregularly shaped object is to measure how much fluid the object displaces.

The girl in **Figure 23** is measuring the volume of a rock by placing it in a graduated cylinder that contains a known quantity of water. The rock displaces some water, which causes the level of the water to rise. The girl can figure out the volume of the rock by subtracting the volume of the water alone from the volume of the water and the rock. Then the volume of water in milliliters displaced by the rock must be converted to cm^3.

Figure 22 *The volume of this aquarium is found by multiplying its length, width, and height. What is its volume?*

 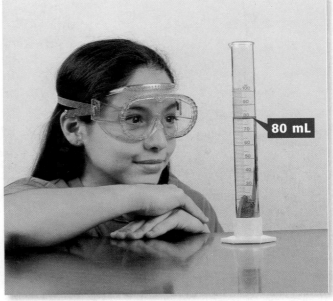

Figure 23 *This graduated cylinder contains 70 mL of water. After the rock was added, the water level moved to 80 mL. Because the rock displaced 10 mL of water and because 1 mL = 1 cm^3, the volume of the rock is 10 cm^3.*

A Massive Undertaking **Mass** is the amount of matter that makes up an object. The kilogram (kg) is the basic unit for mass. The mass of a very large object is described using kilograms (kg) or metric tons. A kilogram equals 1,000 g; therefore, a gram is one-thousandth of a kilogram. A metric ton equals 1,000 kg. Grams are used to describe the mass of small objects. A medium-sized apple has a mass of about 100 g. As shown in **Figure 24,** mass can be measured with a balance.

Figure 24 *The mass of the apple equals the mass of the weights.*

°F		°C	
212°F Water boils	220 200 180 160 140 120	110 100 90 80 70 60 50	100°C Water boils
98.6°F Normal body temperature	100 80 60	40 30 20 10	37°C Normal body temperature
32°F Water freezes	40 20 0	0 -10 -20	0°C Water freezes

Figure 25 *Water freezes at 0°C and boils at 100°C. Your normal body temperature is 37°C, which is equal to 98.6°F.*

Is It Hot Enough for You? How hot does it need to be to kill bacteria? To answer this question, a life scientist would measure the temperature at which bacteria die. **Temperature** is a measure of how hot or cold something is. You may not realize it, but the molecules that make up all matter are constantly moving. When energy is transferred to these molecules, they move even more, which causes the temperature to increase. Temperature, then, can also be defined as a measure of the average energy of the molecules of a substance.

You are probably used to describing temperature using degrees Fahrenheit (°F). Scientists commonly use degrees Celsius (°C), although Kelvins are the official SI units for temperature. You will use °C in this book. The thermometer in **Figure 25** shows the relationship between °F and °C.

Safety Rules!

Life science is exciting and fun, but it can also be dangerous. So don't take any chances! Always follow your teacher's instructions, and don't take shortcuts—even when you think there is little or no danger.

Before starting an experiment, get your teacher's permission and read the lab procedures carefully. Pay particular attention to safety information and caution statements. The diagram below shows the safety symbols used in this book. Get to know these symbols and what they mean. Do this by reading the safety information starting on page 682. **This is important!** If you are still unsure about what a safety symbol means, ask your teacher.

Stay on the safe side by reading the safety information on page 682.
This is a must before doing an experiment!

Safety Symbols

Eye Protection   Clothing Protection   Hand Safety

Heating Safety   Electric Safety   Sharp Object

Chemical Safety   Animal Safety   Plant Safety

REVIEW

1. How is temperature related to energy?

2. If you were going to measure the mass of a fly, which metric unit would be most appropriate?

3. What are two benefits of using the International System of Units?

4. **Understanding Technology** What tool was used to produce the image at right? How can you tell?

internet**connect**

SC*i*LINKS
NSTA

TOPIC: Tools of Life Science, SI Units
GO TO: www.scilinks.org
*sci*LINKS NUMBER: HSTL015, HSTL020

Chapter Highlights

SECTION 1

Vocabulary

life science *(p. 6)*

Section Notes

- Life science is the study of living things. Observations often lead to questions. Questions fuel the study of life science.

- Anyone can become a life scientist. Life scientists work in many different places and investigate a wide variety of questions and problems.

- Life scientists help prevent and treat diseases and help solve environmental problems.

SECTION 2

Vocabulary

scientific method *(p. 10)*

hypothesis *(p. 12)*

controlled experiment *(p. 14)*

variable *(p. 14)*

theory *(p. 18)*

technology *(p. 18)*

Section Notes

- The scientific method is a series of steps that scientists use to answer a question or solve a problem.

- The parts of the scientific method are not always completed in the same order. Steps are sometimes skipped or repeated.

- Scientists perform controlled experiments to test the effects of one factor at a time.

- Scientists must make careful observations, record data accurately, and be creative in finding answers and designing experiments.

- A hypothesis, which is a possible explanation for what has been observed, must be testable.

☑ Skills Check

Math Concepts

UNIT CONVERSIONS Imagine that you are writing a paper on the Empire State Building, in New York City. One source in the library lists the height of the building as 381,000,000 µm. This is a very large number, so you'll probably want to convert it to a more manageable number by using meters instead of micrometers. As you can see in the table on page 22, 1 µm = 0.000 001 m. To convert micrometers to meters, you multiply by 0.000 001.

$$381,000,000 \times 0.000\ 001 = 381 \text{ m}$$

Visual Understanding

HOW BIG? To review what can be seen with different types of microscopes, turn to pages 19 and 20. The Scale of Sizes, on page 23, will also help you visualize sizes decribed using the metric system.

SAFETY FIRST! Make sure that you know and understand the different safety symbols shown on page 27.

SECTION 2

- A theory is a unifying explanation for a broad range of hypotheses and observations that have been supported by testing.

- Scientific knowledge is constantly changing and growing as scientists ask new questions, find different answers to the same questions, and use tools that allow them to gather information in new ways.

Labs

Does It All Add Up? *(p. 686)*

Graphing Data *(p. 688)*

SECTION 3

Vocabulary

compound light microscope *(p. 19)*

electron microscope *(p. 20)*

area *(p. 24)*

volume *(p. 24)*

mass *(p. 26)*

temperature *(p. 26)*

Section Notes

- Life scientists commonly use compound light microscopes and electron microscopes to make observations of organisms or parts of organisms that are too small to be seen with the naked eye.

- X rays, CT scans, and MRI are used to view internal structures of organisms.

- Life scientists use computers to collect, store, organize, analyze, and share data.

- The International System of Units (SI), which is a simple and reliable system of measurement, is used by most scientists.

Labs

A Window to a Hidden World *(p. 689)*

---

 internetconnect

GO TO: go.hrw.com

Visit the **HRW** Web site for a variety of learning tools related to this chapter. Just type in the keyword:

KEYWORD: HSTLIV

 SCI**LINKS**sm

N S T A

GO TO: www.scilinks.org

Visit the **National Science Teachers Association** on-line Web site for Internet resources related to this chapter. Just type in the *sci*LINKS number for more information about the topic:

TOPIC: Scientific Method	*sci*LINKS **NUMBER:** HSTL004
TOPIC: Deformed Frogs	*sci*LINKS **NUMBER:** HSTL005
TOPIC: Careers in Life Science	*sci*LINKS **NUMBER:** HSTL010
TOPIC: Tools of Life Science	*sci*LINKS **NUMBER:** HSTL015
TOPIC: SI Units	*sci*LINKS **NUMBER:** HSTL020

Chapter Review

To complete the following sentences, choose the correct term from each pair of terms listed below:

1. The set of skills or steps that scientists use to answer questions is the __?__. (*controlled experiment* or *scientific method*)

2. After recognizing a problem or asking a question, life scientists form one or more __?__, which are possible explanations for what has been observed. (*predictions* or *hypotheses*)

3. In a controlled experiment, the __?__ is the one factor that differs between the __?__ and the experimental group. (*prediction, variable group* or *variable, control group*)

4. __?__ is a measure of how much surface an object has. (*Area* or *Volume*)

5. Life scientists use __?__ to describe the measurement of an object's mass. (*meters* or *grams*)

UNDERSTANDING CONCEPTS

Multiple Choice

6. Which of the following would *not* be an area of study in life science?
   a. studying how lions and hyenas interact
   b. measuring the rate at which bacteria divide
   c. comparing the reproduction of arctic plants with that of desert plants
   d. studying how volcanoes are formed

7. The steps of the scientific method
   a. must all be used in every scientific investigation.
   b. must always be used in the same order.
   c. are not always used in order.
   d. start with the development of a theory.

8. In a controlled experiment,
   a. a control group is compared with one or more experimental groups.
   b. there are at least two variables.
   c. all factors should be different.
   d. a variable is not needed.

9. When a scientist finds that a hypothesis is wrong, the scientist usually
   a. tries to find another explanation for what has been observed.
   b. stops studying science.
   c. feels that nothing valuable was learned.
   d. adds an additional variable to his or her experiment.

10. What tool would a life scientist use to get a three-dimensional image of a microscopic organism?
    a. CT scan
    b. X ray
    c. scanning electron microscope
    d. magnifying lens

11. The International System of Units
    a. is based on standardized body measurements.
    b. contains units that are based on the number 10.
    c. is useful only for measuring lengths.
    d. is a device used to measure volume.

Short Answer

12. Why do hypotheses need to be testable?

13. What is a prediction?

14. Which SI units can be used to describe the measurement of volume? Which SI units can be used to describe the mass of an object?

Concept Mapping

15. Use the following terms to create a concept map: observations, predictions, questions, controlled experiments, variable, hypothesis.

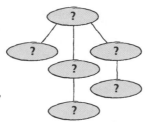

CRITICAL THINKING AND PROBLEM SOLVING

Write one or two sentences to answer the following questions:

16. In a controlled experiment, why should there be several individuals in the control group and several in each of the experimental groups?

17. A scientist who studies mice observes that on the day he feeds the mice vitamins with their meals, they perform better in mazes. What hypothesis would you form to explain this phenomenon?

18. The volume of an egg and water in a graduated beaker is 200 mL. After the egg is removed, the volume of the water is found to be 125 mL. What is the volume of the egg in cm^3?

200 mL   125 mL

MATH IN SCIENCE

19. If you magnified a 5 μm long organism 1,000 ×, how long would that organism appear in millimeters (mm)?

INTERPRETING GRAPHICS

Examine the illustration below of an experiment set up to test the following prediction: **If** bees are more attracted to yellow flowers than to red flowers, **then** bees will visit yellow flowers more often than they will visit red flowers.

11 visits   3 visits   11 visits

2 visits   9 visits   4 visits

20. How many total visits did the yellow flowers receive? How many total visits did the red flowers receive?

21. What is the average number of visits for yellow flowers? What is the average number of visits for red flowers?

22. In what ways might the experimental setup be an unreliable test of the prediction?

NOW What Do You Think?

Take a minute to review your answers to the ScienceLog questions on page 5. Have your answers changed? If necessary, revise your answers based on what you have learned since you began this chapter.

CAREERS

Eric Pianka became interested in lizards when he was 6 years old. "On a trip across the country with my family, I saw a big green lizard at a roadside park," Pianka explains. I tried to catch it, but all I got was the tail. At that moment, I knew I had to find out everything I could about the kind of life it led." Pianka is now a world-famous professor of zoology at the University of Texas, in Austin, Texas.

*O*ne of the things Eric Pianka likes best about his job is being in the wilderness and seeing things that few people have ever seen. "I've been almost everywhere! I've spent a lot of time studying deserts in the western United States. I've been to deserts in southern Africa, India, and Chile. My most current (and oldest) interest is in the deserts of Australia. I haven't had a chance to study the Brazilian Amazon yet, but that's a goal for the future!"

The Ecology of Desert Lizards

In his research as a zoologist, Pianka has focused on the ecology of desert lizards. He goes to a desert, collects lizards, and examines and classifies them. Then he compiles data and interprets them in books or papers. As Pianka puts it, "I try to answer questions like, Why are there more lizards in one place than in another? How do they react with each other and other species? How have they adapted to their environment?"

Recently, Pianka conducted a study to learn about the effects of wildfires on the ecology and diversity of lizard species. He hopes this work will show how lizard species adapted to the large-scale wildfires that at one time occurred regularly in desert areas but that today are usually controlled by humans.

▼ *The collared lizard lives in rocky regions of the southwestern United States.*

Learning from Wildlife

Pianka believes that doing research on lizards and other animals may help us protect our environment. "Everyone always asks, 'Why lizards?' I turn the question around and say, 'Why you?' The general attitude is that everything on Earth has to somehow serve humans. By looking at how other species have lived and died and changed over millions of years, we can gain a better understanding of the world we live in."

Be a Zoologist for a Day

▶ Select a common animal that lives in your area and that can be easily observed. Spend a few hours watching it carefully. Document everything you observe. Did you discover anything you did not already know? Present your findings to the class.

Science Fiction

"The Homesick Chicken"

by Edward D. Hoch

OK, OK, why *did* the chicken cross the road? Oh sure, you know the answer to this old riddle, don't you? Or maybe you just think you do! But "The Homesick Chicken," by Edward D. Hoch, may surprise you. That old chicken may not be exactly what it seems…

You see, one of the chickens at Tangaway Research Farms has escaped—not just flown the coop, mind you, but really escaped. It pecked a hole in a super-strength security fence and then crossed an eight-lane highway to get away. But after all that effort, it just stopped! It was found in a vacant lot across the highway from Tangaway, pecking away contentedly.

Barnabus Rex, a specialist in solving scientific riddles, is called in to work on the mystery. He is intrigued by this escaping chicken. Why would it go to all the trouble to peck through the tough security fence, risk being flattened on the superhighway, and then just stop when it got to the other side?

There are a few clues in the story. As you read it, maybe you can see what Mr. Rex sees. If you know anything about chickens, you might be able to solve the mystery. Escape to the *Holt Anthology of Science Fiction* and read "The Homesick Chicken."

CHAPTER 2

It's Alive!! Or, Is It?

Imagine . . .

The Movile Cave, in Romania, is one of the spookiest, slimiest, and smelliest places on Earth. For more than 5 million years, the cave and its inhabitants were sealed off from the outside world. Many of the creepiest organisms known to science inhabit the Movile Cave.

Poisonous water scorpions lurk in murky pools and breathe through snorkels attached to their stomach. Predatory centipedes zero in on smaller bugs and inject them with a paralyzing toxin. Wolf spiders move on spindly legs in pursuit of millipedes, pill bugs, and even their own young!

Almost all living things get their energy either directly or indirectly from the sun. But what about the inhabitants of the Movile Cave, a place where sunlight never enters? The supply of energy that fuels life in the Movile Cave comes from organisms that can't be seen. These microorganisms don't feed on other creepy crawlies; they feed on hydrogen sulfide. This chemical, which smells like rotten eggs, is abundant in the cave. The hydrogen sulfide provides the microorganisms with the energy they need for life. When the microorganisms are eaten, their energy is transferred to other organisms.

Using energy is just one of the characteristics of life. Read on to find out what else all living things have in common.

What Do You Think?

In your ScienceLog, try to answer the following questions based on what you already know:

1. What characteristics do all living things have in common?

2. What do organisms need in order to stay alive?

Investigate!

TRY at HOME

Lights On!

Responding to change is a characteristic of living things. In this activity, you will work with a partner to see how eyes react to changes in light.

Procedure

1. Observe a classmate's eyes in a room with normal light. Find the pupil, which is the black area in the center of the colored part of the eye. Light enters the eye through the pupil. Notice the size of your classmate's pupils.

Pupil

2. Have your partner keep both eyes open and completely cover each one with a cupped hand so that no light can reach them. Wait about 1 minute.

3. Instruct your partner to quickly pull away both hands. Immediately look at your partner's pupils. Record what happens.

4. Now briefly shine a **flashlight** into your partner's eyes. In your ScienceLog, record how this affects the pupils.
   Caution: Do not use the sun as the source of the light.

5. Change places with your partner, and repeat steps 1–4 so that he or she can observe how your eyes respond to changes in light.

Analysis

6. How did your partner's eyes respond to changes in the level of light?

7. How did changes in the size of your pupils affect your vision? What does this tell you about why pupils change size?

Characteristics of Living Things

Section 1

Terms to Learn

cell
stimulus
homeostasis
asexual
  reproduction

sexual
  reproduction
DNA
heredity
metabolism

What You'll Do

◆ List the characteristics of living things.
◆ Distinguish between asexual reproduction and sexual reproduction.
◆ Define and describe homeostasis.

While out in your yard one day, you notice something strange in the grass. It's slimy, bright yellow, and about the size of a dime. You have no idea what it is. Is it a plant part that fell from a tree? Is it alive? How can you tell?

Even though an amazing variety of living things exist on Earth, they are all alike in several ways. What does a dog have in common with a tree? What does a fish have in common with a mushroom? And what do *you* have in common with a slimy blob (also known as a slime mold)? Read on to find out about the six characteristics that all organisms share.

Slime mold

1 Living Things Have Cells

Every living thing is composed of one or more cells. A **cell** is a membrane-covered structure that contains all of the materials necessary for life. The membrane that surrounds a cell separates the contents of the cell from the cell's environment.

Many organisms, such as those in **Figure 1,** are made up of only one cell. Other organisms, such as the monkeys and trees in **Figure 2,** are made up of trillions of cells. Most cells are too small to be seen with the naked eye.

In an organism with many cells, cells perform specialized functions. For example, your nerve cells are specialized to transport signals, and your muscle cells are specialized for movement.

Figure 1 *Each of these organisms is made of only one cell.*

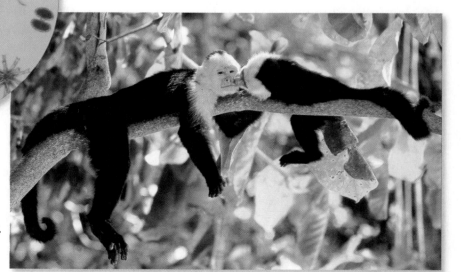

Figure 2 *Trillions of cells make up these organisms.*

2 Living Things Sense and Respond to Change

All organisms have the ability to sense change in their environment and to respond to that change. When your pupils are exposed to light, they respond by becoming smaller. A change in an organism's environment that affects the activity of the organism is called a **stimulus** (plural, *stimuli*).

Stimuli can be chemicals, gravity, darkness, light, sounds, tastes, or anything that causes organisms to respond in some way. A gentle touch causes a response in the plant shown in **Figure 3**.

Self-Check

Is your alarm clock a stimulus? Explain. *(See page 782 to check your answer.)*

 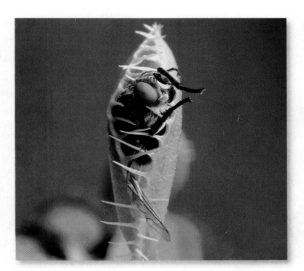

Figure 3 *The touch of an insect triggers the Venus' flytrap to quickly close its leaves.*

Homeostasis Even though an organism's external environment may change, the organism must maintain a stable internal environment to survive. This is because the life processes of organisms involve many different kinds of chemical reactions that can occur only in delicately balanced environments. The maintenance of a stable internal environment is called **homeostasis** (HOH mee OH STAY sis).

Your body maintains a temperature of about 37°C. When you get hot, your body responds by sweating. When you get cold, your muscles twitch in an attempt to generate heat. This causes you to shiver. Whether you are sweating or shivering, your body is trying to return things to normal. Another example of homeostasis is your body's ability to maintain a stable amount of sugar in your blood.

Oceanography CONNECTION

Fish that live in the ice-cold waters off Antarctica make a natural antifreeze that keeps them from freezing.

3 Living Things Reproduce

Organisms make other organisms like themselves. This is accomplished in one of two ways: by asexual reproduction or by sexual reproduction. In **asexual reproduction,** a single parent produces offspring that are identical to the parent. **Figure 4** shows an organism that reproduces asexually. Most single-celled organisms reproduce in this way. **Sexual reproduction,** however, almost always requires two parents to produce offspring that will share characteristics of both parents. Most animals and plants reproduce in this way. The bear cubs in **Figure 5** were produced sexually by their parents.

Figure 4 *The hydra can reproduce asexually by forming buds that will break off and grow into new individuals.*

Figure 5 *Like most animals, bears produce offspring by sexual reproduction.*

4 Living Things Have DNA

The cells of all living things contain a special molecule called **DNA** (**d**eoxyribo**n**ucleic **a**cid). DNA provides instructions for making molecules called *proteins*. Proteins take part in almost all of the activities of an organism's cells. Proteins also determine many of an organism's characteristics.

When organisms reproduce, they pass on copies of their DNA to their offspring. The transmission of characteristics from one generation to the next is called **heredity.** Offspring, such as the children in **Figure 6,** resemble their parents because of heredity.

Figure 6 *Children resemble their parents because of heredity.*

5 Living Things Use Energy

Organisms use energy to carry out the activities of life. These activities include such things as making food, breaking down food, moving materials into and out of cells, and building cells. An organism's **metabolism** (muh TAB uh LIZ uhm) is the total of all of the chemical activities that it performs.

APPLY

Are Computers Alive?

Computers can do all kinds of things, such as storing information and doing complex calculations. Some computers have even been programmed to learn, that is, to get better and faster at solving problems over time. Do you think computers could become so advanced that they should be considered alive? Why or why not?

6 Living Things Grow and Develop

All living things, whether they are made of one cell or many cells, grow during periods of their lives. Growth in single-celled organisms occurs as the cell gets larger. Organisms made of many cells grow mainly by increasing their number of cells.

In addition to getting larger, living things may develop and change as they grow. Just like the organisms in **Figure 7**, you will pass through different stages in your life as you develop into an adult.

Figure 7 *Over time, acorns develop into oak seedlings, which become oak trees.*

REVIEW

1. What characteristics of living things does a river have? Is a river alive?

2. What does the fur coat of a bear have to do with homeostasis?

3. How is reproduction related to heredity?

4. **Applying Concepts** What are some stimuli in your environment? How do you respond to these stimuli?

internet**connect**

SCi*LINKS*
NSTA

TOPIC: Characteristics of Living Things
GO TO: www.scilinks.org
*sci*LINKS NUMBER: HSTL030

Terms to Learn

producer
consumer
decomposer

What You'll Do

◆ Explain why organisms need food, water, air, and living space.
◆ Discuss how living things obtain what they need to live.

The Simple Bare Necessities of Life

Would it surprise you to learn that you have the same basic needs as a tree, a frog, or a fly? In fact, almost every organism has the same basic needs: food, water, air, and living space.

Food

All living things need food. Food provides organisms with the energy and raw materials needed to carry on life processes and to build and repair cells and body parts. But not all organisms get food in the same way. In fact, organisms can be grouped into three different categories based on how they get their food.

Making Food Some organisms, such as plants, are called **producers** because they can produce their own food. Like most producers, plants use energy from the sun to make food from water and carbon dioxide. Some producers, like the microorganisms in Movile Cave, obtain energy and food from the chemicals in their environment.

Getting Food Other organisms are called **consumers** because they must eat (consume) other organisms to get food. The salamander in **Figure 8** is an example of a consumer. It gets the energy it needs by eating insects and other organisms.

Some consumers are decomposers. **Decomposers** are organisms that get their food by breaking down the nutrients in dead organisms or animal wastes.

Figure 8 *The salamander is a consumer. The fungus is a decomposer, and the plants are producers.*

Water

You may have heard that your body is made mostly of water. In fact, your cells and the cells of almost all living organisms are approximately 70 percent water—even the cells of a cactus and a camel. Most of the chemical reactions involved in metabolism require water.

Organisms differ greatly in terms of how much water they need and how they obtain it. You could survive for only about 3 days without water. You obtain water from the fluids you drink and the food you eat. The desert-dwelling kangaroo rat never drinks. It gets all of its water from its food.

Air

Air is a mixture of several different gases, including oxygen and carbon dioxide. Animals, plants, and most other living things use oxygen in the chemical process that releases energy from food. Organisms that live on land get oxygen from the air. Organisms living in fresh water and salt water either take in dissolved oxygen from the water or come to the water's surface to get oxygen from the air. Some organisms, such as the European diving spider in **Figure 9,** go to great lengths to get oxygen.

Green plants, algae, and some bacteria need carbon dioxide gas in addition to oxygen. The food these organisms produce is made from carbon dioxide and water by *photosynthesis* (FOHT oh SIN thuh sis), the process that converts the energy in sunlight to energy stored in food.

Figure 9 *This spider surrounds itself with an air bubble so that it can obtain oxygen underwater.*

A Place to Live

All organisms must have somewhere to live that contains all of the things they need to survive. Some organisms, such as elephants, require a large amount of space. Other organisms, such as bacteria, may live their entire life in a single pore on the tip of your nose.

Because the amount of space on Earth is limited, organisms often compete with each other for food, water, and other necessities. Many animals, including the warbler in **Figure 10,** will claim a particular space and try to keep other animals away. Plants also compete with each other for living space and for access to water and sunlight.

Figure 10 *A warbler's song is more than just a pretty tune. The warbler is protecting its home by telling other warblers to stay out of its territory.*

REVIEW

1. Why are decomposers categorized as consumers? How do they differ from producers?

2. Why are most cells 70 percent water?

3. **Making Inferences** Could life as we know it exist on Earth if air contained only oxygen? Explain.

4. **Identifying Relationships** How might a cave, an ant, and a lake meet the needs of an organism?

■ internet**connect**

SC*i*LINKS.
NSTA

TOPIC: The Necessities of Life
GO TO: www.scilinks.org
*sci*LINKS NUMBER: HSTL035

Terms to Learn

protein   phospholipid
carbohydrate   nucleic acid
lipid   ATP

What You'll Do

◆ Compare and contrast the
  chemical building blocks of cells.
◆ Explain the importance of ATP.

The Chemistry of Life

All living things are made of cells, but what are cells made of? Everything, whether it is living or not, is made up of tiny building blocks called *atoms*. There are about 100 different kinds of atoms.

A substance made up of one type of atom is called an *element*. When two or more atoms join together, they form what's called a *molecule*. Molecules found in living things are usually made of different combinations of six elements: carbon, hydrogen, nitrogen, oxygen, phosphorous, and sulfur. These elements combine to form proteins, carbohydrates, lipids, nucleic acids, and ATP.

Proteins

Almost all of the life processes of a cell involve proteins. After water, proteins are the most abundant materials in cells. **Proteins** are large molecules that are made up of subunits called *amino acids*.

Organisms break down the proteins in food to supply their cells with amino acids. These amino acids are then linked together to form new proteins. Some proteins are made up of only a few amino acids, while others contain more than 10,000 amino acids.

Proteins in Action Proteins have many different functions. Some proteins form structures that are easy to see, such as those in **Figure 11.** Other proteins are at work at the cellular level. The protein *hemoglobin* (HEE moh GLOH bin) in red blood cells attaches to oxygen so that oxygen can be delivered throughout the body. Some proteins help protect cells from foreign materials. And special proteins called *enzymes* make many different chemical reactions in a cell occur quickly.

Figure 11 *Feathers, spider webs, and hair are all made of proteins.*

Carbohydrates

Carbohydrates are a group of compounds made of sugars. Cells use carbohydrates as a source of energy and for energy storage. When an organism needs energy, its cells break down carbohydrates to release the energy stored in the carbohydrates.

There are two types of carbohydrates, simple carbohydrates and complex carbohydrates. Simple carbohydrates are made of one sugar molecule or a few sugar molecules linked together. Table sugar and the sugar in fruits are examples of simple carbohydrates.

Too Much Sugar! When an organism has more sugar than it needs, its extra sugar may be stored in the form of complex carbohydrates. Complex carbohydrates are made of hundreds of sugar molecules linked together. Your body makes some complex carbohydrates and stores them in your liver. Plants make a complex carbohydrate called *starch*. A potato plant, such as the one in **Figure 12,** stores its extra sugar as starch. When you eat mashed potatoes or French fries, you are eating a potato plant's stored starch. Your body can then break down this complex carbohydrate to release the energy stored in it.

÷ 5 ÷ Ω ≤ ∞ +Ω √ 9 ∞ ≤ Σ 2

MATH BREAK

How Much Oxygen?

Each red blood cell carries about 250 million molecules of hemoglobin. How many molecules of oxygen could a single red blood cell deliver throughout the body if every hemoglobin molecule attached to four oxygen molecules?

Sugars

Starch

Figure 12 *Most sugars are simple carbohydrates. The extra sugar in a potato plant is stored in the potato as starch, a complex carbohydrate.*

QuickLab

Starch Search

When **iodine** comes into contact with starch, the iodine turns black. Use this handy trait to find out which **food samples** supplied by your teacher contain starch.

Caution: Iodine can stain clothing. Wear goggles, protective gloves, and an apron.

Lipids

Lipids are compounds that cannot mix with water. Lipids have many important functions in the cell. Like carbohydrates, some lipids store energy. Other lipids form the membranes of cells.

Fats and Oils Fats and oils are lipids that store energy. When an organism has used up most of its carbohydrates, it can obtain energy from these lipids. The structures of fats and oils are almost identical, but at room temperature most fats are solid and oils are liquid. Most of the lipids stored in plants are oils, while most of the lipids stored in animals are fats.

Phospholipids All cells are surrounded by a structure called a *cell membrane.* **Phospholipids** are the molecules that form much of the cell membrane. As you read earlier, water is the most abundant material in a cell. When phospholipids are in water, the tails come together and the heads face out into the water. This happens because the head of a phospholipid molecule is attracted to water, while the tail is not. **Figure 13** shows how phospholipid molecules form two layers when they are in water.

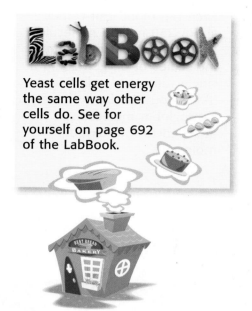

Yeast cells get energy the same way other cells do. See for yourself on page 692 of the LabBook.

Figure 13 *The contents of a cell are surrounded by a membrane of phospholipid molecules.*

Phospholipid molecule

Tail   Head

a *The head of a phospholipid molecule is attracted to water, but the tail is not.*

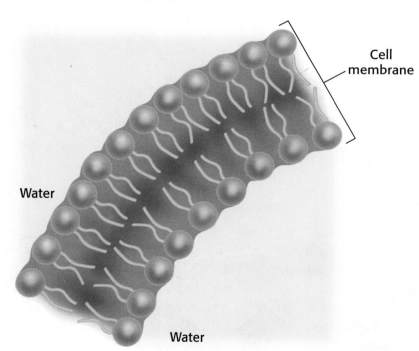

Cell membrane

Water

Water

b *When phospholipid molecules come together in water, they form two layers.*

Nucleic Acids

Nucleic acids are compounds made up of subunits called *nucleotides*. A nucleic acid may contain thousands of nucleotides. Nucleic acids are sometimes called the blueprints of life because they contain all the information needed for the cell to make all of its proteins.

DNA is a nucleic acid. A DNA molecule is like a recipe book titled *How to Make Proteins*. When a cell needs to make a certain protein, it gets information from DNA to direct how amino acids are hooked together to make that protein. You will learn more about DNA later.

The Cell's Fuel

Another molecule that is important to cells is ATP (**a**denosine **tri**phosphate). **ATP** is the major fuel used for all cell activities that require energy.

When food molecules, such as carbohydrates and fats, are broken down, some of the released energy is transferred to ATP molecules, as shown in **Figure 14**. The energy in carbohydrates and lipids must be transferred to ATP before the stored energy can be used by cells to fuel their life processes.

Energy in lipids and carbohydrates

ATP

Energy in adenosine triphosphate

Energy for a cell's activities

Figure 14 *The energy in the carbohydrates and lipids in food must be transferred to ATP molecules before cells can use the energy.*

REVIEW

1. What are the subunits of proteins? of starch? of DNA?

2. What do carbohydrates, fats, and oils have in common?

3. Are all proteins enzymes? Explain your answer.

4. **Making Predictions** What would happen to the supply of ATP in your cells if you did not eat enough carbohydrates? How would this affect your cells?

Chapter Highlights

SECTION 1

Vocabulary

cell (p. 36)

stimulus (p. 37)

homeostasis (p. 37)

asexual reproduction (p. 38)

sexual reproduction (p. 38)

DNA (p. 38)

heredity (p. 38)

metabolism (p. 38)

Section Notes

- All living things share the six characteristics of life.

- Organisms are made of one or more cells.

- Organisms detect and respond to stimuli in their environment.

- Organisms work to keep their internal environment stable so that the chemical activities of their cells are not disrupted. The maintenance of a stable internal environment is called homeostasis.

- Organisms reproduce and make more organisms like themselves. Offspring can be produced asexually or sexually.

- Offspring resemble their parents. The passing of characteristics from parent to offspring is called heredity.

- Organisms grow and may change during their lifetime.

- Organisms use energy to carry out the chemical activities of life. Metabolism is the sum of an organism's chemical activities.

Labs

Roly-Poly Races (p. 690)

SECTION 2

Vocabulary

producer (p. 40)

consumer (p. 40)

decomposer (p. 40)

Section Notes

- Organisms must have food. Producers make their own food. Consumers eat other organisms for food. Decomposers break down the nutrients in dead organisms and animal wastes.

☑ Skills Check

Math Concepts

HOW MANY? In the MathBreak on page 43, you determined how many molecules of oxygen a single red blood cell could carry.

$$\frac{250{,}000{,}000 \text{ molecules of hemoglobin}}{1 \text{ red blood cell}} \times \frac{4 \text{ molecules of oxygen}}{1 \text{ molecule of hemoglobin}}$$

$$= 1{,}000{,}000{,}000 \text{ molecules of oxygen}$$

Visual Understanding

PHOSPHOLIPIDS Look at the illustrations of phospholipids and the cell membrane on page 44. Notice that the fluid inside and outside of the cell contains a lot of water. The head of the phospholipid molecule is attracted to water. Therefore, the phospholipid molecules that form the cell membrane line up with their tails facing away from the water.

SECTION 2

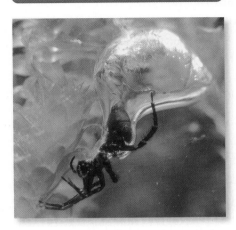

- Organisms depend on water. Water is necessary for maintaining metabolism.

- Organisms need oxygen to release the energy contained in their food. Plants, algae, and some bacteria also need carbon dioxide.

- Organisms must have a place to live where they can obtain the things they need.

SECTION 3

Vocabulary

protein *(p. 42)*

carbohydrate *(p. 43)*

lipid *(p. 44)*

phospholipid *(p. 44)*

nucleic acid *(p. 45)*

ATP *(p. 45)*

Section Notes

- Proteins, carbohydrates, lipids, nucleic acids, and ATP are important to life.

- Cells use carbohydrates for energy storage. Carbohydrates are made of sugars.

- Fats and oils store energy. Phospholipids make cell membranes.

- Proteins are made up of amino acids and have many important functions. Enzymes are proteins that help chemical reactions occur quickly.

- Nucleic acids are made up of nucleotides. DNA is a nucleic acid that contains the information for making proteins.

- Cells use molecules of ATP to fuel their activities.

Labs

The Best-Bread Bakery Dilemma *(p. 692)*

---

internet connect

GO TO: go.hrw.com

Visit the **HRW** Web site for a variety of learning tools related to this chapter. Just type in the keyword:

KEYWORD: HSTALV

GO TO: www.scilinks.org

Visit the **National Science Teachers Association** on-line Web site for Internet resources related to this chapter. Just type in the *sci*LINKS number for more information about the topic:

TOPIC: Characteristics of Living Things   *sci*LINKS NUMBER: HSTL030

TOPIC: The Necessities of Life   *sci*LINKS NUMBER: HSTL035

TOPIC: The Chemistry of Life   *sci*LINKS NUMBER: HSTL040

TOPIC: Is There Life on Other Planets?   *sci*LINKS NUMBER: HSTL045

Chapter Review

USING VOCABULARY

To complete the following sentences, choose the correct term from each pair of terms listed below:

1. The process of maintaining a stable internal environment is known as ___?___. (*metabolism* or *homeostasis*)

2. The resemblance of offspring to their parents is a result of ___?___. (*heredity* or *stimuli*)

3. A ___?___ obtains food by eating other organisms. (*producer* or *consumer*)

4. Starch is a ___?___ and is made up of ___?___. (*carbohydrate/sugars* or *nucleic acid/ nucleotides*)

5. Fats and oils are ___?___ that store energy for an organism. (*proteins* or *lipids*)

UNDERSTANDING CONCEPTS

Multiple Choice

6. Cells are
   a. the structures that contain all of the materials necessary for life.
   b. found in all organisms.
   c. sometimes specialized for particular functions.
   d. All of the above

7. Which of the following is a true statement about all living things?
   a. They cannot sense changes in their external environment.
   b. They have one or more cells.
   c. They do not need to use energy.
   d. They reproduce asexually.

8. Organisms must have food because
   a. food is a source of energy.
   b. food supplies cells with oxygen.
   c. organisms never make their own food.
   d. All of the above

9. A change in an organism's environment that affects the organism's activities is a
   a. response.   c. metabolism.
   b. stimulus.   d. producer.

10. Organisms store energy in
    a. nucleic acids.   c. lipids.
    b. phospholipids.   d. water.

11. The molecule that contains the information on how to make proteins is
    a. ATP.
    b. a carbohydrate.
    c. DNA.
    d. a phospholipid.

12. The subunits of nucleic acids are
    a. nucleotides.   c. sugars.
    b. oils.   d. amino acids.

Short Answer

13. What is the difference between asexual reproduction and sexual reproduction?

14. In one or two sentences, explain why living things must have air.

15. What is ATP, and why is it important to a cell?

Concept Mapping

16. Use the following terms to create a concept map: cell, carbohydrates, protein, enzymes, DNA, sugars, lipids, nucleotides, amino acids, nucleic acid.

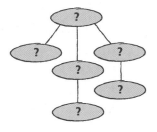

Write one or two sentences to answer the following questions:

17. A flame can move, grow larger, and give off heat. Is a flame alive? Explain.

18. Based on what you know about carbohydrates, lipids, and proteins, why is it important for you to eat a balanced diet?

19. Your friend tells you that the stimulus of music makes his goldfish swim faster. How would you design a controlled experiment to test your friend's claim?

MATH IN SCIENCE

20. An elephant has a mass of 3,900 kg. If 70 percent of the elephant's mass comes from water, how many kilograms of water does the elephant contain?

INTERPRETING GRAPHICS

Take a look at the pictures below, which show the same plant over a time span of 3 days.

Day 1

Day 2

Day 3

21. What is the plant doing?

22. What characteristic(s) of living things is the plant exhibiting?

NOW What Do You Think?

Take a minute to review your answers to the ScienceLog questions on page 35. Have your answers changed? If necessary, revise your answers based on what you have learned since you began this chapter.

Life on Mars?

In late 1996 the headlines read, "Evidence of Life on Mars." What kind of life? Aliens similar to those that we see in sci-fi movies? Some creature completely unlike any we've seen before? Not quite, but the story behind the headlines is no less fascinating!

An Unusual Spaceship

In 1996, a group of researchers led by NASA scientists studied a 3.8-billion-year-old meteorite named ALH84001. These scientists agree that ALH84001 is a potato-sized piece of the planet Mars. They also agree that it fell to Earth about 13,000 years ago. It was discovered in Antarctica in 1984. And according to the NASA team, ALH84001 brought with it evidence that life once existed on Mars.

Life-Form Leftovers

On the surface of ALH84001, scientists found certain kinds of *organic molecules* (molecules containing carbon). These molecules are similar to those left behind when living things break down substances for food. And when these scientists examined the interior of the meteorite, they found the same organic

▲ *This scanning electron micrograph image of a tube-like structure found within meteorite ALH84001 is thought to be evidence of life on Mars.*

molecules throughout. Because these molecules were spread throughout the meteorite, scientists concluded the molecules were not contamination from Earth. The NASA team believes these organic leftovers are strong evidence that tiny organisms similar to bacteria lived, ate, and died on Mars millions of years ago.

Dirty Water or Star Dust

Many scientists disagree that ALH84001 contains evidence of Martian life. Some of them argue that the organic compounds are contaminants from Antarctic meltwater that seeped into the meteorite.

Others argue that the molecules were created by processes involving very high temperatures. These scientists think the compounds were formed during star formation and ended up on Mars when it became a planet. Other supporters of this theory believe that the compounds were created during the formation of rocks on Mars. In either case, they argue that no life-forms could exist at such high temperatures and that these compounds could not be the result of living things.

The Debate Continues

Scientists continue to debate the evidence of ALH84001. They are looking for evidence specific to biological life, such as proteins, nucleic acids, and cellular walls. Other scientists are looking to Mars itself for more evidence. Some hope to find underground water that might have supported life. Others hope to gather soil and rock samples that might hold evidence that Mars was once a living planet. Until scientists have more evidence, the debate will continue.

Think About It

▶ If you went to Mars, what kinds of evidence would you look for to prove that life once existed there? How could the discovery of nucleic or amino acids prove life existed on Mars?

Science Fiction

"They're Made Out of Meat"

by Terry Bisson

Two space travelers millions of light-years from home are visiting an uncharted sector of the universe to find signs of life. Their mission is to contact, welcome, and log any and all beings in this quadrant of the universe. Once they discover a living being, they must find a way to communicate with it.

During their mission they encounter a life-form quite unlike anything they have ever seen before. These unusual beings can think and communicate. They have even built a few simple machines, so they aren't exactly pond scum.

Nevertheless, the explorers have very strong doubts about adding this new species to the list of known life-forms in the universe. The creatures are just too strange and, well, disgusting. They just don't fit on the list. Besides, with their limited abilities, it is unlikely they will make contact with any of the other life-forms that dwell elsewhere in the universe.

Perhaps it might be better if the explorers agreed to pretend that they never encountered these beings at all. But the travelers' official duty is to contact and welcome all life-forms, no matter how ugly they are or what they are made of. Can they bring themselves to perform their official duty? Will anyone believe their story if they do?

You'll find out by reading Terry Bisson's short story "They're Made Out of Meat." This story is in the *Holt Anthology of Science Fiction*.

UNIT 2

C ells are everywhere. Even though most can't be seen with the naked eye, they make up every living thing. Your body alone contains trillions of cells.

In this unit, you will learn about cells. You will learn the difference between animal cells, plant cells, and bacterial cells. You'll learn about the different parts of a cell and see how they work together.

Cells were discovered in 1665, and since then we have learned a lot about cells and the way they work. This timeline shows some of the discoveries that have been made along the way, but there is still a lot to learn about the fascinating world of cells!

Cells

1620
The Pilgrims settle Plymouth Colony.

1665
Robert Hooke discovers cells after observing a thin piece of cork under a microscope.

1937
The Golden Gate Bridge opens in San Francisco.

1873
Anton Schneider observes and accurately describes mitosis.

1941
George Beadle and Edward Tatum discover that genes control the chemical reactions in cells by directing protein production.

1952
Martha Chase and Alfred Hershey demonstrate that DNA, found in the nucleus of cells, is the hereditary material.

1831
Robert Brown discovers the nucleus in a plant cell.

1838
Matthias Schleiden discovers that all plant tissue is made up of cells.

1839
Theodor Schwann shows that all animal tissue is made up of cells.

1861
The American Civil War begins.

1858
Rudolf Virchow determines that all cells are produced from cells.

1971
Lynn Margulis proposes a theory about the origin of cell organelles.

1956
The manufacture of protein in the cell is found to occur in ribosomes.

1997
A sheep named Dolly becomes the first animal to be cloned from a single cell.

3 Cells: The Basic Units of Life

What If . . . ?

Imagine this scene from a horror film. A young man sits down to dinner to find that his mother has made asparagus again. The young man eats the dreaded asparagus stalks. Later, he finds out that instead of being digested, one of the stalks has taken up residence inside his body and is very much alive! Too horrifying to think about? What if the asparagus began to do wonderful things for the young man, such as giving him more energy than he ever dreamed possible? Lynn Margulis, a scientist, thinks that something similar may have happened to certain one-celled organisms that lived more than a billion years ago, giving rise to the kinds of cells that we are made of today.

According to Margulis's theory, about 1.2 billion years ago, some larger cells began eating smaller cells for dinner. Like the white blood cell on this page, these larger cells trapped the smaller cells with extensions of their cell body. But some of these smaller cells resisted being digested. In fact, they began to do very well in their new homes.

The larger cells also benefited from their new guests. The smaller cells released large amounts of energy from food taken in by the larger cells. Other kinds of small cells used the energy in sunlight to make enough food to feed themselves and the larger cell. The energy-producing structures of most cells, including yours, are thought to have descended from these smaller cells. In this chapter, you will learn more about cells and their structures.

What Do You Think?

In your ScienceLog, try to answer the following questions based on what you already know:

1. What is a cell, and where are cells found?

2. Why are there cells, and why are they so small?

Investigate!

What Are Plants Made Of?

As you have already learned, all living things are made of cells, including plants. What do some of these cells look like? Do this activity to find out.

Procedure

1. Wear goggles, protective gloves, and an apron throughout this experiment. Have your teacher place a drop of **Lugol's iodine solution** on your **plastic microscope slide**.
   Caution: Be careful not to get this solution on your skin or clothing. If this happens, rinse it off immediately, and call your teacher.

2. Tear off a small leaf near the tip of an **Elodea sprig.**

3. Using **tweezers,** place the whole leaf in the drop of iodine solution on the slide.

4. Place a **plastic coverslip** on top of the drop. Put one edge on the slide and then slowly lower the coverslip over the drop to prevent air bubbles.

5. Place the slide on your **microscope,** and try to find the cells. In your ScienceLog, draw a picture of what you see.

Analysis

6. What do *Elodea* cells look like? Are they all the same?

7. Do you think the cells in your body look like this? Explain your answer.

Organization of Life

tissue   multicellular
organ   population
organ system   community
organism   ecosystem
unicellular

What You'll Do

◆ Explain how life is organized, from a single cell to an ecosystem.
◆ Describe the difference between unicellular organisms and multicellular organisms.

Imagine that you are going on a trip to Mars. In your suitcase, you should pack everything you will need in order to survive. What would you pack? To start, you'd need food, oxygen, and water. And that's just the beginning. You would probably need a pretty big suitcase, wouldn't you? Actually, you have all of these items inside your body's cells. A cell is smaller than the period at the end of this sentence, yet a single cell has all the items necessary to carry out life's activities.

Every living thing has at least one cell. Many living things exist as a single cell, while others have trillions of cells. To get an idea of what a living thing with nearly 100 trillion cells looks like, just look in the mirror!

Cells: Starting Out Small

Most cells are too small to be seen without a microscope, but you might have one of the world's largest cells in your refrigerator. To find out what it is, see **Figure 1.** The first cell of a chicken is yellow with a tiny white dot in it, and it is surrounded by clear, jellylike fluid called egg white. The white dot divides over and over again to form a chick. The yellow yolk (from the first cell) and the egg white provide nutrients for the developing chick's cells. Like a chicken, you too began as a single egg cell. Look at **Figure 2** to see some of the early stages of your development.

Not all of your cells look or act the same. You have about 200 different kinds of cells, and each type is specialized to do a particular job. Some are bone cells, some are blood cells, and others are skin cells. When someone looks at all of those cells together, they see you.

Figure 1 *The first cell of a chicken is one of the largest cells in the world.*

Figure 2 *You began as a single cell. But after many cell divisions, you are now made of about 100 trillion cells.*

24 hours   40 hours   6 days   4 months

Tissues: Cells Working in Teams

When you look closely at your clothes, you can see that threads have been grouped together (woven) to make cloth that has a function. In the same way, cells are grouped together to make a tissue that has a function. A **tissue** is a group of cells that work together to perform a specific job in the body. The material around and between the cells is also part of the tissue. Some examples of tissues in your body are shown in **Figure 3**.

Organs: Teams Working Together

When two or more tissues work together to perform a specific job, the group of tissues is called an **organ.** Some examples of organs are your stomach, intestines, heart, lungs, and skin. That's right; even your skin is an organ because it contains different kinds of tissues. To get a closer look, see **Figure 4**.

Plants also have different kinds of tissues that work together. A leaf is a plant organ that contains tissue that traps light energy to make food. Other examples of plant organs are stems and roots.

Fat

Red blood cells

Muscle

Figure 3 *Blood, fat, and muscle cells are just a few of the many cells that make tissues in your body.*

Figure 4 *The skin is the body's largest organ. An average-sized person's skin has a mass of about 4.5 kg.*

BRAIN FOOD

The part of the skin, hair, and nails that you can see is dead tissue! Isn't it strange to think that we put so much effort into making sure our dead cells look nice?

Chemistry CONNECTION

On the surface of every person's cells are special proteins that act like identification cards. When a person gets an organ transplant, the cells of the new organ must have most of the same "ID cards" as the person's cells. If too many are different, the person's body will try to reject the new organ.

Organ Systems: A Great Combination

Organs work together in groups to perform particular jobs. These groups are called **organ systems.** Each system has a specific job to do in the body. For example, your digestive system's job is to break down food into very small particles so it can be used by all of your body's cells. Your nervous system's job is to transmit information back and forth between your brain and the other parts of your body. Organ systems in plants include leaf systems, root systems, and stem systems.

Your body has several organ systems. The digestive system is shown in **Figure 5.** Each organ in the digestive system has a job to do. A particular organ is able to do its job because of the different tissues within it.

The organs in an organ system depend on each other. If any part of the system fails, the whole system is affected. And failure of one organ system can affect other organ systems. Just think of what would happen if your digestive system stopped converting food to energy. None of the other organ systems would have energy to function.

Activity

A school system's job is to educate students at all levels. The different schools (elementary, middle, and high school) are like the different organs within an organ system. Groups of teachers at each school work together to teach a specific grade level. If each group of teachers can be thought of as tissue, what would that make each individual teacher? What other examples can you use to represent the parts of an organ system? Explain your answer.

TRY at HOME

Figure 5 *The digestive system is one of the 11 main organ systems. It is made of different organs, which in turn are made of different tissues.*

Organisms: Independent Living

Anything that can live on its own is called an **organism.** All organisms are made up of at least one cell. If a single cell is living on its own, it is called a **unicellular** organism. Most unicellular organisms are so small that you need to use a microscope to see them. Some different kinds of unicellular organisms are shown in **Figure 6.**

You are a **multicellular** organism. This means that you can exist only as a group of cells and that most of your cells can survive only if they remain a part of your body. When you fall down on a sidewalk and scrape your knee, the cells you leave behind on the sidewalk are not able to live on their own. **Figure 7** shows how your cells work together to make a multicellular organism.

Figure 6
Unicellular organisms come in a wide variety of shapes and sizes.

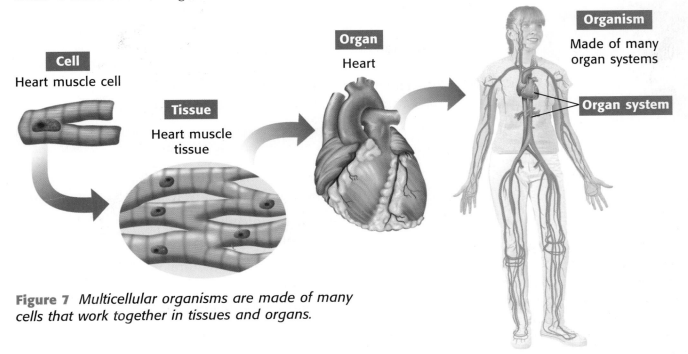

Cell
Heart muscle cell

Tissue
Heart muscle tissue

Organ
Heart

Organism
Made of many organ systems

Organ system

Figure 7 *Multicellular organisms are made of many cells that work together in tissues and organs.*

The Big Picture

Although unicellular organisms and multicellular organisms can live on their own, they usually do not live alone. Organisms interact with each other in many different ways.

Populations A group of organisms that are of the same kind and that live in the same area make up a **population.** All of the ladybird beetles living in the forest shown in **Figure 8** make up the ladybird beetle population of that forest. All of the red oak trees make up the forest's red oak population.

Figure 8 *A population is made up of all of the individuals of the same kind that live in the same area.*

Communities Two or more different populations living in the same area make up a **community.** The populations of foxes, oak trees, lizards, flowers, and other organisms in a forest are all part of a forest community, as shown in **Figure 9.** Your hometown is a community that includes all of the people, dogs, cats, and other organisms living there.

Ecosystems The community and all of the nonliving things that affect it, such as water, soil, rocks, temperature, and light, make up an **ecosystem.** Ecosystems on land are called *terrestrial* ecosystems, and they include forests, deserts, prairies, and your own backyard. Ecosystems in water are called *aquatic* ecosystems, and they include rivers, ponds, lakes, oceans, and even aquariums. The community in Figure 10 lives in a terrestrial ecosystem.

Figure 9 *The fox, flowers, and trees are all part of a forest community.*

REVIEW

1. Complete the following sentence: *Cells* are related to ? in the same way that ? are related to *organ systems.*

2. How do the cells of unicellular organisms differ from the cells of multicellular organisms?

3. **Applying Concepts** Use the picture of an aquarium below to answer the following questions:

    a. How many *different* kinds of organisms are visible?

    b. How many populations are visible?

    c. How many communities are visible?

What You'll Do

- State the parts of the cell theory.
- Explain why cells are so small.
- Calculate a cell's surface-to-volume ratio.
- List the advantages of being multicellular.
- Explain the difference between prokaryotic cells and eukaryotic cells.

The Discovery of Cells

Most cells are so tiny that they are not visible to the naked eye. So how did we find out that cells are the basic unit of all living things? What would make someone think that a rabbit or a tree or a person is made up of tiny parts that cannot be seen? Actually, the first person to see cells was not even looking for them.

Seeing the First Cells

In 1665, a British scientist named Robert Hooke was trying to find something interesting that he could show to other scientists at a meeting. Earlier, he had built a crude microscope that allowed him to look at very tiny objects. One day he decided to look at a thin slice of cork, a soft plant tissue found in the bark of trees like the ones shown in **Figure 10.** To his amazement, the cork looked like hundreds of little boxes, which he described as looking like a honeycomb. He named these tiny boxes *cells,* which means "little rooms" in Latin.

Although Hooke did not realize it, these boxes were actually the outer layers of the cork cells that were left behind after the cells died. Later, he looked at thin slices of plants and saw that they too were made of tiny cells. Some of them were even filled with "juice" (those were living cells). Hooke's microscope and drawings of cork cells are shown in **Figure 11.**

Hooke also used his microscope to look at feathers, fish scales, and the eyes of house flies, but he spent most of his time looking at plants and fungi. Since plant and fungal cells had walls that were easier to see, Hooke thought that cells were found only in those types of organisms and not in animals.

Figure 10 *Cork is a soft material found in trees. Cork cells were the first cells seen with a microscope.*

Figure 11 *This is the compound microscope that Hooke used to see the first cells. Hooke made a drawing of the cork cells that he saw.*

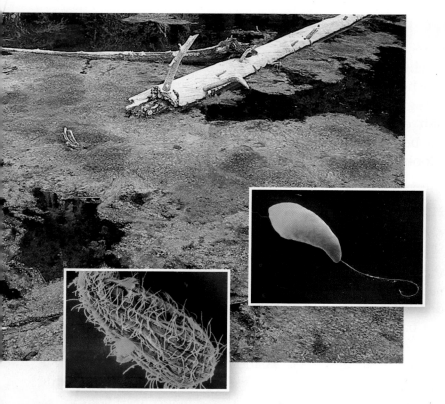

Seeing Cells in Other Life-Forms

In 1673, a few years after Hooke made his observations, a Dutch merchant named Anton van Leeuwenhoek (LAY vuhn hook) used one of his own handmade microscopes to get a closer look at pond scum, similar to that shown in **Figure 12.** He was amazed to see many small creatures swimming around in the slimy ooze; he named the creatures *animalcules,* which means "little animals."

Leeuwenhoek also looked at blood he took from different animals and tartar he scraped off their teeth and his own. He observed that blood cells in fish, birds, and frogs are oval-shaped, while those in humans and dogs are flatter. He was the first person to see bacteria, and he discovered that the yeasts used to make bread dough rise are actually unicellular organisms.

Figure 12 *Leeuwenhoek saw unicellular organisms similar to these, which are found in pond scum.*

The Cell Theory

After Hooke first saw the cork cells, almost two centuries passed before anyone realized that cells are present in *all* living things. Matthias Schleiden, a German scientist, looked at many slides of plant tissues and read about what other scientists had seen under the microscope. In 1838, he concluded that all plant parts are made of cells.

The next year, Theodor Schwann, a German scientist who studied animals, stated that all animal tissues are made of cells. Not long after that, Schwann wrote the first two parts of what is now known as the *cell theory:*

- **All organisms are composed of one or more cells.**

- **The cell is the basic unit of life in all living things.**

About 20 years later, in 1858, Rudolf Virchow, a German doctor, saw that cells could not develop from anything except other cells. He then wrote the third part of the cell theory:

- **All cells come from existing cells.**

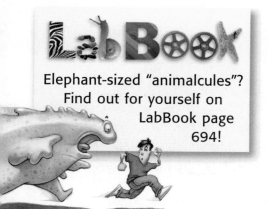

Elephant-sized "animalcules"? Find out for yourself on LabBook page 694!

Cell Similarities

Cells come in many different shapes and sizes and perform a wide variety of functions, but they all have the following things in common:

Cell Membrane All cells are surrounded by a **cell membrane.** This membrane acts as a barrier between the inside of the cell and the cell's environment. It also controls the passage of materials into and out of the cell. **Figure 13** shows the outside of a cell.

Figure 13 *The cell membrane holds the contents of the cell together.*

Hereditary Material Part of the cell theory states that all cells are made from existing cells. When new cells are made, they receive a copy of the hereditary material of the original cells. This material is *DNA* (deoxyribonucleic acid). It controls all of the activities of a cell and contains the information needed for that cell to make new cells.

Cytoplasm and Organelles All cells have chemicals and structures that enable the cell to live, grow, and reproduce. The structures are called **organelles.** Although all cells have organelles, they don't all have the same kind. Some organelles are surrounded by membranes, but others are not. The cell in **Figure 14** has membrane-covered organelles. The chemicals and structures of a cell are surrounded by fluid. This fluid and almost everything in it are collectively called the **cytoplasm.**

Small Size Almost all cells are too small to be seen with the naked eye. You are made up of 100 trillion cells, and it would take 50 of these cells just to cover up the dot on the letter *i*.

Figure 14 *This cell has many organelles. These organelles are surrounded by membranes.*

✓ Self-Check

Why do all cells need DNA? *(See page 782 to check your answer.)*

Giant Amoeba Eats New York City

This is not a headline you are likely to ever see. Why not? Amoebas consist of only a single cell. Most amoebas can't even grow large enough to be seen without a microscope. That's because as a cell gets larger, it needs more food and produces more waste. Therefore, more materials must be able to move into and out of the cell through the cell membrane.

Surface-to-Volume Ratio To keep up with these demands, a growing cell needs a larger surface area through which to exchange materials. As the cell's volume increases, its outer surface grows too. But the volume of a cell (the amount a cell will hold) increases at a faster rate than the area of its outer surface. If a cell gets too large, its surface will have too few openings to allow enough materials into and out of it.

To understand why the volume of a cell increases faster than its surface area, look at the table below. The *surface-to-volume ratio* is the area of a cell's outer surface in relation to its volume. The surface-to-volume ratio decreases as cell size increases. Increasing the number of cells but not their size maintains a high surface-to-volume ratio.

Surface-to-Volume Ratio

Each side of this cell is 1 unit long.	Each side of this cell is 2 units long.	The sides of each of these 8 cells are 1 unit long.
The surface area of one side is **1 square unit.** $(1 \times 1 = 1)$	The surface area of one side is **4 square units.** $(2 \times 2 = 4)$	The combined surface area of these 8 cells is **48 square units.** $(8 \times 6 \text{ square units} = 48)$
The surface area of the cell is **6 square units.** $(1 \times 1 \times 6 = 6)$	This cell has a surface area of **24 square units.** $(2 \times 2 \times 6 = 24)$	The combined volume of these cells is **8 cubic units.** $(8 \times 1 \text{ cubic unit} = 8)$
The volume of this cell is **1 cubic unit.** $(1 \times 1 \times 1 = 1)$	The volume of this larger cell is **8 cubic units.** $(2 \times 2 \times 2 = 8)$	The surface-to-volume ratio of the combined cells is 48:8, or **6:1.**
The surface-to-volume ratio of this cell is **6:1.**	The surface-to-volume ratio of this cell is 24:8, or **3:1.**	

The Benefits of Being Multicellular Do you know now why you are made up of many tiny cells instead of one large cell? A single cell as big as you are would have an incredibly small surface-to-volume ratio. The cell could not survive because its outer surface would be too small to allow in the materials it would need. Multicellular organisms grow by producing more small cells, not larger cells. The elephant in **Figure 15** has cells that are the same size as yours.

Many Kinds of Cells In addition to being able to grow larger, multicellular organisms are able to do lots of other things because they are made up of different kinds of cells. Just as there are teachers who are specialized to teach and mechanics who are specialized to work on cars, different cells are specialized to perform different jobs. A single cell cannot do all the things that many different cells can do. Having many different cells that are specialized for specific jobs allows multicellular organisms to perform more functions than unicellular organisms.

The different kinds of cells can form tissues and organs with different functions. People have specialized cells, such as muscle cells, eye cells, and brain cells, so they can walk, run, watch a movie, think, and do many other activities. If you enjoy doing many different things, be glad you are not a single cell.

Figure 15 *An elephant is larger than a human because it has more cells, not larger cells.*

MATH BREAK

Surface-to-Volume Ratio

The shape of a cell can affect its surface-to-volume ratio. Examine the cells below, and answer the questions that follow:

1. What is the surface area of Cell A? of Cell B?
2. What is the volume of Cell A? of Cell B?
3. Which of the two cells pictured here has the greater surface-to-volume ratio?

A Pet *Paramecium*
Imagine that you have a pet *Paramecium*, a type of unicellular organism. In order to properly care for your pet, you have to figure out how much you need to feed it. The dimensions of your *Paramecium* are roughly 125 μm × 50 μm × 20 μm. If seven food molecules can enter through each square micrometer of surface every minute, how many molecules can it eat in 1 minute? If your pet needs one food molecule per cubic micrometer of volume every minute to survive, how much would you have to feed it every minute?

Self-Check

1. As a cell grows larger, what happens to its surface-to-volume ratio?

2. What does a eukaryotic cell have that a prokaryotic cell does not?

(See page 782 to check your answer.)

Do Bacteria Taste Good?

If they're the kind found in yogurt, they taste great! Using a **cotton swab,** put a small dot of **yogurt** on a **plastic microscope slide.** Add a drop of **water,** and use the cotton swab to stir. Add a **plastic coverslip,** and examine the slide using a **microscope.** Draw what you see.

The masses of rod-shaped bacteria feed on the sugar in milk (lactose) and convert it into lactic acid. Lactic acid causes milk to thicken, which makes yogurt!

Two Types of Cells

The many different kinds of cells that exist can be divided into two groups. As you have already learned, all cells have DNA. In one group, cells have a **nucleus,** which is a membrane-covered organelle that holds the cells' DNA. In the other group, the cells' DNA is not contained in a nucleus. Cells that do not have a nucleus are **prokaryotic,** and cells that have a nucleus are **eukaryotic.**

Prokaryotic Cells Prokaryotic cells are also called **bacteria.** They are the world's smallest cells, and they do not have a nucleus. A prokaryotic cell's DNA is one long, circular molecule shaped sort of like a rubber band.

Bacteria do not have any membrane-covered organelles, but they do have tiny, round organelles called *ribosomes.* These organelles work like little factories to make proteins.

Most bacteria are covered by a hard cell wall outside a softer cell membrane. Think of the membrane pressing against the wall as an inflated balloon pressing against the inside of a glass jar. But unlike the balloon and jar, the membrane and the wall allow food and waste molecules to pass through. **Figure 16** shows a generalized view of a prokaryotic cell.

Bacteria were probably the first type of cells on Earth. The oldest fossils ever found are of prokaryotic cells. Scientists have estimated these fossils to be 3.5 billion years old.

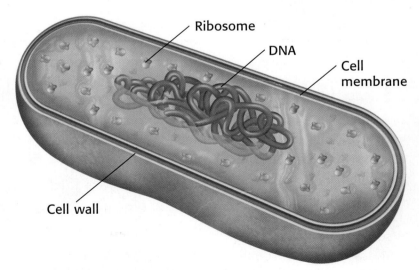

Figure 16 *Prokaryotic cells do not have a nucleus or any other membrane-covered organelles. The circular DNA is bunched up in the cytoplasm.*

Eukaryotic Cells Eukaryotic cells are more complex than prokaryotic cells. Although most eukaryotic cells are about 10 times larger than prokaryotic cells, they still have a high enough surface-to-volume ratio to survive. Fossil evidence suggests that eukaryotic cells first appeared about 2 billion years ago. All living things that are not bacteria are made of one or more eukaryotic cells. This includes plants, animals, fungi, and protists.

Eukaryotic cells have a nucleus and many other membrane-covered organelles. An advantage of having the cell divided into compartments is that it allows many different chemical processes to occur at the same time. A generalized eukaryotic cell is shown in **Figure 17.**

There is more DNA in eukaryotic cells than in prokaryotic cells, and it is stored in the nucleus. Instead of being circular, the DNA molecules in eukaryotic cells are linear.

All eukaryotic cells have a cell membrane, and some of them have a cell wall. Those that have cell walls are found in plants, fungi, and some unicellular organisms. The tables below summarize the differences between eukaryotic and prokaryotic cells.

Nucleus

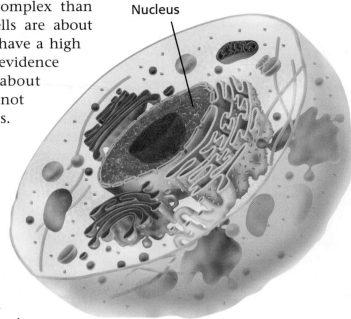

Figure 17 *Eukaryotic cells contain a nucleus and many other organelles.*

Prokaryotic Cells	Eukaryotic Cells
No nucleus	Nucleus
No membrane-covered organelles	Membrane-covered organelles
Circular DNA	Linear DNA
Bacteria	All other cells

Science CONNECTION

A new way to cure sick cells? See page 80.

REVIEW

1. What are the three parts of the cell theory?

2. What do all cells have in common?

3. What are two advantages of being multicellular?

4. If a unicellular organism has a cell wall, ribosomes, and circular DNA, is it eukaryotic or prokaryotic?

5. **Applying Concepts** Which has the greater surface-to-volume ratio, a tennis ball or a basketball? Explain your answer. What could be done to increase the surface-to-volume ratio of both?

internet connect

*sci*LINKS
NSTA

TOPIC: Prokaryotic Cells
GO TO: www.scilinks.org
*sci*LINKS NUMBER: HSTL065

Eukaryotic Cells: The Inside Story

What You'll Do

◆ Explain the function of each part of a eukaryotic cell.

◆ Describe the differences between animal cells and plant cells.

For a long time after the discovery of cells, scientists did not really know what cells were made of. Cells are so small that the details of their structure could not be seen until better methods of magnifying and staining were developed. We now know that cells are very complex, especially eukaryotic cells. Everything, from the structures covering the cells to the organelles inside them, performs a task that helps to keep the cells alive.

Holding It All Together

All cells have outer coverings that separate what is inside the cell from what is outside. One kind of covering, called the cell membrane, surrounds all cells. Some cells have an additional layer outside the cell membrane called the cell wall.

Cell Membrane All cells are covered by a cell membrane. The job of the cell membrane is to keep the cytoplasm inside, to allow nutrients in and waste products out, and to interact with things outside the cell. In **Figure 18,** you can see a close-up view of the cell membrane of a cell that has had its top half cut away.

Phospholipids

Figure 18 *A cell membrane surrounds all cells. Phospholipid molecules form the cell membrane.*

Cell Wall The cells of plants and algae have a hard cell wall made of cellulose. The **cell wall** provides strength and support to the cell membrane. When too much water enters or leaves a plant cell, the cell wall can prevent the membrane from tearing. The strength of billions of cell walls in plants enables a tree to stand tall and its limbs to defy gravity. When you are looking at dried hay, sticks, and wooden boards, you are seeing the cell walls of dead plant cells. The cells of fungi, such as mushrooms, toadstools, mold, and yeasts, have cell walls made of a chemical similar to that found in the hard covering of insects. **Figure 19** shows a cross section of a generalized plant cell and a close-up view of the cell wall.

Cell wall

Cell membrane

Figure 19 *The cell wall surrounds the cell membrane. In plant cells, the cell wall is made of cellulose fibers.*

The Cell's Library

The largest and most visible organelle in a eukaryotic cell is the nucleus. The word *nucleus* means "kernel" or "nut" (maybe it does look sort of like a nut inside a piece of candy). As you can see in **Figure 20,** the nucleus is covered by a membrane through which materials can pass.

The nucleus has often been called the control center of the cell. As you know, it stores the DNA that has information on how to make all of the cell's proteins. Almost every chemical reaction that is important to the cell's life involves some kind of protein. Sometimes a dark spot can be seen inside the nucleus. This spot is called a *nucleolus,* and it looks like a small nucleus inside the big nucleus. The nucleolus stores the materials that will be used later to make ribosomes in the cytoplasm.

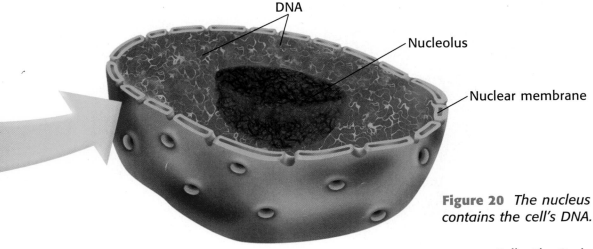

DNA

Nucleolus

Nuclear membrane

Figure 20 *The nucleus contains the cell's DNA.*

Protein Factories

Proteins, the building blocks of all cells, are made up of chemicals known as *amino acids*. These amino acids are hooked together to make proteins at very small organelles called **ribosomes.** Ribosomes are the smallest but most abundant organelles. *All* cells have ribosomes because all cells need protein to live. Unlike most other organelles, ribosomes are not covered with a membrane.

Self-Check

What is the difference between a cell wall and a cell membrane? *(See page 782 to check your answer.)*

The Cell's Delivery System

Eukaryotic cells have an organelle called the endoplasmic (EN doh PLAZ mik) reticulum (ri TIK yuh luhm), which is shown in **Figure 21.** The **endoplasmic reticulum,** or ER, is a membrane-covered compartment that makes lipids and other materials for use inside and outside the cell. It is also the organelle that breaks down drugs and certain other chemicals that could damage the cell. The ER is the internal delivery system of a cell. Substances in the ER can move from one place to another through its many tubular connections, sort of like cars moving through tunnels.

The ER looks like flattened sacks stacked side by side or a cloth folded back and forth. Some ER may be covered with ribosomes that make its surface look rough. The proteins made at those ribosomes pass into the ER. Later the proteins are released from the ER for use elsewhere.

Ribosome

Endoplasmic reticulum

Mitochondria

Endoplasmic reticulum

Figure 21 *The ER is made up of flattened compartments and tubes. Ribosomes are attached to some of the ER.*

The Cell's Power Plants

In today's world, we use many sources of energy, such as oil, gas, and nuclear power. We need this energy to heat our homes, fuel our cars, and cook our food. Cells also need energy to function. Where do they get it?

Mitochondria Inside all cells, food molecules are "burned" (broken down) to release energy. The energy is transferred to a special molecule that the cell uses to get work done. As you learned earlier, this molecule is called ATP.

ATP can be made at several locations in eukaryotic cells, but most of it is produced at bean-shaped organelles called **mitochondria** (MIET oh KAHN dree uh), shown in **Figure 22.** These organelles are surrounded by two membranes. The inner membrane, which has many folds in it, is where most of the ATP is made.

Mitochondria can work only if they have oxygen. The reason you breathe air is to make sure your mitochondria have the oxygen they need to make ATP. Highly active cells, such as those in the heart and liver, may have thousands of mitochondria, while other cells may have only a few.

Outer membrane

Inner membrane

Figure 22 *Mitochondria have two membranes. The inner membrane has many folds.*

Chloroplast

Figure 23 *Chloroplasts, found in plant cells, also have two membranes. The inner membrane forms stacks of flattened sacs.*

Chloroplasts Plants and algae have an additional kind of energy-converting organelle, called a **chloroplast,** which is shown in **Figure 23.** Chloroplasts have two membranes and structures that look like stacks of coins. These are flattened, membrane-covered sacs that contain an important chemical called chlorophyll. Chlorophyll is what makes chloroplasts green. The energy of sunlight is trapped by chlorophyll and used to make sugar. This process is called *photosynthesis.* The sugar that is produced is used by mitochondria to make ATP. You will learn more about photosynthesis in a later chapter.

Outer membrane

Inner membrane

DNA of large cell

Small prokaryotic cell

Large prokaryotic cell

Mitochondria

Small prokaryotic cell that can photosynthesize

DNA enclosed in nucleus

Chloroplast

Figure 24 *Mitochondria and chloroplasts may have originated from energy-producing ancestors that were engulfed by larger cells.*

Where Did They Come From? Many scientists believe that mitochondria and chloroplasts originated as prokaryotic cells that were "eaten" by larger cells. Instead of being digested, the bacteria survived. **Figure 24** shows how bacteria might have become the ancestors of mitochondria and chloroplasts.

What evidence do scientists have that this theory is correct? The first piece of evidence is that mitochondria and chloroplasts are about the same size as bacteria. The second is that both are surrounded by *two membranes.* If the theory is correct, the outer membrane was created when the bacteria were engulfed by the larger cells. Other evidence supports this theory. Mitochondria and chloroplasts have the same kind of ribosomes and circular DNA as bacteria. They also divide like bacteria.

The Cell's Packaging Center

When proteins and other materials need to be processed and shipped out of a eukaryotic cell, the job goes to an organelle called the **Golgi complex.** This structure is named after Camillo Golgi, the Italian scientist who first identified it.

The Golgi complex looks like the ER, but it is located closer to the cell membrane. The Golgi complex of a cell is shown in **Figure 25.** Lipids and proteins from the ER are delivered to the Golgi complex, where they are modified for different functions. The final products are enclosed in a piece of the Golgi complex's membrane that pinches off to form a small compartment. This small compartment transports its contents to other parts of the cell or outside of the cell.

Golgi complex

Figure 25 *The Golgi complex processes, packages, and transports materials sent to it from the ER.*

The Cell's Storage Centers

All eukaryotic cells have membrane-covered compartments called **vesicles.** Some of them form when part of the membrane pinches off the ER or Golgi complex. Others are formed when part of the cell membrane surrounds an object outside the cell. This is how white blood cells engulf other cells in your body, as shown in **Figure 26.**

Vacuoles Most plant cells have a very large membrane-covered chamber called a **vacuole,** as shown in **Figure 27.** Vacuoles store water and other liquids. Vacuoles that are full of water help support the cell. Some plants wilt when their cell vacuoles lose water. If you want crispy lettuce for a salad, all you need to do is fill up the vacuoles by leaving the lettuce in water overnight. Have you ever wondered what makes roses red and violets blue? It is a colorful liquid stored inside vacuoles. Vacuoles also contain the juices you associate with oranges and other fruits.

Some unicellular organisms that live in freshwater environments have a problem with too much water entering the cell. They have a special structure called a contractile vacuole that can squeeze excess water out of the cell. It works in much the same way that a pump removes water from inside a boat.

Figure 26 *The smaller cell is a yeast cell that is being engulfed by a white blood cell.*

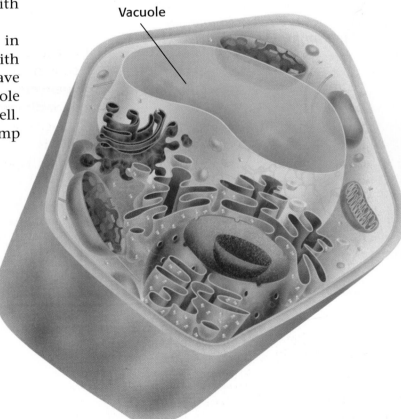

Vacuole

Figure 27 *This plant cell's vacuole is the large structure in the middle of the cell shown in blue. Vacuoles are usually the largest organelles in a plant cell.*

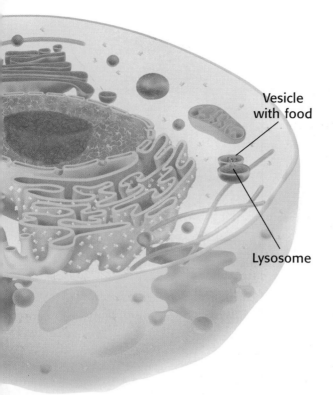

Vesicle
with food

Lysosome

Figure 28 *This lysosome is pouring enzymes into a vesicle that contains food particles. The digested food molecules are released into the cytoplasm for use by the cell.*

Packages of Destruction

What causes most of the cells of a caterpillar to dissolve into ooze inside a cocoon? What causes the tail of a tadpole to shrink and then disappear? Lysosomes, that's what!

Lysosomes are special vesicles in animal cells that contain enzymes. When a cell engulfs a particle and encloses it in a vesicle, lysosomes bump into these vesicles and pour enzymes into them. This is illustrated in **Figure 28.** The particles in the vesicles are digested by the enzymes.

Lysosomes destroy worn-out or damaged organelles. They also get rid of waste materials and protect the cell from foreign invaders.

Sometimes lysosome membranes break, and the enzymes spill into the cytoplasm, killing the cell. This is what must happen for a tadpole to become a frog. Lysosomes cause the cells in a tadpole's tail to die and dissolve as the tadpole becomes a frog. Lysosomes played a similar role in your development! Before you were born, lysosomes caused the destruction of cells that formed the webbing between your fingers. Lysosome destruction of cells may also be one of the factors that contribute to the aging process in humans.

Organelles and Their Functions	
Nucleus contains the cell's DNA and is the control center of the cell	**Chloroplasts** make food using the energy of sunlight
Ribosomes the site where amino acids are hooked together to make proteins	**Golgi complex** processes and transports materials out of the cell
Endoplasmic reticulum makes lipids, breaks down drugs and other substances, packages up proteins for release from the cell	**Vacuole** stores water and other materials
Mitochondria break down food molecules to make ATP	**Lysosomes** digest food particles, wastes, cell parts, and foreign invaders

Plant or Animal?

How can you tell the difference between a plant cell and an animal cell? They both have a cell membrane, and they both have nuclei, ribosomes, mitochondria, endoplasmic reticula, Golgi complexes, and lysosomes. But plant cells have things that animal cells do not have: a cell wall, chloroplasts, and a large vacuole. You can see the differences between plant and animal cells in **Figure 29.**

Found in Plant and Animal Cells	Found Only in Plant Cells

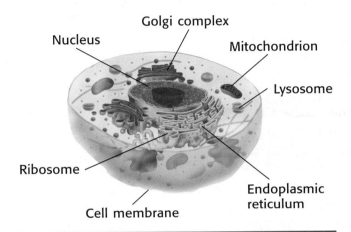

Golgi complex
Nucleus
Mitochondrion
Lysosome
Ribosome
Cell membrane
Endoplasmic reticulum

Chloroplast
Large vacuole
Cell wall

Figure 29 *Animal and plant cells have some structures in common, but they also have some that are unique.*

REVIEW

1. How does the nucleus control the cell's activities?

2. Which of the following would not be found in an animal cell: mitochondria, cell wall, chloroplast, ribosome, endoplasmic reticulum, Golgi complex, large vacuole, DNA, chlorophyll?

3. Use the following words in a sentence: oxygen, ATP, breathing, and mitochondria.

4. **Applying Concepts** You have the job of giving new names to different things in a city. The new names have to be parts of a eukaryotic cell. Write down some things you would see in a city. Assign the name of a cell part that is most appropriate to their function. Explain your choices.

internetconnect

SC*L*INKS.
NSTA

TOPIC: Eukaryotic Cells
GO TO: www.scilinks.org
sciLINKS NUMBER: HSTL070

Chapter Highlights

Vocabulary

tissue (*p. 57*)

organ (*p. 57*)

organ system (*p. 58*)

organism (*p. 59*)

unicellular (*p. 59*)

multicellular (*p. 59*)

population (*p. 59*)

community (*p. 60*)

ecosystem (*p. 60*)

Section Notes

- The cell is the smallest unit of life on Earth. Organisms can be made up of one or more cells.

- In multicellular organisms, groups of cells can work together to form tissue. Organs are formed from different tissues and work together with other organs in organ systems.

- The same kind of organisms living together in the same place at the same time make up a population. Different populations living together in the same area make up a community. An ecosystem includes the community and an area's nonliving parts, such as the water and soil.

Vocabulary

cell membrane (*p. 63*)

organelles (*p. 63*)

cytoplasm (*p. 63*)

nucleus (*p. 66*)

prokaryotic (*p. 66*)

eukaryotic (*p. 66*)

bacteria (*p. 66*)

Section Notes

- The cell theory states that all organisms are made of cells, the cell is the basic unit of life, and all cells come from other cells.

- All cells have a cell membrane, DNA, cytoplasm, and organelles. Most cells are too small to be seen with the naked eye.

☑ Skills Check

Math Concepts

SURFACE-TO-VOLUME RATIO You can determine the surface-to-volume ratio of a cell or other object by dividing surface area by the volume. To determine the surface-to-volume ratio of the rectangle at left, you must first determine the surface area. Surface area is the total area of all the sides. This rectangle has two sides with an area of 6 cm × 3 cm, two sides with an area of 3 cm × 2 cm, and two sides with an area of 6 cm × 2 cm.

6 cm

2 cm

3 cm

surface area = 2(6 cm × 3 cm) + 2(3 cm × 2 cm) + 2(6 cm × 2 cm) = 72 cm²

Next you need to find the volume. The volume is determined by multiplying the length of the three sides.

volume = 6 cm × 3 cm × 2 cm = 36 cm³

To find surface-to-volume ratio, you divide the surface area by the volume:

$$\frac{72}{36} = 2$$

So the surface-to-volume ratio of this rectangle is 2:1.

SECTION 2

- Materials that cells need to take in or release must pass through the cell membrane.

- The surface-to-volume ratio is a comparison of the cell's outer surface to the cell's volume. A cell's surface-to-volume ratio decreases as the cell grows.

  - Eukaryotes have linear DNA enclosed in a nucleus and membrane-covered organelles. Prokaryotic cells have circular DNA and organelles that are not covered by membranes.

Labs
Elephant-Sized Amoebas? (p. 694)

SECTION 3

Vocabulary
cell wall (p. 69)

ribosome (p. 70)

endoplasmic reticulum (p. 70)

mitochondria (p. 71)

chloroplast (p. 71)

Golgi complex (p. 72)

vesicle (p. 73)

vacuole (p. 73)

lysosome (p. 74)

Section Notes

- All cells have a cell membrane that surrounds the contents of the cell. Some cells have a cell wall outside their membrane.

- The nucleus is the control center of the eukaryotic cell. It contains the cell's DNA.

- Ribosomes are the sites where amino acids are strung together to form proteins. Ribosomes are not covered by a membrane.

- The endoplasmic reticulum (ER) and the Golgi complex are membrane-covered compartments in which materials are made and processed before they are transported to other parts of the cell or out of the cell.

- Mitochondria and chloroplasts are energy-producing organelles.

- Vesicles and vacuoles are membrane-covered compartments that store material. Vacuoles are found in plant cells. Lysosomes are vesicles found in animal cells.

Labs
Cells Alive! (p. 696)
Name That Part! (p. 697)

🗗 internet connect

GO TO: go.hrw.com

Visit the **HRW** Web site for a variety of learning tools related to this chapter. Just type in the keyword:

KEYWORD: HSTCEL

GO TO: www.scilinks.org

Visit the **National Science Teachers Association** on-line Web site for Internet resources related to this chapter. Just type in the *sci*LINKS number for more information about the topic:

TOPIC: Organization of Life	***sci*LINKS NUMBER:** HSTL055
TOPIC: Populations, Communities, and Ecosystems	***sci*LINKS NUMBER:** HSTL060
TOPIC: Prokaryotic Cells	***sci*LINKS NUMBER:** HSTL065
TOPIC: Eukaryotic Cells	***sci*LINKS NUMBER:** HSTL070

Chapter Review

To complete the following sentences, choose the correct term from each pair of terms listed below:

1. The cell wall of plant cells is made of ___?___. (*lipids* or *cellulose*)

2. Having membrane-covered organelles is a characteristic of ___?___ cells. (*prokaryotic* or *eukaryotic*)

3. The information for how to make proteins is located in the ___?___. (*Golgi complex* or *nucleus*)

4. The two organelles that can generate ATP in a plant cell are ___?___ and ___?___. (*chloroplasts/ER* or *mitochondria/ chloroplasts*)

5. Vesicles that will transport materials out of the cell are formed at the ___?___. (*Golgi complex* or *cell membrane*)

UNDERSTANDING CONCEPTS

Multiple Choice

6. Which of the following is *not* found in animal cells?
   a. cell wall
   b. cell membrane
   c. lysosomes
   d. vesicle

7. Different ___?___ work together in an organ.
   a. organ systems
   b. tissues
   c. organisms
   d. prokaryotes

8. Which of the following refers to all of the organisms in a particular area?
   a. population
   b. ecosystem
   c. community
   d. organelles

9. The scientist who said that all cells come from cells was named
   a. Virchow.
   b. Schleiden.
   c. Hooke.
   d. Schwann.

10. Which of the following are *not* covered by a membrane?
    a. Golgi complex
    b. mitochondria
    c. ribosomes
    d. none of the above

11. Which of the following contain enzymes that can break down particles in vesicles?
    a. mitochondria
    b. endoplasmic reticulum
    c. lysosomes
    d. none of the above

Short Answer

12. Why are most cells so small?

13. What five characteristics of mitochondria suggest that they may have originated as bacteria?

14. In your own words, list the three parts of the cell theory.

Concept Mapping

15. Use the following terms to create a concept map: ecosystem, cells, organisms, Golgi complex, organ systems, community, organs, endoplasmic reticulum, nucleus, population, tissues.

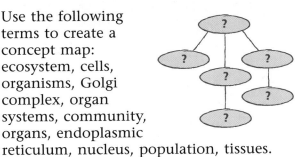

CRITICAL THINKING AND PROBLEM SOLVING

Write one or two sentences to answer the following questions:

16. Explain how the nucleus can control what happens in a lysosome.

17. Even though cellulose is not made at ribosomes, explain how ribosomes in a plant cell are important to the formation of a cell wall.

MATH IN SCIENCE

18. Assume that three food molecules per cubic unit of volume per minute is required for the cell below to survive. If one molecule can enter through each square unit of surface per minute, this cell is
   a. too big and would starve.
   b. too small and would starve.
   c. at a size that would allow it to survive.

3

3   2

INTERPRETING GRAPHICS

Look at the cell diagrams below, and answer the questions that follow:

Cell A

19

Cell B

21

19. Name the organelle labeled "19" in Cell A.

20. Is Cell A a bacterial cell, a plant cell, or an animal cell? Explain your answer.

21. What is the name and function of the organelle labeled "21" in Cell B?

22. Is Cell B a prokaryotic cell or a eukaryotic cell? Explain your answer.

NOW What Do You Think?

Take a minute to review your answers to the ScienceLog questions on page 55. Have your answers changed? If necessary, revise your answers based on what you have learned since you began this chapter.

LIFE SCIENCE • PHYSICAL SCIENCE

Battling Cancer with Pigs' Blood and Laser Light

What do you get when you cross pigs' blood and laser beams? Would you believe a treatment for cancer? Medical researchers have developed an effective new cancer treatment called *photodynamic therapy,* or PDT. It combines high-energy laser beams with a light-sensitive drug derived from pigs' blood to combat the deadly disease.

▲ *Blood from pigs provides substances used to help treat cancer.*

Pigs' Blood to the Rescue

The first step in PDT involves a light-sensitive substance called *porphyrin.* Porphyrins are natural chemicals found in red blood cells that bind to lipoproteins, which carry cholesterol in our blood. All cells use lipoproteins in their cell membranes. But cells that divide quickly, like cancer cells, make membranes faster than normal cells. Since they use more lipoproteins, they also accumulate more porphyrins.

Scientists have developed a synthetic porphyrin, called Photofrin®, made from natural porphyrins found in pigs' blood. Photofrin can absorb energy from light. When Photofrin is injected into a patient's bloodstream, it acts the same way natural porphyrins do—it becomes part of the cell membranes formed by cancer cells. A short time later, the patient visits a surgeon's office for step two of PDT, zapping the diseased tissue with a laser beam.

Hitting the Target

A surgeon threads a long, thin laser-tipped tube into the cancerous area where the Photofrin has accumulated. When the laser beam hits the cancerous tissue, Photofrin absorbs the light energy. Then, in a process similar to photosynthesis, Photofrin releases oxygen. The type of oxygen released damages the proteins, lipids, nucleic acids, and other components of cancer cells. This damage kills off cancer cells in the treated area but doesn't kill healthy cells. Photofrin is more sensitive to certain wavelengths of light than are natural porphyrins. And the intense beam of laser light can be precisely focused on the cancerous tissue without affecting nearby healthy tissue.

An Alternative?

PDT is an important medical development because it kills cancer cells without many of the harmful side effects caused by other cancer therapies, such as chemotherapy. However, PDT does have some side effects. Until the drug wears off, in about 30 days, the patient is susceptible to severe sunburn. Researchers are working to develop a second-generation drug, called BPD (benzoporphyrin derivative), that will have fewer side effects and respond to different wavelengths of lasers. BPD is also being tested for use in certain eye diseases and as a treatment for psoriasis.

Find Out for Yourself

▶ Do some research to find out why scientists used pigs' blood to create Photofrin.

The Scrape of the Future

What did you do the last time you scraped your knee? You probably put a bandage on it, and before you realized it your knee was as good as new. Bandages serve as barriers that help prevent infection and further injury. But what if there were such a thing as a living bandage that actually helped your body heal? It sounds like science fiction, but it's not!

▲ *Dr. Daniel Smith holds the GEBB that he designed.*

The Main Factor

An injury to the skin, such as a scraped knee, triggers skin cells to produce and release a steady stream of proteins that heal the injury. These naturally occurring proteins are called *human growth factors,* or just *growth factors.* Growth factors specialize in rebuilding the body. Some reconstruct connective tissue that provides structure for new skin, some help rebuild blood vessels in a wounded area, and still others stimulate the body's immune system. Thanks to growth factors, scraped skin usually heals in just a few days.

Help from a Living Bandage

Unfortunately, healing isn't always an easy, natural process. Someone with a weakened immune system may be unable to produce enough growth factors to heal a wound properly. For example, someone with severe burns may have lost the ability in the burned area to produce the proteins necessary to rebuild healthy tissues. In these cases, using manufactured human growth factors can greatly assist the healing process.

Recent advances in bio-engineering can help people whose immune system prevents them from healing naturally. The Genetically Engineered Biological Bandage (GEBB) is a special bandage that is actually a bag of living skin cells taken from donors. The cells' DNA is manipulated to produce human growth factors. The GEBB is about 1 cm thick and consists of three layers: a thin gauze layer; a thin, permeable membrane; and a dome-shaped silicone bag containing the growth factors. The bandage is applied to the wound just as a normal bandage is, with the gauze layer closest to the injury. The growth factors leave the silicone bag through the membrane and pass through the gauze into the wound. There they act on the wound just as the body's own growth factors would.

Time-Release Formula

The GEBB also helps heal wounds more quickly. It maximizes the effectiveness of growth hormones by releasing them at a constant rate over 3 to 5 days.

Because the GEBB imitates the body's own healing processes, other versions of the living bandage will likely be used in the future to treat a variety of wounds and skin conditions, such as severe acne.

Think About It

▶ Can you think of other advances in medical technology, such as eyeglasses or a hearing aid, that mimic or enhance what the human body does naturally?

4 The Cell in Action

Happy 140th Birthday!

What If . . . ?

How long would you like to live? What if you could live to be 120 years old? or 150 and beyond? Since ancient times, people have searched in vain for a magical fountain or potion that could give them eternal youth. No one has yet found the secret of immortality, but scientists have recently made a startling discovery that may help extend people's lives.

In January of 1998, researchers at the University of Texas reported that they had found an enzyme in the body that acts like a "cellular fountain of youth." In the laboratory, the enzyme enables human cells to stay young and multiply long past the time when cells would normally stop dividing and die. Researchers hope that the enzyme can someday be used to understand and treat certain cancers and other incurable diseases. Although the so-called immortalizing enzyme won't help people live forever, it may help them live longer, healthier lives.

Every living thing is made of cells. In this chapter you will learn how cells grow and how they make more cells. You will also learn how cells transport materials and obtain the energy they need to survive.

What Do You Think?

In your ScienceLog, try to answer the following questions based on what you already know:

1. How do water, food, and wastes get into and out of a cell?

2. How do cells use food molecules?

3. How does one cell produce many cells?

Cells in Action

Yeast are unicellular fungi that are frequently used in cooking. Yeast cells break down sugar molecules to release energy. In the process, a gas called carbon dioxide (CO_2) is produced. CO_2 bubbles make bread dough rise. The amount of CO_2 produced depends on how much sugar is broken down.

Procedure

1. From your teacher, get a **small plastic cup** that contains **10 mL of a yeast-and-water mixture.**

2. Next fill a **small test tube** with **4 mL of a sugar solution** that has also been prepared by your teacher. Pour it into the cup containing the yeast-and-water mixture. Thoroughly mix the two liquids with a **stirring rod.**

3. Pour the contents of the small plastic cup back into the small test tube.

4. Place a slightly **larger test tube** over the small test tube. The top of the small test tube should touch the bottom of the large test tube.

5. Quickly turn the tubes over. As shown below, most of the yeast-and-water mixture should still be in the small test tube. Some will be in the larger test tube. Use a **ruler** to measure the height of the fluid in the large test tube.

6. Place the test tubes in a **test-tube stand,** and do not disturb them. After 20 minutes, measure the height of the liquid in the outer test tube again.

Analysis

7. What is the difference between the first height measurement and the second?

8. What do you think caused the change in the height of the fluid?

Terms to Learn

diffusion   active transport
osmosis   endocytosis
passive transport exocytosis

What You'll Do

◆ Explain the process of diffusion.
◆ Describe how osmosis occurs.
◆ Compare passive transport with active transport.
◆ Explain how large particles get into and out of cells.

Exchange with the Environment

What would happen to a factory if its power were shut off or its supply of raw materials never arrived? What if it couldn't get rid of its garbage? The factory would stop functioning. Like a factory, a cell must be able to obtain energy and raw materials and get rid of wastes.

The exchange of materials between a cell and its environment takes place at the cell's membrane. To understand how materials move into and out of the cell, you need to know about diffusion, a process that affects the movement of particles.

What Is Diffusion?

What happens if you pour dye into a container of solid gelatin? At first, it is easy to see where the gelatin ends and the dye begins. But over time the line between the two layers will become blurry, as shown in **Figure 1.** Why? Dye and gelatin, like all matter, are made up of tiny particles. The particles are always moving and colliding with each other. The mixing of the different particles causes the layers to blur. This occurs whether matter is in the form of a gas, liquid, or solid.

QuickLab

Bead Diffusion

Arrange three groups of **colored beads** on the bottom of a **plastic bowl.** Each group should have five beads of the same color. Stretch some **clear plastic wrap** tightly over the top of the bowl. Gently shake the bowl for 10 seconds while watching the beads. How is the scattering of the beads like the diffusion of particles? How is it different from the diffusion of particles?

Figure 1 *The particles of the dye and the gelatin slowly begin to mix because of diffusion.*

Particles naturally travel from areas where they are crowded to areas where they are less crowded. **Diffusion** is the movement of particles from an area where their concentration is high to an area where their concentration is low. This movement can occur across cell membranes or outside of cells. Cells do not need to use any energy for diffusion of particles to occur.

Diffusion of Water All organisms need water to live. The cells of living organisms are surrounded by and filled with fluids that are made mostly of water. The diffusion of water through the cell membrane is so important to life processes that it has been given a special name—**osmosis.**

Water, like all matter, is made up of small particles. Pure water has the highest possible concentration of water particles. To lower this concentration, you simply mix water with something else, such as food coloring, sugar, or salt. **Figure 2** shows what happens when osmosis occurs between two different concentrations of water.

The Cell and Osmosis As you have learned, water particles will move from areas of high concentration to areas of lower concentration. This concept is especially important when you look at it in relation to your cells.

For example, **Figure 3** shows the effects of different concentrations of water on a red blood cell. As you can see, osmosis takes place in different directions depending on the concentration of water surrounding the cell. Fortunately for you, your red blood cells are normally surrounded by blood plasma, which is made up of water, salts, sugars, and other particles in the same concentration as they exist inside the red blood cells.

The cells of plants also take in and release water by osmosis. This is why a wilted plant or even a wilted stalk of celery will become firm again if given water.

✓ Self-Check

What would happen to a grape if you placed it in a dish of pure water? in water mixed with a large amount of sugar? (*See page 782 to check your answer.*)

Figure 2 *This container is divided by a barrier. Particles of water are small enough to pass through the barrier, but the particles of food coloring are not.*

1 The side of the container with pure water has the higher concentration of water.

2 During osmosis, water particles move to where they are less concentrated.

This cell has a normal shape because the concentration of water in the cell is the same as the concentration outside the cell.

This cell is in pure water. It is gaining water because the concentration of water particles is lower inside the cell than outside.

Figure 3 *The shape of these red blood cells is affected by the concentration of water outside the cell.*

Moving Small Particles

Help solve The Perfect Taters Mystery on page 698 of the LabBook!

Many particles, such as water and oxygen, can diffuse directly through the cell membrane, which is made of phospholipid molecules. These particles can slip through the molecules of the membrane in part because of their small size. However, not all of the particles a cell needs can pass through the membrane in this way. For example, sugar and amino acids aren't small enough to squeeze between the phospholipid molecules, and they are also repelled by the phospholipids in the membrane. They must travel through protein "doorways" located in the cell membrane in order to enter or leave the cell.

Particles can travel through these proteins either by passive transport or by active transport. **Passive transport,** shown in **Figure 4,** is the diffusion of particles through the proteins. The particles move from an area of high concentration to an area of low concentration. The cell does not need to use any energy to make this happen.

Active transport, shown in **Figure 5,** is the movement of particles through proteins against the normal direction of diffusion. In other words, particles are moved from an area of low concentration to an area of high concentration. The cell must use energy to make this happen. This energy comes from the molecule ATP, which stores energy in a form that cells can use.

Passive Transport

Cell membrane

A particle in an area of high concentration diffuses through a protein.

Figure 4 *In passive transport, particles travel through proteins from areas of high concentration to areas of low concentration.*

Active Transport

ATP

Energy from ATP is used to move a particle through a protein against the direction of diffusion.

Figure 5 *In active transport, cells use energy to move particles from areas of low concentration to areas of high concentration.*

Moving Large Particles

Diffusion, passive transport, and active transport are good methods of moving small particles into and out of cells, but what about moving large particles? The cell membrane has two ways of accomplishing this task: *endocytosis* and *exocytosis*.

Endocytosis In **endocytosis,** the cell membrane surrounds a particle and encloses it in a vesicle. This is how large particles, such as other cells, can be brought into a cell, as shown in **Figure 6.**

1 The cell comes into contact with a particle.

2 The cell membrane begins to wrap around the particle.

3 Once the particle is completely surrounded, a vesicle pinches off.

Figure 6 Endocytosis *means "within the cell."*

Exocytosis When a large particle must be removed from the cell, the cell uses a different process. In **exocytosis,** vesicles are formed at the endoplasmic reticulum or Golgi complex and carry the particles to the cell membrane, as shown in **Figure 7.**

1 Large particles that must leave the cell are packaged in vesicles.

2 The vesicle travels to the cell membrane and fuses with it.

3 The cell releases the particles into its environment.

Figure 7 Exocytosis *means "outside the cell."*

REVIEW

1. During diffusion, how do particles move?

2. How does a cell take in large particles? How does a cell expel large particles?

3. **Making Inferences** The transfer of glucose into a cell does not require ATP. What type of transport supplies a cell with glucose? Explain your answer.

internet**connect**

SCI*LINKS*
NSTA

TOPIC: Osmosis
GO TO: www.scilinks.org
*sci*LINKS NUMBER: HSTL075

Terms to Learn

photosynthesis
cellular respiration
fermentation

What You'll Do

♦ Describe photosynthesis and cellular respiration.
♦ Compare cellular respiration with fermentation.

Cell Energy

Why do you get hungry? Feeling hungry is your body's way of telling you that your cells need energy. Your cells and the cells of all organisms use energy to carry out the chemical activities that allow them to live, grow, and reproduce.

From Sun to Cell

Nearly all of the energy that fuels life comes from the sun. Plants are able to capture light energy from the sun and change it into food through a process called **photosynthesis.** The food that plants make supplies them with energy and also becomes a source of energy for the organisms that eat the plants. Without plants and other producers, consumers would not be able to live.

Photosynthesis Plants have molecules in their cells that absorb the energy of light. These molecules are called *pigments.* Chlorophyll, the main pigment used in photosynthesis, gives plants their green color. In the cells of plants, chlorophyll is found in chloroplasts, which are shown in **Figure 8.**

Plants use the energy captured by chlorophyll to change carbon dioxide (CO_2) and water (H_2O) into food, the simple sugar glucose ($C_6H_{12}O_6$). Glucose is a carbohydrate. When plants make glucose, they are converting the sun's energy into a form of energy that can be stored. The energy in glucose is used by the plant's cells, and some of it may be stored in the form of other carbohydrates or lipids. Photosynthesis also produces oxygen (O_2). Photosynthesis can be summarized by the following equation:

Plant Cell

Chloroplast

$$6CO_2 + 6H_2O + \text{light energy} \longrightarrow C_6H_{12}O_6 + 6O_2$$

Carbon   Water   Glucose   Oxygen
dioxide

Figure 8 *During photosynthesis, plant cells use the energy in sunlight to make food (glucose) from carbon dioxide and water. Photosynthesis takes place in chloroplasts.*

Getting Energy from Food

The food you eat has to be broken down so that the energy it contains can be converted into a form your cells can use. In fact, all organisms must break down food molecules in order to release the stored energy. There are two ways to do this. One way uses oxygen and is called **cellular respiration.** The other way does not use oxygen and is called **fermentation.**

Cellular Respiration The word *respiration* means "breathing," but cellular respiration is not the same thing as breathing. Breathing supplies your cells with the oxygen they need to perform cellular respiration. Breathing also rids your body of carbon dioxide, which is a waste product of cellular respiration.

Most organisms, such as the cow in **Figure 9,** use cellular respiration to obtain energy from food. During cellular respiration, food (glucose) is broken down into CO_2 and H_2O, and energy is released. A lot of the energy is stored in the form of ATP. ATP is the molecule that supplies energy to fuel the activities of cells. Most of the energy released, however, is in the form of heat. In some organisms, including yourself, this heat helps to maintain the body's temperature.

In the cells of eukaryotes, cellular respiration takes place in mitochondria. The process of cellular respiration is summarized in the equation below. Does this equation remind you of the equation for photosynthesis? The diagram on the next page shows how photosynthesis and respiration are related.

$$C_6H_{12}O_6 + 6O_2 \longrightarrow 6CO_2 + 6H_2O + energy\ (ATP)$$

Glucose   Oxygen   Carbon   Water
                      dioxide

Mitochondria

Animal Cell

Figure 9 *The mitochondria in the cells of this cow will use cellular respiration to release the energy stored in the grass.*

The Cell in Action   **89**

Photosynthesis and Respiration: What's the Connection?

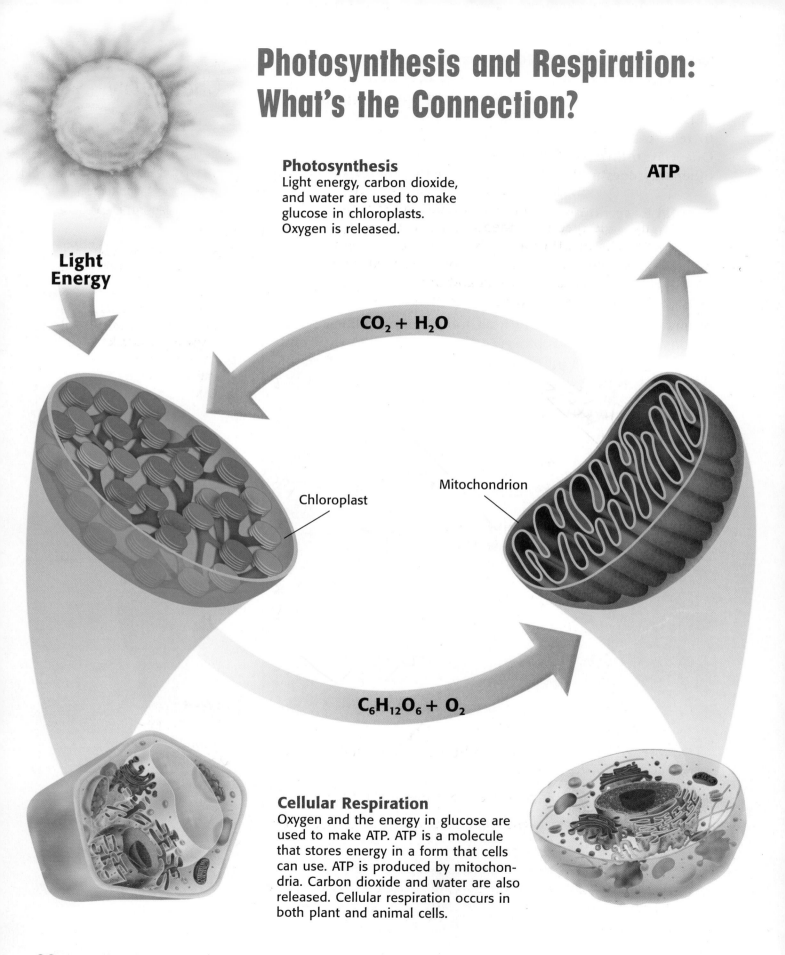

Photosynthesis
Light energy, carbon dioxide, and water are used to make glucose in chloroplasts. Oxygen is released.

ATP

Light Energy

$CO_2 + H_2O$

Chloroplast

Mitochondrion

$C_6H_{12}O_6 + O_2$

Cellular Respiration
Oxygen and the energy in glucose are used to make ATP. ATP is a molecule that stores energy in a form that cells can use. ATP is produced by mitochondria. Carbon dioxide and water are also released. Cellular respiration occurs in both plant and animal cells.

Fermentation Have you ever run so far that you started to feel a burning sensation in your muscles? Well, sometimes your muscle cells can't get the oxygen they need to produce ATP by cellular respiration. When this happens, they use the process of fermentation. Fermentation leads to the production of a small amount of ATP and products from the partial breakdown of glucose.

There are two major types of fermentation. The first type occurs in your muscles. It produces lactic acid, which contributes to muscle fatigue after strenuous activity. This type of fermentation also occurs in the muscle cells of other animals and in some types of fungi and bacteria. The second type of fermentation occurs in certain types of bacteria and in yeast. This type of fermentation is described in **Figure 10.**

Figure 10 *Yeast cells make carbon dioxide and alcohol during the fermentation of sugar. The carbon dioxide causes bubbles to form in bread.*

 APPLY

Fantasy Island

You have been given the assignment of restoring life to a barren island. What types of organisms would you put on the island? If you want to have animals on the island, what other organisms must be on the island as well? Explain your answer.

REVIEW

1. Why are producers important to the survival of all other organisms?

2. How do the processes of photosynthesis and cellular respiration relate to each other?

3. What does breathing have to do with cellular respiration?

4. How are respiration and fermentation similar? How are they different?

5. **Identifying Relationships** In which cells would you expect to find the greater number of mitochondria: cells that are very active or cells that are not very active? Why?

internet**connect**

*sci*LINKS
NSTA

TOPIC: Cell Energy, Photosynthesis
GO TO: www.scilinks.org
***sci*LINKS NUMBER:** HSTL080, HSTL085

Terms to Learn

cell cycle   chromatids
chromosome   centromere
binary fission   mitosis
homologous   cytokinesis
  chromosomes

What You'll Do

◆ Explain how cells produce
  more cells.
◆ Discuss the importance of
  mitosis.
◆ Explain how cell division differs
  in animals and plants.

MATH BREAK

Cell Multiplication

It takes Cell *A* 6 hours to
complete its cell cycle and
produce two cells. The cell
cycle of Cell *B* takes 8 hours.
How many more cells would
be formed from Cell *A* than
from Cell *B* in 24 hours?

The Cell Cycle

In the time that it takes you to read this sentence, your body
will have produced millions of new cells! Producing new cells
allows you to grow and replace cells that have died. For example, the environment in your stomach is so acidic that the
cells lining it must be replaced every few days!

The Life of a Cell

As you grow, you pass through different stages in life. Similarly,
your cells pass through different stages in their life cycle. The
life cycle of a cell is known as the **cell cycle.**

The cell cycle begins when the cell is formed and ends when
the cell divides and forms new cells. Before a cell divides, it
must make a copy of its DNA. DNA contains the information
that tells a cell how to make proteins. The DNA of a cell is organized into structures called **chromosomes.** In some organisms,
chromosomes also contain protein. Copying chromosomes
ensures that each new cell will be able to survive.

How does a cell make more cells? Well, that depends on
whether the cell is prokaryotic or eukaryotic.

Making More Prokaryotic Cells Prokaryotic cells (bacteria)
and their DNA are not very complex. Bacteria have ribosomes
and a single, circular molecule of DNA, but they don't have
any membrane-covered organelles. Because of this, cell division
in bacteria is fairly simple. It is called **binary fission,** which
means "splitting into two parts." Each of the resulting cells contains one copy of the DNA. Some of the bacteria in **Figure 11**
are undergoing binary fission.

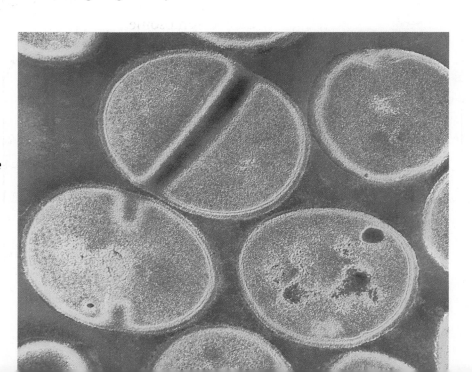

Figure 11 *Bacteria reproduce by pinching in two.*

Eukaryotic Cells and Their DNA Eukaryotic cells are usually much larger and more complex than prokaryotic cells. Because of this, eukaryotic cells have a lot more DNA. The chromosomes of eukaryotes contain DNA and proteins.

The number of chromosomes in the cells of eukaryotes differs from one kind of organism to the next and has nothing to do with the complexity of an organism. For example, fruit flies have 8 chromosomes, potatoes have 48, and humans have 46. **Figure 12** shows the 46 chromosomes of a human body cell lined up in pairs. These pairs are made up of similar chromosomes known as **homologous chromosomes.**

Making More Eukaryotic Cells The eukaryotic cell cycle includes three main stages. In the first stage, the cell grows and copies its organelles and chromosomes. During this time, the strands of DNA and proteins are like loosely coiled pieces of thread. After each chromosome is duplicated, the two copies are called **chromatids.** Chromatids are held together at a region called the **centromere.** The chromatids each twist and coil and condense into an X shape, as shown in **Figure 13.** After this happens, the cell enters the second stage of the cell cycle.

In the second stage, the chromatids separate. The complicated process of chromosome separation is **mitosis.** Mitosis ensures that each new cell receives a copy of each chromosome. Mitosis can be divided into four phases, as shown on the following pages.

In the third stage of the cell cycle, the cell divides and produces two cells that are identical to the original cell. Cell division will be discussed after mitosis has been described.

✓ Self-Check

After duplication, how many chromatids are there in a pair of homologous chromosomes? *(See page 782 to check your answer.)*

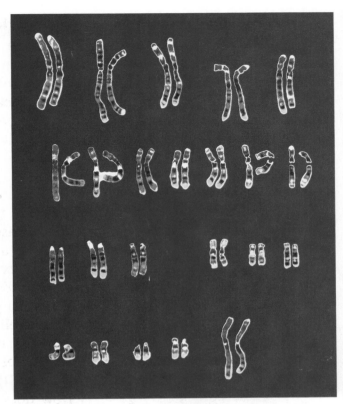

Figure 12 *Human body cells have 46 chromosomes, or 23 pairs of homologous chromosomes.*

Chromatids

Centromere

Figure 13 *Two strands of DNA and protein coiled together to form this duplicated chromosome, which consists of two chromatids.*

Mitosis and the Cell Cycle

The diagram below shows the cell cycle and the phases of mitosis in an animal cell. Although mitosis is a continuous process, it can be divided into the four phases that are shown and described. As you know, different types of living things have different numbers of chromosomes. In this diagram, only four chromosomes are shown to make it easier to see what's happening.

Before mitosis begins, the chromosomes and other cell materials are copied. The pair of *centrioles,* which are two cylindrical structures, are also copied. Each chromosome now consists of two chromatids.

Mitosis Phase 1

Mitosis begins. The nuclear membrane breaks apart. Chromosomes condense into rodlike structures. The two pairs of centrioles move to opposite sides of the cell. Fibers form between the two pairs of centrioles and attach to the centromeres.

Mitosis Phase 2

The chromosomes line up along the equator of the cell.

Mitosis Phase 3

The chromatids separate and are pulled to opposite sides of the cell by the fibers attached to the centrioles.

Mitosis Phase 4

The nuclear membrane forms around the two sets of chromosomes, and they unwind. The fibers disappear. Mitosis is completed.

Once mitosis is completed, the cytoplasm splits in two. This process is called **cytokinesis.** The result is two identical cells that are also identical to the original cell from which they were formed. After cytokinesis, the cell cycle is complete, and the new cells are at the beginning of their next cell cycle.

More About Cytokinesis In animal cells and other eukaryotes that do not have cell walls, division of the cytoplasm begins at the cell membrane. The cell membrane begins to pinch inward to form a groove, which eventually pinches all the way through the cell, and two daughter cells are formed. Cytokinesis in an animal cell is shown above.

Eukaryotic cells that have a cell wall, such as the cells of plants, algae, and fungi, do things a little differently. In these organisms, a *cell plate* forms in the middle of the cell and becomes the new cell membranes that will separate the two new cells. After the cell is split in two, a new cell wall forms between the two membranes. Cytokinesis in a plant cell is shown in **Figure 14.**

Cell plate

Figure 14 *When plant cells divide, a cell plate forms and the cell is split in two.*

REVIEW

1. How are binary fission and mitosis similar? How are they different?

2. Why is it important for chromosomes to be copied before cell division?

3. How does cytokinesis differ in animals and plants?

4. **Applying Concepts** What would happen if cytokinesis occurred without mitosis?

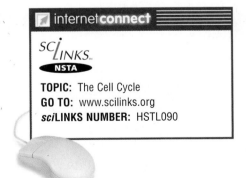

internet**connect**

SC*i*LINKS
NSTA

TOPIC: The Cell Cycle
GO TO: www.scilinks.org
*sci*LINKS NUMBER: HSTL090

Chapter Highlights

Vocabulary

diffusion *(p. 84)*

osmosis *(p. 85)*

passive transport *(p. 86)*

active transport *(p. 86)*

endocytosis *(p. 87)*

exocytosis *(p. 87)*

Section Notes

- A cell can survive only if food molecules are taken into the cell and waste materials are removed. Materials enter and leave the cell by passing through the cell membrane. The cell membrane allows some materials to pass through but prevents others.

- A cell does not need to use energy to move particles from regions of high concentration to regions of low concentration. This type of movement is called diffusion.

- Osmosis is the diffusion of water through a membrane.

- Some substances enter and leave a cell by passing through proteins. During passive transport, substances diffuse through proteins. During active transport, substances are moved from areas of low concentration to areas of high concentration. The cell must supply energy for active transport to occur.

- Particles that are too large to pass easily through the membrane can enter a cell by a process called endocytosis. Large particles can leave a cell by exocytosis.

Labs

The Perfect Taters Mystery *(p. 698)*

☑ Skills Check

Math Concepts

CELL CYCLE It takes 4 hours for a cell to complete its cell cycle and produce 2 cells. How many cells can be produced from this cell in 12 hours? First you must determine how many cell cycles will occur in 12 hours:

12 hours/4 hours = 3

The number of cells doubles after each cycle:

Cycle 1	1 cell × 2 = 2 cells
Cycle 2	2 cells × 2 = 4 cells
Cycle 3	4 cells × 2 = 8 cells

Therefore, after 3 cell cycles (12 hours), 8 cells will have been produced from the original cell.

Visual Understanding

MITOSIS The process of mitosis can be confusing, but looking at illustrations can help. Look at the illustrations of the cell cycle on pp. 94 and 95. Read the label for each phase, and look at the illustrations and photographs for each. Look for the cell structures that are described in the label. Trace the movement of chromosomes through each step. By carefully studying the labels and pictures, you can better understand mitosis.

Vocabulary

photosynthesis *(p. 88)*

cellular respiration *(p. 89)*

fermentation *(p. 89)*

Section Notes

- The sun is the ultimate source of almost all energy needed to fuel the chemical activities of organisms. Most producers use energy from sunlight to make food during the process known as photosynthesis. This food then becomes a source of energy for the producers and for the consumers that eat the producers.

- Cells use cellular respiration or fermentation to release the energy from food to make ATP. Cellular respiration requires oxygen, but fermentation does not.

Labs

Stayin' Alive! *(p. 700)*

Vocabulary

cell cycle *(p. 92)*

chromosome *(p. 92)*

binary fission *(p. 92)*

homologous chromosomes *(p. 93)*

chromatids *(p. 93)*

centromere *(p. 93)*

mitosis *(p. 93)*

cytokinesis *(p. 95)*

Section Notes

- The life cycle of a cell is called the cell cycle. The cell cycle begins when the cell is formed and ends when the cell divides to produce two new cells. Prokaryotic cells produce new cells by binary fission. Eukaryotic cells produce new cells by mitosis and cytokinesis.

- Before mitosis, the chromosomes are copied. During mitosis, chromatids separate, and two new nuclei are formed. During cytokinesis, the cell divides.

---

internet connect

GO TO: go.hrw.com

Visit the **HRW** Web site for a variety of learning tools related to this chapter. Just type in the keyword:

KEYWORD: HSTACT

GO TO: www.scilinks.org

Visit the **National Science Teachers Association** on-line Web site for Internet resources related to this chapter. Just type in the *sci*LINKS number for more information about the topic:

TOPIC:		*sci*LINKS NUMBER:
TOPIC: Osmosis		*sci*LINKS NUMBER: HSTL075
TOPIC: Cell Energy		*sci*LINKS NUMBER: HSTL080
TOPIC: Photosynthesis		*sci*LINKS NUMBER: HSTL085
TOPIC: The Cell Cycle		*sci*LINKS NUMBER: HSTL090
TOPIC: Microbes		*sci*LINKS NUMBER: HSTL095

Chapter Review

To complete the following sentences, choose the correct term from each pair of terms listed below:

1. The diffusion of water through the cell membrane is called __?__. *(osmosis or active transport)*

2. A cell can remove large particles during __?__. *(exocytosis or endocytosis)*

3. Plants use __?__ to make glucose. *(cellular respiration or photosynthesis)*

4. During __?__, food molecules are broken down to form CO_2 and H_2O and release large amounts of energy. *(cellular respiration or fermentation)*

5. In eukaryotes, __?__ creates two nuclei, and __?__ creates two cells. *(cytokinesis or mitosis)*

UNDERSTANDING CONCEPTS

Multiple Choice

6. When particles are moved through a membrane from a region of low concentration to a region of high concentration, the process is called
   a. diffusion.
   b. passive transport.
   c. active transport.
   d. fermentation.

7. An organism with chloroplasts is a
   a. consumer.   c. producer.
   b. prokaryote.   d. centromere.

8. What is produced by mitosis?
   a. two identical cells
   b. two nuclei
   c. chloroplasts
   d. two different cells

9. Before the energy in food can be used by a cell, it must first be transferred to molecules of
   a. proteins.
   b. carbohydrates.
   c. DNA.
   d. ATP.

10. Which one of the following does not perform mitosis?
    a. prokaryotic cell
    b. human body cell
    c. eukaryotic cell
    d. plant cell

11. Which of the following would form a cell plate during the cell cycle?
    a. human cell
    b. prokaryotic cell
    c. plant cell
    d. all of the above

Short Answer

12. What cell structures are needed for photosynthesis? for respiration?

13. How many chromatids are present in a chromosome at the beginning of mitosis?

14. What are the three stages of the cell cycle in a eukaryotic cell?

Concept Mapping

15. Use the following terms to create a concept map: chromosome duplication, cytokinesis, prokaryote, mitosis, cell cycle, binary fission, eukaryote.

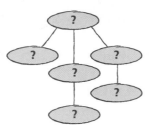

Write one or two sentences to answer the following questions:

16. Which one of the plants below was given water mixed with salt, and which one was given pure water? Explain how you know, and be sure to use the word *osmosis* in your answer.

17. Why would your muscle cells need to be supplied with more food when there is a lack of oxygen than when there is plenty of oxygen present?

18. A parent cell has 10 chromosomes before dividing.
   a. Will the cell go through binary fission or mitosis and cytokinesis to produce new cells?
   b. How many chromosomes will each new cell have after the parent cell divides?

MATH IN SCIENCE

19. A cell has six chromosomes at the beginning of its cell cycle. How many chromatids will line up at the equator of the cell during mitosis?

INTERPRETING GRAPHICS

Look at the cell below to answer the following questions:

20. Is the cell prokaryotic or eukaryotic?

21. In what stage of the cell cycle is this cell?

22. How many chromatids are present? How many pairs of homologous chromosomes are present?

23. How many chromosomes will be present in each of the new cells after the cell divides?

NOW What Do You Think?

Take a minute to review your answers to the ScienceLog questions on page 83. Have your answers changed? If necessary, revise your answers based on what you have learned since you began this chapter.

Electrifying News About Microbes

Your car is out of fuel, and there isn't a service station in sight. No problem! Your car's motor runs on electricity supplied by trillions of micro-organisms—and they're hungry. You pop a handful of sugar cubes into the tank along with some fresh water, and you're on your way. The microbes devour the food and produce enough electricity to get you home safely.

A "Living" Battery

Sound far-fetched? Peter Bennetto and his team of scientists at King's College, in London, don't think so. Chemists there envision "living" batteries that will someday operate everything from wristwatches to entire towns. Although cars won't be using batteries powered by bacteria anytime soon, the London scientists have demonstrated that microorganisms can convert food into usable electrical energy. One test battery that is smaller than 0.5 cm^2 kept a digital clock operating for a day.

Freeing Electrons

For nearly a century, scientists have known that living things produce and use electric charges. But only in the last few decades have they figured out the chemical processes that produce these tiny electric charges. As part of their normal activities, living cells break down starches and sugars, and these chemical reactions release electrons. Scientists produce electricity by harvesting these free electrons from single-celled organisms, such as bacteria.

Bennetto and his colleagues have developed a list of foods that matches the carbohydrates, such as table sugar and molasses, with the microorganisms that digest them the most efficiently. Bennetto explains that there are lazy bacteria and efficient bacteria. An efficient microbe can convert more than 90 percent of its food into compounds that will fuel an

▲ *Bacteria like this can convert carbohydrates to electrical energy.*

electric reaction. A less efficient microbe converts 50 percent or less of its food into electron-yielding compounds.

Feed Them Leftovers

One advantage that batteries powered by microbes have over generators is that microbes do not require nonrenewable resources, such as coal or oil. Microbes can produce electricity by consuming pollutants, such as certain byproducts from the milk and sugar industries. And since the microorganisms reproduce constantly, no battery charging is necessary; just give the battery a bacteria change from time to time. For now, the London scientists are content to speculate on the battery's potential. Other specialists, such as electrical engineers, are needed to make this technology practical.

Project Idea

▶ Imagine that you manage a government agency and you are asked to provide funds for research on batteries powered by microbes. Think of some of the benefits of developing "living batteries." Are there any problems you can think of? As a class, decide whether you would fund the research.

Science Fiction

"Contagion"

by Katherine MacLean

A quarter mile from their spaceship, the *Explorer,* a team of doctors walk carefully along a narrow forest trail. Around them, the forest looks like an Earth forest in the fall—the leaves are green, copper, purple, and fiery red. But it isn't fall. And the team is not on Earth.

Minos is enough like Earth to be the home of another colony of humans. But Minos might also be home to unknown organisms that could cause severe illness or death among the *Explorer*'s crew. These diseases might be enough like Earth diseases to be contagious, yet just different enough to be extremely difficult to treat.

Something large moves among the shadows —it looks like a man. When he suddenly steps out onto the trail, he is taller than any of them, lean and muscled, and darkly tanned with bright red hair. Even more amazing, he speaks.

"Welcome to Minos. The mayor sends greetings from Alexandria."

And so we, and the crew of the *Explorer,* meet red-haired Patrick Mead. According to Patrick, there was once a colony of humans on Minos. About two years after the colony arrived, a terrible plague swept through the colony and killed everyone except the Mead family. But, Patrick tells them, the plague has never come back and there are no other contagions on Minos.

Or are there? What has Patrick hidden from the crew of the *Explorer*? Read Katherine MacLean's "Contagion" in the *Holt Anthology of Science Fiction* to find out.

UNIT 3

Heredity, Evolution, and Classification

The differences and similarities among living things are the subject of this unit. You will learn how characteristics are passed from one generation to another, how living things are classified based on their characteristics, and how these characteristics help living things survive.

Scientists have not always understood these topics, and there is still much to be learned. This timeline will give you an idea of some things that have been learned so far.

1753

Carolus Linnaeus publishes the first of two volumes containing the classification of all known species.

1951

Rosalind Franklin photographs DNA.

1953

James Watson and Francis Crick figure out the structure of DNA.

1960

Louis and Mary Leakey discover fossil bones of the human ancestor *Homo habilis* in Olduvai Gorge, Tanzania.

1969

Apollo 11 lands on the moon. Neil Armstrong becomes the first person to walk on the lunar surface.

1859

Charles Darwin suggests that natural selection is a mechanism of evolution.

1860

Abraham Lincoln is elected the 16th president of the United States.

1865

Gregor Mendel publishes the results of his studies of genetic inheritance in pea plants.

1930

The planet Pluto is discovered.

1905

Nettie Stevens describes how sex is determined by the X and Y chromosomes.

1990

Ashanti DeSilva is given genetically engineered white blood cells to combat disease.

1974

Donald Johanson discovers a fossilized skeleton of one of the first hominids.

2000

The Human Genome Project has identified thousands of human genes and is scheduled to decode the entire human genome by 2003.

5 Heredity

Would You Believe . . . ?

It all started in ancient China. A fisherman caught an unusual carp. Usually these small freshwater fish are drab colored, but this one had a pale golden hue. It was too pretty to eat, so the fisherman took the fish home as a pet.

Months later, the fisherman caught another gold-tinged carp. He kept the two fish in the same bowl. When the fish reproduced, the offspring were even more brightly colored than their parents. The first goldfish had been born!

In the years that followed, people throughout China began keeping and breeding the new, orange-colored pets. Many became goldfish matchmakers, choosing only the most handsome mates for their favorite fish. With each generation of hatchlings, the fish looked more and more distinctive. By A.D. 1500, when the first shipments of goldfish arrived in Japan, goldfish no longer resembled carp. In fact, they were so regal looking that the commoners in Japan were forbidden to keep them as pets.

Without knowing it, these early goldfish breeders were using the principles of genetics to create many new kinds of goldfish. In this chapter you will learn about heredity, the passing of traits from parents to offspring. You'll discover the principles that allowed beautiful goldfish to be bred from rather plain-looking carp.

What Do You Think?

In your ScienceLog, try to answer the following questions based on what you already know:

1. Why don't all humans look exactly alike?

2. What determines whether a human baby will be a boy or a girl?

Clothing Combos

Do you look like your father or your mother? Do you look like your sister or your brother? You may. But chances are you look quite different. Even though you are different, you share some characteristics with your siblings and your parents.

In this activity you will investigate how different characteristics can be combined to make something special and unique, just like you are.

Procedure

1. Your teacher will provide **three boxes.** One box contains **five hats.** One box contains **five gloves,** and one box contains **five scarves.**

2. Without looking in the boxes, five of your classmates will select one hat, one scarf, and one glove. They will put the items on and model them for the class. Then they will put the clothing back into the boxes for the next five students. This process will continue until all students have made their selections.

3. Record the clothing combination you selected in your ScienceLog.

Analysis

4. Were any of the combinations the same? How many different combinations did you have in your class?

5. Do you think you saw all of the possible combinations? Explain your answer.

6. Choose a partner. Using the pieces of clothing you and your partner selected from the box, how many different combinations could you make by giving a third person one hat, one glove, and one scarf? You may want to make a chart like the one below to help you figure it out.

	Hat		Glove		Scarf	
1	X		X		X	
2	X		X			X
3	X					

7. Considering what you have learned from this Investigate, why do you think parents often have children who look very different from each other?

Mendel and His Peas

Terms to Learn

heredity   alleles
dominant trait   genotype
recessive trait   phenotype
genes   probability

What You'll Do

◆ Explain the experiments of Gregor Mendel.
◆ Explain how genes and alleles are related to genotypes and phenotypes.
◆ Use the information in a Punnett square.

There is no one else in the world exactly like you. You are unique. But what sets you apart? If you look around your classroom, you'll see that you share many physical characteristics with your classmates. For example, you all have skin instead of scales and a noticeable lack of antennae. You are a human being very much like all of your fellow human beings.

Yet you are different from everyone else in many ways. The people you most resemble are your parents and your brothers and sisters. But you probably don't look exactly like them either. Read on to find out why this is so.

Why Don't You Look Like a Rhinoceros?

The answer to this question seems simple: Neither of your parents is a rhinoceros. But there's more to this answer than meets the eye. As it turns out, **heredity,** or the passing of traits from parents to offspring, is a very complicated subject. For example, you might have curly hair, while both of your parents have straight hair. You might have blue eyes, even though both of your parents have brown eyes. How does this happen? People have investigated this question for a long time. About 150 years ago, some very important experiments were performed that helped scientists begin to find some answers. The person who performed these experiments was Gregor Mendel.

Who Was Gregor Mendel?

Gregor Mendel was born in 1822 in Heinzendorf, Austria. Growing up on his family's farm, Mendel learned a lot about cultivating flowers and fruit trees. After completing his studies at a university, he entered a monastery. He worked in the monastery garden, where he was able to use plants to study the way traits are passed from parents to offspring. **Figure 1** shows an illustration of Mendel in the monastery garden.

Figure 1 Gregor Mendel

Activity

Imagine that you are planning to meet your pen pal at the airport, but you have never met. How would you describe yourself? Would you say that you are tall or short, have curly hair or straight hair, have brown eyes or green eyes? Make a list. Put a check mark next to traits you think you inherited.

TRY at HOME

Unraveling the Mystery

From his experiences breeding plants, Mendel knew that sometimes the patterns of inheritance seemed simple and sometimes they did not. Mendel wanted to find out why.

Mendel was interested in the way traits are passed from parents to offspring. For example, sometimes a trait that appeared in one generation did not show up in any of the offspring in the next generation. In the third generation, though, the trait showed up again. Mendel noticed similar patterns in people, plants, and many other living things.

To simplify his investigation, Mendel decided to study only one kind of organism. He had already done studies using the garden pea plant, so he chose this as his subject.

How Do You Like Your Peas? Garden peas were a good choice for several reasons. These plants grow quickly, they are usually self-pollinating, and they come in many varieties. A *self-pollinating plant* contains both male and female reproductive structures, like the flower in **Figure 2.** Therefore, pollen from one flower or plant can fertilize the eggs of the same flower or the eggs of another flower on the same plant. **Figure 3** illustrates the parts of a flower and how fertilization takes place in plants.

Figure 2 *This photograph of a flower shows the male and female reproductive structures.*

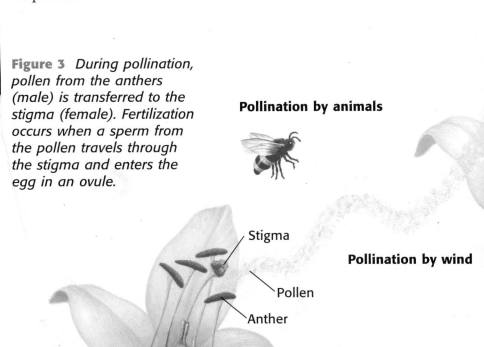

Figure 3 *During pollination, pollen from the anthers (male) is transferred to the stigma (female). Fertilization occurs when a sperm from the pollen travels through the stigma and enters the egg in an ovule.*

Pollination by animals

Pollination by wind

Self-pollination

Stigma

Pollen

Anther

Ovary

Ovule

Petal

Peas Be My Podner

Mendel chose to study only one characteristic, such as plant height or pea color, at a time. That way, he could understand the results. Mendel chose plants that had two forms for each of the characteristics he studied. For example, for the characteristic of plant height, one form always produced tall plar s, and the other form always produced short plants. Some of e characteristics investigated by Mendel are shown in **Figur** The two different traits of each characteristic are also sho

True-Breeding Plants Mendel was very careful to use p. that were true breeding for each of the traits he was study When a *true-breeding plant* self-pollinates, it will always duce offspring with the same trait the parent plant has. example, a tall true-breeding plant will always produce spring that are tall.

Mendel decided to find out what would happen if he cros two plants that had different forms of a single trait. To this, he used a method known as *cross-pollination*. In cros pollination, the anthers of one plant are removed so that th plant cannot self-pollinate. Then pollen from another plant used to fertilize the plant without anthers. This way, Mend could select which pollen would fertilize which plant. Thi technique is illustrated in **Figure 5.**

Seed Shape

Round   Wrinkled

Plant Height

Tall   Short

Flower Color

Purple   White

Figure 4 *These are some of the plant characteristics that Mendel studied.*

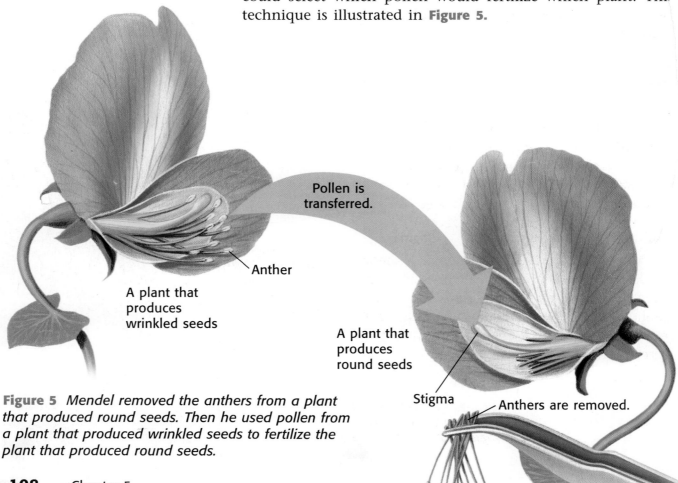

Pollen is transferred.

Anther

A plant that produces wrinkled seeds

A plant that produces round seeds

Stigma

Anthers are removed.

Figure 5 *Mendel removed the anthers from a plant that produced round seeds. Then he used pollen from a plant that produced wrinkled seeds to fertilize the plant that produced round seeds.*

Mendel's First Experiment

In his first experiment, Mendel performed crosses to study seven different characteristics. Each of the crosses was between the two traits of each characteristic. The results of the cross between plants that produce round seeds and plants that produce wrinkled seeds are shown in **Figure 6.** The offspring from this cross are known as the *first generation.* Do the results surprise you? What do you think happened to the trait for wrinkled seeds?

Mendel got similar results for each of the crosses that he made. One trait always appeared, and the other trait seemed to vanish. Mendel chose to call the trait that appeared the **dominant trait.** The other trait seemed to recede into the background, so Mendel called this the **recessive trait.** To find out what might have happened to the recessive trait, Mendel decided to perform another experiment.

Mendel's Second Experiment

Mendel allowed the first generation from each of the seven crosses to self-pollinate. This is also illustrated in Figure 6. This time the plant with the dominant trait for seed shape (which is round) was allowed to self-pollinate. As you can see, the recessive trait for wrinkled seeds showed up again.

Mendel performed this same experiment on the two traits of each of the seven characteristics. No matter which characteristic Mendel investigated, when the first generation was allowed to self-pollinate, the recessive trait reappeared.

Figure 6 *A plant that produces wrinkled seeds is fertilized with pollen from a plant that produces round seeds.*

Parent generation

Pollen transfer

First generation
All round seeds

Growth

First generation
A seed grows into a mature plant that is allowed to self-pollinate.

Second generation
For every three round seeds, there is one wrinkled seed.

Bug Builders, Inc. needs your help to design some new bugs. Turn to page 702 of the LabBook.

A Different Point of View

Mendel then did something that no one else had done before: He decided to count the number of plants with each trait that turned up in the second generation. He hoped that this might help him explain his results. Take a look at Mendel's actual results, shown in the table below.

Mendel's Results			
Characteristic	Dominant trait	Recessive trait	Ratio
Flower color	705 purple	224 white	?
Seed color	6,002 yellow	2,001 green	?
Seed shape	5,474 round	1,850 wrinkled	?
Pod color	428 green	152 yellow	?
Pod shape	882 smooth	299 bumpy	?
Flower position	651 along stem	207 at tip	?
Plant height	787 tall	277 short	?

$\div$ 5 $\div$ Ω $\leq$ ∞ $+\Omega$ $\sqrt{}$ 9 ∞ $\leq$ Σ 2
+

MATH BREAK

Understanding Ratios

A ratio is a way to compare two numbers by using division. The ratio of plants with purple flowers to plants with white flowers can be written as 705 to 224, 705:224, or as a fraction:

$$\frac{705}{224}$$

Reduce this fraction by dividing:

$$\frac{3.15}{1}$$

For every three plants with purple flowers, there will be roughly one plant with white flowers. Try this problem:

In a box of chocolates, there are 18 nougat-filled chocolates and 6 caramel-filled chocolates. What is the ratio of nougat-filled chocolates to caramel-filled chocolates?

As you can see, the recessive trait showed up again, but not as often as the dominant trait showed up. Mendel decided to calculate the *ratio* of dominant traits to recessive traits for each characteristic. Follow in Mendel's footsteps by calculating the dominant-to-recessive ratio for each characteristic. (If you need help, check out the MathBreak at left.) Can you find a pattern among the ratios?

A Brilliant Idea

Mendel realized that his results could be explained only if each plant had two sets of instructions for each characteristic. Each parent donates one set of instructions, now known as **genes,** to the offspring. The fertilized egg would then have two forms of the same gene for every characteristic—one from each parent. The two forms of a gene are known as **alleles.**

The Proof Is in the Punnett Square To understand Mendel's conclusions, we'll use a diagram called a Punnett square. A *Punnett square* is used to visualize all the possible combinations of alleles from the parents. Dominant alleles are symbolized with capital letters, and recessive alleles are symbolized with lowercase letters. Therefore, the alleles for a true-breeding purple-flowered plant are written as *PP.* The alleles for a true-breeding white-flowered plant are written as *pp.* The cross between these two parent plants, as shown in **Figure 7,** is then written as *PP × pp.* The squares contain the allele combinations that could occur in the offspring. The inherited combination of alleles is known as the offspring's **genotype.**

Figure 7 shows that all of the offspring will have the same genotype: *Pp.* The dominant allele, *P,* in each genotype ensures that all of the offspring will be purple-flowered plants. An organism's appearance is known as its **phenotype.** The recessive allele, *p,* may be passed on to the next generation.

A true-breeding white flower *(pp)*

A true-breeding purple flower *(PP)*

Figure 7 *The possible allele combinations in the offspring for this cross are all the same:* **Pp.**

How to Make a Punnett Square

Draw a square, and divide it into four sections. Next, write the letters that represent alleles from one parent along the top of the box. Write the letters that represent alleles from the other parent along the side of the box.

The cross shown at right is between a plant that produces only round seeds, **RR,** and a plant that produces only wrinkled seeds, **rr.** Follow the arrows to see how the inside of the box was filled. The resulting alleles inside the box show all the possible genotypes for the offspring from this cross. What would the phenotypes for these offspring be?

A self-pollinating purple flower

Male alleles

Female alleles

Figure 8 *This Punnett square shows the possible results from the cross* **Pp** × **Pp.**

More Evidence In Mendel's second experiment, he allowed the first-generation plants to self-pollinate. **Figure 8** shows a self-pollination cross of a first-generation plant with the genotype **Pp.** The parental alleles in the cross indicate that the egg and sperm can contain either a **P** allele or a **p** allele.

What might the genotypes of the offspring be? Notice that one square shows the **Pp** combination, while another shows the **pP** combination. These are exactly the same genotype, even though the letters are written in a different order. The other possible genotypes in the offspring are **PP** and **pp.** The combinations **PP, Pp,** and **pP** have the same phenotype—purple flowers—because they each contain at least one dominant allele (**P**). Only one combination, **pp,** produces plants with white flowers. The ratio of dominant to recessive is 3:1, just as Mendel calculated from his data.

What Are the Chances?

It's important to understand that offspring are equally likely to inherit either allele from either parent. Think of a coin toss. There's a 50 percent chance you'll get heads and a 50 percent chance you'll get tails. Like the toss of a coin, the chance of inheriting one allele or another is completely random.

Probability The mathematical chance that an event will occur is known as **probability.** Probability is usually expressed as a fraction or percentage. If you toss a coin, the probability of tossing tails is $\frac{1}{2}$. This means that half the number of times you toss a coin, you will get tails. To express probability as a percentage, divide the numerator of the fraction by the denominator, and then multiply the answer by 100.

$$\frac{1}{2} \times 100 = 50\%$$

To find the probability that you will toss two heads in a row, multiply the probability of the two events.

$$\frac{1}{2} \times \frac{1}{2} = \frac{1}{4}$$

The percentage would be $1 \div 4 \times 100$, which equals 25 percent.

Curly Eared Cats

A curly eared cat, like the one at right, mated with a cat that had normal ears. If half the kittens had the genotype **Cc** and curly ears, and the other half had the genotype **cc** and normal ears, which was the allele for curly ears?

What was the genotype of each parent? (**Hint:** Use a Punnett square to fill in the genotypes of the offspring, and then work backward.)

Genotype Probability The same method is used to calculate the probability that an offspring will inherit a certain genotype. For a pea plant to inherit the white flower trait, it must receive a **p** allele from each parent. There is a 50 percent chance of inheriting either allele from either parent. So the probability of inheriting two **p** alleles from a **Pp** × **Pp** cross is $\frac{1}{2} \times \frac{1}{2}$. This equals $\frac{1}{4}$ or 25 percent.

Gregor Mendel—Gone but Not Forgotten Good ideas are often overlooked or misunderstood when they first appear. This was the fate of Gregor Mendel's ideas. In 1865, he published his findings for the scientific community. Unfortunately, his work didn't get much attention. It wasn't until after his death, more than 30 years later, that Mendel finally got the recognition he deserved. Once Mendel's ideas were rediscovered and understood, the door was opened to modern genetics.

internet connect

*SCi*LINKS.
NSTA

TOPIC: Heredity, Dominant and Recessive Traits
GO TO: www.scilinks.org
sciLINKS NUMBER: HSTL110, HSTL115

REVIEW

1. The allele for a cleft chin, **C,** is dominant among humans. What would be the results from a cross between a woman with the genotype **Cc** and a man with the genotype **cc?** Create a Punnett square showing this cross.

2. Of the possible combinations you found in question 1, what is the ratio of offspring with a cleft chin to offspring without a cleft chin?

3. **Applying Concepts** The Punnett square at right shows the possible combinations of alleles for fur color in rabbits. Black fur, **B,** is dominant over white fur, **b.** Given the combinations shown, what are the genotypes of the parents?

Terms to Learn

sex cells
homologous chromosomes
meiosis
sex chromosomes

What You'll Do

◆ Explain the difference between mitosis and meiosis.
◆ Describe how Mendel's ideas are supported by the process of meiosis.
◆ Explain the difference between male and female sex chromosomes.

Meiosis

In the early 1900s, scientists began doing experiments similar to those done by Gregor Mendel. Excited by their findings, they searched for similar results obtained by others. They came across Mendel's forgotten paper and realized that their discoveries were not new; Mendel had made the same observation 35 years earlier. However, genes were still a mystery. Where were they located, and how did they pass information from one cell to another? Understanding reproduction was the first step in finding the answers to these questions.

Two Kinds of Reproduction

You know that there are two types of reproduction: asexual reproduction and sexual reproduction.

One Makes Two In *asexual reproduction,* only one parent cell is needed for reproduction. First, the internal structures of the cell are copied by a process known as mitosis. The parent cell then divides, producing new cells that are exact copies of the parent cell. Most single-celled organisms reproduce in this way. Most of the cells in your body also reproduce asexually.

Two Make One A different type of reproduction is used to make a new human being or a new pea plant. In *sexual reproduction,* two parent cells join together to form a new individual. The parent cells, known as **sex cells,** are different from ordinary body cells. Human body cells, for example, have 46 chromosomes (or 23 pairs), as shown in **Figure 9.** The chromosomes in each pair are called **homologous chromosomes.** But human sex cells have only 23 chromosomes—half the usual number. Male sex cells are called *sperm.* Female sex cells are called *eggs,* or ova. Each sperm and each egg has only one of the chromosomes from each homologous pair.

Figure 9 *Human body cells have 46 chromosomes, or 23 pairs of homologous chromosomes. One member of a pair of homologous chromosomes is shown at right.*

Less Is More Why is it important that sex cells have half the usual number of chromosomes? When an egg and a sperm join to form a new individual, each parent donates one half of a homologous pair of chromosomes. This ensures that the offspring will receive a normal number of chromosomes in each body cell. Each body cell must have an entire set of 46 chromosomes in order to grow and function properly.

Meiosis to the Rescue Sex cells are made during meiosis, a copying process that is different from mitosis. **Meiosis** produces new cells with half the usual number of chromosomes. When the sex cells are made, the chromosomes are copied once, and then the nucleus divides twice. The resulting sperm and eggs have half the number of chromosomes found in a normal body cell.

Meanwhile, Back at the Lab

What does all of this have to do with the location of genes? Not long after Mendel's paper was rediscovered, a young graduate student named Walter Sutton made an important observation. Sutton was studying sperm cells in grasshoppers. Sutton knew of Mendel's studies, which showed that the egg and sperm must each contribute the same amount of information to the offspring. That was the only way the 3:1 ratio found in the second generation could be explained. Sutton also knew from his own studies that although eggs and sperm were different, they did have something in common: their chromosomes were located inside a nucleus. Using his observations of meiosis, his understanding of Mendel's work, and some creative thinking, Sutton proposed something very important:

Genes are located on chromosomes!

And Sutton was correct, as it turned out. The steps of meiosis are outlined on the next two pages. But first, let's review mitosis so that you can compare the two processes.

Mitosis Revisited

1 Inside a typical cell: each of the long strands (chromosomes) makes a copy of itself.

2 Each chromosome consists of two identical copies called chromatids. The chromosomes thicken and shorten.

3 The nuclear membrane dissolves. The chromosomes line up along the equator (center) of the cell.

4 The chromatids pull apart.

5 The nuclear membrane forms around the separated chromatids. The chromosomes unwind, and the cell divides.

6 The result: two identical copies of the original cell.

Meiosis in Eight Easy Steps

The diagram on these two pages shows each stage of meiosis. Read about each step as you look at the diagram. Different types of living things have different numbers of chromosomes. In this diagram, only four chromosomes are shown.

One pair of homologous chromosomes

Two chromatids

1 Before meiosis begins, the chromosomes are in a threadlike form. Each chromosome makes an identical copy of itself, forming two exact halves called *chromatids.* The chromosomes then thicken and shorten into a form that is visible under a microscope. The nuclear membrane disappears.

2 Each chromosome is now made up of two chromatids, the original and an exact copy. Similar chromosomes pair with one another, forming *homologous chromosome pairs.* The paired homologous chromosomes line up at the equator of the cell.

3 The chromosomes separate from their homologous partners and move to opposite ends of the cell.

4 The nuclear membrane re-forms, and the cell divides. The paired chromatids are still joined.

5 Each cell contains one member of each homologous chromosome pair. The chromosomes are not copied again between the two cell divisions.

6 The chromosomes line up at the equator of each cell.

7 The chromatids pull apart and move to opposite ends of the cell. The nuclear membrane forms around the separated chromosomes, and the cells divide.

8 The result: Four new cells have formed from the original single cell. Each new cell has half the number of chromosomes present in the original cell.

✓ Self-Check

1. How many chromosomes are in the original single cell in the diagram on page 116?

2. How many homologous pairs are shown in the original cell?

3. How many times do the chromosomes make copies of themselves during meiosis? How many times do cells divide during meiosis?

4. How many chromosomes are present in each cell at the end of meiosis? at the end of mitosis?

(See page 782 to check your answers.)

internet connect

SC*L*INKS
NSTA

TOPIC: Cell Division
GO TO: www.scilinks.org
*sci*LINKS NUMBER: HSTL120

Meiosis and Mendel

As Walter Sutton realized, the steps in meiosis explain Mendel's findings. **Figure 10** illustrates what happens to a pair of homologous chromosomes during meiosis and fertilization. The cross is between a plant that is true breeding for round seeds and a plant that is true breeding for wrinkled seeds.

Figure 10 *Meiosis helps explain Mendel's findings.*

Male Parent In the plant cell nucleus below, each homologous chromosome has an allele for seed shape and each allele carries the same instructions: to make wrinkled seeds.

Female Parent In the plant cell nucleus below, each homologous chromosome has an allele for seed shape and each allele carries the same instruction: to make round seeds.

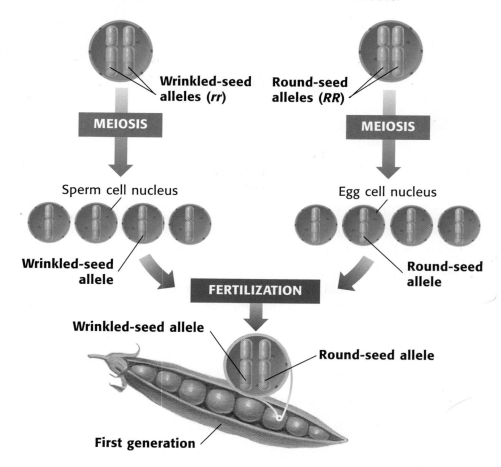

Following **meiosis**, each sperm cell contains a recessive allele for wrinkled seeds and each egg cell contains a dominant allele for round seeds.

Fertilization of any egg by any sperm results in the same genotype (*Rr*) and the same phenotype (round). This is exactly what Mendel found in his studies.

Each fertilized egg in the first generation contained one dominant allele and one recessive allele for seed type. Only one genotype was possible because all sperm formed during meiosis contained the wrinkled-seed allele and all eggs contained the round-seed allele. When the first generation was allowed to self-pollinate, the possible genotypes changed. There are three genotype possibilities for this cross: ***RR, Rr,*** and ***rr.***

Male or Female?

There are many ways that different organisms become male or female. To see how this happens in humans, examine **Figure 11.** Then look back at Figure 9, on page 114. Each figure shows the chromosomes in human body cells. Which chromosome photograph is from a female, and which is from a male? Here's a hint: Females have 23 matched pairs, while males have 22 matched pairs and one unmatched pair.

Sex Chromosomes The chromosomes in Figure 11 are from a male, and the chromosomes in Figure 9 are from a female. **Sex chromosomes** carry genes that determine whether the offspring is male or female. In humans, females have two X chromosomes (the matching pair), and males have one X chromosome and one Y chromosome (the unmatched pair).

During meiosis, one of each of the chromosome pairs ends up in a sex cell. This is also true of the sex chromosomes. Females have two X chromosomes in each body cell. When meiosis produces the egg cells, each egg contains one X chromosome. Males have both an X chromosome and a Y chromosome in each body cell. During meiosis, these chromosomes separate, so each sperm cell contains either an X or a Y chromosome. An egg fertilized by a sperm with an X chromosome will produce a female. If the sperm contains a Y chromosome, the offspring will be male. This is illustrated in **Figure 12.**

Figure 11 *Are these chromosomes from a male or female? How can you tell?*

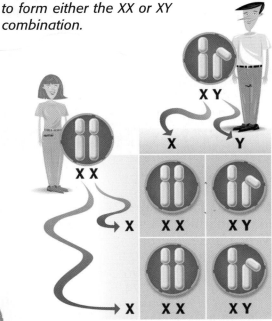

Figure 12 *Egg and sperm combine to form either the XX or XY combination.*

50% females   50% males

REVIEW

1. Explain the difference between sex cells and sex chromosomes.

2. If there are 14 chromosomes in pea plant cells, how many chromosomes are present in a sex cell of a pea?

3. **Interpreting Illustrations** Examine the illustration at right. Does it show a stage of mitosis or meiosis? How can you tell?

Chapter Highlights

Vocabulary

heredity *(p. 106)*

dominant trait *(p. 109)*

recessive trait *(p. 109)*

genes *(p. 111)*

alleles *(p. 111)*

genotype *(p. 111)*

phenotype *(p. 111)*

probability *(p. 112)*

Section Notes

- Heredity is the passing of traits from parents to offspring.

- Traits are inherited forms of characteristics.

- Gregor Mendel used pea plants to study heredity.

- Mendel's pea plants were self-pollinating. They contained both male and female reproductive structures. They were also true breeding, always producing offspring with the same traits as the parents.

- Offspring inherit two sets of instructions for each characteristic, one set from each parent.

- The sets of instructions are known as genes.

- Different versions of the same gene are known as alleles.

- If both the dominant allele and the recessive allele are inherited for a characteristic, only the dominant allele is expressed.

- Recessive traits are apparent only when two recessive alleles for the characteristic are inherited.

- A genotype is the combination of alleles for a particular trait.

- A phenotype is the physical expression of the genotype.

- Probability is the mathematical chance that an event will occur. It is usually expressed as a fraction or as a percentage.

Labs

Bug Builders, Inc. *(p. 702)*

Tracing Traits *(p. 704)*

☑ Skills Check

Math Concepts

RATIOS A jar contains 24 green marbles and 96 red marbles. There are 4 red marbles for every 1 green marble.

$$\frac{96}{24} = \frac{4}{1}$$

This can also be written as follows:

$$4:1$$

Visual Understanding

PUNNETT SQUARES
A Punnett square can help you visualize all the possible combinations of alleles passed from parents to offspring. See page 111 to review how Punnett squares are made.

Vocabulary

sex cells *(p. 114)*

homologous chromosomes *(p. 114)*

meiosis *(p. 115)*

sex chromosomes *(p. 119)*

Section Notes

- Genes are located on chromosomes.

- Most human cells contain 46 chromosomes, or 23 pairs.

- Each pair contains one chromosome donated by the mother and one donated by the father. These pairs are known as homologous chromosomes.

- Meiosis produces sex cells, eggs and sperm.

- Sex cells have half the usual number of chromosomes.

- Sex chromosomes contain genes that determine an offspring's sex.

- Human females have two X chromosomes, and males have one X chromosome and one Y chromosome.

 internetconnect

GO TO: go.hrw.com

Visit the **HRW** Web site for a variety of learning tools related to this chapter. Just type in the keyword:

KEYWORD: HSTHER

GO TO: www.scilinks.org

Visit the **National Science Teachers Association** on-line Web site for Internet resources related to this chapter. Just type in the *sci*LINKS number for more information about the topic:

TOPIC: Gregor Mendel	***sci*LINKS NUMBER:** HSTL105
TOPIC: Heredity	***sci*LINKS NUMBER:** HSTL110
TOPIC: Dominant and Recessive Traits	***sci*LINKS NUMBER:** HSTL115
TOPIC: Cell Division	***sci*LINKS NUMBER:** HSTL120

Chapter Review

USING VOCABULARY

To complete the following sentences, choose the correct term from each pair of terms listed below:

1. Sperm and eggs are known as __?__ . (*sex cells* or *sex chromosomes*)

2. The __?__ , the expression of a trait, is determined by the __?__ , the combination of alleles. (*genotype* or *phenotype*)

3. __?__ produces cells with half the normal number of chromosomes. (*Meiosis* or *Mitosis*)

4. Different versions of the same genes are called __?__ . (*sex cells* or *alleles*)

5. A __?__ plant can pollinate its own eggs. (*self-pollinating* or *true-breeding*)

UNDERSTANDING CONCEPTS

Multiple Choice

6. Genes are found on
   a. chromosomes.
   b. alleles.
   c. proteins.
   d. anthers.

7. The process that produces sex cells is
   a. mitosis.
   b. photosynthesis.
   c. meiosis.
   d. probability.

8. The passing of traits from parents to offspring is
   a. probability.
   b. heredity.
   c. recessive.
   d. meiosis.

9. If you cross a white flower (with the genotype *pp*) with a purple flower (with the genotype *PP*), the possible genotypes in the offspring are:
   a. *PP* and *pp.*
   b. all *Pp.*
   c. all *PP.*
   d. all *pp.*

10. For the above cross, what would the phenotypes be?
    a. all white
    b. all tall
    c. all purple
    d. $\frac{1}{2}$ white, $\frac{1}{2}$ purple

11. In meiosis,
    a. the chromosomes are copied twice.
    b. the nucleus divides once.
    c. four cells are produced from a single cell.
    d. All of the above

12. Probability is
    a. always expressed as a ratio.
    b. a 50% chance that an event will occur.
    c. the mathematical chance that an event will occur.
    d. a 3:1 chance that an event will occur.

Short Answer

13. Which sex chromosomes do females have? Which do males have?

14. In your own words, give a one- or two-sentence definition of the term *recessive trait*.

15. How are sex cells different from other body cells?

Concept Mapping

16. Use the following terms to create a concept map: meiosis, eggs, cell division, X chromosome, sex cells, sperm, mitosis, Y chromosome.

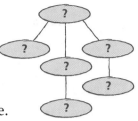

CRITICAL THINKING AND PROBLEM SOLVING

Write one or two sentences to answer the following questions:

17. If a child has blue eyes and both her parents have brown eyes, what does that tell you about the trait for blue eyes? Explain your answer.

18. Why is meiosis important for sexual reproduction?

19. Gregor Mendel used only true-breeding plants. If he had used plants that were not true breeding, do you think he would have discovered dominant and recessive traits? Why or why not?

MATH IN SCIENCE

20. Assume that *Y* is the dominent allele for yellow seeds and *y* is the recessive allele for green seeds. What is the probability that a pea plant with the genotype *Yy* crossed with a pea plant with the genotype *yy* will have offspring with the genotype *yy*?

INTERPRETING GRAPHICS

Examine the Punnett square below, and then answer the following questions:

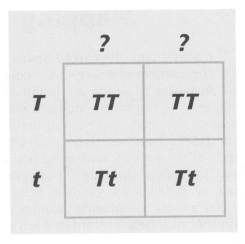

21. What is the unknown genotype?

22. If *T* represents the allele for tall pea plants, and *t* represents the allele for short pea plants, what is the phenotype of each parent and of the offspring?

23. If each of the offspring were allowed to self-fertilize, what are the possible genotypes in the next generation?

24. What is the probability of each genotype in item 23?

NOW What Do You Think?

Take a minute to review your answers to the ScienceLog questions on page 105. Have your answers changed? If necessary, revise your answers based on what you have learned since you began this chapter.

Science, Technology, and Society

Mapping the Human Genome

Scientists with the United States Department of Energy and National Institutes of Health are in the midst of what may be the most ambitious scientific research project ever—the Human Genome Project (HGP). These researchers want to create a map of all the genes found on human chromosomes. The body's complete set of genetic instructions is called the genome. Scientists hope this project will provide valuable information that may help prevent or even cure many genetic diseases.

Whose Genes Are These?

You might be wondering whose genome the scientists are decoding. Actually, it doesn't matter because each person is unique in only about 1 percent of his or her genetic material. The scientists' goal is to identify how tiny differences in that 1 percent of DNA make each of us who we are, and to understand how some changes can cause disease.

Genetic Medicine

The tiny changes that can cause disease, called mutations, are often inherited. Once scientists determine the normal order of our genes, doctors may be able to use this information to help detect mutations in patients. Then doctors would be able to warn patients of an increased risk of a disease before any symptoms appear! For example, a doctor's early warning about a genetic risk of high cholesterol would give a person a chance to eat healthier and exercise more before any serious symptoms were detectable.

Advancing Technology

Scientists organizing the HGP hope to have a complete and accurate sequence of the human

▲ *This scientist is performing one of the many steps involved in the research for the Human Genome Project.*

genome—estimated to have between 50,000 and 100,000 genes—by 2003. One day in the future, scientists may even be able to provide people with a healthy gene to replace a mutated one. This technique, called gene therapy, may eventually be the cure for many genetic diseases.

What Do You Think?

▶ Despite the medical advancements the Human Genome Project will bring, many people continue to debate ethical, social, and legal issues surrounding this controversial project. Look into these issues, and discuss them with your classmates!

WATCH
WATCH
WATCH
Health
WATCH
WATCH
WATCH

Lab Rats with Wings

What's less than 1 mm in length, can be extremely annoying when buzzing around your kitchen, and sometimes grows legs out of its eyes? The answer is *Drosophila melanogaster*—better known as the fruit fly because it feeds on fruit. This tiny insect has played a big role in helping us understand many illnesses, especially those that occur at certain stages of human development. Scientists use fruit flies to find out more about diseases and disorders such as cancer, Alzheimer's disease, muscular dystrophy, and Down's syndrome.

Why a Fly?

Fruit flies are some scientists' favorite research animal. Scientists can raise several generations of fruit flies in just a few months. Because fruit flies have only a two-week life cycle, scientists can alter a fruit-fly gene as part of an experiment and then see the results very quickly.

Another advantage to using these tiny animals is their small size. Thousands of fruit flies can be raised in a relatively small space.

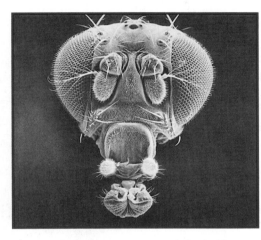

▲ *This is what a normal fruit fly looks like under a scanning electron microscope.*

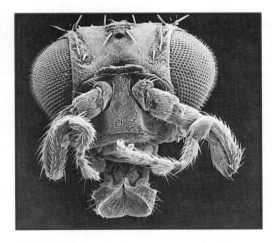

▲ *This fruit fly has legs growing out of its eyes!*

Researchers can afford to buy and maintain a variety of fruit fly strains to use in experiments.

Comparing Codes

Another important reason for using these "lab rats with wings" is that their genetic code is relatively simple and well understood. Fruit flies have 12,000 genes, whereas humans have more than 70,000. Nonetheless, many fruit-fly genes are similar in function to human genes, and scientists have learned to manipulate them to produce genetic mutations. Scientists who study these mutations gain valuable information about genetic mutations in humans. Without fruit flies, some human genetic problems that we now have important information about—such as basal cell carcinoma cancer—might have taken many more years and many more dollars to study.

Where Do You Draw the Line?

▶ Do you think it is acceptable for scientists to perform research on fruit flies? What about on rats, mice, and rabbits? Have a debate with your classmates about conducting scientific experiments on other species.

6 Genes and Gene Technology

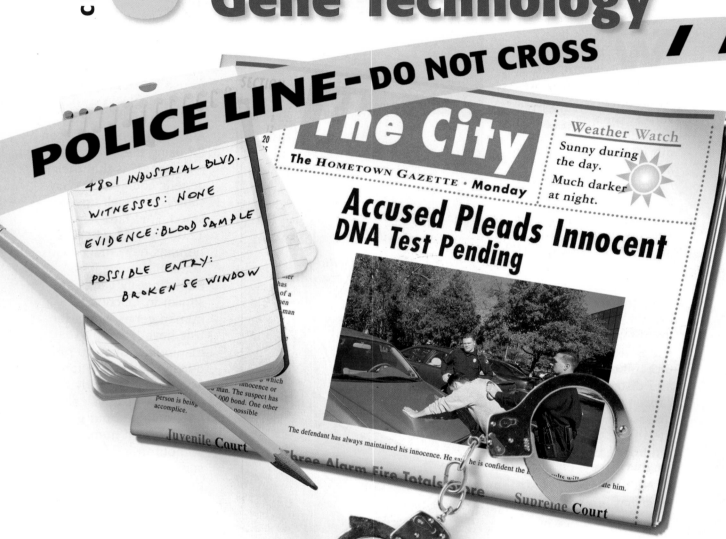

POLICE LINE - DO NOT CROSS

4801 INDUSTRIAL BLVD.

WITNESSES: NONE

EVIDENCE: BLOOD SAMPLE

POSSIBLE ENTRY:
BROKEN SE WINDOW

The City

THE HOMETOWN GAZETTE • Monday

Weather Watch
Sunny during the day.
Much darker at night.

Accused Pleads Innocent
DNA Test Pending

The defendant has always maintained his innocence. He said he is confident the results will vindicate him.

What If . . . ?

Imagine that you are wrongly accused of a crime. A witness at the scene picks you out of a lineup. Your blood type matches blood found at the scene. You were really at home when the crime occurred, but you have no way to prove it. However, there is a witness that can help you—your DNA. DNA is a substance found in nearly every one of your cells.

A technique known as DNA fingerprinting can produce an image of the patterns made by your DNA. Unless you have an identical twin, your DNA fingerprint is like no one else's and can be used to identify you. But what is DNA? Why is yours unique? What does DNA have to do with who you are? In this chapter you will learn the answers to these questions.

What Do You Think?

In your ScienceLog, try to answer the following questions based on what you already know:

1. How are proteins related to the way you look?
2. What are genes? Where are they found?
3. How does knowing about DNA help scientists treat diseases?

Fingerprint Your Friends

One common method of identification is finger-printing. Does it really work? Are everyone's fingerprints different? Try this activity to find out.

Procedure

1. Rub a **piece of charcoal** back and forth across a **piece of tracing paper.** Rub the tip of one of your fingers on the charcoal mark. Then place a **small piece of transparent tape** over the charcoal on your finger. Remove the tape, and stick it on a **piece of white paper.** Do the same for the rest of your fingers.

2. Observe the patterns with a **magnifying lens.** What kinds of patterns do you see? The finger-print patterns shown at right are the most common found among humans. Is the pattern the same on each of your fingers?

Analysis

3. Compare your fingerprints with those of your classmates. How many of each type do you see? Do any two people in your class have the same prints? Try to explain your findings.

Whorl

Arch

Loop

Terms to Learn

DNA   thymine
nucleotide   guanine
adenine   cytosine

What You'll Do

◆ Describe the basic structure of the DNA molecule.
◆ Explain how DNA molecules can be copied.
◆ Explain some of the exceptions to Mendel's heredity principles.

What Do Genes Look Like?

Scientists know that traits are determined by genes and that genes are passed from one generation to another. Scientists also know that genes are located on chromosomes, structures in the nucleus of most cells. Chromosomes are made of protein and **DNA**, short for deoxyribonucleic (dee AHKS ee RIE boh noo KLEE ik) acid. But which type of material makes the genes?

The Pieces of the Puzzle

The gene material must be able to do two things. First it must be able to supply instructions for cell processes and for building cell structures. Second it must be able to be copied each time a cell divides, so that each cell contains an identical set of genes. Early studies of DNA suggested that DNA was a very simple molecule. Because of this, most scientists thought protein probably carried hereditary information. After all, proteins are complex molecules.

In the 1940s, however, scientists discovered that genes of bacteria are made of DNA. How could something so simple hold the key to an organism's characteristics? To find the answer, let's take a closer look at the subunits of a DNA molecule.

Nucleotides—The Subunits of DNA DNA is made of only four subunits, which are known as **nucleotides.** Each nucleotide consists of three different types of material: a sugar, a phosphate, and a base. Nucleotides are identical except for the base. The four bases are **adenine, thymine, guanine,** and **cytosine,** and they each have a slightly different shape. The bases are usually referred to by the first letters in their names, A, T, G, and C. **Figure 1** shows diagrams of the four nucleotides.

Adenine (A)

Nucleotide

Thymine (T)

Figure 1 *Can you imagine how the nucleotides might fit together?*

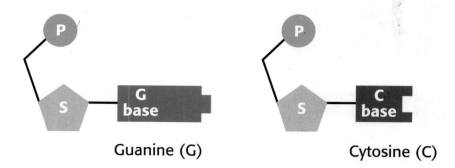

Guanine (G)   Cytosine (C)

Chargaff's Rules In the 1950s, a biochemist named Erwin Chargaff found that the amount of adenine in DNA always equals the amount of thymine, and the amount of guanine always equals the amount of cytosine. His findings are known as Chargaff's rules.

At the time, no one knew quite what to make of Chargaff's findings. How could Chargaff's rules help solve the mysteries of DNA's structure? Read on to find out.

A Picture of DNA

More clues came from the laboratory of British scientist Maurice Wilkins. There, chemist Rosalind Franklin, shown in **Figure 2,** was able to create images of DNA molecules. The process that she used to create these images is known as X-ray diffraction. In this process, X rays bombard the DNA molecule. When the X ray hits a particle within the molecule, the ray bounces off the particle. This creates a pattern that is captured on film. The images that Franklin created suggested that DNA has a spiral shape.

Figure 2 Rosalind Franklin, 1920–1958

Eureka!

Two other young scientists, James Watson and Francis Crick, shown in **Figure 3,** were also investigating the mystery of DNA's structure. Based on the work of others, Watson and Crick built models of DNA using simple materials, such as labeled pieces of cardboard. After seeing the X-ray images of DNA made by Rosalind Franklin, Watson and Crick concluded that DNA resembles a twisted ladder shape known as a *double helix.* Watson and Crick used their DNA model to predict how DNA is copied. Upon making the discovery, Crick is said to have exclaimed, "We have discovered the secret of life!"

Figure 3 *This photo shows James Watson, on the left, and Francis Crick, on the right, with their model of DNA.*

DNA Structure

The twisted ladder, or double helix, shape is represented in **Figure 4.** As you can see in **Figure 5,** the two sides of the ladder are made of alternating sugar molecules and phosphate molecules. The rungs of the ladder are composed of a pair of nucleotide bases. Adenine on one side always pairs up with thymine on the other side. Guanine always pairs up with cytosine in the same way. How might this structure explain Chargaff's findings?

Figure 4 *The structure of DNA can be compared to a twisted ladder.*

Figure 5 *In a DNA molecule, the bases must pair up in a certain way. If a mistake happens and the bases do not pair up correctly, the gene may not carry the correct information.*

Making Copies of DNA

What's so great about DNA? Because adenine always bonds with thymine and guanine always bonds with cytosine, one side of a DNA molecule is *complementary* to the other. For example, a sequence such as ACCG always binds to the sequence TGGC. This allows DNA to make a copy of itself, or *replicate*.

As illustrated in **Figure 6,** a DNA molecule replicates by splitting down the middle where the two bases meet. The bases on each side of the molecule can be used as a template, or pattern, for a new complementary side. This creates two identical molecules of DNA.

÷ 5 ÷ Ω ≤ ∞ +Ω √ 9 ∞ ≤ Σ 2
+

MATH BREAK

Genes and Bases

A human being has about 100,000 genes. If there are about 30,000 bases in each human gene, about how many bases are in all the genes?

Figure 6 *The illustration shows DNA separating down the middle in order to make a copy of itself. Each half of the original molecule serves as a template along which a new complementary strand forms. The photograph shows a DNA molecule that has separated. It is magnified about 1 million times.*

✓ Self-Check

What would the complementary strand of DNA be for the following sequence of bases? ACCTAGTTG *(See page 782 to check your answer.)*

Old   New   New   Old

BRAIN FOOD

If you took all the DNA in your body from all of your cells and stretched it out end to end, it would extend about 610 million kilometers. That's long enough to stretch from Earth to the sun and back—twice!

From Trait to Gene

The Watson-Crick model also explains how DNA can contain so much information. The bases on one side of the molecule can be put in any order, allowing for an enormous variety of genes. Each gene consists of a string of bases. The order of the bases gives the cell information about how to make each trait.

Putting It All Together DNA functions in the same way for all organisms, from bacteria to mosquitoes to whales to humans. DNA unites us all, and at the same time, it makes each of us unique. The journey from trait to DNA base is illustrated in the diagram on these two pages.

2
. . . magnified 10 times

1
The skin of your forehead . . .

3
A cross section of your skin reveals many different types of cells.

4
A typical skin cell is about 0.0025 cm in diameter.

8
A single loop
of DNA . . .

7
Each chromosome
contains an enormous
amount of DNA.

9
. . . contains
even more
coils.

6
Each chromosome
is made of protein
and DNA.

10
Each molecule
of DNA contains
two halves that are
connected down the
center and twisted
like a spiral
staircase.

5
Each skin cell
contains 46
chromosomes.

S C ... G S P

S G ... C S P

S T ... A P

P C ... G S

S A ... T S

DNA
on trial?
Read all about
it on page 146.

Figure 7 *The snapdragon provides a good example of incomplete dominance.*

LabBook

A C G T

Learn the DNA alphabet on page 706.

More News About Traits

As you may have already discovered, things are often more complicated than they first appear to be. Gregor Mendel uncovered the basic principles of how genes are passed from one generation to the next. But as scientists learned more about heredity, they began to find exceptions to Mendel's principles. A few of these exceptions are explained in the following paragraphs.

Incomplete Dominance In his studies with peas, Mendel found that different traits did not blend together to produce an in-between form. Since then, researchers have found that sometimes one trait is not completely dominant over another. These traits do not blend together, but each allele has its own degree of influence. This is known as *incomplete dominance*. One example of this is the snapdragon flower. **Figure 7** shows a cross between a true-breeding red snapdragon (R^1R^1) and a true-breeding white snapdragon (R^2R^2). As you can see, all of the possible phenotypes for their offspring are pink because both alleles of the gene have some degree of influence.

One Gene Can Influence Many Traits Sometimes one gene influences more than one trait. An example of this phenomenon is shown by the white tiger at right. The white fur is caused by a single gene, but this gene influences more than just fur color. Do you see anything else unusual about the tiger? If you look closely, you'll see that the tiger has blue eyes. Here the gene that controls fur color also influences eye color.

Many Genes Can Influence a Single Trait Some traits, such as the color of your skin, hair, and eyes, are the result of several genes acting together. That's why it's difficult to tell if a trait is the result of a dominant or recessive gene. As shown in **Figure 8,** you may have blue eyes, but they are probably a slightly different shade of blue than the blue eyes of a classmate. Different combinations of alleles result in slight differences in the amount of pigment present.

The Importance of Environment It's important to remember that genes aren't the only influences on your development. Many things in your environment also influence how you grow and develop. Consider the importance of a healthy diet, exercise, and examples set by family and friends. For example, your genes may determine that you can grow to be tall, but you must receive the proper nutrients as you grow in order to reach your full potential height. You may have inherited a special talent, but you need to practice.

Figure 8 *At least two genes determine human eye color. That's why so many shades of a single color are possible.*

REVIEW

1. List and describe the parts of a nucleotide.

2. Which bases pair together in a DNA molecule?

3. What shape was suggested by Rosalind Franklin's X-ray images?

4. Explain what is meant by the statement, "DNA unites all organisms."

5. **Doing Calculations** If a sample of DNA were found to contain 20 percent cytosine, what percentage of guanine would be in this sample? Why?

internet connect

sci LINKS
NSTA

TOPIC: DNA, Genes and Traits
GO TO: www.scilinks.org
sciLINKS NUMBER: HSTL130, HSTL135

How DNA Works

Terms to Learn

ribosome   mutagen
mutation   pedigree

What You'll Do

◆ Explain the relationship between genes and proteins.
◆ Outline the basic steps in making a protein.
◆ Define *mutation,* and give an example.
◆ Evaluate the information in a pedigree.

Scientists knew that the order of the bases formed a code that somehow told each cell what to do. The next step in understanding DNA involved breaking this code.

Genes and Proteins

Scientists discovered that the bases in DNA read like a book, from one end to the other and in one direction only. The bases **A, T, G,** and **C** form the alphabet of the code. Groups of three bases code for a specific amino acid. For example, the three bases **CCA** code for the amino acid proline. The bases **AGC** code for the amino acid serine. As you know, proteins are made up of long strings of amino acids. The order of the bases determines the order of amino acids in a protein. Each gene is a set of instructions for making a protein. This is illustrated in **Figure 9.**

NUCLEUS

A copy of a portion of the DNA molecule where a particular gene is located is made and transferred outside of the cell nucleus.

This single strand is a copy of one strand of the original DNA.

Base

Each group of three bases codes for one amino acid.

Figure 9 *A gene is a section of DNA that contains instructions for stringing together amino acids to make a protein.*

Why Proteins? You may be wondering, "What do proteins have to do with who I am or what I look like?" Proteins are found throughout cells. They act as chemical messengers, and they help determine how tall you will grow, what colors you can see, and whether your hair is curly or straight. Human cells contain about 100,000 genes, and each gene spells out sequences of amino acids for specific proteins. Proteins exist in an almost limitless variety. The human body contains about 50,000 different kinds of proteins. Proteins are the reason for the multitude of different shapes, sizes, colors, and textures found in living things, such as antlers, claws, hair, and skin.

The Making of a Protein

As explained in Figure 9, the first step in making a protein is to copy the section of the DNA strand containing a gene. A copy of this section is made with the help of copier enzymes. Messenger molecules take the genetic information from the sections of DNA in the nucleus out into the cytoplasm.

In the cytoplasm, the copy of DNA is fed through a kind of protein assembly line. The "factory" where this assembly line exists is known as a **ribosome.** The copy is fed through the ribosome three bases at a time. Transfer molecules act as translators of the message contained in the copy of DNA. Each transfer molecule picks up a specific amino acid from the cytoplasm. The amino acid is determined by the order of the bases the transfer molecule contains. Like pieces of a puzzle, bases on the transfer molecule then match up with bases on the copy of DNA inside the ribosome. The transfer molecules then drop off their amino acid "suitcases," which are strung together to form a protein. This process is illustrated in **Figure 10.**

✓ Self-Check

1. How many amino acids are present in a protein that requires 3,000 bases in its code?

2. Explain how proteins influence how you look.

(See page 782 to check your answers.)

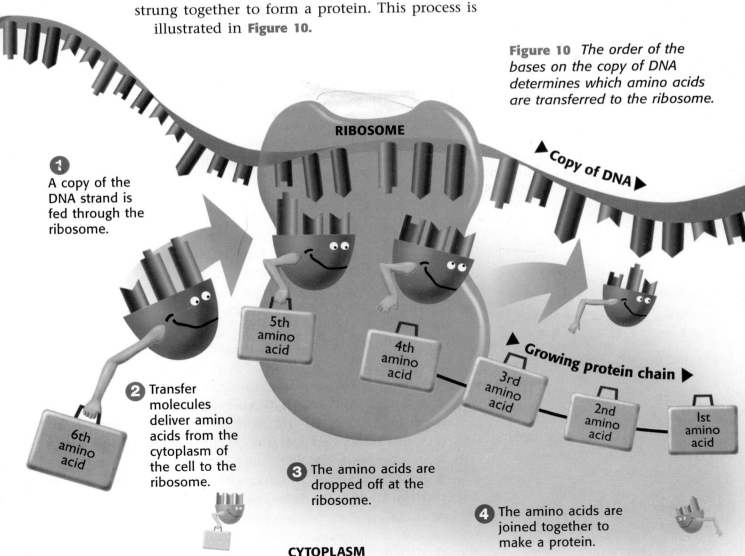

Figure 10 *The order of the bases on the copy of DNA determines which amino acids are transferred to the ribosome.*

RIBOSOME

▲ Copy of DNA ▶

1 A copy of the DNA strand is fed through the ribosome.

2 Transfer molecules deliver amino acids from the cytoplasm of the cell to the ribosome.

3 The amino acids are dropped off at the ribosome.

4 The amino acids are joined together to make a protein.

▲ Growing protein chain ▶

5th amino acid

4th amino acid

3rd amino acid

2nd amino acid

1st amino acid

6th amino acid

CYTOPLASM

Original sequence

a Base pair replaced

b Base pair added

c Base pair removed

Figure 11 *The original base-pair sequence at the top has been changed to illustrate (a) substitution, (b) insertion, and (c) deletion.*

Meteorology

CONNECTION

The layer of ozone in the Earth's atmosphere helps shield the planet's surface from ultraviolet (UV) radiation. UV radiation can cause mutations in skin cells that can lead to cancer. Each year more than 750,000 people get skin cancer. Scientists fear that damage to the ozone layer may greatly increase the number of skin cancers each year.

Changes in Genes

Imagine that you've been invited to ride on a brand-new roller coaster at the state fair. Just before you climb into the front car, you are informed that some of the metal parts on the coaster have been replaced by parts made of a different substance. Would you still want to ride this roller coaster?

Perhaps a stronger metal was substituted. Or perhaps a material not suited to the job was used. Imagine what would happen if cardboard were used instead of metal!

Mutant Molecules Substitutions like this can occur in DNA. They are known as **mutations.** Mutations occur when there is a change in the order of bases in an organism's DNA. Sometimes a base is left out; this is known as a *deletion.* Or an extra base might be added; this is known as an *insertion.* The most common error occurs when an incorrect base replaces a correct base. This is known as a *substitution.* **Figure 11** illustrates these three types of mutations.

Mistakes Happen Fortunately, repair enzymes are continuously on the job, patrolling the DNA molecule for errors. When an error is found, it is usually repaired. But occasionally the repairs are not completely accurate, and the mistakes become part of the genetic message. There are three possible consequences to changes in DNA: an improvement, no change at all, or a harmful change. If the mutation occurs in the sex cells, it can be passed from one generation to the next.

How Can DNA Become Damaged? In addition to random errors that occur when DNA is copied, damage can be caused by physical and chemical agents known as mutagens. A **mutagen** is anything that can cause a mutation in DNA. Examples of mutagens include high-energy radiation from X rays and ultraviolet radiation. Ultraviolet radiation is the type of energy in sunlight that is responsible for suntans and sunburns. Other mutagens include asbestos and the chemicals in cigarette smoke.

An Example of a Substitution

Consider the DNA sequence containing the three bases **GAA**. **GAA** are the three letters that give the instructions: "Put the amino acid glutamic acid here." If a mistake occurs and the sequence is changed to **GTA**, a completely different message is sent: "Put valine here."

This simple change just described can cause the disease *sickle cell anemia*. Sickle cell anemia is a disease that affects red blood cells. When valine is substituted for glutamic acid in a blood protein, as shown in **Figure 12,** the red blood cells become distorted into a sickle shape.

The sickled cells are not as good as normal red blood cells at carrying oxygen. They are also more likely to get stuck in blood vessels, causing painful and dangerous clots.

QuickLab

Mutations

The sentence below contains all three-letter words but has experienced a mutation. Can you find the mutation?

THE IGR EDC ATA TET HEB IGB ADR AT

What kind of mutation did you find? Now what does the sentence say?

TRY at HOME

Normal red blood cell

Substitution

Sickled red blood cell

Figure 12 *The simple change of one base leads to the disease called sickle cell anemia.*

Genetic Counseling

Most hereditary disorders, such as sickle cell anemia, are recessive disorders. This means that the disease occurs only when a child inherits a defective gene from both parents. Some people, called carriers, have only one allele for the disease. Carriers of the gene may pass it along to their children without knowing that they have the mutated gene.

Genetic counseling provides information and counseling to couples who wish to have children but are worried that they might pass a disease to their children. Genetic counselors often make use of a diagram known as a **pedigree,** which is a tool for tracing a trait through generations of a family. By making a pedigree, it is often possible to predict whether a person is a carrier of a hereditary disease. In **Figure 13,** the trait for the disease cystic fibrosis is tracked through four generations. Each generation is numbered with Roman numerals, and each individual is numbered with Arabic numerals.

Figure 13 *Cystic fibrosis is a recessive hereditary disease that affects the respiratory system. A pedigree for cystic fibrosis is shown below.*

 Males ◯ Females

Vertical lines connect children to their parents.

■ or ● A solid square or circle indicates that the person has a certain trait.

◣ or ◐ A half-filled square or circle indicates that the person is a carrier of the trait.

Pedigree and Punnett Squares

The pedigree at right shows the recessive trait of nearsightedness in Jane's family. Jane, her parents, and her brother all have normal vision. Which individuals in the pedigree are nearsighted? What are the possible genotypes of Jane's parents? Jane has two possible genotypes. What are they? Jane is planning to marry a person who has normal vision but carries the trait for nearsightedness. Work two Punnett squares to show the possible genotypes of Jane's future children.

Designer Genes

For thousands of years, humans have been aware of the benefits of selective breeding. In *selective breeding*, organisms with certain desirable characteristics are mated to produce a new breed. You probably have enjoyed the benefits of selective breeding, although you may not have realized it. For example, you may have eaten an egg from a chicken that was bred to produce a large number of eggs. Your pet dog might even be a result of selective breeding. Some kinds of dogs, for example, have a thick coat so that they can retrieve game in icy waters.

Engineering Organisms Scientists now have the ability to produce desired characteristics in some organisms without breeding. They can manipulate individual genes using a technique known as genetic engineering. Like all types of engineering, genetic engineering puts scientific knowledge to practical use. Basically, *genetic engineering* allows scientists to transfer genes from one organism to another. Genetic engineering is already used to manufacture proteins, repair damaged genes, and identify individuals who may carry an allele for a disease. Some other uses are shown in **Figures 14** and **15**.

Figure 14 *Scientists added a gene found in fireflies to this tobacco plant. The plant now produces an enzyme that causes the plant to glow.*

Figure 15 *A sheep called Dolly was the first successfully cloned mammal.*

REVIEW

1. List the three types of mutations. How do they differ?

2. What type of mutation causes sickle cell anemia?

3. How is genetic engineering different from selective breeding?

4. **Applying Concepts** Mutations can occur in sex cells or in body cells. In which cell type might a mutation be passed from generation to generation? Explain.

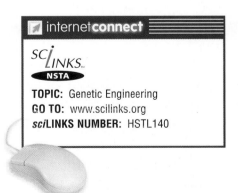

internet**connect**

SC*i*LINKS
NSTA

TOPIC: Genetic Engineering
GO TO: www.scilinks.org
sci*LINKS NUMBER: HSTL140

Chapter Highlights

Vocabulary

DNA *(p. 128)*

nucleotide *(p. 128)*

adenine *(p. 128)*

thymine *(p. 128)*

guanine *(p. 128)*

cytosine *(p. 128)*

Section Notes

- Proteins are made of long strings of amino acids.

- DNA is made of long strings of nucleotides.

- Chromosomes are made of protein and DNA.

- The DNA molecule looks like a twisted ladder. The rungs of the ladder are made of base pairs, either adenine and thymine, or cytosine and guanine.

- DNA carries genetic information in the order of the nucleotide bases.

- DNA can be copied because one strand of the molecule serves as a template for the other side.

Labs

Base-Pair Basics *(p. 706)*

☑ Skills Check

Math Concepts

THE GENETIC CODE The MathBreak on page 131 asks you to calculate the number of bases in all of your genes. If there are about 30,000 bases in each gene and there are 100,000 genes, then multiply to find the answer.

$$30,000 \times 100,000 = 3,000,000,000$$

So, there are about 3 billion bases in all of your genes.

Visual Understanding

COPIES OF DNA Look at Figure 9 on page 136. You can see the nucleus and the pores in its membrane. The copy of DNA emerges through these pores on its way to deliver its coded message to the ribosomes. Why does DNA send a copy out of the nucleus to relay its message? The answer is that DNA is much more protected from factors that might cause a mutation if it stays inside the nucleus. The messenger copy may encounter bad luck, but the master DNA usually stays very safe!

Vocabulary

ribosome *(p. 137)*

mutation *(p. 138)*

mutagen *(p. 138)*

pedigree *(p. 140)*

Section Notes

- A gene is a set of instructions for assembling a protein.

- Each group of three bases in a gene codes for a particular amino acid.

- Genes can become mutated when the order of the bases is changed.

▶ Copy of DNA ▶

5th amino acid

4th amino acid

▶ Growing protein chain ▶

3rd amino acid

2nd amino acid

1st amino acid

6th amino acid

---

internet connect

GO TO: go.hrw.com

Visit the **HRW** Web site for a variety of learning tools related to this chapter. Just type in the keyword:

KEYWORD: HSTDNA

SCi*LINKS*_{SM}

N S T A

GO TO: www.scilinks.org

Visit the **National Science Teachers Association** on-line Web site for Internet resources related to this chapter. Just type in the *sci*LINKS number for more information about the topic:

TOPIC:	DNA	*sci*LINKS NUMBER:	HSTL130
TOPIC:	Genes and Traits	*sci*LINKS NUMBER:	HSTL135
TOPIC:	Genetic Engineering	*sci*LINKS NUMBER:	HSTL140
TOPIC:	DNA Fingerprinting	*sci*LINKS NUMBER:	HSTL145

Chapter Review

USING VOCABULARY

To complete the following sentences, choose the correct term from each pair of terms listed below:

1. A protein is a long string of __?__.
   A strand of DNA is a long string of __?__.
   (*amino acids* or *nucleotides*)

2. A disorder, such as cystic fibrosis, is known as __?__ if the child must receive an allele for the disease from each parent in order to have the disease. (*dominant* or *recessive*)

3. A change in the order of bases in DNA is called a __?__. (*mutation* or *mutagen*)

4. A __?__ is a physical or chemical agent that causes damage to DNA. (*mutagen* or *pedigree*)

UNDERSTANDING CONCEPTS

Multiple Choice

5. In a DNA molecule, which of the following bases pair together?
   a. adenine and cytosine
   b. thymine and adenine
   c. thymine and guanine
   d. cytosine and thymine

6. A gene is
   a. a set of instructions for each trait.
   b. instructions on how to make a protein.
   c. a portion of a strand of DNA.
   d. All of the above

7. DNA
   a. is made up of three subunits.
   b. has a structure like a twisted ladder.
   c. cannot be repaired if it is mutated.
   d. All of the above

8. In incomplete dominance,
   a. a single gene controls many traits.
   b. genes for a trait are all recessive.
   c. each allele for a trait has its own degree of influence.
   d. the environment controls the genes.

9. Watson and Crick
   a. studied the amounts of each base in DNA.
   b. took X-ray pictures of DNA.
   c. made models to determine DNA structure.
   d. discovered that genes were located on chromosomes.

10. Which of the following is NOT a step in making a protein?
    a. Copies of DNA are taken to the cytoplasm.
    b. Transfer molecules deliver amino acids to the nucleus.
    c. Amino acids are joined together at the ribosome to make a protein.
    d. A copy of the DNA is fed through the ribosome.

Short Answer

11. What would the complementary strand of DNA be for the following sequence of bases?

    C T T A G G C T T A C C A

12. How does DNA copy itself? Draw a picture to help explain your answer.

13. If the DNA sequence TGAGCCATGA is changed to TGAGCACATGA, what kind of mutation has occurred?

Concept Mapping

14. Use the following terms to create a concept map: bases, adenine, thymine, nucleotides, guanine, DNA, cytosine.

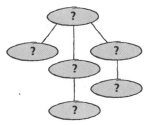

CRITICAL THINKING AND PROBLEM SOLVING

Write one or two sentences to answer the following questions:

15. If neither parent shows signs of having sickle cell anemia, does this fact guarantee that their children will not contract the disease? Explain.

16. How many amino acids does this DNA sequence code for?

    T C A G C C A C C T A T G G A

MATH IN SCIENCE

17. The goal of a project called the Human Genome Project is to discover the location and DNA sequence of all human genes. Scientists estimate that there are 100,000 human genes. In 1998, 38,000 genes had been discovered. How many more genes must the Human Genome Project discover?

18. If scientists find 6,000 genes each year, how many years will it take to finish the project?

19. Of the 38,000 genes discovered, 7,000 have been mapped to their chromosome location. What percentage of the discovered genes have been mapped?

INTERPRETING GRAPHICS

Examine the pedigree for albinism shown below, and then answer the following questions. You may need to use a Punnett square to answer some of these questions. (Albinism is a trait among individuals who produce no pigment in their skin, hair, or eyes.)

20. How many males are represented on this pedigree? How many females?

21. How many individuals in Generation II had albinism? How many were carriers of the trait?

22. Do you think albinism is a dominant trait or a recessive trait? Explain.

NOW What Do You Think?

Take a minute to review your answers to the ScienceLog questions on page 127. Have your answers changed? If necessary, revise your answers based on what you have learned since you began this chapter.

DNA on Trial

The tension in the court-room was so thick you could cut it with a knife. The prosecuting attorney presented the evidence: "DNA analysis indicates that blood found on the defendant's shoes matches the blood of the victim. The odds of this match happening by chance are one in 20 million." The jury members were stunned by these figures. Can there be any doubt that the defendant is guilty?

Next Defendant: DNA

Court battles involving DNA fingerprinting are becoming more and more common. Traditional fingerprinting has been used for more than 100 years, and it has been an extremely important identification tool. Recently, many people have claimed that DNA fingerprinting, also called DNA profiling, will replace the traditional technique. The DNA profiling technique has been used to clear thousands of wrongly accused or convicted individuals. However, the controversy begins when the evidence is used to try to prove a suspect's guilt.

Room for Reasonable Doubt

Critics claim that the DNA fingerprinting process allows too much room for human error.

▲ *This forensic scientist is gathering dead skin cells from an article of clothing in hopes of collecting samples of DNA.*

Handling samples from a crime scene can be tricky—a sample may have been removed from a small area beneath a victim's fingernail or scraped off a dirty sidewalk. Contamination by salt, chemicals, denim, or even a lab person's sneeze can affect the accuracy of the results.

Much of the controversy about DNA fingerprinting surrounds the interpretation of the results. The question becomes, "How likely is it that someone else also has that same DNA profile?" Answers can range from one in three to one in 20 million, depending on the person doing the interpreting, the sample size, and the process used.

Critics also point out that the results may be calculated without regard for certain factors. For instance, individuals belonging to certain ethnic groups are likely to share more characteristics of their DNA with others in their group than with people outside the group.

Beyond a Reasonable Doubt

Those who support DNA evidence point out that the analysis is totally objective because the labs that do the DNA analysis receive samples labeled in code. The data either clear or incriminate a suspect. More-over, DNA evidence alone is rarely used to convict a person. It is one of several forms of evidence, including motive and access to the crime scene, used to reach a verdict.

Supporters of DNA finger-printing say that checks and balances in laboratories help prevent human errors. In addition, recent efforts to standardize both evidence gathering and interpretation of samples have further improved results.

What Do You Think?

▶ Should DNA fingerprinting be admitted as evidence in the courtroom? Do some additional research, and decide for yourself.

Science Fiction

Once upon
in a forewar
land
there
lived a
space

who had a
tic ship
of silver
great
haircut that
was the gala

"Moby James"

by Patricia A. McKillip

Rob Trask has a problem. It's his older brother, James. Rob is convinced that James is not his real brother. Rob and his family live on a space station, and he just knows that his real brother was sent back to Earth. This person who claims to be James is really either some sort of mutant, irradiated plant life or a mutant pair of dirty sweat socks.

Now Rob has another problem—his class is reading Herman Melville's novel *Moby Dick.* At first, Rob just can't get interested in the story. But as he reads more and more, Rob becomes entranced by the story of Captain Ahab and his quest for revenge against the great white whale Moby Dick. Moby Dick had taken something from Ahab—his leg—and Ahab wants to make the whale pay!

Suddenly Rob realizes that his brother is a great white mutant whale—Moby James. As Rob follows Ahab on his search for Moby Dick, Rob begins to understand what he must do to get his real brother back again. So he watches Moby James, trying to catch James in some mistake that will reveal him for the mutant he is. Once Rob catches the fake James, he will be able to get the real James back again.

To find out if Rob is successful in his quest to find his real brother, read "Moby James" in the *Holt Anthology of Science Fiction.*

7 The Evolution of Living Things

SECTION A
Main Street 6
Law & Order 9
Obituaries 11

CENOZOIC TIMES

COMMUNITY NEWS • Saturday June 21

Large Bird Terrorizes Countryside!

Panic Possible

Farmers in the local area reported yesterday seeing a fantastic creature dashing through the trees and trampling crops in their fields. The creature has been described as weighing about 400 lb (about 182 kg), standing about 7 ft (over 2 m) tall, with a huge head, enormous wings, an enormous beak, and ferocious claws.

...ave been no casualties reported. ...acres of corn that was ready for ...appeared! Tracks left behind by ...re are all over the former corn ...corn cobs litter the ground,

...say.

The local agriculture agent reports, "This could be the worst disaster to our corn harvest since the heat wave 10 years ago when all the corn popped in the field." Anyone spotting this creature should stay inside and contact the local ...

Artist's rendering of a marauding monster.

What If . . . ?

The time is 50 million years ago. The place is a swamp in North America. Imagine yourself trekking through the steamy swamp, sidestepping snakes and spiders. Suddenly, out of the trees dashes a 182 kg giant with a huge head, a thick neck, and long, muscular legs.

What is this beast? A velociraptor? A giant sloth? A prehistoric bear? None of the above. It's a *Diatryma*, a kind of flightless bird that was common during the Cenozoic era of prehistory, 57 to 35 million years ago! *Diatryma* stood over 2 m tall and had an enormous beak and sharp claws.

Scientists know about *Diatryma* from many fossils dug up in Wyoming, New Mexico, and New Jersey. *Diatryma* was probably forced out of existence by large mammals. Though the monster bird is long gone, smaller versions of it live in poultry coops around the world. *Diatryma*'s fossils indicate that it was a distant cousin of the present-day chicken!

What Do You Think?

In your ScienceLog, try to answer the following questions based on what you already know:

1. What is evolution?

2. What role does the environment play in the survival of an organism?

Making a Fossil

In this activity, you and a classmate will work together to make two different types of fossils.

Procedure

1. You and your partner will receive a **paper cup,** a **paper plate, modeling clay,** some **petroleum jelly,** and a small item, such as a **leaf,** a **shell,** or a tiny **toy dinosaur.**

2. Pat some modeling clay into the bottom of the paper plate. Press the item into the clay, and then remove it as carefully as possible so that an impression of the object remains in the clay.

3. Pat some clay into the bottom of the cup. Rub petroleum jelly on the item, and place it in the bottom of the cup. (Do not press it into the clay this time.)

4. Have your teacher pour some **plaster of Paris** into the plate and the cup so that the clay and the object are covered. Allow the plaster to dry overnight.

5. The next day, carefully tear the paper plate and cup from the hardened plaster. Remove the clay and the object. You have made two different kinds of fossils—a *mold* and a *cast*. A mold is a cavity (imprint) in the shape of an organism. A cast is a mold filled in with sediment.

Analysis

6. Identify each of your fossils as a mold or a cast.

7. Which of these organisms—a clam, a jellyfish, a crab, or a mushroom—would make good fossils? Which kind of fossil (mold or cast) would you expect to find? Which would not make good fossils? Explain your answers.

Change Over Time

Terms to Learn

adaptation   fossil record
species   vestigial
evolution   structure
fossil

What You'll Do

◆ Explain how fossils provide evidence that organisms have evolved over time.

◆ Identify three ways that organisms can be compared to support the theory of evolution.

If someone asked you to describe a frog, you might say that a frog has long hind legs, eyes that bulge, and a habit of croaking from time to time. Then you might start to think about some of the differences among frogs—differences that set one kind of frog apart from another. Take a look at **Figures 1, 2,** and **3** on this page. These frogs look different from each other, yet they all inhabit a tropical rain forest.

Figure 1 *The red-eyed tree frog hides among a tree's leaves during the day and comes out at night.*

Figure 2 *The smoky jungle frog blends into the forest floor.*

Figure 3 *The strawberry dart-poison frog's bright coloring warns predators that it is poisonous.*

Differences Among Organisms

As you can see, these three frogs have different adaptations that enable them to survive. An **adaptation** is a characteristic that helps an organism survive and reproduce in its environment. Adaptations can include structures and behaviors for finding food, for protection, and for moving from place to place.

Living things that share the same characteristics and adaptations may be members of the same species. A **species** is a group of organisms that can mate with one another to produce fertile offspring. For example, all red-eyed tree frogs are members of the same species and can mate with one another to produce more red-eyed tree frogs.

BRAIN FOOD

Native tribes in Central America rub the poison from the strawberry dart-poison frog on their arrow tips before hunting. The poison helps to paralyze their prey.

Do Species Change over Time? These frogs are just a few of the millions of different species that share the Earth with us. The species on Earth today range from bacteria that lack cell nuclei to multicellular fungi, plants, and animals. Have these same species always existed on Earth?

Earth is a very old planet. Scientists estimate that it is 4.6 billion years old. The planet itself has changed a great deal during that long period of time. Fossil evidence shows that living things have changed as well. Since life first appeared on Earth, a great number of species have died out and have been replaced by newer species. **Figure 4** shows some of the different life-forms that have existed during Earth's history.

What causes species to change? Scientists think that newer species have descended from older species through the process of evolution. **Evolution** is the process by which populations accumulate inherited changes over time. Because of evolution, scientists think that all living things, from daisies to crocodiles to humans, share a common ancestor.

Figure 4 *This spiral diagram represents many changes in life on Earth since the formation of the planet 4.6 billion years ago.*

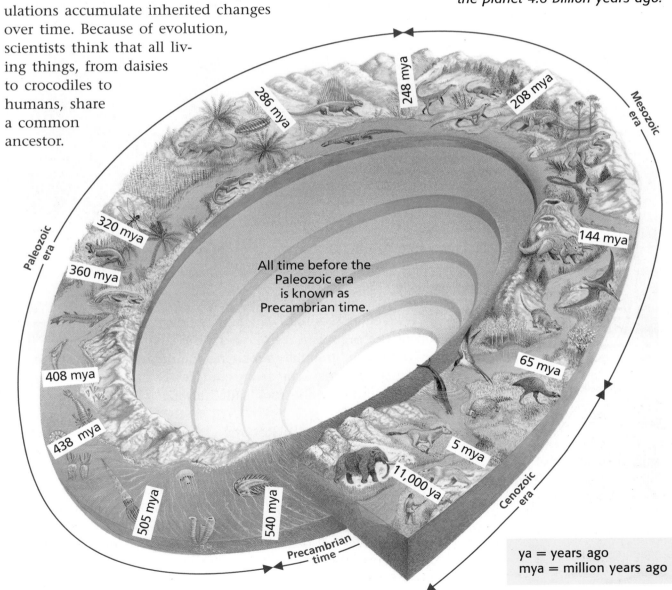

All time before the Paleozoic era is known as Precambrian time.

Mesozoic era

Paleozoic era

Cenozoic era

Precambrian time

286 mya
248 mya
208 mya
144 mya
320 mya
360 mya
408 mya
438 mya
505 mya
540 mya
65 mya
5 mya
11,000 ya

ya = years ago
mya = million years ago

Evidence of Evolution: The Fossil Record

Evidence that living things evolve comes from many different sources. This evidence includes fossils as well as comparisons among different groups of organisms.

Fossils The Earth's crust is arranged in layers, with different kinds of rock and soil stacked on top of one another. These layers are formed when sediments, particles of sand, dust, or soil are carried by wind and water and are deposited in an orderly fashion. Older layers are deposited before newer layers and are buried deeper within the Earth. **Fossils,** the solidified remains or imprints of once-living organisms, are found in these layers. Fossils, like those pictured in **Figure 5,** can be of complete organisms, parts of organisms, or just a set of footprints.

Figure 5 *The fossil on the left is of a trilobite, an ancient aquatic animal. The fossils on the right are of seed ferns.*

Geology

C O N N E C T I O N

Fossils are usually found in layered rock called sedimentary rock. Sedimentary rock usually forms when rock is broken into sediment by wind, water, and other means. The wind and water move the sediment around and deposit it. Over time, layers of sediment pile up. Lower layers are compressed and changed into rock.

Fossils are usually formed when a dead organism is covered by a layer of sediment. Over time, more sediment settles on top of the organism. Minerals in the sediment may seep into the organism, gradually replacing the organism with stone. Or the organism may rot away completely after being covered, leaving a hole in the rock called a *mold.*

Reading the Fossil Record Fossils provide a historical sequence of life known as the **fossil record.** The fossil record supplies evidence about the order in which evolutionary changes have occurred. Fossils found in the upper, or newer, layers of the Earth's crust tend to resemble present-day organisms. This similarity indicates that the fossilized organisms were close relatives of present-day organisms. The deeper in the Earth's crust fossils are found, the less they tend to look like present-day organisms. These fossils are of earlier forms of life that may now be extinct.

Gaps in the Fossil Record If every organism that lived left an imprint behind, the fossil record would resemble a very large evolutionary family tree. **Figure 6** shows a hypothetical fossil record in which all relationships between organisms are clearly mapped.

Although scientists have collected thousands of fossils, gaps remain in the current fossil record, as shown in **Figure 7.** This is because specific conditions are necessary for fossils to form. The organism must be buried in very fine sediment. Also, oxygen—which promotes decay—cannot be present. However, very few places are free of oxygen. Because the conditions needed for fossils to form are rare, fossils are often difficult to find. Nevertheless, scientists have identified some fossils that complete sections of the fossil record.

Vestigial Structures Whales are similar in shape to fish. Yet whales are *mammals*—animals that breathe air, give birth to live young, and produce milk. Although modern whales do not have hind limbs, there are remnants of hind-limb bones inside their bodies, as shown in **Figure 8.** These remnants of once-useful structures are known as **vestigial** (ves TIJ ee uhl) **structures.** Scientists think that over millions of years, whales evolved from doglike land dwellers into sea-dwelling organisms. But scientists have not had the fossil evidence to support their ideas—until now. Read the following case study to learn the story of whale evolution.

The Fossil Record

Figure 6 *This is the way the fossil record might appear if fossils from every species had been found.*

The Fossil Record

Figure 7 *This diagram illustrates the many gaps in the existing fossil record.*

Figure 8 *Remnants of hind-limb bones are embedded deep inside the whale's body.*

Case Study: Evolution of the Whale

Scientists hypothesize that whales evolved from land-dwelling mammals like *Mesonychid* (muh ZOH ni kid), shown below, which returned to the ocean about 55 million years ago. During the 1980s and 1990s, several fossils of whale ancestors were discovered. These discoveries support a theory of whale evolution.

55 million years ago
Mesonychid

Ambulocetus (AM byoo loh CEE tuhs), pictured below, lived in coastal waters. *Ambulocetus* had shorter legs than *Mesonychid*, but it still had feet and toes that could support its weight on land. Although *Ambulocetus* had a tail, scientists think it kicked its legs like an otter in order to swim and used its tail for balance.

50 million years ago
Ambulocetus

46 million years ago
Rodhocetus

Forty-six million years ago, *Rodhocetus* (roh doh CEE tuhs) appeared in the fossil record. This animal more closely resembled modern whales, but it had hind limbs and feet that it retained from its land-dwelling ancestor. Because of its short legs, *Rodhocetus* was restricted to a crocodile-like waddle while on land. Unlike the legs of *Ambulocetus*, these legs were not necessary for swimming. Instead, *Rodhocetus* depended on its massive tail to propel it through the water. While *Ambulocetus* probably pulled itself onto land every night, *Rodhocetus* probably spent most of its time in the water.

Prozeuglodon (pro ZOO gloh dahn), which appeared in the fossil record 6 million years after *Rodhocetus*, was well adapted for life at sea. Although it still had a pair of very small legs, *Prozeuglodon* lived only in the water.

BRAIN FOOD

During their early development, modern whale embryos have four limbs. The rear limbs disappear before birth, and the front limbs develop into flippers.

40 million years ago
Prozeuglodon

Evidence of Evolution: Comparing Organisms

Evidence that life has evolved also comes from comparisons of different groups of organisms. On the following pages, the different kinds of evidence that support the theory of evolution are discussed in greater detail.

Human arm

Cat leg

Dolphin flipper

Bat wing

Figure 9 *The bones in the front limbs of these animals are similar, even though the limbs are used in different ways. Similar bones are shown in the same color.*

Comparing Skeletal Structures What does your arm have in common with the front leg of a cat, the front flipper of a dolphin, or the wing of a bat? At first glance, you might think that they have little in common. After all, these structures don't look very much alike and are not used in the same way. If you look under the surface, however, the structure and order of the bones in the front limbs of these different animals, shown in **Figure 9,** are actually similar to the structure and order of the bones found in your arm.

The similarities indicate that animals as different as a cat, a dolphin, a bat, and a human are all related by a common ancestor. The evolutionary process has modified these bones over millions of years to perform specific functions.

Comparing DNA from Different Species Scientists hypothesize that if all organisms living today evolved from a common ancestor, they should all have the same kind of genetic material. And in fact they do. From microscopic bacteria to giant polar bears, all organisms share the same genetic material—DNA.

In addition, scientists hypothesize that species appearing to be close relatives should have greater similarities in their DNA than species appearing to be distant relatives. For example, chimpanzees and gorillas appear to be close relatives. Chimpanzees and toucans appear to be distant relatives. The DNA of chimpanzees is, in fact, more similar to the DNA of gorillas than to the DNA of toucans.

Comparing Embryonic Structures Can you tell the difference between a chicken, a rabbit, and a human? It's pretty easy when you compare adults from each species. But what about comparing members of these species before they are born? Look at the left side of **Figure 10,** which depicts the very early embryos of a chicken, a rabbit, and a human.

All the organisms shown in the figure are *vertebrates*, or animals that have a backbone. Early in development, human embryos and the embryos of all other vertebrates are similar. These early similarities are evidence that all vertebrates share a common ancestor. Although the embryos look similar to each other in very early stages, none of them look like their adult forms. Embryo development has evolved over millions of years, causing the embryonic structures to grow into many different species of vertebrates. The changes in the process of embryo development therefore produce animals as different as a chicken and a human.

Figure 10 *The embryos of different vertebrates are very similar during the earliest stages of development.*

REVIEW

1. How does the fossil record suggest that species have changed over time?

2. How do the similarities in the fore-limb bones of humans, cats, dolphins, and bats support the theory of evolution?

3. **Interpreting Graphics** The photograph at right shows the layers of sedimentary rock exposed during the construction of a road. Imagine that a species which lived 200 million years ago is found in the layer designated as **b.** Its ancestor, which lived 250 million years ago, would most likely be found in which layer, **a** or **c**? Explain your answer.

How Does Evolution Happen?

Terms to Learn

trait
selective breeding
natural selection
mutation

What You'll Do

◆ Describe the four steps of Darwin's theory of evolution by natural selection.
◆ Explain how mutations are important to evolution.

The early 1800s was a time of great scientific discovery. Geologists realized that the Earth is much older than anyone had previously thought. Evidence showed that gradual processes had shaped the Earth's surface over millions of years. Fossilized remains of bizarre organisms were found. Fossils of familiar things were also found, but some of them were in unusual places. For example, fish fossils and shells were found on the tops of mountains. The Earth suddenly seemed to be a place where great change was possible. Many people thought that evolution occurs, but no one had been able to determine *how* it happens—until Charles Darwin.

Charles Darwin

In 1831, 21-year-old Charles Darwin, shown in **Figure 11,** had just graduated from college. Like many young people just out of college, Darwin didn't know what he wanted to do with his life. His father wanted him to become a doctor. However, Darwin was sickened by watching surgery. Although he eventually earned a degree in theology, he was *really* interested in the study of plants and animals.

Darwin was able to talk his father into letting him sign on for a 5-year voyage around the world. He served as the naturalist (a scientist who studies nature) on a British naval ship, the HMS *Beagle*. During this voyage, Darwin made observations that later became the foundation for his theory of evolution by natural selection.

Figure 11 *Charles Darwin, shown at far left, sailed around the world on a ship very similar to this one.*

Darwin's Excellent Adventure

As the HMS *Beagle* made its way around the world, Darwin collected thousands of plant and animal samples and kept detailed notes of his observations. The *Beagle*'s journey is charted in **Figure 12.** During the journey, the ship visited the Galápagos Islands, shown below, which are 965 km (600 mi) west of Ecuador, a country in South America.

Darwin's Finches

Darwin observed that the animals and plants on the Galápagos Islands were very similar, yet not identical, to the animals and plants on the nearby South American mainland. For example, he noted that the finches living on the Galápagos Islands differed slightly from the finches in Ecuador. The finches on the islands were different not only from the mainland finches but also from each other. As you can see in **Figure 13,** the birds differed from each other mainly in the shape of their beaks and in the food they ate.

Figure 12 *The course of the HMS* Beagle *is noted by the red line.*

Figure 13 *The beaks of these three species of finches are adapted to the different ways the finches obtain food.*

The **large ground finch** has a heavy, strong beak adapted for cracking big, hard seeds. This finch's beak works like a nutcracker.

The **cactus finch** has a tough beak that is good for eating cactus and its nectar. It works like a pair of needle-nosed pliers.

The **warbler finch's** small, pointed beak is adapted for probing into cracks and crevices to obtain small insects. This beak works like a pair of tweezers.

Darwin Does Some Thinking

Darwin's observations raised questions that he couldn't easily answer, such as, "Why are the finches on the islands similar but not identical to the finches on the mainland?" and "Why do the finches from different islands differ from one another?" Darwin thought that perhaps all the finches on the Galápagos Islands descended from finches on the South American mainland. The original population of finches may have been blown from South America to the Galápagos Islands by a storm. Over many generations, the finches that survived may have adapted to various ways of living on the Galápagos Islands.

After Darwin returned to England, he spent many years working on his theory of how evolution happens. During this period, he gathered many ideas from a variety of sources.

Figure 14 *Dogs are a good example of how selective breeding works. Over the past 12,000 years, dogs have been selectively bred to produce more than 150 different breeds.*

Darwin Learned from Farmers and Animal and Plant Breeders

In Darwin's time, many varieties of farm animals and plants had been selectively produced. Farmers chose certain **traits,** distinguishing qualities such as plump corn kernels, and bred only the individuals that had the desired traits. This procedure is called **selective breeding** because humans, not nature, select which traits will be passed along to the next generation. Selective breeding in dogs, shown in **Figure 14,** has exaggerated certain traits to produce more than 150 different breeds.

In your studies of genetics and heredity, you learned that a great variety of traits exists among individuals in a species. Darwin was impressed that farmers and breeders could direct and shape these traits and make such dramatic changes in animals and plants in just a few short generations. He thought that wild animals and plants could change in a similar way but that the process would take much longer because variations would be due to chance.

Have you ever heard of a bank that has no money, only seeds? Read about it on page 172.

Darwin Learned from Geologists

Geologists told Darwin that they had evidence that the Earth was much older than anyone had imagined. He learned from reading *Principles of Geology*, by Charles Lyell, that Earth had been formed by natural processes over a long period of time. Lyell's data were important because Darwin thought that populations of organisms changed very slowly, requiring a lot of time.

Darwin Learned from the Work of Thomas Malthus In his *Essay on the Principle of Population*, Malthus proposed that humans have the potential to reproduce beyond the capacity of their food supplies. However, he also recognized that death caused by starvation, disease, and war affects the size of human populations. Malthus's thoughts are represented in **Figure 15.**

Darwin realized that other animal species are also capable of producing too many offspring. For these animal species, starvation, disease, and predators affect the size of their populations. Only a limited number survive to reproduce. Thus, there must be something special about the survivors. What traits make them better equipped to survive and reproduce? Darwin reasoned that the offspring of the survivors inherit traits that help them survive in their environment.

QuickLab

Could We Run out of Food?

Malthus thought we could. Do the following activity to better understand Malthus's hypothesis. Get **2 empty egg cartons** and a **bag of rice.** Label one carton "Food supply" and the second carton "Population growth." In the food supply carton, place one grain of rice in the first cup. Increase the amount by one in each subsequent cup. Each grain represents a unit of food. In the population growth carton, place one grain of rice in the first cup, and double the number of grains of rice in each subsequent cup. This rice represents people.

1. How many "people" are there in the last cup?
2. How many units of food are there in the last cup?
3. What conclusion can you draw?

TRY at HOME

Malthus's Principle of Population Increase Versus Food Availability

Increase in human population

Increase in food supply

Quantity

Time

Figure 15 *Malthus thought the human population would increase beyond what the available food supply could support.*

Natural Selection

In 1858, about 20 years after he returned from his voyage on the HMS *Beagle*, Darwin received a letter from a naturalist named Alfred Russel Wallace. Wallace had independently arrived at the same theory of evolution that Darwin had been working on for so many years. Darwin and Wallace discussed their research and made plans to present their findings at a meeting later in the year. Then, in 1859, Darwin published his own results in his book called *On the Origin of Species by Means of Natural Selection*. Darwin theorized that evolution occurs through a process he called **natural selection.** This process, examined below, is divided into four parts.

Natural Selection in Four Steps

1 Overproduction Each species produces more offspring than will survive to maturity.

2 Genetic Variation The individuals in a population are slightly different from one another. Each individual has a unique combination of traits, such as size, color, and the ability to find food. Some traits increase the chances that the individual will survive and reproduce. Other traits decrease the chances of survival. These variations are genetic and can be inherited.

3 Struggle to Survive A natural environment does not have enough food, water, and other resources to support all the individuals born. In addition, many individuals are killed by other organisms. Only some of the individuals in a population survive to adulthood.

4 Successful Reproduction Successful reproduction is the key to natural selection. The individuals that are well adapted to their environment, that is, those that have better traits for living in their environment, are more likely to survive and reproduce. The individuals that are not well adapted to their environment are more likely to die early or produce few offspring.

A Breed All Their Own

Imagine that your grandfather has owned a kennel for more than 50 years but has never sold a dog. He cares for the dogs and keeps them in one large pen. Originally there were six labs, six terriers, and six pointers. There are now 76 dogs, and you are surprised that only a few look like pointers, labs, and terriers. The other dogs look similar to each other but not to any of the specific breeds. Your grandfather says that over the past 50 years each generation has looked less like the generation that preceded it.

By the time you visited the kennel, what may have happened to make most of the dogs look similar to each other but not to any specific original breed? Base your answer on what you've learned about selective breeding in this section.

More Evidence of Evolution

One of the observations on which Darwin based his theory of evolution by natural selection is that parents pass traits to their offspring. But Darwin did not know *how* inheritance occurs or *why* individuals vary within a population.

During the 1930s and 1940s, biologists combined the principles of genetic inheritance with Darwin's theory of evolution by natural selection. This combination of principles explained that the variations Darwin observed within a species are caused by **mutation,** or changes in a gene.

Since Darwin's time, new evidence has been collected from many fields of science. Although scientists recognize that other mechanisms may also play a part in the evolution of a species, the theory of evolution by natural selection provides the most thorough explanation for the diversity of life on Earth.

REVIEW

1. Why are some animals more likely to survive to adulthood than other animals?

2. **Summarizing Data** What did Darwin think happened to the first small population of finches that reached the Galápagos Islands from South America?

3. **Doing Calculations** A female cockroach can produce 80 offspring at a time. If half of the offspring were female, and each female produced 80 offspring, how many cockroaches would there be in 3 generations?

internet**connect**

SC*i*LINKS™
NSTA

TOPIC: The Galápagos Islands, Darwin and Natural Selection
GO TO: www.scilinks.org
*sci*LINKS NUMBER: HSTL165, HSTL170

Section

3

Terms to Learn

generation time
speciation

What You'll Do

◆ Give two examples of natural selection in action.
◆ Outline the process of speciation.

Natural Selection in Action

The theory of natural selection explains how a population changes over many generations in response to its environment. In fact, members of a population tend to be well adapted to their environment because natural selection is continuously taking place.

Insecticide Resistance To keep crops safe from certain insects, some farmers use a wide variety of chemical insecticides. However, some insecticides that worked well in the past are no longer as effective. In the 50 years that insecticides have been widely used, more than 500 species of insects have developed resistance to certain insecticides.

Insects quickly develop resistance to insecticides because they produce many offspring and usually have short generation times. A **generation time** is the period between the birth of one generation and the birth of the next generation. Look at **Figure 16** to see how a common household pest, the cockroach, has adapted to become resistant to certain insecticides.

1 An insecticide will kill most insects, but a few may survive. These survivors have genes that make them resistant to the insecticide.

2 The survivors then reproduce, passing the insecticide-resistance genes to their offspring.

3 In time, the replacement population of insects is made up mostly of individuals that have the insecticide-resistance genes.

4 When the same kind of insecticide is used on the insects, only a few are killed because most of them are resistant to that insecticide.

Figure 16 *Variety in a population's characteristics helps ensure that some individuals will be able to survive a change in the environment.*

We're off to hunt the marshmallows! Look on page 710 to find out why.

Adaptation to Pollution   There are two color variations among European peppered moths, as shown in **Figure 17.** Before 1850, the dark peppered moth was considered rare. The pale peppered moth was much more common. After the 1850s, however, dark peppered moths became more abundant in heavily industrialized areas.

Figure 17   *Against a dark tree trunk (above), the pale peppered moth stands out. Against a light tree trunk (right), the dark peppered moth stands out.*

What caused this change in the peppered moth population? Several species of birds eat peppered moths that rest on tree trunks. Before the 1850s, the trees had a gray appearance, and pale peppered moths blended into their surroundings. Dark peppered moths were easier for the birds to see and were eaten more frequently. After the 1850s, soot and smoke from newly developing industrial areas blackened nearby trees. The dark peppered moths became less visible on the dark tree trunks. The pale peppered moths stood out against the dark background and became easy prey for the birds. More dark moths survived and produced more dark offspring. Thus, the population changed from mostly light-colored moths to mostly dark-colored moths.

> ### ✓ Self-Check
>
> If the air pollution in Europe were cleaned up, what do you think would happen to the population of light-colored peppered moths? *(See page 782 to check your answers.)*

Formation of New Species

The process of natural selection can explain how a species can evolve into a new species. A portion of a species' population can become separated from the original population. Over time, the two populations can become so different that they can no longer interbreed. This process is called **speciation.** One way that speciation can occur is shown in the following three steps:

1. Separation The process of speciation often begins when a portion of a population becomes isolated. **Figure 18** shows some of the ways this can happen. A newly formed canyon, mountain range, and lake are a few of the ways that populations can be divided.

Figure 18 *Populations can become separated in a variety of ways.*

2. Adaptation If a population has been divided by one of the changes illustrated above, the environment may also change. This is where natural selection comes in. As the environment changes, so may the population that lives there. Over many generations, the separated groups may adapt to better fit their environment, as shown in **Figure 19.** If the environmental conditions are different for each of the groups, the adaptations in the groups may also be different.

Figure 19 *When a single population becomes divided, the groups may evolve separately and may form separate species.*

3. Division Over many hundreds, thousands, or even millions of generations, the two groups of a population may become so different that they can no longer interbreed, even if the geographical barrier is removed. At this point, the two groups are no longer the same species. Scientists think that the finches on the Galápagos Islands evolved by these three basic steps. **Figure 20** illustrates how this might have happened.

Figure 20 The finches on the Galápagos Islands might have evolved into different species by the process depicted below.

❶ Some finches left the mainland and reached one of the islands (separation).

❷ The finches reproduced and adapted to the environment (adaptation).

❸ Some finches flew to a second island (separation).

❹ The finches reproduced and adapted to the different environment (adaptation).

❺ Some finches flew back to the first island but could no longer interbreed with the finches there (division).

❻ This process may have occurred over and over again as the finches flew to the other islands.

REVIEW

1. Why did the number of dark peppered moths increase after the 1850s?

2. What factor indicates that a population has evolved into two separate species?

3. **Applying Concepts** Most cactuses have spines, which are leaves modified to protect the plant. The spines cover a juicy stem that stores water. Explain how cactus leaves and stems might have changed through the process of natural selection.

internet**connect**

SC*L*INKS
NSTA

TOPIC: Species and Adaptation
GO TO: www.scilinks.org
*sci*LINKS NUMBER: HSTL155

Chapter Highlights

SECTION 1

Vocabulary

adaptation *(p. 150)*

species *(p. 150)*

evolution *(p. 151)*

fossil *(p. 152)*

fossil record *(p. 152)*

vestigial structure *(p. 153)*

Section Notes

- Evolution is the process by which populations change over time. Those changes are inherited.

- Evidence of a common ancestor for all organisms is provided by the following: the fossil record, comparisons of skeletal structures found in related species, comparisons of the embryos of distantly related vertebrates, and the presence of DNA in all living organisms.

- Species that are closely related have DNA that is more alike than DNA of distantly related species.

Labs

Mystery Footprints *(p. 708)*

SECTION 2

Vocabulary

trait *(p. 160)*

selective breeding *(p. 160)*

natural selection *(p. 162)*

mutation *(p. 163)*

Section Notes

- Charles Darwin developed an explanation for evolution after years of studying the organisms he observed on the voyage of the *Beagle*.

- Darwin's study was influenced by the concepts of selective breeding, the age of the Earth, and the idea that some organisms are better equipped to survive than others.

☑ Skills Check

Math Concepts

MALTHUS'S PRINCIPLE The graph on page 161 shows two types of growth. The straight line represents an increase in which the same number is added to the previous number, as in 3, 4, 5, 6, . . . , where 1 is added to each number.

The curved line represents an increase in which each number is multiplied by the same factor, as in 2, 4, 8, 16, . . . , where each number is multiplied by 2. As you can see on the graph, the curved line increases at a much faster rate than the straight line.

Visual Understanding

SKELETAL STRUCTURE Figure 9 on page 156 illustrates skeletal evidence for evolution. By looking at the same-colored bones, you can see how the early mammalian skeletal structure has evolved in certain species to help with specialized tasks such as flying and swimming.

- Darwin explained that evolution occurs through natural selection. Natural selection can be divided into four parts:

  (1) Each species produces more offspring than will survive to reproduce.

  (2) Individuals within a population are slightly different from one another.

  (3) Individuals within a population compete with one another for limited resources.

  (4) Individuals that are better equipped to live in an environment are more likely to survive and reproduce.

- Evolution is explained today by combining the principles of natural selection with the principles of genetic inheritance.

Labs

Survival of the Chocolates
(p. 711)

Vocabulary

generation time (p. 164)
speciation (p. 166)

Section Notes

- Natural selection allows a population to adapt to changes in environmental conditions.

- Evidence of natural selection can be seen by studying generations of organisms that have developed resistance to an insecticide or antibiotic.

- Natural selection also explains how one species may evolve into another through the process of speciation.

Labs

Out-of-Sight Marshmallows
(p. 710)

---

internet connect

GO TO: go.hrw.com

Visit the **HRW** Web site for a variety of learning tools related to this chapter. Just type in the keyword:

KEYWORD: HSTEVO

SC*i*LINKS*ᴿ*

NSTA

GO TO: www.scilinks.org

Visit the **National Science Teachers Association** on-line Web site for Internet resources related to this chapter. Just type in the *sci*LINKS number for more information about the topic:

TOPIC: Species and Adaptation	***sci*LINKS NUMBER:** HSTL155
TOPIC: The Fossil Record	***sci*LINKS NUMBER:** HSTL160
TOPIC: The Galápagos Islands	***sci*LINKS NUMBER:** HSTL165
TOPIC: Darwin and Natural Selection	***sci*LINKS NUMBER:** HSTL170

Chapter Review

USING VOCABULARY

To complete the following sentences, choose the correct term from each pair of terms listed below:

1. One species evolves into another through the process of __?__. (*adaptation* or *speciation*)

2. A group of similar organisms that can mate with one another to produce off-spring is known as a __?__. (*fossil* or *species*)

3. A(n) __?__ helps an organism survive better in its environment. (*adaptation* or *vestigial structure*)

4. __?__ is the process by which populations change over time. (*Natural selection* or *Evolution*)

5. In __?__, humans select traits that will be passed from one generation to another. (*selective breeding* or *natural selection*)

6. A change in a gene at the DNA level is called a __?__. (*mutation* or *trait*)

UNDERSTANDING CONCEPTS

Multiple Choice

7. Although Darwin did not realize it, the variations he observed among the individuals of a population of finches were caused by
   a. genetic resistance.   c. fossils.
   b. mutations.   d. selective breeding.

8. The theory of evolution combines the principles of
   a. natural selection and artificial selection.
   b. natural selection and genetic resistance.
   c. selective breeding and genetic inheritance.
   d. natural selection and genetic inheritance.

9. Fossils are commonly found in
   a. sedimentary rock.
   b. igneous rock.
   c. granite.
   d. loose sand or granite.

10. A human's arm, a cat's front leg, a dolphin's front flipper, and a bat's wing
    a. have similar kinds of bones.
    b. are used in similar ways.
    c. share many similarities with insect wings and jellyfish tentacles.
    d. have nothing in common.

11. The fact that all organisms have DNA as their genetic material is evidence that
    a. natural selection occurred.
    b. all organisms descended from a common ancestor.
    c. selective breeding takes place every day.
    d. genetic resistance rarely occurs.

12. What body part of the Galápagos finches appears to have been most modified by natural selection?
    a. their webbed feet
    b. their beaks
    c. the bone structure of their wings
    d. the color of their eyes

Short Answer

13. Describe the four parts of Darwin's theory of evolution by natural selection.

14. How do the fossils of whales provide evidence that whales have evolved over millions of years?

15. What might account for gaps in the fossil record?

Concept Mapping

16. Use the following terms to create a concept map: struggle to survive, genetic variation, Darwin, overpopulation, natural selection, successful reproduction.

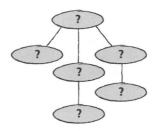

CRITICAL THINKING AND PROBLEM SOLVING

Write one or two sentences to answer the following questions:

17. In selective breeding, humans influence the course of evolution. What determines the course of evolution in natural selection?

18. Many forms of bacteria evolve resistance to antibiotics, drugs that kill bacteria. Based on what you know about how insects evolve to resist insecticides, suggest how bacteria might evolve to resist antibiotics.

19. The two species of squirrels shown below live on opposite sides of the Grand Canyon, in Arizona. The two squirrels look very similar, but they cannot interbreed to produce fertile offspring. Explain how a single species of squirrel might have become two species.

INTERPRETING GRAPHICS

Use the following graphs to answer questions 20, 21, and 22:

Infant Births by Birth Weight

Percentage of births / Weight in pounds

Infant Deaths by Birth Weight

Percentage of deaths / Weight in pounds

20. What is the most common birth weight?

21. What birth weight has the highest survival rate?

22. How do the principles of natural selection help explain why there are more deaths among babies with low birth weights than among babies of average birth weights?

NOW What Do You Think?

Take a minute to review your answers to the ScienceLog questions on page 149. Have your answers changed? If necessary, revise your answers based on what you have learned since you began this chapter.

EYE ON THE ENVIRONMENT

Saving at the Seed Bank

A very unusual laboratory can be found in Fort Collins, Colorado. There, sealed in test tubes, locked in specialized drawers, and even frozen in liquid nitrogen at −196°C, are hundreds of thousands of seeds and plants. Although in storage for now, these organisms may hold the keys to preventing worldwide famine or medicine shortage in the future. Sound serious? Well, it is.

This laboratory is called the National Seed Storage Lab, and it is the largest of a worldwide network of seed banks. The seeds and plant cuttings stored within these seed banks represent almost every plant grown for food, clothing, and medicine.

▲ *To protect tomorrow's wheat fields, we need the genetic diversity of crops stored in seed banks.*

No More Pizza!

Imagine heading out for pizza only to discover a sign on the door that says, "Closed today due to flour shortage." Flour shortage? How can that be? What about burritos? When you get to the burrito stand, the sign is the same, "Closed due to flour shortage." Think this sounds far-fetched? Well, it really isn't.

If wheat crops around the world are ruined by a disease, we could have a flour shortage. And the best way to fight such devastation, and even prevent it, is by breeding new varieties. Through the process of selective breeding, many plants have been improved to increase their yields and their resistance to disease and insects. But to breed new crops, plant breeders need lots of different genetic material. Where do they get this genetic material? At the seed bank, of course!

Why We'll Never Know

But what if some plants never make it to the seed bank? We have the new and improved varieties, so why does it matter if we keep the old ones? It matters because these lost varieties often have important traits, like resistance to disease and drought, that might come in handy in the future. Once a variety of plant is improved, demand for the old variety can dwindle to nothing. If an old variety is no longer grown, it may become extinct if it is not placed in the seed bank. In fact, many varieties of plants have already been lost forever. We'll never know if one of those lost varieties was capable of resisting a severe drought.

It's All in the Bank

Fortunately, seed banks have collected seeds and plants for more than a century. They preserve the genetic diversity of crop plants while allowing farmers to grow the most productive varieties in their fields. As long as there are seed banks across the globe, it is unlikely that there will be a flour shortage. Let's go out for pizza!

Going Further

▶ Many seed banks are in jeopardy. Why? Find out by doing research to learn more about the complicated and costly process of operating a seed bank.

Science Fiction

"The Anatomy Lesson"

by Scott Sanders

You know what it's like. You have an important test tomorrow, or your semester project is due, and you've forgotten your book or just run out of clay. Suddenly things seem very serious.

That's the situation a certain medical student faces in Scott Sanders's "The Anatomy Lesson." The student needs to learn the bones of the human body for an anatomy exam the next day. After arriving at the anatomy library to check out a skeleton-in-a-box, the student finds that all the skeletons have been checked out. Without bones to assemble as practice, the student knows passing the exam will be impossible. So the student asks the librarian to look again. Sure enough, the librarian finds one last box. And that's when things start to get strange.

There are too many bones. They are the wrong shape. They don't fit together just right. Somebody must be playing a joke! The bones fit together, sort of—but not in any way that helps the medical student get ready for the exam. When the student complains to the librarian, the librarian isn't very sympathetic. It seems she has other things on her mind. Now the student is really worried.

Find out what this medical student and a quiet librarian have in common. And find out how they will never be the same after "The Anatomy Lesson." You can read it in *Anthology of Science Fiction.*

Imagine . . .

One day you and your friends learn about a secret underground passage that leads into an old abandoned mansion, and you set out to find it. As you walk around a field in search of the passage, you stumble across a large hole in the ground. Could this be it?

One by one, you and your friends squeeze down into the hole. You slide down the sloping tunnel and finally land. Dusting yourself off, you turn on your flashlight. Instead of finding a passage to an abandoned mansion, you and your friends find yourselves in an immense cavern. Painted high on the cavern's walls are pictures of bulls, cows, horses, and stags. You get the feeling these images have been here for a very long time. Who these paintings?

This adventure actually occurred in southern France in the late 1940s. Four teenage boys went hunting for a passageway to the old manor of Lascaux. Instead of finding a passageway, they stumbled onto a 17,000-year-old connection with our ancestors, the Cro-Magnons. Three of the adventurers are shown below talking to their teacher.

What Do You Think?

Reading Warm-Up

In your ScienceLog, try to answer the following questions based on what you already know:

1. How can you tell how old a fossil is?

2. How long did dinosaurs roam the Earth?

Investigate!

Timeline of Earth's History

To help you understand Earth's history, make a timeline. You will need a **pencil,** a **metric ruler,** and a strip of **adding machine paper** 46 cm long.

Procedure

1. Mark off 10 cm sections of the paper. Divide each 10 cm section into ten 1 cm sections. (Each 1 cm represents 100 million years.)

2. Label each 10 cm section in order from top to bottom as follows: 1 bya (billion years ago), 2 bya, 3 bya, and 4 bya. The timeline begins at 4.6 bya.

3. Label some of the important events of Earth's history listed below:

   a. At the end of the paper (4.6 bya), write "The origin of the Earth."

   b. Measure off 35 cm, and mark the end point (3.5 bya) with your pencil. Write "The earliest cells appear."

   c. Dinosaurs first appeared on Earth about 215 million years ago. Then about 65 million years ago, they became extinct. Mark these two events.

   d. About 100,000 years ago, humans with modern features appeared. Mark this event on your timeline. (**Hint:** 10 million years = 1 mm. So 100,000 years ago would be a small fraction of 1 mm.)

   e. Continue to mark events on your timeline as you learn about them in this chapter.

Analysis

4. The Lascaux cave paintings were done more than 17,000 years ago. Compare that length of time with the length of time Earth existed before the beginning of life.

5. Compare the length of time dinosaurs roamed the Earth with the length of time humans have existed.

The History of Life on Earth **175**

Evidence of the Past

Terms to Learn

fossil   extinct
relative dating   plate tectonics
absolute dating
geologic time
  scale

What You'll Do

◆ Explain how fossils are dated.
◆ Describe the geologic time scale and the information it provides scientists.
◆ Describe the possible causes of mass extinctions.
◆ Explain the theory of plate tectonics.

Some scientists look for clues to help them reconstruct what happened in the past. These scientists are called paleontologists. *Paleontologists*, like the man in **Figure 1,** use fossils to reconstruct the history of life millions of years before humans existed. Fossils show us that life on Earth has changed a great deal. They also provide us with clues to how those changes occurred.

Figure 1 *In 1995, Paul Sereno found this dinosaur fossil in the Sahara Desert. The dinosaur may have been the largest land predator that has ever existed!*

Fossils

Fossils are traces or imprints of living things—such as animals, plants, bacteria, and fungi—that are preserved in rock. Fossils are usually formed when a dead organism is covered by a layer of sediment. These sediments may later be pressed together to form sedimentary rock. **Figure 2** shows one way fossils can be formed in this type of rock.

Figure 2 *The pictures below show one way fossils can form.*

❶ An organism dies and becomes buried in sediment.

❷ The organism gradually dissolves, leaving a hollow impression, or mold, in the sediment.

❸ Over time, the mold fills with sediment that forms a cast of the original organism.

The Age of Fossils

When paleontologists find a fossil, how do they determine its age? They can use one of two methods: relative dating or absolute dating.

Relative Dating A cross section of sedimentary rock shows many layers. The oldest layers are on the bottom, and the newer layers are on the top. If fossils are found in the rock, a scientist could start at the bottom and work upward to examine a sequence of fossils in the order that the organisms existed. This method of ordering fossils to estimate their age is known as **relative dating.**

Absolute Dating How can scientists determine the age of a fossil? The answer lies in particles called *atoms* that make up all matter. Atoms, in turn, are made of smaller particles. These particles are held together by strong forces. If there isn't enough force to hold them together, the atom is said to be unstable. Unstable atoms decay by releasing either energy or particles or both. That way, the atom becomes stable, but it also becomes a different kind of atom.

Each kind of unstable atom decays at its own rate. As shown in **Figure 3,** the time it takes for half of the unstable atoms in a sample to decay is its *half-life*. Half-lives range from fractions of a second to billions of years. By measuring the ratio of unstable atoms to stable atoms, scientists can determine the approximate age of a rock sample and the fossil it contains. This method is called **absolute dating.**

Bananabana bobana is a rare fossil! Turn to page 712 in your LabBook to see it.

Figure 3 *Sometimes volcanic rock will cover a dead organism. By finding the age of the rock, scientists can get a good idea about the age of the fossil.*

Fossil

Volcanic rock

Half-lives

A. The unstable atoms in the sample of volcanic rock have a half-life of 1.3 billion years. The sample contained 4 mg of unstable atoms when the rock formed.

B. After 1.3 billion years, or one half-life, only 2 mg of the unstable atoms will be left in the rock, and 2 mg of its stable decay product will have formed.

C. After another 1.3 billion years (two half-lives), there will only be 1 mg of the unstable atoms and 3 mg of the decay atoms.

D. How many milligrams of unstable atoms are left after 3 half-lives?

Amount of unstable atoms (mg)

4

2

1
0.5

1 half-life   2 half-lives   3 half-lives
Time

● Unstable element   ● Stable decay product

The Geologic Time Scale

When you consider important events that have happened during your lifetime, you usually recall each event in terms of the day, month, or year in which it occurred. These divisions of time make it easier to recall when you were born, when you kicked the winning soccer goal, or when you started the fifth grade. Because the span of time is so great from the formation of the Earth to now, scientists also use a type of calendar to divide the Earth's long history into very long units of time.

The calendar scientists use to outline the history of life on Earth is called the **geologic time scale,** shown in the table at left. After a fossil is dated using relative and absolute dating techniques, a paleontologist can place the fossil in chronological order with other fossils. This forms a picture of the past that shows how organisms have changed over time.

Divisions in the Geologic Time Scale Paleontologists have divided the time scale into large blocks of time called *eras*. Each era has been subdivided into smaller blocks of time as paleontologists have continued to find more fossil information.

Eras are characterized by the type of animal that dominated the Earth at the time. For instance, the Mesozoic era— dominated by dinosaurs and other reptiles—is referred to as the Age of Reptiles. The end of each era is marked by the extinction of certain organisms. The next section analyzes the different eras of the geologic time scale in greater detail.

The Geologic Time Scale

Era	Period	MYA	Representative Organisms
CENOZOIC	Quaternary	1.8	
	Tertiary	65	
MESOZOIC	Cretaceous	144	
	Jurassic	206	
	Triassic	248	
PALEOZOIC	Permian	290	
	Carboniferous	354	
	Devonian	417	
	Silurian	443	
	Ordovician	490	
	Cambrian	540	
PRECAMBRIAN		4,600	

Figure 4 *A meteorite hit Earth about 65 million years ago, perhaps leading to major climatic changes.*

Mass Extinctions Some of the important divisions in the geologic time scale are marked by events that caused many animal and plant species to die out completely, or become **extinct.** Once a species is extinct, it does not reappear. There have been several periods in the Earth's history when a large number of species died out at the same time. These periods of large-scale extinction are called *mass extinctions.*

Scientists are not sure what causes mass extinctions. Mass extinctions may result from major changes in the Earth's climate or atmosphere. Some scientists think the mass extinction of the dinosaurs occurred when a meteorite collided with Earth and caused catastrophic climate changes. An artist's depiction of this event is shown in **Figure 4.** Changes in the climate may have also been caused by the movement of continents. Read on to find out how this is possible.

Scientists estimate that only a small fraction ($1/20$ of 1 percent) of all the species that have ever existed on Earth are living today. All the other species existed in the past and then became extinct.

✓Self-Check

Ten grams of an unstable atom were present in a rock when the rock solidified. In grams, how much of these atoms will be present after one half-life? What amount of the unstable atoms will be present after two half-lives? *(See page 782 to check your answers.)*

The Changing Earth

Do you know that dinosaur fossils have been found on Antarctica? Antarctica, now frozen, must have once had a warm climate to support these large reptiles. How could this be? Antarctica and the other continents have not always been in their present position. Antarctica was once located nearer the equator!

Pangaea If you take a look at a map of the world, you might notice that the shapes of the continents seem to resemble pieces of a puzzle. If you could move the pieces around, you might find that some of them almost fit together. A similar thought occurred to the German scientist Alfred Wegener in the early 1900s. He proposed that long ago the continents were part of one great landmass surrounded by a single gigantic ocean. Wegener called that single landmass *Pangaea* (pan JEE uh), meaning "all Earth."

Wegener thought our present continents were once part of one great supercontinent for three reasons. First, the shapes of the continents seemed to "fit" together. Second, fossils of plants and animals discovered on either side of the Atlantic Ocean were very similar. Third, Wegener noticed that glaciers had existed in places that now have very warm climates. **Figure 5** shows how the continents may have formed from Pangaea.

About **245 million years ago,** the continents were one giant landmass called Pangaea. The grey outlines indicate where the continents are today.

About **180 million years ago,** Pangaea began to divide into two pieces: Laurasia and Gondwanaland.

Figure 5 *Because the continents are moving 1–10 cm per year, the continents will be arranged very differently in 150 million years.*

Even as recently as **65 million years ago,** the location of Earth's continents was very different from their current location.

Do the Continents Move? In the mid-1960s, J. Tuzo Wilson of Canada came up with the idea that it wasn't the continents that were moving. Wilson thought that huge pieces of the Earth's crust are driven back and forth by forces within the planet. Each huge piece of crust is called a *tectonic plate.* Wilson's theory of how these huge pieces of crust move around the globe is called **plate tectonics.**

According to Wilson, the outer crust of the Earth is broken into seven large, rigid plates and several smaller ones, shown in **Figure 6.** The continents and oceans ride on top of these plates. It is the motion of the plates that causes continents to move.

Figure 6 *Scientists think that the tectonic plates, outlined above, have been slowly rearranging the continents since the crust cooled billions of years ago.*

Adaptation in Slow Motion Although tectonic plates move very slowly, the motion of continents affects living organisms. Living things usually have time to adapt, through evolution, to the changes brought about by moving continents. That is why you are able to see living things that are well adapted to the environment they live in. In the same location, however, you may find fossil evidence of very different organisms that could not survive the changes.

REVIEW

1. What information does the geologic time scale provide, and what are the major divisions of time?

2. What is one possible cause of mass extinctions?

3. Explain one way that geological changes in the Earth can cause plants and animals to change.

4. What is the difference between relative dating and absolute dating of fossils?

5. **Understanding Concepts** Fossils of *Mesosaurus,* a small aquatic lizard, shown at right, have been found only in Africa and South America. Using what you know about plate tectonics, how would you explain this finding?

Terms to Learn

Precambrian time
Paleozoic era
Mesozoic era
Cenozoic era

What You'll Do

◆ Outline the major developments that allowed for the existence of life on Earth.
◆ Describe the different types of organisms that arose during the four eras of the geologic time scale.

Eras of the Geologic Time Scale

Look at the photograph of the Grand Canyon shown in **Figure 7.** If you look closely, you will notice that the walls of the canyon are layered with different kinds and colors of rocks. The deeper you go down into the canyon, the older the layer of rocks. It may surprise you to learn that each layer of the Grand Canyon was once the top layer. Billions of years ago the bottom layer was on top!

Each layer tells a story about what was happening on Earth when that layer was on top. The story is told mainly by the types of rocks and fossils found in the layer. In studying these different rocks and fossils, scientists have divided geologic history into four eras: Precambrian time, the Paleozoic era, the Mesozoic era, and the Cenozoic era.

Precambrian Time

If you journey to the bottom of the Grand Canyon, you can see layers of Earth that are over 1 billion years old. These layers are from Precambrian time. **Precambrian time** began when the Earth originated 4.6 billion years ago, and continued until about 540 million years ago. During this time life began and transformed the planet.

Figure 7 *Each rock layer of the Grand Canyon is like a page in the "history book of the Earth."*

The Early Earth Scientists hypothesize that life began when conditions were quite different from Earth's current environment. These conditions included an atmosphere that lacked oxygen but was rich in other gases, such as carbon monoxide, carbon dioxide, hydrogen, and nitrogen. Also, the early Earth, as illustrated in **Figure 8,** was a place of great turmoil. Meteorites crashed into the Earth's surface. Violent thunderstorms and volcanic eruptions were constant on the young planet. Intense radiation, including ultraviolet radiation from the sun, bombarded Earth's surface.

Figure 8 *The early Earth was a violent place.*

How Did Life Begin? Scientists hypothesize that under these conditions, life developed from nonliving matter. In other words, life started from the chemicals that already existed in the environment. These chemicals included water, clay, dissolved minerals in the oceans, and the gases present in the atmosphere. The energy present in the early Earth caused these chemicals to react with one another, forming the complex molecules that made life possible.

Some scientists further hypothesize that for millions of years these small, complex molecules floated in the ancient oceans and joined together to form larger molecules. These larger molecules combined into more-complicated structures. As time passed, complicated structures developed into cell-like structures that eventually became the first true cells, called prokaryotes. *Prokaryotes* are cells that lack a nucleus. Early prokaryotic cells, like the one shown in **Figure 9,** were *anaerobic,* which means they did not require oxygen to survive. Many varieties of anaerobic organisms still live on Earth today. Organisms that need oxygen could not have survived on early Earth because there was no free oxygen in the atmosphere.

Figure 9 *Fossilized prokaryotes (such as the circular structure in the photograph) suggest that life first appeared on Earth more than 3.5 billion years ago.*

Figure 10 *Cyanobacteria are the simplest living organisms that photosynthesize.*

The Earth's First Pollution—Oxygen! As indicated by the fossil record, prokaryotic organisms called cyanobacteria appeared more than 3 billion years ago. Cyanobacteria, pictured in **Figure 10,** are photosynthetic organisms, which means that they use sunlight to produce food. One of the byproducts of this process is oxygen. As cyanobacteria carried out photosynthesis, they released oxygen gas into the oceans. The oxygen then escaped out into the air, changing Earth's atmosphere forever. Over the next several million years, more and more oxygen was added to the atmosphere.

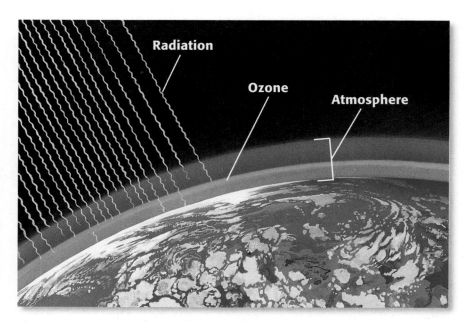

Figure 11 *Oxygen from photosynthesis formed ozone, which helps to absorb ultraviolet radiation.*

Environment

CONNECTION

Ozone depletion in the upper atmosphere is a serious problem. Chemicals, such as those used in refrigerators and air conditioners, are slowly destroying the ozone layer in the Earth's atmosphere. Because of ozone depletion, all living things are exposed to higher levels of radiation, which can cause skin cancer. Some countries have outlawed ozone-depleting chemicals.

Radiation Shield As the atmosphere filled with oxygen, some of the oxygen formed a layer of ozone in the upper atmosphere, as shown in **Figure 11.** *Ozone* is a gas that absorbs ultraviolet (UV) radiation from the sun. UV radiation damages DNA but is absorbed by water. Before ozone formed, therefore, life was restricted to the oceans and underground. But the new ozone blocked out most of the UV radiation. This brought radiation on Earth's surface down to a level that allowed life to move onto dry land.

Life's So Complex The fossil record tells us that after a long period of time, about 1 billion years, more-complex life-forms appeared. These organisms, known as *eukaryotes,* are much larger than prokaryotes. They contain a central nucleus and a complicated internal structure. Scientists think that over the past 2.5 billion years, eukaryotic cells have evolved together to form organisms that are composed of many cells.

The Paleozoic Era

The **Paleozoic era** began about 540 million years ago and ended about 248 million years ago. *Paleozoic* comes from the Greek words meaning "ancient life." Considering how long Precambrian time lasted, the Paleozoic era was relatively recent. Rocks from the Paleozoic era are rich in fossils of animals such as sponges, corals, snails, clams, squids, and trilobites. Fishes, the earliest animals with backbones, also appeared during this era, and ancient sharks became abundant. Some Paleozoic organisms are shown in **Figure 12**.

The Greening of the Earth During the Paleozoic era, plants, fungi, and air-breathing animals colonized dry land over a period of 30 million years. Plants provided the first land animals with food and shelter. By the end of the Paleozoic era, forests of giant ferns, club mosses, horsetails, and conifers covered much of the Earth. All major plant groups except for flowering plants appeared during this era.

Creepers Crawl onto Land Fossils indicate that crawling insects were some of the first animals to appear on land. They were followed by large salamanderlike animals. Near the end of the Paleozoic era, reptiles, winged insects, cockroaches, and dragonflies appeared.

The largest mass extinction known occurred at the end of the Paleozoic era, about 248 million years ago. As many as 90 percent of all marine species died out.

Figure 12 *Organisms that appeared in the Paleozoic era include the first reptiles, amphibians, fishes, worms, and ferns.*

Self-Check

Place the following events in chronological order:

a. The ozone layer formed, and living things moved onto dry land.

b. Gases in the atmosphere and minerals in the oceans combined to form small molecules.

c. The first prokaryotic, anaerobic cells appeared.

d. Cyanobacteria appeared.

(See page 782 to check your answer.)

The Mesozoic Era

The **Mesozoic era** began about 248 million years ago and lasted about 183 million years. *Mesozoic* comes from the Greek words meaning "middle life." Scientists think that, after the extinctions of the Paleozoic era, a burst of evolution occurred among the surviving reptiles, resulting in many different species. Therefore, the Mesozoic era is commonly referred to as the Age of Reptiles.

Life in the Mesozoic Era Dinosaurs are the most well known of the reptiles that evolved during the Mesozoic era. Dinosaurs dominated the Earth for about 150 million years. (Consider that humans and their ancestors have been around for only about 4 million years.) Dinosaurs had a great variety of physical characteristics, such as duck bills and projecting spines. In addition to dinosaurs, there were giant marine lizards that swam in the ocean. The first birds also appeared during the Mesozoic era. The most important plants during the early part of the Mesozoic era were cone-bearing seed plants, which formed large forests. Flowering plants appeared later in the Mesozoic era. Some of the organisms that appeared during the Mesozoic era are shown in **Figure 13.**

A Bad Time for Dinosaurs At the end of the Mesozoic era, 65 million years ago, dinosaurs and many other animal and plant species became extinct. What happened to the dinosaurs? According to one hypothesis, a large meteorite hit the Earth and generated giant dust clouds and enough heat to cause worldwide fires. The dust and smoke from these fires blocked out much of the sunlight, causing many plants to die out. Without enough plants to eat, the plant-eating dinosaurs died out. As a result, the meat-eating dinosaurs that fed on the plant-eating dinosaurs died. Global temperatures may have dropped for many years. Only a few organisms, including some small mammals, were able to survive.

Figure 13 *The Mesozoic era ended with the mass extinction of most of the large animals. Survivors included small mammals and* Archaeopteryx.

The Cenozoic Era

The **Cenozoic era** began about 65 million years ago and continues today. *Cenozoic* comes from the Greek words meaning "recent life." Scientists have more information about the Cenozoic era than about any of the previous eras because fossils from the Cenozoic era are embedded in rock layers that are close to the Earth's surface. This makes them easier to find. During the Cenozoic era, many kinds of mammals, birds, insects, and flowering plants appeared. Some organisms that appeared in the Cenozoic era are shown in **Figure 14.**

A Good Time for Large Mammals The Cenozoic era is sometimes referred to as the Age of Mammals. Mammals came to dominate the Cenozoic era much as reptiles dominated the Mesozoic era. Early Cenozoic mammals were small forest dwellers. Larger mammals appeared later. Some of these larger mammals had long legs for running, teeth that were specialized for eating different kinds of food, and large brains. Cenozoic mammals include mastodons, saber-toothed cats, camels, giant ground sloths, and small horses.

Figure 14 *Many types of mammals evolved during the Cenozoic era.*

REVIEW

1. What is the main difference between the atmosphere 3.5 billion years ago and the atmosphere today?

2. How do prokaryotic cells and eukaryotic cells differ?

3. Explain why cyanobacteria are so important to the development of new life-forms.

4. **Identifying Relationships** Match the organisms to the time period in which they first appeared.

   1. eukaryotes   a. Precambrian time
   2. dinosaurs   b. Paleozoic era
   3. fishes   c. Mesozoic era
   4. flowering plants   d. Cenozoic era
   5. birds

internet**connect**

*SC*LINKS.
NSTA

TOPIC: Mass Extinctions, The Geologic Time Scale
GO TO: www.scilinks.org
*sci*LINKS NUMBER: HSTL185, HSTL190

Terms to Learn

primate   australopithecine
hominid   Neanderthal

What You'll Do

◆ Discuss the shared characteristics of primates.
◆ Describe what is known
about the differences between
hominids.

Human Evolution

After studying thousands of fossilized skeletons and other evidence, scientists theorize that humans evolved over millions
of years from a distant ancestor that is also common to apes
and monkeys. This common ancestor is thought to have lived
more than 30 million years ago. How did we get from that
distant ancestor to who we are today? This section presents
some of the evidence that has been gathered so far.

Primates

To understand human evolution, we must first understand
the characteristics that make us human beings. Humans are
classified as primates. **Primates** are a group of mammals that
includes humans, apes, monkeys, and prosimians.
Primates have the charac-
teristics illustrated below
and in **Figure 15.**

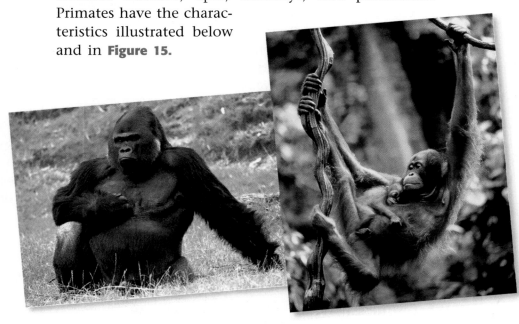

Figure 15 *The gorilla (left)
and these orangutans
(right) have characteristics
that make them nonhuman
primates, including opposable big toes!*

Characteristics of Primates

Most primates have five
flexible fingers—four
fingers plus an opposable
thumb.

This opposable thumb
enables primates to grip
objects.

Both eyes are located
at the front of the head,
providing **binocular,** or
three-dimensional,
vision. Each eye sees a
slightly different image
of the same scene. The
brain merges these two
images to create one
three-dimensional
image.

Based on physical and genetic similarities, the closest living relative of humans is thought to be the chimpanzee. This conclusion does not mean that humans descended from chimpanzees. Rather, it means that humans and chimpanzees share a common ancestor. The ancestor of humans is thought to have diverged from the ancestor of the chimpanzee about 7 million years ago. Since then, humans and chimpanzees have evolved along different paths.

Hominids Humans are assigned to a family separate from other primates, called **hominids.** The word *hominid* refers specifically to humans and their human-like ancestors. The main characteristic that distinguishes hominids from other primates is walking upright on two legs as their main way of moving around. Walking on two legs is called *bipedalism.* Examine **Figure 16** to see some skeletal similarities and differences between a hominid and an ape. Except for present-day humans, all hominid species are now extinct.

Figure 16 *The bones of a gorilla and a human are basically the same in form, but the human pelvis is suited for walking upright.*

The **gorilla pelvis** tilts the large rib cage and heavy neck and head forward. The arms are long to provide balance on the ground while the ape looks forward.

The **human pelvis** is vertical and helps hold the entire skeleton upright.

QuickLab

Thumb Through This

Tape your thumbs to the side of your hands so they cannot be used. Attempt each of the tasks listed below.

- Sharpen a pencil.
- Cut a circle out of a piece of paper using scissors.
- Tie your shoelaces.
- Button several buttons.

After each attempt, answer the following questions:

1. Is the task more difficult with or without an opposable thumb?

2. Without an opposable thumb, do you think you would carry out this task on a regular basis?

TRY at HOME

Hominid Evolution

The first primate ancestors appeared during the Cenozoic era, 55 million years ago, and evolved in several directions. These ancestors are thought to have been mouse-like mammals that were active during the night, lived in trees, and ate insects. When the dinosaurs died out, these mammals survived and gave rise to the first primates called *prosimians,* which means "before monkeys." Only a few species, such as the one pictured in **Figure 17,** survive today. How long after prosimians appeared did the first hominid appear? No one has been able to answer that question, but scientists have discovered fossil bones of hominids that date back to 4.4 million years ago.

Figure 17 *Prosimians, such as this lemur, hunt in trees for insects and small animals.*

Australopithecines Scientists think hominid evolution began in Africa. Among the oldest hominids are **australopithecines** (ah STRA loh PITH uh seens). The word *Australopithecus* means "southern man ape." These early hominids had long arms, short legs, and small brains. Fossil evidence shows that the australopithecines differed from apes in several important ways. For example, they were bipedal. Also, australopithecine brains were generally larger than ape brains, although they were still much smaller than the brains of present-day humans.

In 1976, paleoanthropologist Mary Leakey discovered a series of footprints in Tanzania. Mary Leakey and the footprints are pictured in **Figure 18.** By determining the age of the rock containing the prints, she learned that the footprints were more than 3.6 million years old. The footprints indicated that a group of three hominids had walked in an upright position across the wet volcanic ash-covered plain.

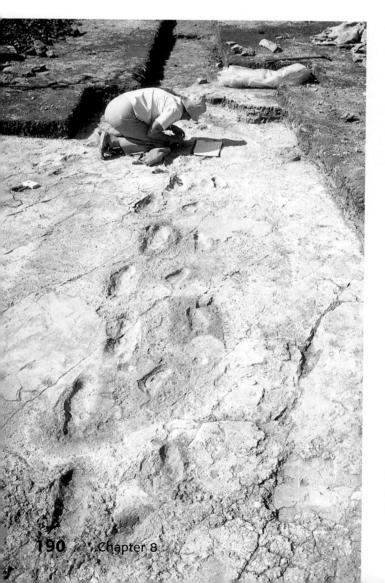

Figure 18 *Mary Leakey is shown here with the 3.6-million-year-old footprints.*

Lucy In 1979, a group of fossils was discovered in Ethiopia. Included in this group was the most complete skeleton of an australopithecine ever found. Nicknamed Lucy, this australopithecine lived about 2 million years ago. Lucy had a sturdy body and stood upright, but her brain was about the size of a chimpanzee's. Fossil discoveries like this one demonstrate that upright posture evolved long before the brain enlarged.

A Face Like Ours Hominids with more humanlike facial features appeared approximately 2.3 million years ago, probably evolving from australopithecine ancestors. This species is known as *Homo habilis.* Its skull is shown in **Figure 19.** Fossils of *Homo habilis* have been found along with crude stone tools. About 2 million years ago, *Homo habilis* was replaced by its larger-brained descendant, *Homo erectus,* pictured in **Figure 20.** *Homo erectus* was larger than *Homo habilis* and had a smaller jaw.

Figure 19 Homo habilis *is called handy man because this group of hominids made stone tools.*

Hominids Go Global Fossil evidence shows that *Homo erectus* may have lived in caves, built fires, and wore clothing. They successfully hunted large animals and butchered them using tools made of flint and bone. The appearance of *Homo erectus* marks the beginning of the expansion of human populations across the globe. *Homo erectus* survived for more than 1 million years, which is longer than any other species of hominid has lived. *Homo erectus* disappeared about 200,000 years ago. This is about the time present-day humans, called *Homo sapiens,* first appear in the fossil record.

Although *Homo erectus* migrated across the globe, it is thought that *Homo sapiens* evolved in Africa and then migrated to Asia and Europe.

Figure 20 Homo erectus *lived about 2 million years ago and may have looked like the sculpture above.*

Neanderthals In the Neander Valley, in Germany, fossils were discovered that belonged to a group of hominids referred to as **Neanderthals** (nee AN duhr TAHLS). They lived in Europe and western Asia beginning about 230,000 years ago.

Neanderthals hunted large animals, made fires, and wore clothing. There is evidence that they also cared for the sick and elderly and buried their dead, sometimes placing food, weapons, and even flowers with the dead bodies. Pictured in **Figure 21** is an artist's idea of how a Neanderthal might have looked. About 30,000 years ago, Neanderthals disappeared; nobody knows what caused their extinction.

Some scientists think the Neanderthals are a separate species, *Homo neanderthalensis*, from present-day humans, *Homo sapiens*. Other scientists think Neanderthals are a race of *Homo sapiens*. There is not yet enough evidence to fully answer this question.

Figure 21 *Neanderthals had heavy brow ridges, like* Homo erectus, *but a larger brain than modern humans.*

Cro-Magnons In 1868, fossil skulls were found in caves in southwestern France. The skulls were about 35,000 years old, and they belonged to a group of *Homo sapiens* with modern features, called *Cro-Magnons*. Cro-Magnons may have existed in Africa 100,000 years ago and migrated from Africa about 40,000 years ago, coexisting with Neanderthals. Compared with Neanderthals, Cro-Magnons had a smaller and flatter face, and their skulls were higher and more rounded, like an artist has modeled in **Figure 22**. The only significant physical difference between Cro-Magnons and present-day humans is that Cro-Magnons had thicker and heavier bones.

Figure 22 *This is an artist's idea of how a Cro-Magnon woman may have looked.*

Activity

Neanderthals made sophisticated spear points and other stone tools. Examine the Neanderthal tools below. Each of these tools was specialized for a particular task. Can you suggest what each stone tool was used for?

TRY at HOME

The chapter introduction discussed the cave paintings made by Cro-Magnons. These paintings are the earliest known examples of human art. In fact, Cro-Magnon culture is marked by an amazing diversity of artistic efforts, including cave paintings, sculptures, and carvings, like the one shown in **Figure 23.** The preserved villages and burial grounds of Cro-Magnon groups also show that they had a complex social organization.

Figure 23 *Cro-Magnons left many kinds of paintings, sculptures, and carvings, such as this carving of a bull.*

New Evidence of Human Evolution Although we know a great deal about our hominid ancestors, much remains to be understood. Each fossil discovery causes great excitement and raises new questions, such as, "Where did *Homo sapiens* evolve?" Current evidence suggests that *Homo sapiens* evolved in Africa. "Which australopithecine gave rise to humans?" Some scientists think *Australopithecus afarensis* is the ancestor of all hominids, including present-day humans. But recent fossil discoveries indicate another australopithecine species gave rise to human ancestors. There is still much to be learned about the evolution of humans.

REVIEW

1. Identify three characteristics of primates.

2. Compare *Homo habilis* with *Homo erectus*. What made the two species different from one another?

3. What evidence suggests Neanderthals were like present-day humans?

4. **Inferring Conclusions** Imagine you are a scientist excavating an ancient campsite. What might you conclude about the people who used the site if you found the charred bones of large animals and various stone blades among human fossils?

internet**connect**

*SCi*LINKS
NSTA

TOPIC: Human Evolution
GO TO: www.scilinks.org
*sci*LINKS NUMBER: HSTL195

Chapter Highlights

Vocabulary

fossil *(p. 176)*

relative dating *(p. 177)*

absolute dating *(p. 177)*

geologic time scale *(p. 178)*

extinct *(p. 179)*

plate tectonics *(p. 181)*

Section Notes

- Paleontologists are scientists who study fossils.

- The age of a fossil can be determined using relative dating and absolute dating. Relative dating is an estimate based on the known age of the sediment layer in which the fossil is found. Absolute dating usually involves the measurement of the rate of decay of the unstable atoms found in the rock surrounding the fossil.

- The geologic time scale is a calendar scientists use to outline the history of Earth and life on Earth.

- Many species existed for a few million years and then became extinct. Mass extinctions have occurred several times in Earth's history.

Labs

Dating the Fossil Record *(p. 712)*

The Half-life of Pennies *(p. 715)*

Vocabulary

Precambrian time *(p. 182)*

Paleozoic era *(p. 185)*

Mesozoic era *(p. 186)*

Cenozoic era *(p. 187)*

Section Notes

- Precambrian time includes the formation of the Earth, the beginning of life, and the evolution of simple multicellular organisms.

✓ Skills Check

Math Concepts

HALF-LIFE To understand half-life better, imagine that you have $10.00 in your pocket. You determine that you are going to spend half of all the money you have in your possession every 30 minutes. How much will you have after 30 minutes? ($5.00) How much will you have after another 30 minutes? ($2.50) How much will you have after 3 hours? (a little more than 15¢)

Visual Understanding

THE GEOLOGIC TIME SCALE You have probably seen old movies or cartoons that show humans and dinosaurs inhabiting the same environment. Can this be possible? Dinosaurs and humans did not exist at the same time. Dinosaurs became extinct 65 million years ago. Humans and their ancestors have been around for less than 4 million years. Review the Geologic Time Scale on page 178.

- The Earth is about 4.6 billion years old. Life formed from nonliving matter on the turbulent early Earth.

- The first cells, prokaryotes, were anaerobic. Later, photosynthetic cyanobacteria evolved and caused oxygen to enter the atmosphere.

- During the Paleozoic era, animals appeared in the oceans, and plants and animals colonized the land.

- Dinosaurs and other reptiles roamed the Earth during the Mesozoic era. Flowering plants, birds, and primitive mammals also appeared.

- Primates evolved during the Cenozoic era, which extends to the present day.

Vocabulary

primate *(p. 188)*

hominid *(p. 189)*

australopithecine *(p. 190)*

Neanderthal *(p. 192)*

Section Notes

- Humans, apes, and monkeys are primates. Primates are distinguished from other mammals by their opposable thumbs and binocular vision.

- Hominids, a subgroup of primates, include humans and their human-like ancestors. The oldest known hominids are australopithecines.

- Neanderthals were a species of humans that disappeared about 30,000 years ago.

- Cro-Magnons did not differ very much from present-day humans.

---

internet**connect**

GO TO: go.hrw.com

Visit the **HRW** Web site for a variety of learning tools related to this chapter. Just type in the keyword:

KEYWORD: HSTHIS

GO TO: www.scilinks.org

Visit the **National Science Teachers Association** on-line Web site for Internet resources related to this chapter. Just type in the *sci*LINKS number for more information about the topic:

TOPIC: Evidence of the Past	***sci*LINKS NUMBER:** HSTL180
TOPIC: Mass Extinctions	***sci*LINKS NUMBER:** HSTL185
TOPIC: The Geologic Time Scale	***sci*LINKS NUMBER:** HSTL190
TOPIC: Human Evolution	***sci*LINKS NUMBER:** HSTL195
TOPIC: Birds and Dinosaurs	***sci*LINKS NUMBER:** HSTL200

Chapter Review

To complete the following sentences, choose the correct term from each pair of terms listed below:

1. During the ___?___ of the Earth's history, life is thought to have originated from nonliving matter. *(Precambrian time period* or *Paleozoic era)*

2. The Age of Mammals refers to the ___?___. *(Mesozoic era* or *Cenozoic era)*

3. The Age of Reptiles refers to the ___?___. *(Paleozoic era* or *Mesozoic era)*

4. Plants colonized dry land during the ___?___. *(Precambrian time* or *Paleozoic era)*

5. The most ancient hominids are called ___?___. *(Neanderthals* or *australopithecines)*

UNDERSTANDING CONCEPTS

Multiple Choice

6. Scientists estimate the age of the Earth to be about
   a. 10 billion years.
   b. 4.6 billion years.
   c. 3.8 billion years.
   d. 4.4 million years.

7. The first cells probably appeared about
   a. 10 billion years ago.
   b. 4.6 billion years ago.
   c. 3.5 billion years ago.
   d. 4.4 million years ago.

8. How is the age of a fossil estimated?
   a. by using the geologic time scale
   b. by measuring unstable elements in the rock that holds the fossil
   c. by studying the relative position of continents
   d. by measuring the amount of oxygen in the fossil rock

9. Plants and air-breathing animals appeared during this time period.
   a. Precambrian time
   b. Paleozoic era
   c. Mesozoic era
   d. Cenozoic era

10. These hominids made sophisticated tools, hunted large animals, wore clothing, and cared for the sick and elderly. Their extinction is a mystery.
    a. australopithecines
    b. hominids in the genus *Homo*
    c. Neanderthals
    d. Cro-Magnons

Short Answer

11. What kinds of information do fossils provide about the evolutionary history of life?

12. Name at least one important biological event that occurred during each of the following geologic eras: Precambrian time, Paleozoic era, Mesozoic era, and Cenozoic era.

13. Why are there usually more fossils from the Cenozoic era than from other geologic eras?

Concept Mapping

14. Use the following terms to create a concept map: Earth's history, humans, Paleozoic era, dinosaurs, Precambrian time, cyanobacteria, Mesozoic era, land plants, Cenozoic era.

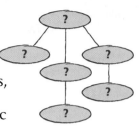

CRITICAL THINKING AND PROBLEM SOLVING

Write one or two sentences to answer the following questions:

15. Why do scientists think the first cells were anaerobic?

16. List three evolutionary changes in early hominids that led to the rise of modern humans.

MATH IN SCIENCE

17. A rock containing a newly discovered fossil is found to contain 5 mg of an unstable form of potassium and 5 mg of the stable element formed from its decay. If the half-life of the unstable form of potassium is 1.3 billion years, how old is the rock? What can you infer about the age of the fossil?

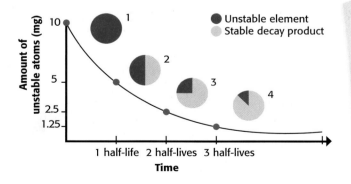

INTERPRETING GRAPHICS

The figure below illustrates the evolutionary relationships between some primates. Examine the figure, and answer the questions.

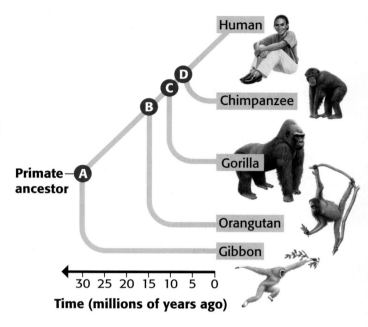

18. Which letter represents when gorillas took a different evolutionary path?

19. About how long ago did orangutans diverge from the human evolutionary line?

20. Which group has been separated from the human line of evolution the longest?

NOW What Do You Think?

Take a minute to review your answers to the ScienceLog questions on page 175. Have your answers changed? If necessary, revise your answers based on what you have learned since you began this chapter.

Windows into the Past

When you think about the history of life on Earth, you may not think of rocks. After all, rocks are nonliving! What can they tell you about life? It may surprise you to learn that a great deal of what we know about life on Earth has been provided by rocks. How? It just so happens that life-forms have been fossilized between layers of rock for million of years—maybe even since life first appeared on Earth. And finding these fossils is like finding an old snapshot of ancient life-forms.

Layers of Rock

Fossils are most likely to be found in sedimentary rock. This is a type of rock that forms as exposed rock surfaces are worn away by wind, rain, and ice. The particles from these rock surfaces then collect in low-lying areas. As these layers build up, their combined weight compacts the particles, and chemical reactions cement them together. After thousands of years, the layers of particles become solid rock—and so do parts of any organism that has been trapped in the layers.

The Rock Cycle

The illustration at right shows how sedimentary rock forms. It also shows how igneous rock and metamorphic rock form. Notice that sedimentary and metamorphic rock can melt and become igneous rock; this happens deep underground. Can you see why fossils would not normally be found in igneous rock?

The rock cycle is a continuous process. All three kinds of rock eventually become another type of rock. Fortunately for life scientists, this process can take millions of years. If this process happened more quickly—and sedimentary rock became either metamorphic or igneous rock at a faster pace—our fossil record would be much shorter. We may not have found out about the dinosaurs!

Cycle This!

▶ Suppose you found several fossils of the same organism. You found some fossils in very deep layers of sedimentary rock and some fossils in very shallow layers of sedimentary rock. What does this say about the organism?

▼ *The Rock Cycle*

CAREERS

PALEOBOTANIST

In school **Bonnie Jacobs** was fascinated by fossils, ancient cultures, and geology. "I have always had an interest in ancient things," she says. To pursue her interests, Jacobs became a paleobotanist. "A paleobotanist is someone who studies fossil plants," she explains. "That means you study fossilized leaves, wood, pollen, flower parts, or anything else that comes from a plant."

Bonnie Jacobs teaches and does research at Southern Methodist University, in Dallas, Texas. As a paleobotanist, she uses special "snapshots" that let her "see" back in time. If you look at these snapshots, you might see an ancient grassland, desert, or rain forest. Jacobs's snapshots might even give you a glimpse of the place where our human family may have started.

Fossil Plants and Ancient Climates

Jacobs and other paleobotanists study present-day plant species and how they grow in different climates. Plants that grow in warm, wet climates today probably grew in the same kind of climate millions of years ago. So when Jacobs finds ancient plant fossils that are similar to plants that exist today, she can determine what the ancient climate was like. But her fossils give more than just a climate report.

Plants and . . . Ancient Bones

Because some of these same plant fossils are found in rocks that also contain bits of bone—some from human ancestors—they may hold clues to human history. "Ideas about the causes of human evolution have a lot to do with changes in the landscape," Jacobs explains. "For instance, many scientists who study human evolution assumed that there was a big change from forested to more-open environments just before the origin of the human family. That assumption needs to be tested. The best way to do that is to go back to the plants themselves."

It's an Adventure!

In doing her research, Jacobs has traveled to many different places and worked with a wide variety of people. "Kiptalam Chepboi, a colleague we worked with in Kenya, grew up in the area where we do fieldwork. He took me to a sweat-bee hive. Sweat bees don't sting. You can take a honeycomb out from under a rock ledge, pop the whole thing in your mouth, and suck out the honey without worrying about getting stung. That was one of the neatest things I did out there."

Making a Modern Record

▶ Make your own plant fossil. Press a leaf part into a piece of clay. Fill the depression with plaster of Paris. Then write a report describing what the fossil tells you about the environment it came from.

▲ *Fossilized leaves*

9 Classification

This Really Happened . . .

Skunks have been thrown out of their family. It wasn't their awful smell that got them thrown out, though. It was their DNA.

Skunks were once thought to be most closely related to weasels, ferrets, minks, badgers, and otters. Those furry, short-legged, long-bodied, meat-eating mammals are grouped together in a family called Mustelidae (moo STEL i dee). *Mustelidae* is from the Latin word for "mouse." Skunks were classified along with weasels and ferrets because they all share several physical characteristics with mice, such as short, round ears and short legs.

However, a researcher at the University of New Mexico's Museum of Southwestern Biology discovered that the DNA of skunks is very different from the DNA of the other

members of Mustelidae. By comparing the DNA of different species, scientists can tell how closely related the species are. The DNA of two closely related animals—a house cat and a tiger, for example—are more similar than the DNA of two animals that are distantly related—such as a house cat and a chicken.

So where does that leave the little striped stinkers? Right in their own, newly created scientific family—Mephitidae (me FIT i dee). *Mephitid* is from the Latin word that means "bad odor"!

In this chapter you will learn why scientific names are important and how scientists classify organisms. You will also learn about the six major kingdoms into which all organisms are classified.

What Do You Think?

In your ScienceLog, try to answer the following questions based on what you already know:

1. What is classification?

2. How do people use classification in their everyday lives?

3. Why do scientists classify living things?

TRY at HOME

Classifying Shoes

In this activity, you will work in small groups to develop a system of classification for shoes.

Procedure

1. Gather **10 different shoes** from members of the class, a secondhand store, or a garage sale. Use a **black marker** to label the sole of each shoe with a number (1 through 10), and place the shoes on a table in the classroom.

2. Form small groups. In your ScienceLog, make a table similar to the one shown below. Make your own list of characteristics using the table as an example. Complete the chart, and then fill it in by describing each shoe.

Characteristics of Shoes				
Left or right	Boy's or girl's	Laced or slip-on	Color	Size
1.				
2.				
3.				
4.				
5.				

3. Use the information in the chart to make a key that can be used to identify each shoe. Your key should be a list of steps. Each step should contain two descriptive statements about the shoes that lead you to another set of statements. For example, step one might be:

1. a. This is a red sandal.   **Shoe #4**
   b. This is not a red sandal.   **Go to step 2.**

Each set of statements should eliminate more shoes until only one shoe exactly fits the description, such as in (a) above. Check the number on the sole of the shoe to see if you are correct.

4. When all the groups have finished, exchange keys with members of another group. See if you can use their key to identify the shoes.

Analysis

5. How was it helpful to list the characteristics of the shoes before making the key?

6. Were you able to identify the shoes using another group's key? If not, what problems did you have?

Terms to Learn

classification   family
kingdom   genus
phylum   species
class   taxonomy
order   dichotomous key

What You'll Do

◆ List the seven levels of classification.

◆ Explain the importance of having scientific names for species.

◆ Explain how scientific names are written.

◆ Describe how dichotomous keys help in identifying organisms.

Classification: Sorting It All Out

Imagine that you live in a tropical rain forest and are responsible for getting your own food, shelter, and clothing from the forest. If you are going to survive, you will need to know which plants you can eat and which are poisonous. You will need to know which animals to eat and which may eat you. You will need to organize the living things around you into categories, or classify them. **Classification** is the arrangement of organisms into orderly groups based on their similarities.

Why Classify?

For thousands of years, humans have classified different kinds of organisms based on their usefulness. For example, the Chácabo people of Bolivia, like the family shown in **Figure 1,** know of 360 species of plants in the forest where they live, and they have uses for 305 of those plants. How many plants can you name that are useful in your life?

Biologists also classify organisms—both living and extinct. Why? There are millions of different living things in the world. Making sense of the sheer number and diversity of living things requires classification. Classifying living things makes it easier for biologists to find the answers to many important questions, including the following:

■ How many known species are there?

■ What are the characteristics of each?

■ What are the relationships between these species?

In order to classify an organism, a biologist must use a system that groups organisms according to shared characteristics and their relationships between one another. There are seven levels of classification used by biologists—kingdom, phylum, class, order, family, genus, and species.

Figure 1 *The Chácabo people have a great amount of knowledge about their environment.*

Levels of Classification

Each organism is classified into one of several **kingdoms,** which are the largest, most general groups. All the organisms in a kingdom are then sorted into several *phyla* (singular, **phylum**). The members of one phylum are more like each other than they are like members of another phylum. Then all the organisms in a given phylum are further sorted into **classes.** Each class is subdivided into one or more **orders,** orders are separated into **families,** families are sorted into *genera* (singular, **genus**), and genera are sorted into **species.**

Examine **Figure 2** to follow the classification of the ordinary house cat from kingdom Animalia to species *Felis domesticus.*

Figure 2 *Kingdom Animalia contains all species of animals, while species* Felis domesticus *contains only one.*

Kingdom Animalia contains all the different phyla of animals.

Phylum Chordata contains animals with a hollow nerve cord.

Class Mammalia contains only animals that have a backbone and nurse their young.

Order Carnivora contains animals with a backbone that nurse their young and whose ancestors had special teeth for tearing meat.

Family Felidae contains animals with a backbone that nurse their young, have well-developed claws and special teeth for tearing meat, and are cats.

Genus *Felis* contains animals that have characteristics of the previous classifications, but they can't roar; they can only purr.

Species *Felis domesticus* contains only one kind of animal, the common house cat. It has characteristics of all the levels above it, but it has other unique characteristics.

Activity

A mnemonic device is a tool to help you remember something. One way to remember the levels of classification is to use a mnemonic device like this sentence: **K**ing **P**hillip **C**ame **O**ver **F**or **G**rape **S**oda.

Invent your own mnemonic device for the levels of classification using words that are meaningful to you.

TRY at HOME

What Is the Basis for Classification?

Carolus Linnaeus (lin AY uhs), pictured in **Figure 3,** was a Swedish physician and botanist who lived in the 1700s. Linnaeus founded **taxonomy,** the science of identifying, classifying, and naming living things.

Linnaeus attempted to classify all known organisms only by their shared characteristics. Later, scientists began to recognize that evolutionary changes form a line of descent from a common ancestor. Taxonomy changed to include these new ideas about evolutionary relationships.

Figure 3 *Carolus Linnaeus classified more than 7,000 species of plants.*

Modern Classification   Today's taxonomists still classify organisms based on presumed evolutionary relationships. Species with a recent common ancestor can be classified together. For example, the platypus, brown bear, lion, and house cat are related because they are thought to have an ancestor in common—an ancient mammal. Because of this relationship, all four animals are grouped into the same class—Mammalia.

A brown bear, lion, and house cat are more closely related to each other than to the platypus. They are all mammals, but only the platypus lays eggs. Brown bears, lions, and house cats share a different common ancestor—an ancient carnivore. Thus, they are classified into the same order—Carnivora.

Branching Diagrams   The close evolutionary relationship between lions and house cats is shown by the branching diagram in **Figure 4.** The characteristics listed on the arrow pointing to the right are the characteristics that make the next animal unique. The house cat and the platypus share the characteristics of hair and mammary glands. But they are different in many ways. The branch that leads to lions is closest to the branch that leads to house cats. The lion and the house cat are closely related because they share the most recent common ancestor—an ancient cat.

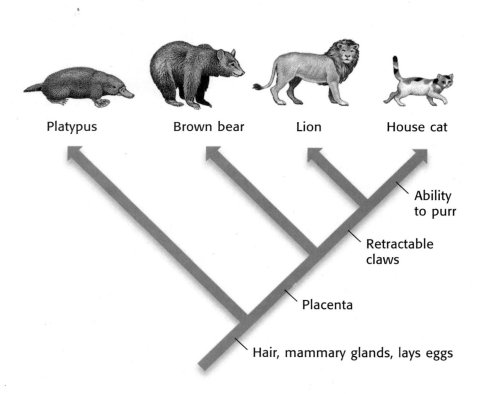

Platypus   Brown bear   Lion   House cat

Ability to purr

Retractable claws

Placenta

Hair, mammary glands, lays eggs

Figure 4 *This branching diagram shows the evolutionary relationships between four mammals.*

Naming Names

By classifying organisms, biologists are also able to give them scientific names. A scientific name is always the same for a specific organism no matter how many common names it might have.

Before Linnaeus's time, scholars used Latin names up to 12 words long to identify species. Linnaeus simplified the naming of organisms by giving each species a two-part scientific name. The first part of the name identifies the genus, and the second part identifies the species. The scientific name for the Indian elephant, for example, is *Elephas maximus*. No other species has this name, and all scientists know that *Elephas maximus* refers to the Indian elephant.

It's All Greek (or Latin) to Me Scientific names might seem difficult to understand because they are in Latin or Greek. Most scientific names, however, are actually full of meaning. Take a look at **Figure 5.** You probably already know this animal's scientific name. It's *Tyrannosaurus rex*! The first word is a combination of two Greek words meaning "tyrant lizard," and the second word is Latin for "king." The genus name always begins with a capital letter, and the species name begins with a lowercase letter. Both words are underlined or italicized. You may have heard *Tyrannosaurus rex* called *T. rex*. This is acceptable in science as long as the genus name is spelled out the first time it is used. The species name is incomplete without the genus name or its abbreviation.

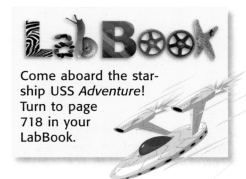

Come aboard the starship USS *Adventure*! Turn to page 718 in your LabBook.

Turn to page 718 in your LabBook.

QuickLab

Evolutionary Diagrams

A branching evolutionary diagram can be used to show evolutionary relationships between different organisms.

Construct a diagram similar to the one on page 204. Use a frog, a snake, a kangaroo, and a rabbit. What do you think is one major evolutionary change between one organism and the next? Write them on your diagram.

TRY at HOME

Figure 5
You would never call Tyrannosaurus rex *just* rex!

Why Are Scientific Names So Important? Examine the cartoon in **Figure 6.** What name do you have for the small black and white and sometimes smelly animal pictured? The skunk is called by several common names in English and has even more names—at least one name in every language! All of these common names can cause quite a bit of confusion for biologists who want to discuss the skunk. Biologists from different parts of the world who are interested in skunks need to know that they are all talking about the same animal, so they use its scientific name, *Mephitis mephitis.* All known living things have a two-part scientific name.

Figure 6 *Using an organism's two-part scientific name is a sure way for scientists to know they are discussing the same organism.*

When and where did the first bird live? Find out about the debate on page 218.

Dichotomous Keys

Taxonomists have developed special guides known as **dichotomous keys** to aid in identifying unknown organisms. A dichotomous key consists of several pairs of descriptive statements that have only two alternative responses. From each pair of statements, the person trying to identify the unknown organism chooses the appropriate statement. From there, the person is directed to another pair of statements. By working through the statements in the key, the person can eventually identify the organism. Using the simple dichotomous key on the next page, try to identify the two animals shown.

Dichotomous Key to 10 Common Mammals in the Eastern United States

1. a. This mammal flies. Its hand is formed into a wing.	**Little brown bat**
b. This mammal does not fly.	**Go to step 2**
2. a. This mammal has a naked (no fur) tail.	**Go to step 3**
b. This mammal doesn't have a naked tail.	**Go to step 4**
3. a. This mammal has a short, naked tail.	**Eastern mole**
b. This mammal has a long, naked tail.	**Go to step 5**
4. a. This mammal has a black mask across its face.	**Raccoon**
b. This mammal does not have a black mask across its face.	**Go to step 6**
5. a. This mammal has a tail that is flattened and shaped like a paddle.	**Beaver**
b. This mammal has a tail that is not flattened or shaped like a paddle.	**Opossum**
6. a. This mammal is brown with a white underbelly.	**Go to step 7**
b. This mammal is not brown with a white underbelly.	**Go to step 8**
7. a. This mammal has a long, furry tail that is black on the tip.	**Longtail weasel**
b. This mammal has a long tail without much fur.	**White-footed mouse**
8. a. This mammal is black with a narrow white stripe on its forehead and broad white stripes on its back.	**Striped skunk**
b. This mammal is not black with white stripes.	**Go to step 9**
9. a. This mammal has long ears and a short, cottony tail.	**Eastern cottontail**
b. This mammal has short ears and a medium-length tail.	**Woodchuck**

REVIEW

1. Why do scientists use scientific names for organisms?

2. Explain the two parts of a scientific name.

3. List the seven levels of classification.

4. Describe how a dichotomous key helps to identify unknown organisms.

5. **Interpreting Illustrations** Study the figure at right. Which plant is the closest relative of the hibiscus? Which plant is most distantly related to the hibiscus? Which plants have seeds?

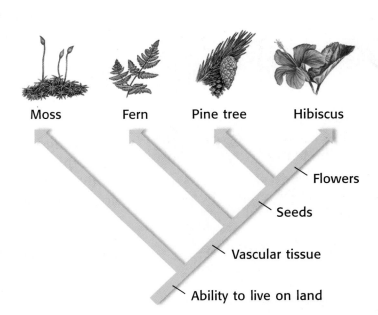

The Six Kingdoms

Terms to Learn

Archaebacteria   Plantae
Eubacteria   Fungi
Protista   Animalia

What You'll Do

◆ Explain how classification schemes for kingdoms developed as greater numbers of different organisms became known.

◆ List the six kingdoms, and provide two characteristics of each.

For hundreds of years, all living things were classified as either plants or animals. These two kingdoms, Plantae and Animalia, worked just fine until organisms like the species *Euglena,* shown in **Figure 7,** were discovered. If you were a taxonomist, how would you classify such an organism?

What Is It?

As you know, organisms are classified by their characteristics. Being the excellent taxonomist that you are, you decide to list the characteristics of *Euglena*:

■ *Euglena* are a species of single-celled organisms that live in pond water.

■ *Euglena* are green and, like most plants, can make their own food through photosynthesis.

"This is easy!" you think to yourself. "*Euglena* are plants." Not so fast! There are other important characteristics to consider:

■ *Euglena* can move about from place to place by whipping their "tails," called flagella.

■ Sometimes *Euglena* use food obtained from other organisms.

Figure 7 *How would you classify this organism?* Euglena, *shown here magnified 1,000 times, has characteristics of both plants and animals.*

Plants don't move around and usually do not eat other organisms. Does this mean that *Euglena* are animals? As you can see, neither category seems to fit. Scientists ran into the same problem, so they decided to add another kingdom for classifying organisms such as *Euglena.* This kingdom is known as Protista.

More Kingdoms As scientists continued to learn more about living things, they added kingdoms in order to account for the differences and similarities between organisms. Currently, most scientists agree that the six-kingdom classification system works best. There is still some disagreement, however, and still more to be learned. In the following pages, you will learn more about each of the kingdoms.

BRAIN FOOD

If *Euglena*'s chloroplasts are shaded from light or removed, it will begin to hunt for food like an animal. If the chloroplasts are shaded long enough, the chloroplasts degenerate and never come back.

The Two Kingdoms of Bacteria

Bacteria are extremely small single-celled organisms. Bacteria are different from all other living things in that they are *prokaryotes*, organisms that do not have nuclei. Many biologists divide bacteria into two kingdoms, **Archaebacteria** (AHR kee bak TEER ee uh) and **Eubacteria** (YOO bak TEER ee uh).

Archaebacteria have been on Earth at least 3 billion years. The prefix *archae* comes from a Greek word meaning "ancient." Today you can find archaebacteria living in places where most organisms could not survive. **Figure 8** shows a hot spring in Yellowstone National Park. The yellow and orange rings around the edge of the hot spring are formed by the billions of archaebacteria that live there.

Most of the other thousands of kinds of bacteria are eubacteria. These microscopic organisms live in the soil, in water, and even on and inside the human body! For example, the eubacterium *Escherichia coli,* pictured in **Figure 9,** is present in great numbers in human intestines, where it produces vitamin K. Another kind of eubacterium converts milk to yogurt, and yet another species causes ear and sinus infections and pneumonia.

Figure 8 *The Grand Prismatic Spring, in Yellowstone National Park, contains water that is about 90°C (194°F). The spring is home to archaebacteria that thrive in its hot water.*

Figure 9 E. coli, shown on the point of a pin, are seen with a scanning electron microscope. These eubacteria live in the intestines of animals, where they decompose undigested food.

Figure 10 Paramecium *usually moves about rapidly.*

Kingdom Protista

Members of the kingdom **Protista,** commonly called protists, are single-celled or simple multicellular organisms. Unlike bacteria, protists are *eukaryotes,* organisms that have cells with a nucleus and membrane-bound organelles. Kingdom Protista contains all eukaryotes that are not plants, animals, or fungi. Scientists think the first protists evolved from ancient bacteria about 2 billion years ago. Much later, protists gave rise to plants, fungi, and animals as well as to modern protists.

As you can see, kingdom Protista contains many different kinds of organisms. Protists include protozoa, which are animal-like protists; algae, which are plantlike protists; and slime molds and water molds, which are funguslike protists. *Euglena,* which were discussed earlier, are also members of kingdom Protista, as are the *Paramecium* and the slime mold pictured in **Figures 10** and **11.** Most protists are single-celled organisms, but some are multicellular, such as the giant kelp shown in **Figure 12.**

Self-Check

1. How are the two kingdoms of bacteria different from all other kingdoms?
2. How would you distinguish Protista from the two kingdoms of bacteria?

(See page 782 to check your answers.)

Figure 11 *A slime mold spreads over a fallen log on the forest floor.*

Figure 12
This giant kelp is a multicellular protist.

Kingdom Plantae

Although plants vary remarkably in size and form, most people easily recognize the members of kingdom **Plantae.** Plants are complex multicellular organisms that are usually green and use the sun's energy to make sugar by a process called *photosynthesis*. The giant sequoias and flowering plants shown in **Figures 13** and **14** are examples of the different organisms classified in the kingdom Plantae.

÷ 5 ÷ Ω ≤ ∞ +Ω √ 9 ∞ ≤ Σ 2

MATH BREAK

Building a Human Chain Around a Giant Sequoia

How many students would it take to join hands and form a human chain around a giant sequoia that is 30 m in circumference? Assume for this calculation that the average student can extend his or her arms about 1.3 m. NOTE: You can't have a fraction of a student, so be sure to round up your answer to the nearest whole number.

Environment CONNECTION

Giant sequoia trees are very rare. They grow only in California and are a protected species. Some of them are over 3,000 years old.

Figure 13 *A giant sequoia can measure 30 m around its base and can grow to more than 91.5 m tall.*

Figure 14 *Plants such as these are common in the rain forest.*

Kingdom Fungi

Molds and mushrooms are examples of the complex multi-cellular members of the kingdom **Fungi**. Fungi (singular, *fungus*) were originally classified as plants, but fungi do not obtain nutrients by photosynthesis. Moreover, fungi do not have many animal characteristics. Because of their unusual combination of characteristics, fungi are classified in a separate kingdom.

Fungi do not perform photosynthesis, as plants do, and they do not eat food, as animals do. Instead, fungi absorb nutrients from their surroundings after breaking them down with digestive juices. **Figure 15** shows a pretty but deadly mushroom, and **Figure 16** shows black bread mold (a fungus) growing on a piece of bread. Have you ever seen this type of mold on bread?

Figure 15 *This beautiful mushroom of the genus* Amanita *is poisonous.*

Figure 16 *This black bread mold can be dangerous if you inhale the spores. Some molds are dangerous, and others produce life-saving antibiotics.*

Classify This!
You and a friend are walking through the forest and you come upon the organism shown at right. You think it is a plant, but you are not sure. It has a flower and seeds, very small leaves, and roots that are growing into a rotting log. But this organism is white from its roots to its petals. To which kingdom do you think this organism belongs? What characteristic is your answer based on? What additional information would you need in order to give a more accurate answer?

Kingdom Animalia

Animals are complex multicellular organisms that belong to the kingdom **Animalia.** Most animals can move about from place to place and have nervous systems that help them sense and react to their surroundings. At the microscopic level, animal cells differ from those of fungi, plants, most protists, and bacteria because animal cells lack cell walls. **Figure 17** shows some members of the kingdom Animalia.

Figure 17 *The kingdom Animalia contains many different organisms, such as eagles, tortoises, beetles, and dolphins.*

REVIEW

1. Name the six kingdoms.

2. Which of the six kingdoms include prokaryotes, and which include eukaryotes?

3. Explain the different ways plants, fungi, and animals obtain nutrients.

4. Why are protists placed in their own kingdom?

5. **Applying Concepts** To which kingdom do humans belong? What characteristics place humans in this kingdom?

🖳 internet**connect**

*SCI*LINKS.
NSTA

TOPIC: The Basis for Classification, The Six Kingdoms
GO TO: www.scilinks.org
*sci***LINKS NUMBER:** HLST205, HSTL220

Chapter Highlights

Vocabulary

classification (p. 202)

kingdom (p. 203)

phylum (p. 203)

class (p. 203)

order (p. 203)

family (p. 203)

genus (p. 203)

species (p. 203)

taxonomy (p. 204)

dichotomous key (p. 206)

Section Notes

• Classification refers to the arrangement of organisms into orderly groups based on their similarities and evolutionary relationships.

• Biologists classify organisms in order to organize the number and diversity of living things and to give them scientific names.

• The classification scheme used today is based on the work of Carolus Linnaeus. Linnaeus founded the science of taxonomy, in which organisms are described, named, and classified.

• Modern classification schemes include evolutionary relationships.

• Today organisms are classified using a seven-level system of organization. The seven levels are kingdom, phylum, class, order, family, genus, and species. The genus and species of an organism compose its two-part scientific name.

• A scientific name is always the same for a specific organism, no matter how many common names it has.

• Dichotomous keys help to identify organisms.

Labs

Shape Island (p. 716)

Voyage of the USS Adventure (p. 718)

☑ Skills Check

Math Concepts

LARGE ORGANISMS The rounding-off rule states: If the number you wish to round is greater than or equal to the midpoint, round the number to the next greater number.

Sometimes when you are working with objects instead of numbers, you have to use a different rule! The MathBreak on page 211 asks you to round up your answer even though the answer includes a fraction that is less than halfway to the next number. Why is that? The answer is that if you don't round up, you won't have enough students to encircle the tree.

Visual Understanding

LEVELS OF CLASSIFICATION If you are still a little unsure about how organisms are grouped into levels of classification, turn back to page 203. Review Figure 2. Notice that the broadest, most inclusive level is kingdom. For example, all animals are grouped into kingdom Animalia. From there, the groups become more and more specific until only one animal is included under the level of species. Working from species up, notice that more and more animals are included in the group as you move toward the level of kingdom.

Vocabulary

Archaebacteria *(p. 209)*

Eubacteria *(p. 209)*

Protista *(p. 210)*

Plantae *(p. 211)*

Fungi *(p. 212)*

Animalia *(p. 213)*

Section Notes

- At first, living things were classified as either plants or animals. As scientists discovered more about living things and discovered more organisms, new kingdoms were added that were more descriptive than the old two-kingdom system.

- Most biologists recognize six kingdoms—Archaebacteria, Eubacteria, Protista, Plantae, Fungi, and Animalia.

- Bacteria are prokaryotes, single-celled organisms that do not contain nuclei. The organisms of all other kingdoms are eukaryotes, organisms that have cells with nuclei.

- Archaebacteria have been on Earth for about 3 billion years and can live where most other organisms cannot survive.

- Most bacteria are eubacteria and live almost everywhere. Some are harmful, and some are beneficial.

- Plants, most fungi, and animals are complex multicellular organisms. Plants perform photosynthesis. Fungi break down material outside their body and then absorb the nutrients. Animals eat food, which is digested inside their body.

---

internetconnect

GO TO: go.hrw.com

Visit the **HRW** Web site for a variety of learning tools related to this chapter. Just type in the keyword:

KEYWORD: HSTCLS

GO TO: www.scilinks.org

Visit the **National Science Teachers Association** on-line Web site for Internet resources related to this chapter. Just type in the *sci*LINKS number for more information about the topic:

TOPIC: The Basis for Classification	*sci*LINKS NUMBER: HSTL205
TOPIC: Levels of Classification	*sci*LINKS NUMBER: HSTL210
TOPIC: Dichotomous Keys	*sci*LINKS NUMBER: HSTL215
TOPIC: The Six Kingdoms	*sci*LINKS NUMBER: HSTL220

Chapter Review

USING VOCABULARY

To complete the following sentences, choose the correct term from each pair of terms listed below:

1. Linnaeus founded the science of __?__ . (*DNA analysis* or *taxonomy*)

2. All of the organisms classified into a single kingdom are then divided into one of several __?__ . (*phyla* or *classes*)

3. The narrowest level of classification is the __?__ . (*genus* or *species*)

4. Linnaeus began naming organisms using __?__ . (*two-part scientific names* or *evolutionary relationships*)

5. Archaebacteria and eubacteria are __?__ . (*prokaryotes* or *eukaryotes*)

UNDERSTANDING CONCEPTS

Multiple Choice

6. When scientists classify organisms, they
   a. arrange them in orderly groups.
   b. give them many common names.
   c. decide whether they are useful.
   d. ignore evolutionary relationships.

7. When the seven levels of classification are listed from broadest to narrowest, which level is in the fifth position?
   a. class
   b. order
   c. genus
   d. family

8. The scientific name for the European white water lily is *Nymphaea alba*. What is the genus to which this plant belongs?
   a. *Nymphaea*   c. water lily
   b. *alba*   d. alba lily

9. "Kings Play Chess On Fine-Grained Sand" is a mnemonic device that helps one remember
   a. the scientific names of different organisms.
   b. the six kingdoms.
   c. the seven levels of classification.
   d. the difference between prokaryotic and eukaryotic cells.

10. Most bacteria are classified in which kingdom?
    a. Archaebacteria   c. Protista
    b. Eubacteria   d. Fungi

11. What kind of organism thrives in hot springs and other extreme environments?
    a. archaebacteria   c. protists
    b. eubacteria   d. fungi

Short Answer

12. Why is the use of scientific names so important in biology?

13. List two kinds of evidence used by modern taxonomists to classify organisms based on evolutionary relationships.

14. Is a eubacterium a type of eukaryote? Explain your answer.

Concept Map

15. Use the following terms to create a concept map: kingdom, fern, lizard, Animalia, Fungi, algae, Protista, Plantae, mushroom.

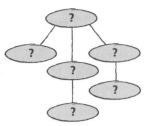

Write one or two sentences to answer the following questions:

16. How are the levels of classification related to evolutionary relationships among organisms?

17. Explain why two species that belong to the same genus, such as white oak *(Quercus alba)* and cork oak *(Quercus suber)*, also belong to the same family.

18. What characteristic do the members of all six kingdoms have in common?

MATH IN SCIENCE

19. Scientists estimate that millions of species are yet to be discovered and classified. If only 1.5 million, or 10 percent, of species have been discovered and classified, how many species do scientists think exist on Earth?

20. Sequoia trees can grow to more than 90 m in height. There are 3.28 ft per meter. How many feet are in 90 m?

INTERPRETING GRAPHICS

The diagram below illustrates the evolutionary relationships among several primates.

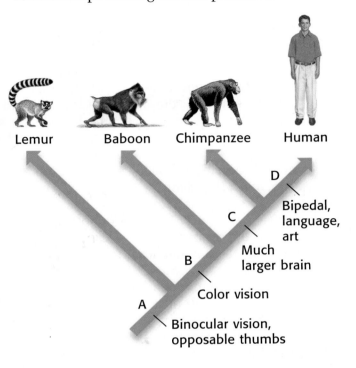

Lemur   Baboon   Chimpanzee   Human

D
Bipedal, language, art
C
Much larger brain
B
Color vision
A
Binocular vision, opposable thumbs

21. Which primate is the closest relative to the common ancestor of all primates?

22. Which primate shares the most traits with humans?

23. Do lemurs share the characteristics listed at point D with humans? Explain your answer.

24. What characteristic do baboons have that lemurs do not have? Explain your answer.

NOW What Do You Think?

Take a minute to review your answers to the ScienceLog questions on page 201. Have your answers changed? If necessary, revise your answers based on what you have learned since you began this chapter.

It's a Bird, It's a Plane, It's a *Dinosaur*?

Think about birds. Parrots, pigeons, buzzards, emus . . . they're everywhere! But once there were no birds. So where did they come from? When did birds evolve? Was it 225 million years ago, just 115 million years ago, or somewhere in between? No one really knows for sure, but the topic has fueled a long-standing debate among scientists.

The debate began when the fossil remains of a 150-million-year-old dinosaur with wings and feathers—*Archaeopteryx*—were found in Germany in 1860 and 1861.

▲ Archaeopteryx *was the first true bird.*

Birds Are Dinosaurs!

Some scientists think that birds evolved from small, carnivorous dinosaurs like *Velociraptor* about 115 million to 150 million years ago. Their idea relies on similarities between modern birds and these small dinosaurs. Particularly important are the size, shape, and number of toes and "fingers"; the location and shape of the breastbone and shoulder; the presence of a hollow bone structure; and the development of wrist bones that "flap" for flight. To many scientists, all this evidence is overwhelming. It can lead to only one conclusion: Modern birds are descendants of dinosaurs.

No They Aren't!

"Not so fast!" say a smaller but equally determined group of scientists who think that birds developed 100 million years before *Velociraptor* and its relatives. They point out that all these dinosaurs were ground dwellers and were the wrong shape and size for flying. They would never get off the ground! Further, these dinosaurs lacked at least one of the bones necessary for flight in today's birds.

This "birds came before dinosaurs" idea rests on fossils of *thecodonts,* small tree-dwelling reptiles that lived about 225 million years ago. One thecodont, a small, four-legged tree dweller called *Megalancosaurus,* had the right bones and body shape—and the right center of gravity—for flight. The evidence is clear, say these scientists, that birds flew long before dinosaurs even existed!

▲ *This small tree-dwelling reptile,* Megalancosaurus, *may have evolved into the birds we know today.*

So Who Is Right?

Both sides are debating fossils 65 million years to 225 million years old. Some species left many fossils, while some left just a few. In the last few years, new fossils discovered in China, Mongolia, and Argentina have just added fuel to the fire. So scientists will continue to study the available evidence and provide their educated guesses. Meanwhile, the debate rages on!

Compare for Yourself

▶ Find photographs of *Sinosauropteryx* and *Archaeopteryx* fossils, and compare them. How are they similar? How are they different? Do you think birds could be modern dinosaurs? Debate your idea with someone who holds the opposite view.

LOBSTER-LIP LIFE-FORM

Have you ever stopped to think about lobsters' lips? Did you even know that lobsters have lips? Oddly enough, they do. And even stranger, scientists have found a tiny animal living on lobsters' lips. Surprised? Although scientists noticed this little critter about 30 years ago, they had never studied it closely. When they finally did, they were astounded! This tiny organism is different from anything else in the world. Meet *Symbion pandora.*

▲ *Although scientists knew of* Symbion pandora's *existence for 30 years, they did not realize how unusual it was.*

A Little Weird

What makes *Symbion pandora* so unusual? As if spending most of its life on lobster lips isn't strange enough, *S. pandora* also seems to combine the traits of very different animals. Here are some of its strange characteristics:

- **Life stages:** *S. pandora*'s life cycle involves many different *stages,* or body forms. The stages are very different from each other. For instance, at certain times in its life, *S. pandora* can swim around, while at other times, it can exist only by attaching to a lobster's mouth.
- **Dwarf males:** Male *S. pandora* are much smaller than the females. Thus, they are called *dwarf males.*

- **Feeding habits:** Dwarf males don't eat; they can only find a female, reproduce, and then die!
- **Budding:** Many individuals are neither male nor female. These animals reproduce through a process called *budding.* In budding, a new, complete animal can sprout out of the adult. In turn, the new offspring can reproduce in the same way.
- **Disappearing guts:** When an adult starts to form a new bud, its digestive and nervous systems disappear! Part of these guts help make the new bud. Then the adult forms new digestive and nervous systems to replace the old ones.

How Unusual Is It?

When scientists discover a new plant or animal, they may conclude that it represents a new species within an existing genus. In that case scientists make up a name for the new species. Usually, the person who finds the new organism gets to name it. If the new organism is *very* unusual, scientists may place it not only in a new species but also in a new genus.

S. *pandora* is so unusual that it was placed not only in a new species and a new genus, but also in a new family, a new order, a new class, and even a new phylum! Such a scientific discovery is extremely rare. In fact, when this discovery was made, in 1995, it was announced in newspapers all over the world!

Where Would You Look?

▶ *S. pandora* was first noticed more than 30 years ago, but no one realized how unusual it was until scientists studied it. Scientists estimate that we've identified less than 10 percent of Earth's organisms. Find out about other new animal species that have been discovered within the last 10 years. Where are some places you would look for new species?

UNIT 4

Simple Organisms, Fungi, and Plants

You are probably familiar with plants. But do you know how important plants are? When plants make food for themselves, they provide oxygen and food for other living things.

Throughout history, people have been trying to understand plants, and in this unit you will join them.

You'll also learn about fascinating organisms that you may not know about—bacteria, protists, and fungi. Although many of these organisms are too small to see, they are just as important as plants. Some cause disease, but others provide food and medicines. Read on, and be amazed!

250 B.C.

Mayan farmers build terraces to control the flow of water to their crops.

1580

Prospero Alpini discovers that plants have both male and female structures.

1898

Martinus Beijerinck gives the name *virus* to infectious material that is smaller than bacteria.

1928

Alexander Fleming observes that certain molds can eliminate bacterial growth, and he discovers penicillin.

1955

Jonas Salk develops a vaccine for the polio virus.

1683

Anton van Leeuwenhoek is the first to describe bacteria.

1763

Joseph Kölreuter studies pollination in plants.

1897

Beatrix Potter, the author of *The Tale of Peter Rabbit*, completes her collection of 270 watercolors of fungi. She is now considered an expert in mycology, the study of fungi.

1864

Louis Pasteur uses heat to eliminate microbes. This process is later called pasteurization.

1995

An outbreak of the deadly Ebola virus occurs in Zaire.

1983

HIV, the virus responsible for AIDS, is isolated.

1972

Ananda Chakrabarty uses genetics to design bacteria that can break down oil in oil spills.

CHAPTER 10 Bacteria and Viruses

Imagine . . .

It was a dark and stormy night—the kind of night where bizarre things happen. Suzanne sat quietly in her bedroom reading her science book. She tried to concentrate, but the constant patter of rain against her window soon lulled her to sleep.

Thunder roared through the air. Suzanne looked down at her hands and suddenly screamed in horror. She was covered from head to toe with creeping, crawling creatures! They clung to her hair, her back, and even her eyelashes! There was nowhere she could go to escape them!

Suzanne woke with a start. What a strange dream! Were these creatures real? Then she remembered what she had just read in her science book. The things she had dreamed about were called bacteria and viruses.

Bacteria and viruses are all around Suzanne, just as they are all around you. They are in the air you breathe and the food you eat. They are inside your body and all over the ground. Most of them are so small that they can only be seen with a high-powered microscope. Despite their tiny size, bacteria and viruses have a huge impact on the world around you. You'll read all about them in this chapter.

222 Chapter 10

What Do You Think?

In your ScienceLog, try to answer the following questions based on what you already know:

1. How many cells make up a bacterium?

2. What do cheese and yogurt have to do with bacteria?

3. Do you think a virus is alive? Explain your answer.

Investigate!

Your Constant Companions

Bacteria are everywhere. They are in the soil, in the air, and even inside you. When grown in a laboratory, microscopic bacteria form easily visible colonies. In this activity, you will see some of the bacteria that share your environment.

Procedure

1. Obtain **three plastic Petri dishes** containing **nutrient agar** from your teacher. Label one dish "Hand," another "Breath," and another "Soil." Wipe your finger across the first one. Breathe onto the second one. Place a small amount of **soil** in the third one.

2. Secure the Petri dish lids with **transparent tape.** Place them in a warm, dark place for about a week.
   Caution: Do not open these Petri dishes after they are sealed.

3. Observe the Petri dishes each day. What do you see? Record your observations in your ScienceLog.

Analysis

4. How does the appearance of the three dishes differ?

5. Which source had the most bacterial growth? Can you guess why this might be?

Bacteria

Bacteria are the smallest and simplest organisms on the planet. They are also the most abundant. A single gram of soil (which is about equal to the mass of your pencil eraser) can contain over 2.5 billion bacteria!

Not all bacteria are that small. The largest known bacteria are a thousand times larger than the *average* bacterium. Can you imagine an animal a thousand times larger than you? The first giant bacteria ever identified were found in the intestines of a surgeonfish like the one in **Figure 1.**

Terms to Learn

binary fission
endospore

What You'll Do

◆ Describe the characteristics of a prokaryotic cell.
◆ Explain how bacteria reproduce.
◆ Compare and contrast eubacteria and archaebacteria.

Figure 1 *The giant bacteria inside this fish are 0.6 mm long. That's big enough to be seen with the naked eye.*

$$\div \;\; 5 \;\; \div \;\; \Omega \;\; \infty \;\; +\Omega \;\; \sqrt{} \;\; 9 \;\; \leq \;\; \Sigma \;\; 2$$
$$+$$

MATH BREAK

Airborne Organisms

Air typically has around 4,000 bacteria per cubic meter. Cindy's bedroom is 3 m long and 4 m wide. Her ceiling is 2.5 m high. That means there are 30 m³ in her bedroom (3 m × 4 m × 2.5 m). About how many bacteria are in her bedroom's air? About how many bacteria are in the air of your classroom?

Classifying Bacteria

All organisms fit into one of the six kingdoms: Protista, Plantae, Fungi, Animalia, Eubacteria, and Archaebacteria. Bacteria make up the kingdoms Eubacteria (YOO bak TIR ee uh) and Archaebacteria (AHR kee bak TIR ee uh). These two kingdoms contain the oldest forms of life on Earth. In fact, for over 2 billion years, they were the *only* forms of life on Earth.

Look, Mom! No Nucleus! Bacteria are single-celled organisms that do not have nuclei. A cell with no nucleus is called a *prokaryote*. A prokaryote is able to use cellular respiration, move around, and reproduce. Because a prokaryote has these abilities, it can function as an independent organism.

Bacterial Reproduction

Most bacteria reproduce by a type of simple cell division known as **binary fission,** illustrated in **Figures 2** and **3.** In binary fission, a prokaryote's DNA is replicated before cell division. The DNA and its copy attach to the inside of the cell membrane. As the cell grows and the membrane grows longer, the loops of DNA become separated. When the cell is about double in size, the membrane pinches inward. A new cell wall forms, separating the two new cells and their DNA.

Figure 2 Binary Fission

❶ *The cell grows.*

❷ *The DNA replicates and attaches to the cell membrane.*

❸ *The DNA and its copy separate as the cell grows even larger.*

❹ *The cell splits in two. Each new cell has a copy of the DNA.*

Figure 3 *This bacterium is about to complete binary fission.*

Endospores Each species of bacteria reproduces best at a certain temperature and with a certain amount of moisture. Most species thrive in warm, moist environments. If the environment is unfavorable, some species will be unable to survive. Others will survive by growing a thick protective membrane. These bacteria are then called **endospores.**

Many endospores can survive boiling, freezing, and extremely dry environments. When conditions become favorable again, the endospores will break open, and the bacteria will become active. Scientists have found endospores in the digestive tract of an insect that had been preserved in amber for 30 million years. A similar piece of amber can be seen in **Figure 4.** When the endospores were moistened in a laboratory, the bacteria began to grow!

Figure 4 *Endospores found in a preserved insect indicate that bacteria can survive for millions of years.*

Spying on Spirilla

Use a **microscope** to observe prepared **slides of bacteria.** What shapes can you see? What are these shapes called? Draw and label the bacteria in your ScienceLog.

The Shape of Bacteria

Almost all bacteria have a rigid cell wall that gives the organism its characteristic shape. Bacteria have a great variety of shapes. The three most common shapes are illustrated below. Each shape provides a different advantage. Can you guess what the advantage of each shape might be?

Whipping Something Up Some bacteria have hairlike structures called flagella (singular, *flagellum*) that help them move around. *Flagellum* means "whip" in Latin. A flagellum spins like a corkscrew, propelling a bacterium through liquid.

The Most Common Shapes of Bacteria

◀ *Bacilli* (buh SIL ie) *are rod-shaped bacteria. Rod-shaped bacteria have a large surface area, which helps them absorb nutrients, but they can also dry out easily.*

▲ *Spirilla* (spie RI luh) *are long, spiral-shaped bacteria. This is the least common shape for a bacterium. Spirilla move easily in a corkscrew motion, using flagella at both ends.*

▲ *Cocci* (KAHK sie) *are spherical bacteria. They are more resistant to drying out than rod-shaped bacteria.*

Kingdom Eubacteria

Most bacteria are eubacteria. The kingdom Eubacteria has more individual organisms than any of the other five kingdoms. Eubacteria have existed for over 3.5 billion years.

Eu Are What Eu Eat Eubacteria are classified by the way they get food. *Consumers* obtain nutrients from other organisms. Most eubacteria, like those helping to decay the leaf in **Figure 5,** are consumers. Many consumers are *decomposers,* which feed on dead organic matter. Other consumers are *parasitic,* which means they invade the body of another organism to obtain food.

Eubacteria that make their own food are *producers.* Some producers are photosynthetic. Like green plants, they convert the energy of the sun into food. These bacteria contain the green pigment *chlorophyll* that is needed for photosynthesis.

Plant Predecessor? Some bacterial producers are *cyanobacteria* (SIE uh noh bak TIR ee uh). Cyanobacteria live in many different types of water environments, such as the one shown in **Figure 6.** It may be that billions of years ago photosynthetic bacteria similar to these began to live inside certain cells with nuclei. The photosynthetic bacteria made food, and the host provided a protected environment for the bacteria. This might be how the first plants came to be.

Figure 5 *Decomposers, like the ones helping to decay this leaf, return nutrients to the ecosystem.*

✓ Self-Check

Cyanobacteria were once classified as plants. Can you explain why? *(See page 782 to check your answer.)*

Figure 6 *Cyanobacteria in this hot spring excrete chemicals that help form the chalky terraces.*

Kingdom Archaebacteria

Archaebacteria thrive in places where no other living things are found. Scientists have found archaebacteria in the hot springs at Yellowstone National Park and beneath 430 m of ice in Antarctica. They have even been found living 8 km below the Earth's surface!

Archaebacteria are genetically different from eubacteria. Not all archaebacteria have cell walls. The cell walls of archaebacteria—when they do have them—are chemically different from those of all other organisms.

Pass the Salt There are three main types of archaebacteria: methane makers, heat lovers, and salt lovers. Methane makers excrete methane gas. They are found in many places including swamps. Heat lovers live in places like ocean rift vents where temperatures are over 360°C. Salt lovers live in places where the concentration of salt is very high, such as the Dead Sea, shown in **Figure 7.**

Figure 7 *The Dead Sea is so salty that only archaebacteria can survive in it. Fish carried into the Dead Sea by the Jordan River die instantly.*

internetconnect

SCiLINKS
NSTA

TOPIC: Bacteria, Archaebacteria
GO TO: www.scilinks.org
*sci*LINKS NUMBER: HSTL230, HSTL235

REVIEW

1. Draw and label the three main shapes of bacteria.

2. Describe the four steps of binary fission.

3. How do eubacteria and archaebacteria differ?

4. **Analyzing Concepts** Many bacteria cannot reproduce in cooler temperatures and are destroyed at high temperatures. How do humans take advantage of this when preparing and storing food?

Terms to Learn

bioremediation
antibiotic
pathogenic bacteria

What You'll Do

- Explain why life on Earth depends on bacteria.
- List five ways bacteria are useful to people.
- Describe why some bacteria are harmful to people.

Bacteria's Role in the World

Bacteria may be invisible to us, but their effects on the planet are not. Because many types of bacteria cause disease, bacteria have gotten a bad reputation. However, they also do many things that are important to humans.

Good for the Environment

Life as we know it could not exist without bacteria. They are vital to our environment, and we benefit from them in several ways.

Nitrogen-Fixing Nitrogen is an essential chemical for all organisms because it is a component of proteins and DNA. Plants must have nitrogen in order to grow properly. You might think getting nitrogen would be easy because nitrogen gas makes up more than 75 percent of the air. But most plants cannot use nitrogen from the air. They need to take in a different form of nitrogen. *Nitrogen-fixing bacteria* consume nitrogen in the air and change it into a form that plants can use. This process is described in **Figure 8.**

Recycling Have you ever seen dead leaves and twigs on a forest floor? The leaves and twigs will be recycled over time with the help of bacteria. By breaking down dead organic matter, decomposing bacteria make nutrients available again to living things.

Figure 8 **Bacteria's Role in the Nitrogen Cycle.**

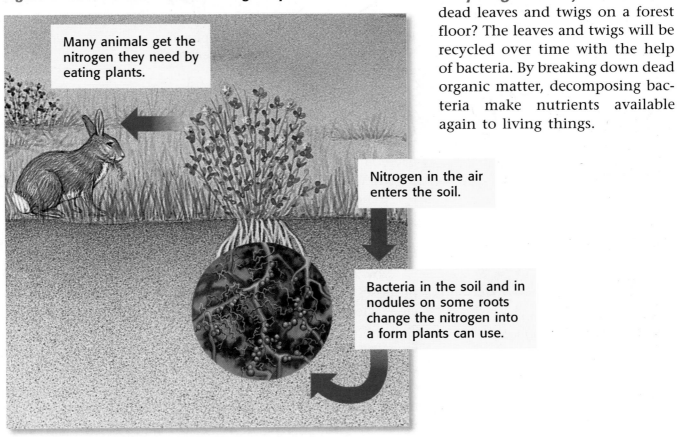

Many animals get the nitrogen they need by eating plants.

Nitrogen in the air enters the soil.

Bacteria in the soil and in nodules on some roots change the nitrogen into a form plants can use.

Cleaning Up Recently bacteria have been used to combat pollution. **Bioremediation** (BIE oh ri MEE dee AY shuhn) is the use of bacteria and other microorganisms to change pollutants into harmless chemicals. Bioremediation is used to clean up industrial, agricultural, and municipal wastes, as well as oil spills. The workers in **Figure 9** are using bioremediation to remove toxins from the soil.

Figure 9 *Bioremediating bacteria are added to soil to consume pollutants and excrete them as harmless chemicals.*

Figure 10 *Genes from the Xenopus frog were used to produce the first genetically engineered bacteria.*

Good for People

Scientists are constantly searching for new ways to use bacteria to better the lives of humans. People have been able to genetically engineer bacteria since 1973. It was then that researchers inserted genes from a frog like the one in **Figure 10** into the bacterium *Escherichia coli* (ES uhr RI shee uh COHL ie). The bacterium started reproducing the frog genes. Never before had such a genetically altered organism existed.

Now scientists can genetically engineer bacteria for many purposes, including the production of medicines, insecticides, cleansers, adhesives, foods, and many other products.

Fighting Bacteria with Bacteria Although some bacteria cause diseases, others make chemicals that treat diseases. **Antibiotics** are medicines used to kill bacteria and other microoganisms. Many bacteria have been genetically engineered to make antibiotics in large quantities.

BRAIN FOOD

Alexander Fleming, the Scottish scientist who discovered antibiotics, created a microbial growth shaped like the British flag in honor of the queen's visit to his lab. She was *not* amused.

APPLY

Ingenious Engineering!

Ralph specializes in genetically engineering bacteria. He has engineered many different types of bacteria to help solve medical and environmental problems, but today he is completely out of ideas. He needs you to help him think of a design for a new bacterium that will either treat a disease or help the environment. What would you want this new bacterium to do? What kinds of traits would you give it?

Insulin Scientists have created genetically engineered bacteria that can produce other medicines, such as insulin. Insulin is a substance needed by the body to properly use sugars and other carbohydrates. People who have *diabetes* cannot produce the insulin they need. They must take insulin daily. In the late 1970s, scientists put genes carrying the genetic code for human insulin into *E. coli* bacteria. The bacteria produced human insulin, which can be separated from the bacteria and given to diabetics.

Feeding Time! Believe it or not, people breed bacteria for food! Every time you eat cheese, yogurt, buttermilk, or sour cream, you also eat a lot of lactic-acid bacteria. *Lactic-acid bacteria* digest the milk sugar lactose and convert it into lactic acid. The lactic acid acts as a preservative and adds flavor to the food. The foods in **Figure 11** could not be made without bacteria.

Activity

Create a week's meal plan without any foods made with bacteria. What would your diet be like without prokaryotes?

TRY at HOME

Figure 11 *Bacteria are used to make many different types of food, including sauerkraut, sourdough bread, some kinds of sausages, pickles, and dairy products.*

Harmful Bacteria

We couldn't survive without bacteria, but they are also capable of doing incredible damage. Scientists realized in the mid-1800s that some bacteria are pathogenic. **Pathogenic bacteria** cause diseases, such as the one illustrated in **Figure 12.** These bacteria invade a host organism and obtain nutrients from the host's cells. In the process, they cause damage to the host. Today, almost all bacterial diseases can be treated with antibiotics. Many can also be prevented with vaccines. Some diseases caused by bacteria are shown in the table below.

Figure 12 *Between the years 1346 and 1350, the bubonic plague killed 25 million people. That was one-third of Europe's population at the time.*

Bacterial Diseases

• Dental cavities	• Lyme disease
• Ulcers	• Tuberculosis
• Strep throat	• Leprosy
• Food poisoning	• Typhoid fever
• Bacterial pneumonia	• Bubonic plague

Enough Diseases to Go Around Bacteria cause diseases in other organisms as well as in people. Have you ever seen a plant with discolored spots or soft rot? If so, you've seen bacterial damage to another organism.

Pathogenic bacteria attack plants, animals, protists, fungi, and even other bacteria. They can cause considerable damage to grain, fruit, and vegetable crops. The branch of a pear tree in **Figure 13** shows the effects of pathogenic bacteria.

Figure 13 *This branch of a pear tree has fire blight, a bacterial disease.*

REVIEW

1. List three different products bacteria are used to make.

2. What are two ways that bacteria affect plants?

3. How can bacteria both cause and cure diseases?

4. **Analyzing Relationships** Describe some of the problems humans would face if there were no bacteria.

What You'll Do

◆ Explain how viruses are similar to and different from living things.
◆ List the four major virus shapes.
◆ Describe the two kinds of viral reproduction.

Viruses

Viruses have been called the greatest threat to the survival of humanity. But what are they? A **virus** is a microscopic particle that invades a cell and often destroys it. They are everywhere, and for humans they are mostly one big headache. That's because many diseases are caused by viruses, including the common cold, flu, and acquired immune deficiency syndrome (AIDS). AIDS is caused by the human immunodeficiency virus (HIV).

It's a Small World

Viruses are incredibly tiny. They are even smaller than the smallest bacteria. About 5 billion of them can fit into a single drop of blood. Because of viruses' small size and ever-changing nature, scientists don't know how many types of viruses exist. The number may be in the billions or higher!

Are They Living?

Like living things, viruses contain protein and nucleic acids. But viruses, such as the ones shown in **Figure 14,** don't eat, grow, breathe, or perform other biological functions. A virus cannot "live" on its own, although it can reproduce inside a living organism that serves as its host. A **host** is an organism that supports a parasite. Using a host's cell as a miniature factory, viruses instruct the cell to produce viruses rather than healthy new cells.

$\div$ 5 $\div$ Ω $\leq$ ∞ $+\Omega$ $\sqrt{}$ 9 ∞ $\leq$ Σ 2
$+$

MATH **BREAK**

Sizing Up a Virus

If you enlarged an average virus 600,000 times, it would be about the size of a small pea. How tall would you be if you were enlarged 600,000 times?

LabBook

Get a leg up on viruses. Turn to page 721 in your LabBook.

Figure 14 *Viruses are not cells. They do not have cytoplasm or organelles.*

Classifying Viruses

Viruses can be grouped by the type of disease they cause, their life cycle, or the type of genetic material they contain. Viruses can also be classified by their basic shape, as illustrated below. No matter what its structure is, every virus is basically some form of genetic material enclosed in a protein coat.

The Basic Shapes of Viruses

▲ **Crystals** The polio virus is shaped like the crystals shown here.

▲ **Spheres** Influenza viruses look like spheres. HIV is another virus with this structure.

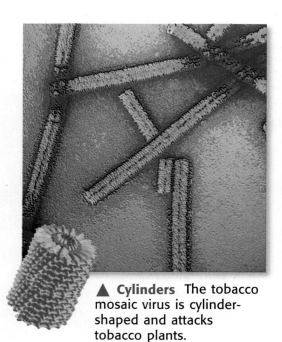

▲ **Cylinders** The tobacco mosaic virus is cylinder-shaped and attacks tobacco plants.

▲ **Spacecraft** One group of viruses attacks only bacteria. Many of these look almost like spacecraft.

A Destructive House Guest

The one function that viruses share with living things is that they reproduce. They do this by infecting living cells and turning them into virus factories. This is called the *lytic cycle,* as shown in **Figure 15.**

Figure 15 **The Lytic Cycle**

1 The virus finds a host cell.

2 The virus enters the cell, or in some cases, the virus's genes are injected into the cell.

3 Once the virus's genes are inside, they take over the direction of the host cell, turning it into a virus factory.

4 The new viruses break out of the host cell ready to find a new host and repeat the cycle.

A Ticking Time Bomb   Some viruses don't go straight into the lytic cycle. These viruses insert their genes into the host cell, but no new viruses are made immediately. When the host cell divides, each new cell has a copy of the virus's genes. This is called the *lysogenic cycle.* The viral genes can remain inactive for long periods of time until a change in the environment or stress to the organism causes the genes to launch into the lytic cycle.

REVIEW

1. What would happen if one generation of measles viruses never found a host?

2. Describe the four steps in the lytic cycle.

3. **Analyzing Relationships**   Do you think modern transportation has had an effect on the way viruses are spread? Explain your answer.

internet connect

SCI LINKS
NSTA

TOPIC: Viruses
GO TO: www.scilinks.org
*sci*LINKS NUMBER: HSTL245

Chapter Highlights

Vocabulary

binary fission (*p. 225*)

endospore (*p. 225*)

Section Notes

- Bacteria are classified as eubacteria or archaebacteria. Both are prokaryotes.

- Most bacteria have one of three shapes. Bacilli are rod-shaped. Cocci are spherical, and spirilla are long, spiral rods.

- Most bacteria reproduce by binary fission. Some produce endospores that can survive for thousands of years.

- Many eubacteria are decomposers. They obtain their energy from dead organic matter. Others are parasites.

- Many bacterial producers, including cyanobacteria, contain chlorophyll.

- Archaebacteria live in places where no other organisms can survive. Many are grouped as salt lovers, methane makers, and heat lovers.

☑ Skills Check

Math Concepts

MULTIPLYING MICROORGANISMS Some bacteria can divide every 20 minutes in an ideal growing environment. That means that if you start out with just one bacterium, in an hour there will be eight bacteria. There will be 512 bacteria in 3 hours, 32,768 in 5 hours, and 1,073,741,824 bacteria in 10 hours!

Visual Understanding

BACTERIA VERSUS VIRUSES The diagrams on pp. 225 and 235 illustrate the way some bacteria and viruses reproduce. Make sure you under-

stand how each process works. Viruses use their hosts' cells to reproduce. Think about how this is different from the way pathogenic bacteria use a host's cell.

SECTION 2

Vocabulary

bioremediation *(p. 230)*

antibiotic *(p. 230)*

pathogenic bacteria *(p. 232)*

Section Notes

- Bacteria are important to the planet. Some act as decomposers. Others convert nitrogen gas to a form that plants can use.

- Bacteria are used in making a variety of foods, medicines, and pesticides. They are also used to clean up pollution.

- Pathogenic bacteria cause diseases in humans as well as other organisms.

Labs

Aunt Flossie and the Intruder *(p. 720)*

SECTION 3

Vocabulary

virus *(p. 233)*

host *(p. 233)*

Section Notes

- Viruses have characteristics of both living and nonliving things. They can reproduce only inside a living cell.

- Viruses may be classified by their structure, the kind of disease they cause, or their life cycle.

- In order for a virus to reproduce, it must enter a cell, reproduce itself, and then break open the cell. This is called the lytic cycle.

- The genes of a virus are incorporated into the genes of the host cell in the lysogenic cycle. The virus's genes may remain inactive for years.

Labs

Viral Decorations *(p. 721)*

Chapter Review

USING VOCABULARY

To complete the following sentences, choose the correct term from each pair of terms listed below:

1. Rod-shaped bacteria are called __?__. (*bacilli* or *cocci*)

2. Most bacteria reproduce by __?__. (*endospores* or *binary fission*)

3. Bacterial infections can be treated with __?__. (*antibiotics* or *bioremediation*)

4. A virus needs a __?__ to reproduce. (*crystal* or *host*)

5. Without __?__ bacteria, life on Earth could not exist. (*pathogenic* or *nitrogen-fixing*)

6. __?__ make their own food. (*Consumers* or *Producers*)

UNDERSTANDING CONCEPTS

Multiple Choice

7. Bacteria are used for all of the following except
   a. making certain foods.
   b. making antibiotics.
   c. cleaning up oil spills.
   d. preserving fruit.

8. In the lytic cycle
   a. the host cell is destroyed.
   b. the host cell destroys the virus.
   c. the host cell becomes a virus.
   d. the host cell undergoes cell division.

9. A bacterial cell
   a. is an endospore.
   b. has a loop of DNA.
   c. has a distinct nucleus.
   d. is a eukaryote.

10. Eubacteria
    a. include methane makers.
    b. include decomposers.
    c. all have chlorophyll.
    d. are all rod-shaped.

11. Cyanobacteria
    a. are consumers.
    b. are parasites.
    c. contain chlorophyll.
    d. are decomposers.

12. Archaebacteria
    a. are a special type of eubacteria.
    b. live only in places without oxygen.
    c. are primarily lactic-acid bacteria.
    d. can live in hostile environments.

13. Viruses
    a. are about the same size as bacteria.
    b. have nuclei.
    c. can reproduce only within a host cell.
    d. don't infect plants.

14. Bacteria are important to the planet as
    a. decomposers of dead organic matter.
    b. processors of nitrogen.
    c. makers of medicine.
    d. All of the above

Short Answer

15. How are the functions of nitrogen-fixing bacteria and decomposers similar?

16. What is the difference between the lytic cycle and the lysogenic cycle?

Concept Mapping

17. Use the following terms to create a concept map: eubacteria, bacilli, cocci, spirilla, parasites, consumers, producers, cyanobacteria.

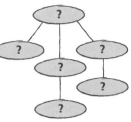

Write one or two sentences to answer the following questions:

18. Describe some of the problems you think bacteria might face if there were no humans.

19. A nuclear power plant explodes and wipes out every living thing within a 30 km radius. What kind of organism do you think might colonize the radioactive area first? Why?

MATH IN SCIENCE

20. An ounce is equal to about 28 g. If 1 g of soil contains 2.5 billion bacteria, how many bacteria are in 1 oz?

21. A bacterial cell infected by a virus divides every 20 minutes. After 10,000 divisions, the virus breaks loose from its host cell. About how many weeks will this take?

INTERPRETING GRAPHICS

The following diagram illustrates the stages of binary fission. Match each statement with the correct stage.

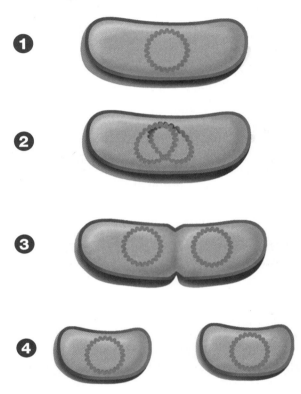

22. The DNA loops separate.

23. The DNA loop replicates.

24. The parent cell starts to expand.

25. The DNA attaches to the cell membrane.

NOW What Do You Think?

Take a minute to review your answers to the ScienceLog questions on page 223. Have your answers changed? If necessary, revise your answers based on what you have learned since you began this chapter.

Science, Technology, and Society

Edible Vaccines

No one likes getting a shot, right? Unfortunately, though, shots are a necessary part of life. This is because people in this country are protected from life-threatening diseases by vaccinations. But vaccination shots are expensive, may require refrigeration, and require trained medical professionals to administer them. These facts often keep people in developing countries from getting vaccinated.

▲ *Banana vaccines may soon replace a shot in the arm!*

Pass the Banana, Please

Edible vaccines would have several important advantages over traditional injected vaccines. First of all, they wouldn't require a painful shot! But more important, these vaccines will be cheaper to produce and may not require refrigeration or trained medical professionals. Plants like bananas are easily grown in fields and greenhouses in many Third World countries. One banana could even carry vaccines for several diseases at one time! But just how could a banana do this?

Add Some DNA

Scientists have made DNA that closely resembles the "fingerprints" of specific disease particles. They can insert this DNA into banana genes that code for proteins. Scientists hope they can trick the human immune system into recognizing these proteins as invaders and producing the necessary antibodies to fight diseases. Unlike traditional vaccines, these transgenic bananas (bananas containing foreign DNA) do not carry the risk of infection because they do not contain any viral particles.

Transgenic plants aren't all that new. Agricultural scientists make transgenic plants to improve crops. Scientists have introduced new DNA into fruits and vegetables so that they are more resistant to pests and drought; have larger, sweeter, and more colorful fruit; and ripen more quickly.

Important Questions

Unfortunately, edible vaccines will not be available for several years. Some safety concerns must still be addressed before these vaccines can be given to people. Do edible vaccines have side effects? How long will the resistance last? What happens if someone eats too many bananas? Research labs are testing the vaccines to answer these questions.

Check It Out!

▶ The milk of transgenic animals is also being tested as a potential vaccine carrier. Scientists hope that goat's milk containing malarialike proteins will prevent as many as 3 million deaths each year. Investigate for yourself how the malaria vaccine will work.

Health

Helpful Viruses

Less than 100 years ago, people had no way to treat bacterial infections. If you became ill from contact with pathogenic bacteria, you could only hope that your immune system would be able to defeat the invaders. But in 1928 a Scottish scientist named Alexander Fleming discovered the first antibiotic, or bacteria-killing drug. This first antibiotic was called penicillin.

Using Viruses to Fight Bacteria

Since Fleming's discovery, people have used antibiotics to treat infections and to purify water supplies. But scientists are now realizing that many bacteria are becoming resistant to existing antibiotics. It is quite possible that the overuse of antibiotics will make all current antibiotics ineffective in the near future. So what will people use to fight bacterial infections? Some scientists think viruses might be the answer! You might be thinking that viruses can only cause diseases, not cure them, but there is a particular type of virus, called a bacteriophage, that attacks only bacteria.

How Do They Do This?

Bacteriophages destroy bacteria cells in the same way other viruses can destroy animal or plant cells. Each kind of bacteriophage can only infect a particular species of bacteria. This can make an extremely effective antibiotic. Existing antibiotics kill not only harmful bacteria but also bacteria that people need to stay healthy. This can make people treated with antibiotics very sick, causing a breakdown in their immune system or digestive process. Because bacteriophages would kill only specific harmful bacteria, using bacteriophages could eliminate antibiotics' damaging side effects.

Current Uses

Bacteriophages are not yet used as antibiotics because the immune system destroys the viruses before they can infect the pathogenic bacteria. Scientists are still researching ways to use bacteriophages effectively.

Bacteriophages are currently used to diagnose bacterial infections quickly. Diagnoses can be made by injecting many different types of bacteriophages into a patient. Blood tests then indicate which virus was able to reproduce, in turn determining the type of bacterial infection the patient has. Scientists are also able to use bacteriophages in the same way to detect bacterial contamination of food and water supplies. Perhaps one day in the future, your doctor will give you a helpful virus instead of an antibiotic to fight the harmful bacteria that make you sick!

◀ *Some bacteriophages look more like machines than living organisms.*

Going Further

▶ Bacteriophages aren't always so helpful. Sometimes they can do more harm than good. Can you think of ways bacteriophages can cause trouble for humans ?

11 Protists and Fungi

The Potato Eaters, van Gogh, 1885

This Really Happened . . .

The year is 1846, and the country is Ireland. The weather is cold and rainy, and the situation is desperate. Disease has swept through the potato fields. In just a few weeks, it destroyed almost the entire crop.

The Irish depend on potatoes for food. Every day, hundreds of people die of starvation. With no other hope for survival, tens of thousands are fleeing their country. Most head for the United States.

During the hungry years of the Great Potato Famine, from 1845–1852, Ireland lost one-third of its population. Two million people left the country. One million people died. What was the cause of all this death and devastation? A simple organism called a water mold was to blame.

Water molds are protists. This particular water mold changed the course of Irish history. It also changed the American population. Do you have Irish ancestry? If so, a water mold may have brought your family to this country.

But don't get the wrong idea. Not all protists are harmful. Some are very helpful. You'll learn about protists in this chapter.

What Do You Think?

In your ScienceLog, try to answer the following questions based on what you already know:

1. What is seaweed?

2. What is a fungus?

3. Do mushrooms have roots?

Investigate!

A Microscopic World

Protists are small, simple organisms. In this activity, you will observe some common protists in pond water or in a solution called a *hay infusion.* Hay infusion is made by adding pond water to grass or hay. The hay is dried, and without water, microscopic pond organisms enter a resting state. With the addition of more water, these pond organisms become active again and use the hay for food.

Procedure

1. Using a **plastic eyedropper,** place one drop of the **pond water** or **hay infusion** onto a **microscope slide.**

2. Add one drop of **ProtoSlo**™ to the drop on the slide.

3. Add a **plastic coverslip** by putting one edge on the slide and then slowly lowering it over the drop to prevent air bubbles.

4. Observe the slide under low power of a **microscope.** Once you've located an organism, try high power for a closer look.

5. Sketch the organisms you see in your ScienceLog.

Analysis

6. How many different organisms do you see?

7. What clues suggest that what you are observing is alive?

8. How many cells does each organism appear to have?

Terms to Learn

protist
funguslike
  protist
parasite

host
algae
phytoplankton
protozoa

What You'll Do

◆ Describe the characteristics of protists.
◆ Name the three groups of protists, and give examples of each.
◆ Explain how protists reproduce.

Protists

Some are so tiny they cannot be seen without a microscope, and others grow many meters long. Some are poisonous, and others provide food. Some are like plants. Some are like animals. And some are nothing like plants or animals. Despite their differences, all of these organisms are related. What are they? They are all members of the kingdom Protista and are called **protists.** Look at **Figure 1** to see some of the variety of protists.

Zooflagellate

Paramecium

Ulva

Figure 1 *Protists have many different shapes and sizes.*

Pretzel slime mold

General Characteristics

All protists are *eukaryotic.* That means their cells have a nucleus. Most protists are single-celled organisms, but some are multicellular. Scientists generally agree that the more complex eukaryotic organisms—plants, animals, and fungi—all originated from primitive protists.

Some protists are *producers.* Like plants, they get their energy from the sun through *photosynthesis.* Others are *consumers.* They cannot obtain energy from sunlight and must get food from their environment. Protists are often classified by the way they obtain energy. This method groups these organisms into funguslike protists, plantlike protists, or animal-like protists.

Funguslike Protists

A fungus is an organism that obtains its food from dead organic matter or from the body of another organism. You will learn more about fungi in the next section. The protists that get food this way are called **funguslike protists.** The funguslike protists are consumers that secrete digestive juices into the food source and then absorb the digested nutrients. These protists also reproduce like fungi. Two types of funguslike protists will be discussed in this chapter—slime molds and water molds.

It's Slime! *Slime molds* are thin masses of living matter. They look like colorful, shapeless globs of slime. Many slime molds live as single-celled organisms. But during times of environmental stress, these single organisms come together to form a group of cells with many nuclei and a single cytoplasm. Slime molds live in cool, shady, moist places in the woods and in fresh water. **Figure 2** shows a slime mold growing over a log.

Slime molds eat bacteria, yeast, and small bits of decaying plant and animal matter. They surround food particles and digest them. As long as food and water are available, a slime mold will continue to grow. It may cover an area more than 1 m across!

When growth conditions are unfavorable, a slime mold develops stalklike structures with rounded knobs at the top. You can see this in **Figure 3.** The knobs contain *spores.* The spores can survive for a long time without water or nutrients. When conditions improve, the spores will develop into new slime molds.

Figure 2 *Slime molds, like this scrambled egg slime mold, are consumers.*

Figure 3 *The spore-containing knobs of a slime mold are called sporangia.*

Moldy Water? Another type of funguslike protist is the *water mold*. Most water molds are small, single-celled organisms. Water molds live in water, moist soil, or other organisms.

Some water molds are *decomposers* and eat dead organic matter. But many water molds are parasites. **Parasites** invade the body of another organism to obtain the nutrients they need. The organism a parasite invades is called a **host**. Hosts can be living plants, animals, algae, or fungi. A parasitic water mold is shown in **Figure 4.**

Some parasitic water molds cause diseases. A water mold causes "late blight" of potatoes, the disease that led to the Great Potato Famine. Another water mold attacks grapes and threatened the French wine industry in the late 1800s. These protists still endanger crops today, but fortunately methods now exist to control them.

Figure 4 *Parasitic water molds attack various organisms, including fish.*

Self-Check

Are all funguslike protists decomposers? Explain. *(See page 782 to check your answers.)*

Plantlike Protists: Algae

A second group of protists are producers. Like plants, they use the sun's energy to make food through photosynthesis. These plantlike protists are also known as **algae** (AL JEE). All algae (singular, *alga*) have the green pigment chlorophyll, which is used for photosynthesis. But most algae also have other pigments that give them a specific color. Almost all algae live in water. You can see some examples of algae in **Figure 5.**

Some algae are multicellular. These algae generally live in shallow water along the shore. You may know these as *seaweed* or *kelp*. Some of these algae can grow to many meters in length.

Figure 5 *Algae range in size from giant seaweeds to single-celled organisms.*

Spirogyra

Kelp

Single-celled algae cannot be seen without a microscope. They usually float near the water's surface. The single-celled algae make up **phytoplankton** (FITE oh PLANK tuhn). Phytoplankton are producers that provide food for most other water-dwelling organisms. They also produce most of the world's oxygen.

The plantlike protists are divided into phyla based on their color and cell structure. We will discuss six of the phyla here: red algae, brown algae, green algae, diatoms, dinoflagellates, and euglenoids.

Red Algae Most of the world's seaweeds are red algae. They contain chlorophyll and a red pigment that gives them their color. These multicellular protists live mainly in tropical marine waters, attached to rocks or other algae. Their red pigment allows them to absorb the light that filters deep into the clear water of the Tropics. Red algae can grow as much as 260 m below the surface of the water but are usually less than 1 m in length.

Brown Algae Most of the seaweeds found in cool climates are brown algae. They attach to rocks or form large floating beds in ocean waters. Brown algae have chlorophyll and a yellow-brown pigment. Many are very large—some grow 60 m in just one growing season! The tops of these gigantic algae are exposed to sunlight. The food made here by photosynthesis is transported to the parts of the algae that are too deep in the water to receive sunlight. An example of a brown alga can be seen in **Figure 6.**

Figure 6 Laminaria *is a brown alga.*

Green Algae The green algae are the most diverse group of plantlike protists. They are green because chlorophyll is the main pigment they contain. Most live in water or moist soil, but others are found in melting snow, on tree trunks, and even inside other organisms.

Many green algae are single-celled, microscopic organisms. Others are multicellular. These species may grow up to 8 m long. Individual cells of some species of green algae live in groups called colonies. **Figure 7** shows colonies of *Volvox.*

Figure 7 Volvox *is a green alga that grows in round colonies.*

Diatoms Diatoms (DIE e TAHMZ) are single-celled organisms. They are found in both salt water and fresh water. As with all algae, diatoms get their energy from photosynthesis. They make up a large percentage of phytoplankton.

As you can see in **Figure 8,** many diatoms have unusual shapes. Their cell walls contain cellulose and silica, a rigid, glasslike substance. The cells are enclosed in a shell with two parts that fit neatly together. Piles of diatom shells deposited over millions of years form a fine, crumbly substance that is used in silver polish, toothpaste, filters, and insulation.

Figure 8 *Although most diatoms are free floating, many cling to plants, shellfish, sea turtles, and whales.*

Dinoflagellates Most dinoflagellates (DIE noh FLAJ uh lits) are single-celled algae. They live primarily in salt water, although a few species live in fresh water, and some are even found in snow. Dinoflagellates have two whiplike strands called *flagella* (singular, *flagellum*). The beating of these flagella causes the cells to spin through the water. For this reason they are sometimes called spinning flagellates.

Most dinoflagellates get energy from photosynthesis, but a few are consumers, decomposers, or parasites. Some dinoflagellates are red and produce a strong poison. If these algae multiply rapidly, they can turn the water red, causing a dangerous condition known as *red tide*. When shellfish eat these algae, the poison is concentrated in their bodies. The shellfish are then toxic to humans and other vertebrates who eat them. A red tide is shown in **Figure 9.**

Chemistry
C O N N E C T I O N

Some dinoflagellates give off light. A chemical reaction in the cells produces light that is similar to the light produced by fireflies. Water filled with these dinoflagellates glows like a twinkling neon light.

Figure 9 *Red tides occur throughout the world and are common in the Gulf of Mexico.*

Euglenoids Euglenoids (yoo GLEE NOYDZ) are single-celled protists that live primarily in fresh water. Most euglenoids have characteristics of both plants and animals. Like plants, they use photosynthesis. But when light is too low for photosynthesis, they can become consumers, like animals. Euglenoids can also move like animals. Flagella propel the organisms through the water. The structure of a euglenoid is shown in **Figure 10.**

Some euglenoids do not have chloroplasts for photosynthesis. These species either consume other small protists or absorb dissolved nutrients.

Most euglenoids have two **flagella,** one long and one short. The long flagellum is used to move the organism through water.

Chloroplasts are needed for photosynthesis. These structures contain the green pigment chlorophyll.

Nucleus

Euglenoids can't see, but they have **eyespots** that respond to light.

A special structure called a **contractile vacuole** collects excess water and removes it from the cell.

Figure 10 *Euglenoids have both plant and animal characteristics.*

REVIEW

1. How does a slime mold survive when food and water are limited?

2. Which plantlike protists move? How?

3. Add the following terms to the concept map at right: consumer, water mold, diatom, euglenoid.

4. Look at the picture of a euglenoid on this page. Which cell structures are plantlike? Which are animal-like?

5. **Analyzing Relationships** How do funguslike protists differ from plantlike protists?

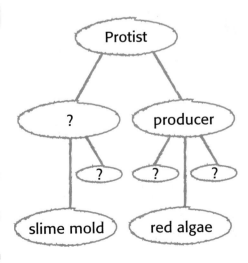

Animal-Like Protists: Protozoa

The animal-like protists are single-celled consumers. These protists are also known as **protozoa.** Some are parasites. Many can move. Scientists do not agree on how to group protozoa, but they are often divided into four phyla: amoebalike protists, flagellates, ciliates, and spore-forming protists.

Amoebalike Protists An amoeba (uh MEE buh) is a soft, jellylike protozoan. Amoebas are found in both fresh and salt water, in soil, or as parasites in animals. Although an amoeba looks shapeless, it is actually a highly structured cell. Like euglenoids, amoebas have contractile vacuoles to get rid of excess water. Amoebas move with *pseudopodia* (soo doh POH dee uh). *Pseudopodia* means "false feet." You can see how an amoeba uses pseudopodia to move in **Figure 11.**

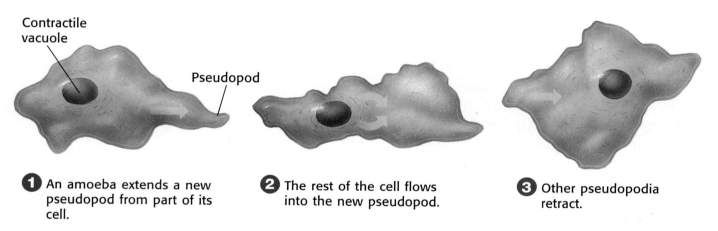

Contractile vacuole

Pseudopod

1 An amoeba extends a new pseudopod from part of its cell.

2 The rest of the cell flows into the new pseudopod.

3 Other pseudopodia retract.

Figure 11 *The shape of an amoeba changes constantly as new pseudopodia form.*

Prey

Pseudopodia

Figure 12 *An amoeba engulfs its prey with its pseudopodia.*

Feeding Amoebas Like slime molds, amoebas feed by engulfing food. An amoeba senses the presence of another single-celled organism and moves toward it. It surrounds a bacterium or small protist with its pseudopodia, forming a *food vacuole.* Enzymes move into the vacuole to digest the food, and the digested food passes out of the vacuole into the cytoplasm of the amoeba. To get rid of wastes, an amoeba reverses the process. A waste-filled vacuole is moved to the edge of the cell and is released. **Figure 12** shows an amoeba feeding.

Some amoebas are parasites. Certain species live in the human intestine and cause amebic dysentery, a painful condition that can involve bleeding ulcers.

Protozoa with Shells Not all amoebalike protozoa look like amoebas. Some have an outer shell. *Radiolarians* (RAY dee oh LER ee uhnz) have shells made of silica that look like glass ornaments. This type of protozoan is shown in **Figure 13.** *Foraminiferans* (fuh RAM uh NIF uhr uhnz) have snail-like shells made of calcium carbonate.

Flagellates Flagellates (FLAJ uh LITS) are protozoa that use flagella to move. The flagella wave back and forth to propel the organism forward. Some flagellates live in water. Others are parasites that can cause disease.

The flagellate parasite, *Giardia lamblia,* lives in the digestive tracts of humans and other vertebrates. This parasite is shown in **Figure 14.** In an inactive form, *Giardia* (JEE ar DEE uh) can survive in water. Hikers or others who drink water infected with *Giardia* can get diarrhea and severe stomach cramps, but the disease is usually not fatal.

Some flagellates live in symbiosis with vertebrates or invertebrates. In *symbiosis,* one organism lives closely with another organism, and each organism helps the other survive. One symbiotic flagellate lives in the guts of termites and digests the cellulose in the wood that the termites eat. Without the protozoa, the termites could not completely digest the cellulose.

Figure 13 *Radiolarians are amoebalike protozoa with shells.*

Geology
CONNECTION

Foraminiferans have existed for over 600 million years. During this time, the shells of dead foraminiferans have been sinking to the bottom of the ocean. Millions of years ago, foraminiferan shells formed a thick layer of sediment of limestone and chalk deposits. The chalk deposits known as the White Cliffs of Dover in England were formed this way.

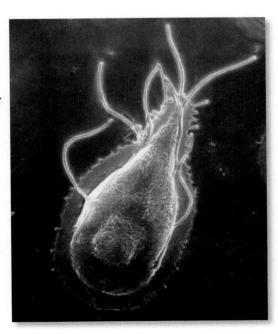

Figure 14 *The parasitic protist,* Giardia lamblia, *is a primitive cell. Can you see why it is a flagellate?*

Explore the different shapes of protists on page 722 of your LabBook.

Ciliates Ciliates (SIL ee its) are the most complex protozoa. Ciliates have hundreds of tiny hairlike structures known as *cilia*. The cilia move a protozoan forward by beating back and forth. Cilia can beat up to 60 times a second! In some species, clumps of cilia form bristlelike structures used for movement. Cilia are also important for feeding. Ciliates use their cilia to sweep food through the water toward them. The best known ciliate is *Paramecium* (PAR uh MEE see uhm), shown in **Figure 15.**

Ciliates have two kinds of nuclei. A large nucleus called a *macronucleus* controls the functions of the cell. A smaller nucleus, the *micronucleus,* passes genetic material to another individual during sexual reproduction.

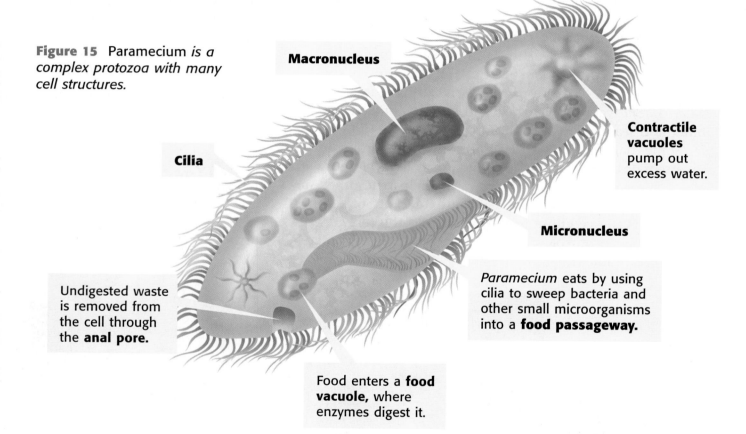

Figure 15 Paramecium *is a complex protozoa with many cell structures.*

Macronucleus

Cilia

Contractile vacuoles pump out excess water.

Micronucleus

Paramecium eats by using cilia to sweep bacteria and other small microorganisms into a **food passageway.**

Undigested waste is removed from the cell through the **anal pore.**

Food enters a **food vacuole,** where enzymes digest it.

✓ Self-Check

1. What are the functions of cilia?
2. Why are the ciliates classified as animal-like protists?

(See page 782 to check your answers.)

Spore-Forming Protists The spore-forming protozoa are all parasites that absorb nutrients from their hosts. They have no cilia or flagella, and they cannot move on their own. Spore-forming protozoa have complicated life cycles that usually involve two or more different hosts.

Plasmodium (plaz MOH dee uhm) *vivax* (VIE VAKS) is the spore-forming protist that causes malaria. Malaria is a serious disease that is carried by mosquitoes in tropical areas. Although malaria can be treated with drugs, more than 2 million people die from malaria each year.

The Life Cycle of *Plasmodium vivax*

Plasmodium vivax is a parasite that has two different hosts, mosquitoes and humans. It needs both hosts to survive. Once a human is bitten by an infected mosquito, *Plasmodium* spores enter the liver. The spores multiply and change form.

They then enter red blood cells and multiply, causing the red blood cells to burst. If the malaria victim is bitten by another mosquito, the disease can then be carried to another human.

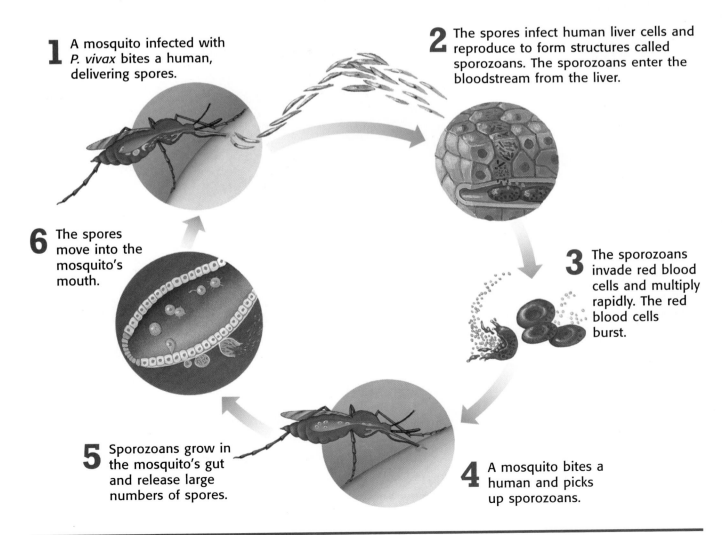

1 A mosquito infected with *P. vivax* bites a human, delivering spores.

2 The spores infect human liver cells and reproduce to form structures called sporozoans. The sporozoans enter the bloodstream from the liver.

3 The sporozoans invade red blood cells and multiply rapidly. The red blood cells burst.

4 A mosquito bites a human and picks up sporozoans.

5 Sporozoans grow in the mosquito's gut and release large numbers of spores.

6 The spores move into the mosquito's mouth.

Reproduction of Protists

Some protists reproduce asexually. In asexual reproduction, the offspring come from just one parent. Both animal-like amoebas and plantlike *Euglena* reproduce asexually by fission, as shown in **Figure 16**.

Some protists can also reproduce sexually. Sexual reproduction requires two parents. Animal-like *Paramecium* sometimes reproduces sexually by a process called conjugation. During conjugation, two *Paramecium* join together and exchange genetic material using their micronuclei. Then they divide to produce four organisms with new combinations of genetic material. Conjugation is shown in **Figure 17.**

Many protists reproduce both asexually and sexually. In some algae, asexual reproduction and sexual reproduction alternate from one generation to the next.

Figure 16 *During fission,* Euglena *divides lengthwise.*

Figure 17 *Conjugation in* Paramecium *is a type of sexual reproduction.*

REVIEW

1. Name the three main groups of protists, and give the characteristics of each.

2. What are three ways that flagella and cilia differ?

3. **Making Inferences** Killing mosquitoes is one method of controlling malaria. Using what you know about the organism that causes malaria, explain why this method works.

Terms to Learn

fungus   spore
hyphae   mold
mycelium   lichen

What You'll Do

◆ Describe the characteristics of fungi.
◆ Distinguish between the four main groups of fungi.
◆ Describe how fungi can be helpful or harmful.
◆ Define *lichen*.

Fungi

Have you ever heard someone say, "A fungus is among us"? This statement has more truth in it than you may realize. The mushrooms on pizza are a type of fungus (plural, *fungi*). The yeast used to make bread is a fungus. Fungi are also used to produce cheeses, antibiotics, and soy sauce. And if you've ever had athlete's foot, you can thank a fungus. Fungi are everywhere!

Characteristics of Fungi

Fungi are eukaryotic consumers, but they are so different from other organisms that they are placed in their own kingdom. As you can see in **Figure 18,** fungi come in a variety of shapes, sizes, and colors. But all fungi have similar ways of obtaining food and reproducing.

Figure 18 *Fungi vary in their size and shape.*

Straight coral fungus

Ascomycetus

Bird's nest fungus

Witch's hat fungus

Food for Fungi   Fungi are consumers, but they cannot eat or engulf food. Fungi must live on or near their food supply. Most fungi obtain nutrients by secreting digestive juices onto a food source, then absorbing the dissolved substances. Many fungi are *decomposers*. This means that they feed on dead plant or animal matter. Other fungi are parasites.

Some fungi live in symbiotic relationships with other organisms. For example, many types of fungi grow on the roots of plants. They release an acid that changes minerals in the soil into forms that plants can use. The fungi also protect the plant from some disease-causing organisms.

Self-Check

1. In what ways are fungi and fungus-like protists alike?
2. How are hyphae and mycelia related?

(See page 782 to check your answer.)

Hidden from View All fungi are made of eukaryotic cells, which have nuclei. Some fungi are single-celled, but most fungi are multicellular. Multicellular fungi are made up of chains of cells called **hyphae** (HIE fee). Hyphae are fungal filaments that are similar to plant roots. These filaments are made of cells. But unlike plant root cells, the hyphae cells have openings in their cell walls that allow cytoplasm to move freely between the cells. The hyphae grow together to form a twisted mass called the **mycelium** (mie SEE lee uhm). The mycelium is the major part of the fungus, but it is often hidden from view underneath the ground. **Figure 19** shows the hyphae and mycelium of a fungus.

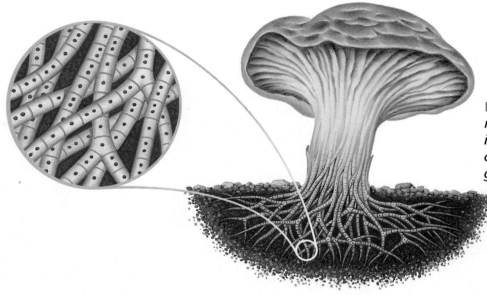

Figure 19 *The mycelium of a fungus is formed by hyphae and is often underground.*

Making More Fungi Reproduction in fungi may be either asexual or sexual. Asexual reproduction occurs in two ways. In one type of asexual reproduction, the hyphae break apart and each new piece becomes a new individual. Asexual reproduction can also occur by the production of spores. **Spores** are small reproductive cells protected by a thick cell wall. Spores are light and easily spread by the wind. See for yourself in **Figure 20.** If the growing conditions where it lands are right, a spore will produce a new fungus.

Sexual reproduction occurs in fungi when special structures form to make sex cells. The sex cells join to produce sexual spores that grow into a new fungus.

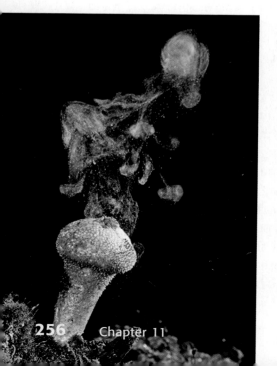

Figure 20 *This puffball is releasing spores that can produce new fungi.*

Kinds of Fungi

Fungi are divided into four main groups: threadlike fungi, sac fungi, club fungi, and imperfect fungi. A fungus is classified into a particular group based on its shape and the way it reproduces.

Threadlike Fungi   Have you ever seen fuzzy black mold growing on bread? **Molds** are shapeless fuzzy fungi, as shown in **Figure 21.** This particular mold belongs to a group of fungi called *threadlike fungi.* Most of the fungi in this group live in the soil and are usually decomposers, although some are parasites.

Threadlike fungi can reproduce asexually. Extensions of the hyphae grow into the air and form round spore cases at the tips called *sporangia* (spoh RAN jee uh). These sporangia are shown in **Figure 22.** When the sporangia break open, many tiny spores are released into the air.

Threadlike fungi can also reproduce sexually. Two hyphae from different individuals join and develop into specialized sporangia. These sporangia can survive periods of cold or drought. When conditions become more favorable, these specialized sporangia release spores that can grow into new fungi.

Figure 21 *Black bread mold is a soft, cottony mass that grows on bread and fruit.*

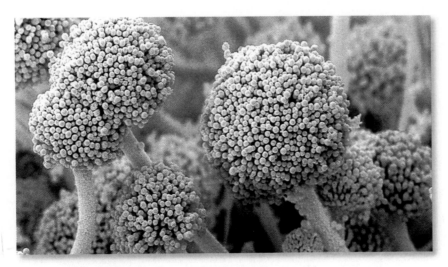

Figure 22 *Each of the round sporangia contains thousands of spores.*

Self-Check

What is the relationship between spores and sporangia? *(See page 782 to check your answers.)*

QuickLab

Moldy Bread

If you took a **slice of bread,** moistened it with a few drops of **water,** and then sealed it in a **plastic bag** for 1 week, what do you think would happen? Would the bread get moldy? Why or why not? Where would mold spores come from? How would these spores grow? Design an experiment to check your predictions. How many pieces of bread will you use? Will you treat them the same or differently? Why? If your teacher approves, try your experiment. Did it answer your questions? If not, what changes could you make to get the answers?

Figure 23 *Many people think truffles are delicious. Would you eat them?*

Sac Fungi *Sac fungi* form the largest group of fungi. Sac fungi include yeasts, powdery mildews, truffles, and morels. Truffles are shown in **Figure 23.**

Sexual reproduction in these fungi involves the formation of a sac called an *ascus.* These sacs give the sac fungi their name. Sexually produced spores develop within the ascus. During their life cycles, sac fungi usually reproduce both sexually and asexually.

Most sac fungi are multicellular, but *yeasts* are single-celled sac fungi. Yeasts reproduce asexually by *budding.* In budding, a new cell pinches off from an existing cell. A yeast is budding in **Figure 24.** Yeasts are the only fungi to reproduce by budding.

Figure 24 *Yeasts reproduce by budding. A round scar forms where a bud breaks off of a parent cell. How many times has the larger cell reproduced?*

÷ 5 ÷ Ω ∞ +Ω $\sqrt{\ }$ 9 ∞ $^{\leq}$ Σ 2
+ ≤

MATH BREAK

Multiplying Yeasts

Under ideal conditions, a yeast will produce a new cell by budding in about 30 minutes. Suppose a beaker contains 100 yeast cells. How many cells will it contain after 30 minutes? after 1 hour? after 2 hours? Make a graph to show the increase in size of the yeast population over a period of 5 hours.

Some sac fungi are very useful to humans. One example is yeasts, which are used in making bread. Yeasts use sugar as food and produce carbon dioxide gas and alcohol as waste products. Trapped bubbles of carbon dioxide cause the dough to rise and make bread light and fluffy. Other sac fungi are sources of antibiotics and vitamins. Truffles and morels are prized edible fungi.

Many sac fungi are parasites. They cause plant diseases, such as chestnut blight and Dutch elm disease, shown in **Figure 25.**

Figure 25 *Dutch elm disease is a fungal disease that has killed thousands of elm trees in North America.*

Club Fungi The umbrella-shaped mushrooms are the most commonly known fungi. They belong to a group of fungi called *club fungi.* During sexual reproduction, special hyphae develop and produce clublike structures called *basidia* (buh SID ee uh), the Greek word for "clubs." Sexual spores develop inside the basidia.

What you think of as a mushroom is only the sexual spore-producing part of the organism. The mass of hyphae from which mushrooms are produced may grow 35 m across. Since mushrooms usually grow at the outer edges of the mass of hyphae, they often appear in circles, as shown in **Figure 26.**

The most familiar mushrooms are known as gill fungi because the basidia develop in the grooves, or *gills,* under the cap. Some varieties are grown commercially and sold in supermarkets, but not all gill fungi are edible. The white destroying angel is one type that is very poisonous. Simply a taste of this mushroom can be fatal. See if you can pick out the poisonous fungus in **Figure 27.**

Figure 26 *A ring of mushrooms can appear overnight. In European folk legends, these were known as "fairy rings."*

Figure 27 *Many poisonous mushrooms look good to eat. The mushrooms on the left are edible, but the ones on the right are poisonous.*

 Quick Lab

Observe a Mushroom

1. Identify the stalk, cap, and gills on a **mushroom** that your teacher has provided.

2. Carefully twist or cut off the cap, and cut it open with a **knife.** Observe the gills with a **magnifying lens.** Look for spores.

3. Observe the other parts of the mushroom with the magnifying lens. The mycelium begins at the bottom of the stalk. Try to find individual hyphae.

4. Sketch the mushroom, and label the parts.

 APPLY

A Mushroom Omelet
A friend wants to make a mushroom omelet, but he has no mushrooms. He recently got a mushroom book that has pictures of all the poisonous and edible mushrooms. Using the book, he picks some mushrooms in the woods behind his house. He uses the wild mushrooms to make an omelet. Do you think he should eat the omelet? Why or why not?

Mushrooms are not the only club fungi. Bracket fungi, puffballs, smuts, and rusts are also in this group of fungi. Bracket fungi grow outward from wood, forming small shelves or brackets, as shown in **Figure 28.** Smuts and rusts are common plant parasites. They often attack crops such as corn and wheat. This can be seen in **Figure 29.**

Figure 28 *Bracket fungi look like shelves on trees. Spores are found on the underside of the bracket.*

Figure 29 *This corn crop is infected with a club fungus called a smut.*

BRAIN FOOD

Did you know that stone-washed jeans aren't really washed with stones? They get their faded look from a fungus! Jeans are soaked in a solution containing the fungus *Trichoderma.* This fungus produces enzymes that partially digest the cotton fibers to give jeans a stone-washed appearance.

Imperfect Fungi The *imperfect fungi* group includes all the species of fungi that do not quite fit in the other groups. These fungi do not reproduce sexually. Most are parasites that cause diseases in plants and animals. One common human disease caused by these fungi is athlete's foot, a skin disease. Another fungus from this group produces a poison called *aflatoxin,* which can cause cancer.

Some imperfect fungi are useful. *Penicillium,* shown in **Figure 30,** is the source of the antibiotic penicillin. Other imperfect fungi are also used to produce medicines. Some imperfect fungi are used to produce cheeses, soy sauce, and the citric acid used in cola drinks.

Figure 30 *The fungus* Penicillium *produces a substance that kills certain bacteria.*

Lichens

A **lichen** is a combination of a fungus and an alga that grow intertwined. The alga actually lives inside the protective walls of the fungus. The resulting organism is different from either of the two organisms growing alone. The merging of the two organisms to form a lichen is so complete that scientists give lichens their own scientific names. **Figure 31** shows examples of lichens.

Unlike fungi, lichens are producers. The algae in the lichens produce food through photosynthesis. Unlike algae, lichens can withstand drying out because of the protective walls of the fungus. Lichens are found in almost every type of terrestrial environment. They can even grow in extreme environments like dry deserts and the Arctic.

Lichens need only air, light, and minerals to grow. This is why lichens can grow on rocks. They produce acids that break down the rock and cause cracks. Bits of rock and dead lichens fill the cracks, making soil that other organisms can grow on.

Lichens absorb water and minerals from the air. As a result, they are easily affected by air pollution. Thus, the presence or absence of lichens is a good measure of air quality in an area.

Jewel lichen

Fruticose lichen

British soldier lichen

Figure 31 *These are some of the many types of lichens.*

REVIEW

1. How are fungi able to withstand periods of cold or drought?

2. Why are fungi such an important part of the natural world?

3. What are the four main groups of fungi? Give a characteristic of each.

4. **Making Inferences** Why are lichens an example of symbiosis?

internet**connect**

*SC*LINKS
NSTA

TOPIC: Fungi, Lichens
GO TO: www.scilinks.org
*sci*LINKS NUMBER: HSTL265, HSTL270

Chapter Highlights

Vocabulary

protist (p. 244)

funguslike protist (p. 245)

parasite (p. 246)

host (p. 246)

algae (p. 246)

phytoplankton (p. 247)

protozoa (p. 250)

Section Notes

• The protists are a diverse group of single-celled and multicellular organisms. They are grouped in their own kingdom because they differ from other organisms in many ways.

• Funguslike protists are consumers that obtain their food from dead organic matter or from the body of another organism.

• Slime molds and water molds are two groups of funguslike protists.

• Plantlike protists are producers that are also known as algae. Most are aquatic.

• Among the plantlike protists are red algae, brown algae, green algae, diatoms, dinoflagellates, and euglenoids.

• The animal-like protists are single-celled consumers also known as protozoa. Most can move.

• The protozoa include amoebalike protists, flagellates, ciliates, and spore-forming protists.

• Some protists reproduce sexually, some asexually, and some both sexually and asexually.

Labs

Making a Protist Mobile (p. 722)

☑ Skills Check

Math Concepts

MICROBE MULTIPLICATION Suppose an amoeba can reproduce by fission once every 30 minutes. If you start with 50 amoebas, after 30 minutes you will have twice as many because each amoeba has divided.

$$2 \times 50 = 100 \text{ amoebas}$$

After 1 hour (30 minutes later) the number of amoebas will double again.

$$2 \times 100 = 200 \text{ amoebas}$$

Visual Understanding

PROTIST STRUCTURE Look at the illustration of *Paramecium* on page 252. Carefully read the labels, and look at each part described. Now do the same thing with the illustration of the euglenoid on page 249. Notice what the two cells have in common and how they differ.

Vocabulary

fungus *(p. 255)*

hyphae *(p. 256)*

mycelium *(p. 256)*

spore *(p. 256)*

mold *(p. 257)*

lichen *(p. 261)*

Section Notes

- Fungi are consumers. They can be decomposers or parasites, or they can live in symbiotic relationships with other organisms.

- Most fungi are made up of chains of cells called hyphae. Many hyphae join together to form a mycelium.

- The four main groups of fungi are threadlike fungi, sac fungi, club fungi, and imperfect fungi.

- Threadlike fungi are primarily decomposers that form sporangia to hold spores.

- Molds are shapeless, fuzzy fungi.

- During sexual reproduction, sac fungi form little sacs in which sexual spores develop.

- Club fungi form structures called basidia during sexual reproduction.

- The imperfect fungi include all the species that do not quite fit anywhere else. Most are parasites that reproduce only by asexual reproduction.

- A lichen is a combination of a specific fungus and a specific alga that is different from either organism growing alone.

Labs

There's a Fungus Among Us! *(p. 723)*

 internetconnect

GO TO: go.hrw.com

Visit the **HRW** Web site for a variety of learning tools related to this chapter. Just type in the keyword:

KEYWORD: HSTPRO

GO TO: www.scilinks.org

Visit the **National Science Teachers Association** on-line Web site for Internet resources related to this chapter. Just type in the *sci*LINKS number for more information about the topic:

TOPIC: Algae	*sci***LINKS NUMBER:** HSTL255
TOPIC: Protozoa	*sci***LINKS NUMBER:** HSTL260
TOPIC: Fungi	*sci***LINKS NUMBER:** HSTL265
TOPIC: Lichens	*sci***LINKS NUMBER:** HSTL270

Chapter Review

To complete the following sentences, choose the correct term from each pair of terms listed below:

1. Protists that get energy from photosynthesis are ___?___. *(algae* or *amoebas)*

2. *Paramecium* reproduces sexually by ___?___. *(budding* or *conjugation)*

3. The structure containing spores in a sac fungi is called ___?___. *(an ascus* or *a basidium)*

4. ___?___ live on dead organic matter. *(Parasites* or *Decomposers)*

5. Animal-like protists are also called ___?___. *(protozoa* or *algae)*

6. A parasite gets its nutrients from its ___?___. *(host* or *spores)*

UNDERSTANDING CONCEPTS

Multiple Choice

7. Plantlike protists include
   a. euglenoids and ciliates.
   b. lichens and flagellates.
   c. spore-forming protists and smuts.
   d. dinoflagellates and diatoms.

8. Funguslike protists
   a. are consumers or decomposers.
   b. are made of chains of cells called hyphae.
   c. are divided into four major groups.
   d. are always parasites.

9. A euglenoid has
   a. a micronucleus.
   b. pseudopodia.
   c. two flagella.
   d. cilia.

10. Fungi
    a. are producers.
    b. cannot eat or engulf food.
    c. are found only in the soil.
    d. are primarily single-celled.

11. A lichen
    a. is a parasite.
    b. is made up of an alga and a fungus that live intertwined together.
    c. can live only where there is plenty of water.
    d. is a consumer.

12. Animal-like protists
    a. are also known as protozoa.
    b. include amoebas and *Paramecium*.
    c. may be either free living or parasitic.
    d. All of the above

13. A contractile vacuole
    a. is a food passageway.
    b. pumps out excess water.
    c. is the location of food digestion.
    d. can be found in any animal-like protist.

Short Answer

14. How are fungi helpful to humans? How are they harmful?

15. What is the function of cilia in *Paramecium*?

16. What is a red tide?

17. How are slime molds and amoebas similar?

Concept Mapping

18. Use the following terms to create a concept map: fungi, ascus, club fungi, basidia, bread mold, yeast, threadlike fungi, mushrooms.

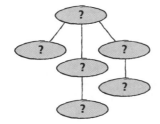

CRITICAL THINKING AND PROBLEM SOLVING

Write one or two sentences to answer the following questions:

19. What might happen if all the protists on Earth died?

20. Water can pass easily through a cell membrane, but too much water can cause a cell to burst. Single-celled amoebas and *Paramecium* have thin cell membranes, and they also live in water. Why don't these organisms burst?

21. You discover some mushrooms in your backyard one morning, and you pull them out of the ground. But the next day you find even more mushrooms. They seem to be growing in a line. Where did the new mushrooms come from?

MATH IN SCIENCE

22. You and your classmates are studying the growth of *Euglena*. Using a microscope, you count the number of organisms in a small container each day. Your teacher says you can expect the number of *Euglena* to double in 1.5 days. If you started out with five *Euglena,* how many *Euglena* do you think you will see on the third day?

INTERPRETING GRAPHICS

Look at the pictures of fungi below, and answer the following questions:

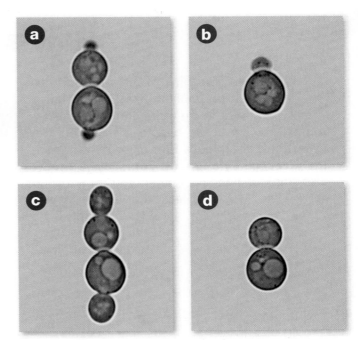

23. What kind of fungus is shown here?

24. What cellular process is shown in these pictures?

25. Which picture was taken first? last? Arrange the pictures in order.

26. Which is the original parent cell? How do you know?

NOW What Do You Think?

Take a minute to review your answers to the ScienceLog questions on page 243. Have your answers changed? If necessary, revise your answers based on what you have learned since you began this chapter.

Science, Technology, and Society

Moldy Bandages

When you think of the word *fungus,* you probably think of moldy leftovers in the refrigerator or mushrooms growing at the base of a tree. You may even think of athlete's foot or some other ailment caused by a fungus. Someday you may also think of bandages when you think of fungi. At least that is the hope of Paul Hamlyn and his colleagues at the British Textile Technology Group (BTTG).

▲ *Would you believe that fungi like this may someday be used in surgical bandages?*

Fungi Versus Infection

The scientists at BTTG, along with scientists at the Welsh School of Pharmacy, have discovered that the cell walls of fungi contain polymers that promote the growth of the human cells responsible for rebuilding tissue around a wound. These human healing cells are called fibroblasts, and studies show that the fungal polymers attract and help bind the fibroblasts at a wound. Researchers believe that the polymers react with oxygen to produce hydrogen peroxide. The hydrogen peroxide activates white blood cells and promotes the growth of the fibroblasts. The white blood cells help fight infection around the wound.

From Crab Shells to Wound Healing

Until recently, the only sources of these polymers were crab and prawn shells. The quality and quantity of polymers found in the shells of crabs and prawns vary with weather conditions and with the seasons. Hamlyn's studies have shown that fungi can provide a more consistent product. For even more consistent results, scientists are able to grow fungi in the laboratory in a liquid growth medium.

Where Do We Go from Here?

Although his work is still in the research stage, Hamlyn is working toward a commercial application of the wound-healing fungi. He is researching the possibility of manufacturing two types of bandages from fungi. The first would be made by freeze-drying pieces of the fungi to create an absorbent dressing. This could be used for patients with deep wounds. The second type would be used to help patients with bed sores or diabetic skin ulcers. This bandage would involve a wet dressing of fungi that could be placed over sores or abrasions on the surface of the skin. The fungi would help accelerate the healing process.

Fungi Find the Cure

▶ Fungal products have long been used in the field of medicine. One modern use is cyclosporin. It is a drug used to help prevent the rejection of transplanted organs in humans. Other uses for fungi include a popular folk remedy—placing moldy bread on a wound to promote healing. Research these or other types of medicines that are made from fungi to discover how they work.

It's Alive!

The Maya of Mexico and their descendants believe that Cueva de Villa Luz (the Cave of the Lighted House) is inhabited by powerful spirits. For centuries, they have walked past slimy globs that drip from the cave's ceiling without even thinking about them. When scientists decided to analyze these slime balls, they discovered that the formations are home to billions of microscopic organisms! They nick-named these colonies "snot-tites" because they resemble mucus.

Life in Battery Acid

As people climb down into the pitch-dark pas-sages of Cueva de Villa Luz, they are greeted by the stench of rotten eggs, an odor rarely found in caves and quickly recognized as potentially deadly hydrogen sulfide gas. This foul and dangerous gas is emitted by the snot-tites! Because it is not safe to remain inside the caverns if there is too much hydrogen sulfide, explorers must constantly monitor the level of the gas in the air.

A closer inspection of snot-tite drippings reveals that they contain sulfuric acid. When sulfuric acid dripped on some of the explorers' clothes, the clothes dissolved right off of their backs!

How do the organisms live in such harsh conditions? It turns out that snot-tites can actually get energy from sulfur, which is toxic to most organisms. And since snot-tites do not have to rely on photosynthesis for energy, they can live in absolute darkness.

A Unique Ecosystem

During dry seasons, the Mayan people feast on tiny fish called mollies that are abundant in the milky-white streams that flow through Cueva de Villa Luz. It's very rare to find so many fish in cave streams. Why are there fish in this cave?

Scientists have discovered that the snot-tites are part of a complex underground ecosystem, possibly unlike any other on Earth. When snot-tites use the sulfur found in the cave, they produce a nutritionally rich waste product. This waste drips into the streams below, where hungry fish can eat it.

Life on Mars?

Many scientists argue that conditions on Mars are too harsh to support any form of life. However, Martian rocks have a large amount of sulfur and scientists know that Mars has caves. Snot-tites have proven that life can exist in these harsh conditions. Someday a space trav-eler might find a similar organism on Mars!

Going to Extremes

▶ Snot-tites have adapted to extreme environ-mental conditions that would kill other organ-isms. Such organisms are called extremophiles. Investigate to find out about other extremophiles. Why are scien-tists so interested in extremophiles?

◀ *Several billion sul-fur-eating microbes can live in a single cubic centimeter of these slimy, gooey snot-tites!*

12 Introduction to Plants

This Really Happened . . .

A lone scientist trudges through a remote rain forest. Peering into a steep, narrow canyon, he notices something unusual. On closer inspection, he discovers that it is a species of tree that has survived from the days when *Tyrannosaurus rex* and *Velociraptor* walked the Earth!

No, this isn't a scene out of *Jurassic Park.* This really happened in an Australian rain forest in 1994. The scientist's name was David Noble. He discovered a tree species that dates back to the Cretaceous period, between 144 million and 65 million years ago.

The trees, called Wollemi pines, have large, bladelike leaves and knobby brown bark. They grow as tall as 35 m, and their trunks can grow as wide as 1 m.

Since the discovery of the trees, scientists at the Royal Botanic Gardens in Sydney, Australia, have been planting seeds of the Wollemi pines and growing seedlings. Soon Wollemi pines will be made available to gardeners so they can transform their yards into their own Cretaceous parks.

In this chapter, you will learn more about the mysterious world of plants. You will see that plants are complex organisms that challenge our understanding of nature.

What Do You Think?

In your ScienceLog, try to answer the following questions based on what you already know:

1. How do plants use flowers and fruits?

2. How are plants different from animals?

TRY at HOME

2 c. of flour
1 tsp. of salt
1 tsp. of baking soda
$1\frac{1}{2}$ c. of sugar
1 tsp. of vanilla
2 eggs
2 c. of chocolate chips
$\frac{1}{2}$ c. of margarine

Cookie Calamity

One morning, a bakery receives an order for hundreds of chocolate chip cookies that must be made as soon as possible. When the baker goes to get the ingredients for the cookies, he finds that the bakery has run out of all the ingredients that come directly and indirectly from plants. Can he still make the cookies?

Procedure

1. Examine the ingredients listed in the cookie recipe.

2. Determine which ingredients come from plants, either directly or indirectly.

3. Identify the plant or plants involved in each ingredient.

Analysis

4. Suppose the recipe called for butter instead of margarine. Would that be of any help to the baker? Why or why not?

5. If you took all the plant ingredients out of chocolate chip cookies, what would you be eating?

Terms to Learn

sporophyte   vascular plant
gametophyte   gymnosperm
nonvascular plant   angiosperm

What You'll Do

◆ Identify the characteristics that all plants share.
◆ Discuss the origin of plants.
◆ Explain how the four main groups of plants differ.

What Makes a Plant a Plant?

Imagine spending a day without anything made from plants. Not only would it be impossible to make chocolate chip cookies, it would be impossible to do many other things, too. You couldn't wear jeans or any clothes made of cotton or linen. You couldn't use any furniture constructed of wood. You couldn't write with wooden pencils or use paper in any form, including money. You couldn't eat anything because almost all food is made from plants or from animals that eat plants. Spending a day without plants would be very hard to do. In fact, life as we know it would be impossible if plants did not exist!

Fern

Sugar maple

Plant Characteristics

Plants come in many different shapes and sizes. What do cactuses, water lilies, ferns, and all other plants have in common? Although one plant may seem very different from another, all plants share certain characteristics.

Plants Make Their Own Food One thing that you have probably noticed about plants is that most of them are green. This is because plant cells have chloroplasts. As you learned earlier, chloroplasts are organelles that contain the green pigment *chlorophyll*. Chlorophyll absorbs light energy from the sun. Plants then use this energy to make food molecules, such as glucose. You may recall that this process is called *photosynthesis*.

Plants Have a Cuticle A *cuticle* is a waxy layer that coats the surface of stems, leaves, and other plant parts exposed to air. Most plants live on dry land, and the cuticle is an adaptation that helps keep plants from drying out.

Prickly pear cactus

Plant Cells Have Cell Walls Plant cells are surrounded by a cell membrane and a rigid cell wall. The cell wall lies outside the cell membrane, as shown in **Figure 1.** The cell wall helps support and protect the plant. Cell walls contain complex carbohydrates and proteins that form a hard material. When the cell reaches its full size, a tough secondary cell wall may develop. Once this wall is formed, a plant cell cannot grow any larger.

Plants Reproduce with Spores and Sex Cells A plant's life cycle can be divided into two parts. Plants spend one part of their lives in the stage that produces spores and the other part in the stage that produces sex cells (egg and sperm cells). The spore-producing stage is called a **sporophyte** (SPOH roh FIET). The stage that produces egg cells and sperm cells is called a **gametophyte** (guh MEET oh FIET). A diagram of the plant life cycle is shown in **Figure 2.**

Spores and sex cells are tiny reproductive cells. Spores that land in a suitable environment, such as damp soil, can grow into new plants. In contrast, sex cells cannot grow directly into new plants. Instead, a male sex cell (sperm cell) must join with a female sex cell (egg cell). The fertilized egg that results may grow into a new plant.

Cell membrane

Cell wall

Figure 1 *In addition to the cell membrane, a cell wall surrounds plant cells.*

Figure 2 Plant Life Cycle

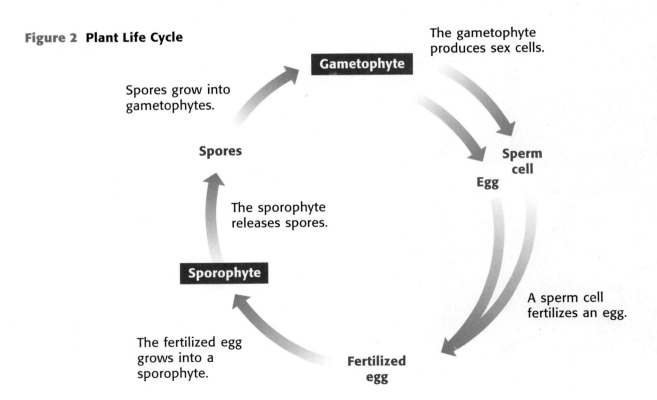

Spores grow into gametophytes.

Gametophyte

The gametophyte produces sex cells.

Spores

Sperm cell

Egg

The sporophyte releases spores.

A sperm cell fertilizes an egg.

Sporophyte

The fertilized egg grows into a sporophyte.

Fertilized egg

The Origin of Plants

If you were to travel back in time 440 million years, Earth would seem like a strange, bare, and unfriendly place. For one thing, no plants lived on land. Where did plants come from?

Take a look at the photographs in **Figure 3.** On the left is an organism called green algae. Plants and green algae are similar in color, but their similarities go beyond color. Green algae and plants contain the same kind of chlorophyll and have similar cell walls. They both store their energy in the form of starch. Like plants, green algae also have a two-part life cycle. These similarities suggest that ancient green algae that lived in the oceans were the ancestors of all plants.

Green algae

Plant

Figure 3 *The similarities between modern green algae and plants suggest that both may have originated from an ancient species of green algae.*

How Are Plants Classified?

There are more than 260,000 species of plants living on Earth today. Although all plants share the basic characteristics discussed earlier, they can be divided into two groups—vascular plants and nonvascular plants.

Plants Without "Plumbing" The nonvascular plants, mosses and liverworts, are shown in **Figure 4.** **Nonvascular plants** have no "pipes" to transport water and nutrients. They depend on diffusion and osmosis to move materials from one part of the plant to another. This is possible because nonvascular plants are small. If they were large—the size of trees, for example—there would be no way to deliver the needed materials to all the cells by diffusion and osmosis.

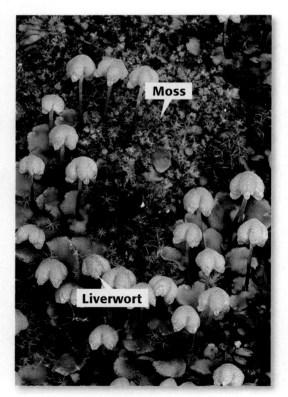

Moss

Liverwort

Figure 4 *Mosses and liverworts are examples of nonvascular plants.*

> ### ✓ Self-Check
>
> Green algae cells do not have a cuticle surrounding them. Why do plants need a cuticle, while algae do not? *(See page 782 to check your answer.)*

Plants with "Plumbing" Vascular plants do not rely solely on diffusion and osmosis to deliver needed materials to their cells. **Vascular plants** have tissues that deliver needed materials throughout a plant, much as pipes deliver water to faucets in your home. These tissues are called *vascular tissues*. Because vascular tissues can carry needed materials long distances within the plant body, vascular plants can be almost any size.

Vascular plants can be divided into two groups—plants that produce seeds and plants that do not. Plants that do not produce seeds include ferns, horsetails, and club mosses. Plants that produce seeds also fall into two groups—those that produce flowers and those that do not. Nonflowering plants are called **gymnosperms** (JIM noh SPUHRMZ). Flowering plants are called **angiosperms** (AN jee oh SPUHRMZ). The four main groups of living plants are shown in **Figure 5**.

MATH BREAK

Practice with Percents

The following list gives an estimate of the number of species in each plant group:

Mosses
and liverworts   15,000
Ferns, horsetails,
and club mosses   12,000
Gymnosperms   760
Angiosperms   235,000

What percentage of plants do not produce seeds?

Figure 5 The Main Groups of Living Plants

Nonvascular	Vascular		
	No seeds	Seeds	
		Nonflowering	Flowering
Mosses and liverworts	Ferns, horsetails, and club mosses	Gymnosperms	Angiosperms

REVIEW

1. What are two characteristics that all plants have in common?

2. What type of organism is thought to be the ancestor of all plants? Why?

3. How are ferns, horsetails, and club mosses different from angiosperms?

4. **Applying Concepts** How would you decide whether an unknown organism is a type of green algae or a plant?

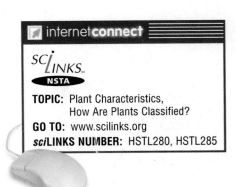

internet connect

SC_i_**LINKS**
NSTA

TOPIC: Plant Characteristics,
How Are Plants Classified?
GO TO: www.scilinks.org
*sci*LINKS NUMBER: HSTL280, HSTL285

Terms to Learn

rhizoid
rhizome

What You'll Do

◆ Describe the features of mosses and liverworts.
◆ Describe the features of ferns, horsetails, and club mosses.
◆ Explain how plants without seeds are important to humans and to the environment.

Seedless Plants

Two groups of plants don't make seeds. One group of seedless plants is the nonvascular plants—mosses and liverworts. The other group is made up of several vascular plants—ferns, horsetails, and club mosses.

Mosses and Liverworts

Mosses and liverworts are small. They grow on soil, the bark of trees, and rocks. Because they lack a vascular system, these plants usually live in places that are always wet. Each cell of the plant must absorb water directly from the environment or from a neighboring cell.

Mosses and liverworts don't have true stems, roots, or leaves. They do, however, have structures that carry out the activities of stems, roots, and leaves.

Rock-to-Rock Carpeting Mosses typically live together in large groups, covering soil or rocks with a mat of tiny green plants. Each moss plant has slender, hairlike threads of cells called **rhizoids.** Like roots, rhizoids help hold the plant in place. Each moss plant also has a leafy stalk. The life cycle of the moss alternates between the gametophyte and the sporophyte, as shown in **Figure 6.**

Figure 6 Moss Life Cycle

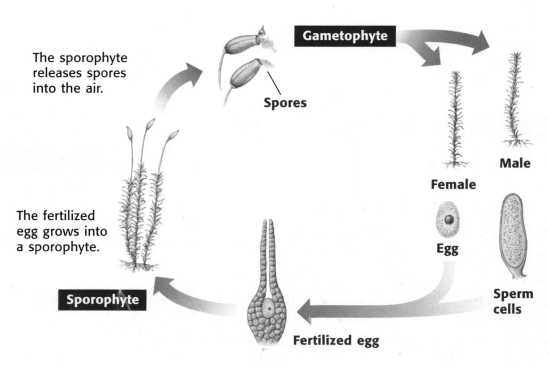

The sporophyte releases spores into the air.

Spores

Gametophyte

Spores land in a moist place, crack open, and grow into leafy gametophytes.

Male

Female

Egg

Sperm cells

Water carries sperm cells from the male gametophyte to the egg in the female gametophyte, where fertilization occurs.

The fertilized egg grows into a sporophyte.

Sporophyte

Fertilized egg

Liverworts Like mosses, liverworts are small, nonvascular plants that usually live in damp or moist places. Liverworts have a life cycle similar to that of mosses. The gameto-phytes of liverworts can be leafy and mosslike or broad and flattened, like those shown in **Figure 7.** Rhizoids extend out of the lower side of the liverwort body and help anchor the plant.

The Importance of Mosses and Liverworts

Although nonvascular plants are small, they play an important role in the environment. They are usually the first plants to inhabit a new environment, such as newly exposed rock. When the mosses and liverworts die, they form a thin layer of soil in which new plants can grow. New mosses and liverworts cover the soil and help hold it in place. This reduces soil erosion. Mosses also provide nest-ing materials for birds.

Peat mosses are important to humans. Peat mosses grow in bogs and other wet places. In certain locations, such as Ireland, dead peat mosses have built up thick deposits in bogs. This peat can be taken from the bog, dried, and burned as a fuel.

Figure 7 *This liverwort has a broad, flattened gametophyte. The sporophyte looks like a tiny palm tree or umbrella.*

Ferns, Horsetails, and Club Mosses

Unlike most of their modern descendants, ancient ferns, horsetails, and club mosses grew to be quite tall. The first forests were made up of 40 m high club mosses, 18 m high horsetails, and 8 m high ferns. **Figure 8** shows how these forests may have looked. These plants had vascular systems and could therefore grow taller than nonvascular plants.

Moss Mass

Determine the mass of a small sample of **dry sphag-num moss.** Place this sample in a **large beaker of water** for 10–15 minutes. What do you think the mass will be after soaking in water? Remove the wet moss from the beaker, and determine its mass. How much mass did the moss gain? Compare your findings with your predictions. What could this absorbent plant be used for? Do some research to find out.

Figure 8 *Vascular tissue allowed the ancestors of modern ferns, horsetails, and club mosses to grow tall.*

Ferns Ferns grow in many places, from the cold Arctic to warm, humid tropical forests. Although most ferns are relatively small plants, some tree ferns in the tropics grow as tall as 23 m.

Figure 9 shows a typical fern. Most ferns have an underground stem, called a **rhizome,** that produces leaves called *fronds* and wiry roots. Young fronds are tightly coiled. They are called *fiddleheads* because they look like the end of a violin, or fiddle.

Like the life cycles of all other plants, the life cycle of ferns, shown in **Figure 10,** is divided into two parts. You are probably most familiar with the sporophyte. The fern gametophyte is a tiny plant about the size of half of one of your fingernails. It is green and flat, and it is usually shaped like a tiny heart. The fern gametophyte has male structures that produce sperm cells and female structures that produce eggs. If a thin film of water is on the ground, the sperm cells can swim through it to an egg.

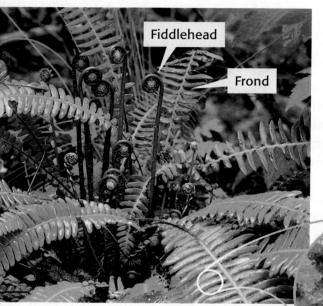

Figure 9 *This fern produces spores in spore cases on the underside of fronds. Fiddleheads grow into new fronds.*

Fiddlehead

Frond

Cluster of spore cases

Figure 10 Fern Life Cycle

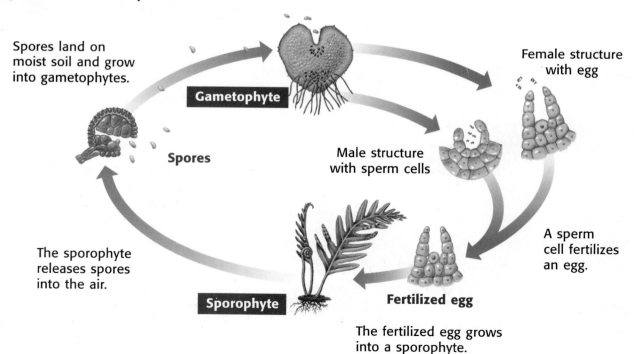

Spores land on moist soil and grow into gametophytes.

Gametophyte

Spores

The sporophyte releases spores into the air.

Male structure with sperm cells

Female structure with egg

A sperm cell fertilizes an egg.

Sporophyte

Fertilized egg

The fertilized egg grows into a sporophyte.

276   Chapter 12

Horsetails Horsetails were common plants millions of years ago, but only about 15 species have survived to the present. Modern horsetails, shown in **Figure 11,** are small vascular plants usually less than 1.3 m tall. They grow in wet, marshy places. Their stems are hollow and contain silica. Because of this, they feel gritty. In fact, pioneers of the early United States called horsetails "scouring rushes" and used them to scrub pots and pans. The life cycle of horsetails is similar to that of ferns.

Figure 11 *The conelike tips of horsetails contain spores.*

Club Mosses Club mosses, shown in **Figure 12,** are about 25 cm tall and grow in woodlands. Club mosses are not actually mosses. Unlike true mosses, club mosses have vascular tissue. Like horsetails, club mosses were common plants millions of years ago.

The Importance of Seedless Vascular Plants Seedless vascular plants play important roles in the environment. Like nonvascular plants, the ferns, horsetails, and club mosses help form soil. They also hold the soil in place, preventing soil erosion.

Ferns are popular as houseplants because of their beautiful leaves. The fiddleheads of some ferns are harvested in early spring, cooked, and eaten.

For humans, some of the most important seedless vascular plants lived and died about 300 million years ago. The remains of these ancient ferns, horsetails, and club mosses formed coal, a fossil fuel that we now extract from the Earth's crust.

Figure 12 *Club mosses release spores from their conelike tips.*

REVIEW

1. What is the connection between coal and seedless vascular plants?

2. How are horsetails and club mosses similar to ferns?

3. List two ways that seedless vascular plants are important to the environment.

4. **Applying Concepts** Why don't mosses ever grow as large as ferns?

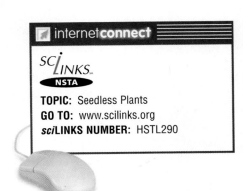

internetconnect

SCILINKS
NSTA

TOPIC: Seedless Plants
GO TO: www.scilinks.org
*sci*LINKS NUMBER: HSTL290

Plants with Seeds

Do the plants on this page look familiar to you? They are all seed plants.

As you read earlier, there are two groups of vascular plants that produce seeds—the gymnosperms and the angiosperms. Gymnosperms are trees and shrubs that produce seeds in cones or fleshy structures on stems. Pine, spruce, fir, and ginkgo trees are examples of gymnosperms. Angiosperms, or flowering plants, produce their seeds within a fruit. Peach trees, grasses, oak trees, rose bushes, and buttercups are all examples of angiosperms.

Peaches

Characteristics of Seed Plants

Just like the life cycle of other plants, the life cycle of seed plants alternates between two stages. During part of the cycle, the seed plants are called sporophytes. During another stage, the seed plants are called gametophytes. Gametophytes produce sex cells. But seed plants differ from other plants in the following ways:

■ Seed plants produce seeds, structures in which young sporophytes are nourished and protected.

■ Unlike the gametophytes of seedless plants, the gametophytes of seed plants do not live independently of the sporophyte. Gametophytes of seed plants are tiny and are always found protected in the reproductive structures of the sporophyte.

■ The male gametophytes of seed plants do not need water to travel to the female gametophytes. Male gametophytes develop inside tiny structures that can be transported by the wind or by animals. These dustlike structures are called **pollen.**

These characteristics allow seed plants to live just about anywhere. That is why seed plants are the most common plants on Earth today.

Desert yucca

English elm

What's So Great About Seeds?

A seed develops after fertilization takes place. Fertilization is the union of an egg and a sperm cell. A seed is made up of three parts: a young plant (the sporophyte), stored food, and a tough seed coat that surrounds and protects the young plant. These parts are shown in **Figure 13.**

Did you know that seeds like to travel far from home? See how on page 726 of your LabBook.

Figure 13 *A seed contains stored food and a young plant. A seed is surrounded and protected by a seed coat.*

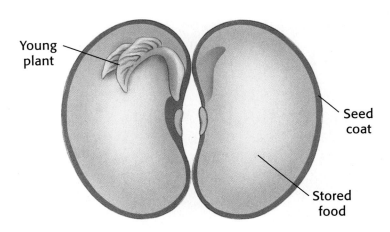

Young plant

Seed coat

Stored food

Plants that reproduce by seeds have several advantages over spore-forming seedless plants. For example, when a seed *germinates,* or begins to grow, the young plant is nourished by the food stored in the seed. By the time the young plant uses up these food reserves, it is able to make all the food it needs by photosynthesis. In contrast, the gametophyte that develops from a spore must be in an environment where it can begin photosynthesis as soon as it begins to grow.

Environment
C O N N E C T I O N

Animals need plants to live, but some plants need animals, too. These plants produce seeds with tough seed coats that can't begin to grow into new plants until they have been eaten by an animal. When the seed is exposed to the acids and enzymes of the animal's digestive system, the seed coat wears down. After the seed passes out of the animal's digestive tract, it is able to absorb water, germinate, and grow.

The Accidental Garden

During the summer, Patrick and his sister love to sit out on the porch munching away on juicy watermelon. One year they held a contest to see who could spit the seeds the farthest. The next spring, Patrick noticed some new plants growing in their yard. When he examined them closely, he realized little watermelons were growing on the plants. Patrick and his sister had no idea that they were starting a watermelon garden. Think about the eating habits of animals in the wild. How might they start a garden?

Gymnosperms: Seed Plants Without Flowers

The seeds of gymnosperms are not enclosed in a fruit. The word *gymnosperm* is Greek for "naked seed." There are four groups of gymnosperms: conifers, ginkgoes, cycads, and gnetophytes (NEE toh FIETS). Examples are shown in **Figure 14**.

Figure 14 *Gymnosperms do not produce flowers or fruits.*

◄ The **ginkgoes** contain only one living species, the ginkgo tree. Ginkgo seeds are produced in fleshy structures that are attached directly to branches.

▲ The **conifers,** with about 550 species, make up the largest group of gymnosperms. Most conifers are evergreen and keep their needle-shaped leaves all year. Conifer seeds develop in cones. Pines, spruces, firs, and hemlocks are examples of conifers.

▲ The **cycads** were more common millions of years ago. Today there are only about 140 species. These plants grow in the tropics. Like seeds of conifers, seeds of cycads develop in cones.

▲ The **gnetophytes** consist of about 70 species of very unusual plants. This gnetophyte is a shrub that grows in dry areas. Its seeds are formed in cones.

Gymnosperm Life Cycle The gymnosperms that are most familiar to you are probably the conifers. The name *conifer* comes from Greek and Latin words that mean "carry cones." Conifers have two kinds of cones—male and female. These are shown in **Figure 15.** Male spores are produced in the male cones, and female spores are produced in the female cones. The spores develop into gametophytes. The male gametophytes are pollen, dustlike particles that produce sperm cells. The female gametophyte produces eggs. Wind carries pollen from the male cones to the female cones on the same plant or on different plants. The transfer of pollen is called **pollination.**

After the egg is fertilized, it develops into a seed within the female cone. When the seed is mature, it is released by the cone and falls to the ground. The seed then germinates and grows into a new tree. The life cycle of a pine tree is shown in **Figure 16.**

The Importance of Gymnosperms Conifers are the most economically important group of gymnosperms. People harvest conifers and use the wood for building materials and paper products. Pine trees produce a sticky fluid called resin, which is used to make soap, turpentine, paint, and ink.

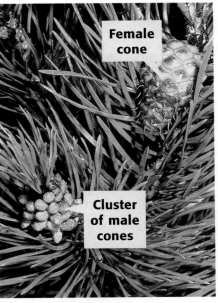

Figure 15 *A pine tree has male cones and female cones.*

Figure 16 **Pine Life Cycle**

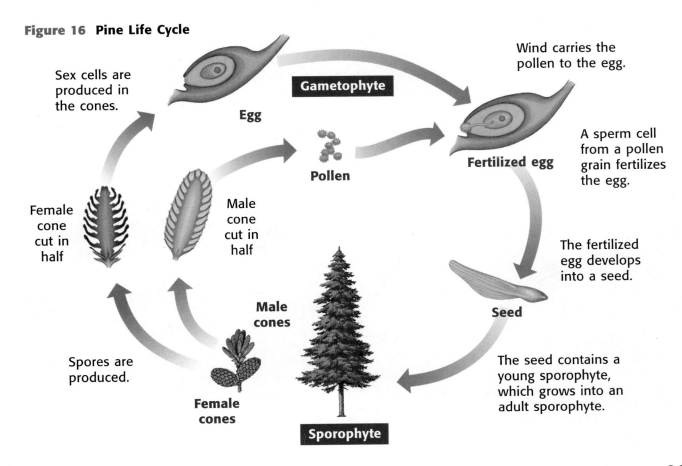

Sex cells are produced in the cones.

Wind carries the pollen to the egg.

Gametophyte

Egg

A sperm cell from a pollen grain fertilizes the egg.

Pollen

Fertilized egg

Female cone cut in half

Male cone cut in half

The fertilized egg develops into a seed.

Seed

Spores are produced.

Male cones

The seed contains a young sporophyte, which grows into an adult sporophyte.

Female cones

Sporophyte

Introduction to Plants   **281**

Angiosperms: Seed Plants with Flowers

Flowering plants, or angiosperms, are the most abundant plants today. Angiosperms can be found in almost every environment on land. There are at least 235,000 species of flowering plants, many more than all other plant species combined. Angiosperms come in a wide variety of sizes and shapes, from dandelions and water lilies to prickly-pear cactuses and oak trees.

All angiosperms are vascular plants that produce flowers and fruits. Tulips and roses are examples of flowering plants with large flowers. Other flowering plants, such as grasses and maple trees, have small flowers. After fertilization, angiosperms produce seeds within fruits. Peaches, lemons, and grapes are fruits, as are tomatoes, cucumbers, and many other foods we think of as vegetables.

What Are Flowers For? Flowers help angiosperms reproduce. Some angiosperms depend on the wind for pollination, but others have flowers that attract animals. As shown in **Figure 17,** when animals visit different flowers, they may carry pollen from flower to flower.

What Are Fruits For? Fruits are also important structures for reproduction in angiosperms. They help to ensure that seeds survive as they are transported to areas where new plants can grow. Fruits surround and protect seeds. Some fruits and seeds, such as those shown in **Figure 18,** have structures that help the wind carry them short or long distances. Other fruits may attract animals that eat the fruits and discard the seeds some distance from the parent plant. Prickly burrs are fruits that are carried from place to place by sticking to the fur of animals or to the clothes and shoes of people.

Figure 17 *This bee is on its way to another squash flower, where it will leave some of the pollen it is carrying.*

Figure 18 *Special structures allow some fruits and seeds to float or drift through the air.*

Dandelion

Maple

Milkweed

Monocots and Dicots Angiosperms are divided into two classes—monocots and dicots. The two classes differ in the number of cotyledons in their seeds. A **cotyledon** (KAHT uh LEED uhn) is a seed leaf found inside a seed. Monocot seeds have one cotyledon, and dicot seeds have two cotyledons. Other differences between monocots and dicots are summarized in **Figure 19.** Monocots include grasses, orchids, onions, lilies, and palms. Dicots include roses, cactuses, sunflowers, peanuts, and peas.

The Importance of Angiosperms

Flowering plants provide animals that live on land with the food they need to survive. A deer nibbling on meadow grass is using flowering plants directly as food. An owl that consumes a field mouse is using flowering plants indirectly as food because the field mouse ate seeds and berries.

Humans depend on flowering plants and use them in many ways. All of our major food crops, such as corn, wheat, and rice, are flowering plants. Some flowering plants, such as oak trees, are used to make furniture and toys. Others, such as cotton and flax, supply fibers for clothing and rope. Flowering plants are used to make many medicines as well as cork, rubber, and perfume oils.

Figure 19   Two Classes of Angiosperms

Monocots

Flower parts in threes

Leaves with parallel veins

One cotyledon (seed leaf)

Bundles of vascular tissue are scattered

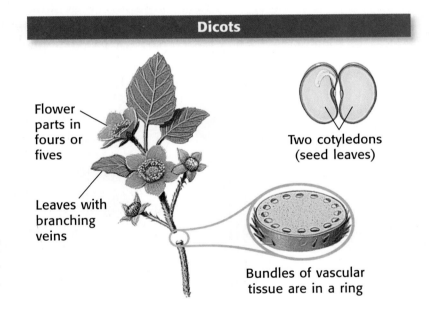

Dicots

Flower parts in fours or fives

Leaves with branching veins

Two cotyledons (seed leaves)

Bundles of vascular tissue are in a ring

REVIEW

1. What are two differences between a seed and a spore?

2. Briefly describe the four groups of gymnosperms. Which group is the largest and most economically important?

3. How do monocots and dicots differ from each other?

4. **Identifying Relationships** In what ways are flowers and fruits adaptations that help angiosperms reproduce?

internet**connect**

SC*L*INKS
NSTA

TOPIC: Plants with Seeds
GO TO: www.scilinks.org
*sci*LINKS NUMBER: HSTL295

The Structures of Seed Plants

Terms to Learn

xylem	stamen
phloem	pistil
sepal	stigma
petal	ovary

What You'll Do

- Describe the functions of roots.
- Describe the functions of stems.
- Explain how the structure of leaves is related to their function.
- Identify the parts of a flower and their functions.

You have different body systems that carry out a variety of functions. For example, your cardiovascular system transports materials throughout your body, and your skeletal system provides support and protection. Similarly, plants have systems too—a root system, a shoot system, and a reproductive system.

Plant Systems

A plant's root system and shoot system supply the plant with needed resources that are found underground and above ground. The root system is made up of roots. The shoot system is made up of stems and leaves.

The root system and the shoot system are dependent on each other. The vascular tissues of the two systems are connected, as shown in **Figure 20.** There are two kinds of vascular tissue—xylem (ZIE luhm) and phloem (FLOH EM). **Xylem** transports water and minerals through the plant. **Phloem** transports sugar molecules. Xylem and phloem are found in all parts of vascular plants.

Vascular tissue

Figure 20 *The vascular tissues of the roots and shoots are connected.*

The Root of the Matter

Because most roots are underground, many people do not realize how extensive a plant's root system can be. For example, a 2.5 m tall corn plant can have roots that grow 2.5 m deep and 1.2 m out away from the stem!

Root Functions The main functions of roots are as follows:

- **Roots supply plants with water and dissolved minerals that have been absorbed from the soil.** These materials are transported throughout the plant in the xylem.

- **Roots support and anchor plants.** Roots hold plants securely in the soil.

- **Roots often store surplus food made during photosynthesis.** This food is produced in the leaves and transported as sugar in the phloem to the roots. There the surplus food is usually stored as sugar or starch.

Root Structure The structures of a root are shown in **Figure 21.** Like the cells in the outer-most layer of your skin, the layer of cells that covers the surface of roots is called the *epidermis.* Some cells of the root epidermis extend out from the root. These cells, called *root hairs,* increase the amount of surface area through which roots can absorb water and minerals.

After water and minerals are absorbed by the epidermis, they diffuse into the center of the root, where the vascular tissue is located. Roots grow longer at their tips. A group of cells called the *root cap* protects the tip of a root and produces a slimy substance that makes it easier for the root to grow through soil.

Root Types There are two types of roots—taproots and fibrous roots. Examples of each are shown in **Figure 22.**

A *taproot* consists of one main root that grows downward, with many smaller branch roots coming out of it. Taproots can usually obtain water located deep underground. Dicots and gymnosperms have taproots.

A *fibrous root* has several roots of the same size that spread out from the base of the stem. Fibrous roots typically obtain water that is close to the soil surface. Monocots have fibrous roots.

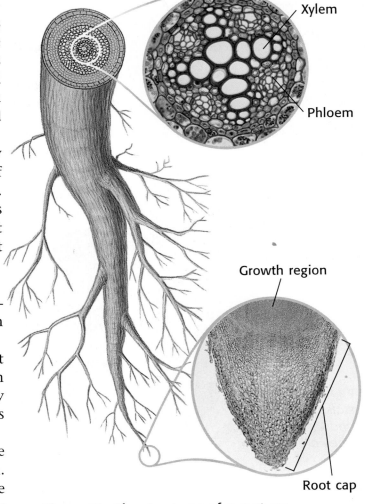

Xylem

Phloem

Growth region

Root cap

Figure 21 *The structures of a root are labeled above.*

Figure 22 *The onion has a fibrous root, and the dandelions and carrots have taproots.*

Fibrous roots

Taproot

Taproots

What's the Holdup?

As shown in **Figure 23,** stems vary greatly in shape and size. Stems are usually located above ground, although many plants have underground stems.

Stem Functions A stem connects a plant's roots to its leaves and flowers and performs these main functions:

- **Stems support the plant body.** Leaves are arranged on stems so that each leaf can absorb the sunlight it needs for photosynthesis. Stems hold up flowers and display them to pollinators.

- **Stems transport materials between the root system and the shoot system.** Xylem carries water and dissolved minerals upward from the roots to the leaves and other shoot parts. Phloem carries the glucose produced during photosynthesis to roots and other parts of the plant.

- **Some stems store materials.** For example, the stems of the plants in **Figure 24** are adapted for water storage.

Valley oak

Figure 23 *The stalks of daisies and the trunks of trees are stems.*

Daisy

BRAIN FOOD

Root or shoot? Even though potatoes grow in the ground, they're not roots. The white potato is an underground stem adapted to store starch.

Figure 24 *Baobab trees store large quantities of water and starch in their massive trunks. Cactuses store water in their thick, green stems.*

Stem Structures

Herbaceous Stems

Phloem

Xylem

Woody Stems

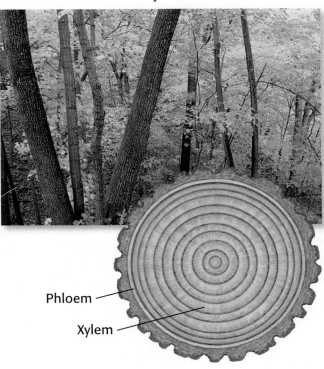

Phloem

Xylem

The plants in this group have stems that are soft, thin, and flexible. These stems are called *herbaceous* stems. Examples of plants with herbaceous (her BAY shuhs) stems include wildflowers, such as clovers and poppies, and many vegetable crops, such as beans, tomatoes, and corn. Some plants with herbaceous stems live only 1 or 2 years. A cross section of one kind of herbaceous stem is shown above.

Trees and shrubs have rigid stems made of wood and bark. Their stems are called *woody* stems. If a tree or a shrub lives in an area with cold winters, the plant has a growing period and a dormant period.

At the beginning of each spring growing period, large xylem cells are produced. As fall approaches, the plants produce smaller xylem cells, which appear darker. In the fall and winter, the plants stop producing new cells. The cycle begins again when the spring growing season begins. A ring of dark cells surrounding a ring of light cells make up a growth ring.

REVIEW

1. What are three functions of roots?

2. What are three functions of stems?

3. **Applying Concepts** Suppose the cross section of a tree reveals 12 light-colored rings and 12 dark-colored rings. How many years of growth are represented?

A Plant's Food Factories

Leaves vary greatly in shape and size. They may be round, narrow, heart-shaped, or fan-shaped. The raffia palm, shown in **Figure 25,** has leaves that may be six times longer than you are tall. A leaf of the duckweed, a tiny aquatic plant also shown in Figure 25, is so small that several can fit on your fingernail.

Sweet gum

Leaf Function The main function of leaves is to make food for the plant. Leaves capture the energy in sunlight and absorb carbon dioxide from the air. Light energy, carbon dioxide, and water are needed to carry out photosynthesis. During photosynthesis, plants use light energy to make food (sugar) from carbon dioxide and water.

Figure 25 *Even though the leaves of these plants are very different, they serve the same purpose.*

Raffia palm

Mimosa

Duckweed

Self-Check

How is the function of stems related to the function of leaves? *(See page 782 to check your answers.)*

Leaf Structure The structure of leaves is related to their main function—photosynthesis. **Figure 26** shows a cutaway view of a small block of leaf tissue. The top and bottom surfaces of the leaf are covered with a single layer of cells called the epidermis. Light can easily pass through the thin epidermis to the leaf's interior. Notice the tiny pores in the epidermis. These pores, called *stomata* (singular, *stoma*), allow carbon dioxide to enter the leaf. *Guard cells* open and close the stomata.

The middle of a leaf, which is where photosynthesis takes place, has two layers. The upper layer is the *palisade layer,* and the lower layer is the *spongy layer.* Cells in the palisade layer contain many chloroplasts, the green organelles that carry out photosynthesis. Cells in the spongy layer are spread farther apart than cells in the palisade layer. The air spaces between these cells allow carbon dioxide to diffuse more freely throughout the leaf.

The veins of a leaf contain xylem and phloem surrounded by supporting tissue. Xylem transports water and minerals to the leaf. Phloem conducts the sugar made during photosynthesis from the leaf to the rest of the plant.

Leaf Adaptations Some leaves have functions other than photosynthesis. For example, the leaves on a cactus plant are modified as spines. These hard, pointed leaves discourage animals from eating the succulent cactus stem. **Figure 27** shows leaves with a most unusual function. The leaves of a sundew are modified to catch insects. Sundews grow in soil that does not contain enough nitrogen to meet the plants' needs. By catching and digesting insects, a sundew is able to meet its nitrogen requirement.

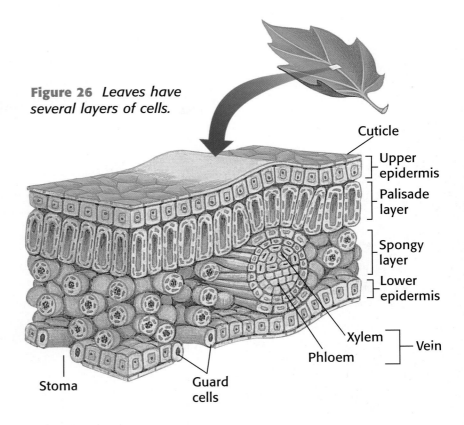

Figure 26 *Leaves have several layers of cells.*

Cuticle
Upper epidermis
Palisade layer
Spongy layer
Lower epidermis
Xylem
Phloem
Vein
Stoma
Guard cells

Figure 27 *This damselfly is trapped in the sticky fluid of a sundew flower.*

Flowers

Most people admire the beauty of flowers, such as roses or lilies, without stopping to think about *why* plants have flowers. Flowers are adaptations for sexual reproduction. Flowers come in many different shapes, colors, and fragrances that attract pollinators or catch the wind. Flowers usually contain the following parts: sepals, petals, stamens, and one or more pistils. The flower parts are usually arranged in rings around the central pistil. **Figure 28** shows the parts of a typical flower.

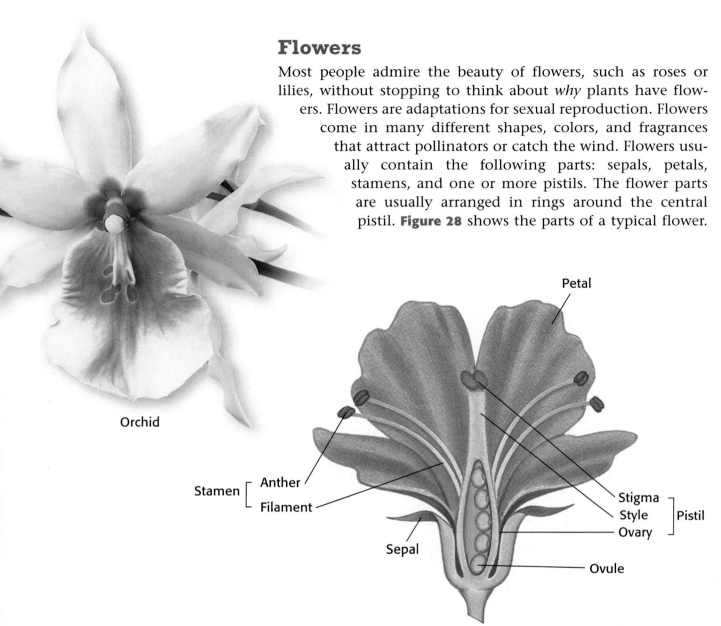

Orchid

Figure 28 *The stamens, which produce pollen, and the pistil, which produces eggs, are surrounded by the petals and the sepals.*

Build a flower of your very own on page 727.

Sepals make up the bottom ring of flower parts. They are often green like leaves. The main function of sepals is to cover and protect the immature flower when it is a bud. As the blossom opens, the sepals fold back so that the petals can enlarge and become visible.

Petals are broad, flat, and thin, like sepals, but they vary in shape and color. Petals may attract insects or other animals to the flower. These animals help plants reproduce by transferring pollen from flower to flower.

Just above the petals is a circle of **stamens,** which are the male reproductive structures. Each stamen consists of a thin stalk called a *filament,* and each stamen is topped by an *anther.* Anthers are saclike structures that produce pollen grains.

In the center of most flowers is one or more **pistils,** the female reproductive structures. The tip of the pistil is called the **stigma.** Pollen grains collect on stigmas, which are often sticky or feathery. The long, slender part of the pistil is the *style.* The rounded base of the pistil is called the **ovary.** As shown in **Figure 29,** the ovary contains one or more *ovules.* Each ovule contains an egg. If fertilization occurs, the ovule develops into a seed, and the ovary develops into a fruit.

Flowers that have brightly colored petals and aromas usually depend on animals for pollination. Plants without bright colors and aromas, such as the grass flowers shown in **Figure 30,** depend on wind to spread pollen.

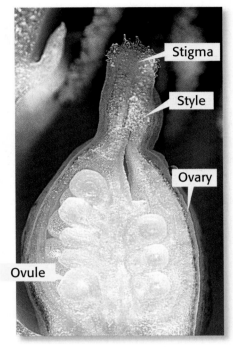

Figure 29 *This hyacinth ovary contains many ovules.*

Figure 30 *The tall stems of these pampas grass flowers allow their pollen to be picked up by the wind.*

REVIEW

1. Describe the internal structure of a typical leaf. How is a leaf's structure related to its function?

2. Which flower structure produces pollen?

3. **Identifying Relationships** Compare the functions of xylem and phloem in roots, stems, leaves, and flowers.

internet connect

SC*i*LINKS.
NSTA

TOPIC: The Structure of Seed Plants
GO TO: www.scilinks.org
sci*LINKS NUMBER: HSTL300

Chapter Highlights

Vocabulary

sporophyte *(p. 271)*

gametophyte *(p. 271)*

nonvascular plant *(p. 272)*

vascular plant *(p. 273)*

gymnosperm *(p. 273)*

angiosperm *(p. 273)*

Section Notes

• Plants use photosynthesis to make food. Plant cells have cell walls. Plants are covered by a waxy cuticle.

• The life cycle of a plant includes a spore-producing stage (the sporophyte) and a sex-cell-producing stage (the gametophyte).

• Plants probably evolved from a type of ancient green algae.

• Vascular plants have tissues that carry materials throughout a plant. Nonvascular plants do not have vascular tissues and must depend on diffusion and osmosis to move materials.

Vocabulary

rhizoid *(p. 274)*

rhizome *(p. 276)*

Section Notes

• There are two groups of plants that do not make seeds.

• Mosses and liverworts are small, nonvascular plants. They are small because they lack xylem and phloem. Mosses and liverworts need water to transport sperm cells to eggs.

• Ferns, horsetails, and club mosses are vascular plants. They can grow larger than nonvascular plants. Ferns, horsetails, and club mosses need water to transport sperm cells to eggs.

☑ Skills Check

Math Concepts

DO THE PERCENTAGES ADD UP? If 38 percent of the plants in a forest are flowering plants, what percentage of the plants are not flowering plants? The two groups together make up 100 percent. So subtract 38 percent from 100.

100 percent – 38 percent = 62 percent

Look again at the MathBreak on page 273. You can calculate the percentage of plants that do produce seeds by subtracting your MathBreak answer from 100 percent.

Visual Understanding

SEEDS This image shows the two cotyledons of a dicot seed. The seed has been split, and the two cotyledons laid open like two halves of a hamburger bun. You are looking at the inside surfaces of the two cotyledons. Open a peanut and see for yourself. In peanuts, the two cotyledons come apart very easily. You can even see the young delicate plant inside.

SECTION 3

Vocabulary
pollen *(p. 278)*
pollination *(p. 281)*
cotyledon *(p. 283)*

Section Notes

- Seed plants are vascular plants that produce seeds. The sperm cells of seed plants develop inside pollen.

- Gymnosperms are seed plants that produce their seeds in cones or in fleshy structures attached to branches. The four groups of gymnosperms are conifers, ginkgoes, cycads, and gnetophytes.

- Angiosperms are seed plants that produce their seeds in flowers. The two groups of flowering plants are monocots and dicots.

Labs
Travelin' Seeds *(p. 726)*

SECTION 4

Vocabulary
xylem *(p. 284)*
phloem *(p. 284)*
sepal *(p. 290)*
petal *(p. 290)*
stamen *(p. 291)*
pistil *(p. 291)*
stigma *(p. 291)*
ovary *(p. 291)*

Section Notes

- Roots generally grow underground. Roots anchor the plant, absorb water and minerals, and store food.

- Stems connect roots and leaves. Stems support leaves and other structures; transport water, minerals, and food; and store water and food.

- The main function of leaves is photosynthesis. Leaf structure is related to this function.

- Flowers usually have four parts—sepals, petals, stamens, and pistils. Stamens produce sperm cells in pollen. The ovary in the pistil contains ovules. Each ovule contains an egg. Ovules become seeds after fertilization.

Labs
Leaf Me Alone! *(p. 724)*
Build a Flower *(p. 727)*

---

internet**connect**

GO TO: go.hrw.com

Visit the **HRW** Web site for a variety of learning tools related to this chapter. Just type in the keyword:

KEYWORD: HSTPL1

GO TO: www.scilinks.org

Visit the **National Science Teachers Association** on-line Web site for Internet resources related to this chapter. Just type in the *sci*LINKS number for more information about the topic:

TOPIC:		*sci*LINKS NUMBER:
TOPIC: Plant Characteristics		*sci***LINKS NUMBER:** HSTL280
TOPIC: How Are Plants Classified?		*sci***LINKS NUMBER:** HSTL285
TOPIC: Seedless Plants		*sci***LINKS NUMBER:** HSTL290
TOPIC: Plants with Seeds		*sci***LINKS NUMBER:** HSTL295
TOPIC: The Structure of Seed Plants		*sci***LINKS NUMBER:** HSTL300

Chapter Review

To complete the following sentences, choose the correct term from each pair of terms listed below:

1. The __?__ is a waxy layer that coats the surface of stems and leaves. *(stomata* or *cuticle)*

2. During the plant life cycle, eggs and sperm cells are produced by the __?__. *(sporophyte* or *gametophyte)*

3. In vascular plants, __?__ transports water and minerals, and __?__ transports food molecules, such as sugar. *(xylem/phloem* or *phloem/xylem)*

4. Seedless vascular plants include ferns, horsetails, and __?__. *(club mosses* or *liverworts)*

5. A __?__ is a seed leaf found inside a seed. *(cotyledon* or *sepal)*

6. In a flower, the __?__ are the male reproductive structures. *(pistils* or *stamens)*

UNDERSTANDING CONCEPTS

Multiple Choice

7. Which of the following plants is nonvascular?
   a. fern   c. conifer
   b. moss   d. monocot

8. Coal formed millions of years ago from the remains of
   a. nonvascular plants.
   b. flowering plants.
   c. green algae.
   d. seedless vascular plants.

9. The largest group of gymnosperms is the
   a. conifers.   c. cycads.
   b. ginkgoes.   d. gnetophytes.

10. Roots
    a. absorb water and minerals.
    b. store surplus food.
    c. anchor the plant.
    d. All of the above

11. Woody stems
    a. are soft, green, and flexible.
    b. include the stems of daisies.
    c. contain wood and bark.
    d. All of the above

12. The veins of a leaf contain
    a. xylem and phloem.
    b. stomata.
    c. epidermis and cuticle.
    d. xylem only.

13. In a flower, petals function to
    a. produce ovules.
    b. attract pollinators.
    c. protect the flower bud.
    d. produce pollen.

14. Monocots have
    a. flower parts in fours or fives.
    b. two cotyledons in the seed.
    c. parallel veins in leaves.
    d. All of the above

Short Answer

15. What advantages does a seed have over a spore?

16. How is water important to the reproduction of mosses and ferns?

Concept Map

17. Use the following terms to create a concept map: nonvascular plants, vascular plants, xylem, phloem, ferns, seeds in cones, plants, gymnosperms, spores, angiosperms, seeds in flowers.

CRITICAL THINKING AND PROBLEM SOLVING

Write one or two sentences to answer the following questions:

18. Plants that are pollinated by wind produce much more pollen than plants that are pollinated by animals. Why do you suppose this is so?

19. If plants did not possess a cuticle, where would they have to live? Why?

20. Grasses do not have strong aromas or bright colors. How might this be related to the way these plants are pollinated?

21. Imagine that a seed and a spore are beginning to grow in a deep, dark crack in a rock. Which reproductive structure—the seed or the spore—is more likely to survive and develop into an adult plant after it begins to grow? Explain your answer.

MATH IN SCIENCE

22. One year a maple tree produced 1,056 seeds. If only 15 percent of those seeds germinated and grew into seedlings, how many seedlings would there be?

INTERPRETING GRAPHICS

23. Examine the cross section of the flower below to answer the following questions:
    a. Which letter corresponds to the structure in which pollen is produced? What is the name of this structure?
    b. Which letter corresponds to the structure that contains ovules? What is the name of this structure?

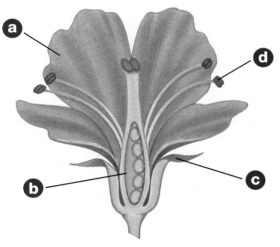

24. In a woody stem, a ring of dark cells and a ring of light cells represent 1 year of growth. Examine the cross section of a tree trunk below, and determine the age of the tree.

NOW What Do You Think?

Take a minute to review your answers to the ScienceLog questions on page 269. Have your answers changed? If necessary, revise your answers based on what you have learned since you began this chapter.

Science, Technology, and Society

Supersquash or Frankenfruit?

The fruits and vegetables you buy at the supermarket may not be exactly what they seem. Scientists may have genetically altered these foods to make them look and taste better, contain more nutrients, or have a longer shelf life.

From Bullets to Bacteria

Through genetic engineering, scientists are now able to duplicate one organism's DNA and place a certain gene from the DNA into the cells of another species of plant or animal. This technology enables scientists to give plants and animals a new trait. The new trait can then be passed along to the organism's offspring and future generations.

Scientists alter plants by inserting a gene with a certain property into a plant's cells. The DNA is usually inserted by one of two methods. In one method, new DNA is first placed inside a special bacterium, and the bacterium carries the DNA into the plant cell. In another method, microscopic particles of metal coated with the new DNA are fired into the plant cells with a special "gene gun."

High-tech Food

During the past decade, scientists have inserted genes into more than 50 different kinds of plants. In most cases, the new trait from the inserted gene makes the plants more disease resistant or more marketable in some way. For example, scientists have added genes from a caterpillar-attacking bacterium to cotton, tomato, and potato plants. The altered plants produce proteins that kill the crop-eating caterpillars. Scientists are also trying to develop genetically altered peas and red peppers that stay sweeter longer. A genetically altered tomato that lasts longer and tastes better is already in many supermarkets. One day it may even be possible to create a caffeine-free coffee bean.

Are We Ready?

As promising as these genetically engineered foods seem to be, they are not without controversy. Some scientists are afraid that genes introduced to crop plants could be released into the environment or that foods may be changed in ways that endanger human health. For example, could people who are allergic to peanuts become sick from eating a tomato plant that contains certain peanut genes? All of these concerns will have to be addressed before the genetically altered food products are widely accepted.

Find Out for Yourself

▶ Are genetically altered foods controversial in your area? Survey a few people to get their opinions about genetically altered foods. Do they think grocery stores should carry these foods? Why or why not?

◀ *A scientist uses a "gene gun" to insert DNA into plant cells.*

CAREERS

ETHNOBOTANIST

Paul Cox is an *ethnobotanist.* He travels to remote places to look for plants that can help cure diseases. He seeks the advice of shamans and other native healers in his search. In 1984, Cox made a trip to Samoa to observe healers. While there he met a 78-year-old Samoan healer named Epenesa. She was able to identify more than 200 medicinal plants, and she astounded Cox with her knowledge. Epenesa had an accurate understanding of human anatomy, and she dispensed medicines with great care and accuracy.

In Samoan culture, the healer is one of the most valued members of the community. After all, the healer has the knowledge to treat diseases. In some cases, Samoan healers know about ancient treatments that Western medicine has yet to discover. Recently, some researchers have turned to Samoan healers to ask them about their medical secrets.

Blending Polynesian and Western Medicine

After Cox spent months observing Epenesa as she treated patients, Epenesa gave him her treatment for yellow fever—a tea made from the wood of a rain-forest tree. Cox brought the yellow-fever remedy to the United States, and in 1986 researchers at the National Cancer Institute (NCI) began studying the plant. They found that the plant contains a virus-fighting chemical called *prostratin.* Further research by NCI indicates that prostratin may also have potential as a treatment for AIDS.

Another compound from Samoan healers treats inflammation. The healers apply the bark of a local tree to the inflamed skin. When a team of scientists evaluated the bark, they found that the healers were absolutely correct. The active compound in the bark, *flavanone,* is now being researched for its medicinal properties. Some day Western doctors may prescribe medicine containing flavanone.

Preserving Their Knowledge

When two of the healers Cox observed in Samoa died in 1993, generations of medical knowledge died with them. The healers' deaths point out the urgency of recording the ancient wisdom before all of the healers are gone. Cox and other ethnobotanists must work hard to gather information from healers as quickly as they can.

The Feel of Natural Healing

▶ The next time you have a mosquito bite or a mild sunburn, consider a treatment that comes from the experience of Native American healers. Aloe vera, another plant product, is found in a variety of lotions and ointments. Find out how well it works for you!

▶ *These plant parts from Samoa may one day be used in medicines to treat a variety of diseases.*

13 Plant Processes

Strange but True!

It's war every day in the cornfield. When beet armyworm caterpillars attack the corn, the corn fights back. The corn somehow manages to send out SOS signals. Soon, parasitic wasps swoop in, attack the caterpillars, and save the day!

How can a plant send out a distress signal? When a corn plant is being munched on by a caterpillar, chemicals in the mouth of the caterpillar cause the corn plant to release a second chemical into the air. Wasps sense the corn's response and make a beeline for the infested plant.

Like an airborne cavalry, the wasps dive for the caterpillars and lay eggs under their skin. The eggs hatch in a short time, and the wasp larvae devour the insides of the caterpillars.

Jim Tumlinson, the scientist who discovered this partnership between corn and wasps, says it probably occurred by chance. Many plants release special chemicals when attacked by pests. The wasps have a natural attraction for the chemical released by corn plants.

Tumlinson hopes to breed other plants so that they release insect-attracting chemicals. Attracting plant-friendly wasps could decrease the need for poisonous pesticides.

Making and releasing special chemicals are processes that occur in many plants. In this chapter you will learn about other plant processes.

What Do You Think?

In your ScienceLog, try to answer the following questions based on what you already know:

1. How do plants respond to changes in their environment?

2. Why do plants need light?

Observing Plant Growth

When planting a garden, you bury seeds in the ground, water them, and then wait for tiny sprouts to poke through the soil. What happens to the seeds while they're underneath the soil? How do seeds grow into plants?

Procedure

1. Your instructor will supply you with the materials you need: the bottom half of a **clear 2 L soda bottle, potting soil, three or four bean seeds,** and **aluminum foil.**

2. Fill the soda bottle to within 8 cm of the top with potting soil.

3. Press the seeds into the soil and against the wall of the soda bottle, as shown above. The top of the seeds should be level with the surface of the potting soil. Add an additional 5 cm of potting soil.

4. Cover the sides of the soda bottle with aluminum foil to keep out light. Leave the top uncovered.

5. Water the seeds with about **60 mL of water.** Add more water whenever the top 1 cm of the soil is completely dry.

6. Once every day, remove the aluminum foil from the soda bottle for a few minutes and check on your seeds. Keep a record in your ScienceLog of how the seeds grow.

Analysis

7. How long did it take for the seeds to start growing? How many seeds grew?

8. Where do the seeds get the energy to start growing?

The Reproduction of Flowering Plants

Terms to Learn

dormant

What You'll Do

◆ Describe the roles of pollination and fertilization in sexual reproduction.
◆ Describe how fruits are formed from flowers.
◆ Explain the difference between sexual and asexual reproduction in plants.

If you went outside right now and made a list of all the different kinds of plants you could see, most of the plants on your list would probably be flowering plants. Flowering plants are the largest and the most diverse group of plants in the world. Their success is partly due to their flowers, which are adaptations for sexual reproduction. During sexual reproduction, an egg is fertilized by a sperm cell. In flowering plants, fertilization takes place within the flower and leads to the formation of one or more seeds within a fruit.

How Does Fertilization Occur?

In order for fertilization to occur, sperm cells must be able to reach eggs. The sperm cells of a flowering plant are contained in pollen grains. Pollination occurs when pollen grains are transported from anthers to stigmas. This is the beginning of fertilization, as shown in **Figure 1.** After the pollen lands on the stigma, a tube grows from the pollen grain through the style to the ovary. Inside the ovary are ovules. Each ovule contains an egg.

Sperm cells within the pollen grain move down the pollen tube and into an ovule. Fertilization occurs as one of the sperm cells fuses with the egg inside the ovule.

Figure 1 *Fertilization occurs after pollination.*

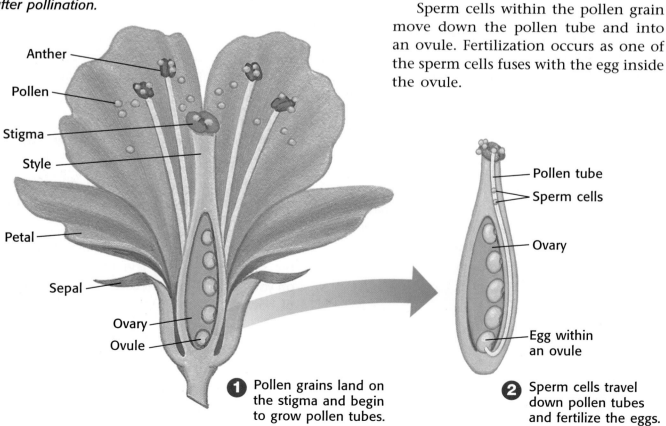

Anther
Pollen
Stigma
Style
Petal
Sepal
Ovary
Ovule

Pollen tube
Sperm cells
Ovary
Egg within an ovule

❶ Pollen grains land on the stigma and begin to grow pollen tubes.

❷ Sperm cells travel down pollen tubes and fertilize the eggs.

From Flower to Fruit

After fertilization takes place, the ovule develops into a seed that contains a tiny, undeveloped plant. The ovary surrounding the ovule develops into a fruit. **Figure 2** shows how the ovary and ovules of a flower develop into a fruit and seeds.

Figure 2 *Fertilization leads to the development of fruit and seeds.*

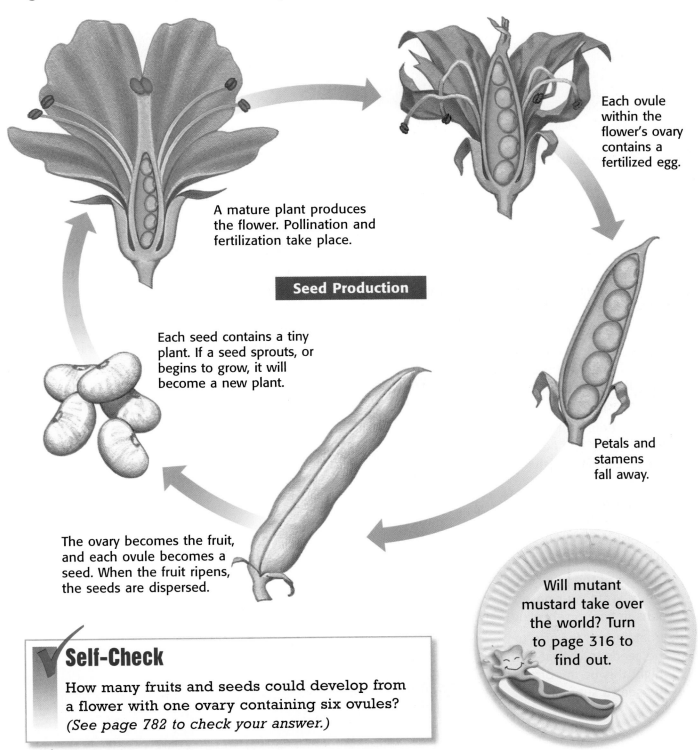

A mature plant produces the flower. Pollination and fertilization take place.

Seed Production

Each ovule within the flower's ovary contains a fertilized egg.

Petals and stamens fall away.

Each seed contains a tiny plant. If a seed sprouts, or begins to grow, it will become a new plant.

The ovary becomes the fruit, and each ovule becomes a seed. When the fruit ripens, the seeds are dispersed.

✓ Self-Check

How many fruits and seeds could develop from a flower with one ovary containing six ovules? *(See page 782 to check your answer.)*

Will mutant mustard take over the world? Turn to page 316 to find out.

Familiar Fruits

While the ovules are developing into seeds, the ovary is developing into the fruit. As the fruit swells and ripens, it holds and protects the developing seeds. Look below to see which parts of the fruits developed from a flower's ovary and ovules.

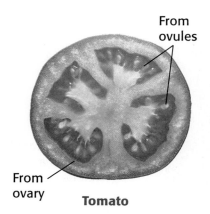

From ovules

From ovary

Tomato

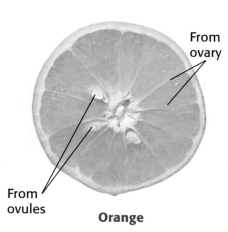

From ovary

From ovules

Orange

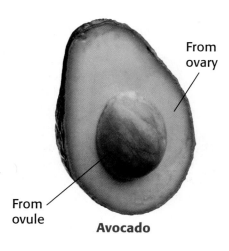

From ovary

From ovule

Avocado

Seeds Become New Plants

Once a seed is fully developed, the young plant inside the seed stops growing. The seed may become dormant. When seeds are **dormant,** they are inactive. Dormant seeds can often survive long periods of drought or freezing temperatures. Some seeds need extreme conditions such as cold winters or even forest fires to break their dormancy.

When a seed is dropped or planted in an environment that has water, oxygen, and a suitable temperature, the seed sprouts. Each plant species has an ideal temperature at which most of its seeds will begin to grow. For most plants, the ideal temperature for growth is about 27°C (80.6°F). **Figure 3** shows the *germination,* or sprouting, of a bean seed and the early stages of growth in a young bean plant.

Figure 3 *Sexual reproduction produces seeds that grow into new plants.*

QuickLab

Thirsty Seeds

1. Obtain **12 dry bean seeds, 2 Petri dishes,** a **wax pencil,** and **water** from your teacher.

2. Fill one Petri dish two-thirds full of water and add six seeds. Label the dish "Water."

3. Add the remaining seeds to the dry Petri dish. Label this dish "Control."

4. The next day, compare the size of the two sets of seeds. Write your observations in your ScienceLog.

5. What caused the size of the seeds to change? Why might this be important to the seed's survival?

Other Methods of Reproduction

Many flowering plants can also reproduce asexually. Asexual reproduction in plants does not involve the formation of flowers, seeds, and fruits. In asexual reproduction, a part of a plant, such as a stem or root, produces a new plant. Several examples of asexual reproduction are shown below in **Figure 4**.

Figure 4 *Asexual reproduction can occur in several different ways. Some examples are shown here.*

▼ The strawberry plant produces runners, stems that run horizontally along the ground. Buds along runners grow into new plants.

▲ The "eyes" of potatoes are buds that can grow asexually into new plants.

Kalanchoe plants produce plantlets, ▶ tiny plants along the margins of their leaves. Plantlets eventually fall off and root in the soil as separate plants.

REVIEW

1. How does pollination differ from fertilization?

2. Which part of a flower develops into a fruit?

3. **Relating Concepts** What do flowers and runners have in common? How are they different?

4. **Identifying Relationships** When might asexual reproduction be important for the survival of some flowering plants?

internet **connect**

SC*L*INKS.
NSTA

TOPIC: Reproduction of Plants
GO TO: www.scilinks.org
*sci*LINKS NUMBER: HSTL305

What You'll Do

◆ Describe the process of photosynthesis.
◆ Discuss the relationship between photosynthesis and cellular respiration.
◆ Explain the importance of stomata in the processes of photosynthesis and transpiration.

The Ins and Outs of Making Food

Plants do not have lungs, but they need air just like you. Air is a mixture of oxygen, carbon dioxide, and other gases. Plants must have carbon dioxide to carry out photosynthesis, which is how they make their own food.

What Happens During Photosynthesis?

Plants need sunlight to produce food. During photosynthesis, the energy in sunlight is used to make food in the form of the sugar glucose ($C_6H_{12}O_6$) from carbon dioxide (CO_2) and water (H_2O). How does this happen?

Capturing Light Energy Plant cells have organelles called chloroplasts. Chloroplasts contain **chlorophyll,** a green pigment that absorbs light energy. You may not know it, but sunlight is actually a mixture of all the colors of the rainbow. **Figure 5** shows how light from the sun can be separated into different colors when passed through a triangular piece of glass called a prism. Chlorophyll absorbs all of the colors in light except green. Plants look green because chlorophyll reflects green light.

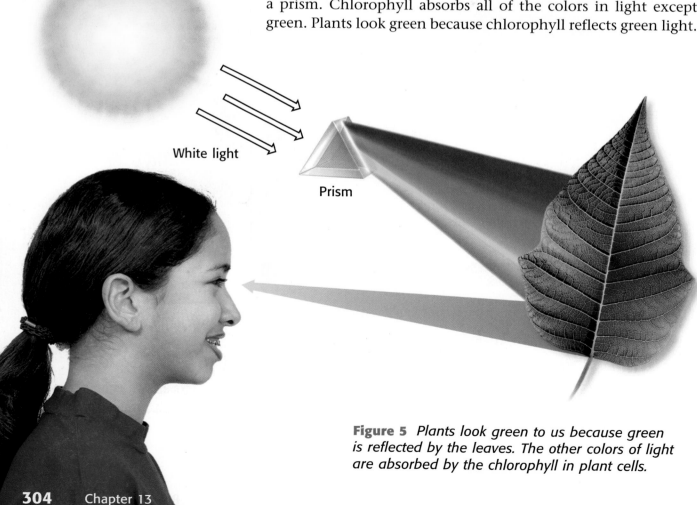

White light

Prism

Figure 5 *Plants look green to us because green is reflected by the leaves. The other colors of light are absorbed by the chlorophyll in plant cells.*

Making Sugar The light energy absorbed by chlorophyll is used to break water (H_2O) down into hydrogen (H) and oxygen (O). The hydrogen is then combined with carbon dioxide (CO_2) from the air to make a sugar called glucose ($C_6H_{12}O_6$). Oxygen is given off as a byproduct. The process of photosynthesis is summarized in the following chemical equation:

$$6CO_2 + 6H_2O \xrightarrow{\text{light energy}} C_6H_{12}O_6 + 6O_2$$

The equation shows that it takes six molecules of carbon dioxide and six molecules of water to produce one molecule of glucose and six molecules of oxygen. The process is illustrated in **Figure 6.**

The energy stored in food molecules is used by plant cells to carry out their life processes. Within each living cell, glucose and other food molecules are broken down in a process called cellular respiration. **Cellular respiration** converts the energy stored in food into a form of energy that cells can use. During this process, the plant uses oxygen and releases carbon dioxide and water.

What do plants produce that is necessary for life as we know it? Find out on page 728 of your LabBook.

Self-Check

What is the original source of the energy stored in the sugar produced by plant cells? *(See page 782 to check your answer.)*

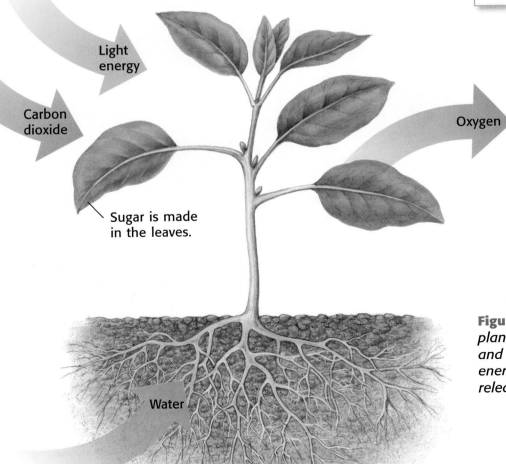

Light energy

Carbon dioxide

Oxygen

Sugar is made in the leaves.

Water

Figure 6 *During photosynthesis, plants take in carbon dioxide and water and absorb light energy. They make sugar and release oxygen.*

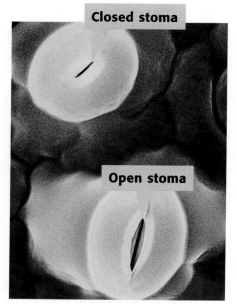

Closed stoma

Open stoma

Figure 7 *When light is available for photosynthesis, the stomata are usually open. When it's dark, the stomata close to conserve water.*

Gas Exchange

All above ground plant surfaces are covered by a waxy cuticle. How does a plant obtain carbon dioxide through this barrier? Carbon dioxide enters the plant's leaves through the **stomata** (singular, *stoma*). A stoma is an opening in the leaf's epidermis and cuticle. Each stoma is surrounded by two *guard cells,* which act like double doors, opening and closing the gap. You can see open and closed stomata in **Figure 7.** The function of stomata is shown in **Figure 8.**

When the stomata are open, carbon dioxide diffuses into the leaf. The oxygen produced during photosynthesis diffuses out of the leaf cells and exits the leaf through the stomata.

When the stomata are open, water vapor also exits the leaf. The loss of water from leaves is called **transpiration.** Most of the water absorbed by a plant's roots is needed to replace water lost during transpiration. When a plant wilts, it is usually because more water is being lost through its leaves than is being absorbed by its roots.

Figure 8 *Plants take in carbon dioxide and release oxygen and water through the stomata in their leaves.*

Cuticle

Vein

Guard cells

Stoma

CO_2 enters through stoma

H_2O and O_2 leave through stoma

internetconnect

SC*i*LINKS
NSTA

TOPIC: Photosynthesis
GO TO: www.scilinks.org
*sci*LINKS NUMBER: HSTL310

REVIEW

1. What three things do plants need to carry out photosynthesis?

2. Why must plant cells carry out cellular respiration?

3. **Identifying Relationships** How are the opening and closing of stomata related to transpiration? When does transpiration occur?

Terms to Learn

tropism   evergreen
phototropism   deciduous
gravitropism

What You'll Do

◆ Describe how plants may respond to light and gravity.
◆ Explain how some plants flower in response to night length.
◆ Describe how some plants are adapted to survive cold weather.

MATH BREAK

Bending by Degrees

Suppose a plant has a positive phototropism and bends toward the light at a rate of 0.3 degrees per minute. How many hours will it take the plant to bend 90 degrees?

Plant Responses to the Environment

What happens when you get really cold? Do your teeth chatter as you shiver uncontrollably? If so, your brain is responding to the stimulus of cold by causing your muscles to twitch rapidly and generate warmth. Anything that causes a reaction in an organ or tissue is a stimulus. Do plant tissues respond to stimuli? They sure do! Examples of stimuli to which plants respond include light, gravity, and changing seasons.

Plant Tropisms

Some plants respond to an environmental stimulus, such as light or gravity, by growing in a particular direction. Growth in response to a stimulus is called a **tropism.** Tropisms are either positive or negative, depending on whether the plant grows toward or away from the stimulus. Plant growth toward a stimulus is a positive tropism. Plant growth away from a stimulus is a negative tropism. Two examples of tropisms are phototropism and gravitropism.

Sensing Light If you place a houseplant so that it gets light from only one direction, such as from a window, the shoot tips bend toward the light. A change in the growth of a plant that is caused by light is called **phototropism** (foh TAH troh PIZ uhm). As shown in **Figure 9,** the bending occurs when cells on one side of the shoot grow longer than cells on the other side of the shoot.

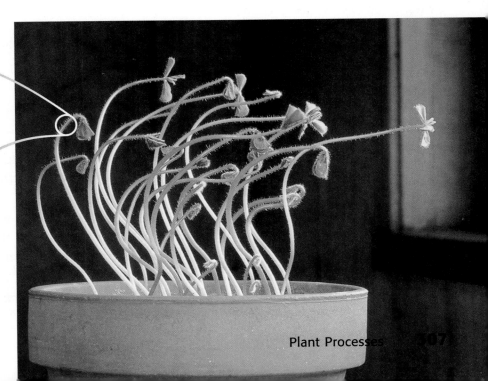

Figure 9 *The plant cells on the dark side of the shoot grow longer than the cells on the other side. This causes the shoot to bend toward the light.*

Which Way Is Up? When the growth of a plant changes direction in response to the direction of gravity, the change is called **gravitropism** (GRAV i TROH PIZ uhm). The effect of gravitropism is demonstrated by the plants in **Figure 10.** A few days after a plant is placed on its side or turned upside down, the roots and shoots show a change in their direction of growth. Most shoot tips have negative gravitropism—they grow upward, away from the center of the Earth. In contrast, most root tips have positive gravitropism—they grow downward, toward the center of the Earth.

Figure 10 *Gravity is a stimulus that causes plants to change their direction of growth.*

▲ To grow away from the pull of gravity, this plant has grown upward.

This plant has recently ▶ been upside down.

Quick Lab

Which Way Is Up?

Will a potted plant grow sideways? You will need **several potted plants** to find out. Use **duct tape** to secure **cardboard** around the base of each plant so that the soil will not fall out. Turn the plants on their sides and observe what happens over the next few days. Describe two stimuli that might have influenced the direction of growth. How might gravitropism benefit a plant?

✓ Self-Check

1. Use the following terms to create a concept map: tropism, stimuli, light, gravity, phototropism, and gravitropism.
2. Imagine a plant in which light causes a negative phototropism. Will the plant bend to the left or to the right when light is shining only on the plant's right side?

(See page 782 to check your answers.)

Seasonal Responses

What would happen if a plant living in an area that has severe winters flowered in December? Would the plant be able to successfully produce seeds and fruits? If your answer is no, you're correct. If the plant produced any flowers at all, the flowers would probably freeze and die before they had the chance to produce mature seeds. Plants living in regions with cold winters can detect the change in seasons. How do plants do this?

As Different as Night and Day Think about what happens as the seasons change. For example, what happens to the length of the days and the nights? As autumn and winter approach, the days get shorter and the nights get longer. The opposite happens when spring and summer approach.

The difference between day length and night length is an important environmental stimulus for many plants. This stimulus can cause plants to begin reproducing. Some plants flower only in late summer or early autumn, when the night length is long. These plants are called short-day plants. Examples of short-day plants include poinsettias (shown in **Figure 11**), ragweed, and chrysanthemums. Other plants flower in spring or early summer, when night length is short. These plants are called long-day plants. Clover, spinach, and lettuce are examples of long-day plants.

Astronomy CONNECTION

Summer | Winter
Sun

The seasons are caused by Earth's tilt and its orbit around the sun. We have summer when the Northern Hemisphere is tilted toward the sun and the sun's energy falls more directly on the Northern Hemisphere. While the Northern Hemisphere experiences the warm season, the Southern Hemisphere experiences the cold season. The opposite of this occurs when the Northern Hemisphere is tilted away from the sun.

Figure 11 *Night length determines when poinsettias flower.*

Early summer

In the early summer, night length is short. At this time, poinsettia leaves are all green, and there are no flowers.

Late fall

Poinsettias flower in the fall, when nights are longer. The leaves surrounding the flower clusters turn red. Professional growers use artificial lighting to control the timing of the color change.

Can Trees Tell Time?

One fall afternoon, Holly looks into her backyard. She notices that a tree that was full of leaves the week before is now completely bare. What caused the tree to drop all its leaves?

Holly came up with the following hypothesis:

Each leaf on the tree was able to sense day length. When the day length became short enough, each leaf responded by falling.

Design an experiment that would test Holly's hypothesis.

Seasonal Changes in Leaves All trees lose their leaves at some time. Some trees, such as pine and holly, shed some of their leaves year-round so that some leaves are always present on the tree. These trees are called **evergreen.** Evergreen trees have leaves adapted to survive throughout the year.

Other trees, such as the maple tree in **Figure 12,** are **deciduous** and lose all their leaves at the same time each year. Deciduous trees usually lose their leaves before winter begins. In tropical climates that have wet and dry seasons, deciduous trees lose their leaves before the dry season. Having bare branches during the winter or during the dry season may reduce the water lost by transpiration. The loss of leaves helps plants survive low temperatures or long periods without rain.

Figure 12 *The leaves of some deciduous trees, like the maple shown here, change from green to orange in autumn. In winter, the maple is bare.*

As shown in **Figure 13,** leaves often change color before they fall. As autumn approaches, chlorophyll, the green pigment used in photosynthesis, breaks down. As chlorophyll is lost from leaves, other yellow and orange pigments are revealed. These pigments were always present in the leaves but were hidden by the green chlorophyll. Some leaves also have red pigments, which also become visible when chlorophyll is broken down.

BRAIN FOOD

In autumn, trees growing near streetlights keep their leaves longer than their rural counterparts.

Summer

Amount

Pigment color

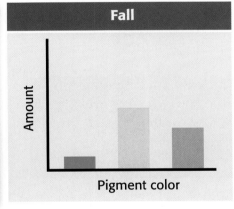

Fall

Amount

Pigment color

Figure 13 *The breakdown of chlorophyll in the autumn is a seasonal response in many trees. As the amount of chlorophyll in leaves decreases, other pigments become visible.*

REVIEW

1. What are the effects of the tropisms caused by light and gravity?

2. What is the difference between a short-day plant and a long-day plant?

3. How does the loss of leaves help a plant survive winter or long periods without rain?

4. **Applying Concepts** If a plant does not flower when exposed to 12 hours of daylight but does flower when exposed to 15 hours of daylight, is it a short-day plant or a long-day plant?

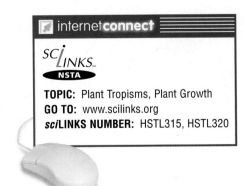

internet**connect**

SCiLINKS.
NSTA

TOPIC: Plant Tropisms, Plant Growth
GO TO: www.scilinks.org
*sci***LINKS NUMBER:** HSTL315, HSTL320

Chapter Highlights

Vocabulary

dormant (*p. 302*)

Section Notes

• Sexual reproduction in flowering plants requires pollination and fertilization. Fertilization is the joining of an egg and a sperm cell.

• After fertilization has occurred, the ovules develop into seeds that contain plant embryos. The ovary develops into a fruit.

• Once seeds mature, they may become dormant. Seeds sprout when they are in an environment with the proper temperature and the proper amounts of water and oxygen.

• Many flowering plants can reproduce asexually without flowers.

Vocabulary

chlorophyll (*p. 304*)
cellular respiration (*p. 305*)
stomata (*p. 306*)
transpiration (*p. 306*)

Section Notes

• During photosynthesis, leaves absorb sunlight and form glucose from carbon dioxide and water.

• During cellular respiration, a plant uses oxygen and releases carbon dioxide and water. Glucose is converted into a form of energy that cells can use.

• Plants take in carbon dioxide and release oxygen and water through stomata in their leaves.

Labs

Food Factory Waste (*p. 728*)
Weepy Weeds (*p. 730*)

☑ Skills Check

Visual Understanding

CIRCLE GRAPH A circle graph is a great visual for illustrating fractions without using numbers. Each circle graph on page 309 represents a 24-hour period. The blue area represents the fraction of time in which there is no sunlight, and the gold area represents the fraction of time in which there is light. As shown by the graph, early summer is about two-thirds day and one-third night.

BAR GRAPHS As shown on page 311, bar graphs are often used to compare numbers. The graph at right compares the success rate of flower seeds from five seed producers. As shown by the bar height, company D, at about 88 percent, had the highest rate of success.

Vocabulary

tropism *(p. 307)*

phototropism *(p. 307)*

gravitropism *(p. 308)*

evergreen *(p. 310)*

deciduous *(p. 310)*

Section Notes

- A tropism is plant growth in response to an environmental stimulus, such as light or gravity. Plant growth toward a stimulus is a positive tropism. Plant growth away from a stimulus is a negative tropism.

- Phototropism is growth in response to the direction of light. Gravitropism is growth in response to the direction of gravity.

- The change in the amount of daylight and darkness that occurs with changing seasons often controls plant reproduction.

- Evergreen plants have leaves adapted to survive throughout the year. Deciduous plants lose their leaves before cold or dry seasons. The loss of leaves helps deciduous plants survive low temperatures and dry periods.

internetconnect

GO TO: go.hrw.com

Visit the **HRW** Web site for a variety of learning tools related to this chapter. Just type in the keyword:

KEYWORD: HSTPL2

*sci*LINKS.

N S T A

GO TO: www.scilinks.org

Visit the **National Science Teachers Association** on-line Web site for Internet resources related to this chapter. Just type in the *sci*LINKS number for more information about the topic:

TOPIC: Reproduction of Plants	*sci*LINKS NUMBER: HSTL305
TOPIC: Photosynthesis	*sci*LINKS NUMBER: HSTL310
TOPIC: Plant Tropisms	*sci*LINKS NUMBER: HSTL315
TOPIC: Plant Growth	*sci*LINKS NUMBER: HSTL320

Chapter Review

USING VOCABULARY

To complete the following sentences, choose the correct term from each pair of terms listed below:

1. After seeds develop fully, and before they sprout, they may become __?__. (*deciduous* or *dormant*)

2. During __?__, energy from sunlight is used to make sugar. (*photosynthesis* or *phototropism*)

3. The loss of water through stomata is called __?__. (*transpiration* or *tropism*)

4. A change in plant growth in response to the direction of light is called __?__. (*gravitropism* or *phototropism*)

5. Plants that have leaves year-round are __?__. (*deciduous* or *evergreen*)

UNDERSTANDING CONCEPTS

Multiple Choice

6. The cells that open and close the stomata are the
   a. guard cells.
   b. xylem cells.
   c. cuticle cells.
   d. mesophyll cells.

7. Plant cells need carbon dioxide, which is used for
   a. cellular respiration.   c. fertilization.
   b. phototropism.   d. photosynthesis.

8. When chlorophyll breaks down,
   a. pollination occurs.
   b. other pigments become visible.
   c. red pigments disappear.
   d. photosynthesis occurs.

9. Which of the following sequences shows the correct order of events that occur after an insect brings pollen to a flower?
   a. germination, fertilization, pollination
   b. fertilization, germination, pollination
   c. pollination, germination, fertilization
   d. pollination, fertilization, germination

10. When the amount of water transpired from a plant's leaves is greater than the amount absorbed by its roots,
   a. the cuticle conserves water.
   b. the stem exhibits positive gravitropism.
   c. the plant wilts.
   d. the plant recovers from wilting.

11. Ovules develop into
   a. fruits.   c. flowers.
   b. ovaries.   d. seeds.

Short Answer

12. What is the relationship between transpiration, the cuticle, and the stomata?

13. What is the stimulus in phototropism? What is the plant's response to the stimulus?

14. Give an example of a positive tropism and a negative tropism.

Concept Mapping

15. Use the following terms to create a concept map: plantlets, flower, seeds, ovules, plant reproduction, asexual, runners.

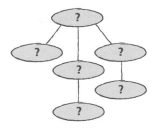

CRITICAL THINKING AND PROBLEM SOLVING

Write one or two sentences to answer the following questions:

16. Many plants that live in regions that experience severe winters have seeds that will not germinate at any temperature unless the seeds have been exposed first to a long period of cold. How might this characteristic help new plants survive?

17. If you wanted to make poinsettias bloom and turn red in the summer, what would you have to do?

18. What benefit is there for a plant's shoots to have positive phototropism? What benefit is there for its roots to have positive gravitropism?

MATH IN SCIENCE

19. If a particular leaf has a surface area of 8 cm^2, what is its surface area in square millimeters? (Hint: 1 cm^2 = 100 mm^2.)

20. Leaves have an average of 100 stomata per square millimeter of surface area. How many stomata would you expect the leaf in question 19 to possess?

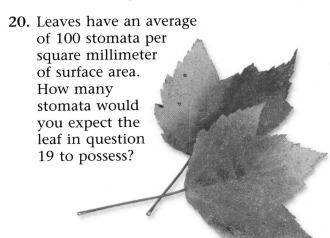

INTERPRETING GRAPHICS

Look at the illustrations below, and then answer the questions that follow. The illustration shows part of an experiment on phototropism in young plants. In part (1), the young plants have just been placed in the light after being in the dark. The shoot tip of one plant is cut off. The other tip is not cut. In part (2), the plants from part (1) are exposed to light from one direction.

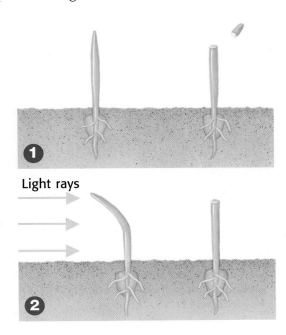

Light rays

21. Why did the plant with the intact tip bend toward the light?

22. Why did the plant with the removed tip remain straight?

NOW What Do You Think?

Take a minute to review your answers to the ScienceLog questions on page 299. Have your answers changed? If necessary, revise your answers based on what you have learned since you began this chapter.

MUTANT MUSTARD

The tiny mustard flowers grown by Elliot Meyerowitz are horribly deformed. You may think they are the result of a terrible accident, but Meyerowitz created these mutants on purpose. In fact, he is very proud of these flowers because they may help him solve an important biological mystery.

▲ *Elliot Meyerowitz, shown here in his laboratory, has raised about a million individual specimens of a mustard variety known as* Arabidopsis thaliana.

Normal and Abnormal Flowers

Normally, mustard flowers have four distinct parts that are arranged in a specific way. Many of the plants grown by Meyerowitz and his colleagues, however, are far from normal. Some have leaves in the center of their flowers. Others have seed-producing ovaries where the petals should be. At first glance, the arrangement of the parts seems random, but the structure of each flower has actually been determined by a small number of genes.

A Simple Model

After many years of careful studies, Meyerowitz and his colleagues have identified most of the genes that control the mustard flower's development. With this information, Meyerowitz has discovered patterns that have led to a surprisingly simple model. The model points to just three classes of genes that determine what happens to the various parts of a flower as it develops. He learned that if one or more of those gene classes is inactivated, a mutant mustard plant results.

Pieces of an Old Puzzle

By understanding how genes shape the growth of flowers, Meyerowitz hopes to add pieces to a long-standing puzzle involving the origin of flowering plants. Scientists estimate that flowering plants first appeared on Earth about 125 million years ago and that they quickly spread to become the dominant plants on Earth. By studying which genes produce flowers in present-day plants, Meyerowitz and his colleagues hope to learn how flowering plants evolved in the first place.

Meyerowitz's mutant plants are well qualified to add to our understanding of plant genetics. But don't look for these mustard plants in your local flower shop. These strange mutants won't win any prizes for beauty!

▲ *Meyerowitz alters the genes of a mustard plant so that it develops a mutant flower. The inset shows a normal flower.*

Think About It

▶ It is possible to genetically change a plant. What are some possible risks of such a practice?

EYE ON THE ENVIRONMENT

A Rainbow of Cotton

Think about your favorite T-shirt. Chances are, it's made of cotton and brightly colored. The fibers in cotton plants, however, are naturally white. They must be dyed with chemicals—often toxic ones—to create the bright colors seen in T-shirts and other fabrics. To minimize the use of toxic chemicals, an ingenious woman named Sally Fox had an idea: What if you could grow the cotton *already colored*?

Learning from the Past

Cotton fibers come from the plant's seed pods, or *bolls.* Bolls are a little bigger than a golf ball and open at maturity to reveal a fuzzy mass of fibers and seeds. Once the seeds are removed, the fibers can be twisted into yarn and used to make many kinds of fabric. Sally Fox began her career as an *entomologist,* a scientist who studies insects. She first found out about colored cotton while studying pest resistance. Although most of the cotton grown for textiles is white, different shades of cotton have been harvested by Native Americans for centuries. These types of cotton showed some resistance to pests but had fibers too short to be used by the textile industry.

In 1982, Fox began the very slow process of crossbreeding different varieties of cotton to produce strains that were both colored *and* long-fibered. Her cotton is registered under the name FoxFibre® and has earned her high praise.

Solutions to Environmental Problems

The textile industry is the source of two major environmental hazards. The first hazard is the dyes used for cotton fabrics. The second is the pesticides that are required for growing cotton. These pesticides, like the dyes, can cause damage to both living things and natural resources, such as water and land.

Fox's cotton represents a solution to both of these problems. First, since the cotton is naturally colored, no dyes are necessary. Second, the native strains of cotton from which she bred her plants passed on their natural pest resistance. Thus, fewer pesticides are necessary to grow her cotton successfully.

Sally Fox's efforts demonstrate that with ingenuity and patience, science and agriculture can work together in new ways to offer solutions to environmental problems.

▲ *Sally Fox in a field of colored cotton*

Some Detective Work

▶ Like Fox's cotton, many types of plants and breeds of domesticated animals have been created through artificial selection. Research to find out where and when your favorite fruit or breed of dog was first established.

317

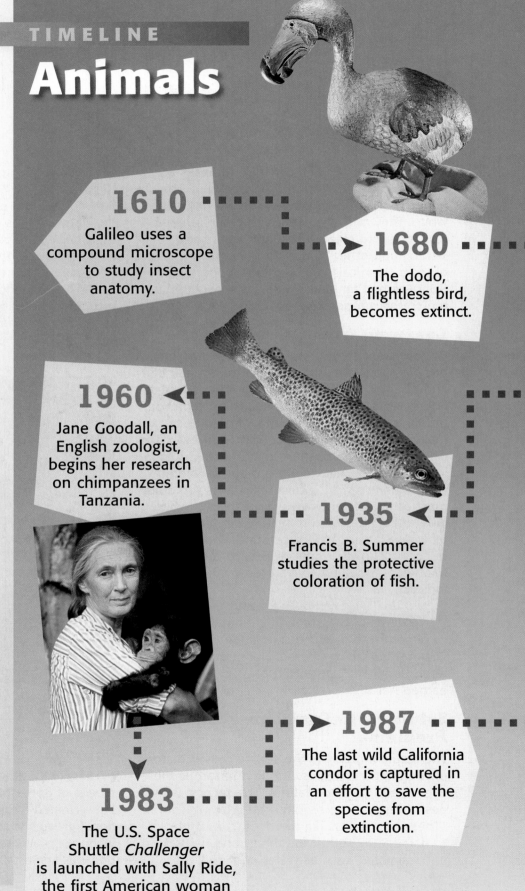

UNIT 5

Have you ever been to a zoo or watched a wild-animal program on television? If so, you have some idea of the many different types of animals found on Earth—from tiny insects to massive whales.

Animals are fascinating, in part because of their variety in appearance and behavior. They also teach us about ourselves because we humans are also classified as animals. Humans have always observed and interacted with their fellow animals.

In this unit you will learn about many different types of animals, maybe even some that you never knew existed. So get ready for an animal adventure!

1610
Galileo uses a compound microscope to study insect anatomy.

1680
The dodo, a flightless bird, becomes extinct.

1960
Jane Goodall, an English zoologist, begins her research on chimpanzees in Tanzania.

1935
Francis B. Summer studies the protective coloration of fish.

1987
The last wild California condor is captured in an effort to save the species from extinction.

1983
The U.S. Space Shuttle *Challenger* is launched with Sally Ride, the first American woman in space, on board.

1693

John Ray correctly identifies whales as mammals.

1761

The first veterinary school is founded in Lyons, France.

1775

J. C. Fabricius develops a system for the classification of insects.

1827

John James Audubon publishes the first edition of *Birds of North America.*

1882

Research on the ship *The Albatross* helps to increase our knowledge of marine life.

1839

The first bicycle is constructed.

1995

Fourteen Canadian gray wolves are reintroduced to Yellowstone National Park.

1998

Keiko, the killer-whale star of the movie *Free Willy*, is taught to catch fish so that he can be released from captivity.

14 Animals and Behavior

This Really Happened . . .

Robert S. Ridgely and Lelis Navarette are ornithologists, people who study birds. In November 1997, they were hiking in the Andes mountains of Ecuador and recording bird songs. Suddenly they heard a sound that was a cross between the hoot of an owl and the bark of a dog. Even though they both had spent a lot of time in the woods, neither of the scientists had ever heard such a sound before.

What was in the woods? They kept hiking, and almost 40 minutes later, they heard the sound again. This time, Ridgely, shown below, taped the sound and quickly played it back. The creature answered and came rushing through the woods toward them. It was a bird! But neither of the experts had ever seen a bird like it.

It turned out to be a species that no one had ever seen before! The bird is about 25 cm long, with long legs and a short tail. It has a broad white stripe across its face and a crown of black. It hops on the forest floor and eats large insects. So far, the bird does not have a name, but Ridgely and Navarette have been studying it and will name it soon.

For centuries, people like Robert Ridgely and Lelis Navarette have used their observation skills to study animals and their behavior. We now know of over 1 million animal species, and we have learned much about how animals live and interact with other animals. But there are always more discoveries to be made!

What Do You Think?

In your ScienceLog, try to answer the following questions based on what you already know:

1. What characteristics make an animal different from a plant?

2. How do animals know when to migrate?

3. Write down everything you notice about each animal. What kind of animal is it? What does it look like? You may want to draw a picture of it. How big is it? What is it doing? Why? Is it moving? How does it move? Is it eating? What is it eating?

Analysis

4. Compare the two animals you studied. How are they similar? How are they different?

5. How do the animals move? Do the ways they move give you clues about how they defend themselves or communicate with other animals?

6. Can you tell what each animal eats? What characteristics of these animals help them find or catch food?

Go on a Safari!

You don't have to travel far to see interesting animals. You can see ants walking along a sidewalk. Look for flowers, and you'll probably see bees. Turn over some soil, and you may find earthworms. Look up, and you might see birds. If you are near a stream, you may see fish and salamanders and maybe a few mosquitoes. And don't forget household pets!

Procedure

1. Go outside and find **two different animals** to observe, or use the animals that your teacher supplies.

2. Without disturbing the animals, sit quietly and watch them for a few minutes from a distance. You may want to use **binoculars** or a **magnifying lens** to help you get a closer look. **Caution:** Always be careful around animals that may bite or sting.

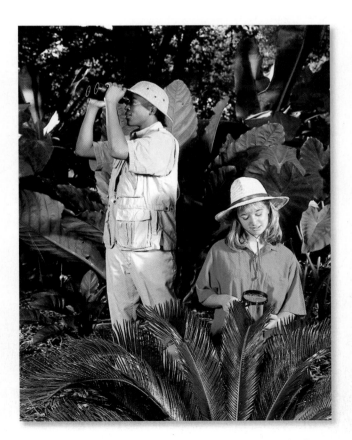

Terms to Learn

vertebrate   tissue
invertebrate   organ
embryo   consumer

What You'll Do

◆ Describe the differences between vertebrates and invertebrates.
◆ Explain the characteristics of animals.

What Is an Animal?

What do you think of when you hear the word *animal*? You may think of your dog or cat. You may think about giraffes or grizzly bears or other creatures you've seen in zoos or on television. But would you think about a sponge? Natural bath sponges, like the one in **Figure 1,** are the remains of an animal that lived in the ocean!

Animals come in many different shapes and sizes. Some have four legs and fur, but most do not. Some are too small to be seen without a microscope, and others are bigger than a car. But they are all part of the fascinating world of animals.

The Animal Kingdom

Scientists have named about 1 million species of animals. How many different kinds of animals do you see in **Figure 2**? It may surprise you to learn that in addition to sponges, sea anemones and corals are also animals. So are spiders, fish, birds, and dolphins. Slugs, whales, kangaroos, and humans are animals too. Scientists have divided all these animal species into about 35 phyla and classes.

Most animals look nothing like humans. However, we do share characteristics with a group of animals called vertebrates. Any animal with a skull and a backbone is a **vertebrate.** Vertebrates include fishes, amphibians, reptiles, birds, and mammals.

Figure 1 *This natural sponge used to be alive.*

Figure 2 *All of the living things in this picture are classified as animals. Do they look like animals to you?*

Even though you are probably most familiar with vertebrates, we are definitely the minority among living things. Less than five percent of known animal species are vertebrates. Take a look at **Figure 3.** As you can see, the great majority of known animal species are insects, snails, jellyfish, worms, and other **invertebrates,** animals without backbones. In fact, more than one-fourth of all animal species are beetles!

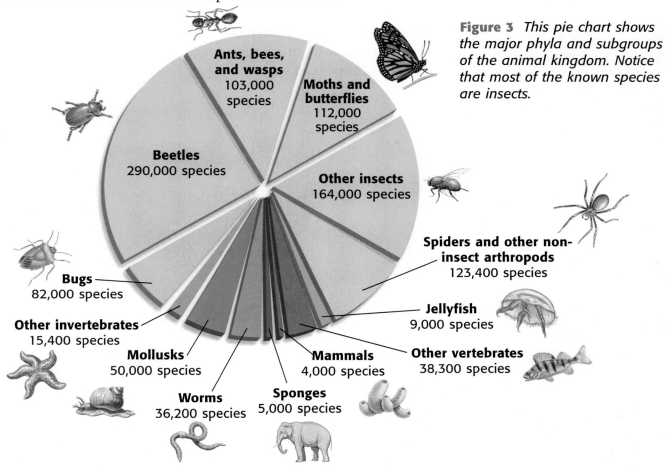

Figure 3 *This pie chart shows the major phyla and subgroups of the animal kingdom. Notice that most of the known species are insects.*

Ants, bees, and wasps
103,000 species

Moths and butterflies
112,000 species

Beetles
290,000 species

Other insects
164,000 species

Spiders and other non-insect arthropods
123,400 species

Jellyfish
9,000 species

Other vertebrates
38,300 species

Mammals
4,000 species

Sponges
5,000 species

Worms
36,200 species

Mollusks
50,000 species

Other invertebrates
15,400 species

Bugs
82,000 species

That's an Animal?

Sponges don't look like other animals. Indeed, until about 200 years ago, most people thought sponges were plants. Earthworms don't look anything like penguins, and no one would confuse a frog for a lion. So why do we say all these things are animals? What determines whether something is an animal, a plant, or something else?

There is no single answer. But all animals share characteristics that set them apart from all other living things.

Animals have many cells. All animals are *multicellular,* which means they are made of many cells. Your own body contains about 13 trillion cells. Animal cells are eukaryotic, and they do not have cell walls. Animal cells are surrounded by cell membranes only.

Figure 4 *Several sperm surround an egg. Only one sperm can fuse with the egg to form a new individual.*

Self-Check

Why are humans classified as vertebrates? *(See page 782 to check your answer.)*

Animals usually reproduce by sexual reproduction. Animals make sex cells, eggs or sperm. When an egg and a sperm come together at fertilization, they form the first cell of a new individual. **Figure 4** shows an egg surrounded by sperm during fertilization. Some animals, like sponges and sea stars, can also reproduce asexually, by budding or fragmentation.

Animals develop from embryos. The fertilized egg cell divides into many different cells to form an embryo. An **embryo** is an organism in the earliest stage of development. A mouse embryo is shown in **Figure 5.**

Head — Tail — Hind leg — Front leg

Figure 5 A Mouse Embryo

Animals have many specialized parts. An animal's body has distinct parts that do different things. When a fertilized egg cell divides into many cells to form an embryo, the cells become different from each other. Some may become skin cells. Others may become muscle cells, nerve cells, or bone cells. These different kinds of cells arrange themselves to form **tissues,** which are collections of similar cells. For example, muscle cells form muscle tissue, and nerve cells form nerve tissue.

Most animals also have organs. An **organ** is a combination of two or more tissues. Your heart, lungs, and kidneys are all organs. All animals, including the shark shown in **Figure 6,** have different organs for different jobs.

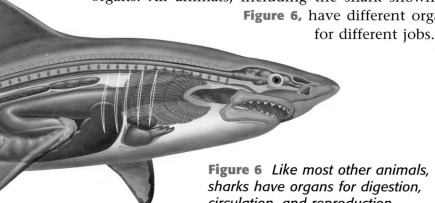

Figure 6 *Like most other animals, sharks have organs for digestion, circulation, and reproduction.*

Animals move. Most animals can move from place to place. As shown in **Figure 7**, they fly, run, swim, and jump. While it's true that other organisms move, animals are more likely to move quickly in a single direction. Some animals do not move much, though. Sea anemones and clams, for example, attach to rocks or the ocean floor and wait for food to arrive. But most animals are active.

Figure 7 *Animals move in many different ways.*

Animals are consumers. Animals cannot make their own food. All animals survive by eating other organisms, parts of other organisms, or the products of other organisms. In other words, animals are consumers. A **consumer** is an organism that eats other organisms. This trait sets animals apart from plants. Except for the Venus' flytrap and a handful of other plants, plants do not eat other living things. Plants make their own food.

Animal food is as varied as animals themselves. Rabbits and caterpillars eat plants. Lions and spiders eat other animals. Reindeer eat lichens. Mosquitoes drink blood. Butterflies drink nectar from flowers.

internet**connect**

*SC*LINKS
NSTA

TOPIC: Vertebrates and Invertebrates
GO TO: www.scilinks.org
*sci*LINKS NUMBER: HSTL330

REVIEW

1. What characteristics separate animals from plants?

2. How are tissues and organs related?

3. **Interpreting Illustrations** What characteristics of the chameleon shown at far right tell you it is an animal?

Animal Behavior

In the last section, you learned the characteristics that help us recognize an animal. One characteristic of most animals is that they move. Animals jump, run, fly, dart, scurry, slither, and glide. But animals don't move just for the sake of moving. They move for a reason. They run from enemies. They climb for food. They build homes. Even the tiniest mite can actively stalk its dinner, battle for territory, or migrate. All of these activities are known as behavior.

What You'll Do

◆ Explain the difference between learned and innate behavior.
◆ Explain the difference between hibernation and estivation.
◆ Give examples of how a biological clock influences behavior.
◆ Describe circadian rhythms.
◆ Explain how animals navigate.

Survival Behavior

In order to stay alive, an animal has to do many things. It must find food and water, avoid being eaten, and have a place to live. Animals have many behaviors that help them accomplish these tasks.

Looking for Lunch Animals use many different methods to find or catch food. Owls swoop down on unsuspecting mice. Bees fly from flower to flower collecting nectar. Koala bears climb trees to get eucalyptus leaves. Jellyfish harpoon and lasso their prey with their tentacles. Some animals, such as the chimpanzee shown in **Figure 8,** use tools to get dinner. Whatever the meal of choice, animals have adapted to their surroundings so that they can obtain the most food using the least amount of energy.

How to Avoid Being Eaten Animals that eat other animals are known as **predators.** The animal being eaten is the **prey.** At any given moment, an animal *diner* can become another animal's *dinner.* Therefore, animals looking for food often have to think about other things besides which food looks or tastes the best. Animals will pass up a good meal if it's too dangerous to get. But being careful is just one method of defense. Keep reading to find out what other things animals do to stay alive.

Figure 8 *Chimpanzees make and use tools in order to get ants and other food out of hard-to-reach places.*

Hiding Out One way to avoid being eaten is to be hard to see. A rabbit often "freezes" so that its natural color blends into a background of shrubs or grass. Blending in with the background is called *camouflage*. Many animals mimic twigs, leaves, stones, bark, or other materials in their environment. The insect called a walking stick looks just like a twig. Some walking sticks even sway a bit, as though a breeze were blowing. See **Figure 9** for another example of camouflage.

In Your Face The horns of a bull and the spines of a porcupine clearly signal trouble to a potential predator, but other defenses may not be as obvious. For example, animals may defend themselves with chemicals. The skunk and the bombardier beetle both spray predators with irritating chemicals. Bees, ants, and wasps inject a powerful acid into their attackers. The skin of both the South American dart-poison frog and the hooded pito-hui bird of New Guinea contains a deadly toxin. Any predator that eats, or even tries to eat, one of these animals will likely die.

Warning! Animals with a chemical defense need a way to warn predators that they should look elsewhere for a meal. Their chemical weapons are often advertised by the animal's outer covering, which has a bright design called *warning coloration*, as shown in **Figure 10.** Predators will avoid any animal with the colors and patterns they associate with pain, illness, or other unpleasant experiences. The most common warning colors are vivid shades of red, yellow, orange, black, and white.

Figure 9 *This is a picture of a caterpillar camouflaged as a twig. Can you find the caterpillar?*

Octopuses are camouflage experts. They can change the color of their entire body in less than 1 second.

Figure 10 *The warning coloration of the hooded pitohui warns predators that it is poisonous. The yellow and black stripes of the stinging yellow jacket are another example.*

Why Do They Behave That Way?

How do animals know when a situation is dangerous? How do predators know which warning coloration to avoid? Sometimes animals instinctively know what to do, but sometimes they have to learn. Biologists call these two kinds of animal behavior innate behavior and learned behavior.

It's in the Genes Behavior that doesn't depend on learning or experience is known as **innate behavior.** Innate behaviors are influenced by genes. Humans inherit genes that give us the ability to walk. Puppies inherit the tendency to chew, bees the tendency to fly, and earthworms the tendency to burrow.

Some innate behaviors are present at birth. Newborn whales all have the innate ability to swim. Other innate behaviors develop months or years after birth. For example, the tendency of a bird to sing is innate. But a bird does not sing until it is nearly grown.

What did the bumblebee do to Aunt Flossie? Find out on page 734.

Animal School Just because a behavior is innate does not mean that it cannot be modified. Learning can change innate behavior. **Learned behavior** is behavior that has been learned from experience or from observing other animals. Humans inherit the tendency to speak. But the language we speak is not inherited. We might learn English, Spanish, Chinese, or Tagalog.

Humans are not the only animals that modify inherited behaviors through learning. Nearly all animals can learn. For example, many young animals learn by watching their parents. **Figure 11** shows a monkey that learned a new behavior by observation.

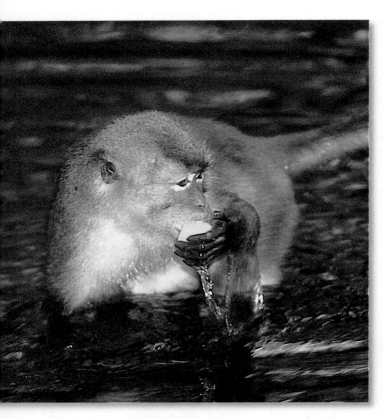

Figure 11 *One Japanese macaque washed the sand off a sweet potato it found on the beach. Now all of the macaques on the island wash their potatoes.*

REVIEW

1. How do innate behavior and learned behavior differ?

2. **Applying Concepts** How does the effectiveness of warning coloration for protection depend on learning?

Seasonal Behavior

In many places, animals must deal with the winter hardships of little food and bitter cold. Some avoid winter by traveling to places that are warmer. Others collect and store food. Frogs bury themselves in mud, and insects burrow into the ground.

World Travelers When food is scarce because of winter or drought, many animals migrate. To *migrate* is to travel from one place to another. Animals migrate to find food, water, or safe nesting grounds. Whales, salmon, bats, and even chimpanzees migrate. Each winter, monarch butterflies, shown in **Figure 12,** gather in central Mexico from all over North America to wait for spring. And each year, birds in the Northern Hemisphere fly thousands of kilometers south. In the spring, they return north to nest.

Slowing Down Some animals deal with food and water shortages by hibernating. **Hibernation** is a period of inactivity and decreased body temperature that some animals experience in winter. Hibernating animals survive on stored body fat. Many animals hibernate, including mice, squirrels, and skunks. While an animal hibernates, its temperature, heart rate, and breathing rate drop. Some hibernating animals drop their body temperature to a few degrees above freezing and do not wake for weeks at a time. Other animals, like the polar bears in **Figure 13,** do not enter deep hibernation. Their body temperature does not drop as severely, and they sleep for shorter periods of time.

Winter is not the only time that resources can be scarce. Many desert squirrels and mice experience a similar internal slowdown in the hottest part of the summer, when they run low on water and food. This period of reduced activity in the summer is called **estivation.**

Figure 12 *When the monarchs gather in Mexico, there can be as many as 4 million butterflies per acre!*

Don't wake the bats!
Read about the effects of humans on bat hibernation on page 340.

Figure 13 *Bears do not enter deep hibernation. However, they have periods of inactivity in which they do not eat, and their body functions slow down.*

QuickLab

How Long Is a Minute?

Do you have an internal clock that helps you keep track of time? Pair up with a classmate. Your partner will start a **stopwatch** and say, "Go." When you think a minute has passed, say, "Stop!" Check the time. Try several times, and keep a record of your results. Then trade places and let your partner try. Were the recorded times close to a minute? Did your performance improve? Try again, using your pulse or your breathing as a guide. Were these times closer? Do you think you have an internal clock? Explain.

The Rhythms of Life

Humans need clocks and calendars to tell us when to get up and go to school, when a movie starts, and when it is someone's birthday. Other animals need to know when to store food and when to fly south for the winter. The internal clocks and calendars that animals use are called biological clocks. A **biological clock** is the internal control of natural cycles. Animals may use clues from their surroundings, such as the length of the day and the temperature, to set their clocks.

Some biological clocks keep track of very small amounts of time. Other biological clocks control daily cycles. These daily cycles are called **circadian rhythms.** *Circadian* means "around the day." Most animals wake up at about the same time each day and get sleepy at about the same time each night. This is an example of a circadian rhythm.

Some biological clocks control even longer cycles. Seasonal cycles are nearly universal among animals. Animals hibernate at certain times of the year and breed at other times. And every spring, migrating birds head north. Biological clocks control all of these cycles.

How Do Animals Find Their Way?

If you were planning a trip, you'd probably consult a map. If you were hiking, you might rely on a compass or trail markers to find your way. When it's time to migrate, how do animals, such as the arctic terns in **Figure 14,** know which way to go? They must *navigate,* or find their way from one place to another.

Figure 14 *Each year, arctic terns make a 38,000 km round trip from the Northern Hemisphere to Antarctica.*

APPLY

Jet Lag

When people travel to places that are in a different time zone, they frequently suffer from "jet lag." Here's an example: New York time is 6 hours behind Paris time. A traveler from New York who is staying in Paris is suffering from jet lag. She goes to bed at 10 P.M., Paris time, but she wakes up at midnight, unable to fall back asleep. She lies awake all night and finally falls asleep at about 6 A.M., one hour before her alarm rings. How might circadian rhythms explain her jet lag? When it is 10 P.M. in Paris, what time is it in New York?

Take a Left at the Post Office For short trips, many animals, including humans, use landmarks to navigate. *Landmarks* are fixed objects that an animal uses to find its way. For example, once you see the corner gas station six blocks from your house, you know how to go the rest of the way. The gas station is a landmark for you.

Bees and pigeons have a kind of mental map of landmarks in their home territory. Birds use mountain ranges, rivers, and coastlines to find their way home. Humans and other animals also navigate short distances by using a mental image of an area. Not all landmarks are visual. Blind people can navigate precisely through a familiar house because they know where everything is and how long it takes to cross a room. Pigeons navigate in their home area based on smell as well as sight.

Compass Anyone? Like human sailors, animals use the position of the sun and stars as a map. But some animals, such as migratory birds, have other methods of finding their way. They navigate using the Earth's magnetic field. You can read about this in the Physics Connection at right.

Physics
CONNECTION

Earth's core acts as a giant magnet, with magnetic north and south poles. The strength and direction of the Earth's magnetic field varies from place to place, and many birds use this variation as a map. Some migratory birds have tiny magnetic crystals of magnetite in their heads above their nostrils. Biologists think that the crystals somehow move or stimulate nerves so that a bird knows its position.

REVIEW

1. Why do animals migrate?

2. What are three methods animals use to navigate?

3. How are hibernation and estivation similar? How are they different?

4. **Applying Concepts** Some research suggests that jet lag can be overcome by getting plenty of exposure to sunlight in the new time zone. Why might this method work?

internet**connect**

SC*i*LINKS.
NSTA

TOPIC: Animal Behavior, The Rhythms of Life
GO TO: www.scilinks.org
*sci*LINKS NUMBER: HSTL335, HSTL340

Terms to Learn

social behavior
communication
territory
pheromone

What You'll Do

◆ Discuss ways that animals communicate.
◆ List the advantages and disadvantages of living in groups.

Living Together

Most animals do not live alone; they associate with other animals. When animals interact, it may be in large groups or one on one. Animals may work together, or they may compete with one another. All of this behavior is called social behavior. **Social behavior** is the interaction between animals of the same species. Whether friendly or hostile, all social behavior requires communication.

Communication

Imagine what life would be like if people could not talk or read. There would be no telephones, no televisions, no books, and no Internet. The world would certainly be a lot different! Language is an important way for humans to communicate. In **communication,** a signal must travel from one animal to another, and the receiver of the signal must respond in some way.

Communication helps animals live together, find food, avoid enemies, and protect their homes. Animals communicate to warn others of danger, to identify family members, to frighten predators, and to find mates. Some of the most dramatic uses of communication are courtship displays. *Courtship* is special behavior by animals of the same species that leads to mating. **Figure 15** shows two cranes performing a courtship display.

Animals also communicate to protect their living space. Many animals defend a **territory,** an area that is occupied by one animal or a group of animals and that other members of the species are excluded from. Many species, such as the wolves in **Figure 16,** use their territories for mating, finding food, and raising young.

Figure 15 *Japanese ground cranes perform an elaborate courtship dance.*

Figure 16 *These wolves are howling to discourage neighboring wolves from invading their territory.*

How Do Animals Communicate?

Animals communicate by signaling intentions and information to other animals through smell, sound, vision, and touch. Most animal signals tend to be simple compared with those that we use. But no matter which signal is used, it must convey specific information.

Do You Smell Trouble? One method of communication is chemical. Even single-celled organisms communicate with one another by means of chemicals. In animals, these chemicals are called **pheromones.**

Ants and other insects secrete a variety of pheromones. For example, alarm substances released into the air alert other members of the species to danger. Trail substances are left along a path so that others can follow to find food and return to the nest. Recognition odors on an ant's body announce which colony an ant is from. Such a message signals both friends and enemies, depending on who is receiving the message.

Many animals, including vertebrates, use pheromones to attract or influence members of the opposite sex. Amazingly, elephants and insects use some of the same pheromones to attract mates. Queen butterflies, like the one in **Figure 17,** use pheromones during their courtship displays.

Figure 17 *Queen butterflies use pheromones as part of their courtship display.*

Do You Hear What I Hear? Animals also communicate by making noises. Wolves howl. Dolphins and whales use whistles and complex clicking noises to communicate with others. Male birds may sing songs in the spring to claim their territory or attract a mate.

Sound is a signal that can reach a large number of animals over a large area. Elephants communicate with other elephants kilometers away using rumbles at a frequency too low for most humans to hear, as described in **Figure 18.** Humpback whales sing songs that can be heard for kilometers.

Figure 18 *Elephants communicate with low-pitched sounds that humans cannot hear. When an elephant is communicating this way, the skin on its forehead flutters.*

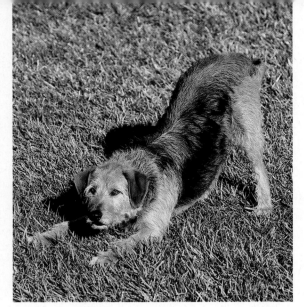

Figure 19 *When dogs want to play, they drop down on their forelegs.*

Showing Off Many forms of communication are visual. When we wink at a friend or frown at an opponent, we are communicating with *body language.* Other animals are no different. **Figure 19** shows one way dogs use body language.

An animal that wants to scare another animal may do something that makes it appear larger. It may ruffle its feathers or fur or open its mouth and show its teeth. Visual displays are also important in courtship. Fireflies blink complex signals in the dark to attract one another.

Getting in Touch An animal may also use touch to communicate, like the honeybee does. A honeybee that finds a patch of flowers rich in nectar returns to its hive to tell fellow workers where the flowers are. Inside the dark hive, the bee communicates by performing a complex figure-eight dance, as shown below, which the other bees learn by observation and touch.

The Dance of the Bees

Honeybees do a "waggle dance" to tell other bees where they've found nectar. As the bee goes through the middle of the figure eight, it communicates two things: the direction of the nectar and the distance to the nectar from the hive. Other worker bees gather closely around the dancing bee to learn the dance. By learning the dance, the bees learn the direction to the nectar.

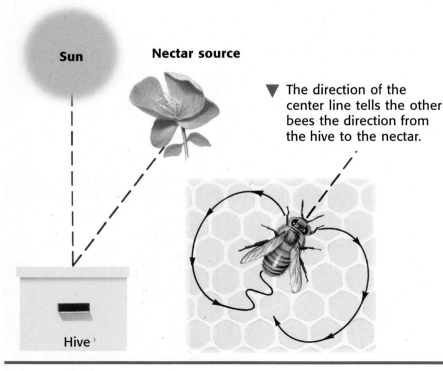

Sun

Nectar source

▼ The direction of the center line tells the other bees the direction from the hive to the nectar.

Hive

▲ As the bee goes through the center, it waggles its abdomen. The number of waggles tells the other bees how far away the nectar is.

Part of the Family

Tigers live alone. Except for the time a mother tiger spends with her cubs, a tiger meets other tigers rarely and for very short periods. Yet the tiger's closest relative, the lion, is rarely alone. Lions live in groups called prides. The members of a pride sleep together, hunt together, and raise their cubs together. **Figure 20** shows two lions at work. Why do some animals live in groups, while others live apart?

Figure 20 *This pair of lions cooperates to hunt a gazelle.*

The Benefits of Living in a Group Living with other animals is much safer than living alone. Large groups can spot a predator or other dangers quickly, and groups of animals can cooperate to defend themselves. For example, if a predator threatens them, a herd of musk oxen will circle their young with their horns pointed outward. Honeybees attack by the thousands when another animal tries to take their honey.

Living together can also help animals find food. Tigers and other animals that hunt alone can usually kill only animals that are smaller than themselves. In contrast, lions, wolves, hyenas, and other predators that hunt cooperatively can kill much larger prey.

The Downside of Living in a Group Living in groups causes problems as well. Animals living in groups attract predators, so they must always be on the lookout, as shown in **Figure 21.** Groups of animals need more food, and animals in groups compete with each other for food and for mates. Individuals in groups can also give each other diseases.

Figure 21 *A ground squirrel whistles a loud alarm to alert other ground squirrels that danger is near.*

REVIEW

1. Scientists have discovered pheromones in humans. Name three other types of animal communication used by humans.

2. Why is communication important? Name three reasons.

3. **Applying Concepts** Considering what you have learned about group living, list two advantages and two disadvantages to living in a group of humans.

internet**connect**

SC*i*LINKS.
NSTA

TOPIC: Communication in the Animal Kingdom
GO TO: www.scilinks.org
*sci*LINKS NUMBER: HSTL345

Chapter Highlights

SECTION 1

Vocabulary

vertebrate (p. 322)
invertebrate (p. 323)
embryo (p. 324)
tissue (p. 324)
organ (p. 324)
consumer (p. 325)

Section Notes

- Animals with a skull and a backbone are vertebrates. Animals without a backbone are invertebrates.

- Animals are multicellular. Their cells are eukaryotic and lack a cell wall.

- Most animals reproduce sexually and develop from embryos.

- Most animals have tissues and organs.

- Most animals move.

- Animals are consumers.

SECTION 2

Vocabulary

predator (p. 326)
prey (p. 326)
innate behavior (p. 328)
learned behavior (p. 328)
hibernation (p. 329)
estivation (p. 329)
biological clock (p. 330)
circadian rhythm (p. 330)

Section Notes

- Many animals use camouflage, chemicals, or both to defend themselves against predators.

- Behavior may be classified as innate or learned. The potential for innate behavior is inherited. Learned behavior depends on experience.

- Some animals migrate to find food, water, or safe nesting grounds.

- Some animals hibernate in the winter, and some estivate in the summer.

☑ Skills Check

Math Concepts

TIME DIFFERENCE In the Apply on page 331, you considered how the time difference between New York and Paris could explain jet lag. Paris time is 6 hours later than New York time. If it is 10 P.M. in Paris, subtract 6 hours to get New York time.

$$10 - 6 = 4$$

It is 4 P.M. in New York. Similarly, when it is 7 A.M. in Paris, it is 1 A.M. in New York.

Visual Understanding

THE DANCE OF THE BEES The illustration on page 334 shows how bees use the waggle dance to communicate the location of a nectar source. Notice the position of the sun in relation to the hive and the nectar source. The bee communicates this information by the direction of the center line in the dance.

SECTION 2

- Animals have internal biological clocks to control natural cycles.
- Daily cycles are called circadian rhythms.
- Some biological clocks are regulated by cues from an animal's environment.
- Animals navigate close to home using landmarks and a mental image of their home area.
- Some animals use the positions of the sun and stars or Earth's magnetic field to navigate.

Labs

Wet, Wiggly Worms! *(p. 732)*

Aunt Flossie and the Bumblebee *(p. 734)*

SECTION 3

Vocabulary

social behavior *(p. 332)*

communication *(p. 332)*

territory *(p. 332)*

pheromone *(p. 333)*

Section Notes

- Communication must include both a signal and a response.
- Two important kinds of communication are courtship and territorial displays.
- Animals communicate through sight, sound, touch, and smell.
- Group living allows animals to spot both prey and predators more easily.

- Groups of animals are more visible to predators than are individuals, and animals in groups must compete with one another for food and mates.

---

 internet connect

GO TO: go.hrw.com

Visit the **HRW** Web site for a variety of learning tools related to this chapter. Just type in the keyword:

KEYWORD: HSTANM

 SCiLINKSSM
NSTA
GO TO: www.scilinks.org

Visit the **National Science Teachers Association** on-line Web site for Internet resources related to this chapter. Just type in the *sci*LINKS number for more information about the topic:

TOPIC: Vertebrates and Invertebrates	*sci*LINKS NUMBER: HSTL330
TOPIC: Animal Behavior	*sci*LINKS NUMBER: HSTL335
TOPIC: The Rhythms of Life	*sci*LINKS NUMBER: HSTL340
TOPIC: Communication in the Animal Kingdom	*sci*LINKS NUMBER: HSTL345

Chapter Review

USING VOCABULARY

To complete the following sentences, choose the correct term from each pair of terms listed below:

1. An animal with a skull and a backbone is __?__. An animal with no backbone is __?__. *(an invertebrate* or *a vertebrate)*

2. A behavior that does not depend on experience is __?__. *(innate* or *learned)*

3. In the summer, an animal enters a state of reduced activity. The animal is __?__. *(estivating* or *hibernating)*

4. Daily cycles are known as __?__. *(biological clocks* or *circadian rhythms)*

5. When an egg and a sperm come together, they form __?__. *(an embryo* or *an organ)*

UNDERSTANDING CONCEPTS

Multiple Choice

6. Which characteristic is not true of animals?
   a. They are multicellular.
   b. They usually reproduce sexually.
   c. They make their own food.
   d. They have tissues.

7. Living in groups
   a. attracts predators.
   b. helps prey spot predators.
   c. helps animals find food.
   d. All of the above

8. Warning coloration is
   a. a kind of camouflage.
   b. a way to warn predators away.
   c. always black and white.
   d. always a sign that an animal is poisonous to eat.

9. Some birds use Earth's magnetic field
   a. to attract mates.
   b. to navigate.
   c. to set their biological clocks.
   d. to defend their territory.

10. To defend against predators, an animal might use
    a. camouflage.   c. toxins.
    b. warning coloration. d. All of the above

Short Answer

11. How are pheromones used in communication?

12. What is a territory? Give an example of a territory from your own environment.

13. What landmarks help you navigate your way home from school?

14. What do migration and hibernation have in common?

Concept Mapping

15. Use the following terms to create a concept map: estivation, circadian rhythms, seasonal behaviors, hibernation, migration, biological clocks.

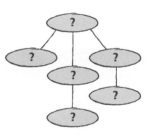

Write one or two sentences to answer the following questions:

16. If you smell a skunk while riding in a car and you shut the car window, has the skunk communicated with you? Explain.

17. Flying is an innate behavior in birds. Is it an innate behavior or a learned behavior in humans? Why?

18. Ants depend on pheromones and touch for communication, but birds depend more on sight and sound. Why might these two types of animals communicate differently?

INTERPRETING GRAPHICS

The pie chart below shows the major phyla of the animal species on Earth. Use the chart to answer the questions that follow.

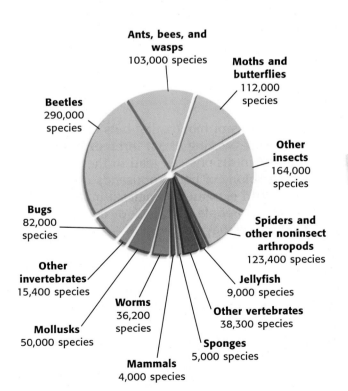

Ants, bees, and wasps 103,000 species

Moths and butterflies 112,000 species

Beetles 290,000 species

Other insects 164,000 species

Bugs 82,000 species

Spiders and other noninsect arthropods 123,400 species

Other invertebrates 15,400 species

Jellyfish 9,000 species

Worms 36,200 species

Other vertebrates 38,300 species

Mollusks 50,000 species

Sponges 5,000 species

Mammals 4,000 species

19. What group of animals has the most species? How is this shown on the chart?

20. How many species of beetles are on Earth? How does that compare with the number of mammal species?

21. How many species of vertebrates are known?

22. Scientists are still discovering new species. Which pie wedges are most likely to increase? Why do you think so?

MATH IN SCIENCE

Use the data from the pie chart to answer the following questions:

23. What is the total number of animal species on Earth?

24. How many different species of moths and butterflies are on Earth?

25. What percentage of all animal species are moths and butterflies?

26. What percentage of all animal species are vertebrates?

NOW What Do You Think?

Take a minute to review your answers to the ScienceLog questions on page 321. Have your answers changed? If necessary, revise your answers based on what you have learned since you began this chapter.

EYE ON THE ENVIRONMENT

Do Not Disturb!

Did you know that bats are the only mammals that can fly? Unlike many birds, most bat species in the northern and central parts of the United States don't fly south for the winter. Instead of migrating, many bat species go into hibernation. But if their sleep is disturbed too often, the bats may die.

Long Winter's Nap

Most bats eat insects, but winter is a time of food shortage. In late summer, many North American bats begin to store up extra fat. These fat reserves help them survive the winter. For the stored fat to last until spring, bats must hibernate. They travel to caves where winter temperatures are low enough—0°C to 9.5°C—and stable enough for the bats to hibernate comfortably.

Hibernating bats' body temperature drops to almost the same temperature as the surrounding cave. Their heart rate, normally about 400 beats per minute, slows to about 25 beats per minute. With these changes, the stored fat will usually last all winter, unless human visitors wake the bats from their deep sleep. If that happens, the bats may starve to death.

No Admittance!

Even with their slowed metabolism, bats must wake up occasionally. They still need to drink water every so often. Sometimes they move to a warmer or cooler spot in the cave. But bats usually have enough fat stored so that they can wake up a few times each winter and then go back to sleep.

People visiting the caves force the bats to wake up unnecessarily. This causes the bats to use up the fat they have stored faster than they can afford. For example, a little brown bat consumes 67 days worth of stored fat each time it awakes. And with no insects around to eat, it cannot build up its fat reserve again.

▲ *These little brown bats are roosting in a cave.*

Most species of hibernating bats can survive the winter after waking about three extra times. But frequent intrusions can lead to the death of a whole colony of bats. Thousands of these interesting and extremely beneficial mammals may die when people carelessly or deliberately disturb them as they hibernate.

Increase Your Knowledge

▶ Using the Internet or the library, find out more about bats. Learn how they are beneficial to the environment and what threatens their survival. Discuss with your classmates some ways to protect bats and their habitats.

WEIRD SCIENCE

ANIMAL CANNIBALS

Competing, surviving, and reproducing are all part of life. And in some species, so is *cannibalism* (eating members of one's own species). But how does cannibalism relate to competing, surviving, and reproducing? It turns out that sometimes an animal's choice of food is a factor in whether its genes get passed on or not.

Picky Eaters

Tiger salamanders start life by eating zooplankton, aquatic insect larvae, and sometimes tadpoles. If conditions in their small pond include intense competition with members of their own species, some of the larger salamanders become cannibals!

Scientists are not sure why tiger salamanders become cannibals or why they usually eat nonrelatives. Scientists hypothesize that this behavior eliminates competition. By eating other salamanders, a tiger salamander reduces competition for food and improves the chances of its own survival. That increases the chances its genes will be passed on to the next generation. And eating nonrelatives helps to ensure that genes coming from the same family are more likely to be passed on to the next generation.

The Ultimate Sacrifice

Male Australian redback spiders take a different approach to making sure their genes are

▲ *During mating, male Australian redback spiders offer themselves as food to their mates.*

passed on. During mating, the male spider tumbles his body over, does a hand-stand, and waves his abdomen near the female's mouth, offering himself to her as a meal. The female accepts the dinner invitation if she is hungry. And it seems that about 65 percent of the time she is hungry!

Male spiders want to pass on their genes, so they compete fiercely for the females. A female redback spider wants to make sure that as many of her eggs are fertilized as possible, so she often mates with two different males. If the female eats the first male, studies show that she will not mate with a second male as often as she would if she had not eaten the first suitor. Because eating the male takes some time, more eggs are fertilized by the mate who also becomes dinner. The male spider who offers himself as a meal may then have more of his genes passed to the next generation.

On Your Own

▶ Other animals devour members of their own species. Scientists believe there are a variety of reasons for the behavior. Using the Internet or the library, research cannibalism in different animals, such as praying mantises, blue crabs, stickleback fish, black widow spiders, spadefoot toad tadpoles, and lions. Present your findings to the class.

15 Invertebrates

Strange but True!

In 1995, researchers in Germany made a computer chip that could send signals to a single nerve cell in a living leech. Even more amazing, the leech's nerve cell could send signals back to the computer chip. What is so amazing about having a "mind link" with a leech? The answer may surprise you.

In the United States alone, accidents result in more than 10,000 spinal-cord injuries a year. In severe cases, a person can lose muscle control, particularly in the arms and legs. But what does this have to do with leeches?

Giant leeches from South America, like the one shown here on the scientist's arm, have only a few nerve cells. By studying leech nerves, biologists are learning how to communicate directly with nerve cells.

The scientists hope that communicating with leech nerves using a computer chip will one day help them communicate with human nerve cells. In the future, people with spinal-cord injuries may be able to use computers to communicate with the nerve cells in their body and move their muscles.

Scientists still have a lot to learn, but who would have expected such a promising breakthrough with an animal that doesn't even have a backbone? In this chapter, you will learn about many spineless critters, the invertebrates.

What Do You Think?

In your ScienceLog, try to answer the following questions based on what you already know:

1. How are sponges different from other invertebrates?

2. How are you different from an octopus? How are you similar?

Crab

Fly

Octopus

Slug

Classify It!

The animal kingdom is divided into a number of groups called phyla. The phyla are divided into subgroups called classes.

When we classify animals, we have to decide which characteristics to use. All of the animals' features, including their internal features, are observed carefully. In this activity, you will try your hand at classification.

Millipede

Spider

Crayfish

Procedure

1. Take a look at the pictures on this page. All of these animals are grouped together because they do not have a backbone.

2. Try dividing these animals into phyla and classes. Which ones are the most similar? Put these in the same phyla. For animals in the same phylum, determine which are the most similar. Put these in classes within the same phylum.

3. Draw a chart to show which animals you have grouped together.

Snail

Analysis

4. What characteristics did you use to classify these animals into different phyla? Explain why you think these characteristics are the most important.

5. What characteristics did you use to group these animals into classes?

6. What descriptive names could you give to your phyla and classes?

Simple Invertebrates

Animals without backbones, also known as **invertebrates,** make up an estimated 97 percent of all animal species. So far, more than 1 million invertebrates have been named. Most biologists think that millions more remain undiscovered.

Tiger beetle

No Backbones Here!

Invertebrates come in many different shapes and sizes. Grasshoppers, clams, earthworms, and jellyfish are all invertebrates, and they are all very different from each other. But one thing invertebrates have in common is that they don't have backbones.

The differences and similarities among all animals, including invertebrates, can be compared by looking at several characteristics. These characteristics include the type of body plan, the presence or absence of a head, and the way food is digested and absorbed.

Morpho butterfly

Horned flatworm

Harlequin shrimp

Body Plans Invertebrates have two basic body plans, or types of *symmetry*. Symmetry can be bilateral or radial. Animal body plans are shown on the next page.

Most animals have bilateral symmetry. An animal with **bilateral symmetry** has a body with two similar halves. For example, if you draw an imaginary line down the middle of an ant, you see the same features on each side of the line.

Some invertebrates have radial symmetry. In an animal with **radial symmetry,** the body parts are arranged in a circle around a central point. If you were to draw an imaginary line across the top of a sea anemone, you would see that both halves look the same. But you could draw the line in any direction and still see two similar halves.

The simplest invertebrates, the sponges, have no symmetry at all. Animals without symmetry are **asymmetrical.**

Animal Body Plans

This ant has **bilateral symmetry.** The two halves of its body mirror each other. On each side you see one eye, one antenna, and three legs.

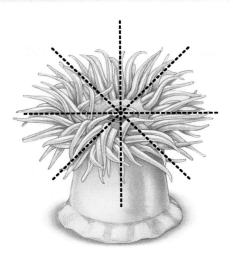

This sea anemone has **radial symmetry.** Animals with radial symmetry have a body organized around the center, like spokes on a wheel.

This sponge is **asymmetrical.** You cannot draw a straight line so that its body is divided into two equal halves.

Getting a Head All animals except sponges have fibers called *nerves* that carry signals to control the movements of their body. Simple invertebrates have nerves arranged in networks or in nerve cords throughout their body. These simple animals have no brain or head.

In some invertebrates, dozens of nerve cells come together in groups called **ganglia** (singular, *ganglion*). Ganglia occur throughout the body, controlling different body parts. **Figure 1** shows one of the ganglia, the brain, and nerve cords of a leech.

More-complex animals have a brain and a head, where the brain is stored. The brain controls many different nerves in different parts of the body.

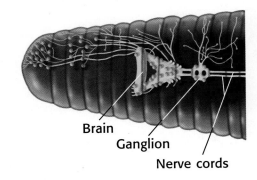

Figure 1 *Leeches have a simple brain and ganglia. A pair of nerve cords connects the brain and ganglia.*

Don't You Have Any Guts? Almost all animals digest food in a central gut. The **gut** is a pouch lined with cells that release powerful enzymes. These enzymes break down food into small particles that cells can then absorb. Your gut is your digestive tract.

Complex animals have a special space in the body for the gut. This space is the **coelom** (SEE luhm), shown in **Figure 2.** The coelum allows the gut to move food without interference from the movements of the body. Other organs, such as the heart and lungs, are also in the coelom, but they are separated from the gut.

Figure 2 *This is the coelom of an earthworm. The gut and organs are in this special cavity.*

Invertebrates **345**

Sponges

Sponges are the simplest animals. They have no symmetry, no head or nerves, and no gut. Although sponges can move, they are so slow that their movement is very difficult to see. In fact, sponges were once thought to be plants. But sponges cannot make their own food and must eat other organisms. That's one reason they are classified as animals.

Kinds of Sponges All sponges live in water, and most are found in the ocean. As shown in **Figure 3,** they come in beautiful colors and a variety of shapes.

Most sponges have a skeleton made of needlelike splinters called *spicules,* as shown in **Figure 4.** Spicules come in many shapes, from simple, straight needles to curved rods and complex star shapes. The skeleton supports the body of the sponge and helps protect it from predators.

Sponges are divided into classes according to the type of spicules they have. The largest class of sponges contain spicules made of silicate, the material we use to make glass. Bath sponges are similar to silica sponges, but they lack spicules. Instead of spicules, they have a skeleton made of a protein called *spongin.* That is why they are soft. Another group of sponges have spicules made of calcium carbonate, the material that makes up the shells of shellfish.

Re-form and Replace If a sponge's body is broken apart by being forced through a sieve, the separate cells will come back together and re-form the same sponge. In addition, new sponges can form from pieces broken off another sponge. Unlike most animals, a sponge can also replace its body parts, or *regenerate.*

Giant barrel sponge

Tube sponge

Figure 3 *Sponges come in a variety of shapes, sizes, and colors.*

Figure 4 *This is the skeleton of a glass sponge.*

How Do Sponges Eat? Sponges belong to the phylum Porifera. The name refers to the thousands of holes, or *pores,* on the outside of sponges. The sponge pumps water into its body through these pores. Inside the body, cells called *collar cells* filter food particles and microorganisms from the water. The rest of the water flows into a central cavity and out a hole at the top of the sponge, like smoke going up a chimney. The hole at the top is called the *osculum.* **Figure 5** shows this process.

Sponges don't have a gut. Instead, each collar cell digests its own particles of food. No other animal has anything like collar cells.

Collar cells line the central cavity of a sponge. Each collar cell filters particles of food from the water and digests them.

Pore cells are used to pump water into a sponge.

Osculum

Water flow

Pores

Figure 5 *A sponge filters particles of food from water using collar cells and then pumps the water out the osculum. A sponge can filter up to 22 L of water a day.*

REVIEW

1. Why are collar cells important in classifying sponges as animals?

2. What is a coelom?

3. **Interpreting Graphics** Does the animal shown at right have radial symmetry, bilateral symmetry, or no symmetry? Explain your answer.

Jellyfish

Cnidarians

Take a look at the organisms shown in **Figure 6.** They look very different, but all of these animals belong to the phylum Cnidaria (ni DER ee uh).

The word *cnidaria* comes from the Greek word for "nettle." Nettles are plants that release stinging barbs into the skin. Cnidarians do the same. All cnidarians have stinging cells. Do you know anyone who has been stung by a jellyfish? It is a very painful experience!

Cnidarians are more complex than sponges. Cnidarians have complex tissues, a gut for digesting food, and a nervous system. However, some species of cnidarians do share a characteristic with sponges. If the cells of the body are separated, they can come back together to form the cnidarian.

The Medusa and the Polyp Cnidarians come in two forms, the medusa and the polyp. They are shown in **Figure 7.** The *medusa* looks like a mushroom with tentacles streaming down from below. A well-known medusa is the jellyfish. As a medusa's body, or bell, contracts and relaxes, the medusa swims through the water.

The other cnidarian body form is the *polyp.* Polyps are shaped like vases and usually live attached to a surface.

Some cnidarians are polyps and medusas at different times in their life. But most cnidarians spend their life as a polyp.

Hydra

Figure 6 *These three organisms are cnidarians. Why are they in the same phylum?*

Sea anemone

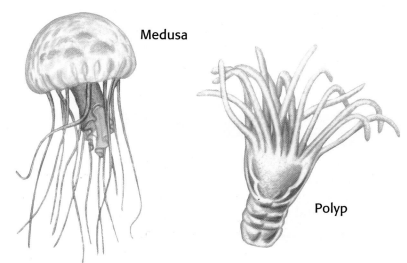
Medusa

Polyp

Figure 7 *Both the medusa and the polyp have radial symmetry. Can you see why?*

Kinds of Cnidarians There are three classes of cnidarians: hydras, jellyfish, and sea anemones and corals. Hydras are common cnidarians that live in fresh water. They spend their entire life in the polyp form. Jellyfish spend most of their life as a medusa.

Sea anemones and corals are polyps all their life. They look like brightly colored flowers. Corals are tiny cnidarians that live in colonies. These colonies build huge skeletons of calcium carbonate. Each new generation of corals builds on top of the last generation. Over thousands of years, these tiny animals build massive underwater reefs. Coral reefs can be found in warm tropical waters throughout the world.

Catching Lunch All cnidarians have long tentacles covered with special stinging cells. When a small fish or other organism brushes against the tentacles of a cnidarian, hundreds of stinging cells fire into the organism and release a paralyzing toxin. Each stinging cell uses water pressure to fire a tiny barbed spear called a *nematocyst* (ne MA toh sist). **Figure 8** shows a nematocyst before and after firing.

Figure 8 *Each stinging cell contains a nematocyst.*

Before firing Coiled inside each stinging cell is a tiny barbed harpoon.

After firing When the nematocyst is fired, the long barbed strand ejects into the water. Larger barbs also cover the base of the strand.

You've Got Some Nerve Cnidarians have a simple network of nerve cells called a *nerve net*. The nerve net controls the movements of the body and the tentacles.

A medusa has a *nerve ring* in the center of its nerve net. This ring of nerve cells coordinates the swimming of a jellyfish in the same way that our spinal cord coordinates walking. The nerve ring is not a brain, however. Cnidarians do not think or plan in the way that more-complex animals do.

✓ Self-Check

Medusas have a nerve ring, but polyps do not. How does the way medusas move explain their more complex nervous system? *(See page 782 to check your answer.)*

Flatworms

When you think of worms, you probably think of earthworms. But there are many other types of worms, and most of them are too tiny to see. The simplest group of worms are the flatworms.

Look at the flatworm shown in **Figure 9.** Unlike the invertebrates you have studied so far, flatworms have bilateral symmetry. Most flatworms also have a clearly defined head and two large, unblinking eyespots. Even though the eyespots cannot focus, a flatworm knows the direction that light is coming from. A flatworm also has two bumps on each side of its head. These are *sensory lobes* and are used for detecting food.

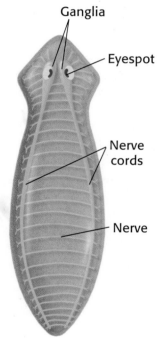

Figure 9 *This flatworm is called a planarian. It has a head with eyespots and sensory lobes.*

Planarians Flatworms are divided into three classes. The big-eyed flatworms we have been discussing are called *planarians.* Most of these flatworms are small; their length is less than the length of a fingernail. They live in water and on land. Most planarians are predators. They eat other animals or parts of other animals and digest food in their gut. The planarian's head, eyespots, and sensory lobes are clues that it has a brain for processing information. **Figure 10** shows a diagram of the nervous system of a planarian.

Flukes and Tapeworms The two other groups of flatworms are *flukes* and *tapeworms.* A fluke is shown in **Figure 11.** These animals are parasites. A *parasite* is an organism that feeds on another living creature, called the *host.* The host is usually not killed. Most flukes and all tapeworms find their way inside the bodies of other animals, where they live and reproduce. Fertilized eggs pass out of the host's body with the body's waste. If these fertilized eggs end up in drinking water or on food, they can be eaten by another host, where they will develop into a new fluke or tapeworm.

Ganglia

Eyespot

Nerve cords

Nerve

Figure 10 *The nervous system of a flatworm has nerves connecting two parallel nerve cords. Ganglia make up a primitive brain.*

Figure 11 *Flukes use suckers to attach to their host.*

Flukes and tapeworms have tiny heads without eyespots or sensory lobes. They have special suckers and hooks for attaching to the host. Those flatworms that live inside the gut of their host have special skin that resists digestion by the stomach enzymes of the host. Tapeworms are so specialized that they have no gut at all. These creatures simply absorb nutrients from the intestines of their host. **Figure 12** shows a tapeworm that can infect humans.

Roundworms

Roundworms, or nematodes, are round when viewed in cross section and are long and slender. Like other worms, they have bilateral symmetry. Most species of roundworms are tiny. A single rotten apple lying on the ground in an orchard could contain 100,000 roundworms. These tiny creatures break down the dead tissues of plants and animals and help build rich soils. **Figure 13** shows a roundworm.

Roundworms have a simple nervous system. A ring of ganglia forms a primitive brain, and parallel nerve cords run the length of their body.

Most roundworms are parasites. Roundworms that infect humans include pinworms and hookworms. Another roundworm is passed from infected pork to humans and causes trichinosis (TRIK i NOH sis), a severe illness. Cooking pork thoroughly will kill the roundworms.

Figure 12 *Tapeworms can reach enormous sizes. Some can grow longer than a school bus!*

Figure 13 *Roundworms have a fluid-filled body cavity.*

REVIEW

1. What characteristic gives cnidarians their name?

2. What are two characteristics of flatworms that make them different from cnidarians?

3. **Analyzing Relationships** Both predators and parasites live off the tissues of other animals. Explain the difference between a predator and a parasite.

internet**connect**

SCiLINKS
NSTA

TOPIC: Sponges, Roundworms
GO TO: www.scilinks.org
*sci*LINKS NUMBER: HSTL355, HSTL360

Earthworm

Terms to Learn

open circulatory system
closed circulatory system
segment

What You'll Do

◆ Describe the body parts of a mollusk.

◆ Explain the difference between an open circulatory system and a closed circulatory system.

◆ Describe segmentation.

Mollusks and Annelid Worms

Have you ever eaten clam chowder or calamari? Have you ever seen worms on the sidewalk after it rains? If you have, then you have encountered the invertebrates discussed in this section—mollusks and annelid worms. These invertebrates are more complex than the invertebrates you have read about so far. Mollusks and annelid worms have a coelom and a circulatory system. And they have more-complex nervous systems than those of the flatworms and roundworms.

Mollusks

The phylum Mollusca includes snails, slugs, clams, oysters, squids, and octopuses. The mollusks are the second largest phylum of animals. Most mollusks are in three classes: *gastropods* (slugs and snails), *bivalves* (clams and other two-shelled shellfish), and *cephalopods* (squids and octopuses). **Figure 14** shows some of the variety of mollusks.

Snails

Squid

Clam

Figure 14 *A snail, a squid, and a clam are all mollusks. Snails are gastropods; squids are cephalopods; and clams are bivalves.*

Most mollusks live in the ocean, but some live in freshwater habitats. Other mollusks, such as slugs and snails, have adapted to life on land.

Mollusks range in size from 1 mm long snails to the giant squid, which can reach up to 18 m in length. Most mollusks move slowly, but some squids can swim up to 40 km/h and leap more than 4 m above the water.

$\div \ 5 \div \ \Omega \ \leq \ \infty \ + \Omega \ \sqrt{} \ 9 \ \infty^{\leq} \ \Sigma \ 2$

MATH BREAK

Speeding Squid

If a squid is swimming at 30 km/h, how far can it go in 1 minute?

How Do You Know a Mollusk When You See One? A snail, a clam, and a squid look quite different from one another. Yet on closer inspection, the bodies of all mollusks are almost the same. The body parts shared by mollusks are described in **Figure 15.**

Figure 15 *A mollusk has a soft body, usually covered by a shell. All mollusks also have a foot, a visceral mass, and a mantle.*

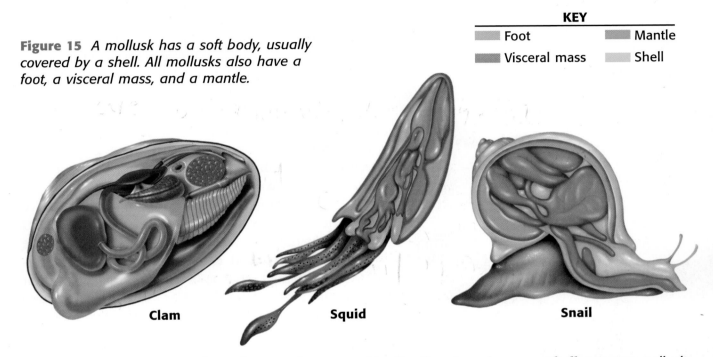

KEY

Foot	Mantle
Visceral mass	Shell

Clam   **Squid**   **Snail**

Foot The most obvious feature of a mollusk is a broad, muscular foot. A mollusk uses its foot to move. In gastropods, the foot secretes mucus that it slides along.

Visceral mass The visceral (VIS uhr uhl) mass contains the gills, gut, and other organs. It is located in a mollusk's coelom.

Mantle The visceral mass is covered by a layer of tissue called the mantle. The mantle protects the body of mollusks that do not have a shell.

Shell In most mollusks, the outside of the mantle secretes a shell. The shell protects the mollusk from predators and keeps land mollusks from drying out.

How Do Mollusks Eat? Each type of mollusk has its own way of eating. Clams and other bivalves sit in one place and filter tiny plants, bacteria, and other particles from the water around them. Snails and slugs eat with a ribbonlike tongue covered with curved teeth, called a *radula* (RAJ oo luh). **Figure 16** shows a close-up of a slug's radula. Slugs and snails use the radula to scrape algae off rocks, chunks of tissue from seaweed, or pieces from the leaves of plants. Predatory snails and slugs often have large teeth on their radula that they use to attack their prey. And parasitic snails pierce their victims much as a mosquito does. Octopuses and squids use tentacles to grab their prey and place it in their powerful jaws, just as we can use our fingers to eat.

Figure 16 *The rows of teeth on a slug's radula help to scrape food from surfaces.*

Have a Heart Unlike simpler invertebrates, mollusks have a circulatory system. Most mollusks have an **open circulatory system.** In this system, a simple heart pumps blood through blood vessels that empty into spaces in the animal's body called *sinuses*. This is very different from our own circulatory system, which is a **closed circulatory system.** In a closed circulatory system, a heart circulates blood through a network of blood vessels that form a closed loop. Cephalopods (squids and octopuses) also have a closed circulatory system, although it is much simpler than ours.

It's a Brain! Mollusks have complex ganglia. In most mollusks, these ganglia occur throughout the body. Mollusks have ganglia that control breathing, ganglia that move the foot, and ganglia that control digestion.

Cephalopods, like the one in **Figure 17,** have a more complex nervous system than the other mollusks have. In fact, octopuses and squids have the most advanced nervous system of all invertebrates. They have a brain, where all of their ganglia are connected. Not surprisingly, these animals are the smartest of all invertebrates. Octopuses, for example, can learn to navigate a maze and can distinguish between different shapes and colors. If they are given bricks or stones, they will build a cave to hide in.

Figure 17 *An octopus has a large brain. The brain coordinates the movement of its eight long arms.*

REVIEW

1. What are the four main parts of a mollusk's body?

2. What is the difference between an open circulatory system and a closed circulatory system?

3. **Analyzing Relationships** What two features do cephalopods share with humans that other mollusks do not?

Annelid Worms

You have probably seen earthworms, like the one in **Figure 18.** Earthworms belong to the phylum Annelida. Annelid worms are often called segmented worms because their body has segments. **Segments** are identical, or almost identical, repeating body parts.

These worms are much more complex than flatworms and roundworms. Annelid worms have a coelom and a closed circulatory system. They also have a nervous system that includes ganglia in each segment and a brain in the head. A nerve cord connects the brain and the ganglia.

Kinds of Annelid Worms The annelid worms include three classes: earthworms, bristle worms, and leeches. Annelid worms live in salt water, in fresh water, or on land. They may scavenge anything edible, or they may prey on other organisms as predators or as parasites.

More than Just Bait Earthworms are the most common annelid worms. An earthworm has 100 to 175 segments, most of which are identical. Some segments are specialized for eating and reproduction. Earthworms eat soil. They break down organic matter in the soil and excrete wastes called *castings*. Castings provide nutrients that plants can use. Earthworms also improve the soil by burrowing tunnels, which allow air and water to reach deep into the soil.

Earthworms have stiff bristles on the outside of their body to help them move. The bristles hold one part of the worm in place while the other part pushes through the soil.

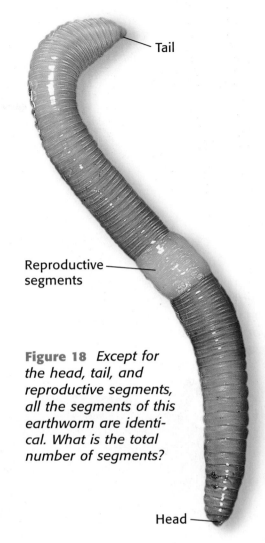

Tail

Reproductive segments

Head

Figure 18 *Except for the head, tail, and reproductive segments, all the segments of this earthworm are identical. What is the total number of segments?*

Do Worms Make Good Neighbors?

A friend of yours is worried because his garden is full of earthworms. He wants to find a way to get rid of the worms. Do you think this is a good idea? Why? Write a letter to your friend explaining what you think he should do.

Figure 19 *This bristle worm feeds by filtering particles from the water with its bristles. Can you see the segments on this worm?*

Bristles Can Be Beautiful If there were a beauty contest for worms, bristle worms would win. These remarkable worms come in many varieties and in brilliant colors. **Figure 19** shows a bristle worm. All bristle worms live in water. Some burrow through soggy sand and mud, eating whatever small creatures and particles they meet. Others crawl along the bottom, eating mollusks and other small animals.

Blood Suckers and More Leeches are known mostly as parasites that suck other animals' blood. This is true of some leeches, but not all. Other leeches are scavengers that eat dead animals. Still others are predators that prey on insects, slugs, and snails. Leeches that are parasites feed on the blood of other animals.

But leeches aren't all bad. Until the twentieth century, doctors regularly used leeches in medical treatments. Doctors attached leeches to a sick person to drain "bad" blood from the body. Although this practice is not accepted today, leeches are still used in medicine. After surgery, doctors sometimes use leeches to prevent dangerous swelling near a wound, as shown in **Figure 20**. Leeches also make a chemical that keeps blood from forming clots. Modern doctors give heart attack patients medicines that contain this chemical to keep blood clots from blocking arteries.

Figure 20 *Modern doctors sometimes use leeches to reduce swelling after surgery.*

📷 internet**connect**

SCI*LINKS*
NSTA

TOPIC: Mollusks and Annelid Worms
GO TO: www.scilinks.org
*sci***LINKS NUMBER:** HSTL365

REVIEW

1. Name the three types of annelid worms. How are they alike? How are they different?

2. **Making Inferences** Why would a chemical that keeps blood from clotting be beneficial to leeches?

3. **Analyzing Relationships** How are annelid worms different from flatworms and roundworms? What characteristics do all worms share?

Arthropods

Fiddler crab

Terms to Learn

exoskeleton   mandible
compound eye   metamorphosis
antennae

What You'll Do

◆ List the four main characteristics of arthropods.

◆ Describe the different body parts of the four kinds of arthropods.

◆ Explain the two types of metamorphosis in insects.

They have lived here for hundreds of millions of years and have adapted to nearly all environments. An acre of land contains millions of them. You know them by more common names, such as insects, spiders, crabs, and centipedes. They are *arthropods,* the largest group of animals on Earth.

Seventy-five percent of all animal species are arthropods. The world population of humans is about 6 billion. Biologists estimate the world population of arthropods to be about a billion billion.

Characteristics of Arthropods

All arthropods share four characteristics: jointed limbs, a segmented body with specialized parts, an exoskeleton, and a well-developed nervous system.

Jointed Limbs   Jointed limbs give arthropods their name. *Arthro* means "joint," and *pod* means "foot." Jointed limbs are arms, legs, or other similar body parts that bend at joints. Jointed limbs allow arthropods to move easily.

Segmented and Specialized   Like annelid worms, arthropods are *segmented.* In some arthropods, such as the centipedes, nearly every segment is identical. Only the segments at the head and tail are different from the rest. Most other species of arthropods have segments that include very specialized parts, such as wings, antennae, gills, pincers, and claws.   Many of these special parts form during the animal's development, when two or three segments grow together to form a *head,* a *thorax,* and an *abdomen.* These parts are labeled on the grasshopper pictured in **Figure 21.**

Mosquito

Tarantula

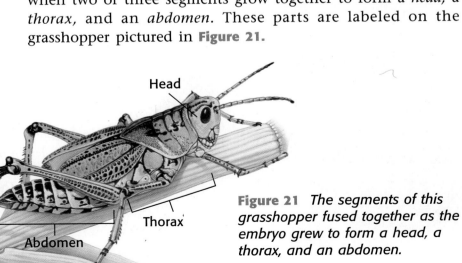

Head

Thorax

Abdomen

Figure 21 *The segments of this grasshopper fused together as the embryo grew to form a head, a thorax, and an abdomen.*

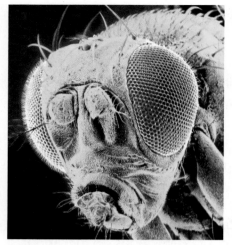

Figure 22 *Compound eyes consist of many individual light-sensitive cells that work together.*

Knights in Shining . . . Chitin? Arthropods have a hard **exoskeleton,** an external skeleton made of protein and a special substance called *chitin* (KIE tin). The exoskeleton does some of the same things an internal skeleton does. It provides a stiff frame that supports the animal's body. The exoskeleton also allows the animal to move. All of the muscles attach to different parts of the skeleton. When the muscles contract, they move the exoskeleton, which moves the parts of the animal.

But the exoskeleton also does things that internal skeletons don't do well. The exoskeleton acts like a suit of armor to protect internal organs and muscles. It also allows arthropods to live on land without drying out.

They've Got Smarts All arthropods have a head and a well-developed brain. The brain coordinates information from many sense organs, including eyes and bristles on the exoskeleton. Bristles sense movement, vibration, pressure, and chemicals. The eyes of some arthropods are very simple; they can detect light but cannot form an image. But most arthropods have compound eyes, which allow them to see images, although not as well as we do. A **compound eye** is made of many identical light-sensitive cells, as shown in **Figure 22.**

Kinds of Arthropods

Arthropods are classified according to the kinds of body parts they have. You can also tell the difference between arthropods by looking at the number of legs, eyes, and antennae they have. **Antennae** are feelers that respond to touch, taste, and smell.

Centipedes and Millipedes Centipedes and millipedes have a single pair of antennae, jaws called **mandibles,** and a hard *head capsule.* The easiest way to tell a centipede from a millipede is to count the number of legs per segment. Centipedes have one pair of legs per segment. Millipedes have two pairs of legs per segment. Take a look at **Figure 23.** How many legs can you count?

Figure 23 *Centipedes have one pair of legs per segment. The number of legs can range from 30 to 354. Millipedes have two pairs of legs per segment. The record number of legs on a millipede is 752!*

Crustaceans Crustaceans include pillbugs, shrimps, barnacles, crabs, and lobsters. Nearly all crustaceans are aquatic and have *gills* for breathing underwater. All crustaceans have mandibles and two pairs of antennae. Crustaceans have two compound eyes, usually on the end of stalks. The lobster in **Figure 24** shows all of these traits. The double antennae of crustaceans set them apart from all other arthropods.

✓ Self-Check

What is the difference between a segmented worm and a centipede? (See page 782 to check your answer.)

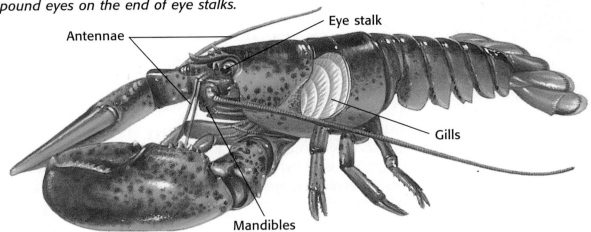

Figure 24 *A lobster is a crustacean. It has compound eyes on the end of eye stalks.*

Antennae

Eye stalk

Gills

Mandibles

Arachnids Spiders, scorpions, mites, ticks, and daddy long-legs are all arachnids. **Figure 25** shows that an arachnid has two main body parts, the cephalothorax (SEF uh loh THOR AKS) and the abdomen. The *cephalothorax* consists of both a head and a thorax and usually has four pairs of walking legs. Arachnids have no antennae and no mandibles. Instead of mandibles, they have special mouthparts called *chelicerae* (kuh LIS uh ree), as illustrated in Figure 25. Some chelicerae look like pincers or fangs.

The eyes of arachnids are distinctive. While crustaceans and insects have compound eyes, arachnids do not. Spiders, for example, have eight simple eyes arranged in two rows at the front of the head. Count the eyes for yourself in **Figure 26.**

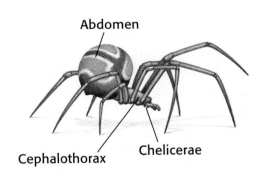

Abdomen

Cephalothorax

Chelicerae

Figure 25 *Arachnids have two main body parts and special mouthparts called chelicerae.*

Figure 26 *In addition to eight legs, spiders have eight eyes!*

Figure 27 American Dog Tick

Spiders and Ticks   Spiders do not carry diseases and are enormously useful to humans. They kill more insect pests than any other animal, including birds. Several arachnids have painful bites or stings. But the fangs of small garden spiders cannot pierce human skin. In the United States, just three species of spiders—the black widow and two species of brown spider—have bites poisonous enough to kill a person. However, with proper medical treatment, they are not fatal.

Ticks live in forests, brushy areas, and even country lawns. **Figure 27** shows an American dog tick. Ticks that bite humans sometimes carry Lyme disease, Rocky Mountain spotted fever, and other diseases. Many people wear long pants and hats when going into areas where ticks live, and they check themselves for ticks after being outdoors. Fortunately, most people who are bitten by ticks do not get sick.

Insects   The largest group of arthropods is insects. If you put all of the insects in the world together, they would weigh more than all other animals combined! **Figure 28** shows some of the wide variety of insects.

Quick Lab

Sticky Webs

Some spiders spin webs of sticky silk to trap their prey. Why don't spiders stick to their own webs? This experiment will show you the answer. Place a piece of **tape** on your desk sticky side up. The tape represents a web. Your fingers will represent an insect. Holding the tape in place by the edges, "walk" your fingers across the tape. What happens? Dip your fingers in **cooking oil,** and "walk" them across the tape again. What happens this time? Why? How might this experiment explain why spiders don't get stuck in their webs?

TRY at HOME

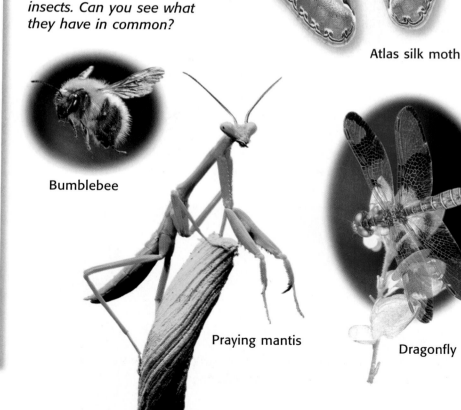

Figure 28 *These are a few of the many varieties of insects. Can you see what they have in common?*

Atlas silk moth

Bumblebee

Praying mantis

Dragonfly

Insects Are Everywhere (Almost) Insects live on land, in every freshwater environment, and at the edges of the sea. The only place on Earth insects do not live is in the ocean.

Many insects are beneficial. Most flowering plants depend on bees, butterflies, and other insects to carry pollen from one plant to another. Farmers depend on insects to pollinate hundreds of fruit crops, such as apples, cherries, tomatoes, and pumpkins.

Many insects are also pests. Fleas, lice, mosquitoes, and flies burrow into our flesh, suck our blood, or carry diseases. Plant-eating insects consume up to one-third of crops in this country, despite the application of pesticides.

Insect Bodies An insect's body has three parts: the head, the thorax, and the abdomen, as shown in **Figure 29.** On the head, insects have one pair of antennae and two compound eyes. They also have three pairs of mouthparts, including one pair of mandibles. The thorax is made of three segments, each with one pair of legs.

In many insects, the second and third segments of the thorax have a pair of wings. Some insects have no wings, and some have two pairs of wings.

Insect Development As an insect develops from an egg to an adult, it changes form. This process is called **metamorphosis.** There are two main types of metamorphosis, incomplete and complete. Primitive insects, such as grasshoppers and cockroaches, go through incomplete metamorphosis. In this metamorphosis there are only three stages: egg, nymph, and adult, as shown in **Figure 30.**

Figure 29 *Wasps have the same body parts as all other insects.*

Head

Thorax

Abdomen

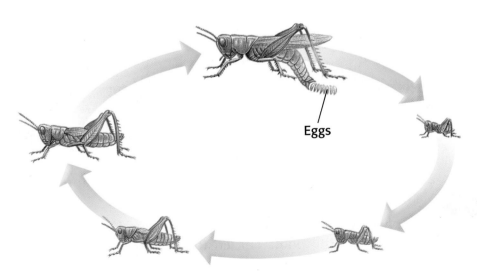

Eggs

Figure 30 *In incomplete metamorphosis, the larvae, called nymphs, look like smaller adults.*

Does a cricket like cold climates? Find out on page 737 of your LabBook.

Changing Form—Complete Metamorphosis

In complete metamorphosis, there are four stages: egg, larva, pupa, and adult. Butterflies, beetles, flies, bees, wasps, and ants go through this process. In complete metamorphosis, the larva looks very different from the adult.

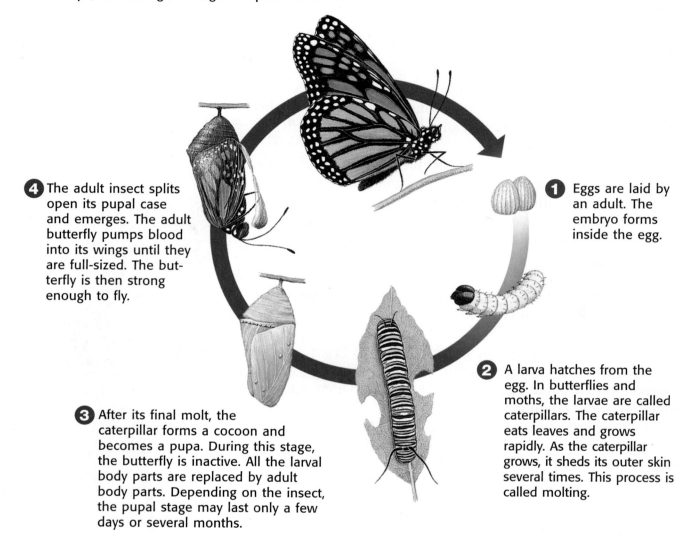

4 The adult insect splits open its pupal case and emerges. The adult butterfly pumps blood into its wings until they are full-sized. The butterfly is then strong enough to fly.

1 Eggs are laid by an adult. The embryo forms inside the egg.

3 After its final molt, the caterpillar forms a cocoon and becomes a pupa. During this stage, the butterfly is inactive. All the larval body parts are replaced by adult body parts. Depending on the insect, the pupal stage may last only a few days or several months.

2 A larva hatches from the egg. In butterflies and moths, the larvae are called caterpillars. The caterpillar eats leaves and grows rapidly. As the caterpillar grows, it sheds its outer skin several times. This process is called molting.

REVIEW

1. Name the four kinds of arthropods. How are their bodies different?

2. What is the difference between complete metamorphosis and incomplete metamorphosis?

3. **Applying Concepts** Suppose you have found an arthropod in a swimming pool. The creature has compound eyes, antennae, and wings. Is it a crustacean? Why or why not?

Terms to Learn

endoskeleton
water vascular system

What You'll Do

◆ Describe three main characteristics of echinoderms.
◆ Describe the water vascular system.

Echinoderms

Brittle star

The last major phylum of invertebrates is Echinodermata. All echinoderms (ee KI noh DUHRMS) are marine animals. They include sea stars (starfish), sea urchins, sea lilies, sea cucumbers, brittle stars, and sand dollars. The smallest echinoderms are only a few millimeters across. The largest is a sea star that grows to 1 m in diameter.

Echinoderms live on the sea floor in all parts of the world's oceans. Some echinoderms prey on oysters and other shellfish, some are scavengers, and others scrape algae off rocky surfaces.

Sea star

Sea lily

Spiny Skinned

The name *echinoderm* means "spiny skinned." The surface of the animal is not the spiny part, however. The body of the echinoderm contains an **endoskeleton,** an internal skeleton similar to the kind that vertebrates have. The hard, bony skeleton is usually covered with spines. The spines may be no more than sharp bumps, as in many sea stars. Or they may be long and pointed, as in sea urchins. All of the spines are covered by the outer skin of the animal.

Bilateral or Radial?

Adult echinoderms have radial symmetry. But sea stars, sea urchins, sand dollars, and other echinoderms all develop from larvae with bilateral symmetry. **Figure 31** shows a sea urchin larva. Notice how the two sides are similar.

When echinoderm embryos first begin to develop, they form a mouth in the same way the embryos of vertebrates do. This is one of the reasons biologists think that vertebrates are more closely related to echinoderms than to other invertebrates.

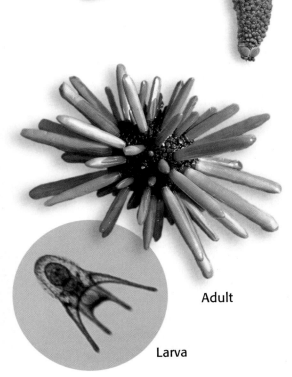

Adult

Larva

Figure 31 *The sea urchin larva has bilateral symmetry. The adult sea urchin has radial symmetry.*

The Nervous System

All echinoderms have a simple nervous system similar to that of a jellyfish. Around the mouth is a circle of nerve fibers called the *nerve ring*. In sea stars, a *radial nerve* runs from the nerve ring to the tip of each arm, as shown in **Figure 32.** The radial nerves control the movements of the sea star's arms.

At the tip of each arm is a simple eye that senses light. The rest of the body is covered with cells that are sensitive to touch and to chemical signals in the water.

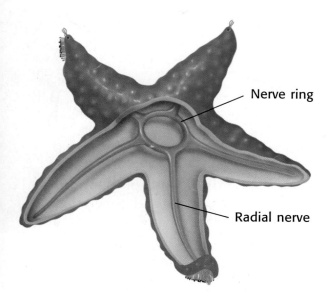

Figure 32 *Sea stars have simple nervous systems.*

Nerve ring

Radial nerve

Water Vascular System

One system that is unique to echinoderms is the **water vascular system.** This system uses water pumps to help the animal move, eat, breathe, and sense its environment. **Figure 33** shows the water vascular system of a sea star. Notice how water pressure from the water vascular system is used for a variety of functions.

Figure 33 *A water vascular system allows sea stars and all echinoderms to move, eat, and breathe.*

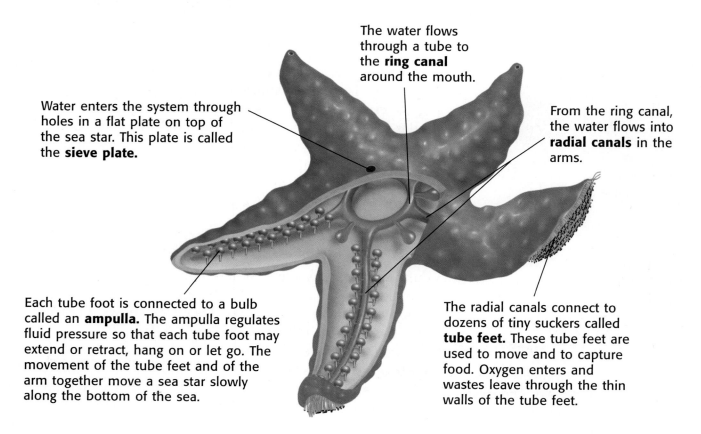

The water flows through a tube to the **ring canal** around the mouth.

Water enters the system through holes in a flat plate on top of the sea star. This plate is called the **sieve plate.**

From the ring canal, the water flows into **radial canals** in the arms.

Each tube foot is connected to a bulb called an **ampulla.** The ampulla regulates fluid pressure so that each tube foot may extend or retract, hang on or let go. The movement of the tube feet and of the arm together move a sea star slowly along the bottom of the sea.

The radial canals connect to dozens of tiny suckers called **tube feet.** These tube feet are used to move and to capture food. Oxygen enters and wastes leave through the thin walls of the tube feet.

Kinds of Echinoderms

Scientists divide echinoderms into several classes. Sea stars are the most familiar echinoderms, and they make up one class. But there are three classes of echinoderms that may not be as familiar to you.

Brittle Stars and Basket Stars The brittle stars and basket stars look like sea stars with long slender arms. These delicate creatures tend to be smaller than sea stars. **Figure 34** shows a basket star.

Sea Urchins and Sand Dollars Sea urchins and sand dollars are round, and their skeletons form a solid internal shell. They have no arms, but they use their tube feet to move in the same way as sea stars. Some sea urchins also walk on their spines. Sea urchins feed on algae they scrape from the surface of rocks and other objects and chew with special teeth. Sand dollars burrow into soft sand or mud, as shown in **Figure 35,** and eat tiny particles of food they find in the sand.

Sea Cucumbers Like sea urchins and sand dollars, sea cucumbers lack arms. A sea cucumber has a soft, leathery body. Unlike sea urchins, sea cucumbers are long and have a wormlike shape. **Figure 36** shows a sea cucumber.

Figure 34 *Basket stars have longer arms than sea stars.*

Figure 35 *Sand dollars burrow in the sand.*

Figure 36 *Like other echinoderms, sea cucumbers move with tube feet.*

REVIEW

1. How are sea cucumbers different from other echinoderms?

2. What is the path taken by water as it flows through the parts of the water vascular system?

3. **Applying Concepts** How are echinoderms different from other invertebrates?

internet**connect**

SC*i*LINKS.
NSTA

TOPIC: Echinoderms
GO TO: www.scilinks.org
*sci*LINKS NUMBER: HSTL375

Chapter Highlights

SECTION 1

Vocabulary

invertebrate *(p. 344)*

bilateral symmetry *(p. 344)*

radial symmetry *(p. 344)*

asymmetrical *(p. 344)*

ganglia *(p. 345)*

gut *(p. 345)*

coelom *(p. 345)*

Section Notes

- Invertebrates are animals without a backbone.

- Most animals have radial symmetry or bilateral symmetry.

- Unlike other animals, sponges have no symmetry.

- A coelom is a space inside the body. The gut hangs inside the coelom.

- Ganglia are clumps of nerves that help control the parts of the body.

- Sponges have special cells called collar cells to digest their food.

- Cnidarians have special stinging cells to catch their prey.

- Cnidarians have two body forms, the polyp and the medusa.

- Tapeworms and flukes are parasitic flatworms.

Labs

Porifera's Porosity *(p. 736)*

SECTION 2

Vocabulary

open circulatory system *(p. 354)*

closed circulatory system *(p. 354)*

segment *(p. 355)*

Section Notes

- All mollusks have a foot, a visceral mass, and a mantle. Most mollusks also have a shell.

- Mollusks and annelid worms have both a coelom and a circulatory system.

- In an open circulatory system, the heart pumps blood through vessels into spaces called sinuses. In a closed circulatory system, the blood is pumped through a closed network of vessels.

- Segments are identical or nearly identical repeating body parts.

☑ Skills Check

Math Concepts

SPEED AND DISTANCE If a snail is moving at 30 cm/h, how far can it travel in 1 minute? There are 60 minutes in 1 hour:

$$\frac{30 \text{ cm}}{60 \text{ min}} = 0.5 \text{ cm/min}$$

In 1 minute the snail will travel 0.5 cm.

Visual Understanding

METAMORPHOSIS Some insects go through incomplete metamorphosis, and some go through complete metamorphosis. Look at the illustrations on pages 361 and 362 to see the difference between these two types of metamorphosis.

SECTION 3

Vocabulary

exoskeleton *(p. 358)*

compound eye *(p. 358)*

antennae *(p. 358)*

mandible *(p. 358)*

metamorphosis *(p. 361)*

Section Notes

- Seventy-five percent of all animals are arthropods.

- The four main characteristics of arthropods are jointed limbs, an exoskeleton, segments, and a well-developed nervous system.

- Arthropods are classified by the type of body parts they have.

- The four kinds of arthropods are centipedes and millipedes, crustaceans, arachnids, and insects.

- Insects can undergo complete or incomplete metamorphosis.

Labs

The Cricket Caper *(p. 737)*

SECTION 4

Vocabulary

endoskeleton *(p. 363)*

water vascular system *(p. 364)*

Section Notes

- Echinoderms are marine animals that have an endoskeleton and a water vascular system.

- Most echinoderms have bilateral symmetry as larvae and radial symmetry as adults.

- The water vascular system allows echinoderms to move around by means of tube feet, which act like suction cups.

- Echinoderms have a simple nervous system consisting of a nerve ring and radial nerves.

Chapter Review

USING VOCABULARY

To complete the following sentences, choose the correct term from each pair of terms listed below:

1. Animals without a backbone are called __?__. (*invertebrates* or *vertebrates*)

2. A sponge uses __?__ to pull water in and releases water out through __?__. (*an osculum* or *pores*)

3. Cnidarians have __?__ symmetry and flatworms have __?__ symmetry. (*radial* or *bilateral*)

4. The shell of a snail is secreted by the __?__. (*radula* or *mantle*)

5. Annelid worms have __?__. (*jointed limbs* or *segments*)

6. An ampulla regulates __?__. (*water pressure in a tube foot* or *blood pressure in a closed circulatory system*)

UNDERSTANDING CONCEPTS

Multiple Choice

7. Invertebrates make up what percentage of all animals?
   a. 4 percent
   b. 50 percent
   c. 85 percent
   d. 97 percent

8. Which of the following describes the body plan of a sponge:
   a. radial symmetry
   b. bilateral symmetry
   c. asymmetry
   d. partial symmetry

9. What cells do sponges have that no other animal has?
   a. blood cells
   b. nerve cells
   c. collar cells
   d. none of the above

10. Which of the following animals do not have ganglia?
    a. annelid worms
    b. cnidarians
    c. flatworms
    d. mollusks

11. Which of the following animals has a coelom?
    a. sponge
    b. cnidarian
    c. flatworm
    d. mollusk

12. Both tapeworms and leeches are
    a. annelid worms.
    b. parasites.
    c. flatworms.
    d. predators.

13. Some arthropods do not have
    a. jointed limbs.
    b. an exoskeleton.
    c. antennae.
    d. segments.

14. Echinoderms live
    a. on land.
    b. in fresh water.
    c. in salt water.
    d. All of the above

15. *Echinoderm* means
    a. "jointed limbs."
    b. "spiny skinned."
    c. "endoskeleton."
    d. "shiny tube foot."

16. Echinoderm larvae have
    a. radial symmetry.
    b. bilateral symmetry.
    c. no symmetry.
    d. radial and bilateral symmetry.

Short Answer

17. What is a gut?

18. How are arachnids different from insects?

19. Which animal phylum contains the most species?

20. How does an echinoderm move?

Concept Mapping

21. Use the following terms to create a concept map: insect, sponges, sea anemone, invertebrates, arachnid, sea cucumber, crustacean, centipede, cnidarians, arthropods, echinoderms.

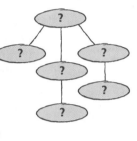

CRITICAL THINKING AND PROBLEM SOLVING

Write one or two sentences to answer the following questions:

22. You have discovered a strange new animal that has bilateral symmetry, a coelom, and nerves. Will this animal be classified in the Cnidaria phylum? Why or why not?

23. Unlike other mollusks, cephalopods can move rapidly. Based on what you know about the body parts of mollusks, why do you think cephalopods have this ability?

24. Roundworms, flatworms, and annelid worms belong to different phyla. Why aren't all the worms grouped in the same phylum?

MATH IN SCIENCE

25. If 75 percent of all animals are arthropods and 40 percent of all arthropods are beetles, what percentage of all animals are beetles?

INTERPRETING GRAPHICS

Below is an evolutionary tree showing how the different phyla of animals may be related to one another. The "trunk" of the tree is on the left. Use the tree to answer the questions that follow.

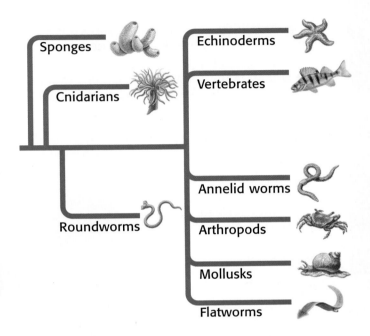

26. Which phylum is the oldest?

27. Are mollusks more closely related to roundworms or flatworms?

28. What phylum is most closely related to the vertebrates?

NOW What Do You Think?

Take a minute to review your answers to the ScienceLog questions on page 343. Have your answers changed? If necessary, revise your answers based on what you have learned since you began this chapter.

WEIRD SCIENCE

WATER BEARS

You're alive and you know it, but how? Well, eating, breathing, and moving around are all pretty sure signs of life. And once something stops eating or breathing, the end is near. Or is it? Oddly enough, this doesn't seem to be the case for one group of invertebrates—the water bears.

Grin and Bear It

When conditions get really rough—too hot, too cold, but mostly too dry to survive—a water bear will shut down its body processes. It's similar to a bear going into hibernation, but it is even more extreme. When a water bear can't find water, it dries itself out and forms a sugar that coats its cells. Scientists think this may keep the water bear's cells from breaking down, and it may be the key to its survival.

During this hibernation-like state, called *cryptobiosis* (CRIP toh bie OH sis), the water bear doesn't eat, move, or breathe. And amazingly, it doesn't die either. Once you add water, the water bear will come right back to normal life!

Water Bear

Hard to Put a Finger On

Officially called tardigrades (TAHR di graydz), water bears have been difficult to classify. But the 700 different species of water bears are probably most closely related to arthropods. Most make their homes on wet mosses and lichens. Some water bears feed on nematodes (a tiny, unsegmented worm) and rotifers (a tiny wormlike or spherical animal). Most feed on the fluids from mosses found near their homes.

From the tropics to the Arctic, the world is full of water bears. None are much larger than a grain of sand, but all have a slow, stomping walk. Some tardigrades live as deep as the bottom of the ocean, more than 4,700 m below sea level. Other water bears live at elevations of 6,600 m above sea level, well above the tree line. It is a wonder how water bears can withstand the range of temperatures found in these places, from 151°C to −270°C.

On Your Own

► What do you think people can learn from an organism like the water bear? Write down at least one reason why it is worthwhile to study these special creatures.

EYE ON THE ENVIRONMENT

Sizable Squid

"Before my eyes was a horrible monster . . . It swam crossways in the direction of the *Nautilus* with great speed, watching us with its enormous staring green eyes. The monster's mouth, a horned beak like a parrot's, opened and shut vertically." So wrote Jules Verne in his science-fiction story *Twenty Thousand Leagues Under the Sea.* But what was this horrible monster that was about to attack the submarine *Nautilus*? Believe it or not, it was a creature that actually exists—a giant squid!

▲ *This giant squid was already dead when it was caught in a fishing net off the coast of New Zealand.*

Squid Facts

As the largest of all invertebrates, giant squids range from 8 m to 25 m long and weigh as much as 2,000 kg. It's hard to know for sure, though, because no one has ever studied a living giant squid. Scientists have studied only dead or dying giant squids that have washed ashore or have been trapped in fishing nets.

Giant squids are very similar to their much smaller relatives. They have a torpedo-shaped body, two tentacles, eight arms, a mantle, a funnel, and a beak. All their body parts are much larger, though! A giant squid's eyes, for instance, may be as large as a volleyball! And like adult squids of smaller species, giant squids feed not only on fish but also on smaller squids. Given the size of giant squids, it's hard to imagine that they have any enemies in the ocean, but they do.

A Hungry Enemy

Weighing in at 20 tons, toothed sperm whales eat giant squids. How do we know this? As many as 10,000 squid beaks have been found in the stomach of a single sperm whale. The hard beaks of giant squids are indigestible. It seems that giant squids are a regular meal for sperm whales. Yet this meal can result in some battle scars. Many whales bear ring marks on their forehead and fins that match the size of the suckers found on giant squids.

Fact or Fiction?

▶ Read Chapter 18 of Jules Verne's *Twenty Thousand Leagues Under the Sea,* and then try to find other stories about squids. Write your own story about a giant squid, and share it with the class.

16 Fishes, Amphibians, and Reptiles

Would You Believe...?

In December 1938, a museum curator living on the coast of South Africa made one of her regular visits to a local fishing dock. Marjorie Courtenay Latimer searched the fishermen's catch for interesting fish. There, beneath a pile of rays and sharks, was the shining fin of the most unusual fish she'd ever seen.

The creature was huge—1.5 m long—and the taxicab driver who took Latimer back to the museum was none too happy to have it in his back seat! After checking several books, Latimer decided the fish might be a coelacanth (SEE luh kahnth). Scientists had thought that coelacanths became extinct with the dinosaurs, about 70 million years ago!

Whatever the fish was, it was beginning to rot. To preserve the fish, Latimer had it mounted. But first she drew a quick sketch of the fish and mailed the drawing to a friend named J.L.B. Smith, an expert on fish. Smith saw right away that the sketch was of a coelacanth.

The preserved fish made Smith and Latimer famous overnight. Latimer's giant fish with thick fins was one of the most fascinating finds of the twentieth century. Smith named the coelacanth *Latimeria* in his friend's honor.

Marjorie Courtenay Latimer discovered a living coelacanth.

In your ScienceLog, try to answer the following questions based on what you already know:

1. What does it mean to say an animal is coldblooded?

2. What is the difference between a reptile and an amphibian?

Unscrambling an Egg

The embryos of fish, amphibians, and reptiles all develop in eggs. Fish and amphibians lay their eggs in water or in very moist areas, but most reptiles lay their eggs on dry land. Modern reptiles have eggs with shells. The shells may be hard or leathery, but the eggs are similar to the eggs that birds have. In this activity, you'll uncover the parts of an egg with a shell. What you learn about chicken eggs will also be true for most reptile eggs.

Procedure

1. Get a **hard-boiled chicken egg** from your teacher.

2. Using a **pencil**, draw an outline of your egg on a **piece of paper.**

3. Gently crack the egg, and peel away the shell. Look for a thin membrane between the shell and the white, and look for an air space on the larger end of the egg. Draw all the parts of the egg as you take it apart.

4. Use a **knife** to carefully cut the egg in half lengthwise. Look for a very thin membrane between the white and the yolk. Add the parts you see to your egg diagram.

Analysis

5. Compare your diagram with the illustration below. Did you find all the parts? Label your diagram with the names of the parts.

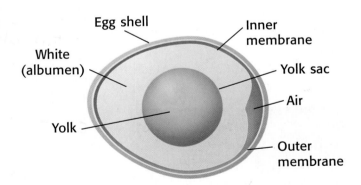

6. Why do you think there is an air space in the egg?

7. Why do you think hard-shelled eggs helped reptiles adapt to life on land?

8. Would the parts be easier or harder to find in a raw egg? Why?

What You'll Do

◆ List the four characteristics of chordates.

◆ Describe the main characteristics of vertebrates.

◆ Explain the difference between an ectotherm and an endotherm.

What Are Vertebrates?

Have you ever seen a dinosaur skeleton at a museum? Fossilized dinosaur bones were put back together to show what the animal looked like. Most dinosaur skeletons are huge compared with the skeletons of the humans who view them. But humans have many of the same kinds of bones that dinosaurs had; ours are just smaller. Your backbone is very much like the one in a dinosaur skeleton, as shown in **Figure 1.** Animals with a backbone are called **vertebrates.**

Figure 1 *Humans and dinosaurs are both vertebrates.*

Chordates

Vertebrates belong to the phylum Chordata. Members of this phylum are called *chordates.* Vertebrates make up the largest group of chordates, but there are two other groups of chordates—lancelets and tunicates. These are shown in **Figure 2.** These chordates do not have a backbone or a well-developed head. They are very simple compared with vertebrates. But all three groups share chordate characteristics.

At some point in their life, all chordates have four special body parts: a *notochord,* a *hollow nerve cord, pharyngeal* (fuh RIN jee uhl) *pouches,* and a *tail.* These are shown in **Figure 3** on the next page.

Figure 2 *Both tunicates, like the sea squirts at left, and the lancelet, shown above, are marine organisms.*

A stiff but flexible rod called a **notochord** gives the body support. In most vertebrates, the embryo's notochord disappears and a backbone grows in its place.

A **hollow nerve cord** runs along the back and is full of fluid. In vertebrates, this nerve cord is called the *spinal cord,* and it is filled with *spinal fluid.*

Chordates have a **tail** that begins behind the anus. Some chordates have a tail in only the embryo stage.

Pharyngeal pouches are found in all chordate embryos. These develop into gills or other body parts as the embryo matures.

Figure 3 *The chordate characteristics in a lancelet are shown here. All chordates have these four characteristics at some point in their life.*

Getting a Backbone

Most chordates are vertebrates. Vertebrates have many traits that set them apart from the lancelets and tunicates. For example, vertebrates have a backbone. The backbone is a segmented column of bones. These bones are called **vertebrae** (VUHR tuh BRAY). You can see the vertebrae of a human in **Figure 4.** The vertebrae surround the nerve cord and protect it. Vertebrates also have a well-developed head protected by a skull. The skull and vertebrae are made of either cartilage or bone. *Cartilage* is the tough material that the flexible parts of our ears and nose are made of.

The skeletons of all vertebrate embryos are made of cartilage. But as most vertebrates grow, the cartilage is usually replaced by bone. Bone is much harder than cartilage.

Because bone is so hard, it can easily be fossilized. Many fossils of vertebrates have been discovered, and they have provided valuable information about relationships among organisms.

Vertebrae

Figure 4 *The vertebrae interlock to form a strong but flexible column of bone. The backbone protects the spinal cord and supports the rest of the body.*

Are Vertebrates Warm or Cold?

Most animals need to stay warm. The chemical reactions that take place in their body cells occur only at certain temperatures. An animal's body temperature cannot be too high or too low. But some animals control their body temperature more than others.

Staying Warm   Birds and mammals warm their body by capturing the heat released by the chemical reactions in their cells. Their body temperature stays nearly constant even as the temperature of their environment changes. Animals that maintain a constant body temperature are called **endotherms.** Endotherms are sometimes called *warmblooded* animals. Because of their constant body temperature, endotherms can live in cold environments.

Cold Blood?   On sunny days, lizards, like the one in **Figure 5,** bask in the sun. As they become warm, they also become more active. They are able to hunt for food and escape predators. But when the temperature drops, lizards slow down.

Lizards and other animals that do not control their body temperature through the chemical reactions of their cells are called **ectotherms.** Their body temperature fluctuates with the temperature of their environment. Nearly all fishes, amphibians, and reptiles are ectotherms. Ectotherms are sometimes called *coldblooded* animals.

Figure 5 *Lizards bask in the sun to absorb heat.*

TOPIC: Vertebrates
GO TO: www.scilinks.org
*sci*LINKS NUMBER: HSTL380

REVIEW

1. How are vertebrates the same as other chordates? How are they different?

2. How are endotherms and ectotherms different?

3. **Applying Concepts**   Your pet lizard is not moving very much. The veterinarian tells you to put a heat lamp in the cage. Why might this help?

Fishes

Terms to Learn

fins   gills
scales   denticles
lateral line swim bladder
  system

What You'll Do

◆ Describe the three classes of
  living fishes, and give an
  example of each.
◆ Describe the function of a swim
  bladder and an oily liver.
◆ Explain the difference between
  internal fertilization and external
  fertilization.

Find a body of water, and you'll probably find fish. Fishes live in almost every water environment, from shallow ponds and streams to the depths of the oceans. You can find fishes in cold arctic waters and in warm tropical seas. Fishes can be found in rivers, lakes, marshes, and even in water-filled caves.

Fish were the first vertebrates on Earth. Fossil evidence indicates that fish appeared about 500 million years ago. Today Earth's marine and freshwater fishes make up more species than all other vertebrates combined. There are more than 25,000 species of fishes, and more are being discovered. A few are shown in **Figure 6.**

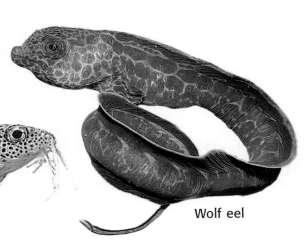

Angelfish

Figure 6 These are just some of the many species of fishes. Do any look familiar?

Surgeonfish

Catfish

Wolf eel

Sea horse

Fish Characteristics

Although the fishes on this page look very different from each other, they share many characteristics that help them live in water.

Many fishes are predators of other animals. Others are herbivores. Because they must actively search for food, they need a strong body, well-developed senses, and a brain.

Born to Swim Fishes have many body parts that help them swim. Strong muscles attached to the backbone allow fishes to swim vigorously after their prey. Fishes swim through the water by moving their fins. **Fins** are fanlike structures that help fish move, steer, stop, and balance. Many fishes have bodies covered by **scales,** which protect the body and reduce friction as they swim through the water. **Figure 7** shows some of the external features of a typical fish.

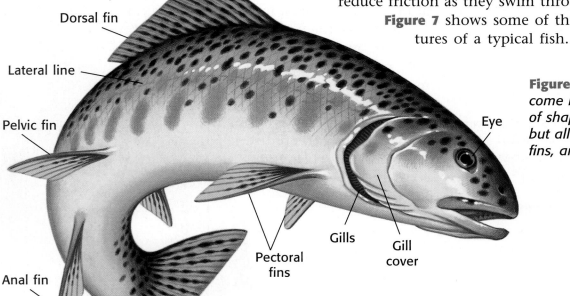

Dorsal fin

Lateral line

Pelvic fin

Anal fin

Tail fin

Pectoral fins

Gills

Gill cover

Eye

Figure 7 *Fishes come in a variety of shapes and sizes, but all have gills, fins, and a tail.*

Making Sense of the World Fishes have well-developed vision, hearing, and sense of smell. Most fishes also have a lateral line system. The **lateral line system** is a row or rows of tiny sense organs along each side of the body that often extend onto the head. This system detects water vibrations, such as those caused by another fish swimming by. Fishes have a brain that keeps track of all the information coming in from these senses. A tough skull protects the brain.

Underwater Breathing Fishes breathe with gills. **Gills** are organs that remove oxygen from the water. Oxygen in the water passes through the thin membrane of the gills to the blood. The blood then carries oxygen throughout the body. Gills are also used to remove carbon dioxide from the blood.

Making More Fish Most fishes reproduce by *external fertilization.* The female lays unfertilized eggs in the water, and the male drops sperm on them. But some species of fish reproduce by internal fertilization. In *internal fertilization,* the male deposits sperm inside the female. In most cases the female then lays eggs that contain the developing embryos. Baby fish hatch from the eggs. But in some species, the embryos develop inside the mother, and the baby fish are born live.

Physics

C O N N E C T I O N

When you look at an object through a magnifying glass, you have to move the lens back and forth in front of your eye to bring the object into focus. The same thing happens in fish eyes. Fish have special muscles to change the position of the lenses of their eyes. By moving the eye lenses, fish can bring objects into focus.

Types of Fishes

Fishes include five very different classes of animals. Two classes are now extinct. We know about them only because of fossils. The three classes of fishes living today are *jawless fishes, cartilaginous fishes,* and *bony fishes.*

Jawless Fishes The first fishes did not have jaws. You might think that having no jaws would make it hard to eat and would lead to extinction. But the jawless fishes have thrived for half a billion years. Today there are about 60 species of jawless fishes.

Modern jawless fishes include lampreys, as shown in **Figure 8,** and hagfish. These fishes are eel-like, and they have smooth, slimy skin and a round, jawless mouth. Their skeleton is made of cartilage, and they have a notochord but no backbone. These fishes have a skull, a brain, and eyes.

Figure 8 *Lampreys are parasites that live by attaching themselves to other fishes.*

Cartilaginous Fishes Did you know that a shark is a fish? Sharks, like the one in **Figure 9,** belong to a class of fishes called cartilaginous (KART'l AJ uh nuhs) fishes. In most vertebrates, soft cartilage in the embryo is gradually replaced by bone. In sharks, skates, and rays, however, the skeleton never changes from cartilage to bone. That is why they are called cartilaginous fishes.

Sharks are the most well-known cartilaginous fishes, but they are not the only ones. Another group includes skates and rays. A sting ray is shown in **Figure 10.**

As any shark lover knows, cartilaginous fishes have fully functional jaws. These fishes are strong swimmers and expert predators. Like most predators, they have keen senses. Many have excellent senses of sight and smell, and they have a lateral line system.

Figure 9 *Sharks, like this hammerhead, rarely prey on humans. They prefer to eat their regular food, which is fish.*

Figure 10 *Rays, like this sting ray, usually feed on shellfish and worms on the sea floor.*

Figure 11 *A shark's denticles and human teeth are made of the same materials.*

Figure 12 *A goldfish is a bony fish.*

A Lot of Bones

If there are 25,000 species of fishes and 95 percent of all fishes are bony fishes, how many species of bony fishes are there?

The skin of cartilaginous fishes is covered with small tooth-like **denticles** that give it the feel of sandpaper. If you rub your hand on a shark's skin from head to tail, it feels smooth. But if you rub your hand from tail to head, you can get cut! Look at the magnified denticles in **Figure 11.**

To stay afloat, cartilaginous fishes store a lot of oil in their liver. See why in the QuickLab on the next page. Even with oily livers, these fishes are heavier than water. They have to keep moving in order to stay afloat. Once they stop swimming, they gradually glide to the bottom.

Cartilaginous fishes do not swim just to keep from sinking, however. Some must swim to maintain the flow of water over their gills. If these fishes stop swimming, they will suffocate. Others do not have to swim. They can lie on the ocean floor and pump water across their gills.

Bony Fishes When you think of a fish, you probably think of something like the fish shown in **Figure 12.** Goldfish, tuna, trout, catfish, and cod are all bony fishes, the largest class of fishes. Ninety-five percent of all fishes are bony fishes. They range in size from 1 cm long to more than 6 m long.

As their name implies, bony fishes have a skeleton made of bone instead of cartilage. The body of a bony fish is covered by bony scales.

Unlike cartilaginous fishes, bony fishes can float in one place without swimming. This is because they have a swim bladder that keeps them from sinking. The **swim bladder** is a balloonlike organ that is filled with oxygen and other gases from the bloodstream. It gives fish *buoyancy,* or the ability to float in water. The swim bladder and other body parts of bony fishes are shown in **Figure 13.**

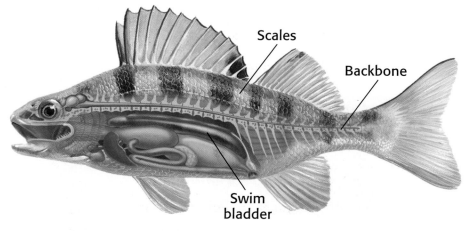

Scales

Backbone

Swim bladder

Figure 13 *Bony fishes have a swim bladder, a bony skeleton, and scales.*

There are two main groups of bony fishes. Almost all bony fishes are *ray-finned fishes*. Ray-finned fishes have paired fins supported by thin rays of bone. Ray-finned fishes include many familiar fishes, such as eels, herrings, trout, minnows, and perch. **Figure 14** shows a ray-finned fish.

Lobe-finned fishes and *lungfishes* make up a second group of bony fishes. Lobe-finned fishes have fins that are muscular and thick. The coelacanths, which were described at the beginning of the chapter, are lobe-finned fishes. There are six known species of modern lungfishes. You can see a lungfish in **Figure 15**. Scientists think that ancient fishes from this group were the ancestors of amphibians.

Figure 14 *Ray-finned fishes are some of the fastest swimmers in the world. A pike, like this one, can swim as fast as the fastest human runners can run, about 48 km/h.*

Figure 15 *Lungfishes have air sacs, or lungs, and can gulp air. They are found in Africa, Australia, and South America and live in shallow waters that often dry up in the summer.*

REVIEW

1. What are the three types of fishes? Which type are the coelacanths?

2. Most bony fishes reproduce by external fertilization. What does this mean?

3. What is the lateral line system, and what is its function?

4. **Analyzing Relationships** Compare the ways that cartilaginous fishes and bony fishes maintain buoyancy.

Quick Lab

Oil on Troubled Waters

Are you wondering how an oily liver can keep a shark afloat? This experiment will help you understand. Measure out equal amounts of **water** and **cooking oil**. Fill a **balloon** with the water. Fill another balloon with the cooking oil. Tie the balloons so that no air remains inside. Float each balloon in a **bowl** half full of water. What happens? How does the oily liver of a cartilaginous fish keep the fish from sinking?

Amphibians

Terms to Learn

lung   metamorphosis
tadpole

What You'll Do

◆ Describe the importance of amphibians in evolution.
◆ Explain how amphibians breathe.
◆ Describe metamorphosis in amphibians.

By the end of the Devonian period, 350 million years ago, fishes lived wherever there was water. But none of these vertebrates could live on land. And the land was a wonderful place for a vertebrate. It had lush green forests, many tasty insects, and few predators. But for vertebrates to adapt to life on land, they needed lungs for breathing and legs for walking. How did these changes occur?

Moving to Land

Most of the amphibians living on Earth today are frogs or salamanders, like those in **Figure 16.** But the early amphibians looked much different. Fossil evidence indicates that the first amphibians evolved from ancient ancestors of modern lungfishes. These fishes developed lungs to get oxygen from the air. A **lung** is a saclike organ that takes oxygen from the air and delivers it to the blood. The fins of these ancient fishes became strong enough to support the fishes' body weight and eventually became legs.

Fossils show that the first amphibians looked like a cross between a fish and a salamander, as shown in **Figure 17.** The early amphibians were the first vertebrates to live most of their life on land, and they were very successful. Many were very large—up to 10 m long—and could stay on dry land longer than today's amphibians can. But early amphibians still had to return to the water to keep from drying out, to avoid overheating, and to lay their eggs.

Figure 16 Modern amphibians include frogs and salamanders.

Barred leaf frog

Sierra Nevada salamander

Figure 17 *Ancient amphibians probably looked something like this.*

Characteristics of Amphibians

Amphibian means "double life." Most amphibians have two parts to their life. Because amphibian eggs do not have a shell and a special membrane to prevent water loss, the embryos must develop in a very wet environment. After amphibians emerge from an egg, they live in the water, like fishes do. Later they develop into animals that can live on land. But even adult amphibians are only partly adapted to life on land, and they must always live near water.

Amphibians are ectotherms. Like the body of a fish, the body of an amphibian changes temperature according to the temperature of its environment.

Thin-Skinned Most amphibians do not have scales. Their skin is thin, smooth, and moist. They do not drink water. Instead, they absorb it through their skin. Amphibians can breathe by gulping air into their lungs. But many also absorb oxygen through their skin, which is full of blood vessels. Some salamanders, like the one in **Figure 18,** breathe only through their skin. Because amphibian skin is so thin and moist, these animals can lose water through their skin and become dehydrated. For this reason, most amphibians live in water or in damp habitats.

The skin of many amphibians is brilliantly colored. The colors are often a warning to predators because the skin of many amphibians contains poison glands. These poisons may simply be irritating or they may be deadly. The skin of the dart-poison frog, shown in **Figure 19,** contains one of the most deadly toxins known.

Figure 18 *The four-toed salamander has no lungs. It gets all of its oxygen through its skin.*

Self-Check

How is amphibian skin like a lung? *(See page 782 to check your answers.)*

Figure 19 *The skin of this dart-poison frog is full of poison glands. In South America, hunters rub the tips of their arrows in the deadly toxin.*

Leading a Double Life The amphibian embryo usually develops into an aquatic larva called a **tadpole.** The tadpole can live only in wet environments. It obtains oxygen through gills and uses its long tail to swim. Later the tadpole loses its gills and develops lungs and limbs. This change from a larval form to an adult form is called **metamorphosis** and is shown in **Figure 20.** Adult amphibians are capable of surviving on land.

Figure 20
Most frogs and salamanders go through metamorphosis.

Adult frog

The tail and gills disappear, and lungs become functional.

Fertilized eggs

A newly hatched tadpole feeds on yolk stored in its body and breathes with gills.

The tadpole begins to feed and grow legs.

A few amphibians skip the aquatic stage and develop directly into adult frogs or salamanders. For example, one species of frog lays eggs on moist ground. Male adults guard the developing embryos. When an embryo begins to move, a male frog quickly takes it into its mouth and protects it inside its vocal sacs. When the embryo finishes developing, the adult frog opens its mouth, and a tiny frog jumps out. You can see this frog in **Figure 21.**

Figure 21 *Darwin frogs live in Chile and Argentina. A male frog may carry 5 to 15 embryos in its vocal sacs until the young are about 1.5 cm in length.*

Kinds of Amphibians

It is estimated that there are 4,600 species of amphibians alive today. These belong to three groups: caecilians (see SIL yuhns), salamanders, and frogs and toads.

Caecilians Most people are not familiar with caecilians. These amphibians do not have legs and are shaped like worms or snakes, as shown in **Figure 22.** But they have the thin, moist skin of amphibians. Unlike other amphibians, some caecilians have bony scales. Many caecilians have very small eyes underneath their skin and are blind. Caecilians live in the tropical areas of Asia, Africa, and South America. About 160 species are known.

Figure 22 *Caecilians are legless amphibians that live in damp soil in the tropics. Caecilians eat small invertebrates in the soil.*

Salamanders Of modern amphibians, salamanders are the most like prehistoric amphibians. Although salamanders are much smaller than their ancient ancestors, they have a similar body shape, a long tail, and four strong legs. They range in size from a few centimeters long to 1.5 m long.

There are about 390 known species of salamanders. Most of them live under stones and logs in the damp woods of North America. They eat small invertebrates. A few, such as the axolotl (AK suh LAHT 'l), shown in **Figure 23,** do not go through metamorphosis. They live their entire life in the water.

Figure 23 *This axolotl is an unusual salamander. It retains its gills and never leaves the water.*

APPLY

Ecological Indicators

Amphibians are often called ecological indicators. When large numbers of amphibians begin to die or show deformities, this may indicate a problem with the environment.

Sometimes deformities are caused by parasites, but amphibians are also extremely sensitive to chemical changes in their environment. Based on what you know about amphibians, why do you think they are sensitive to water pollution and air pollution?

Frogs and Toads Ninety percent of all amphibians are frogs or toads. They are found all over the world, from deserts to rain forests. Frogs and toads are very similar to each other, as you can see in **Figure 24.** In fact, toads are a type of frog.

Frog

Toad

Figure 24 *Frogs have smooth, moist skin. Toads spend less time in water than frogs do, and their skin is drier and bumpier.*

Frogs and toads are highly adapted for life on land. Adults have powerful leg muscles for jumping. They have well-developed ears for hearing, and they have vocal cords for calling. They also have extendible, sticky tongues. The tongue is attached to the front of the mouth so that it can be flipped out quickly to catch insects.

Singing Frogs Frogs are well known for their nighttime choruses, but many frogs sing in the daytime too. Like humans, they force air from their lungs across vocal cords in the throat. But frogs have something we lack. Surrounding their vocal cords is a thin sac of skin called the *vocal sac.* When frogs vocalize, the sac inflates with air, like a balloon does, and vibrates. You can see this in **Figure 25.** The vibrations of the sac increase the volume of the song so that it can be heard over long distances.

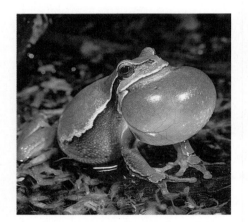

Figure 25 *Most frogs that sing are males, and their songs have different meanings.*

REVIEW

1. Describe metamorphosis in amphibians.

2. Why do amphibians have to be near water or in a very wet habitat?

3. What adaptations allow amphibians to live on land?

4. Name the three types of amphibians. How are they similar? How are they different?

5. **Analyzing Relationships** Describe the relationship between lungfishes and amphibians. What characteristics do they share? How do they differ?

Examine the princely characteristics of a friendly frog on page 742 of your LabBook.

Terms to Learn

therapsid
amniotic egg

What You'll Do

◆ Explain the adaptations that allow reptiles to live on land.
◆ Name the three main groups of vertebrates that evolved from reptiles.
◆ Describe the characteristics of an amniotic egg.
◆ Name the three orders of modern reptiles.

Reptiles

About 35 million years after the first amphibians colonized the land, some of them evolved special traits that prepared them for life in an even drier environment. These animals developed thick, dry skin that protected them from water loss. Their legs became stronger and more vertical, so they were better able to walk. And they evolved a special egg that could be laid on dry land. These animals were reptiles, the first animals to live completely out of the water.

Reptile History

Fossils show that soon after the first reptiles appeared, they split into groups. This can be shown in a family tree of the reptiles, as illustrated in **Figure 26.**

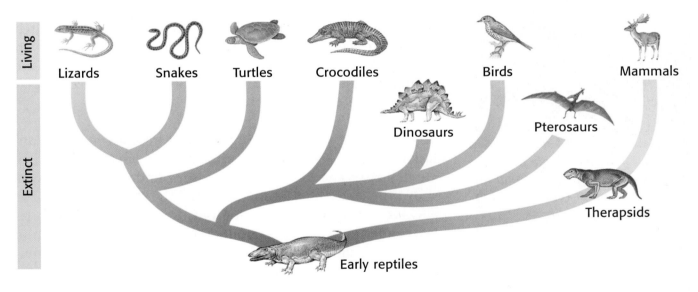

Figure 26 *Early reptiles were the ancestors of modern reptiles, birds, and mammals.*

Many of the most fascinating reptiles are now extinct. When we think of extinct reptiles, we usually think of dinosaurs. But only a fraction of the reptiles living in prehistoric times were land-dwelling dinosaurs. Many were swimming reptiles. A few were flying pterosaurs. And there were turtles, lizards, snakes, and crocodiles. In addition, there was a group of mammal-like reptiles called therapsids. As you can see in Figure 26, **therapsids** (thuh RAP sidz) were the ancestors of mammals.

Characteristics of Reptiles

Reptiles are adapted for life on land. Although crocodiles, turtles, and a few species of snakes live in the water, all of these animals are descended from reptiles that lived on land. All reptiles use lungs to breathe air, just as you do.

Thick-Skinned A very important adaptation for life on land is thick, dry skin, which forms a watertight layer. This thick skin keeps cells from losing water by evaporation. Most reptiles cannot breathe through their skin the way amphibians can. Most depend entirely on their lungs for oxygen and carbon dioxide exchange. Check out the snake's skin in **Figure 27.**

Figure 27 *Many people think snakes are slimy, but the skin of snakes and other reptiles is scaly and dry.*

Coldblooded? Like fishes and amphibians, reptiles are ectotherms. That means that they usually cannot maintain a constant body temperature. Reptiles are active when their environment is warm, and they slow down when their environment is cool.

A few reptiles can generate some heat from their own body. For example, some lizards in the southwestern United States can keep their body temperature at about 34°C, even when the air temperature is cool. Still, modern reptiles are limited to mild climates. They cannot tolerate the cold polar regions, where many mammals and birds thrive.

The Amazing Amniotic Egg Among reptiles' many adaptations to land life, the most critical is the amniotic (AM nee AH tik) egg. The **amniotic egg** is surrounded by a shell, as shown in **Figure 28.** The shell protects the developing embryo and keeps the egg from drying out. An amniotic egg can be laid under rocks, in the ground, in forests, or even in the desert. The amniotic egg is so well adapted to a dry environment that even crocodiles and turtles return to land to lay their eggs.

Figure 28 *Compare the amphibian eggs at left with the reptile eggs at right. What differences can you see?*

Parts of an Amniotic Egg The shell is just one important part of an amniotic egg. The other parts of an amniotic egg are illustrated in **Figure 29.** The egg protects the developing embryo from predators, bacterial infections, and dehydration.

Figure 29 An Amniotic Egg

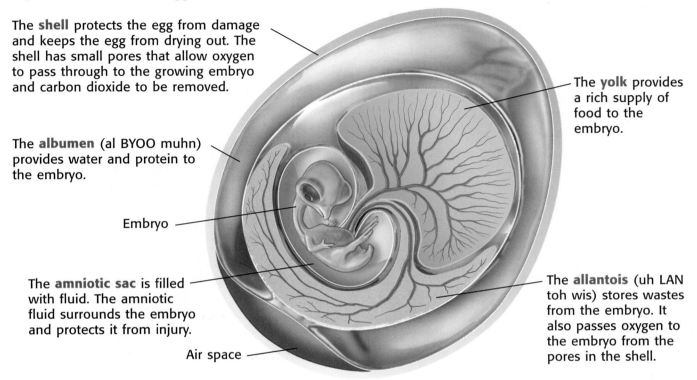

The **shell** protects the egg from damage and keeps the egg from drying out. The shell has small pores that allow oxygen to pass through to the growing embryo and carbon dioxide to be removed.

The **albumen** (al BYOO muhn) provides water and protein to the embryo.

Embryo

The **amniotic sac** is filled with fluid. The amniotic fluid surrounds the embryo and protects it from injury.

Air space

The **yolk** provides a rich supply of food to the embryo.

The **allantois** (uh LAN toh wis) stores wastes from the embryo. It also passes oxygen to the embryo from the pores in the shell.

Reptile Reproduction The amniotic egg is fertilized inside the female. A shell then forms around the egg, and the female lays the egg. Because of the shell, reptiles can reproduce only by internal fertilization.

Most reptiles lay their eggs in soil or sand. A few do not lay eggs. Instead the embryos develop inside the mother's reproductive passages, and the young are born live. In either case, the embryo develops into a tiny young reptile. Reptiles do not have a larval stage and do not undergo metamorphosis.

Types of Reptiles

In the age of the dinosaurs, from 300 million years ago until about 65 million years ago, most land vertebrates were reptiles. Today the 6,000 species of living reptiles represent only a handful of the many species of reptiles that once lived.

Modern reptiles include turtles and tortoises, crocodiles and alligators, and lizards and snakes.

Self-Check

1. What adaptations of reptiles are important for living on dry land?

2. Why must animals that lay eggs with shells reproduce by internal fertilization?

(See page 782 to check your answers.)

Turtles and Tortoises

The 250 species of turtles and tortoises are only distantly related to the rest of the reptiles.

The trait that makes turtles and tortoises unique is their shell. The shell makes a turtle slow and inflexible, so outrunning its predators is highly unlikely. On the other hand, many turtles can draw their head and limbs into the armorlike shell to protect themselves, as the box turtle shown in **Figure 30** is doing.

Most turtles spend some or all of their life in water. The front legs of sea turtles have evolved into flippers, as shown in **Figure 31.** Female sea turtles come ashore only to lay their eggs on sandy beaches. Desert tortoises are different from other turtles. They live only on land.

Figure 30 *The bottom shell of a box turtle is hinged on both ends so the turtle can pull it snug against the top shell.*

Figure 31 *Sea turtles have a streamlined shell to help them swim and turn rapidly.*

Crocodiles and Alligators

The 22 species of crocodiles and alligators are all carnivores. They eat water bugs, fish, turtles, birds, and mammals. These reptiles spend most of their time in the water. Because their eyes and nostrils are on the top of their flat head, they can watch their surroundings while most of their body is hidden underwater. This gives them a great advantage over their prey. How can you tell the difference between an alligator and a crocodile? See for yourself in **Figure 32.**

Figure 32 *An alligator has a broad head and a rounded snout. A crocodile has a narrow head and a pointed snout.*

Alligator

Crocodile

Lizards Most of the species of modern reptiles are lizards and snakes. There are about 4,000 known species of lizards and about 1,600 known species of snakes.

Figure 33 *Komodo dragons eat deer, pigs, and goats. They have even been known to eat humans in rare cases.*

Lizards live in deserts, forests, grasslands, and jungles. Chameleons, geckos, skinks, and iguanas are some of the amazing variety of lizards. Most lizards eat small invertebrates, but many are herbivores. The largest lizard is the 3 m long, 140 kg Komodo dragon of Indonesia, shown in **Figure 33.** But most lizards are less than 30 cm long.

Snakes The most obvious characteristic of snakes is their lack of legs. Snakes move by contractions of their muscular body. On smooth surfaces, scales on their belly grip the surface and help pull the snake forward.

All snakes are carnivores. They eat small animals and eggs. Snakes swallow their prey whole, as shown in **Figure 34.** Snakes have special jaws with five joints that allow them to open their mouth wide and swallow very large prey. Some snakes, such as pythons and boas, kill their prey by squeezing it until it suffocates. Other snakes have poison glands and special fangs for injecting venom into their prey. The venom kills or stuns the prey and contains powerful enzymes that begin digesting it.

Figure 34 *This common egg eater snake is swallowing a bird's egg.*

Snakes do not see or hear well, but they can smell extremely well. When a snake flicks its forked tongue out of its mouth, it is sampling the air. Tiny particles and molecules stick to the tongue. When the snake pulls its tongue inside its mouth, it places the tips of its tongue into two openings in the roof of its mouth, where the molecules are sensed.

REVIEW

1. What characteristics set turtles apart from other reptiles?

2. What special adaptations do snakes have for eating?

3. **Applying Concepts** Like reptiles, mammals have an amniotic egg. But mammals give birth to live young. The embryo develops from a fertilized egg inside the female's body. Which parts of a reptilian amniotic egg do you think a mammal could do without? Explain your answer.

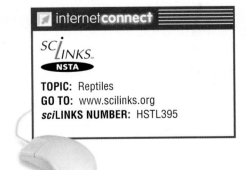

internet connect

SCi*LINKS*
NSTA

TOPIC: Reptiles
GO TO: www.scilinks.org
*sci*LINKS NUMBER: HSTL395

Chapter Highlights

SECTION 1

Vocabulary

vertebrate (*p. 374*)

vertebrae (*p. 375*)

endotherm (*p. 376*)

ectotherm (*p. 376*)

Section Notes

- At some point during their development, chordates have a notochord, a hollow nerve cord, pharyngeal pouches, and a tail.

- Chordates include lancelets, tunicates, and vertebrates. Most chordates are vertebrates.

- Vertebrates differ from the other chordates in that they have a backbone and skull made of bone or cartilage.

- The backbone is composed of units called vertebrae.

- Vertebrates may be ectotherms or endotherms.

- Endotherms control their body temperature through the chemical reactions of their cells. Ectotherms do not.

SECTION 2

Vocabulary

fins (*p. 378*)

scales (*p. 378*)

lateral line system (*p. 378*)

gills (*p. 378*)

denticles (*p. 380*)

swim bladder (*p. 380*)

Section Notes

- There are three groups of living fishes: jawless fishes, cartilaginous fishes, and bony fishes.

- The cartilaginous fishes have an oily liver that helps them float.

☑ Skills Check

Math Concepts

HOW MANY SPECIES? If there are 6,000 species of reptiles and 67 percent of all reptiles are lizards, how many species of lizards are there?

Sixty-seven percent of 6,000 is:

$$6{,}000 \times 0.67 = 4{,}020$$

There are 4,020 species of lizards.

Visual Understanding

METAMORPHOSIS Most amphibians go through metamorphosis. They change form as they develop into an adult. Figure 20 on page 384 illustrates the metamorphosis of a frog. Follow the arrows to see how a frog develops from an egg to a tadpole to an adult.

SECTION 2

- Most bony fishes have a swim bladder. The swim bladder is a balloonlike organ that gives bony fishes buoyancy.

- In external fertilization, eggs are fertilized outside the female's body. In internal fertilization, eggs are fertilized inside the female's body.

Labs

Floating a Pipe Fish (p. 740)

SECTION 3

Vocabulary

lung (p. 382)
tadpole (p. 384)
metamorphosis (p. 384)

Section Notes

- Amphibians were the first vertebrates to live on land.

- Amphibians breathe by gulping air into their lungs and by absorbing oxygen through their skin.

- Amphibians start life in water, where they breathe through gills. During metamorphosis, they lose their gills and develop lungs and legs that allow them to live on land.

- Modern amphibians include caecilians, salamanders, and frogs and toads.

Labs

A Prince of a Frog (p. 742)

SECTION 4

Vocabulary

therapsid (p. 387)
amniotic egg (p. 388)

Section Notes

- Reptiles evolved from amphibians by adapting to life on dry land.

- Reptiles have thick, scaly skin that protects them from drying out.

- A tough shell keeps the amniotic egg from drying out and protects the embryo.

- Amniotic fluid surrounds and protects the embryo in an amniotic egg.

- Vertebrates that evolved from early reptiles are reptiles, birds, and mammals.

- Modern reptiles include turtles and tortoises, lizards and snakes, and crocodiles and alligators.

---

internet connect

GO TO: go.hrw.com

Visit the **HRW** Web site for a variety of learning tools related to this chapter. Just type in the keyword:

KEYWORD: HSTVR1

GO TO: www.scilinks.org

Visit the **National Science Teachers Association** on-line Web site for Internet resources related to this chapter. Just type in the *sci*LINKS number for more information about the topic:

TOPIC: Vertebrates	*sci*LINKS NUMBER: HSTL380
TOPIC: Fishes	*sci*LINKS NUMBER: HSTL385
TOPIC: Amphibians	*sci*LINKS NUMBER: HSTL390
TOPIC: Reptiles	*sci*LINKS NUMBER: HSTL395

Chapter Review

To complete the following sentences, choose the correct term from each pair of terms listed below:

1. At some point in their development, all chordates have __?__. (*lungs and a notochord* or *a hollow nerve cord and a tail*)

2. Mammals evolved from early ancestors called __?__. (*therapsids* or *dinosaurs*)

3. Fish are __?__. (*endotherms* or *ectotherms*)

4. When a frog lays eggs that are later fertilized by sperm, it is an example of __?__ fertilization. (*internal* or *external*)

5. The vertebrae wrap around and protect the __?__ of vertebrates. (*notochord* or *hollow nerve cord*)

UNDERSTANDING CONCEPTS

Multiple Choice

6. Which of the following is not a vertebrate?
   a. tadpole
   b. lizard
   c. lamprey
   d. tunicate

7. Tadpoles change into frogs by the process of
   a. evolution.
   b. internal fertilization.
   c. metamorphosis.
   d. temperature regulation.

8. The swim bladder is found in
   a. jawless fishes.
   b. cartilaginous fishes.
   c. bony fishes.
   d. lancelets.

9. The amniotic egg first evolved in
   a. bony fishes.   c. reptiles.
   b. birds.   d. mammals.

10. The yolk holds
    a. food for the embryo.
    b. amniotic fluid.
    c. wastes.
    d. oxygen.

11. Both bony fishes and cartilaginous fishes have
    a. denticles.
    b. fins.
    c. an oily liver.
    d. a swim bladder.

12. Reptiles are adapted to a life on land because
    a. they can breathe through their skin.
    b. they are ectotherms.
    c. they have thick, moist skin.
    d. they have an amniotic egg.

Short Answer

13. How do amphibians breathe?

14. What characteristics allow fish to live in the water?

15. How does an embryo in an amniotic egg get oxygen?

Concept Mapping

16. Use the following terms to create a concept map: dinosaur, turtle, reptiles, amphibians, fishes, shark, salamander, vertebrates.

Write one or two sentences to answer the following questions:

17. Suppose you have found an animal that has a backbone and gills, but you can't find a notochord. Is it a chordate? How can you be sure?

18. Suppose you have found a shark that lacks the muscles needed to pump water over its gills. What does that tell you about the shark's lifestyle?

19. A rattlesnake does not see very well, but it can detect a temperature change of as little as three-thousandths of a degree Celsius. How is this ability useful to a rattlesnake?

20. It's 43°C outside, and the normal body temperature of a velociraptor is 38°C. Would you most likely find the raptor in the sun or in the shade? Explain.

MATH IN SCIENCE

21. A Costa Rican viper can eat a mouse that has one-third more mass than the viper. How much can you eat? Write down your mass in kilograms. To find your mass in kilograms, divide your mass in pounds by 2.2. If you were to eat a meal with a mass one-third larger than your mass, what would the mass of the meal be in kilograms?

INTERPRETING GRAPHICS

Examine the graph of body temperatures below, and answer the questions that follow.

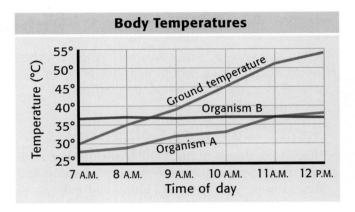

Body Temperatures

22. How do the body temperatures of organism A and organism B change with the ground temperature?

23. Which of these organisms is most likely an ectotherm? Why?

24. Which of these organisms is most likely an endotherm? Why?

NOW What Do You Think?

Take a minute to review your answers to the ScienceLog questions on page 373. Have your answers changed? If necessary, revise your answers based on what you have learned since you began this chapter.

LIFE SCIENCE • PHYSICAL SCIENCE

Robot Fish

When is a fish tail not a fish tail? When it's the tail of RoboTuna, a robotic fish designed by scientists at the Massachusetts Institute of Technology.

Something Fishy Going On

There's no doubt about it—fish are quicker and much more maneuverable than most ships and submarines. So why aren't ships and submarines built more like fish—with tails that flap back and forth? This question caught the imagination of some scientists at MIT and inspired them to build RoboTuna, a model of a bluefin tuna. This robot fish is 124 cm long and is composed of six motors, a skin of foam and Lycra™, and a skeleton of aluminum ribs and hinges connected by pulleys and strings.

A Tail of Force and Motion

The MIT scientists propose that if ships were designed to more closely resemble fish, the ships would use much less energy and thus save money. A ship moving through water leaves a trail of little whirlpools called *vortices*

behind it. These vortices increase the friction between the ship and the water. A fish, however, senses the vortices and responds by flapping its tail, creating vortices of its own. The fish's vortices counteract the effects of the original vortices, and the fish is propelled forward with much less effort.

RoboTuna has special sensors that measure changes in water pressure in much the same way that a living tuna senses vortices. Then the robot fish flaps its vortex-producing tail, allowing it to swim like a living fish. As strange as it may seem, RoboTuna may represent the beginning of a new era in nautical design.

Viewing Vortices

▶ Fill a roasting pan three-quarters full with water. Wait long enough for the water to stop moving. Then tie a 6 cm piece of yarn or ribbon to the end of a pencil. Drag the pencil through the water with the yarn or ribbon trailing behind it. How does the yarn or ribbon respond? Where are the vortices?

▶ *Inner Workings of MIT's RoboTuna*

1. A strut supports the robot, encloses the tendons, and conveys control and sensor information.

3. A skin of foam and Lycra is smooth enough to eliminate wrinkles or bulges and prevent the stray turbulence they cause.

2. Ribs and flexible beams hold the skin in place while allowing the body to flex continuously.

WARM BRAINS IN COLD WATER

Of the world's 30,000 kinds of fish, only a few carry around their own brain heaters. *Brain heaters?* Why would a fish need a special heater just for its brain? Before you can answer that question, you have to think about how fish keep warm in the cold water of the ocean.

A Question of Temperature

Most fish and marine organisms are ectotherms. An ectotherm's body temperature closely matches the temperature of its surroundings. Endotherms, on the other hand, maintain a steady body temperature regardless of the temperature of their surroundings. Humans are endotherms. Other mammals, such as dogs, elephants, whales, and birds, are also endotherms. But only a few kinds of fish—tuna, for example—are endotherms. These fish are still coldblooded, but they can heat certain parts of their bodies. Endothermic fish can hunt for prey in extremely chilly water. Yet these fish pay a high price for their ability to inhabit very cold areas—they use a lot of energy.

Being endothermic requires far more energy than being ectothermic. Some fish, such as swordfish, marlin, and sailfish, have adaptations that let them heat only part of their body. Instead of using large amounts of energy to warm the entire body, they warm only their eyes and brain. That's right—they have special brain heaters!

▶ *Why do you think it is important to protect the brain and eyes from extreme cold?*

Warming the Brain

In a "brain-warming" fish, a small mass of muscle attached to each eye acts as a thermostat. It adjusts the temperature of the brain and eyes as the fish swims through different temperature zones. These "heater muscles" help maintain delicate nerve functions that are important to finding prey.

Heater muscles allow the swordfish, for example, to swim in both warm surface waters of the ocean and depths of 485 m, where the temperature drops to near freezing. This adaptation has an obvious advantage: It gives the fish a large range of places to look for food.

Ectotherms in Action

▶ Contact a local pet store that sells various kinds of fish. Find out what water temperature is best for different fish from different regions of the Earth. For example, compare the ideal water temperatures for goldfish, discus fish, and angelfish. Why do you think fish-tank temperatures must be carefully controlled?

Brain
Heater muscles
Eye

17 Birds and Mammals

Would You Believe . . . ?

Would it surprise you to know that the pigeons in your schoolyard are related to velociraptors? A pigeon's waddling gait might not make you think of the fierce prehistoric animal, but most biologists now agree that birds are descendants of dinosaurs.

The first piece of evidence to link reptiles and birds was the fossil of *Archaeopteryx* (ark ee AHP tuhr iks). *Archaeopteryx* fossils were first discovered in Germany almost 150 years ago. Like a dinosaur, *Archaeopteryx* had heavy bones and teeth, but like a bird, it had feathered wings.

Many scientists were skeptical about the link between dinosaurs and birds. For one thing, some research suggested that *Archaeopteryx* wasn't a true dinosaur.

Then in 1998, Chinese scientists discovered fossils of true dinosaurs that had wings and feathers. These feathers share some characteristics of modern bird feathers. So far, no one knows how feathers might have helped the dinosaurs. Their wings were too short for flight. The feathers may have been insulation against cold. Or maybe males used them to attract female dinosaurs.

The discovery of these winged dinosaurs helped to convince some scientists that birds are descendants of dinosaurs. A few scientists go even further. They say the dinosaurs never went extinct because birds *are* dinosaurs.

You'll learn more about birds in this chapter. You'll also learn about another group of vertebrates—mammals.

Archaeopteryx fossil

Winged dinosaur fossils

What Do You Think?

In your ScienceLog, try to answer the following questions based on what you already know:

1. What holds a bird or plane up when it flies?

2. How do kangaroos differ from most other mammals?

3. Can mammals lay eggs? Can they fly?

Archaeopteryx

Investigate!

Let's Fly!

Humans have always been fascinated by birds and their ability to fly. Throughout history, humans have tried to fly too. Leonardo da Vinci designed flying machines in the fifteenth century. And Orville and Wilbur Wright finally got off the ground when they flew the first airplane, in 1903. How do birds and airplanes fly? This Investigate will give you a few hints.

Procedure

1. Carefully fold a **piece of paper** to make a paper airplane. Make the folds symmetrical and the creases sharp.

2. Throw the plane very slowly. What happened?

3. Take the same plane, and throw it more forcefully. Did anything change?

4. Reduce the size of the wings by cutting them with **scissors.** Make sure the two wings are the same size and are symmetrical.

5. Throw the airplane again, both slowly and with more force. What happened each time?

6. Record all your results in your ScienceLog.

Analysis

7. What happened when you threw the original paper airplane slowly? forcefully?

8. What effect does speed have on plane flight? Do you think this is true of bird flight?

9. What happened when the wings were made smaller? Why do you think this happened? Do you think wing size affects the way a bird flies?

10. Based on your experiments, how would you design and throw the perfect paper airplane? Explain your answer.

Terms to Learn

down feather   lift
contour feather   brooding
preening

What You'll Do

◆ Name two characteristics that birds share with reptiles.

◆ Describe the characteristics of birds that make them well suited for flight.

◆ Explain *lift.*

◆ List some advantages of migration.

Birds

Great blue heron

Have you ever fed pigeons in a city park or watched a hawk fly in circles in the sky? Humans have always been birdwatchers, perhaps because birds are easier to recognize than almost any other animal. Unlike other animals, all birds have feathers. Birds are also well known for their ability to fly. Birds belong to the class Aves. The word *aves* comes from the Latin word for bird. In fact, the word *aviation*—the science of flying airplanes—comes from the same word.

Figure 1 *There are almost 9,000 species of birds on Earth today.*

Toucan

Hummingbird

Bird Characteristics

The first birds appeared on Earth about 150 million years ago. As you learned at the beginning of this chapter, birds are thought to be descendants of dinosaurs.

Even today birds share some characteristics with reptiles. Like reptiles, birds are vertebrates. The legs and feet of birds are covered by thick, dry scales, like those of reptiles. Even the skin around their beaks is scaly. Like reptiles, birds have *amniotic eggs,* that is, eggs with an amniotic sac and a shell. However, the shells of bird eggs are generally harder than the leathery shells of turtles and lizards.

Birds also have many characteristics that set them apart from the rest of the animal kingdom. They have beaks instead of teeth and jaws, and they have feathers, wings, and many other adaptations for flight.

Birds of a Feather Birds have two main types of feathers— down feathers and contour feathers. Examples of each are shown in **Figure 2.** Because feathers wear out, birds shed their worn feathers and grow new ones.

Figure 2 *Birds have light, fluffy down feathers and leaf-shaped contour feathers.*

Down feathers are fluffy, insulating feathers that lie next to a bird's body. To keep from losing heat, birds fluff up their down feathers to form a layer of insulation. Air trapped in the feathers helps keep birds warm. **Contour feathers** are made of a stiff central *shaft* with many side branches, called *barbs*. The barbs link together to form a smooth surface, as can be seen in **Figure 3.** Contour feathers cover the body and wings of birds to form a streamlined flying surface.

Birds take good care of their feathers. They use their beaks to spread oil on their feathers in a process called **preening.** The oil is secreted by a gland near the bird's tail. The oil helps make the feathers water repellent and keeps them clean.

High-Energy Animals Birds need a lot of energy in order to fly. To get this energy, they have a high metabolism, which generates a lot of body heat. In fact, the average body temperature of a bird is 40°C, warmer than yours! If birds are too hot, they lay their feathers flat and pant like dogs do. Birds cannot sweat to cool their bodies.

Eat Like a Bird? Because of their high metabolism, birds eat large amounts of food in proportion to their body weight. Some small birds eat almost constantly to maintain their energy! Most birds eat a high-protein, high-fat diet of insects, nuts, seeds, or meat. This kind of diet requires only a small digestive tract. A few birds, such as geese, eat the leaves of plants.

Birds don't have teeth, so they can't chew their food. Instead, food goes directly from the mouth to the *crop,* where it is stored. Birds also have an organ called a *gizzard,* which often contains small stones. The stones in the gizzard grind up the food so that it can be easily digested by the intestine. A bird's digestive system is shown in **Figure 4.**

Figure 3 *The barbs of a contour feather have cross branches called barbules. Barbs and barbules give the feather strength and shape.*

Figure 4 *The digestive system of a bird allows food to be rapidly converted into usable energy.*

Crop

Gizzard

Intestine

Self-Check

1. Why don't birds have wings made of down feathers?
2. Why do birds eat large quantities of food?

(See page 782 to check your answers.)

Up, Up, and Away

Most birds are flyers. Even flightless birds, such as ostriches, are descended from ancestors that could fly.

Birds have a long list of adaptations for flight. Birds must take in a large amount of energy from the food they eat and a large amount of oxygen from the air they breathe in order to fly. Feathers and wings are also important, as are strong muscles. Birds have lightweight bodies so that they can get off the ground. **Figure 5** on these two pages explains many of the bird characteristics that are important for flight.

Figure 5 Flight Adaptations of Birds

Most birds have **large eyes** and excellent eyesight. This allows them to see objects and food from a distance. Some birds, like hawks and eagles, can see eight times better than humans!

Air sacs

Lung

The **heart** of a bird beats rapidly. This ensures that the flight muscles get as much oxygen as the blood can carry. In small birds, the heart beats almost 1,000 times a minute! Your heart beats about 70 times a minute.

Birds have special organs called **air sacs** attached to their lungs. The air sacs increase the amount of oxygen that a bird can take in and allow air to flow constantly in one direction through the lungs.

The shape of a bird's **wings** is related to the kind of flying it does. Short, rounded wings allow rapid maneuvers, like the movements of a fighter plane. Long narrow wings are best for soaring, like the movement of a glider.

Bird skeletons are compact and strong. Some of the vertebrae, ribs, and hip bones are fused together. This makes the skeleton of birds more rigid than that of other vertebrates. The **rigid skeleton** lets a bird move its wings powerfully and efficiently.

Science
C O N N E C T I O N

These characteristics help birds fly, but how do airplanes fly? Find out on page 428.

Keel

Birds that fly have powerful **flight muscles** attached to a large breastbone called a **keel**. These muscles move the wings.

Bone is a heavy material, but birds have much **lighter skeletons** than those of other vertebrates because their bones are hollow. But bird bones are still very strong because they have thin cross-supports that provide strength, much like the trusses of a bridge do.

Getting off the Ground

How do birds overcome gravity and fly? Birds flap their wings to get into the air and to push themselves through the air. Wings provide lift. **Lift** is the upward pressure on the wing that keeps a bird in the air.

When air flows past a wing, some of the air is forced over the top of the wing, and some is forced underneath. A bird's wing is curved on top. As shown in **Figure 6,** the air on top has to move *farther* than the air underneath. As a result, the air on top moves *faster* than the air underneath. The fast-moving air on top creates low pressure in the air. This is called the *Bernoulli effect.* The air pressure under the wing is higher and pushes the wing up.

Figure 6 *A bird's wing is shaped to produce lift. Air moving over the top of the wing moves faster than air moving underneath the wing. This creates a difference in air pressure that keeps a bird in the air.*

Lift

Air flow

Lift

Birds generate extra lift by flapping their wings. The faster a bird flies, the greater the lift. Another factor that affects lift is wing size. The larger the wing, the greater the lift. This is why birds with large wings can soar long distances without flapping their wings. An albatross, like the one in **Figure 7,** can glide over the ocean for many hours without flapping its wings.

Figure 7 *The wandering albatross has a wingspan of 3.5 m, the largest of any living bird. Its large wings allow the albatross to glide for very long periods of time. An albatross comes ashore only to lay its eggs.*

Fly Away

It is sometimes said that when the going gets tough, the tough get going. If that's true, birds must be some of the toughest animals in the world. For when times are hard, some birds get going faster and farther than any other animal. Because they are able to fly great distances, birds are able to migrate great distances.

Some birds have good reasons to migrate. By migrating, they can find better territories with more food. For example, in the far north in the summer, the Arctic sun is up nearly 24 hours a day. Plants, insects, and other organisms increase explosively, providing lots of food. It's a great place for birds to raise their young. However, the winters are long and harsh, and there is little to eat. So when winter comes, birds fly south to find better feeding grounds.

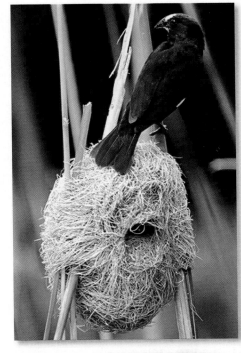

Bringing Up Baby

Like reptiles, birds reproduce by internal fertilization and lay amniotic eggs with the developing embryo inside. But unlike most reptiles, birds must keep their eggs warm for the embryo to develop.

Most birds build elaborate nests and lay their eggs inside them. **Figure 8** shows a few of the many different kinds of bird nests. Birds sit on their eggs until the eggs hatch, using their body heat to keep the eggs warm. This is called **brooding.** Some birds, such as gulls, share brooding duties equally between males and females. But among songbirds, the female is in charge of brooding the eggs, and the male brings her food.

Raising young birds is hard work. Some birds, such as cuckoos and cowbirds, have found a way to make other birds do their work for them. A cuckoo lays its eggs in the nest of another species of bird. When the cuckoo egg hatches, the young cuckoo is fed and protected by the foster parents.

Figure 8 *There are many different types of bird nests. Birds use grass, branches, mud, hair, feathers, and many other building materials.*

Figure 9 *Precocial chicks learn to recognize their parents right after they hatch. But if their parents are not there, the chicks will follow the first moving thing they see, even a person.*

Ready to Go Some baby birds hatch from the egg ready to run around and eat bugs. Chicks that hatch fully active are *precocial* (pree KOH shuhl). Chickens, ducks, and shorebirds all hatch precocial chicks. Precocial chicks are covered with downy feathers and follow their parents as soon as they can stand up. You can see some precocial chicks following a stand-in parent in **Figure 9.** Precocial chicks depend on their mother for warmth and protection, but they can walk, swim, and feed themselves.

Help Wanted The chicks of hawks, songbirds, and many other birds hatch weak, naked, and helpless. These chicks are *altricial* (al TRISH uhl). Their eyes are closed when they are born. Newly hatched altricial chicks cannot walk or fly. Their parents must keep them warm and feed them for several weeks. **Figure 10** shows altricial chicks being fed by a parent.

When altricial chicks grow their first flight feathers, they begin learning to fly. This takes days, however, and the chicks often end up walking around on the ground. The parents must work feverishly to distract cats, weasels, and other predators and protect their young.

REVIEW

1. List three ways birds are similar to reptiles and three ways they are different.

2. Explain the difference between precocial chicks and altricial chicks.

3. People use the phrase "eats like a bird" to describe someone who eats very little. Is this saying appropriate? Why or why not?

4. Name some of the adaptations that make bird bodies lightweight.

5. **Understanding Technology** Would an airplane wing that is not curved on top generate lift? Draw a picture to illustrate your explanation.

Figure 10 *Both parents of altricial chicks leave the nest in search of food. They return to the nest with food every few minutes, sometimes making 1,000 trips a day between the two of them!*

Kinds of Birds

There are almost 9,000 species of birds on Earth. Birds range in size from the 1.6 g bee hummingbird to the 125 kg North African ostrich. The bodies of birds have different characteristics too, depending on where they live and what they eat. Because of their great diversity, birds are classified into 29 different orders. That can be confusing, so birds are often grouped into four nonscientific categories: flightless birds, water birds, birds of prey, and perching birds. These categories don't include all birds, but they do show how different birds can be.

BRAIN FOOD

An ostrich egg has a mass of about 1.4 kg. A single ostrich egg is big enough to provide scrambled eggs for a family of four every morning for several days.

Flightless Birds

Ostriches, kiwis, emus, and other flightless birds do not have a large keel for flight. Though they cannot fly, many flightless birds are fast runners.

▲ The **kiwi,** of New Zealand, is a forest bird about the size of a chicken. Its feathers are soft and hair-like. Kiwis sleep during the day. At night, they hunt for worms, caterpillars, and berries.

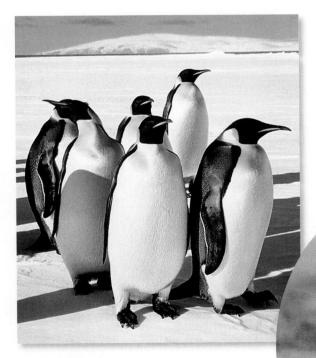

▲ **Penguins** are unique flightless birds. They have a large keel and very strong flight muscles, but their wings have been modified into flippers. They flap these wings to swim underwater. Although penguins are graceful swimmers, they walk clumsily on land.

◄ The **ostrich** is the largest living bird. Ostriches can reach a height of 2.5 m and a mass of 125 kg. An ostrich's two-toed feet look almost like hoofs, and these birds can run up to 64 km/h (40 mi/h).

Water Birds

Water birds are sometimes called *waterfowl*. These include cranes, ducks, geese, swans, pelicans, loons, and many other species. These birds usually have webbed feet for swimming, but they are also strong flyers.

Male **wood ducks** have beautiful ▶ plumage to attract females. Like all ducks, they are strong swimmers and flyers.

◀ The **blue-footed booby** is a tropical water bird. These birds have an elaborate courtship dance that includes raising their feet one at a time.

The **common loon** is the ▶ most primitive of modern birds. It can remain underwater for several minutes while searching for fish.

Birds of Prey

Eagles, hawks, falcons, and other birds of prey are meat eaters. They may eat mammals, fish, reptiles, birds, or other animals. The sharp claws on their feet and their sharp, curved beaks help these birds catch and eat their prey. They also have very good vision. Most birds of prey hunt during the day.

◀ Owls, like this **northern spotted owl,** are the only birds of prey that hunt at night. They have a keen sense of hearing to help them find their prey.

▲ **Ospreys** are fish eaters. They fly over the water and catch fish with their feet.

Perching Birds

Songbirds, like robins, wrens, warblers, and sparrows, are perching birds. These birds have special adaptations for perching on a branch. When a perching bird lands on a branch, its feet automatically close around the branch. So even if the bird falls asleep, it will not fall off.

▲ **Parrots** are not songbirds, but they have special feet for perching and climbing. Their strong, hooked beak allows them to open seeds and slice fruit.

▲ **Chickadees** are lively little birds that frequently flock to garden feeders. They often dangle underneath a branch while hunting for insects, seeds, or fruits.

Most tanagers are tropical birds, ▶ but the **scarlet tanager** spends the summer in North America. The male is red, but the female is a yellow-green color that blends into the trees.

REVIEW

1. How did perching birds get their name?

2. Birds of prey have extremely good eyesight. Why is good vision important for these birds?

3. **Interpreting Illustrations** Look at the illustrations of bird feet at right. Which foot belongs to a water bird? a perching bird? Explain your answers.

Terms to Learn

mammary glands   placental
diaphragm   mammal
monotreme   gestation period
marsupial

What You'll Do

◆ Describe common characteristics of mammals.
◆ Explain the differences between monotremes, marsupials, and placental mammals.
◆ Give some examples of each type of mammal.

Mandrill baboon

Figure 12 *Therapsids had characteristics of both reptiles and mammals and may have looked something like this.*

Mammals

Of all the vertebrates, we seem most interested in mammals. Maybe that's because we are mammals ourselves. But with about 4,500 species, mammals are actually a small class of animals. Mollusks, for example, include more than 90,000 species.

Mammals come in many different forms—from the tiniest bats, which weigh less than a cracker, to the largest whales. The blue whale, with a mass of more than 90,000 kg, is the largest animal—vertebrate or invertebrate—that has ever lived. You can find mammals in the coldest oceans, in the hottest deserts, and in every climate in between. You can see some of the variety of mammals in **Figure 11.**

Rhinoceros

Figure 11 *Even though they look very different, all of these animals are mammals.*

Beluga whale

The Origin of Mammals

Fossil evidence suggests that about 280 million years ago, mammal-like reptiles called therapsids appeared. *Therapsids* (thuh RAP sidz) were the early ancestors of mammals. An artist's rendition of a therapsid is shown in **Figure 12.**

About 200 million years ago, the first mammals appeared in the fossil record. These mammals were about the size of mice. The early mammals were endotherms. Because they did not depend on their surroundings for heat, they could forage at night and avoid their dinosaur predators during the day.

When the dinosaurs became extinct, there was more land and food available for the mammals. Mammals began to diversify and live in many different environments.

Characteristics of Mammals

Dolphins and elephants are mammals, and so are monkeys, horses, and rabbits. You are a mammal, too! These animals are very different, but all mammals share many distinctive traits.

Mamma! All mammals have mammary glands; this sets them apart from other animals. **Mammary glands** secrete a nutritious fluid called milk. All female mammals supply milk to their young. Female mammals usually bear live young and care for their offspring, as illustrated in **Figure 13.** Although only mature female mammals make milk, male mammals also have small inactive mammary glands.

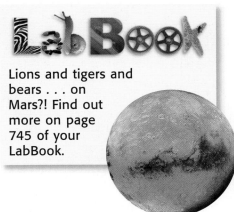

Lions and tigers and bears . . . on Mars?! Find out more on page 745 of your LabBook.

Figure 13 *Like all mammals, this calf gets its first meals from its mother's milk.*

All milk is made of water, protein, fat, and sugar. But the milk from different mammals has varying amounts of each nutrient. For example, human milk has half as much fat as cow's milk but twice as much sugar. The milk of seals may be more than one-half fat. At birth, elephant seals have a mass of 45 kg. After drinking this rich milk for just 3 weeks, their mass is 180 kg!

Cozy and Warm If you've ever had a dog fall asleep in your lap, you already know that mammals are really warm! All mammals are endotherms. Like birds, mammals require a lot of energy from the food they eat. Mammals quickly break down food in their bodies and use the energy released from their cells to keep their bodies warm. Usually a mammal keeps its body temperature constant. Only when a mammal is hibernating, estivating, or running a fever does its body temperature change.

Figure 14 *Mammals feel warm to the touch because they are endotherms.*

Figure 15 *The thick fur of this arctic fox keeps its body warm in even the coldest winters.*

Figure 16
Mountain lions have sharp canine teeth for grabbing their prey. Donkeys have sharp incisors in front for cutting plants and flat grinding teeth in the back of their mouth.

Staying Warm Mammals have adaptations to help them keep warm. One way they stay warm is by having a thick coat, and many mammals have luxurious coats of fur. All mammals, even whales, have hair somewhere on their body. This is another trait that sets mammals apart from other animals. Mammals that live in cold climates usually have thick coats of hair, such as the fox in **Figure 15.** But large mammals that live in warm climates, like elephants, have less hair. Gorillas and humans have similar amounts of hair on their bodies, but human hair is finer and shorter.

Most mammals also have a layer of fat under the skin that acts as insulation. Whales and other mammals that live in cold oceans depend on a layer of fat called *blubber* to keep them warm.

Crunch! Another trait that sets mammals apart from other animals is their teeth. Birds don't even have teeth! And although fish and reptiles have teeth, their teeth tend to be all alike. In contrast, most mammals' teeth are specialized. They have different shapes and sizes for different functions.

Let's look at your teeth, for example. The teeth in the front of your mouth are cutting teeth, called *incisors.* Most people have four on top and four on the bottom. The next teeth are stabbing teeth, called *canines.* Canines help you grab food and hold onto it. Farther back in your mouth are flat teeth called *molars* that help grind up food.

The kinds of teeth a mammal has reflect its diet. Dogs, cats, wolves, foxes, and other meat-eating mammals have large canines. Molars are better developed in animals that eat plants. **Figure 16** shows the teeth of different mammals.

Unlike other vertebrates, mammals have two sets of teeth. A young mammal's first small teeth are called *milk teeth.* These are replaced by a set of permanent adult teeth after the mammal begins eating solid food and its jaw grows larger.

Getting Oxygen Just as a fire needs oxygen in order to burn, all animals need oxygen to efficiently "burn," or break down, the food they eat. Like birds and reptiles, mammals use lungs to get oxygen from the air. But mammals also have a large muscle to help bring air into their lungs. This muscle is called the **diaphragm,** and it lies at the bottom of the rib cage.

Large Brains The brain of a mammal is much larger than the brain of another animal the same size. This allows mammals to learn, move, and think quickly. A mammal's highly developed brain also helps it keep track of what is going on in its environment and respond quickly.

Mammals depend on five major senses to provide them with information about their environment: vision, hearing, smell, touch, and taste. The importance of each sense for any given mammal often depends on the mammal's environment. For example, mammals that are active at night rely more heavily on their ability to hear than on their ability to see.

Mammal Parents All mammals reproduce sexually. Like birds and reptiles, mammals reproduce by internal fertilization. Most mammals give birth to live young, and all mammals nurse their young. Mammal parents are very protective, with one or both parents caring for their young until they are grown. **Figure 17** shows a brown bear caring for its young.

Figure 17 *A mother bear will attack anything that threatens her cubs.*

Activity

Like all mammals, you have a diaphragm. Place your hand underneath your rib cage. What happens as you breathe in and out? You are feeling the motion of your abdominal muscles, which are connected to your diaphragm. Contract and relax your abdominal muscles. What happens?

TRY at HOME

REVIEW

1. Name three characteristics that are unique to mammals.

2. What is the purpose of a diaphragm?

3. **Making Inferences** Suppose you found a mammal skull on an archaeological dig. How would the teeth give you clues about the mammal's diet?

Kinds of Mammals

Mammals are divided into three groups based on the way their young develop. These groups are monotremes, marsupials, and placental mammals.

Monotremes Mammals that lay eggs are called **monotremes.** Monotremes are the only mammals that lay eggs, and early scientists called them "furred reptiles." But monotremes are not reptiles; they have all the mammal traits. They have mammary glands and a thick fur coat, and they are endotherms.

Figure 18 *Echidnas are about the size of a house cat. They have large claws and long snouts that help them dig ants and termites out of their nests.*

A female monotreme lays eggs with thick, leathery shells. Like bird and reptile eggs, monotreme eggs have a yolk and albumen to feed the developing embryo. The female incubates the eggs with her body heat. Newly hatched young are not fully developed. The mother protects her young and feeds them milk. Unlike other mammals, monotremes do not have nipples, and the babies cannot suck. Instead, the tiny monotremes nurse by licking milk from the skin and hair around their mother's mammary glands.

Two Kinds of Monotremes Monotremes are found only in Australia and New Guinea, and just three species of monotremes are alive today. Two are echidnas (ee KID nuhs), spine-covered animals with long snouts. Echidnas have long sticky tongues for catching ants and termites. You can see an echidna in **Figure 18.**

The third monotreme is the duckbilled platypus, shown in **Figure 19.** The duckbilled platypus is a swimming mammal that lives and feeds in rivers and ponds. It has webbed feet and a flat tail to help it move through the water. It also has a flat, rubbery bill that it uses to dig for food and to dig long tunnels in riverbanks to lay its eggs.

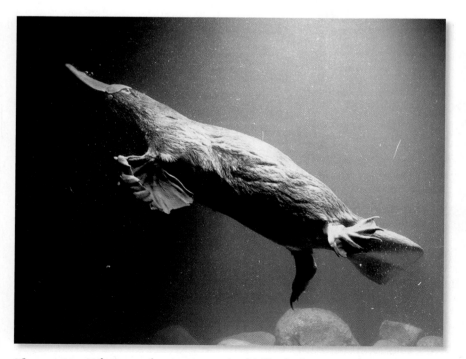

Figure 19 *When underwater, a duckbilled platypus closes its eyes and ears. It uses its sensitive bill to find food.*

Marsupials You probably know that kangaroos, like those in **Figure 20,** have pouches. Kangaroos are **marsupials,** mammals with pouches. Like all mammals, marsupials are endotherms. They have mammary glands, fur, and teeth. Unlike the monotremes, marsupials do not lay eggs. They give birth to live young.

Like newly hatched monotremes, marsupial infants are not fully developed. At birth, the tiny embryos of a kangaroo are no larger than bumblebees. Shortly after birth, they drag themselves through their mother's fur until they reach a pouch on her abdomen. Inside the pouch are mammary glands. The young kangaroo climbs in, latches onto a nipple, and drinks milk until it is able to move around by itself and leave the pouch for short periods. Young kangaroos are called joeys.

There are about 280 species of marsupials. The only marsupial in North America north of Mexico is the opossum (uh PAHS suhm), shown in **Figure 21.** Other marsupials include koalas, shown in **Figure 22,** Tasmanian devils, and wallabies. Most marsupials live in Australia, New Guinea, and South America.

Figure 20 *After birth, a kangaroo continues to develop in its mother's pouch. Older joeys leave the pouch but return if there is any sign of danger.*

Figure 21 *When in danger, an opossum will lie perfectly still and pretend to be dead so predators will tend to ignore it.*

Figure 22 *Koalas sleep in trees during the day and are active at night. They eat nothing but eucalyptus leaves.*

BRAIN FOOD

When a kangaroo first climbs into its mother's pouch, the mother's milk is nonfat. Later, the milk is about 20 percent fat. A mother kangaroo with two babies that are different ages supplies nonfat milk to the baby and fat milk to the older one. Each youngster nurses from a different nipple.

Ants for Dinner!

The giant anteater can stick its tongue out 150 times a minute. Count how many times you can stick out your tongue in a minute. Imagine that you are an anteater and you need 1,800 Calories a day. If you need to eat 50 ants to get 1 Calorie, how many ants would you have to eat per day? If you could catch two ants every time you stuck your tongue out, how many times a day would you have to stick out your tongue? How many hours a day would you have to eat?

Placental Mammals Most mammals are placental mammals. In **placental mammals,** the embryos stay inside the mother's body and develop in an organ called the *uterus.* Placental embryos form a special attachment to the uterus of their mother called a *placenta.* The placenta supplies food and oxygen from the mother's blood to the growing embryo. The placenta also removes wastes from the embryo.

The time during which an embryo develops within the mother is called the **gestation period.** Gestation (jeh STAY shuhn) periods in placental animals range from a few weeks in mice to as long as 23 months in elephants. Humans have a gestation period of about 9 months.

Self-Check

Explain the difference between a monotreme, a marsupial, and a placental mammal. *(See page 782 to check your answer.)*

Kinds of Placental Mammals

Over 90 percent of all the mammals on Earth are placental mammals. Living placental mammals are classified into 18 orders. The characteristics of the most common orders are given on the following pages.

Toothless Mammals

This group includes anteaters, armadillos, aardvarks, pangolins, and sloths. Although these mammals are called "toothless," only the anteaters are completely tooth-less. The others have small teeth. Most toothless mammals feed on insects they catch with their long sticky tongues.

Armadillos eat ▶ insects, frogs, mushrooms, and roots. When threatened, an armadillo rolls up into a ball and is protected by its tough plates.

▲ The largest anteater is the 40 kg **giant anteater** of South America. Anteaters never destroy the nests of their prey. They open the nests, eat a few ants or termites, and then move on to another nest.

Insect Eaters

Insect eaters, or *insectivores,* live on every continent except Australia and Antarctica. Most insectivores are small, and most have long pointed noses to dig into the soil for food. Compared with other mammals, they have a very small brain and few specialized teeth. Insectivores include moles, shrews, and hedgehogs.

◄ The **star-nosed mole** has sensitive feelers on its nose to help it find insects and feel its way while burrowing underground. Although they have tiny eyes, moles cannot see.

▲ **Hedgehogs** live throughout Europe, Asia, and Africa. Their spines keep them safe from most predators.

Rodents

More than one-third of all mammalian species are rodents, and they can be found on every continent except Antarctica. Rodents include squirrels, mice, rats, guinea pigs, porcupines, and chinchillas. Most rodents are small animals with long, sensitive whiskers. Rodents are chewers and gnawers. All rodents have sharp front teeth for gnawing. Because rodents chew so much, their teeth wear down. So a rodent's incisors grow continuously, just like your fingernails do.

▲ The **capybaras** (KAP i BAH ruhs) of South America are the largest rodents in the world. A female can have a mass of 70 kg—as much as a grown man.

▲ Like all rodents, **beavers** have gnawing teeth. They use these teeth to cut down trees.

Lagomorphs

Rabbits, hares, and pikas belong to a group of placental mammals called lagomorphs. Like rodents, they have sharp gnawing teeth. But unlike rodents, they have two sets of incisors in their upper jaw and short tails. Rabbits and hares have long, powerful hind legs for jumping. To detect their many predators, they have sensitive noses and large ears and eyes.

◀ **Pikas** are small animals that live high in the mountains. Pikas gather plants and mound them in "haystacks" to dry. In the winter, they use the dry plants for food and insulation.

▲ The large ears of this **black-tailed jack rabbit** help it hear well.

Flying Mammals

Bats are the only mammals that can fly. Bats are active at night and sleep in sheltered areas during the day. Most bats eat insects. But some bats eat fruit, and three species of vampire bats drink the blood of other animals.

Most bats hunt for insects at night. They find their way using echolocation. Bats make clicking noises when they fly. Trees, rocks, insects, and other objects reflect the sound back to the bat, making an echo.

Echoes from a big, hard tree sound very different from those reflecting off a soft, tasty moth. Bats that echolocate often have enormous ears to help them hear the echoes of their own clicks.

In many Asian countries, **bats** ▶ are symbols of good luck, long life, and happiness.

Bats and Submarines

What do bats have in common with submarines? Submarines use a form of echolocation called sonar to find and avoid objects underwater. Based on what you know about echolocation, what kind of instruments do you think are needed to navigate a submarine with sonar?

Carnivores

Carnivores are a group of mammals that have large canines and special teeth for slicing meat. The name *carnivore* means "meat eater"—the mammals in this group primarily eat meat. Carnivorous mammals include lions, wolves, weasels, otters, bears, raccoons, and hyenas. Carnivores also include a group of fish-eating marine mammals called *pinnipeds.* The pinnipeds include seals, sea lions, and walruses. Some carnivores also eat plants. For example, black bears eat grass, nuts, and berries and only rarely eat meat. But many carnivores eat nothing but other animals.

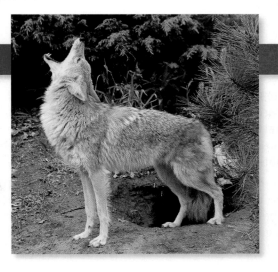

▲ **Coyotes** are members of the dog family. They live throughout North America and in parts of Central America.

▼ **Raccoons** have handlike paws that help them catch fish and hold their food. They can handle objects almost as well as monkeys can.

▲ Cats are divided into two groups, big cats and small cats. All the big cats can roar. The largest of the big cats is the **Siberian tiger,** with a mass of up to 300 kg.

◀ **Walruses** are pinnipeds. Unlike other carnivores, walruses do not use their canines for tearing food. Instead, they use them to defend themselves, to dig for food, and to climb on ice.

Hoofed Mammals

Horses, pigs, deer, and rhinoceroses are just a few of the many mammals that have thick hoofs. Most hoofed mammals are adapted for swift running. Because they are plant eaters, they have large, flat molars to help them grind plant material.

Hoofed mammals are divided into groups based on the number of toes they have. Odd-toed hoofed mammals have one or three toes. Horses and zebras have a single large hoof, or toe. Other odd-toed hoofed mammals include rhinoceroses and tapirs. Even-toed hoofed mammals have two or four toes. These mammals include pigs, cows, camels, deer, hippopotamuses, and giraffes.

▲ **Giraffes** are the tallest living mammals. They have long necks, long legs, and an even number of toes.

▲ **Tapirs** are large, three-toed mammals that live in forests. Tapirs can be found in Central America, South America, and Southeast Asia.

Camels are even- ▶ toed mammals. The hump of a camel is a large lump of fat that provides energy for the camel when food is scarce.

Trunk-Nosed Mammals

Elephants are the only mammals with a trunk. The trunk is an elongated and muscular combination of the upper lip and nose. Elephants use their trunk the same way we use our hands, lips, and nose. The trunk is powerful enough to lift a tree yet agile enough to pick small fruits one at a time. Elephants use their trunk to place food in their mouth and to spray their back with water to cool off.

There are two species of elephants, African elephants and Asian elephants. African elephants are larger and have bigger ears and tusks than Asian elephants. Both species eat plants. Because they are so large, elephants eat up to 18 hours a day to get enough food.

Elephants are the largest land animals. Male African elephants can reach a mass of 7,500 kg! Elephants are very intelligent and may live more than 60 years.

▼ **Elephants** are social animals. They live in herds of related females and their offspring. The whole family helps take care of young.

Self-Check

1. Why are bats classified as mammals and not as birds?
2. How are rodents and lagomorphs similar? How are they different?

(See page 782 to check your answers.)

Environment CONNECTION

Both species of elephants are endangered. For centuries, humans have hunted elephants for their long teeth, called tusks. Elephant tusks are made of ivory, a hard material used for carving. Because of the high demand for ivory, much of the elephant population has been wiped out. Today elephant hunting is illegal.

Cetaceans

Whales, dolphins, and porpoises make up a group of water-dwelling mammals called cetaceans (see TAY shuhns). At first glance, whales and their relatives may look more like fish than mammals. But like all mammals, cetaceans are endotherms, have lungs, and nurse their young. Most of the largest whales are toothless whales that strain tiny, shrimp-like animals from sea water. But dolphins, porpoises, sperm whales, and killer whales have teeth, which they use to eat fish and other animals.

▲ **Spinner dolphins** spin like a football when they leap from the water. Like all dolphins, they are intelligent and highly social.

◀ Like bats, cetaceans use echolocation to "see" their surroundings. **Sperm whales,** like this one, use loud blasts of sound to stun fish, making them easier to catch.

Sirenia

The smallest group of water-dwelling mammals is called sirenia (sie REE nee uh). It includes just four species—three kinds of manatees and the dugong. These mammals are completely aquatic; they live along coasts and in large rivers. They are quiet animals that eat seaweed and water plants.

Manatees are also ▶ called sea cows.

Primates

Prosimians, monkeys, apes, and humans all belong to a group of mammals called *primates.* There are about 160 species of primates. All primates have the eyes facing forward, enabling both eyes to focus on a single point. Most primates have five fingers on each hand and five toes on each foot, with flat fingernails instead of claws. Primates' fingers and opposable thumbs are able to make complicated movements, like grasping objects. Primates have a large brain in proportion to their body size and are considered some of the most intelligent mammals.

Many primates live in trees. Their flexible shoulder joints and grasping hands and feet enable them to climb trees and swing from branch to branch. Most primates eat a diet of leaves and fruits, but some also eat animals.

◀ **Spider monkeys,** like most monkeys, have grasping tails. Their long arms, legs, and tails help them move among the trees.

▲ **Orangutans** and other apes frequently walk upright. Apes usually have larger brains and bodies than monkeys.

REVIEW

1. If you saw only the feet of a hippopotamus and a rhinoceros, could you tell the difference between the two animals? Explain your answer.

2. How are monotremes different from all other mammals? How are they similar?

3. To what group of placental mammals do dogs belong? How do you know?

4. **Making Inferences** What is a gestation period? Why do elephants have a longer gestation period than do mice?

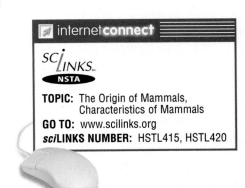

internet**connect**

SC*LINKS.*
NSTA

TOPIC: The Origin of Mammals, Characteristics of Mammals
GO TO: www.scilinks.org
*sci*LINKS NUMBER: HSTL415, HSTL420

Chapter Highlights

Vocabulary

down feather *(p. 401)*

contour feather *(p. 401)*

preening *(p. 401)*

lift *(p. 404)*

brooding *(p. 405)*

Section Notes

- Like reptiles, birds lay amniotic eggs and have thick, dry scales.

- Unlike reptiles, birds are endotherms and are covered with feathers.

- Because flying requires a lot of energy, birds must eat a high-energy diet and breathe efficiently.

- Birds' wings are shaped so that they generate lift. Lift is air pressure beneath the wings that keeps a bird in the air.

- Birds are lightweight. Their feathers are strong but lightweight, and their skeleton is relatively rigid, compact, and hollow.

- Because birds can fly, they can migrate great distances. They can nest in one habitat and winter in another. Migrating birds can take advantage of food supplies and avoid predators.

Labs

What? No Dentist Bills? *(p. 744)*

☑ Skills Check

Visual Understanding

LIFT The diagram on page 404 helps explain the concept of lift. Looking at this illustration, you can see that air must travel a greater distance over a curved wing than under a curved wing. The air above the wing must move faster than the air underneath in order to cover the greater distance in the same amount of time. Faster-moving air creates lower pressure above the wing. The higher pressure under the wing forces it up, creating lift.

Lift

Air flow

Lift

Vocabulary

mammary glands (*p. 411*)

diaphragm (*p. 413*)

monotreme (*p. 414*)

marsupial (*p. 415*)

placental mammal (*p. 416*)

gestation period (*p. 416*)

Section Notes

- All mammals have mammary glands; in females, mammary glands produce milk. Milk is a highly nutritious fluid fed to the young.

- Like birds, mammals are endotherms.

- Mammals maintain their high metabolism by eating a lot of food and breathing efficiently.

- Mammals have a diaphragm that helps them draw air into their lungs.

- Mammals have highly specialized teeth for chewing different kinds of food. Mammals that eat plants have incisors and molars for cutting and grinding plants. Carnivores have canines for seizing and tearing their prey.

- Mammals are the only vertebrates that have mammary glands, fur, and two sets of teeth.

- Mammals are divided into three groups: monotremes, marsupials, and placental mammals.

- Monotremes lay eggs instead of bearing live young. Monotremes produce milk but do not have nipples or a placenta.

- Marsupials give birth to live young, but the young are born as embryos. The embryos climb into their mother's pouch, where they drink milk until they are more developed.

- Placental mammals develop inside of the mother for a period of time called a gestation period. Placental mothers nurse their young after birth.

Labs

Wanted: Mammals on Mars (*p. 745*)

 internetconnect

GO TO: go.hrw.com

Visit the **HRW** Web site for a variety of learning tools related to this chapter. Just type in the keyword:

KEYWORD: HSTVR2

 SCiLINKS **NSTA**

GO TO: www.scilinks.org

Visit the **National Science Teachers Association** on-line Web site for Internet resources related to this chapter. Just type in the *sci*LINKS number for more information about the topic:

TOPIC:	Bird Characteristics	*sci*LINKS NUMBER: HSTL405
TOPIC:	Kinds of Birds	*sci*LINKS NUMBER: HSTL410
TOPIC:	The Origin of Mammals	*sci*LINKS NUMBER: HSTL415
TOPIC:	Characteristics of Mammals	*sci*LINKS NUMBER: HSTL420

Chapter Review

To complete the following sentences, choose the correct term from each pair of terms listed below:

1. __?__ chicks can run after their mother soon after they hatch. __?__ chicks can barely stretch their neck out to be fed when they first hatch. (*Altricial* or *Precocial*)

2. The __?__ helps mammals breathe. (*diaphragm* or *air sac*)

3. The __?__ allows some mammals to supply nutrients to young in the mother's uterus. (*mammary gland* or *placenta*)

4. Birds take care of their feathers by __?__. (*brooding* or *preening*)

5. A lion belongs to a group of mammals called __?__. (*carnivores* or *primates*)

6. __?__ are fluffy feathers that help keep birds warm. (*Contour feathers* or *Down feathers*)

UNDERSTANDING CONCEPTS

Multiple Choice

7. Both birds and reptiles
   a. lay eggs.
   b. brood their young.
   c. have air sacs.
   d. have feathers.

8. Flight requires
   a. a lot of energy and oxygen.
   b. a lightweight body.
   c. strong flight muscles.
   d. All of the above

9. Only mammals
   a. have glands.
   b. nurse their young.
   c. lay eggs.
   d. have teeth.

10. Monotremes do not
    a. have mammary glands.
    b. care for their young.
    c. have pouches.
    d. have fur.

11. Lift
    a. is air that travels over the top of a wing.
    b. is provided by air sacs.
    c. is the upward force on a wing that keeps a bird in the air.
    d. is created by pressure from the diaphragm.

12. Which of the following is not a primate?
    a. a lemur   c. a pika
    b. a human   d. a chimpanzee

Short Answer

13. How are marsupials different from other mammals? How are they similar?

14. Both birds and mammals are endotherms. How do they stay warm?

15. What is the Bernoulli effect?

16. Why do some bats have large ears?

Concept Mapping

17. Use the following terms to create a concept map: monotremes, endotherms, birds, mammals, mammary glands, placental mammals, marsupials, feathers, hair.

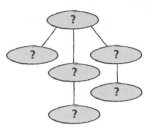

CRITICAL THINKING AND PROBLEM SOLVING

Write one or two sentences to answer the following questions:

18. Unlike bird and monotreme eggs, the eggs of placental mammals and marsupials do not have a yolk. How do developing embryos of marsupials and placental mammals get the nutrition they need?

19. Most bats and cetaceans use echolocation. Why don't these mammals rely solely on sight to find their prey and examine their surroundings?

20. Suppose you are working at a museum and are making a display of bird skeletons. Unfortunately, the skeletons have lost their labels. How can you separate the skeletons of flightless birds from those of birds that fly? Will you be able to tell which birds flew rapidly and which birds could soar? Explain your answer.

MATH IN SCIENCE

21. A bird is flying at a speed of 35 km/h. At this speed, its body consumes 60 Calories per gram of body mass per hour. If the bird has a mass of 50 g, how many Calories will it use if it flies for 30 minutes at this speed?

INTERPRETING GRAPHICS

Endotherms use a lot of energy when they run or fly. The graph below shows how many Calories a small dog uses while running at different speeds. Use this graph to answer the questions below.

22. As the dog runs faster, how does the amount of energy it consumes per hour change?

23. How much energy per hour will this dog consume if it is running at 4 km/h? at 9 km/h?

24. Energy consumed is given in Calories per kilogram of body mass per hour. If the dog has a mass of 6 kg and is running at 7 km/h, how many Calories per hour will it use?

NOW What Do You Think?

Take a minute to review your answers to the ScienceLog questions on page 399. Have your answers changed? If necessary, revise your answers based on what you have learned since you began this chapter.

The Aerodynamics of Flight

For centuries people have tried to imitate a spectacular feat that birds perfected millions of years ago—flight! It was not until 1903 that the Wright brothers were able to fly in a heavier-than-air flying machine. Their first flight lasted only 12 seconds, and they only traveled 37 m. Although modern air-planes are much more sophisticated, they still rely on the same principles of flight.

Fighting Gravity

The sleek body of a jet is shaped to battle drag, while the wings are shaped to battle Earth's gravity. In order to take off, airplanes must pull upward with a force greater than gravitational force. This upward force is called *lift*. Where does an airplane get lift? The top of an airplane wing is curved, and the bottom is flat. As the wing moves through the air, air must travel farther and faster above the wing than below it. This difference causes the pressure above the wing to be less than the pressure below the wing. This difference pulls the airplane upward.

Push and Pull

The shape of its wing is not enough to get an airplane off the ground. Wings require air to flow past them in order to create lift. Airplanes also rely on *thrust*, the force that gives an airplane forward motion. Powerful engines and propellers provide airplanes with thrust. As airplanes move faster, more air rushes past the wings, and lift increases.

Airplanes usually take off into a head wind, which pushes against the airplane as it travels. Any force that pushes against an airplane's motion, like a head wind, is called *drag* and can slow an airplane down. The body of an airplane has smooth curves to minimize drag. A tail wind is an airflow that pushes the airplane from the rear and shortens travel time. In order to increase speed, engineers design airplanes with streamlined bodies to reduce drag. Wings can also be designed to increase lift. A rounded and longer wing provides greater lift, but it also produces more drag. Engineers must consider such trade-offs when they design airplanes. Athletes also consider drag when they choose equipment. For example, runners and cyclists wear tight-fitting clothing to reduce drag.

Think About It!

▶ Airplanes have a variety of shapes and sizes and are designed for many purposes, including transport, travel, and combat. Some planes are designed to fly fast, and others are designed to carry heavy loads. Do some research, and then describe how the aerodynamics differ.

▲ *The design of airplanes got a boost from our feathered friends.*

Earth Science   Life Science

WEIRD SCIENCE

NAKED MOLE-RATS

What do you call a nearly blind rodent that is 7 cm long and looks like a hot dog that has been left in the microwave too long? A naked mole-rat. For more than 150 years, this mammal—which is native to hot, dry regions of Kenya, Ethiopia, and Somalia—has puzzled scientists by its strange appearance and peculiar habits.

What's Hair Got to Do with It?

Naked mole-rats have such strange characteristics that you might wonder whether they are really mammals at all. Their grayish pink skin hangs loosely, allowing them to maneuver through the narrow underground tunnel systems they call home. At first glance, the naked mole-rats appear to be hairless, and hair is a key characteristic of mammals. However, naked mole-rats are not hairless, but they do lack fur. In fact, they have whiskers to guide them through the dark passages and hair between their toes to sweep up loose dirt like tiny brooms. Believe it or not, they also have hair on their lips to prevent dirt from entering their mouth as their massive teeth dig new passages through the dirt!

Is It Cold in Here?

Naked mole-rats have the poorest endothermic capacity of any mammal. Their body temperature remains close to the temperature of the air in their tunnels—a cool 31°C (more than 5°C cooler than the body temperature of humans). At night these animals minimize heat loss by huddling close together. Fortunately, the temperature does not change very much in their native habitat.

Who's in Charge?

Naked mole-rats are the only mammals known to form communities similar to those formed by social insects, such as honey bees. A community of naked mole-rats is made up of between 20 and 300 individuals that divide up tasks much like bees, wasps, and termites do. Each community has one breeding female, called the queen, and up to three breeding males. All females are biologically capable of reproducing, but only one does. When a female becomes a queen, she actually grows longer!

Think About It!

▶ At first glance, naked mole-rats appear to be missing several key characteristics of mammals. Do further research to find out what characteristics they have that classifies them as mammals.

◀ *Naked mole-rats are so unique that they have become a popular attraction at zoos.*

UNIT 6

Ecology

What did you have for breakfast this morning? Whatever you ate, your breakfast was a direct result of living things working together. For example, milk comes from a cow. The cow eats plants to gain energy. Bacteria help the plants obtain nutrients from the soil. And the soil has nutrients because fungi break down dead trees.

All living things on Earth are interconnected. Our actions have an impact on our environment, and our environment has an impact on us. In this unit you will study ecology, the interaction of Earth's living things. This timeline shows some of the ways humans have studied and affected the Earth.

1661

John Evelyn publishes a book condemning air pollution in London, England.

→ 1771

Joseph Priestley experiments with plants and finds that they use carbon dioxide and release oxygen.

1970 ◄

The Environmental Protection Agency (EPA) is formed to set and enforce pollution control standards in the United States.

1973

The U.S. Congress passes the Endangered Species Act.

■■■➤ 1990

In order to save dolphins from being caught in fishing nets, United States tuna processors announce that they will not accept tuna caught in nets that can kill dolphins.

1852

The United States imports sparrows from Germany to defend against crop-damaging caterpillars.

1854

Henry David Thoreau's *Walden* is published. In it, Thoreau asserts that people should live in harmony with nature.

1872

The first United States national park, Yellowstone, is established by Congress.

1933

The Civilian Conservation Corps is established. The corps plants trees, fights forest fires, and builds dams to control floods.

1962

Rachel Carson's book *Silent Spring,* which describes the wasteful use of pesticides and their destruction of the environment, is published.

1993

Americans recycle 59.5 billion aluminum cans (two out of every three cans).

1996

The Glen Canyon Dam is opened, purposefully flooding the Grand Canyon. The flooding helps maintain the ecological balance by restoring beaches and sandbars and rejuvenating marshes.

18 Interactions of Living Things

Strange but True!

A small fish swims through the darkest part of the ocean in search of its next meal. Food is scarce at this depth, but suddenly a glowing morsel comes into view. The tiny fish swims quickly to it, but just as the little fish is about to nab its meal, large jaws rimmed with needle-sharp teeth appear out of nowhere. Before the fish can escape, it is swallowed whole.

This is how the deep-sea anglerfish—the one with the needle-sharp teeth—catches its food. The anglerfish has a unique way of fooling unsuspecting prey. The anglerfish is equipped with its own "fishing pole," a special branchlike body part that hangs over its head. Attached to the tip of the "fishing pole" is the

the bait, a small mass of bacteria that glow in the dark. The anglerfish is only about 7 cm long and is hard to see in the murky depths of the ocean. Fish attracted to the bright bait do not notice the lurking anglerfish until it is too late.

The anglerfish and the glowing bacteria are involved in a relationship that benefits both of them. In exchange for providing the anglerfish with a lure to catch fish, the bacteria get to live in a protected and mobile home. In this chapter you will learn more about the diverse ways living things interact with each other and with their environment. Some of these relationships are almost too strange to believe!

What Do You Think?

In your ScienceLog, try to answer the following questions based on what you already know:

1. Imagine a deer living in a meadow. What does the deer eat? What eats the deer? When the deer dies, what happens to its remains?

2. What is the source of energy for plants?

Analysis

5. How does the arrangement of who eats whom compare with the arrangement of the number of individuals?

6. What might happen to the other organisms if the algae were removed from this group? What might happen if the killer whales were removed?

7. Are there any organisms in this group that eat more than one kind of food? How would you change the order of your cards to reflect this information?

Investigate!

TRY at HOME

Leopard seal

Cod

Who Eats Whom?

In this activity, you will learn how certain organisms interact when finding (or becoming) the next meal. You will need **five index cards.**

Procedure

1. On each index card, print the name of one of the organisms shown at right. All these organisms live in the cold ocean water near Antarctica.

2. Arrange the cards on your desk to show who eats whom. (**Hint:** Algae are small organisms that use the sun's energy to make food. Therefore, the algae card belongs at the bottom of your arrangement.)

3. Draw your card arrangement in your ScienceLog, beginning with the algae card.

4. In its natural habitat, which organism exists in the greatest number? Arrange the cards in order of most to fewest individuals.

Krill

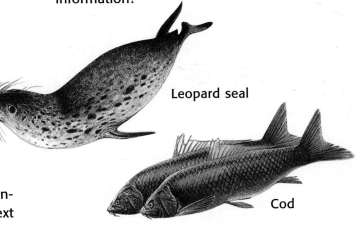

Algae

Killer whale

Everything Is Connected

Terms to Learn

ecology   community
biotic   ecosystem
abiotic   biosphere
population

What You'll Do

◆ Distinguish between the biotic and abiotic environment.
◆ Explain how populations, communities, ecosystems, and the biosphere are related.
◆ Explain how the abiotic environment relates to communities.

Look at **Figure 1** below. An alligator drifts in a weedy Florida river, watching a long, thin fish called a gar. The gar swims too close to the alligator. Suddenly, in a rush of snapping jaws and splashing water, the gar becomes a meal for the alligator.

It is clear that these two organisms have just interacted with one another. But organisms have many interactions other than simply "who eats whom." For example, alligators dig underwater holes to escape from the heat. Later, after the alligators abandon these holes, fish and other aquatic organisms live in them when the water level gets low during a drought. Alligators also build nest mounds in which to lay their eggs, and they enlarge these mounds each year. Eventually, the mounds become small islands where trees and other plants grow. Herons, egrets, and other birds build their nests in the trees. It is easy to see that alligators affect many organisms, not just the gars that they eat.

Studying the Web of Life

All living things are connected in a web of life. Scientists who study the connections among living things specialize in the science of ecology. **Ecology** is the study of the interactions between organisms and their environment.

An Environment Has Two Parts An organism's environment is anything that affects the organism. An environment consists of two parts. The **biotic** part of the environment is all of the organisms that live together and interact with one another. The **abiotic** part of the environment includes all of the physical factors—such as water, soil, light, and temperature—that affect organisms living in a particular area.

Take another look at Figure 1. How many biotic parts and abiotic parts can you see?

Figure 1 *The alligator affects, and is affected by, many organisms in its environment.*

Organization in the Environment At first glance, the environment may seem disorganized. To ecologists, however, the environment can be arranged into different levels, as shown in **Figure 2.** The first level contains the individual organism. The second level contains similar organisms, forming a population. The third contains different populations, forming a community. The fourth contains a community and its abiotic environment, forming an ecosystem. Finally, the fifth level contains all ecosystems, forming the biosphere. Turn the page and examine **Figure 3** to see these levels in a salt marsh.

Figure 2 The Five Levels of Environmental Organization

Organism

Population

Community

Ecosystem

Biosphere

QuickLab

The Human Population

1. Using a **sheet of graph paper,** a **pencil,** and a **ruler,** draw and label a graph as shown below.

Number of people

Year

2. Plot the following points on your graph:
   (1800, 1 billion people)
   (1930, 2 billion people)
   (1960, 3 billion people)
   (1975, 4 billion people)
   (1987, 5 billion people)
   (1999, 6 billion people)

3. Draw a line connecting the points.

4. Answer the following questions in your ScienceLog.

   a. What does the curve that you have drawn indicate about human population growth?

   b. Do you think the human population can continue to grow indefinitely? Why or why not?

   TRY at HOME

Figure 3 *Examine the picture of a salt marsh below. See if you can find examples of each level of organization in this environment.*

Populations A salt marsh is a coastal area where grasslike plants grow. A **population** is a group of individuals of the same species that live together in the same area at the same time. For example, all of the seaside sparrows that live together in a salt marsh are members of a population. The individuals in the population compete with one another for food, nesting space, and mates.

Communities A **community** consists of all of the populations of different species that live and interact in an area. The various animals and plants you see below form a salt-marsh community. The different populations in a community depend on each other for food, shelter, and many other things.

Ecosystems An **ecosystem** is made up of a community of organisms and its abiotic environment. An ecologist studying the salt-marsh ecosystem would examine how the ecosystem's organisms interact with each other and how temperature, precipitation, and soil characteristics affect the organisms. For example, the rivers and streams that empty into the salt marsh carry nutrients, such as nitrogen, from the land. These nutrients influence how the cordgrass and algae grow.

Laughing gull

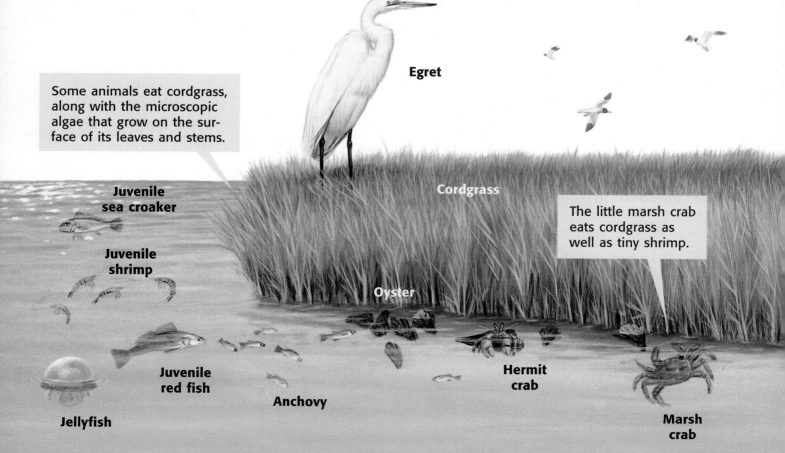

Some animals eat cordgrass, along with the microscopic algae that grow on the surface of its leaves and stems.

Egret

Cordgrass

The little marsh crab eats cordgrass as well as tiny shrimp.

Juvenile sea croaker

Juvenile shrimp

Oyster

Juvenile red fish

Hermit crab

Anchovy

Jellyfish

Marsh crab

The Biosphere The **biosphere** is the part of Earth where life exists. It extends from the deepest parts of the ocean to very high in the atmosphere, where tiny insects and plant spores drift, and it includes every ecosystem. Ecologists study the biosphere to learn how organisms interact with the abiotic environment—Earth's gaseous atmosphere, water, soil, and rock. The water in the abiotic environment includes both fresh water and salt water as well as water that is frozen in polar icecaps and glaciers.

REVIEW

1. What is ecology?

2. Give two examples of biotic and abiotic factors in the salt-marsh ecosystem.

3. Using the salt-marsh example, distinguish between populations, communities, ecosystems, and the biosphere.

4. **Analyzing Relationships** What do you think would happen to the other organisms in the salt-marsh ecosystem if the cordgrass were to suddenly die?

internet **connect**

SCLINKS
NSTA

TOPIC: Biotic and Abiotic Factors, Organization in the Environment
GO TO: www.scilinks.org
*sci*LINKS NUMBER: HSTL430, HSTL435

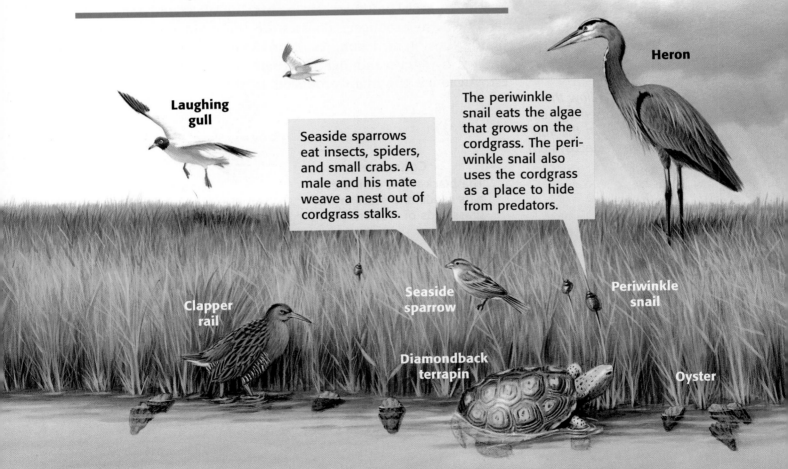

Heron

Laughing gull

Seaside sparrows eat insects, spiders, and small crabs. A male and his mate weave a nest out of cordgrass stalks.

The periwinkle snail eats the algae that grows on the cordgrass. The periwinkle snail also uses the cordgrass as a place to hide from predators.

Clapper rail

Seaside sparrow

Periwinkle snail

Diamondback terrapin

Oyster

What You'll Do

◆ Describe the functions of producers, consumers, and decomposers in an ecosystem.

◆ Distinguish between a food chain and a food web.

◆ Explain how energy flows through a food web.

◆ Distinguish between an organism's habitat and its niche.

Living Things Need Energy

All living things need energy to survive. For example, black-tailed prairie dogs, which live in the grasslands of North America, eat grass and seeds to get the energy they need. They use this energy to grow, move, heal injuries, and reproduce. In fact, everything a prairie dog does requires energy. The same is true for the plants that grow in the grasslands where the prairie dogs live. Coyotes that stalk prairie dogs, as well as the bacteria and fungi that live in the soil, all need energy.

The Energy Connection

Organisms in a prairie or any community can be divided into three groups based on how they obtain energy. These groups are producers, consumers, and decomposers. Examine **Figure 4** to see how energy passes through these groups in an ecosystem.

Producers Organisms that use sunlight directly to make food are called *producers*. They do this using a process called photosynthesis. Most producers are plants, but algae and some bacteria are also producers. Grasses are the main producers in a prairie ecosystem. Examples of producers in other ecosystems include cordgrass and algae in a salt marsh and trees in a forest. Algae are the main producers in the ocean.

Figure 4 *Follow the pathway of energy as it moves from the sun through the ecosystem.*

Energy
Sunlight is the source of energy for almost all living things.

Producer
Plants use the energy in sunlight to make food.

Consumer
The black-tailed prairie dog eats seeds and grass in the grasslands of western North America.

Herbivore

Consumer
All of the prairie dogs in a colony watch for enemies, such as coyotes, hawks, and badgers. Occasionally, a prairie dog is killed and eaten by a coyote.

Carnivore

Consumers Organisms that eat producers or other organisms for energy are called *consumers*. They cannot use the sun's energy directly like producers can. Instead, consumers must eat producers or other animals to obtain energy. There are several kinds of consumers. A **herbivore** is a consumer that eats plants. Herbivores in the prairie ecosystem include grasshoppers, gophers, prairie dogs, bison, and pronghorn antelope. A **carnivore** is a consumer that eats animals. Carnivores in the prairie ecosystem include coyotes, hawks, badgers, and owls. Consumers known as **omnivores** eat a variety of organisms, both plants and animals. The grasshopper mouse is an example of an omnivore in the prairie ecosystem. It eats insects, scorpions, lizards, and grass seeds. **Scavengers** are animals that feed on the bodies of dead animals. The turkey vulture is a scavenger in the prairie ecosystem. Examples of scavengers in aquatic ecosystems include crayfish, snails, clams, worms, and crabs.

Decomposers Organisms that get energy by breaking down the remains of dead organisms are called *decomposers*. Bacteria and fungi are examples of decomposers. These organisms extract the last bit of energy from dead organisms and produce simpler materials, such as water and carbon dioxide. These materials can then be reused by plants and other living things. Decomposers are an essential part of any ecosystem because they are nature's recyclers.

BRAIN FOOD

Prairie dogs are not really dogs. They are rodents. They are called dogs because their warning calls sound like the barking of dogs.

Self-Check

Are you a herbivore, a carnivore, or an omnivore? Explain. (*See page 782 to check your answer.*)

Consumer
A turkey vulture may eat some of the coyote's leftovers. A scavenger can pick bones completely clean.

Decomposer
Any prairie dog remains not eaten by the coyote or the turkey vulture are broken down by bacteria and fungi that live in the soil.

Scavenger

Recycler

Food Chains and Food Webs

Self-Check

How is a food web different from a food chain? *(See page 782 to check your answer.)*

Figure 4, on pages 438–439, shows a **food chain,** which represents how the energy in food molecules flows from one organism to the next. But because few organisms eat just one kind of organism, simple food chains rarely occur in nature. The many energy pathways possible are more accurately shown by a **food web.** **Figure 5** shows a simple food web for a woodland ecosystem.

Find the fox and the rabbit in the figure below. Notice that the arrow goes from the rabbit to the fox, showing that the rabbit is food for the fox. The rabbit is also food for the owl. Neither the fox nor the owl is ever food for the rabbit. Energy moves from one organism to the next in a one-way direction, even in a food web. Any energy not immediately used by an organism is stored in its tissues. Only the energy stored in an organism's tissues can be used by the next consumer.

Figure 5 *Energy moves through an ecosystem in complex ways. Most consumers eat a variety of foods and can be eaten by a variety of other consumers.*

Energy Pyramids

A grass plant uses most of the energy it obtains from the sun for its own life processes. But some of the energy is stored in its tissues and is left over for prairie dogs and other animals that eat the grass. Prairie dogs need a lot of energy and have to eat a lot of grass. Each prairie dog uses most of the energy it obtains from eating grass and stores only a little of it in its tissues. Coyotes need even more energy than prairie dogs, so they must eat many prairie dogs to survive. There must be many more prairie dogs in the community than there are coyotes that eat prairie dogs.

The loss of energy at each level of the food chain can be represented by an **energy pyramid,** as shown in **Figure 6.** You can see that the energy pyramid has a large base and becomes smaller at the top. The amount of available energy is reduced at higher levels because most of the energy is either used by the organism or given off as heat. Only energy stored in the tissues of an organism can be transferred to the next level.

MATH BREAK

Energy Pyramids

Draw an energy pyramid for a river ecosystem that contains four levels—aquatic plants, insect larvae, bluegill fish, and a largemouth bass. The plants obtain 10,000 units of energy from the sun. If each level uses 90 percent of the energy it receives from the previous level, how many units of energy are available to the bass?

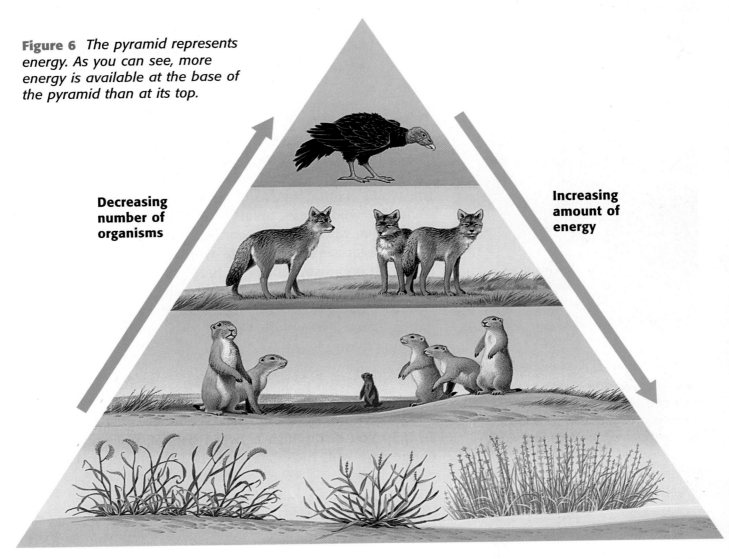

Figure 6 *The pyramid represents energy. As you can see, more energy is available at the base of the pyramid than at its top.*

Decreasing number of organisms

Increasing amount of energy

Figure 7 *As the wilderness was settled, the gray wolf population in the United States declined.*

Wolves and the Energy Pyramid

A single species can be very important to the flow of energy in an environment. Gray wolves, for example, are a consumer species that can control the populations of many other species. The diet of gray wolves can include anything from a lizard to an elk.

Once common throughout much of the United States, gray wolves were almost wiped out as the wilderness was settled. You can see a pair of gray wolves in **Figure 7**. Without wolves, certain other species, such as elk, were no longer controlled. The overpopulation of elk in some areas led to overgrazing and starvation.

Gray wolves were recently restored to the United States at Yellowstone National Park, as shown in **Figure 8**. The U.S. Fish and Wildlife Service hopes this action will restore the natural energy flow in this wilderness area. Not everyone approves, however. Ranchers near Yellowstone are concerned about the safety of their livestock.

Figure 8 *Members of the U.S. Fish and Wildlife Service are moving a caged wolf to a location in Yellowstone National Park.*

Habitat and Niche

An organism's **habitat** is the environment in which it lives. The wolf's habitat was originally very extensive. It included forests, grasslands, deserts, and the northern tundra. Today the wolf's habitat in North America is much smaller. It includes wilderness areas in Montana, Washington, Minnesota, Michigan, Wisconsin, and Canada.

An organism's way of life within an ecosystem is its **niche.** An organism's niche includes its habitat, its food, its predators, and the organisms with which it competes. An organism's niche also includes how the organism affects and is affected by abiotic factors in its environment, such as temperature, light, and moisture.

The Niche of the Gray Wolf

A complete description of a species' niche is very complex. To help you distinguish between habitat and niche, parts of the gray wolf niche are described on the next page.

Gray Wolves Are Consumers Wolves are carnivores. Their diet includes large animals, such as deer, moose, reindeer, sheep, and elk, as well as small animals, such as birds, lizards, snakes, and fish.

Gray Wolves Have a Social Structure Wolves live and hunt in packs, which are groups of about six animals that are usually members of the same family. Each member of the pack has a particular rank within the pack. The pack has two leaders that help defend the pack against enemies, such as other wolf packs or bears.

Gray Wolves Nurture and Teach Their Young A female wolf, shown in **Figure 9,** has five to seven pups and nurses her babies for about 2 months. The entire pack help bring the pups food and baby-sit when the parents are away from the den. It takes about 2 years for the young wolves to learn to hunt. At that time, some young wolves leave the pack to find mates and start their own pack.

Figure 9 *In small wolf packs, only the alpha female has pups. They are well cared for, however, by all of the males and females in the pack.*

Gray Wolves Are Needed in the Food Web If wolves become reestablished at Yellowstone National Park, they will reduce the elk population by killing the old, injured, and diseased elk. This in turn will allow more plants to grow, which will allow animals that eat the plants, such as snowshoe hares, and the animals that eat the hares, such as foxes, to increase in number.

REVIEW

1. How are producers, consumers (herbivores, carnivores, and scavengers), and decomposers linked in a food chain?

2. How do food chains link together to form a food web?

3. Distinguish between an organism's habitat and its niche using the prairie dog as an example.

4. **Applying Concepts** Is it possible for an inverted energy pyramid to exist, as shown in the figure at right? Explain why or why not.

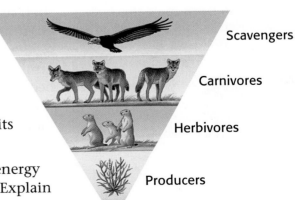

Types of Interactions

What You'll Do

◆ Distinguish between the two types of competition.
◆ Give examples of predators and prey.
◆ Distinguish between mutualism, commensalism, and parasitism.
◆ Define *coevolution,* and give an example.

Look at the seaweed forest shown in **Figure 10** below. Notice that some types of organisms are more numerous than others. In natural communities, populations of different organisms vary greatly. The interactions between these populations affect the size of each population.

Figure 10 *This seaweed forest is home to a large number of interacting species.*

Where on Earth could this bird live? Find out on page 746 of your LabBook.

Interactions with the Environment

Most living things produce more offspring than will survive. A female frog, for example, might lay hundreds of eggs in a small pond. In a few months, the population of frogs in that pond will be about the same as it was the year before. Why won't the pond become overrun with frogs? An organism, such as a frog, interacts with biotic or abiotic factors in its environment that can control the size of its population.

Limiting Factors Populations cannot grow indefinitely because the environment contains only so much food, water, living space, and other needed resources. When one or more of those resources becomes scarce, it is said to be a *limiting factor.* For example, food becomes a limiting factor when a population becomes too large for the amount of food available. Any single resource can be a limiting factor to population size.

Carrying Capacity The largest population that a given environment can support over a long period of time is known as the environment's **carrying capacity.** When a population grows larger than its carrying capacity, limiting factors in the environment cause the population to get smaller. For example, after a very rainy growing season in an environment, plants may produce a large crop of leaves and seeds. This may cause a herbivore population to grow large because of the unlimited food supply. If the next year has less rainfall than usual, there won't be enough food to support the large herbivore population. In this way, a population may temporarily exceed the carrying capacity. But a limiting factor will cause the population to die back. The population will return to a size that the environment can support over a long period of time.

Self-Check

1. Explain how water can limit the growth of a population.
2. Describe how the carrying capacity for deer in a forest ecosystem might be affected by weather.

(See page 782 to check your answers.)

Interactions Among Organisms

Populations contain interacting individuals of a single species, such as a group of rabbits feeding in the same area. Communities contain interacting populations of several species, such as a coral reef community with many species trying to find living space. Ecologists have described four main ways that species and individuals affect each other: competition, predators and prey, certain symbiotic relationships, and coevolution.

Competition

When two or more individuals or populations try to use the same limited resource, such as food, water, shelter, space, or sunlight, it is called *competition*. Because resources are in limited supply in the environment, their use by one individual or population decreases the amount available to other organisms.

Competition can occur among individuals *within* a population. The elks in Yellowstone National Park are herbivores that compete with each other for the same food plants in the park. This is a big problem for this species in winter. Competition can also occur *between* populations of different species. The different species of trees in **Figure 11** are competing with each other for sunlight and space.

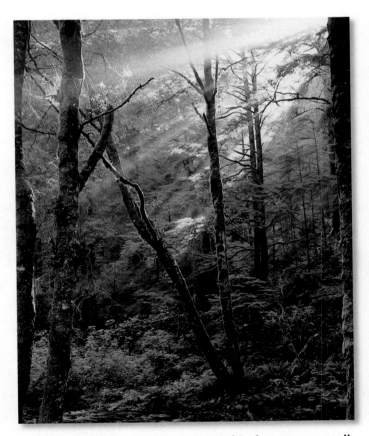

Figure 11 *Some of the trees in this forest grow tall in order to reach sunlight, reducing the amount of sunlight available to shorter trees nearby.*

Predators and Prey

Many interactions among species occur because one organism eats another. The organism that is eaten is called the **prey.** The organism that eats the prey is called the **predator.** When a bird eats a worm, the worm is the prey and the bird is the predator.

Predator Adaptations In order to survive, predators must be able to catch their prey. Predators have a wide variety of methods and abilities for doing this. The cheetah, for example, is able to run at great speed to catch its prey. Other predators, such as the goldenrod spider, shown in **Figure 12,** ambush their prey. The goldenrod spider blends in so well with the goldenrod flower that all it has to do is wait for its next insect meal to arrive.

Prey Adaptations Prey organisms have their own methods and abilities to keep from being eaten. Prey are able to run away, stay in groups, or camouflage themselves. Some prey organisms are poisonous to predators. They may advertise their poison with bright colors to warn predators to stay away. The fire salamander, shown in **Figure 13,** sprays a poison that burns. Predators quickly learn to recognize its warning coloration.

Many animals run away from predators. Prairie dogs run to their underground burrows when a predator approaches. Many small fishes, such as anchovies, swim in groups called schools. Antelopes and buffaloes stay in herds. All the eyes, ears, and noses of the individuals in the group are watching, listening, and smelling for predators. This behavior increases the likelihood of spotting a potential predator.

Some prey species hide from predators by using camouflage. Certain insects resemble leaves so closely that you would never guess they are animals.

Figure 12 *The goldenrod spider is difficult for its insect prey to see. Can you see it?*

Figure 13 *Experienced predators know better than to eat the fire salamander! This colorful animal will make an unlucky predator very sick.*

Symbiosis

Some species have very close interactions with other species. **Symbiosis** is a close, long-term association between two or more species. The individuals in a symbiotic relationship can benefit from, be unaffected by, or be harmed by the relationship. Often, one species lives in or on the other species. The thousands of symbiotic relationships that occur in nature are often classified into three groups: mutualism, commensalism, and parasitism.

Mutualism A symbiotic relationship in which both organisms benefit is called **mutualism.** For example, you and a species of bacteria that lives in your intestines benefit each other! The bacteria get a plentiful food supply from you, and in return you get vitamins that the bacteria produce.

Another example of mutualism occurs between coral and algae. The living corals near the surface of the water provide a home for the algae. The algae produce food through photosynthesis that is used by the corals. When a coral dies, its skeleton serves as a foundation for other corals. Over a long period of time, these skeletons build up large, rocklike formations that lie just beneath the surface of warm, sunny seas, as shown in **Figure 14.**

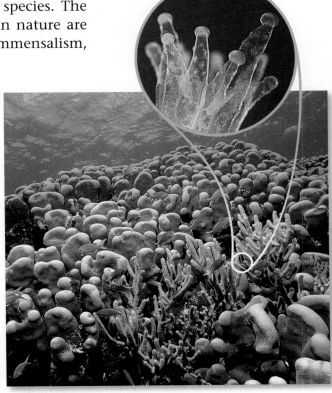

Figure 14 *In the smaller photo above, you can see the gold-colored algae inside the coral.*

Commensalism A symbiotic relationship in which one organism benefits and the other is unaffected is called **commensalism.** One example of commensalism is the relationship between sharks and remoras. **Figure 15** shows a shark with a remora attached to its body. Remoras "hitch a ride" and feed on scraps of food left by sharks. The remoras benefit from this relationship, while sharks are unaffected.

Figure 15 *The remora attached to the shark benefits from the relationship. The shark is neither benefited nor harmed.*

Parasitism A symbiotic association in which one organism benefits while the other is harmed is called **parasitism.** The organism that benefits is called the *parasite*. The organism that is harmed is called the *host*. The parasite gets nourishment from its host, which is weakened in the process. Sometimes a host organism becomes so weak that it dies. Some parasites, such as ticks, live outside the host's body. Other parasites, such as tapeworms, live inside the host's body.

Figure 16 shows a bright green caterpillar called a tomato hornworm. A female wasp laid tiny eggs on the caterpillar. When the eggs hatch, each young wasp will burrow into the caterpillar's body. The young wasps will actually eat the caterpillar alive! In a short time, the caterpillar will be almost completely consumed and will die. When that occurs, the mature wasps will fly away.

In this example of parasitism, the host dies. Most parasites, however, do not kill their hosts. Can you think of reasons why?

Figure 16 *The tomato hornworm is being parasitized by young wasps. Do you see their cocoons?*

Coevolution

Symbiotic relationships and other interactions among organisms in an ecosystem may cause coevolution. **Coevolution** is a long-term change that takes place in two species because of their close interactions with one another.

Coevolution sometimes occurs between herbivores and the plants on which they feed. For example, the ants shown in **Figure 17** have coevolved with a tropical tree called the acacia. The ants protect the tree on which they live by attacking any other herbivore that approaches the tree. The plant has coevolved special structures on its stems that produce food for the ants. The ants live in other structures also made by the tree.

Figure 17 *Ants collect food made by the acacia tree and store the food in their shelter, also made by the tree.*

Coevolution in Australia

In 1859, settlers released 12 rabbits in Australia. There were no predators or parasites to control the rabbit population, and there was plenty of food. The rabbit population increased so fast that the country was soon overrun by rabbits. To control the rabbit population, the Australian government introduced a virus that makes rabbits sick. The first time the virus was used, more than 99 percent of the rabbits died. The survivors reproduced, and the rabbit population grew large again. The second time the virus was used, about 90 percent of the rabbits died. Once again, the rabbit population increased. The third time the virus was used, only about 50 percent of the rabbits died. Suggest what changes might have occurred in the rabbits and the virus.

Coevolution and Flowers Some of the most amazing examples of coevolution are between flowers and their pollinators. (An organism that carries pollen from flower to flower is called a *pollinator*.) When the pollinator travels to the next flower to feed, some of the pollen is left behind on the female part of the flower and more pollen is picked up. Because of pollination, reproduction can take place in the plant. Organisms such as bees, bats, and hummingbirds are attracted to a flower because of its colors, odors, and nectar.

During the course of evolution, hummingbird-pollinated flowers, for example, developed nectar with just the right amount of sugar for their pollinators. The hummingbird's long, thin tongue and beak coevolved to fit into the flowers so that they could reach the nectar. As the hummingbird, like the one shown in **Figure 18,** feeds on the nectar, its head and body become smeared with pollen.

Figure 18 *The bird is attracted to the flower's nectar and picks up the flower's pollen as it feeds.*

REVIEW

1. Briefly describe one example of a predator-prey relationship. Identify the predator and the prey.

2. Name and define the three kinds of symbiosis.

3. **Analyzing Relationships** Explain the probable relationship between the giant *Rafflesia* flower, which smells like rotting meat, and the carrion flies that buzz around it. HINT: *carrion* means "rotting flesh."

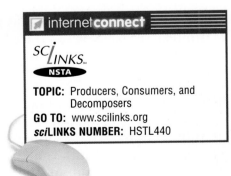

internet**connect**

SC*L*INKS.
NSTA

TOPIC: Producers, Consumers, and Decomposers
GO TO: www.scilinks.org
*sci*LINKS NUMBER: HSTL440

Chapter Highlights

SECTION 1

Vocabulary

ecology *(p. 434)*

biotic *(p. 434)*

abiotic *(p. 434)*

population *(p. 436)*

community *(p. 436)*

ecosystem *(p. 436)*

biosphere *(p. 437)*

Section Notes

• Ecology is the study of the interactions between organisms and their environment.

• The environment consists of both biotic (living) and abiotic (nonliving) parts.

• A population is a group of the same species living in the same place at the same time. A community is all of the populations of different species living together. An ecosystem is a community and its abiotic environment. The biosphere consists of all of Earth's ecosystems.

Labs

Capturing the Wild Bean *(p. 748)*

SECTION 2

Vocabulary

herbivore *(p. 439)*

carnivore *(p. 439)*

omnivore *(p. 439)*

scavenger *(p. 439)*

food chain *(p. 440)*

food web *(p. 440)*

energy pyramid *(p. 441)*

habitat *(p. 442)*

niche *(p. 442)*

Section Notes

• Organisms that use sunlight directly to make food are called producers. Consumers are organisms that eat other organisms to obtain energy. Decomposers are bacteria and fungi that break down the remains of dead organisms to obtain energy.

☑ Skills Check

Math Concepts

ENERGY PYRAMIDS Try calculating the MathBreak on page 441 as if each unit of energy were $1.00. If you have $10,000.00, but you spend 90 percent, how much do you have left to leave in your will? ($1,000.00) If your heir spends 90 percent of that, how much can your heir leave? ($100.00) After four generations, how much will the inheritance be? ($1.00) Not much, huh? That's why there are very few large organisms at the top of the energy pyramid.

Visual Understanding

FOOD WEBS Several food pathways are shown in the food web in Figure 5 on page 440. However, an actual food web in a woodland ecosystem is much more complex because hundreds of species live there. Find the mouse in Figure 5. How many organisms feed on the mouse? How many organisms feed on the butterfly? What might happen to this ecosystem if these animals were eliminated?

- A food chain shows how energy flows from one organism to the next.

- Because most organisms eat more than one kind of food, there are many energy pathways possible; these are represented by a food web.

- Energy pyramids demonstrate that most of the energy at each level of the food chain is used up at that level and is unavailable for organisms higher on the food chain.

- An organism's habitat is the environment in which it lives. An organism's niche is its role in the ecosystem.

Vocabulary

carrying capacity (p. 445)

prey (p. 446)

predator (p. 446)

symbiosis (p. 447)

mutualism (p. 447)

commensalism (p. 447)

parasitism (p. 448)

coevolution (p. 448)

Section Notes

- Population size changes over time.

- Limiting factors slow the growth of a population. The largest population that an environment can support over a long period of time is called the carrying capacity.

- When one organism eats another, the organism that is eaten is the prey, and the organism that eats the prey is the predator.

- Symbiosis is a close, long-term association between two or more species. There are three general types of symbiosis: mutualism, commensalism, and parasitism.

- Coevolution involves the long-term changes that take place in two species because of their close interactions with one another.

Labs

Adaptation: It's a Way of Life (p. 746)

internet**connect**

GO TO: go.hrw.com

Visit the **HRW** Web site for a variety of learning tools related to this chapter. Just type in the keyword:

KEYWORD: HSTINT

GO TO: www.scilinks.org

Visit the **National Science Teachers Association** on-line Web site for Internet resources related to this chapter. Just type in the *sci*LINKS number for more information about the topic:

TOPIC:	*sci*LINKS NUMBER:
Biotic and Abiotic Factors	HSTL430
Organization in the Environment	HSTL435
Producers, Consumers, and Decomposers	HSTL440
Food Chains and Food Webs	HSTL445
Habitats and Niches	HSTL450

Chapter Review

USING VOCABULARY

To complete the following sentences, choose the correct term from each pair of terms listed below:

1. An organism's environment has two parts, the __?__, or living, and the __?__, or nonliving. *(biotic* or *abiotic)*

2. A __?__ is a group of individuals of the same species that live in the same area at the same time. *(community* or *population)*

3. A community and its abiotic environment make up a(n) __?__. *(ecosystem* or *food web)*

4. Organisms that use photosynthesis to obtain energy are called __?__. *(producers* or *decomposers)*

5. The environment in which an organism lives is its __?__, and the role the organism plays in an ecosystem is its __?__. *(niche* or *habitat)*

UNDERSTANDING CONCEPTS

Multiple Choice

6. A tick sucks blood from a dog. In this relationship, the tick is the __?__ and the dog is the __?__.
   a. parasite, prey
   b. predator, host
   c. parasite, host
   d. host, parasite

7. Resources such as water, food, or sunlight are more likely to be limiting factors
   a. when population size is decreasing.
   b. when predators eat their prey.
   c. when the population is small.
   d. when a population is approaching the carrying capacity.

8. "Nature's recyclers" are
   a. predators.
   b. decomposers.
   c. producers.
   d. omnivores.

9. A beneficial association between coral and algae is an example of
   a. commensalism.
   b. parasitism.
   c. mutualism.
   d. predation.

10. How energy moves through an ecosystem can be represented by
    a. food chains.
    b. energy pyramids.
    c. food webs.
    d. All of the above

11. The base of an energy pyramid represents which organisms in an ecosystem?
    a. producers
    b. carnivores
    c. herbivores
    d. scavengers

12. Which of the following is the correct order in a food chain?
    a. sun → producers → herbivores → scavengers → carnivores
    b. sun → consumers → predators → parasites → hosts
    c. sun → producers → decomposers → consumers → omnivores
    d. sun → producers → herbivores → carnivores → scavengers

13. Remoras and sharks have a relationship best described as
    a. mutualism.
    b. commensalism.
    c. predator and prey.
    d. parasitism.

Short Answer

14. Briefly describe the habitat and niche of the gray wolf.

15. What might different species of trees in a forest compete for?

16. How do limiting factors affect the carrying capacity of an environment?

17. What is coevolution?

Concept Mapping

18. Use the following terms to create a concept map: individual organisms, producers, populations, ecosystems, consumers, herbivores, communities, carnivores, the biosphere.

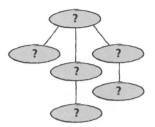

CRITICAL THINKING AND PROBLEM SOLVING

Write one or two sentences to answer the following questions:

19. Could a balanced ecosystem contain producers and consumers but no decomposers? Why or why not?

20. Some biologists think that certain species, such as alligators and wolves, help maintain biological diversity in their ecosystems. Predict what might happen to other species, such as gar fish or herons, if alligators were to become extinct in the Florida Everglades.

21. Does the Earth have a carrying capacity for humans? Explain your answer.

22. Explain why it is important to have a variety of organisms in a community of interacting species. Give an example.

MATH IN SCIENCE

23. The plants in each square meter of an ecosystem obtained 20,810 Calories of the sun's energy by photosynthesis per year. The herbivores in that ecosystem ate all of the plants, but they obtained only 3,370 Calories of energy. How much energy did the plants use for their own life processes?

INTERPRETING GRAPHICS

Examine the following graph, which shows the population growth of a species of *Paramecium*, a slipper-shaped, single-celled microorganism, over a period of 18 days. Food was occasionally added to the test tube in which the paramecia were grown. Answer the following questions:

24. What is the carrying capacity of the test tube as long as food is added?

25. Predict what will happen to the population if the researcher stops adding food to the test tube.

26. What keeps the number of *Paramecium* at a steady level?

27. Predict what might happen if the amount of water is doubled and the food supply stays the same.

Paramecium caudatum Growth

(graph: Number of Paramecium per mL vs. Days)

NOW What Do You Think?

Take a minute to review your answers to the ScienceLog questions on page 433. Have your answers changed? If necessary, revise your answers based on what you have learned since you began this chapter.

Health

An Unusual Guest

What has a tiny tubelike body and short stumpy legs and lives upside down in your eyebrows and eyelashes? Would you believe a small animal? It's called a follicle mite, and humans are its host organism. Like all large animals, human beings are hosts to a variety of smaller creatures. They live in or on our bodies and share our bodies' resources. But none of our guests are stranger than follicle mites. They feed on oil and dead cells from your skin.

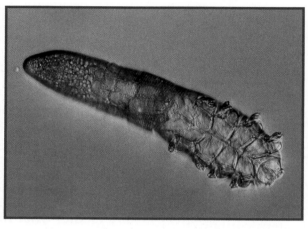

▲ *A follicle mite is smaller than the period at the end of this sentence.*

What Are They?

Follicle mites are arachnids—relatives of spiders. They are about 0.4 mm long, and they live in hair follicles all over your body. Usually they like to live in areas around the nose, cheek, forehead, chin, eyebrows, and eyelashes.

Follicle Mites Don't Bite

These tiny guests are almost always harmless, and they seldom live on children and adolescents. And you probably wouldn't even know they were there. Studies reveal that between 97 percent and 100 percent of all adults have these mites. Except in rare cases, follicle mites in adults are also pretty harmless.

Some Health Concerns

Although follicle mites rarely cause problems, they are sometimes responsible for an acnelike condition around the nose, eyebrows, and eyelashes. A large number of mites (up to 25) may live in the same follicle. This can cause an inflammation of the follicle. The follicle does not swell like acne; instead it becomes red and itchy.

Mites living in eyelashes and on eyelids can irritate those areas. The inflammation causes itchy eyelids or eyebrows. But such inflammations are rare, and the condition clears up very quickly when suitable medication is applied. So while follicle mites may be one of the strangest guests living on human skin, they are almost never a problem.

Other Companions

Many tiny organisms make their home in humans' bodies. Bacteria within the body may help maintain proper pH levels. Even *Escherichia coli,* a type of bacterium that can cause severe health problems, lives in the human colon. Without *E. coli,* a person would be unable to produce enough vitamin K or folic acid.

On Your Own

▶ Do some more research on follicle mites. Search for *Demodex folliculorum* or *Demodex brevis.* Find out more about some of the other strange organisms that rely on humans' bodies for food and shelter. Report on your findings, or write a story from the organism's point of view.

EYE ON THE ENVIRONMENT

Alien Invasion

A group of tiny aliens left their ship in Mobile, Alabama. Their bodies were red and shiny, and they walked on six legs. The aliens looked around and then quietly crawled off to make homes in the new land.

Westward Ho!

In 1918, fire ants were accidentally imported into the United States by a freighter ship from South America. In the United States, fire ants have no natural predators or competitors. In addition, these ants are extremely aggressive, and their colonies can harbor many queens, instead of just one queen, like many other ant species. With all these advantages, it is not surprising that the ants have spread like wildfire. By 1965, fire-ant mounds were popping up on the southeastern coast and as far west as Texas. Today they are found in at least 10 southern states and may soon reach as far west as California.

▲ *Three types of fire ants are found in a colony: the queen, workers, and males. Notice how the queen ant dwarfs the worker ants.*

Jaws of Destruction

Imported fire ants have done a lot of damage as they have spread across the United States. Because they are attracted to electrical currents, they chew through wire insulation, causing shorts in electrical circuits. The invaders have also managed to disturb the natural balance of native ecosystems. In some areas, they have killed off 70 percent of the native ant species and 40 percent of other native insect species. Each year, about 25,000 people seek medical attention for painful fire-ant bites.

Fighting Fire

Eighty years after the fire ants' introduction into the United States, the destructive ants continue to multiply. About 157 chemical products, including ammonia, gasoline, extracts from manure, and harsh pesticides, are registered for use against fire ants, but most have little or no success. Unfortunately, many of these remedies also harm the environment. By 1995, the government had approved only one fire-ant bait for large-scale use.

An Ant-Farm Census

▶ How many total offspring does a single fire-ant queen produce if she lives for 5 years and produces 1,000 eggs a day? If a mound contains 300,000 ants, how many mounds will her offspring fill?

Cycles in Nature

This Really Happened . . .

The sun came up over the desert horizon and woke the scientist. She had a full day ahead of her. Today she would start out working in the fields with the other seven scientists. The small fields of food crops had to recycle all of the water and nutrients that the plants used. These crops were the scientists' only source of food in this tightly sealed environment.

Later, the scientist would jog over to the rain forest, where she would observe a water-recycling experiment. After a swim in the ocean, she planned to walk through the mangrove forest and be home by lunchtime. After lunch, she would go to the computer lab. From the lab, she could monitor the sensors that would alert her if any part of the ecosystem failed to cycle properly. This

monitoring was very important to the scientists because their lives depended on the health of their sealed environment. Several weeks ago, the sensors began to detect trouble . . .

This was an actual day in the life of one of eight scientists who lived in the largest artificial biosphere ever constructed, called Biosphere 2. The goal was to develop an enclosed system where water and air could be recycled and food could be grown and harvested. But modeling Biosphere 1 (the Earth's natural biosphere) wasn't easy. The experiment failed because the correct oxygen level could not be maintained.

In this chapter you will learn how the Earth, a biosphere enclosed in space, recycles matter.

What Do You Think?

In your ScienceLog, try to answer the following questions based on what you already know:

1. What is meant by *recycling*?

2. What happens to rainwater after it falls to Earth?

A Classroom Aquarium

The first large, stable, sealed ecosystems were developed by NASA. They looked similar to an aquarium inside a glass sphere. Everything inside the sphere recycled as long as there was enough light on the sphere for photosynthesis to take place.

In this activity, you will set up an aquarium in your classroom. A typical aquarium is an enclosed, but not sealed, ecosystem. As you study this chapter on cycles in nature, you will observe your aquarium and make the adjustments needed to keep the environment balanced.

Procedure

1. Acquire an **aquarium** from your teacher. Check the Internet, your library, or a pet store to find complete instructions on the proper way to clean and prepare the aquarium.

2. Investigate the kinds of **plants** and **animals** that you can include in your aquarium.

3. Decide on the best location for your aquarium.

4. Check your plans with your teacher and then set up the aquarium.

Analysis

5. Your aquarium will thrive if you add about 2 L of water from an aquarium that is already established. What might this water contain?

6. If your aquarium water turns green, you can add some water fleas *(Daphnia)* to the tank. After a few days, the water will turn clear. Why is the water green? Why would it turn clear after the water fleas are added?

7. If you add two snails for every 3 L of water, the glass of your aquarium will stay clean. How do you think the snails keep the glass clean?

The Cycles of Matter

Terms to Learn

precipitation   decomposition
evaporation   combustion
ground water

What You'll Do

◆ Trace the cycle of water between the atmosphere, land, and oceans.
◆ Diagram the carbon cycle, and explain its importance to living things.
◆ Diagram the nitrogen cycle, and explain its importance to living things.

The matter in your body has been on Earth since the planet was formed billions of years ago! *Matter,* which is anything that occupies space and has mass, is used over and over again. Each kind of matter has its own cycle. In these cycles, matter moves among the environment and living things.

The Water Cycle

The movement of water among the oceans, atmosphere, land, and living things is known as the *water cycle*. Locate each part of the water cycle in **Figure 1** as it is discussed.

Precipitation Water moves from the atmosphere to the land and oceans as **precipitation,** which includes rain, snow, sleet, and hail. About 91 percent of precipitation falls into the ocean. The rest falls on land, renewing the supply of fresh water.

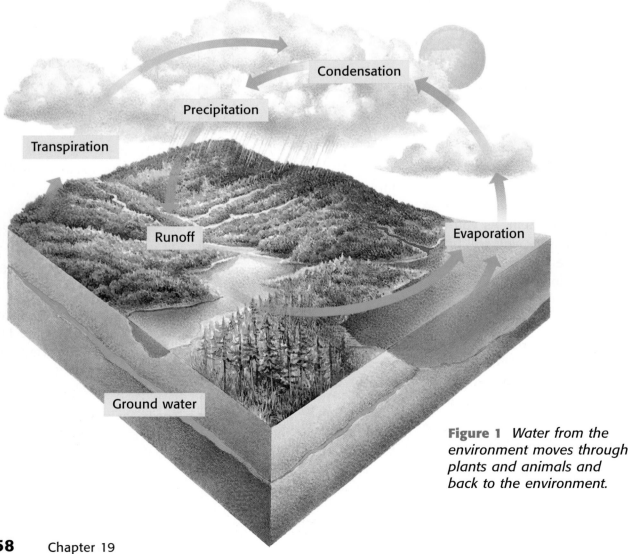

Condensation

Precipitation

Transpiration

Runoff

Evaporation

Ground water

Figure 1 *Water from the environment moves through plants and animals and back to the environment.*

Evaporation Water cycles back to the atmosphere through evaporation. During **evaporation,** the sun's heat causes water to change from liquid to vapor. When the water vapor cools during the process of *condensation,* it forms a liquid that can fall to the Earth as precipitation.

Ground Water Some precipitation seeps into the ground, where it is stored in underground caverns or in porous rock. This water, known as **ground water,** may stay in the ground for hundreds or even thousands of years. Ground water provides water to the soil, streams, rivers, and oceans.

Water and Life All organisms, from tiny bacteria to animals and plants, contain a lot of water. Your body is composed of about 70 percent water. Water carries waste products away from body tissues. Water also helps regulate body temperature through perspiration and evaporation, returning water to the environment in a process called *transpiration.* Without water, there would be no life on Earth.

The Carbon Cycle

Carbon is essential to living things because it is part of all biological molecules. The movement of carbon from the environment into living things and back into the environment is known as the *carbon cycle,* shown in **Figure 2.**

Figure 2 *Carbon may remain in the environment for millions of years before becoming available to living things.*

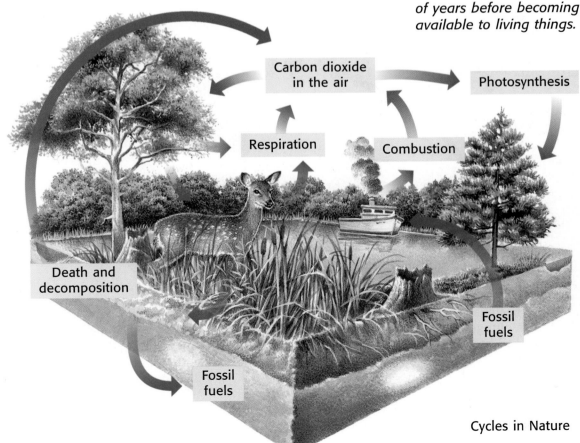

Carbon dioxide in the air

Photosynthesis

Respiration

Combustion

Death and decomposition

Fossil fuels

Fossil fuels

Photosynthesis Photosynthesis is the process by which carbon cycles from the environment into living things. During photosynthesis, plants use carbon dioxide from the air to make sugars. Most animals get the carbon they need by eating plants.

Respiration How does carbon return to the environment? Animals and plants both respire. During *respiration*, sugar molecules are broken down to release energy. Carbon dioxide and water are released as byproducts.

Decomposition The breakdown of dead materials into carbon dioxide and water is called **decomposition.** When fungi and bacteria decompose organic matter, they return carbon to the environment.

Combustion The carbon in coal, oil, and natural gas returns to the atmosphere as carbon dioxide when these fuels are burned. The process of burning fuel is known as **combustion.** Combustion provides much of the fuel people need to drive cars, heat homes, and make electricity.

The Nitrogen Cycle

The movement of nitrogen from the environment to living things and back again is called the *nitrogen cycle,* shown in Figure 3.

Figure 3 *Without bacteria, nitrogen could not enter living things or be returned to the atmosphere.*

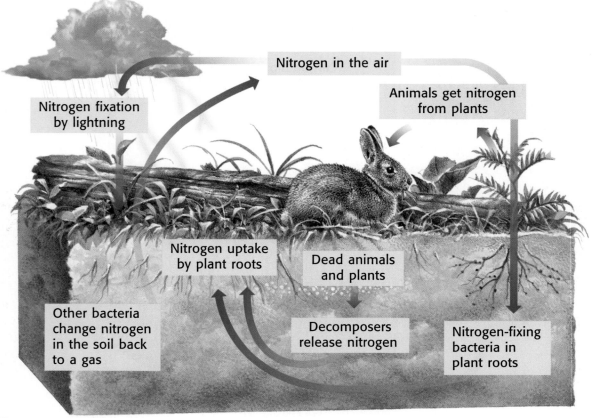

Nitrogen in the air

Nitrogen fixation by lightning

Animals get nitrogen from plants

Nitrogen uptake by plant roots

Dead animals and plants

Other bacteria change nitrogen in the soil back to a gas

Decomposers release nitrogen

Nitrogen-fixing bacteria in plant roots

A Sea of Nitrogen About 78 percent of the Earth's atmosphere is nitrogen gas. However, most organisms cannot use nitrogen gas to obtain the nitrogen they need to build proteins and DNA. But bacteria in the soil are able to change nitrogen gas into forms that can be used by plants. This is called *nitrogen fixation*. Most animals get the nitrogen they need by eating plants.

Back to Gas The final step of the nitrogen cycle is also performed by bacteria in the soil. These bacteria are different species than the bacteria that fix nitrogen. The bacteria break down dead organisms and animal wastes. This process produces nitrogen gas, which is returned to the atmosphere.

MATH BREAK

Gallons Galore

An average person in the United States uses about 78 gal of water each day. How many liters is this? How many cubic centimeters? Remember: 1 gal = 3.79 L and 1 mL = 1 cm^3.

The Pollution Cycle

Isabel read an article about how power plants near her home emit sulfur dioxide into the atmosphere. When sulfur dioxide mixes with water, it forms sulfuric acid, which is extremely toxic to living things. Isabel also learned that sulfur dioxide from these power plants has killed all the fish in a lake hundreds of kilometers away. Trees growing near the lake were also killed. Using what you know about the water cycle, write a letter to Isabel explaining how this could happen.

REVIEW

1. How are precipitation, evaporation, and ground water involved in the water cycle?

2. Draw a simple diagram of the nitrogen cycle. Make sure you include how animals get nitrogen.

3. **Analyzing Relationships** How is decomposition related to the carbon cycle?

internet**connect**

SCI*LINKS*
NSTA

TOPIC: The Water Cycle,
The Nitrogen Cycle
GO TO: www.scilinks.org
***sci*LINKS NUMBER:** HSTL455, HSTL465

Terms to Learn

succession
pioneer species

What You'll Do

◆ Define *succession*.
◆ Contrast primary and secondary succession.

Ecological Succession

Imagine you have a time machine that can take you back to the summer of 1988. If you had visited Yellowstone National Park during that year, you would have found large areas of the park burned to the ground. When the fires were put out, a layer of gray ash blanketed the forest floor. Most of the trees were dead, although many of them were still standing, as shown in **Figure 4.**

Figure 4 *Parts of Yellowstone National Park burned in 1988.*

Figure 5 *In the spring of 1989, regrowth was evident in the burned parts of Yellowstone National Park.*

Regrowth of a Forest

The following spring, the appearance of the "dead" forest began to change. In **Figure 5,** you can see that some of the dead trees are beginning to fall over, and small, green plants have begun to grow in large numbers. National Park foresters report that the number and kinds of plants growing in the recovering area have increased each year since the fire.

A gradual development of a community over time, such as the regrowth of the burned areas of Yellowstone National Park, is called **succession.** Succession takes place in all communities, not just those affected by disturbances such as forest fires. Succession occurs through predictable stages over time, as described on the following pages.

Primary Succession

Sometimes a small community of living things starts to live in an area that did not previously contain any plants or other organisms. There is no soil in this area, usually just bare rock. Over a very long time, a series of organisms live and die on the rock, and the rock is slowly transformed into soil. This process is called *primary succession.*

1 A slowly retreating glacier exposes bare rock where nothing lives, and primary succession begins.

2 Most primary succession begins with lichens. Acids from the lichens begin breaking the rocks into small particles. These particles mix with the remains of dead lichens to start forming soil. Because lichens are the first organisms to live on the rock, they are called **pioneer species.**

3 After many years, the soil is deep enough for mosses to grow. The mosses eventually replace the lichens. Other tiny organisms, such as insects, also make their home among the lichens and mosses. When they die, their remains add to the soil.

4 Over time, the soil layer thickens, and the moss community is replaced by ferns. The ferns in turn may be replaced by grasses and wildflowers. Once there is sufficient soil, shrubs and small trees come into the area.

5 After hundreds or even thousands of years, the soil may be deep enough to support a forest.

Sometimes an existing community is destroyed by a natural disaster, such as fire or flood. Or, a farmer might stop growing crops in an area that had been cleared. In either case, if soil is left intact, the original plant community may regrow through a series of stages called *secondary succession.*

1 The first year after a farmer stops growing crops, or after some other major disturbance, many weeds grow. Crabgrass is usually the most common weed during the first year.

2 By the second year, new weedy plants appear. Their seeds may have blown into the field by the wind, or insects may have carried them. One of the most common weeds during the second year is horseweed.

3 In 5 to 15 years, small pine trees may start growing among the weeds. The pines continue to grow, and, after about 100 years, a forest may form.

4 As older pines die, they may be replaced by hardwoods if the climate can support them.

✓ Self-Check

Describe the differences between primary succession and secondary succession.
(See page 782 to check your answer.)

Where Does It All End? In the early stages of succession only a few species grow in an area. These species grow fast and make many seeds that scatter easily. Because there are only a few species, they are open to invasion by other, longer-lasting species, disease, and other disturbances. In later stages of succession there are usually many more species present. Because of this, there are more pathways available to absorb disturbances. For example, in a mature forest, many species will survive an invasion by insects if these insects prefer to eat only one species of plant.

Eventually, if an area experiences no fires or other disturbances, it will reach a more or less stable stage. Communities change over time even though they are considered to be stable. A stable community may not always be a hardwood forest. Look at **Figure 6.** Why might a stable hardwood forest not develop there? The answer is that the area does not have the kind of climate that will support a stable hardwood forest. The climate in this area supports a desert community.

Figure 6 *This is how a stable community in the Sonoran Desert in Arizona looks in spring.*

REVIEW

1. Define *succession*.

2. Describe succession in an abandoned field.

3. **Applying Concepts** Explain why soil formation is always the first stage of primary succession. Does soil formation stop when trees begin to grow? Why or why not?

Chapter Highlights

Vocabulary

precipitation *(p. 458)*
evaporation *(p. 459)*
ground water *(p. 459)*
decomposition *(p. 460)*
combustion *(p. 460)*

Section Notes

- Materials used by living things continually cycle through ecosystems.

- In the water cycle, water moves through the ocean, atmosphere, land, and living things.

- Precipitation, evaporation, transpiration, and condensation are important processes in the water cycle.

- Water that falls is held in soil or porous rocks as ground water.

- Photosynthesis, respiration, decomposition, and combustion are important steps in the carbon cycle.

- Carbon enters plants from the nonliving environment as carbon dioxide.

- The process of changing nitrogen gas into forms that plants can use is called nitrogen fixation.

Labs

Nitrogen Needs *(p. 750)*

☑ Skills Check

Math Concepts

SAVING WATER Flushing the toilet accounts for almost half the water a person uses in a day. Some toilets use up to 6 gal per flush. More-efficient toilets use about 1.5 gal per flush. How many liters of water can you save using a more-efficient toilet if you flush five times a day?

> 6 gal − 1.5 gal = 4.5 gal
> 4.5 gal × 5 flushes = 22.5 gal
> 1 gal is equal to 3.79 L
> 3.79 L × 22.5 gal = 85.275 L of water saved

Visual Understanding

SOIL FORMATION The formation of soil is part of every stage of primary succession. Look at page 463 to review how soil forms.

Vocabulary

succession *(p. 462)*

pioneer species *(p. 463)*

Section Notes

- Ecological succession is the gradual development of communities over time. Often a series of stages is observed during succession.

- Primary succession occurs in an area that was not previously inhabited by living things; no soil is present.

- Secondary succession occurs in an area where an earlier community was disturbed by fire, landslides, floods, or plowing for crops; soil is present.

Labs

A Passel o' Pioneers *(p. 752)*

 internetconnect

GO TO: go.hrw.com

Visit the **HRW** Web site for a variety of learning tools related to this chapter. Just type in the keyword:

KEYWORD: HSTCYC

SCiLINKS
NSTA

GO TO: www.scilinks.org

Visit the **National Science Teachers Association** on-line Web site for Internet resources related to this chapter. Just type in the *sci*LINKS number for more information about the topic:

TOPIC:	The Water Cycle	*sci*LINKS NUMBER:	HSTL455
TOPIC:	The Carbon Cycle	*sci*LINKS NUMBER:	HSTL460
TOPIC:	The Nitrogen Cycle	*sci*LINKS NUMBER:	HSTL465
TOPIC:	Succession	*sci*LINKS NUMBER:	HSTL470

Chapter Review

USING VOCABULARY

To complete the following sentences, choose the correct term from each pair of terms listed below:

1. During __?__, water moves from the atmosphere to the land and ocean. *(evaporation* or *precipitation)*

2. All biological molecules contain __?__. *(carbon* or *carbon dioxide)*

3. The combustion of coal, oil, and natural gas is part of the __?__. *(nitrogen cycle* or *carbon cycle)*

4. The development of a community on bare, exposed rock is an example of __?__. *(primary succession* or *secondary succession)*

5. The recovery of Yellowstone National Park following the fires of 1988 is an example of __?__. *(primary succession* or *secondary succession)*

UNDERSTANDING CONCEPTS

Multiple Choice

6. Water changes from a liquid to a vapor during
   a. precipitation.
   b. respiration.
   c. evaporation.
   d. decomposition.

7. The process of burning fuel, such as oil and coal, is
   a. combustion.
   b. respiration.
   c. decomposition.
   d. photosynthesis.

8. One of the most common plants in a recently abandoned farm field is
   a. horseweed.
   b. young pine trees.
   c. young oak and hickory trees.
   d. crabgrass.

9. Which of the following statements about ground water is true?
   a. It stays underground for a few days.
   b. It is stored in underground caverns or porous rock.
   c. It is salty like ocean water.
   d. It never reenters the water cycle.

10. Which of the following processes produces carbon dioxide?
   a. decomposition
   b. respiration
   c. combustion
   d. all of the above

11. During nitrogen fixation, nitrogen gas is converted into a form that __?__ can use.
   a. plants
   b. animals
   c. fungi
   d. all of the above

12. Bacteria are essential to
   a. combustion.
   b. photosynthesis.
   c. nitrogen fixation.
   d. evaporation.

13. The pioneer species on bare rock are usually
   a. ferns.
   b. pine trees.
   c. mosses.
   d. lichens.

Short Answer

14. Is snow a part of the water cycle? Why or why not?

15. Can a single scientist observe all of the stages of secondary succession on an abandoned field? Explain your answer.

Concept Mapping

16. Use the following terms to create a concept map: abandoned farmland, lichens, bare rock, soil formation, horseweed, succession, forest fire, primary succession, secondary succession, pioneer species.

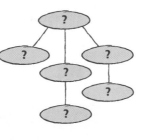

CRITICAL THINKING AND PROBLEM SOLVING

Write one or two sentences to answer the following questions:

17. Explain how living things would be affected if the water on our planet suddenly stopped evaporating.

18. How would living things be affected if there were no decomposers to cycle carbon back to the atmosphere?

19. Explain how living things would be affected if the bacteria responsible for nitrogen fixation were to die.

20. Describe why a lawn doesn't go through succession.

MATH IN SCIENCE

In 1996, 129 million metric tons of fertilizer were used world-wide. Use the following information to answer items 21, 22, and 23: 1996 world population = 5.7 billion; 1 metric ton = 1,000 kg; 1 kg = 2.2 lb.

21. Write out the number corresponding to 5.7 billion. How many zeros are in the number?

22. How many kilograms of fertilizer were used per person in 1996?

23. How many pounds of fertilizer were used per person?

INTERPRETING GRAPHICS

The following graph illustrates the concentration of carbon dioxide in the atmosphere from 1958 to 1994:

24. What was the concentration of carbon dioxide in parts per million in 1960? in 1994?

25. Is the concentration of carbon dioxide increasing or decreasing? Explain.

26. If the level of carbon dioxide continues to change at the same steady rate, what might be the concentration in 2010?

NOW What Do You Think?

Take a minute to review your answers to the ScienceLog questions on page 457. Have your answers changed? If necessary, revise your answers based on what you have learned since you began this chapter.

WEIRD SCIENCE

WEATHER FROM FIRE

As a wildfire burned near Santa Barbara, California, in 1993, huge storm clouds formed overhead. Fiery whirlwinds danced over the ground. The fire not only was destroying everything in its path—it was also creating its own weather!

Fire-Made Clouds

Hot air rising from a forest fire can create tremendous updrafts. Surrounding air rushes in underneath the rising air, stirring up columns of ash, smoke, hot air, and noxious gases. Cool, dry air normally sinks down and stops these columns from developing any further. But if the conditions are just right, a surprising thing happens.

If the upper atmosphere contains warm, moist air, the moisture begins to condense on the ash and smoke. These droplets can develop into clouds. As the clouds grow, the droplets begin to collide and combine until they are heavy enough to fall as rain. The result is an isolated rainstorm, complete with thunder and lightning.

Whirlwinds of Fire

Forest fires can also create whirlwinds. These small, tornado-like funnels can be extremely dangerous. Whirlwinds are similar to dust devils that dance across desert sands. Their circular motion is created by an updraft that is forced to turn after striking an obstacle, such as a cliff or hill. Whirlwinds move across the ground at 8–11 km/h, sometimes growing up to 120 m high and 15 m wide.

Most whirlwinds last less than a minute, but they can cause some big problems. Fire-

▲ *This towering whirlwind is lifting burning debris from a forest fire in Idaho.*

fighters caught in the path of whirlwinds have been severely injured and even killed. Also, if a whirlwind is hot enough, it can suck up tremendous amounts of air. The resulting updraft can pull burning debris up through the whirlwind. In some cases, burning trees have been uprooted and shot into the air. When the debris lands, it often starts new fires hundreds of meters away.

Think About It

▶ Fires are a natural part of the growth of a forest. For example, some tree seeds are released only under the extreme temperatures of a fire. Some scientists believe that forest fires should be allowed to run their natural course. Others argue that forest fires cause too much damage and should be extinguished as soon as possible. Do some additional research and then decide what you think.

EYE ON THE ENVIRONMENT

The Mysterious Dead Zone

Every summer, millions of fish are killed in an area in the Gulf of Mexico called a hypoxia region. Hypoxia is a condition that occurs when there is an unusually low level of oxygen in the water. The area is often referred to as the "dead zone" because almost every fish and crustacean in the area dies. In 1995, this zone covered more than 18,000 km^2, and almost 1 million fish were killed in a single week. Why does this happen? Can it be stopped?

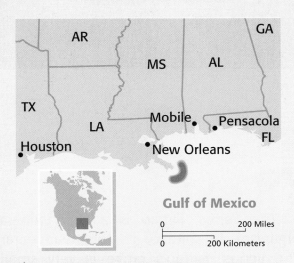

▲ *The Gulf of Mexico hypoxia region grew to the size of New Jersey in 1995.*

What's Going On?

When the oxygen levels in water drop drastically, the fish die. In the Gulf of Mexico hypoxia region, the water contains unusually high amounts of nitrogen and phosphorus. The nitrogen and phosphorus act as nutrients for the growth of algae. When the algae die, their bodies are decomposed by a large number of oxygen-consuming bacteria.

Scientists think the excess nitrogen and phosphate is from animal waste and runoff from farms and developments. The pollution may also be caused in part by the overfertilization of crops. The extra fertilizer runs into the rivers, which empty into the Gulf Coast.

Ecosystem Models Suggest Solutions

All along the Gulf Coast, marine scientists and Earth scientists are trying to find methods to reduce or eliminate the "dead zone." They have made physical and computer models of the Mississippi River ecosystem that have accurately predicted the data that has since been collected. The scientists have changed the models to see what happens. For example, wetlands are one of nature's best filters. They take up a lot of the chemicals present in water. Scientists predict that adding wetlands to the Mississippi River watershed could reduce the chemicals reaching the Gulf of Mexico. Although scientific models support this hypothesis, they also indicate that adding wetlands to the Mississippi River watershed would not be enough to completely prevent the "dead zone."

Find Some Solutions

▶ The Gulf of Mexico is not the only place that suffers from a hypoxia region. Research other bodies of water to find out how widespread the problem is. Have scientists found ways to reduce or eliminate the hypoxia regions elsewhere? How could this information be used to improve the situation in the Gulf of Mexico?

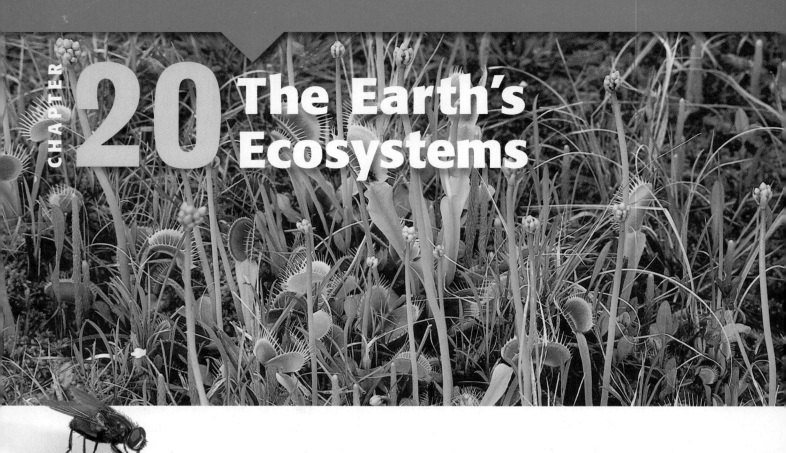

20 The Earth's Ecosystems

Would You Believe . . . ?

A Venus' flytrap waits. Before long, an unsuspecting fly bumps into one of the flytrap's sensitive hairs. Whack! The flytrap's two hinged doors snap shut! The victim is trapped. The more it struggles, the tighter the trap closes. The creature's fate is sealed.

Is this some weird animal? No, the Venus' flytrap is a plant, although an unusual one. As you know, most plants get nutrients they need to survive from the soil. In areas known as wetlands, the soil contains few of the nutrients plants need. Yet plants such as the Venus' flytrap thrive there. They get their nutrients from a different source. Once the flytrap captures a fly or other small animal, it secretes digestive juices, and the insect is slowly digested.

The Venus' flytrap is a very vulnerable organism, in spite of its tough appearance. The Venus' flytrap's range is very small; it grows only in certain areas of North Carolina and South Carolina. Lawn and farm fertilizers cause problems for the Venus' flytrap because it is adapted to areas of low nutrients.

In this chapter you will learn that the Earth contains many areas that are very different from one another. Different plants and animals are especially adapted for survival in each area.

Investigate!

A Mini-Ecosystem

In this activity, you will build and observe a miniature ecosystem.

Procedure

1. Place a layer of **gravel** in the bottom of a **large widemouth jar** or a **2 L soda bottle** with the top cut off. Add a layer of **soil.**

2. Add a variety of **plants** that require similar growing conditions. Choose small plants that will not grow too quickly.

3. Spray **water** inside the jar to moisten the soil.

4. Cover the jar, and place it in indirect light. Describe the appearance of your ecosystem in your ScienceLog.

5. Observe your mini-ecosystem every week. Record all of your observations.

What Do You Think?

In your ScienceLog, try to answer the following questions based on what you already know:

1. What are the main differences between a desert and a rain forest?

2. Where does the water in a lake come from?

3. Which has more species of plants and animals—the open ocean or a swamp? Why?

Analysis

6. List the nonliving factors that make up the ecosystem you have created.

7. How is your mini-ecosystem similar to a real ecosystem? How is it different?

Terms to Learn

abiotic   desert
biome   tundra
savanna   permafrost

What You'll Do

◆ Define *biome.*
◆ Describe three different forest biomes.
◆ Distinguish between temperate grasslands and savannas.
◆ Describe the importance of permafrost to the arctic tundra biome.

Land Ecosystems

Imagine that you are planning a camping trip. You go to a travel agency, where you find a virtual-reality machine that can let you experience different places before you go. You put on the virtual-reality gear, and suddenly you are transported. At first your eyes hurt from the bright sunlight. The wind that hits your face is very hot and very dry. As your eyes grow accustomed to the light, you see a large cactus to your right and some small, bushy plants in the distance. A startled jack rabbit runs across the dry, dusty ground. A lizard basks on a rock. Where are you?

You may not be able to pinpoint your exact location, but you probably realize that you are in a desert. That's because most deserts are hot and dry. These **abiotic,** or nonliving, factors influence the types of plants and animals that live in the area.

The Earth's Biomes

A desert is one of Earth's biomes. A **biome** is a geographic area characterized by certain types of plant and animal communities. A biome contains a number of smaller but related ecosystems. For example, a tropical rain forest is a biome that contains river ecosystems, treetop ecosystems, forest-floor ecosystems, and many others. A biome is not a specific place. For example, a desert biome does not refer to a particular desert. A desert biome refers to any and all desert ecosystems on Earth. The major biomes of Earth are shown in **Figure 1.**

Figure 1 *Rainfall and temperature are the main factors that determine what biome is found in a region. What kind of biome do you live in?*

Polar ice	Temperate grassland
Tundra	Savanna
Coniferous forest	Desert
Tropical rain forest	Chaparral
Temperate deciduous forest	Mountains

Forests

Forest biomes develop where there is enough rain and where the temperature is not too hot in the summer or too cold in the winter. There are three main types of forest biomes—temperate deciduous forests, coniferous forests, and tropical rain forests. The type of forest that develops depends on the area's temperature and rainfall.

Temperate Deciduous Forests In the autumn, have you seen leaves that change colors and fall from trees? If so, you have seen trees that are *deciduous,* which comes from a Latin word meaning "to fall off." By losing their leaves in the fall, deciduous trees are able to conserve water during the winter. **Figure 2** shows a temperate deciduous forest. Most of these forests contain several different species of trees. Temperate deciduous forests also support a variety of animals, such as bears and woodpeckers.

Temperate Deciduous Forest

Average Yearly Rainfall
75–125 cm (29.5–49 in.)

Average Temperatures
Summer: 28°C (82.4°F)
Winter: 6°C (42.8°F)

Figure 2 *In a temperate deciduous forest, mammals, birds, and reptiles thrive on the abundance of leaves, seeds, nuts, and insects.*

In forests, plant growth occurs in layers. The leafy tops of the trees reach high above the forest floor, where they receive full sunlight.

Beneath the tree layer, woody shrubs and bushes catch the light that filters through the trees.

Grasses, herbs, ferns, and mosses are scattered across the forest floor. Most of the flowering plants bloom, and produce seeds in early spring, before the trees grow new leaves.

Average Yearly Rainfall
35–75 cm (14–29.5 in.)

Average Temperatures
Summer: 14°C (57.2°F)
Winter: −10°C (14°F)

Coniferous Forests Coniferous forests do not change very much from summer to winter. They are found in areas with long, cold winters. These forests consist mainly of *evergreen* trees, which are trees that don't lose their leaves and stay green all year. Most of these trees are *conifers*, which means that they produce seeds in cones. You have probably seen a pine cone. Pine trees are common conifers.

Most conifers can also be identified by their compact, needlelike leaves. These leaves, or needles, have a thick waxy coating that prevents them from drying out and being damaged during winter.

Figure 3 shows a coniferous forest and some of the animals that live there. Notice that not many large plants grow beneath the conifers, partly because very little light reaches the ground.

Figure 3 *Many animals that live in a coniferous forest survive the harsh winters by hibernating or migrating to a warmer climate for the winter.*

A coniferous forest is home to many insects and to birds that eat them.

Herbivores that live in the coniferous forest include moose, deer, porcupines, and chipmunks.

These conifer leaves are adapted to conserve water.

Carnivores of the coniferous forest include foxes and lynxes.

Tropical Rain Forests The tropical rain forest has more biological *diversity* than any other biome on the planet; that is, it contains more species than any other biome. As many as 100 species of trees may live in an area about one-fourth the size of a football field. Although some animals live on the ground, the treetops, or *canopy,* are the preferred living site. A huge variety of animals live in the canopy. If you counted the birds in the canopy of a rain forest, you would find up to 1,400 species! **Figure 4** shows some of the diversity of the tropical rain forest biome.

Most of the nutrients in a tropical rain forest biome are in the vegetation. The topsoil is actually very thin and poor in nutrients. Farmers who cut down the forest to grow crops must move their crops to freshly cleared land after about 2 years.

Average Yearly Rainfall
Up to 400 cm (157.5 in.)

Average Temperatures
Daytime: 34°C (93°F)
Nighttime: 20°C (68°F)

Figure 4 **A Tropical Rain Forest Biome**

Trees of various heights form a continuous green roof, called the canopy, that may extend 60 m above the forest floor.

Woody vines climb the tree trunks to reach sunlight.

Little light reaches the ground. Low-growing plants of the rain forest don't require a lot of light.

Grasslands

Plains, steppes, savannas, prairies, pampas—these are names for regions where grasses are the major type of vegetation. Grasslands are found between forests and deserts. They exist on every continent. Most grasslands are flat or have gently rolling hills.

Temperate Grasslands Temperate grassland vegetation is mainly grasses mixed with a variety of flowering plants. There are few trees because fires prevent the growth of most slow-growing plants. The world's temperate grasslands support small, seed-eating mammals, such as prairie dogs and mice, and large herbivores, such as the bison of North America, shown in **Figure 5.**

Figure 5 *Bison roamed the temperate grasslands in great herds before they were hunted nearly to extinction.*

Savanna The **savanna** is a tropical grassland with scattered clumps of trees. During the dry season, the grasses die back, but the deep roots survive even through months of drought. During the wet season, the savanna may receive as much as 150 cm of rain. The savannas of Africa are inhabited by the most abundant and diverse groups of large herbivores in the world, like those shown in **Figure 6.** These include elephants, giraffes, zebras, gazelles, and wildebeests.

Figure 6 *Carnivores, such as lions and leopards, prey on herbivores, such as these zebras and wildebeests. Hyenas and vultures usually "clean up" after the carnivores.*

Self-Check

Use the map in Figure 1 to compare the locations of deciduous and coniferous forests. Explain the differences in location between the two biomes. *(See page 782 to check your answers.)*

How do animals survive in the heat of the desert? Quite nicely, thank you! See how on page 754 of your LabBook.

Deserts

Deserts are hot, dry regions that support a variety of plants and animals. In a desert, most of the water that falls to the ground evaporates. Organisms have evolved in specialized ways to survive extreme temperatures with very little water. For example, plants grow far apart to reduce competition for the limited water supply. Some plants have shallow, widespread roots that absorb water quickly during a storm, while others may have very deep roots that reach ground water.

Animals also have adaptations for survival in the desert. Most are active only at night, when temperatures are cooler. Tortoises eat the flowers or leaves of plants and store the water under their shells for months. **Figure 7** shows how some desert plants and animals survive in the heat with little water.

Desert
Average Yearly Rainfall Less than 25 cm (10 in.)
Average Temperatures Summer: 38°C (100°F) Winter: 7°C (45°F)

Figure 7 *There are many well-adapted residents of the desert biome.*

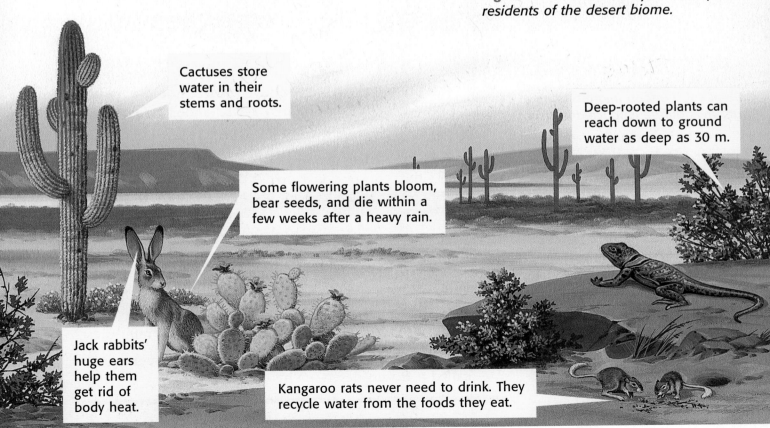

Cactuses store water in their stems and roots.

Deep-rooted plants can reach down to ground water as deep as 30 m.

Some flowering plants bloom, bear seeds, and die within a few weeks after a heavy rain.

Jack rabbits' huge ears help them get rid of body heat.

Kangaroo rats never need to drink. They recycle water from the foods they eat.

Tundra

In the far north and on the tops of high mountains, the climate is so cold that no trees can grow. A biome called the **tundra** is found there.

Arctic Tundra   The major feature of the arctic tundra is permafrost. During the short growing season, only the surface of the soil thaws. The soil below the surface, the **permafrost,** stays frozen all the time. Even though there is little rainfall, water is not in short supply. That's because the permafrost prevents the rain that does fall from draining, and the surface soil stays wet and soggy. Lakes and ponds are common.

The layer of unfrozen soil above the permafrost is too shallow for deep-rooted plants to survive. Grasses, sedges, rushes, and small woody shrubs are common. A layer of mosses and lichens grows beneath these plants on the surface of the ground. Tundra animals, like the one shown in **Figure 8,** include large mammals such as caribous, musk oxen, and wolves, as well as smaller animals, such as lemmings, shrews, and hares. Migratory birds are abundant in summer.

Figure 8 *Caribou migrate to more plentiful grazing grounds during long, cold winters in the tundra.*

Alpine Tundra   Another tundra biome is found above the tree line of very high mountains. These areas, called alpine tundra, receive a lot of sunlight and precipitation, mostly in the form of snow.

MATH BREAK

Rainfall

In 1 year, what is the difference in the rainfall amounts in a coniferous forest, a tropical rain forest, a desert, and a savanna? To compare, create a bar graph of the rainfall in each biome from the data given in this section.

REVIEW

1. How is the climate of temperate grasslands different from that of savannas?

2. Describe three ways that plants and animals are adapted to the desert climate.

3. Where are most of the nutrients in a tropical rain forest?

4. **Applying Concepts**   Could arctic tundra accurately be called a frozen desert? Why or why not?

Marine Ecosystems

Terms to Learn

marine   zooplankton
phytoplankton   estuary

What You'll Do

◆ Distinguish between the different areas of the ocean.
◆ Explain the importance of plankton in marine ecosystems.
◆ Describe coral reefs and intertidal areas.

They cover almost three-quarters of Earth's surface and contain almost 97 percent of Earth's water supply. The largest animals on Earth inhabit them, along with billions of microscopic creatures, shown in **Figure 9.** Their habitats range from dark, cold, high-pressure depths to warm sandy beaches; from icy polar waters to rocky coastlines. They are oceans and seas. Wherever these salty waters are found, marine ecosystems are found. A **marine** ecosystem is one that is based on salty water. This abiotic factor has a strong influence on the ecosystems of oceans and seas.

Abiotic Factors Rule

Like terrestrial biomes, marine biomes are shaped by abiotic factors. These include temperature, the amount of sunlight penetrating the water, the distance from land, and the depth of the water. These abiotic factors are used to define certain areas of the ocean. As with terrestrial biomes, marine biomes occur all over Earth and can contain many ecosystems.

Sunny Waters Water absorbs light, so sunlight can penetrate only about 200 m below the ocean's surface, even in the clearest water. As you know, most producers use photosynthesis to make their own food. Because photosynthesis requires light, most producers are found only where light penetrates. The most abundant producers in the ocean are called **phytoplankton.** Phytoplankton are microscopic photosynthetic organisms that float near the surface of the water. Using the energy of sunlight, these organisms make their own food just as plants that live on land do. **Zooplankton** are the consumers that feed on the phytoplankton. They are small animals that, along with phytoplankton, form the base of the oceans' feeding relationships.

Figure 9 *Marine ecosystems support a broad diversity of life, from the humpback whale to microscopic phytoplankton.*

Wonderful Watery Biomes

Unique and beautiful biomes exist in every part of oceans and seas. These biomes are home to many unusually adapted organisms. The major ocean areas and some of the organisms that live in them are shown below in **Figure 10.**

A **The Intertidal Zone** The intertidal zone is the area where the ocean meets the land. This area is above water part of the day, when the tide is out, and is often battered by waves. Mud flats, rocky shores, and sandy beaches are all in the intertidal area.

B **The Neritic Zone** Moving seaward, the water becomes gradually deeper toward the edge of the continental shelf. Water in this area is generally less than 200 m deep and usually receives a lot of sunlight. Diverse and colorful coral reefs exist in the waters over the continental shelf, where the water is warm, clear, and sunny.

Figure 10 *The life in a particular area depends on how much light the area receives, how far the area is from land, and how far the area is beneath the surface.*

A Sea grasses, periwinkle snails, and herons are common in a mud flat intertidal area. You will find sea stars and anemones on the rocky shores, while clams, crabs, and the shells of snails and conchs are common on the sandy beaches.

B Although phytoplankton are the major producers in this area, seaweeds are common too. Animals, such as sea turtles and dolphins, live in the area over the continental shelf. Corals, sponges, and colorful fish contribute to the vivid seascape.

C The Oceanic Zone Past the continental shelf, the sea floor drops sharply. This is the deep water of the open ocean. To a depth of about 200 m, phytoplankton are the producers. At greater depths, no light penetrates, so most organisms obtain energy by consuming organic material that falls from the surface.

D The Benthic Zone The benthic zone is the sea floor. It extends from the upper edge of the intertidal zone to the bottom of the deepest ocean waters. Organisms that live on the deep-sea floor obtain food mostly by consuming material that filters from above. Some bacteria are *chemosynthetic*, which means they use chemicals in the water near thermal vents to make food. A thermal vent is a place on the ocean floor where heat escapes through a crack in the Earth's crust.

C Many unusual animals are adapted for the darkness and high pressures of great ocean depths. Here you will see whales, squids, and fishes that glow in very deep, dark water.

D Organisms such as bacteria, worms, and sea urchins thrive on the deep-sea floor.

Figure 11 *A coral reef is one of the most biologically diverse biomes.*

A Closer Look

Marine environments provide most of the water for Earth's rainfall through evaporation and precipitation. Ocean temperatures and currents have major effects on world climates and wind patterns. Humans harvest enormous amounts of food from the oceans and dump enormous amounts of waste into them. Let's take a closer look at some of the special environments that thrive in the ocean.

Coral Reefs In some sunny tropical waters, the sea floor contains coral reefs. Corals live in a close relationship with single-celled algae. The algae produce organic nutrients through photosynthesis. This provides food for the coral. The coral provide a place in the sun for the algae to live. The foundation of the reef is formed from coral skeletons that have built up over thousands of years. Coral reefs, like the one in **Figure 11,** are home to many marine species, including a large variety of brightly colored fish and organisms such as sponges and sea urchins.

Figure 12 *The Sargasso Sea is a spawning place for eels and home to a rich diversity of organisms.*

The Sargasso Sea In the middle of the Atlantic Ocean is a large ecosystem with no land boundaries. It is called the Sargasso Sea. *Sargassum* is a type of algae usually found attached to rocks on the shores of North America, but it forms huge floating rafts in the Sargasso Sea. Animals adapted to this environment live among the algae. Most of the animals are the same color as the *Sargassum*. Some even look like it! Why do you think this is so? Can you find a fish in **Figure 12**?

✓ Self-Check

1. List three factors that characterize marine biomes.
2. Describe one way organisms obtain energy at great depths in the open ocean.

(See page 782 to check your answers.)

Polar Ice The Arctic Ocean and the open waters surrounding Antarctica make up a very unusual marine biome—one that includes ice!

The icy waters are rich in nutrients from the surrounding landmasses. These nutrients support large populations of plankton. The plankton in turn support a great diversity of fish, birds, and mammals, as shown in **Figure 13.**

Figure 13 *Sea lions and penguins are some of the animals found on the shores of Antarctica.*

Estuaries An area where fresh water from streams and rivers spills into the ocean is called an **estuary.** The fresh water constantly mixes with the salt water of the sea. The amount of salt in an estuary changes frequently. When the tide rises, the salt content of the water rises. When the tide recedes, the water becomes fresher. The fresh water that spills into an estuary is rich in nutrients that are carried by water running off the land. Because estuaries are so nutrient-rich, they support large numbers of plankton, which provide food for many larger animals.

Intertidal Areas Intertidal areas include mudflats, sandy beaches, and rocky shores. Mud flats are home to many worms and crabs and the shorebirds that feed on them. Sandy beaches are also home to worms, clams, crabs, and plankton that live among the sand grains.

On rocky shores, organisms either have tough holdfasts or are able to cement themselves to a rock to avoid being swept away by crashing waves. **Figure 14** shows some of these animals.

Figure 14 *Sea stars can wedge themselves under a rock to keep from being washed out to sea.*

REVIEW

1. Explain how a coral reef is both living and dead.

2. Why do estuaries support such an abundance of life?

3. **Analyzing Relationships** Explain how the amount of light an area receives determines the kinds of organisms that live in the open ocean.

internet connect

SCi**LINKS**
NSTA

TOPIC: Marine Ecosystems
GO TO: www.scilinks.org
sciLINKS NUMBER: HSTL490

Freshwater Ecosystems

Terms to Learn

tributary · wetland
littoral zone · marsh
open-water zone · swamp
deep-water zone

What You'll Do

◆ List the characteristics of rivers and streams.
◆ Describe the littoral zone of a pond.
◆ Distinguish between two types of wetlands.

A mountain brook bubbles over rocks down a mountainside. A mighty river thunders through a canyon. A small pond teems with life. A lake tosses boats during a heavy storm. A dense swamp echoes with the sounds of frogs and birds.

What do all of these places have in common? They are freshwater ecosystems. Like other ecosystems, freshwater ecosystems are characterized by abiotic factors, primarily the speed at which the water is moving.

Water on the Move

Brooks, streams, and rivers are ecosystems based on moving water. The water may begin flowing from melting ice or snow. Or it may come from a spring, where water flows up to the surface of the Earth. Each trickle or stream of water that joins a larger trickle or stream is a **tributary.**

Fast-Moving Water As more tributaries join a stream, the stream becomes larger and wider, forming a river. Aquatic plants line the edge of the river. Fishes live in the open waters. In the mud at the bottom, burrowers, such as freshwater clams and mussels, make their home.

Organisms that live in moving water require special adaptations to avoid being swept away with the current. Producers, such as algae and moss, cling to rocks. Consumers, such as insect larvae, live under rocks in the shallow water. Some consumers, such as tadpoles, use suction disks to hold themselves to rocks.

Slowing Down As a river grows wider and slower, it may *meander* back and forth across the landscape. Organic material and sediment may be deposited on the bottom, building *deltas*. Dragonflies, water striders, and other invertebrates live in and on slow-moving water. Eventually, the moving water empties into a lake or an ocean. **Figure 15** shows how a river can grow from melted snow.

Melting snow
Stream
Rapids
Waterfall
Tributary
Meander
Marsh
Delta
To lake or ocean

Figure 15 *This figure shows the features of a typical river. Where is the water moving rapidly? Where is it moving slowly?*

Still Waters

Ponds and lakes have different ecosystems than streams and rivers have. Lake Superior, the largest lake in the world, has more in common with a small beaver pond than with a river. **Figure 16** shows a cross section of a typical lake. In looking at this illustration, you will notice that the lake has been divided into three zones. As you read on, you will learn about these zones and the ecosystems they contain.

Where Water Meets Land Look at Figure 16 again, and locate the **littoral zone.** It is the zone closest to the edge of the land. This zone has many inhabitants. Plants that grow in the water closest to the shore include cattails and rushes. Farther from the shore are floating leaf plants, such as water lilies. Still farther out are submerged pond weeds that grow beneath the surface of the water.

The plants of the littoral zone provide a home for small animals, such as snails, small arthropods, and insect larvae. Clams, worms, and other organisms burrow in the mud. Frogs, salamanders, water turtles, various kinds of fishes, and water snakes also live in this area.

Life at the Top Look again at Figure 16. This time locate the **open-water zone.** This zone extends from the littoral zone across the top of the water. The open-water zone only goes as deep as light can reach. This is the habitat of bass, blue gills, lake trout, and other fish. Phytoplankton are the most abundant photosynthetic organisms in the open-water zone of a lake.

Life at the Bottom Now look at Figure 16 and find the **deep-water zone.** This zone is below the open-water zone, where no light reaches. Catfish, carp, worms, insect larvae, crustaceans, fungi, and bacteria live here. These organisms feed on dead organic material that falls down from above.

Pond Food Connections

1. On **index cards**, write the names of the animals and plants that live in a typical freshwater pond or small lake. Write one type of organism on each card.

2. Use **yarn** or **string** to connect each organism to its food sources.

3. In your ScienceLog, describe the food relationships in the pond.

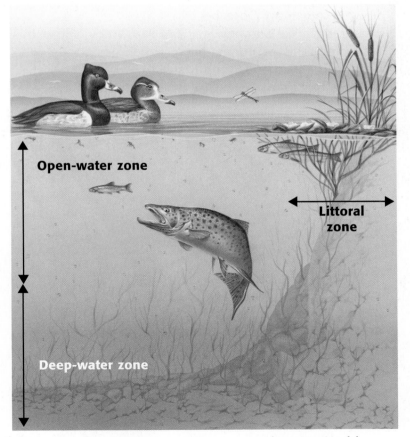

Open-water zone

Littoral zone

Deep-water zone

Figure 16 *Freshwater ecosystems are characterized by abiotic factors that determine which organisms live there.*

A Trip to Lake Superior
Suppose you are a life scientist who specializes in the plants that live in and near Lake Superior. You are preparing for a yearlong expedition to Thunder Bay, on the Canadian shore of Lake Superior.

You will stay "in the wild." Based on what you have learned about ecosystems, answer the following questions: How will you live while you are there? What will you bring along? What problems will you encounter? How will you overcome them?

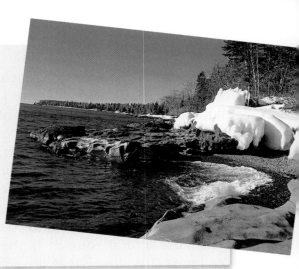

Activity

While exploring in a wetland, you have discovered a new organism. In your ScienceLog, draw the organism. Describe what it looks like and how it is adapted to its environment. Trade with a partner. Is your partner's organism believable?

Wetlands

A **wetland** is an area of land where the water level is near or above the surface of the ground for most of the year. Wetlands support a variety of plant and animal life. They also play an important role in flood control. During heavy rains or spring snow melt, wetlands soak up large amounts of water. The water in wetlands also seeps into the ground, replenishing underground water supplies.

Marshes A **marsh** is a treeless wetland ecosystem where plants such as cattails and rushes grow. A freshwater marsh is shown in **Figure 17**. Freshwater marshes are found in shallow waters along the shores of lakes, ponds, rivers, and streams. The plants in a marsh vary depending on the depth of the water and the location of the marsh. Grasses, reeds, bulrushes, and wild rice are common marsh plants. Muskrats, turtles, frogs, and redwing blackbirds can be found living in marshes.

Figure 17 *Turtles find a lot of places to escape from predators in a freshwater marsh. Many species raise their young in these protected areas.*

Swamps A **swamp** is a wetland eco-system where trees and vines grow. Swamps occur in low-lying areas and beside slow-moving rivers. Most swamps are flooded only part of the year, depending on the rainfall. Trees may include willows, bald cypresses, water tupelos, oaks, and elms. Vines such as poison ivy grow up trees, and Spanish moss hangs from the branches. Water lilies and other lake plants may grow in open-water areas. Swamps, like the one in **Figure 18,** provide a home for a variety of fish, snakes, and birds.

Figure 18 *The bases of the trunks of these trees are adapted to give the tree more support in the wet, soft sediment under the water in this swamp.*

From Lake to Forest

How can a lake or pond, like the one in **Figure 19,** disappear? Water entering a standing body of water usually carries nutrients and sediment along with it. These materials then settle to the bottom. Dead leaves from overhanging trees and decaying plant and animal life also settle to the bottom. Gradually, the pond or lake fills in. Plants grow in the newly filled areas, closer and closer toward the center. With time, the standing body of water becomes a marsh. Eventually, the marsh turns into a forest.

Figure 19 *Eventually decaying organic matter, along with sediment in the runoff from land, will fill in this pond.*

REVIEW

1. Describe some adaptations of organisms that live in moving water.

2. Compare the littoral zone with the open-water zone of a pond.

3. How is a swamp different from a marsh?

4. **Analyzing Concepts** The center of a pond is 10 m deep. Near the shore it is 0–1 m deep. Describe the types of organisms that might live in each zone.

internet**connect**

*SCi*LINKS
NSTA

TOPIC: Freshwater Ecosystems
GO TO: www.scilinks.org
*sci*LINKS **NUMBER:** HSTL495

Chapter Highlights

Vocabulary

abiotic *(p. 474)*

biome *(p. 474)*

savanna *(p. 478)*

desert *(p. 479)*

tundra *(p. 480)*

permafrost *(p. 480)*

Section Notes

- Rainfall and temperature are the main factors that determine what kind of biome is found in a region.

- The three main forest biomes are the temperate deciduous forest and the coniferous forest, which experience warm summers and cold winters, and the tropical rain forest, where temperatures stay warm.

- Grasslands receive more rain than deserts and receive less rain than forests. Temperate grasslands have hot summers and cold winters. Savannas have wet and dry seasons.

- Deserts receive less than 25 cm of rain a year. Plants and animals competing for the limited water supply have developed special adaptations for survival.

- The tundra biome is found mainly in the Arctic region. Arctic tundra is characterized by permafrost.

Labs

Life in the Desert *(p. 754)*

Vocabulary

marine *(p. 481)*

phytoplankton *(p. 481)*

zooplankton *(p. 481)*

estuary *(p. 485)*

Section Notes

- The kinds of marine organisms that inhabit an area vary depending on the water depth, the temperature, the amount of light, and the distance from shore.

- The intertidal area is the area where sea and land meet.

- The sea floor is home to biomes as different as coral reefs and thermal vents.

- The open ocean includes unique biomes, including the Sargasso Sea and the cold water oceans around the poles.

☑ Skills Check

Math Concepts

RAINFALL Using a meterstick, measure 400 cm on the floor of your classroom. This distance represents the depth of rainfall a rain forest receives per year. Next measure 25 cm. This measurement represents the amount of rainfall a desert receives per year. Compare these two quantities. Express your comparison as a ratio.

$$\frac{25}{400} = \frac{1}{16}$$

In 1 year, a desert receives $\frac{1}{16}$ the rainfall that a rain forest receives.

Visual Understanding

RAIN FOREST Look at Figure 4, on page 477. There are three layers of a rain forest—the upper story, the middle story, and the ground story. The upper story is the canopy, where most rain forest species live and where there is the most sunlight. The middle story is under the canopy and above the ground. The ground story is dark in most parts of the forest. Most plants in the rain forest grow very tall to compete for light in the canopy. Growth of plants on the ground story is not very dense due to the lack of available light.

- An estuary is a region where fresh water from rivers spills into the ocean and the fresh and salt water mix with the rising and falling of the tides.

Labs

Discovering Mini-Ecosystems (p. 755)

Vocabulary

tributary (p. 486)

littoral zone (p. 487)

open-water zone (p. 487)

deep-water zone (p. 487)

wetland (p. 488)

marsh (p. 488)

swamp (p. 489)

Section Notes

- Freshwater ecosystems are classified according to whether they have running water or standing water. Brooks, rivers, and streams contain running water. Lakes and ponds contain standing water.

- As tributaries join a stream between its source and the ocean, the volume of water in the stream increases, the nutrient content increases, and the speed decreases.

- The types of organisms found in a stream or river are determined mainly by how quickly the current is moving.

- The littoral zone of a lake is inhabited by floating plants. These plants provide a home for a rich diversity of animal life.

- Wetlands include marshes, which are treeless, and swamps, where trees and vines grow.

Labs

Too Much of a Good Thing? (p. 756)

internet connect

GO TO: go.hrw.com

Visit the **HRW** Web site for a variety of learning tools related to this chapter. Just type in the keyword:

KEYWORD: HSTECO

GO TO: www.scilinks.org

Visit the **National Science Teachers Association** on-line Web site for Internet resources related to this chapter. Just type in the *sci*LINKS number for more information about the topic:

TOPIC: Forests	*sci*LINKS NUMBER: HSTL480
TOPIC: Grasslands	*sci*LINKS NUMBER: HSTL485
TOPIC: Marine Ecosystems	*sci*LINKS NUMBER: HSTL490
TOPIC: Freshwater Ecosystems	*sci*LINKS NUMBER: HSTL495

Chapter Review

To complete the following sentences, choose the correct term from each pair of terms listed below:

1. At the edge of the __?__ , the open ocean begins. *(continental shelf* or *Sargasso Sea)*

2. __?__ are tiny consumers that live in water. *(Phytoplankton* or *Zooplankton)*

3. A __?__ is a treeless wetland. *(swamp* or *marsh)*

4. __?__ lose their leaves in order to conserve water. *(Deciduous trees* or *Conifers)*

5. The major feature of the __?__ biome is permafrost. *(desert* or *tundra)*

6. Each major type of plant community and its associated animal communities make up a(n)__?__. *(estuary* or *biome)*

UNDERSTANDING CONCEPTS

Multiple Choice

7. The most numerous organisms in the oceans are the
   a. plankton.
   b. *Sargassum.*
   c. coral animals.
   d. marine mammals.

8. Marine ecosystems at the poles are unusual because
   a. animals spend time both in and out of the water.
   b. plankton are rare.
   c. they contain ice.
   d. the salt content of the water is very high.

9. The major factor that determines the types of organisms that live in a stream or river is
   a. the water temperature.
   b. the speed of the current.
   c. the depth of the water.
   d. the width of the stream or river.

10. Marine ecosystems
    a. contain the largest animals in the world.
    b. exist in all ocean zones.
    c. include environments where organisms survive without light.
    d. All of the above

11. Two major factors that determine what kind of a biome is found in a region are
    a. the amount of rainfall and the temperature.
    b. the depth of water and the distance from land.
    c. the wave action and the salt content of the water.
    d. All of the above

Short Answer

12. Describe how a stream changes as it moves from its source toward the ocean.

13. Describe two adaptations of animals to the desert environment.

14. Are wetlands always wet? Explain.

15. Explain how the salt content in an estuary changes constantly.

Concept Mapping

16. Use the following terms to create a concept map: tropical rain forest, deep-rooted plants, coral reef, canopy, biomes, permafrost, desert, continental shelf, tundra, ecosystems.

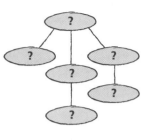

CRITICAL THINKING AND PROBLEM SOLVING

Write one or two sentences to answer the following questions:

17. While excavating a region now covered by grasslands, paleontologists discover the fossil remains of ancient fish and shellfish. What might they conclude?

18. In order to build a new shopping center, developers fill in a wetland. Afterward, flooding becomes a problem in this area. How can this be explained?

19. Explain why most desert flowering plants bloom, bear seeds, and die within a few weeks, while some tropical flowering plants remain in bloom for a much longer time.

MATH IN SCIENCE

20. What is the average difference in rainfall between a temperate deciduous forest and a coniferous forest?

21. An area of Brazilian rain forest received 347 cm of rain in one year. Using the following formula, calculate this amount of rainfall in inches.

    0.394 (the number of inches in a centimeter)

    $\times$ 347 cm

    _____ ? in.

INTERPRETING GRAPHICS

The graphs below show the monthly temperatures and rainfall in a region during 1 year.

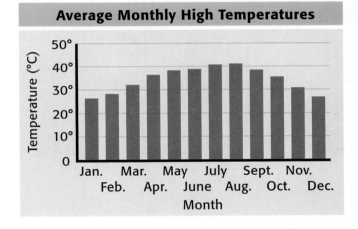

22. What kind of biome is probably found in the region represented by these graphs?

23. Would you expect to find bulrushes in the region represented by these graphs? Why or why not?

NOW What Do You Think?

Take a minute to review your answers to the ScienceLog questions on page 473. Have your answers changed? If necessary, revise your answers based on what you have learned since you began this chapter.

L I F E   S C I E N C E   •   C H E M I S T R Y

Ocean Vents

▲ *"They're very slim, fuzzy, flattened-out worms. Really hairy,"* says scientist Bob Feldman about tubeworms.

Picture the extreme depths of the ocean. There is no light at all, and it is very cold. But in the cracks between the plates on the bottom of the ocean floor, sea water trickles deep into the Earth. On the way back up from these cracks, the heated water collects metals, sulfuric gases, and enough heat to raise the temperature of the chilly ocean to 360°C. That is hot enough to melt lead! This heated sea water blasts up into the ocean through volcanic vents. And when this hot and toxic brew collides with icy ocean waters, the metals and sulfuric gases *precipitate,* that is, settle out of the heated ocean water as solids.

These solids form tubes, called black smokers, that extend up through the ocean floor. To humans, this dark, cold, and toxic environment would be deadly. But to a community of 300 species, including certain bacteria, clams, mussels, and tube worms, it is home. For these species, black smokers make life possible.

Life Without Photosynthesis

For a long time, scientists believed that energy from sunlight was the basis for the Earth's food chains and for life itself. But in the last 15 years, researchers have discovered ecosystems that challenge this belief. We now know of organisms around black smokers that can live without sunlight. One type of bacteria uses toxic gases from a black smoker in the same way that plants use sunlight. In a process called *chemosynthesis,* these bacteria convert sulfur into energy.

These bacteria are producers, and the mussels and clams are the consumers in this deep-sea food web. The bacteria use the mussels and clams as a sturdy place to live. The mussels and clams, in turn, feed off the bacteria. This kind of relationship between organisms is called *symbiosis.* The closer to the vent the clams and mussels are, the more likely the bacteria are to grow. Because of this, the mussels and clams frequently move to find good spots near the black smokers.

What Do You Think?

► Conditions near black smokers are similar to conditions on other planets. Do some research on these extreme environments, both on Earth and elsewhere. Then discuss with your classmates where and how you think life on Earth may have started.

CAREERS

ECOLOGIST

Most winters **Alfonso Alonso-Mejía** climbs up to the few remote sites in central Mexico where about 150 million monarch butterflies spend the winter. He is researching the monarchs because he wants to help preserve their habitat.

onarch butterflies are famous for their long-distance migration. Those that eventually find their way to Mexico come from as far away as the northeastern United States and southern Canada. Some of them travel 3,200 km before reaching central Mexico.

Human Threats to Habitats

Unfortunately, the monarchs' habitat is increasingly threatened by logging and other human activities. Only nine of the monarchs' wintering sites remain. Five of the sites are set aside as sanctuaries for the butterflies, but even those are endangered by people who cut down fir trees for firewood or for commercial purposes.

Research to the Rescue

Alonso-Mejía's work is helping Mexican conservationists better understand and protect monarch butterflies. Especially important is his discovery that monarchs depend on bushlike vegetation that grows beneath the fir trees, called understory vegetation.

Alonso-Mejía's research showed that when the temperature dips below freezing, as it often does at the high-altitude sites where the monarchs winter, some monarchs depend on understory vegetation for survival. This is because low temperatures (−1°C to 4°C) limit the monarchs' movement—the butterflies are not even able to crawl. At extremely cold temperatures (−7°C to −1°C), monarchs resting on the forest floor are in danger of freezing to death. But where there is understory vegetation, the monarchs can slowly climb the vegetation until they are at least 10 cm above the ground. This tiny difference in elevation can provide a microclimate that is warm enough to ensure the monarchs' survival.

The importance of understory vegetation was not known before Alonso-Mejía did his research. Now, thanks to his work, Mexican conservationists will better protect the understory vegetation.

Get Involved!

▶ If you are interested in a nationwide tagging program to help scientists learn more about the monarchs' migration route, write to Monarch Watch, Department of Entomology, 7005 Howorth Hall, University of Kansas, Lawrence, Kansas 66045.

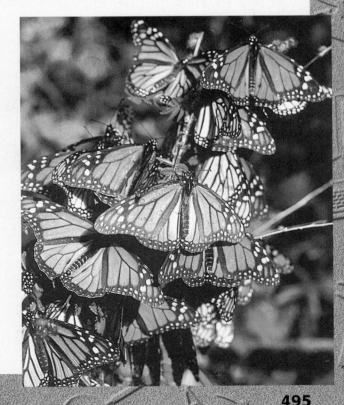

21 Environmental Problems and Solutions

Imagine . . .

Fifteen-year-old Haifa Aldorasi loves science and is concerned about the environment. She knows that today's paper is made by cutting down trees, making them into a pulp, and adding chemicals. Haifa is also fascinated by American history. She knows that the colonists made paper from linen and cotton rags. Their paper had no chemicals, yet some of it is still in good condition today. Haifa knows that today's paper will not last nearly as long as the colonists' paper did.

At age 13, Haifa put her knowledge of history, her love of science, and her concern about the environment together with a variety of vegetables, two years of research and experiments, and a whole lot of patience. The result? Haifa produced good-quality paper without cutting a single branch from a tree

or using a single chemical. Her paper will last for centuries.

Haifa hasn't stopped her research. Hoping to develop a process that can be used to manufacture large amounts of paper without cutting any trees, she continues to perfect her technique. She hopes to eventually present her product to major paper companies. In the meantime, Haifa sells a paper-making kit she developed so that other people can make a good quality paper without using wood or chemicals.

In this chapter, you will learn about some environmental problems and what you can do to help, including making your own paper!

What Do You Think?

In your ScienceLog, try to answer the following questions based on what you already know:

1. Name three ways people damage the Earth.

2. Name three ways people are trying to prevent further damage to the Earth.

Recycling Paper

You can make paper, too. This method doesn't require cutting down trees. Instead, you reuse paper you would otherwise throw away.

Procedure

1. Tear up **two sheets of old newspaper** into small pieces. Put the pieces in a **blender.** Add **1 L of water.** Cover. Blend until you have a soupy pulp. At this point, you may also add small bits of orange peel, carrot peel, or flower petals. Blend again.

2. Cover the bottom of a **large square pan** with **2–3 cm of water.** Place a **wire screen** in the pan. Pour 250 mL of paper pulp onto the screen, as shown below. Spread it evenly into a thin layer with a **spatula** or a **wooden spoon.**

3. To separate the pulp from the water, lift out the screen with the pulp on it. Allow the water to drip off into the pan. Place the screen and the pulp inside a **section of newspaper.**

4. Close the newspaper. Carefully turn it over so that the screen is on top of the pulp. Cover the newspaper with **a flat board.** Press on the board to squeeze out the excess water.

5. Open the newspaper and carefully remove the screen, leaving the layer of pulp behind. Allow the pulp to dry completely. Then carefully peel it off the newspaper.

6. Use your recycled paper to write a note to a friend or to draw a picture.

Analysis

7. In what ways is your paper like regular paper? How is it different?

8. What could you do to improve your paper-making methods?

Terms to Learn

pollution
renewable resource
nonrenewable resource

overpopulation
biodiversity
biodegradable

What You'll Do

◆ Describe the major types of pollution.
◆ Distinguish between renewable and nonrenewable resources.
◆ Explain how habitat destruction affects organisms.
◆ Explain the impact of human population growth.

First the Bad News

You've probably heard it before. The air is unhealthy to breathe. The water is harmful to drink. The soil is filled with poisons. The message is that Earth is sick and in great danger.

Pollution

Pollution is the presence of harmful substances in the environment. These harmful substances, known as *pollutants,* take many forms. They may be solid materials, chemicals, noise, or even heat. Often, pollutants damage or kill the plants and animals living in the affected habitat, as shown in **Figure 1.** Pollutants may also harm humans.

Figure 1 *The water poured into the river by this factory is polluted with chemicals and heat. The smoke contains harmful chemicals that pollute the air.*

Figure 2 *Every year, we throw away 150 million metric tons of garbage.*

Piles of Garbage Americans produce more household waste than any other nation. If stacked up, the beverage cans we use in one year could reach the moon 17 times! The average American throws away 12 kg of trash a week, which usually winds up in a landfill like the one in **Figure 2.** Businesses, mines, and industries also produce large amounts of wastes.

Billions of kilograms of this waste are classified as *hazardous waste,* which means it's harmful to humans and the environment. Many industries produce hazardous wastes, including paper mills, nuclear power plants, oil refineries, and plastic and metal processing plants. Hospitals and laboratories produce hazardous medical wastes. But industry shouldn't get all the blame. Hazardous wastes also come from homes. Old cars, paints, batteries, medical wastes, and detergents all pollute the environment.

Where Does It All Go?   Most of our household waste goes into giant landfills. Hazardous wastes are buried in landfills specially designed to contain them. However, some companies illegally dispose of their hazardous wastes by dumping them into rivers and lakes. Some wastes are burned in incinerators designed to reduce the amount of pollutants that enter the atmosphere. But if wastes are burned improperly, they add to the pollution of the air.

Chemicals Are Everywhere   Chemicals are used to treat diseases. They are also used in plastics, thermometers, paints, hair sprays, and preserved foods. In fact, chemicals are everywhere. We can't get along without chemicals. Sometimes, though, we cannot get along *with* them. Chemical pesticides used to kill crop-destroying insects also pollute the soil and water. Rachel Carson, shown in **Figure 3,** wrote about the dangers of pesticides more than three decades ago.

Figure 3   *Rachel Carson's book* Silent Spring, *published in 1962, made people aware of the environmental dangers of pesticides, especially to birds.*

A class of chemicals called CFCs was once used in aerosol sprays, refrigerators, and plastics. These uses of CFCs have been banned. CFCs rise high into the atmosphere and can cause the destruction of ozone. Ozone protects the Earth from harmful ultraviolet light.

Another class of chemicals, called PCBs, was once used as insulation as well as in paints, household appliances, and other products. Then scientists learned that PCBs are *toxic,* or poisonous. PCBs are now banned, but they have not gone away. They break down very slowly in the environment, and they still pollute even the most remote areas on Earth, as shown in **Figure 4.**

High-Powered Wastes   Nuclear power plants produce electricity for millions of homes and businesses. They also produce *radioactive wastes,* special kinds of hazardous wastes that take hundreds or thousands of years to become harmless. These "hot" wastes can cause cancer, leukemia, and birth defects in humans. Radioactive wastes can have harmful effects on all living things.

Figure 4   *PCBs and other pollutants have even been found in remote parts of the Arctic.*

Chemistry
C O N N E C T I O N

Ozone in the stratosphere absorbs most of the ultraviolet light that comes from the sun. Ozone is destroyed by CFCs. This image of the hole in the ozone layer (the gray area in the center) was taken in 1998.

Exposure to high levels of ultraviolet light can lead to blindness, rapid skin aging, skin cancer, and a weakened immune system.

Too Much Heat The Earth is surrounded by a mixture of gases, including carbon dioxide, that make up the atmosphere. The atmosphere acts as a protective blanket, keeping the Earth warm enough for life to exist. Since the late 1800s, however, the amount of carbon dioxide in the air has increased by 25 percent. Carbon dioxide and certain pollutants in the air act like a greenhouse. Most scientists think the increase in carbon dioxide and other pollutants has caused a significant increase in global temperatures. If the temperatures continue to rise, the polar icecaps could melt, raising the level of the world's oceans. Some scientists think the sea level could rise 10 cm to 1.2 m by the year 2100. A 1 m rise would flood coastal areas, pollute underground water supplies, and cause present shorelines to disappear.

It's Way Too Noisy! Some pollutants affect the senses. These include bad odors and loud noises. Too much noise is not just annoying; it affects the ability to hear and think. If construction workers and others who work in noisy environments do not protect their ears, they can slowly lose their hearing. The students shown in **Figure 5** are listening to music at a sensible volume so that their hearing will not be damaged.

Figure 5 *Listening to music at a sensible volume will help prevent hearing loss.*

internet**connect**

SC*i*LINKS
NSTA

TOPIC: Air Pollution
GO TO: www.scilinks.org
*sci*LINKS NUMBER: HSTL505

REVIEW

1. Describe two ways pollution can be harmful.

2. Explain how loud noise can be considered pollution.

3. **Applying Concepts** Explain how each of the following can help people but harm the environment: hospitals, refrigerators, and road construction.

Resource Depletion

Another problem for our environment is that we are using up, or depleting, natural resources. Some of the Earth's resources are renewable, but others are nonrenewable. A **renewable resource** is one that can be used again and again or has an unlimited supply. Fresh water and solar energy are renewable resources, as are some kinds of trees. A **nonrenewable resource** is one that can be used only once. Most minerals are nonrenewable. Fossil fuels, such as oil and coal, are also nonrenewable resources.

Some nonrenewable resources, such as petroleum, are probably not in danger of running out in your lifetime. But we use more and more nonrenewable resources every year, and they cannot last forever. Plus, the removal of some materials from the Earth carries a high price tag in the form of oil spills, loss of habitat, and damage from mining, as shown in **Figure 6**.

Figure 6 *This area has been mined for coal using a method called strip mining.*

MATH BREAK

Water Depletion

An underground water supply has a depth of 200 m of water. Water seeps in at the rate of 4 cm/year. Water is pumped out at the rate of 1 m/year. How long will this water supply last?

To find the net water loss from an underground water supply, subtract the amount that seeps into the water supply from the amount removed from the water supply.

How long will the water supply last if water seeps in at the rate of 10 cm/year and is removed at the rate of 10 cm/year?

Nonrenewable or Renewable? Some resources once thought to be renewable are becoming nonrenewable. Ecosystems, such as tropical rain forests, are being polluted and destroyed, resulting in huge losses of habitat. Around the world, rich soil is being eroded away and polluted. A few centimeters of soil takes thousands of years to form and can be washed away in less than a year. Underground water needed for drinking and irrigation is used faster than it is replaced. Several centimeters of water may seep into an underground source each year, but in the same amount of time, *meters* of water are being pumped out.

✓ Self-Check

1. In what ways do you use nonrenewable resources?

2. Why would it not be a good idea to use up a nonrenewable resource?

(See page 782 to check your answers.)

Figure 7 *The zebra mussel is an alien invader that is clogging water treatment plants in the Great Lakes region.*

Alien Species

People are constantly on the move. Without knowing it, we take along passengers. Boats, airplanes, and cars carry plant seeds, animal eggs, and adult organisms from one part of the world to another. An organism that makes a home for itself in a new place is an *alien*. One reason alien species often thrive in foreign lands is that they are free from the predators in their native habitats.

Alien species often become pests and drive out native species. The zebra mussel, shown in **Figure 7**, hitched a ride on ships sailing from Europe to the United States in the 1980s. The purple loosestrife, shown in **Figure 8**, arrived long ago from Europe. Today it is crowding out native vegetation and threatening rare plant species in much of North America. Many organisms, such as the dandelion, are so common and have been here so long that it is easy to forget they don't belong.

Human Population Growth

In 1800, there were 1 billion people on Earth. In 1990, there were 5.2 billion. By 2100, there may be 14 billion. Today, one out of ten people goes to bed hungry every night, and millions die each year from hunger-related causes. Some people believe that the human population is already too high for the Earth to support.

More people require more resources, and the human population is growing rapidly. **Overpopulation** occurs when the number of individuals becomes so large that they can't get all the food, water, and other resources they need on an ongoing basis.

Figure 9 shows that it took most of human history for the human population to reach 1 billion. Will the planet be able to support 14 billion people?

Figure 8 *The purple loosestrife from Europe is choking out natural vegetation in North America.*

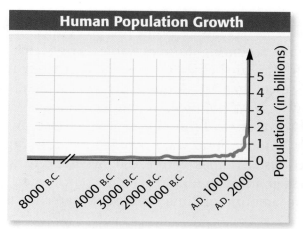

Figure 9 *The Earth's human population is now doubling every few decades.*

Habitat Destruction

The term **biodiversity** means "variety of life." It refers to the many different species found in a particular habitat all across the planet.

Every habitat has its own diverse combination of occupants. Every time a bulldozer digs or a chainsaw buzzes, every time hazardous wastes are dumped, a habitat is damaged, changed, or destroyed. And every time a habitat is destroyed, biodiversity is lost.

Forests Trees give us oxygen, furniture, fuel, fruits and nuts, rubber, alcohol, paper, turpentine, pencils, and telephone poles. Once trees covered twice as much land as they do today. *Deforestation,* such as that in **Figure 10,** is the clearing of forest lands. Tropical forests are cut for mines, dams, and roads. They are also cleared for paper, fuel, and building materials. But after tropical rain forests are cleared, little can grow on the land. Tropical soil doesn't have many nutrients, so it cannot be used for farming and is often abandoned.

Figure 10 *Temperate forests are destroyed for many of the same reasons that tropical rain forests are destroyed.*

Wetlands Wetlands were once considered unimportant. But as you know, that's not true. Wetlands help control flooding by soaking up the water from overflowing rivers. They filter pollutants from flowing water and provide breeding grounds for animals. They help prevent soil erosion and restore underground water supplies. Yet wetlands are often drained and filled to provide land for farms, homes, and shopping malls. They are dredged to keep passages open for ships and boats. Wetland habitats can also be destroyed by pollution.

Activity

Look around the room. How many objects can you find that are made of wood? List them in your ScienceLog. Add all the products you can think of that come from trees.

TRY at HOME

Marine Habitats Oil is a major contributor to marine habitat loss. Oil from cities and industries is sometimes dumped into the ocean. Accidental spills and waste from oil tankers add more oil to the oceans. Spilled oil contaminates both open waters and coastal habitats, as shown in **Figure 11.** All the oceans are connected, so pollutants from one ocean can be carried around the world.

Figure 11 *Oil from the* Exxon Valdez *damaged more than 2,300 km² of the Alaskan coast.*

Balloons Aloft

Your town is about to celebrate its 200th birthday. A giant birthday party is planned. As part of the celebration, the town plans to release 1,000 helium balloons that say "Happy Birthday to Our Town." Why is this not a good idea? What can you do to convince town officials to change their plans?

Figure 12 *This sea bird has become entangled in a plastic six-pack holder.*

BRAIN FOOD

If humans became extinct, other organisms would go on living. But if all the insects became extinct, many plants could not reproduce. Animals would lose their food supply. The organisms we depend on, and eventually all of us, would disappear from the face of the Earth.

Plastics are often dumped into marine habitats. They are lightweight and float on the surface. They are not **biodegradable,** so they are not broken down by the environment. Animals, such as the bird in **Figure 12,** try to eat them and often get tangled in them and die. Dumping plastics into the ocean is against the law, but it is difficult to enforce.

Effects on Humans

Trees and sea creatures are not the only organisms affected by pollution, global warming, and habitat destruction. The damage we do to the Earth affects us too. Sometimes the effect is immediate. If you drink polluted water, you may immediately get sick or even die. But sometimes the damage is not apparent right away. Some chemicals cause cancers 20 or 30 years after a person is exposed to them. Your children or grandchildren may have to deal with depleted resources.

Anything that endangers other organisms will eventually endanger us too. Taking good care of the environment requires being concerned about what is happening right now. It also requires looking ahead to the future.

REVIEW

1. Why do alien species often thrive?

2. Explain how human population growth is related to pollution problems.

3. **Applying Concepts**   How can the destruction of wetland habitats affect humans?

Section 2

Terms to Learn

conservation
recycling
resource recovery

What You'll Do

◆ Explain the importance of conservation.
◆ Describe the three Rs and their importance.
◆ Explain how habitats can be protected.
◆ List ways you can help protect the Earth.

The Good News: Solutions

As you've seen, the news is bad. But it isn't *all* bad. In fact, there is plenty of good news. The good news is about what people can do—and are doing—to save the Earth. It is about what *you* can do to save the Earth. Just as people are responsible for damaging the Earth, people can also take responsiblity for helping to heal and preserve the Earth.

Conservation

One major way to help save the Earth is conservation. **Conservation** is the wise use of and the preservation of natural resources. If you ride your bike to your friend's house, you conserve fuel. At the same time, you prevent air pollution. If you use organic compost instead of chemical fertilizer on your garden, you conserve the resources needed to make the fertilizer. You also prevent soil and water pollution.

Practicing conservation means using fewer natural resources. It also means reducing waste. The three Rs, shown in **Figure 13,** describe three ways to conserve resources and reduce damage to the Earth: **R**educe, **R**euse, and **R**ecycle.

Figure 13 *These teenagers are observing the three Rs by using a cloth shopping bag, donating outgrown clothing to be reused, and recycling plastic.*

Reduce

Reuse

Recycle

Reduce

The most obvious way to conserve the Earth's resources is to use less. This will also help reduce pollution and wastes. Some companies have started using a variety of strategies to conserve resources. They often save money in the process.

Reducing Waste and Pollution One-third of the waste from cities and towns is packaging. To conserve resources and reduce waste, products can be wrapped in less paper and plastic. Fast foods can be wrapped in thin paper instead of large plastic containers that are not biodegradable. You can choose to take your purchases without a sack if you don't need one. Scientists, such as the ones in **Figure 14,** are working to make better biodegradable plastics.

Some companies are searching for less hazardous materials to use in making products. For example, some farmers refuse to use pesticides and chemical fertilizers. They practice organic farming. They use mulch, compost, manure, and natural pesticides. Agricultural specialists are also developing new farming techniques that are better for the environment.

Figure 14 *These scientists are studying ways to use waste products to make biodegradable plastics.*

Reducing Use of Nonrenewable Resources Scientists are searching for alternative sources of energy. They want to avoid burning fuels and using nuclear energy. In some parts of the world solar energy heats water and powers homes, such as those shown in **Figure 15.** Engineers are working to make solar-powered cars practical. Other scientists are investigating the use of alternative power sources, such as wind, tides, and falling water.

It's Everyone's Responsibility Using fewer resources and reducing waste is not the job of industry and agriculture alone. Individuals use plenty of manufactured products and plenty of energy. They also produce large quantities of waste. Each United States citizen produces 40 times more waste than a citizen of a developing country. Why do you think this is so? What could you do to reduce the amount of trash that you produce? Everyone can take responsibility for helping to conserve the Earth's resources.

Figure 15 *Rooftop solar panels provide most of the energy used in this neighborhood in Rotterdam, Holland.*

Reuse

Do you get hand-me-down clothes from an older sibling? Do you try to fix broken sports equipment instead of thowing it away? If so, you are helping preserve the Earth by *reusing* products.

Reusing Products Every time someone reuses a plastic bag, one less bag needs to be made, and one less bag pollutes the Earth. Every time someone uses a rechargeable battery, one less battery needs to be made, and one less battery will pollute the Earth. Reusing is an important way to conserve resources and prevent pollution.

Reusing Water About 85 percent of the water used in homes goes down the drain. Communities with water shortages are experimenting with reclaiming and reusing this waste water. Some use green plants or filter-feeding animals such as clams to clean the water. The water isn't pure enough to drink, but it is fine for watering lawns and golf courses, such as the one shown in **Figure 16**.

Recycle

Recycling is a form of reuse. **Recycling** requires breaking down trash and using it again. Sometimes recycled products are used to make the same kind of products. Sometimes they are made into different products. The park bench in **Figure 17** was made from plastic foam cups, hamburger boxes, and plastic bottles that once held detergent, yogurt, and margarine. All of the containers pictured in **Figure 18** can be easily recycled.

Figure 16 *This golf course is being watered with reclaimed water.*

✓ Self-Check

1. How can you reduce the amount of electricity you use?
2. List five products that can be reused easily.

(See page 782 to check your answers.)

Figure 17 *This park bench is made of melted, remolded, and reused plastic.*

Figure 18 *These containers are examples of common household trash that can be recycled.*

Recycling Trash Plastics, paper, aluminum cans, waste wood, glass, and cardboard are some examples of materials that can be recycled. Every week, half a million trees are needed to make Sunday newspapers. Recycling newspapers could save many trees. Recycling aluminum foil and cans saves 95 percent of the energy needed to change raw ore into aluminum. Glass makes up 8 percent of all our waste. It can be remelted to make new bottles and jars. Lead batteries can be recycled into new batteries.

Some cities, such as Austin, Texas, make recycling easy. Special containers for glass, plastic, aluminum, and paper are provided to each city customer. Each week trash to be recycled is collected in special trucks, such as the one shown in **Figure 19,** at the same time other waste is collected.

Figure 19 *Each kind of recycled material is sorted into its own bin and then delivered to a recycling plant for processing.*

Recycling Resources Waste that can be burned can also be used to generate electricity in factories like the one shown in **Figure 20.** The process of transforming garbage to electricity is called **resource recovery.** The waste collected by all the cities and towns in the United States could produce about the same amount of electricity as 15 large nuclear power plants. Some companies are beginning to do this with their own waste. It saves them money, and it is responsible management.

Recycling is not difficult. Yet in the United States, only about 11 percent of the garbage is recycled. This compares with about 30 percent in Europe and 50 percent in Japan.

Figure 20 *A waste-to-energy plant can provide electricity to many homes and businesses.*

REVIEW

1. Define and explain *conservation.*

2. Describe the three main ways to conserve natural resources.

3. **Analyzing Relationships** How does conservation of resources also reduce pollution and other damage to the Earth?

Maintaining Biodiversity

Imagine a forest with just one kind of tree. If a disease hits that species, the entire forest might be wiped out. Now imagine a forest with 10 different kinds of trees. If a disease hits one kind of tree, nine different species will remain. Look at **Figure 21.** This field is growing a very important crop—cotton. But it is not very diverse. For the crop to thrive, the farmer must carefully manage the crop with weedkillers, pesticides, and fertilizers. Biodiversity helps to keep communities naturally stable.

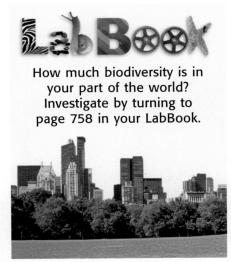

How much biodiversity is in your part of the world? Investigate by turning to page 758 in your LabBook.

Figure 21 *What could happen if a cotton disease hits this cotton field? Biodiversity is low in fields of crops like this one.*

Species variety is also important because each species makes a unique contribution to an ecosystem. In addition, many species are important to humans. They provide many things, such as foods, medicines, natural pest control, beauty, and companionship, to name just a few.

Species Protection One way to maintain biodiversity is through the protection of individual species. In the United States, the Endangered Species Act is designed to do just that. Endangered organisms are included in a special list. The law forbids activities that would damage a plant or animal on the endangered species list. It also requires the development of programs to help endangered populations recover. Some endangered species are now increasing in number, such as the California condor in **Figure 22.**

Unfortunately, the process of getting a species on the endangered list takes a long time. Many new species need to be added to the list. Many species become extinct even before they are listed!

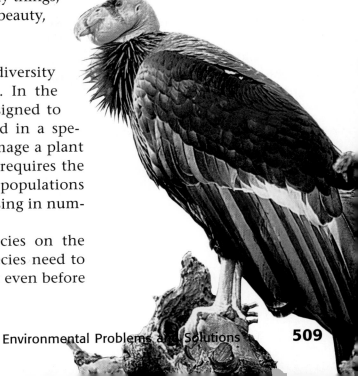

Figure 22 *The California condor is returning from the verge of extinction thanks to careful captive breeding.*

Figure 23 *Setting aside public lands for wildlife is one way to protect habitats.*

Habitat Protection Waiting until a species is almost extinct to begin protecting it is like waiting until your teeth are rotting to begin brushing them. Scientists want to prevent species from becoming endangered as well as from becoming extinct.

Plants, animals, and microorganisms do not live independently. Each is part of a huge interconnected web of organisms. To protect the entire web and to avoid disrupting the worldwide balance of nature, complete habitats, not just individual species, must be preserved. *All* species, not just those that are endangered, must be protected. All of the species that live in the nature preserve pictured in **Figure 23** are protected because the entire habitat is protected.

Strategies

Laws have been enacted to help conserve the Earth's environment. The purposes of such laws are listed below along with some of the ways citizens can help achieve these goals.

- **Reduce pesticide use.**
  Spray only pesticides that are targeted specifically for harmful insects. Use natural pesticides that interfere with the ways certain insects grow, develop, and live. Develop more biodegradable pesticides that will not injure birds, animals, or plants.

- **Reduce pollution.**
  Regulations prohibit the dumping of toxic substances and solid wastes into rivers, streams, lakes, and oceans and onto farmland and forests.

- **Protect habitats.**
  Conserve wetlands. Reduce deforestation. Practice logging techniques that consider the environment. Use resources at a rate that allows them to be replenished. Protect entire habitats.

- **Enforce the Endangered Species Act.**
  Speed up the process of getting endangered organisms listed.

- **Develop alternative energy sources.**
  Increase the use of solar power, wind power, and other renewable energy sources.

Trash Check

Keep track of all the trash you produce in one day. Classify it into groups. How much is food scraps? What might be considered a hazardous waste? What can be recycled? What can be reused? How can you reduce the amount of trash you produce?

TRY at HOME

What *You* Can Do

Reduce, reuse, recycle. Protect the Earth. These are jobs for everyone. Children as well as adults can help to save the Earth. The following list offers some suggestions for how *you* can help. How many of these things do you already do? What can you add to the list?

1. Buy things in packages that can be recycled.
2. Give away your old toys.
3. Use recycled paper.
4. Fill up both sides of a sheet of paper.
5. If you can't use permanent dishes, use paper instead of plastic-foam cups and plates.
6. Recycle glass, plastics, paper, aluminum, and batteries.
7. Don't buy anything made from an endangered animal.
8. Use rechargeable batteries.
9. Turn off lights, CD players, and computers when not in use.
10. Wear hand-me-downs.
11. Share books with friends, or use the library.
12. Walk, ride a bicycle, or use public transportation.
13. Carry a reusable cloth shopping bag to the store.
14. Use a lunch box or reuse your paper lunch bags.
15. Turn off the water while you brush your teeth.
16. Make a compost heap.
17. Buy products made from biodegradable plastic.
18. Use cloth napkins and kitchen towels.
19. Buy products with little or no packaging.
20. Repair leaking faucets.

REVIEW

1. Describe why biodiversity is important.

2. Why is it important to protect entire habitats?

3. **Applying Concepts** In the list above, identify which suggestions involve reducing, reusing, or recycling. Some suggestions will involve more than one of the three Rs.

internet connect

*sci*LINKS
NSTA

TOPIC: Recycling, Maintaining Biodiversity
GO TO: www.scilinks.org
*sci*LINKS NUMBER: HSTL520,HSTL525

Chapter Highlights

SECTION 1

Vocabulary

pollution *(p. 498)*

renewable resource *(p. 501)*

nonrenewable resource *(p. 501)*

overpopulation *(p. 502)*

biodiversity *(p. 503)*

biodegradable *(p. 504)*

Section Notes

- The Earth is being polluted by solid wastes, hazardous chemicals, radioactive materials, noise, and heat.

- Some of the Earth's resources renew themselves, and others do not. Some of the non-renewable resources are being used up.

- Alien species often invade foreign lands, where they may thrive, become pests, and threaten native species.

- The human population is in danger of reaching numbers that the Earth cannot support.

- The Earth's habitats are being destroyed in a variety of ways, including deforestation, the filling of wetlands, and pollution.

- Deforestation may cause the extinction of species and often leaves the soil infertile.

- Air, water, and soil pollution can damage or kill animals, plants, and microorganisms.

- Humans depend on many different kinds of organisms. Pollution, global warming, habitat destruction—anything that affects other organisms will eventually affect humans too.

✓ Skills Check

Math Concepts

NET WATER LOSS Suppose that water seeps into an underground water supply at the rate of 10 cm/year. The underground water supply is 100 m deep, but it is being pumped out at about 2 m/year. How long will the water last?

First convert all measurements to centimeters.

(100 m = 10,000 cm; 2 m = 200 cm)

Then find the net loss of water per year.

200 cm – 10 cm = 190 cm (net loss per year)

Now divide the depth of the underground water supply by the net loss per year to find out how many years this water supply will last.

10,000 cm ÷ 190 cm = 52.6 years

Visual Understanding

THINGS YOU CAN DO Obviously, the strategies listed on page 510 to help preserve the Earth's habitats are strategies that scientists and other professionals are developing. To help you understand some of the things that you can do now, review the list on page 511.

Vocabulary

conservation *(p. 505)*
recycling *(p. 507)*
resource recovery *(p. 508)*

Section Notes

- Conservation is the wise use of and preservation of the Earth's natural resources. By practicing conservation, people can reduce pollution and ensure that resources will be available to people in the future.

- Conservation involves the three Rs: Reduce, Reuse, and Recycle. Reducing means using fewer resources to begin with. Reusing means using materials and products over and over. Recycling involves breaking down used products and making them into new ones.

- Biodiversity is the variety of life on Earth. It is vital for maintaining stable, healthy, and functioning ecosystems.

- Habitats can be protected by using fewer pesticides, reducing pollution, avoiding habitat destruction, protecting species, and using alternative renewable sources of energy.

- Everyone can help to save the Earth by practicing the three Rs in their daily life.

Labs

Biodiversity—What a Disturbing Thought! *(p. 758)*

Deciding About Environmental Issues *(p. 760)*

---

internet connect

GO TO: go.hrw.com

Visit the **HRW** Web site for a variety of learning tools related to this chapter. Just type in the keyword:

KEYWORD: HSTENV

GO TO: www.scilinks.org

Visit the **National Science Teachers Association** on-line Web site for Internet resources related to this chapter. Just type in the *sci*LINKS number for more information about the topic:

TOPIC:	sciLINKS NUMBER:
Air Pollution	HSTL505
Resource Depletion	HSTL510
Population Growth	HSTL515
Recycling	HSTL520
Maintaining Biodiversity	HSTL525

Chapter Review

To complete the following sentences, choose the correct term from each pair of terms listed below:

1. ___?___ is the presence of harmful substances in the environment. *(Pollution or Biodiversity)*

2. ___?___ is a type of pollution produced by nuclear power plants. *(CFC or Radioactive waste)*

3. A ___?___ resource can be used only once. *(nuclear or nonrenewable)*

4. ___?___ is the variety of forms among living things. *(Biodegradable or Biodiversity)*

5. ___?___ is the breaking down of trash and using it to make a new product. *(Recycling or Reuse)*

UNDERSTANDING CONCEPTS

Multiple Choice

6. Habitat protection is important because
   a. organisms do not live independently.
   b. protecting habitats is a way to protect species.
   c. without it the balance of nature could be disrupted.
   d. All of the above

7. The Earth's resources can be conserved
   a. only by the actions of industry.
   b. by reducing the use of nonrenewable resources.
   c. if people do whatever they want to do.
   d. by throwing away all our trash.

8. Endangered species
   a. are those that are extinct.
   b. are found only in tropical rain forests.
   c. can sometimes be brought back from near extinction.
   d. are all protected by the Endangered Species Act.

9. Global warming is a danger
   a. only to people living in warm climates.
   b. to organisms all over the planet.
   c. only to life at the poles.
   d. to the amount of carbon dioxide in the air.

10. Overpopulation
    a. does not occur among human beings.
    b. helps keep pollution levels down.
    c. occurs when a species cannot get all the food, water, and other resources it needs.
    d. occurs only in large cities.

11. Biodiversity
    a. is of no concern to scientists.
    b. helps to keep ecosystems stable.
    c. causes diseases to destroy populations.
    d. is found only in temperate forests.

Short Answer

12. Describe how you can help to conserve resources. Include strategies from all of the three Rs.

13. Describe the connection between alien species and endangered species.

Concept Mapping

14. Use the following terms to create a concept map: pollution, pollutants, CFCs, cancer, PCBs, toxic, radioactive wastes, global warming.

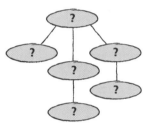

CRITICAL THINKING AND PROBLEM SOLVING

Write one or two sentences to answer the following question:

15. Suppose that the supply of fossil fuels were going to run out in 10 years. What would happen if we ran out without being prepared? What could be done to prepare for such an event?

MATH IN SCIENCE

16. If each person in a city of 150,000 throws away 12 kg of trash every week, how many metric tons of trash does the city produce per year? (There are 52 weeks in a year and 1,000 kg in a metric ton.)

INTERPRETING GRAPHICS

The illustration above shows how people in one home use natural resources.

17. Identify ways in which the people in this picture are wasting natural resources. Describe at least three examples, and tell what could be done to conserve resources.

18. Identify which resources in this picture are renewable.

19. Identify any sources of hazardous waste in this picture.

20. Explain how the girl wearing headphones is reducing pollution in the air. How could such a choice cause her harm?

NOW What Do You Think?

Take a minute to review your answers to the ScienceLog questions on page 497. Have your answers changed? If necessary, revise your answers based on what you have learned since you began this chapter.

CAREERS

BIOLOGIST

Dagmar Werner works at the Carara Biological Preserve, in Costa Rica, protecting green iguanas. Suffering from the effects of hunting, pollution, and habitat destruction, the iguana was nearly extinct. Since the 1980s, Werner has improved the iguanas' chances of survival by breeding them and releasing thousands of young iguanas into the wild. She also trains other people to do the same.

At Werner's "iguana ranch" preserve, female iguanas lay their eggs in artificial nests. After they hatch, the young lizards are placed in a temperature- and humidity-controlled incubator and given a special diet. As a result, the iguanas grow faster and stronger and are better protected from predators than their wild counterparts. Ordinarily, less than 2 percent of all iguanas survive to adulthood, but Werner's iguanas have an 80 percent survival rate. Once the iguanas are released into the wild, Werner tracks and monitors them to determine whether they have successfully adapted to their less-controlled environment.

Chicken of the Trees

Because she knew the iguana was close to extinction, Werner took an immediate and drastic approach to saving the lizards. She combined her captive-breeding program at the preserve with an education program that shows farmers a new way to make money from the rain forest. Instead of cutting down rain forest to raise cattle, Werner encourages farmers to raise iguanas. The iguanas can be released into the wild or sold for food. Known as "chicken of the trees," this lizard has been a favored source of meat among rain-forest inhabitants for thousands of years.

With Werner's methods, farmers can protect iguanas and still earn a living. But convincing farmers hasn't been easy. According to Werner, "Many locals have never thought of wild animals as creatures that must be protected in order to survive." To help, Werner has established the Fundación Pro Iguana Verde (the Green Iguana Foundation), which sponsors festivals and education seminars. These activities promote the traditional appeal of the iguana, increase pride in the animal, and heighten awareness about the iguana's economic importance.

Find Other Solutions

▶ The green iguana is just one animal that is nearing extinction in the rain forest. Research another endangered species and find out what scientists and local communities are doing to protect the species. Does it seem to be working?

▶ *A green Iguana at Carara Biological Preserve, in Costa Rica*

Where Should the Wolves Roam?

The U.S. Fish and Wildlife Service has listed the gray wolf as an endangered species throughout most of the United States and has devised a plan to reintroduce the wolf to Yellowstone National Park, central Idaho, and northwestern Montana. The goal is to establish a population of at least 100 wolves at each location. If the project continues as planned, wolves may be removed from the endangered species list by 2002. But some ranchers and hunters are uneasy about the plan, and some environmentalists and wolf enthusiasts think that the plan doesn't go far enough to protect wolves.

Does the Plan Risk Livestock?

Ranchers are concerned that the wolves will kill livestock. These losses could result in a tremendous financial burden to ranchers. There is a compensation program currently established that will pay ranchers if wolves kill their livestock. But this program will end if the wolf is removed from the endangered species list. Ranchers point out that the threat to their livestock will not end when the wolf is removed from the list. In fact, the threat will increase, but ranchers will no longer receive any compensation.

On the other hand, some biologists offer evidence that wolves living near areas with adequate populations of deer, elk, moose, and other prey do not attack livestock. In fact, fewer than five wolf attacks on livestock were reported between 1995 and 1997.

Are Wolves a Threat to Wildlife?

Many scientists believe that the reintroduction plan would bring these regions into ecological balance for the first time in 60 years. They believe that the wolves will eliminate old and weak elk, moose, and deer and help keep these populations from growing too large.

Hunters fear that the wolves will kill many of the game animals in these areas. They cite studies that say large game animal populations cannot survive hunting by both humans and wolves. Hunting plays a significant role in the economy of the western states.

Are the People Safe?

Some people fear that wolves will attack people. However, there has never been a documented attack on humans by healthy wolves in North America. Supporters say that wolves are shy animals that prefer to keep their distance from people.

Most wolf enthusiasts admit that there are places where wolves belong and places where wolves do not belong. They believe that these reintroduction zones offer places for wolves to thrive without creating problems.

What Do You Think?

▶ Some people argue that stories about "the big, bad wolf" give the wolf its ferocious reputation. Do you think people's fears are based on myth, or do you think that the wolf is a danger to people and livestock living in the reintroduction zones? Do some research and provide examples to support your opinion.

◀ *A Gray Wolf in Montana*

UNIT 7

Human Body Systems

Your body is made up of many systems that all work together like a finely tuned machine. Your lungs take in oxygen. Your heart pumps blood that delivers the oxygen to your tissues. Your brain reacts to things you see, hear, and smell, and sends signals through your nervous system that cause you to react to those things. Your digestive system converts the food you eat into energy that the cells of your body can use. And those are just a few things that your body can do!

In this unit, you will study the systems of your body. You'll discover how the parts of your body work together so that you can complete all your daily activities.

3000 B.C.
Ancient Egyptian doctors are the first to study the human body scientifically.

1824
Prevost and Dumas prove that sperm is essential for fertilization.

1893
Daniel Hale Williams, an African American surgeon, becomes the first to repair a tear in the pericardium, the sac around the heart.

1930
Karl Landsteiner receives a Nobel Prize for his discovery of the four human blood types.

1922
Insulin is discovered.

500 B.C.

Indian surgeon Susrata performs operations to remove cataracts.

1492

Christopher Columbus lands in the West Indies.

1543

Andreas Versalius publishes the first complete description of the structure of the human body.

1766

Albrecht von Haller determines that nerves control muscle movement and that all nerves are connected to the spinal cord or to the brain.

1619

William Harvey discovers that blood circulates and that the heart acts as a pump.

1982

Dr. Robert Jarvik implants an artificial heart in Barney Clark.

1941

During World War II in Italy, Rita Levi-Montalcini is forced to leave her work at a medical school laboratory because she is Jewish. She sets up a laboratory in her bedroom and studies the development of the nervous system.

1998

The first hand transplant is performed in France.

22 Body Organization and Structure

This Really Happened . . .

On April 14, 1912, at 11:40 P.M., the British steamship *Titanic,* the largest and most luxurious steamship ever built, struck an iceberg. Jack Thayer, a 17-year-old from Pennsylvania, felt the impact in his cabin and went on deck to see what had happened. To his horror, he found that the ship was sinking and that there were not enough lifeboats for the 2,207 passengers and crew. Jack watched as the last of the lifeboats, filled with women and children, were launched. Just before the ship slid beneath the icy water, Jack jumped. The pain of the cold felt like knives stabbing every inch of his body. He swam to an overturned lifeboat and climbed on.

Jack Thayer was among the survivors who were able to keep themselves dry enough to survive until help arrived, at 4 A.M. An estimated 1,500 people died. Even those who were wearing life jackets couldn't survive the extreme temperature of the water. The freezing water caused their body systems to fail. Breathing became difficult, and muscles no longer functioned. Finally, they lost consciousness and their hearts stopped.

The water around the *Titanic* was just too cold for human survival.

Under normal circumstances, our bodies are able to maintain a constant internal temperature. Read on to find out about this and other interesting information on how our bodies work.

Investigate!

TRY at HOME

Too Cold for Comfort

Did you know that your nervous system sends you continuous messages about your body's cells? For example, the pain you experience when someone steps on your toe is a message that you need to move your toe to safety. Try the following to see what message you get from your nervous system.

Procedure

1. Clutch **a few pieces of ice** in the palm of one hand. Allow the melting water to drip into **a dish.** Hold the ice until the cold is uncomfortable, and then release the ice into the dish.

2. What message did you receive from your nervous system? Did the sensations make you want to drop the ice and warm your hand?

3. Look at the hand that held the ice, and then look at your other hand. What changes in your skin do you observe? How quickly does the cold hand return to normal?

Analysis

4. What organ systems do you think were involved in restoring your hand to normal?

5. Think of a time in your life when your nervous system sent you a message, such as an uncomfortable feeling of heat or cold or a time when you felt pain. How did your body react? Which organ systems do you think were involved? Share your story with a classmate.

6. The arctic explorer above looks really cold. Use the Internet or library resources to find out how arctic explorers cope with subfreezing temperatures.

Body Organization

Terms to Learn

homeostasis
tissue
epithelial tissue
nervous tissue

muscle tissue
connective
  tissue
organ

What You'll Do

◆ Identify the major tissues found in the body.
◆ Compare an organ with an organ system.
◆ Describe a major function of each organ system.

Your body has an amazing ability to survive, even in the face of harsh conditions. How did Jack Thayer stay alive even though the environment around him was so cold? A short answer is that his body did not allow its internal conditions to change enough to stop his cells from working properly. The maintenance of a stable internal environment is called **homeostasis** (HOH mee OH STAY sis). If homeostasis is disrupted, cells suffer and sometimes die.

Four Types of Tissue

Making sure your internal environment remains stable enough to support healthy cells is not an easy task. Many different "jobs" must be done to maintain homeostasis. Fortunately, not every cell has to do all those jobs because the cells are organized into different teams. Just as each member of a soccer team has a special role in the game, each cell in your body has a specific job in maintaining homeostasis. A group of similar cells working together forms a **tissue.** Your body contains four main types of tissue—epithelial tissue, connective tissue, muscle tissue, and nervous tissue, as shown in **Figure 1.**

Figure 1 *Your body has four types of tissue, and each type has a special function in your body.*

Epithelial tissue covers and protects underlying tissue. When you look at the surface of your skin, you see epithelial tissue. The cells stick tightly and form a continuous sheet.

Nervous tissue sends electrical signals through the body. It is found in the brain, nerves, and sense organs.

Tissues Form Organs

Two or more tissues working together form an **organ.** One type of tissue alone cannot do all the things that several types working together can do. Your stomach, as shown in **Figure 2,** uses several different types of tissue to carry out digestion.

Organs Form Systems

Your stomach does much to help you digest your food, but it doesn't do it all. It works together with other organs, such as the small intestine and large intestine, to digest your food. Organs working together make up an *organ system*. The failure of any part can affect the entire system. Your body has 11 major organ systems, which are illustrated on the next two pages. Are there any that you have not heard of before?

The Stomach Is an Organ

Nervous tissue in the stomach partly controls the production of acids that aid in the digestion of food. Nervous tissue signals when the stomach is full.

Epithelial tissue lines the stomach.

Layers of **muscle tissue** break up stomach contents.

Blood and a **connective tissue** called collagen are found in the wall of the stomach.

Figure 2 *The four types of tissue work together so that the stomach can carry out digestion.*

Muscle tissue is made of cells that can contract and relax to produce movement.

Connective tissue joins, supports, protects, insulates, nourishes, and cushions organs. It also keeps organs from falling apart.

Organ Systems

Integumentary system

Your skin, hair, and nails protect underlying tissue.

Muscular system

Your skeletal muscles move your bones.

Skeletal system

Your bones provide a frame to support and protect body parts.

Cardiovascular system

Your heart pumps blood through all your blood vessels.

Respiratory system

Your lungs absorb oxygen and release carbon dioxide.

Urinary system

Your urinary system removes wastes from the blood and regulates the body's fluids.

Reproductive system (male)

The male reproductive system produces and delivers sperm.

Reproductive system (female)

The female reproductive system produces eggs and nourishes and shelters the unborn baby.

Organ Systems

Nervous system

It is the role of the nervous system to receive and send electrical messages throughout the body.

Lymphatic system

Your lymphatic system returns leaked fluids to blood vessels. It also helps you get rid of germs that can harm you.

Digestive system

Your digestive system breaks down the food you eat into nutrients that can be absorbed into your body.

Endocrine system

Glands regulate body functions by sending out chemical messengers. The ovaries, in females, and testes, in males, are part of this system.

REVIEW

1. Explain the relationship between cells, tissues, organs, and organ systems.

2. Compare the four kinds of tissue found in the human body.

3. **Using Graphics** Make a chart that lists the major organ systems and their functions.

4. **Relating Concepts** Describe a time when homeostasis was disrupted in your body. Which body systems do you think were affected?

internet**connect**

*sci*LINKS
NSTA

TOPIC: Tissues and Organs, Body Systems
GO TO: www.scilinks.org
*sci*LINKS NUMBER: HSTL530, HSTL535

The Skeletal System

Terms to Learn

skeletal system   cartilage
compact bone   joint
spongy bone   ligament

What You'll Do

◆ Identify the major organs of the skeletal system.
◆ Describe the functions of bones.
◆ Illustrate the internal structure of bones.
◆ Compare three types of joints.
◆ Discuss how bones function as levers.

When you hear the word *skeleton,* you may think of the remains of something that has died. But your skeleton is not dead; it is very much alive. Your bones are not dry and brittle. They are just as alive and active as the muscles that are attached to them. Bones, cartilage, and the special structures that connect them make up your **skeletal system.**

The Burden of Being a Bone

Bones do a lot more than just hold you up. Your bones perform several important functions inside your body. The names of some of your bones are identified in **Figure 3.**

Protection Your heart and lungs are shielded by your ribs, your spinal cord is protected by your vertebrae, and your brain is protected by your skull.

Storage Bones store minerals that help the nerves and muscles function properly. Your arm and leg bones also store fat that can be used for energy.

Movement Skeletal muscles pull on the bones to produce movement. Without bones, you would not be able to sit, stand, walk, or run.

Blood Cell Formation Some of your bones are filled with a special material that makes blood cells.

Figure 3 *The adult human skeleton has approximately 206 bones. Several major bones are identified in this skeleton.*

What's in a Bone?

A bone may seem lifeless, but it is a living organ made of several different tissues. Bone is composed of connective tissue and minerals that are deposited by living cells called *osteoblasts*.

If you look inside a bone, you will notice there are two different kinds of bone tissue. If the tissue does not have any visible open spaces, it is called **compact bone.** Bone tissue that has many open spaces is called **spongy bone.** Spongy bone provides most of the strength and support for a bone. It acts like the trusses of a bridge.

Down to the Marrow Bones contain a soft tissue called *marrow*. Red marrow, sometimes found in spongy bone, produces red blood cells. Yellow marrow, found in the central cavity of long bones, stores fat. Tiny canals within the compact bone contain small blood vessels. **Figure 4** shows a cross section of a femur.

QuickLab

Pickled Bones

This activity lets you see how a bone changes when it is exposed to an acid, such as vinegar. Place a **clean chicken bone** in a **jar of vinegar.** After 1 week, remove the bone and rinse it with water. Make a list of changes that you can see or feel. How has the bone's strength changed? What did the vinegar remove?

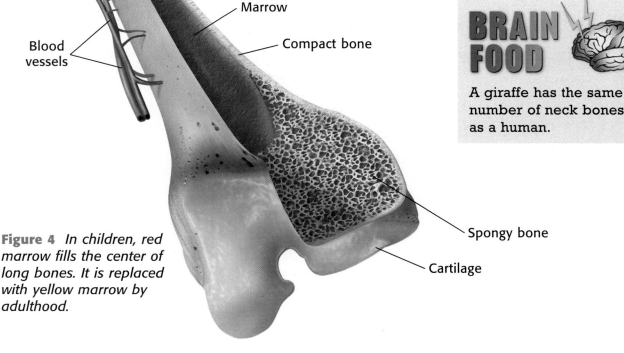

Blood vessels

Marrow

Compact bone

Spongy bone

Cartilage

BRAIN FOOD

A giraffe has the same number of neck bones as a human.

Figure 4 *In children, red marrow fills the center of long bones. It is replaced with yellow marrow by adulthood.*

Growing Bones

Did you know that most of your skeleton used to be soft and rubbery? Most bones start out as a soft, flexible tissue called **cartilage.** When you were born, you had little true bone. But as you grew, the cartilage was replaced by bone. During childhood, growth plates of cartilage remain in most bones, providing a place for those bones to continue to grow.

Feel the end of your nose, or bend the top of your ear. As shown in **Figure 5,** some areas, like these, never become bone. The flexible material beneath your skin in these areas is cartilage.

Figure 5 *The skull and neck bones in this computer-colored X ray are shown mostly in blue.*

What's the Point of a Joint?

The place where two or more bones connect is called a **joint.** Your joints have special designs that allow your body to move when your muscles contract. Some joints allow a lot of movement, while other joints are fixed, which means they allow little or no movement. For example, the joints in the skull are fixed. Joints that have a wide range of movement tend to be more susceptible to injury than those that are less flexible. Some examples of movable joints are shown in **Figure 6.**

Figure 6 *Joints are shaped according to their function in the body.*

Sliding joint

Sliding joints allow bones in the hand to glide over one another, giving some flexibility to the area.

Ball-and-socket joint

Like a joystick on a computer game, the shoulder enables your arm to move freely in all directions.

Hinge joint

Like a hinge on a door, the knee enables you to flex and extend your lower leg.

Bone to Bone Joints are kept together with strong elastic bands of connective tissue called **ligaments.** If a ligament is stretched too far, it becomes strained. A strained ligament will usually heal with time, but a torn ligament will not. A torn ligament must be repaired surgically. Cartilage helps cushion the area where two bones meet. If cartilage wears away, the joint becomes arthritic.

Can Levers Lessen Your Load?

You may not think of your limbs as being machines, but they are. The action of a muscle pulling on a bone often works like a type of simple machine called a *lever*. A lever is a rigid bar that moves on a fixed point known as a *fulcrum*. Any force applied to the lever is called the *effort*. A force that resists the motion of the lever, such as the downward force exerted by a weight on the bar, is called the *load* or the *resistance*. **Figure 7** shows how three types of levers are used in the human body.

Figure 7 There are three classes of levers, based on the location of the fulcrum, the load, and the effort.

REVIEW

1. Describe four important functions of bones.

2. Draw a bone, and label the inside and outside structures. Use colored pencils to color and label spongy bone, blood vessels, marrow cavity, compact bone, and cartilage.

3. List three hinge joints in your body.

4. **Interpreting Models** Study the models of levers pictured in Figure 7. Use a small box (load), a ruler (bar), and a pencil (fulcrum) to create models of each type of lever.

First-class lever

The fulcrum lies between the load and the effort.

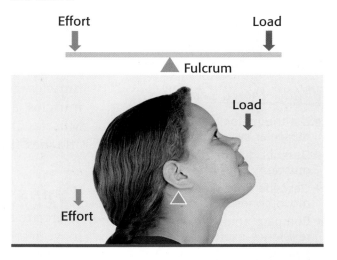

Second-class lever

The load lies between the fulcrum and the effort.

Third-class lever

The effort lies between the fulcrum and the load.

The Muscular System

Terms to Learn

muscular system   skeletal muscle
smooth muscle   tendon
cardiac muscle

What You'll Do

◆ List the major parts of the muscular system.
◆ Describe the different types of muscle.
◆ Describe how skeletal muscles move bones.
◆ Compare aerobic exercise with resistance exercise.
◆ Give an example of a muscle injury.

Have you ever tried to be perfectly still for just 1 minute? Try as you might, you just can't do it. Somewhere in your body, certain muscles are always working. For example, muscles continuously push blood through your blood vessels. A muscle makes you breathe. And muscles hold you upright. If all your muscles rested at the same time, you would collapse. Your muscles are made of muscle tissue and connective tissue. Muscles that attach to bones and the connective tissue that attaches them make up the **muscular system.**

Types of Muscle

There are three types of muscle tissue that make up the muscles in your body. **Smooth muscle** is found in the digestive tract and the blood vessels. **Cardiac muscle** is a special type of muscle found only in your heart. **Skeletal muscles** are attached to your bones for movement, and they help protect your inner organs. The three types of muscles are shown in **Figure 8.**

Muscle action can be voluntary or involuntary. Muscle action that is under your control is *voluntary.* Muscle action that is not under your control is *involuntary.* The actions of smooth muscle and cardiac muscle are involuntary. The actions of skeletal muscles can be both voluntary and involuntary. For example, you can blink your eyes any time you want to, but your eyes will also blink automatically if you do not think about it.

Figure 8 *Your body has smooth muscle, cardiac muscle, and skeletal muscle.*

Skeletal muscle enables bones to move.

Smooth muscle moves food through the digestive system.

Cardiac muscle causes the heart to beat.

Making Your Move

Skeletal muscles produce hundreds of different voluntary movements. This is demonstrated by a ballet dancer, a swimmer, or even someone making a funny face, as shown in **Figure 9.** When you want to make a movement, you cause electrical signals to travel from the brain to the skeletal muscle cells. The muscle cells respond to these signals by contracting or getting shorter.

Figure 9 *It takes an average of 13 muscles to smile and an average of 43 muscles to frown.*

Muscles to Bones Strands of tough connective tissue called **tendons** connect your skeletal muscles to your bones. When a muscle gets shorter, a pulling action occurs, bringing the bones closer to each other. For example, the biceps muscle, shown in **Figure 10,** is attached by tendons to a bone in your shoulder and to another bone in your forearm. When the biceps contracts, your arm bends.

Working in Pairs Your skeletal muscles work in pairs to cause smooth, controlled movements. Many basic movements are the result of muscle pairs that cause bending and straightening. If a muscle bends part of your body, then that muscle is called a *flexor.* If the muscle straightens part of your body, then it is called an *extensor.* The flexor muscle of the arm is the biceps. The extensor muscle of the arm is the triceps. Discover some of your own flexor and extensor muscles by doing the QuickLab at right.

Biceps muscle

Triceps muscle

Flexor

Extensor

Figure 10 *Skeletal muscles, such as the biceps and triceps muscles, work in pairs. When the biceps muscle contracts, the elbow bends. When the triceps muscle contracts, the elbow straightens.*

QuickLab

Power in Pairs

1. While sitting in a chair, place one of your hands palm up under the edge of a **table.** Apply gentle upward pressure.

2. With your free hand, feel the front and back of your upper arm.

3. Next place your hand palm down on top of the table. Apply pressure downward.

4. Again with your free hand, feel the front and back of your upper arm.

5. What did you notice when you were pressing up? when you were pressing down?

TRY at HOME

CONNECTION

Body chemistry is very important for healthy muscle functioning. If there is a chemical imbalance in a muscle due to excessive sweating, poor diet, tension, or illness, spasms or cramping may occur. Sodium, calcium, and potassium—three chemicals called *electrolytes*—must be in proper balance to avoid cramps and spasms. Relaxation and massage usually help the muscle restore its chemical balance.

Use It or Lose It

When someone breaks an arm and has to wear a cast, the muscles surrounding the injured bone change. That's because these muscles are not exercised, and they become smaller and weaker. On the other hand, exercised muscles are stronger and larger. Certain exercises can give muscles more endurance. This means they're able to work longer without getting tired. Strong muscles benefit other systems in your body too. When a muscle contracts, blood vessels in that muscle get squeezed. This helps push blood along, increasing blood flow without demanding more work from the heart.

Resistance Exercises To develop the size and strength of your skeletal muscles, resistance exercises are the most effective form of exercise. Resistance exercises require muscles to overcome the resistance (weight) of another object. Some resistance exercises, like the bent knee curl-up shown in **Figure 11,** require you to overcome your own weight.

Figure 11 *Resistance exercises are tough, but they can really help you build strong muscles.*

Aerobic Exercise Steady, moderate-intensity activity, such as jogging, cycling, skating, swimming laps, or walking, is called aerobic exercise. Aerobic exercise increases the size and strength of your skeletal muscles somewhat, but mostly it strengthens the heart while increasing the endurance of your skeletal muscles. Many people, like the girl in **Figure 12,** enjoy doing aerobic exercise.

Figure 12 *Aerobic exercise is a great way to have fun while strengthening your heart.*

Self-Check

Which kind of skeletal muscle do you use to perform a curl-up? Which kind do you use to do a push-up? *(See page 782 to check your answers.)*

Chapter 22

Muscle Injury

Any exercise program should be started gradually so that the muscles gain strength and endurance without injury. Muscles should also be warmed up gradually to reduce the risk of injury. However, as shown in **Figure 13,** the muscular system can experience damage. A muscle strain, commonly called a pulled muscle, is the overstretching or even tearing of a muscle. Muscle strain often occurs because the muscle has not been properly conditioned for the work it is doing.

Tendons, as well as muscles, can get injured from overuse. A damaged tendon can become hot or inflamed as your body tries to repair it. This painful condition is called tendinitis, and an extended period of rest is often required for the tendon to heal.

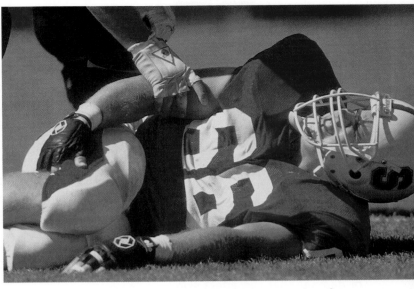

Figure 13 *A pulled hamstring is a tear or strain of one of the muscles or tendons on the back of the thigh.*

The Dangers of Anabolic Steroids Some people try to make their muscles larger and stronger by taking hormones called *anabolic steroids*. Anabolic steroids are powerful chemicals that resemble testosterone, a male sex hormone. Using anabolic steroids not only gives athletes an unfair advantage in competition but also puts the user at risk for serious long-term health problems. The use of anabolic steroids threatens the heart, liver, and kidneys, and it can cause high blood pressure. If taken before the skeleton is mature, anabolic steroids can cause the bones to stop growing.

MATH BREAK

Runner's Time

Jan, who has been a runner for several years, has decided to enter a race. She now runs 5 km in 30 minutes. She would like to decrease her time by 15 percent before the race. What will her time be when she meets her goal?

REVIEW

1. List three types of muscle tissue, and describe their functions in the body.

2. Compare aerobic exercise with resistance exercise, and give two examples of each.

3. **Applying Concepts** Describe the muscle action required to pick up a book. Make a sketch that illustrates the muscle action.

internetconnect

SCiLINKS
NSTA

TOPIC: The Muscular System
GO TO: www.scilinks.org
*sci*LINKS NUMBER: HSTL540

Terms to Learn

integumentary system
sweat glands
melanin
epidermis
dermis
hair follicle

What You'll Do

◆ Describe the major functions of the integumentary system.
◆ List the major parts of the skin, and discuss their functions.
◆ Describe the structure and function of hair and nails.
◆ Describe some common types of damage that can affect skin.

The Integumentary System

Here's a quiz for you. What part of your body has to be partly dead to keep you alive? Here are some clues: it comes in a variety of colors, it is the largest organ in the body, and it protects you from the outside world. Oh, and guess what—it is showing right now. Did you guess your skin? If you did, you guessed correctly.

Your skin, hair, and nails make up your **integumentary** (in TEG yoo MEN tuhr ee) **system.** (*Integument* means "covering.") Like all organ systems, the integumentary system helps your body maintain a healthy internal environment.

The Skin: More than Just a "Coat"

Why do you need skin? Here are four good reasons:

■ Skin protects you by keeping moisture in your body and foreign particles out of your body.

■ Skin keeps you "in touch" with the outside world. The nerve endings in your skin allow you to feel what's around you.

■ Skin helps regulate your body's temperature. For example, small organs in the skin called **sweat glands** produce sweat, a salty liquid that flows to the surface of the skin. As sweat evaporates, the skin cools.

■ Skin helps get rid of wastes. Several types of waste chemicals can leave the bloodstream and be removed in sweat.

What Determines Skin Color? A darkening chemical in skin called **melanin** determines skin color, as shown in **Figure 14.** If a lot of melanin is present, the skin is very dark. If only a little melanin is produced, the skin is very light. Melanin in the upper layer of the skin absorbs much of the harmful radiation from the sun, reducing DNA damage that can lead to cancer. However, *all* skin is vulnerable to cancer and therefore should be protected from sun exposure whenever possible.

Figure 14 *Variety in skin color is caused by the pigment melanin. The amount of melanin varies from person to person.*

A Tale of Two Layers

As you already know, the skin is the largest organ of your body. In fact, the skin of an adult covers an area of about 2 m²! However, there's a lot more to skin than meets the eye. The skin has two main layers: the dermis and the epidermis. The **epidermis** is the thinner layer of the two. It's what you see when you look at your skin. (*Epi* means "on top of.") The deeper, thicker layer is known as the **dermis.**

Epidermis The epidermis is composed of a type of epithelial tissue. Even though the epidermis has many layers of cells, it is only as thick as two sheets of notebook paper over most of the body. It is thicker in the palms of your hands and the soles of your feet. Most epidermal cells are dead and are filled with a protein called keratin, which helps make the skin tough.

Dermis The dermis lies underneath the epidermis. It is mostly connective tissue, and it contains many fibers made of a protein called collagen. The fibers provide strength and allow skin to bend without tearing. The dermis also contains a variety of small structures, as shown in **Figure 15.**

Self-Check

To what system do the skin's blood vessels belong? (*See page 782 to check your answer.*)

Your epidermis is showing!

Figure 15 *Beneath the surface, your skin is a complex organ made of blood vessels, nerves, glands, and muscles.*

Blood vessels transport substances and help regulate body temperature.

Nerves carry messages to and from the brain.

Muscle fibers attached to a hair follicle can contract, causing the hair to stand up.

Hair follicles in the dermis produce hair.

Oil glands release oil that keeps hair flexible and helps waterproof the epidermis.

Sweat glands release sweat. As sweat evaporates, heat is removed from the skin, and the body is cooled. Sweat also contains waste materials taken out of the body.

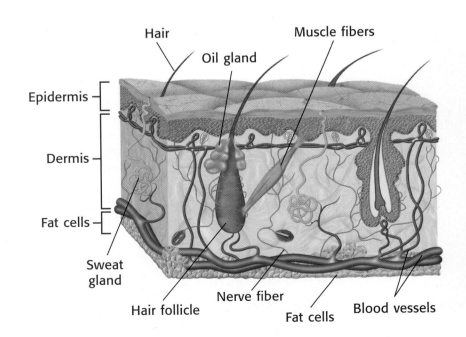

Hair and Nails

A hair, shown in **Figure 16,** is formed at the bottom of a tiny sac called a **hair follicle.** The hair grows as new cells are added at the hair follicle and older cells get pushed upward. The only living cells in a hair are in the hair follicle, where the hair is produced.

How fast do your fingernails grow? Find out on page 763.

Letting Your Hair Down Hairs protect skin from ultraviolet light and can help keep particles, such as dust and insects, out of your eyes and nose. Like skin, hair gets its color from the pigment melanin. Dark hair contains more melanin than blond hair. In most mammals, hair also helps regulate body temperature. A contraction of a tiny muscle attached to the hair follicle causes the follicle to bend. In humans, the bending follicle pushes up the epidermis to make a goose bump. If the follicle contains a hair, the hair "stands up." The lifted hairs function like a sweater to trap warm air around the body.

Figure 16 *A hair is actually layers of dead, tightly packed, keratin-filled cells.*

Hair

A Nail Tale Nails protect the tips of your fingers and toes so that they can remain soft and sensitive. This allows you to have a keen sense of touch. Nails form from *nail roots* under the skin at the base and sides of nails. As new cells form, the nail grows longer. The parts of a nail are shown in **Figure 17.**

Figure 17 *In nails, new cells are produced in the nail root, just beneath the lunula. The new cells push older cells toward the outer edge of the nail.*

Free edge

Nail body

Lunula

Living in Harm's Way

Skin is often damaged. The damage may be minor—a blister, an insect bite, or a small cut. Fortunately, your skin has an amazing ability to repair itself, as shown in **Figure 18.**

Figure 18 How Skin Heals

Scab

Blood clot

Bacteria fighting cells

① When you get a cut, a blood clot forms to prevent bacteria from entering the wound. Bacteria-fighting cells then come to the area to kill bacteria.

New cells

② Damaged cells are replaced through cell division. Eventually, all that is left on the surface is a scar.

Other damage to the skin is very serious. Damage to the genetic material in skin cells can result in uncontrolled cell division, producing a mass of skin cells called a tumor. The term *cancer* is used to describe a tumor that invades other tissue. Darkened areas on the skin, such as moles, should be watched carefully for signs of cancer. **Figure 19** shows an example of a mole that has possibly become cancerous.

Your skin may also be affected by hormones that cause the oil glands in your skin to produce excess oil. This oil combines with dead skin cells and bacteria to clog hair follicles and cause infections. Proper cleansing and daily skin care can be helpful in decreasing the amount of infections.

Figure 19 *This mole has two halves that do not match, a characteristic that might indicate skin cancer.*

REVIEW

1. Why does skin color vary from person to person?

2. List six structures found in the dermis and the function of each one.

3. **Making Inferences** Why do you feel pain when you pull on your hair or nails but not when you cut them?

Chapter Highlights

Vocabulary

homeostasis *(p. 522)*

tissue *(p. 522)*

epithelial tissue *(p. 522)*

nervous tissue *(p. 522)*

muscle tissue *(p. 523)*

connective tissue *(p. 523)*

organ *(p. 523)*

Section Notes

• Your body maintains a stable internal environment called homeostasis.

• Four types of tissues work to maintain homeostasis. Each tissue has a special job to do.

• Tissues work together to form organs.

• A group of organs working together for a common purpose is called an organ system.

• There are 11 major organ systems in the human body.

Vocabulary

skeletal system *(p. 526)*

compact bone *(p. 527)*

spongy bone *(p. 527)*

cartilage *(p. 528)*

joint *(p. 528)*

ligament *(p. 529)*

Section Notes

• The skeletal system includes bones, cartilage, and ligaments.

• Bones support and protect the body, store minerals and fat, and produce blood cells.

• A typical bone contains marrow, spongy bone, compact bone, blood vessels, and cartilage.

☑ Skills Check

Math Concepts

CALCULATING A PERCENTAGE In the MathBreak on page 533 you were asked to calculate a percentage of a number. To do this, first express the percentage as a decimal or a fraction. Then multiply it by the number. For example, 25 percent can be written as 0.25 or $25 \div 100$. To find 25 percent of 48, multiply by either 0.25 or $25 \div 100$.

$$0.25 \times 48 = 12$$
$$\text{or}$$
$$(25 \div 100) \times 48 = 12$$

Visual Understanding

MOVING WITH JOINTS Take another look at the three kinds of joints on page 528. Consider how your joints work when you throw a ball or walk up stairs. The hinge joint in your knee can move freely in only two directions. The ball-and-socket joint in your shoulder can move in many directions. The sliding joints in your hand allow bones to glide over one another.

SECTION 2

- A joint is where two bones meet. Some joints allow a lot of movement, and some allow little or no movement.

- Bones are attached to bones by connective tissue called ligaments.

- The action of muscle on bone and joints often works like a simple machine called a lever.

SECTION 3

Vocabulary

muscular system (*p. 530*)

smooth muscle (*p. 530*)

cardiac muscle (*p. 530*)

skeletal muscle (*p. 530*)

tendon (*p. 531*)

Section Notes

- Skeletal muscles and tendons make up the muscular system.

- You have three types of muscle: smooth, cardiac, and skeletal.

- Muscles are attached to bones by tendons.

- Exercise helps keep your muscular system healthy.

Labs

Muscles at Work (*p. 762*)

SECTION 4

Vocabulary

integumentary system (*p. 534*)

sweat glands (*p. 534*)

melanin (*p. 534*)

epidermis (*p. 535*)

dermis (*p. 535*)

hair follicle (*p. 536*)

Section Notes

- Your skin, hair, and nails make up your integumentary system.

- Your skin has two layers that contain a variety of small organs.

- Your hair and nails help protect your body.

- Skin can be damaged, but it has an amazing ability to repair itself.

Labs

Seeing Is Believing (*p. 763*)

---

 internetconnect

GO TO: go.hrw.com

Visit the **HRW** Web site for a variety of learning tools related to this chapter. Just type in the keyword:

KEYWORD: HSTBD1

 N S T A

GO TO: www.scilinks.org

Visit the **National Science Teachers Association** on-line Web site for Internet resources related to this chapter. Just type in the *sci*LINKS number for more information about the topic:

TOPIC: Tissues and Organs	*sci*LINKS NUMBER: HSTL530
TOPIC: Body Systems	*sci*LINKS NUMBER: HSTL535
TOPIC: Skeletal System	*sci*LINKS NUMBER: HSTL537
TOPIC: The Muscular System	*sci*LINKS NUMBER: HSTL540
TOPIC: Integumentary System	*sci*LINKS NUMBER: HSTL545

Chapter Review

To complete the following sentences, choose the correct term from each pair of terms listed below:

1. Electrical signals are sent throughout the body by the ___?___ tissue. *(epithelial or nervous)*

2. Your ___?___ system is made up of skin, hair, and nails. *(integumentary or muscular)*

3. Bones are moved by ___?___ muscle. *(smooth or skeletal)*

4. When ___?___ muscles contract, they cause parts of the body to bend. *(extensor or flexor)*

5. Most of the skeleton starts out as ___?___, which is later replaced by bone. *(cartilage or ligaments)*

UNDERSTANDING CONCEPTS

Multiple Choice

6. Which of the following is made up of cells that can contract and relax?
   a. skeletal tissue
   b. muscle tissue
   c. connective tissue
   d. nervous tissue

7. The organ system that provides support and protection for body parts is the
   a. endocrine system.
   b. circulatory system.
   c. skeletal system.
   d. respiratory system.

8. The epidermis is composed of
   a. dermis.
   b. epithelial tissue.
   c. connective tissue.
   d. true skin.

9. The fixed point in a lever is the
   a. effort.
   b. load.
   c. fulcrum.
   d. mechanical advantage.

10. Muscles cause bones to move when
    a. the muscles stretch.
    b. the muscles grow between bones.
    c. the muscles pull on bones.
    d. the muscles push bones apart.

11. Ligaments are the connective tissue that attaches
    a. bones to muscles.
    b. bones to other bones.
    c. muscles to other muscles.
    d. muscles to dermis.

Short Answer

12. Summarize the functions of the four types of tissues, and draw a sketch of each type.

13. How does the skin help protect the body?

14. What is a goose bump?

15. What are two ways skeletal muscle differs from cardiac muscle?

16. How do the functions of the skeletal system relate to the functions of the muscular system?

Concept Mapping

17. Use the following terms to create a concept map: bones, marrow, skeletal system, spongy bone, compact bone, cartilage.

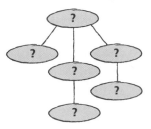

CRITICAL THINKING AND PROBLEM SOLVING

Write one or two sentences to answer the following questions:

18. Why do some muscles not work when a bone is broken?

19. Unlike human bones, some bird bones have air-filled cavities. What advantage does this give birds?

20. Compare the shapes of the bones of the human skull with the shapes of the bones of the human leg. Why is their shape important?

21. Compare the texture and sensitivity of the skin on your elbows with those of the skin on your fingertips. How can you explain the differences?

MATH IN SCIENCE

22. Your muscles make up about 40 percent of your overall mass. What is the muscle mass of a person whose total body mass is 60 kg?

23. The average person blinks 700 times an hour. How many times would the average person blink in a week if he or she were awake for 16 hours each day?

INTERPRETING GRAPHICS

Look at the picture below, and answer the questions that follow.

24. What is *D* called? What type of tissue is most abundant in this layer?

25. What is the name and function of *A*?

26. What is the name and function of *B*?

27. What part of the skin is made up of epithelial tissue that contains dead cells?

28. How does skin help regulate body temperature?

NOW What Do You Think?

Take a minute to review your answers to the ScienceLog questions on page 521. Have your answers changed? If necessary, revise your answers based on what you have learned since you began this chapter.

Science, Technology, and Society

Engineered Skin

Your skin is more than just a well-fitting suit—it's your first line of defense against the outside world. Your skin keeps you safe from dehydration and infection, and the oil glands in your skin keep you waterproof. But what happens when a significant portion of skin is damaged?

More Skin Is the Answer

Sometimes doctors perform a skin graft, transferring some of a person's healthy skin to a damaged area of skin. This is because skin is really the best "bandage" for a wound. It protects the wound but still allows it to breathe. And unlike manufactured cloth or plastic bandages, skin can regenerate itself as it covers a wound. Sometimes, though, a person's skin is so severely damaged (as often occurs in burn victims) that the person doesn't have enough skin to spare.

Tissue Engineering

In the past few years, scientists have been studying tissue engineering to learn more about how the human body heals itself naturally. Using a small piece of young, healthy human skin and some collagen from cows, scientists can now engineer human skin. During the engineering process, cells form the dermal and epidermal layers of skin just as they would if they were still on the body. The living human skin that results can even heal itself if it is cut before it is used for a skin graft. Because it is living, the skin must be kept on a medium that provides it with nutrients until it is placed on a wound. Over time, the color of the grafted skin changes to match the color of the skin that surrounds it.

A Woven Dermis

Tissue engineers have also created another kind of skin, except this one has an unusual dermal

▲ *This is a piece of engineered skin used for grafting.*

and epidermal layer. In this skin, the dermis is made of woven collagen fibers. The wounded area digests these fibers and uses them as a guide to create a new dermis. The epidermal layer is a temporary layer of silicone. It shields the body from infection and protects against dehydration while new skin is being made.

After a new dermal layer forms under the protective silicone epidermis, the body is in better condition to accept a skin graft. Doctors can also graft a thinner portion of skin. A thinner graft is better for the body in the long run because it is easier to take from another part of the body. The new dermal layer also gives the body more time to strengthen on its own before the trauma of transplanting healthy skin to other areas.

On Your Own

▶ In the past, doctors have harvested skin from the bodies of people who, before they died, chose to be organ donors. What kinds of problems could arise if this harvested skin were used on burn victims?

Eureka!

Hairy Oil Spills

Oil and water don't mix, right? Oil floats on the surface of water and is clearly visible to the naked eye. Proving this in your kitchen isn't difficult, nor is it dangerous. But what happens when the water is the ocean and the oil is crude oil? You have an environmental disaster that costs millions of dollars to clean up. The worst example in American waters was in 1989 when the *Exxon Valdez* oil tanker spilled nearly 42 million liters of crude oil into the waters of Prince William Sound on the Alaskan coast.

▲ *Phil McCrory among bags of discarded human hair.*

▲ *This otter was drenched with oil spilled from the* Exxon Valdez.

Backyard Testing

A Huntsville, Alabama, hairdresser asked a brilliant question when he saw an otter whose fur was drenched with oil from the *Valdez* spill. If the otter's fur soaked up all the oil, why wouldn't human hair do the same? The hairdresser, Phil McCrory, gathered hair from the floor of his salon and took it home to perform his own experiments. He stuffed 2.2 kg of hair into a pair of his wife's pantyhose and tied the ankles together to form a bagel-shaped bundle. After filling his son's wading pool with water, McCrory floated the bundle in the pool. Next, McCrory poured used motor oil into the center of the ring. When he pulled the ring closed, not a drop of oil remained in the water!

How Does Hair Do This?

What McCrory discovered was that hair *adsorbs* oil instead of *absorbing* it. To adsorb means to collect a liquid or gas in layers on a surface. Because tiny cuticles cover every hair shaft like fish scales, the oil can bind to the surface of hair. Compare this process with the way a sponge works. A sponge completely absorbs a liquid. This means it is wet throughout, not just on the surface.

McCrory approached the National Aeronautics and Space Administration (NASA) with his discovery. In controlled tests performed by NASA, hair proved to be the fastest adsorber around. A little more than 1 kg of hair can adsorb over 3.5 L of oil in just 2 minutes!

It is estimated that within a week, 64 million kilograms of hair in reusable mesh pillows could have soaked up *all* of the oil spilled by the *Valdez.* Unfortunately, the $2 billion spent on the cleanup removed only about 12 percent of the spill. Did you ever think that the hair from your head could have a purpose beyond keeping your head warm?

Compare the Facts

▶ Research how McCrory's discovery compares with the methods currently used to clean up oil spills. Share your findings with the class.

23 Circulation and Respiration

This Really Happened . . .

The human heart is normally a very dependable organ. It may beat more than 100,000 times per day for a person's entire life. During this time it pumps millions of liters of blood through the body. When there is a serious problem with the heart, it is life threatening.

In the past, heart failure resulted in immediate death. But in 1969, Dr. Denton Cooley, of the Texas Heart Institute, kept a patient alive for 5 days after the patient's heart failed. How did he do it? He used an artificial heart that he designed himself.

The design of artificial hearts has improved considerably since Dr. Cooley's first model. The electric artificial heart shown above right

is one of the more recent test models. Its mass is about 680 g—only a little heavier than a real human heart. Newer test models are even smaller and lighter. These artificial hearts have special sensors and microprocessors that regulate the beat and respond to changes in blood pressure.

Currently, there is no artificial heart that can permanently replace the human heart. The human heart is a sophisticated organ that serves the cardiovascular system, one of the body's pathways for circulating fluids. In this chapter you will also read about the lymphatic system and the respiratory system and how all of these systems are related.

Investigate!

Exercise and Your Heart

How does your heart respond to exercise? You can determine this by measuring how fast your heart beats before and after exercise. Your heart pumps blood through your blood vessels. With each heartbeat, your blood vessels expand and then return to their original position. This produces a throbbing called a *pulse.* You can take your pulse by placing your index and middle fingers on the inside of your wrist just below your thumb.

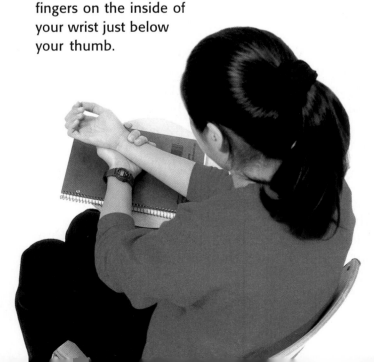

Procedure

1. Take your pulse while remaining still. Using a **watch with a second hand,** count the number of beats in 15 seconds. Then multiply this number by four to calculate the number of beats in 1 minute.

$$\text{Number of beats in 15 seconds} \times 4 = \text{Number of beats in 1 minute}$$

2. Do jumping jacks or jog in place for 30 seconds, and then stop and calculate your heart rate again.
   Caution: Do not perform this exercise if you have difficulty breathing, have high blood pressure, or get dizzy easily.

3. After resting for 5 minutes, determine your pulse again.

Analysis

4. How did exercise affect your heart rate? Why do you think this happened?

5. Why do you think your heart rate returned to normal after you rested?

Circulation and Respiration **545**

Terms to Learn

cardiovascular
  system
blood
arteries
capillaries
veins

pulmonary
  circulation
systemic
  circulation
blood pressure

What You'll Do

◆ Describe the functions of the cardiovascular system.
◆ Compare and contrast the three types of blood vessels.
◆ Describe the path that blood travels as it circulates through the body.
◆ Distinguish between blood types.

The Cardiovascular System

When you hear the word *heart,* what do you think of first? Many people think of romance. But the heart is much more than a symbol of love. It's the pump that drives your cardiovascular system. The **cardiovascular system** transports materials to and from your cells. The word *cardio* means "heart," and the word *vascular* means "vessel." The cardiovascular system, which is shown in **Figure 1,** is made up of three parts: blood, the heart, and blood vessels.

What Is Blood?

The human body contains about 5 L of blood. **Blood** is a connective tissue made up of two types of cells, cell parts, and plasma. *Plasma* is the fluid part of blood. It is a mixture of water, minerals, nutrients, sugars, proteins, and other substances. Red blood cells, white blood cells, and platelets float in the plasma.

**Figure 1
The Cardiovascular System**

Figure 2 *Red blood cells deliver oxygen.*

Red Blood Cells Red blood cells, or RBCs, are the most abundant cells in blood. RBCs, shown in **Figure 2,** supply your cells with oxygen. As you have learned, cells need oxygen to carry out cellular respiration. Each RBC contains a protein called *hemoglobin* (HEE moh GLOH bin). Hemoglobin, which gives RBCs their red color, clings to the oxygen you inhale. This allows RBCs to transport oxygen throughout the body. The shape of RBCs gives them a large amount of surface area for absorbing and releasing oxygen.

RBCs are made in the bone marrow. Before RBCs enter the bloodstream, they lose their nucleus and other organelles. Without a nucleus, which contains DNA, the RBCs cannot replace worn-out proteins. RBCs therefore can live only about 4 months.

White Blood Cells Sometimes *pathogens*—bacteria, viruses, and other microscopic particles that can make you sick—are able to enter your body. When they do, they often encounter your white blood cells, or WBCs. WBCs, shown in **Figure 3,** help you stay healthy by destroying pathogens and helping to clean wounds.

WBCs fight pathogens in several ways. Some squeeze out of vessels and move around in tissues, searching for pathogens. When they find a pathogen, they engulf it. Other WBCs release chemicals called *antibodies,* which help destroy pathogens. WBCs also keep you healthy by engulfing body cells that have died or been damaged. WBCs are made in bone marrow. Some of them mature in lymphatic organs, which will be discussed later.

Platelets Drifting among the blood cells are tiny particles called platelets. *Platelets* are pieces of larger cells found in bone marrow. These larger cells remain in the bone marrow, but they pinch off fragments of themselves, which enter the blood. Although platelets last for only 5 to 10 days, they are an important part of blood. When you cut or scrape your skin, you bleed because blood vessels have been opened. As soon as bleeding occurs, platelets begin to clump together in the damaged area and form a plug that helps reduce blood loss, as shown in **Figure 4.** Platelets also release a variety of chemicals that react with proteins in the plasma and cause tiny fibers to form. The fibers create a blood clot.

Figure 3 *White blood cells defend the body against pathogens. These white blood cells have been colored yellow to make their shape easier to see.*

Figure 4 *Platelets release chemicals in damaged vessels and cause fibers to form. The fibers make a "net" that traps blood cells and stops bleeding.*

Red blood cell

Platelet

Fibers

Figure 5 *The heart is a four-chambered organ that pumps blood through cardiovascular vessels. The vessels carrying oxygen-rich blood are shown in red. The vessels carrying oxygen-poor blood are shown in blue.*

Right atrium

Left atrium

Valves

Valves

Right ventricle

Left ventricle

Have a Heart

Your heart is a muscular organ about the size of your fist. It is found in the center of your chest cavity. The heart pumps oxygen-poor blood to the lungs and oxygen-rich blood to the body. Like the hearts of all mammals, your heart has a left side and a right side that are separated by a thick wall. As you can see in **Figure 5,** each side has an upper chamber and a lower chamber. Each upper chamber is called an *atrium* (plural, *atria*). Each lower chamber is called a *ventricle.*

Flaplike structures called *valves* are located between the atria and ventricles and also where large arteries are attached to the heart. As blood moves through the heart, the valves close and prevent blood from going backward. The lub-dub, lub-dub sound that a beating heart makes is caused by the closing of the valves. The flow of blood through the heart is shown in the diagram below.

The Flow of Blood Through the Heart

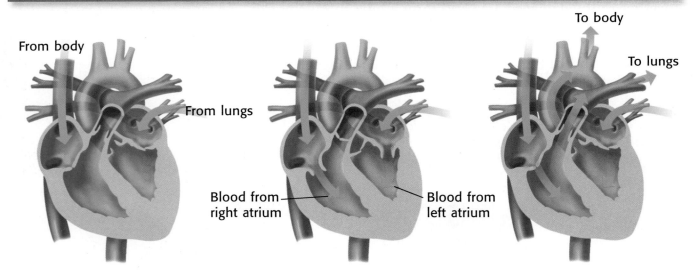

From body

From lungs

Blood from right atrium

Blood from left atrium

To body

To lungs

1 Blood enters the atria first. The left atrium receives oxygen-rich blood from the lungs. The right atrium receives oxygen-poor blood from the body.

2 When the atria contract, blood is squeezed into the ventricles.

3 While the atria relax, the ventricles contract and push blood out of the heart. Blood from the right ventricle goes to the lungs. Blood from the left ventricle goes to the rest of the body.

Blood Vessels

Blood travels throughout your body in blood vessels. A blood vessel is a hollow tube that transports blood. There are three types of blood vessels—arteries, capillaries, and veins. Their structures and their relationship to each other are shown in **Figure 6.**

Figure 6 *Large arteries branch into smaller arteries, which branch into capillaries. Capillaries join small veins, which join to form large veins.*

To heart

From heart

Vein

Capillaries

Artery

Arteries **Arteries** are blood vessels that direct blood away from the heart. Arteries have thick elastic walls that contain a layer of smooth muscle. Each time the heart beats, blood is pumped out of the heart at high pressure. The thick walls of arteries have the strength to withstand this pressure. The rhythmic change in blood pressure is called a *pulse.*

Capillaries A strand of hair is about 10 times wider than a capillary. **Capillaries** are the smallest blood vessels in your body. Capillary walls are only one cell thick. As shown in **Figure 7,** capillaries are so narrow that blood cells must pass through them in single file. The simple structure of a capillary allows nutrients, oxygen, and many other kinds of substances to diffuse easily through capillary walls. No cell in the body is more than three or four cells away from a capillary.

Veins After leaving capillaries, the blood enters veins. **Veins** are blood vessels that direct the blood back to the heart. As blood travels through veins, valves keep the blood from flowing backward. When skeletal muscles contract, they squeeze nearby veins and help push blood toward the heart.

Figure 7 *These red blood cells are traveling through a capillary.*

BRAIN FOOD

If all the blood vessels in your body were strung together, the total length would be more than twice the circumference of the Earth.

Going with the Flow

As you read earlier, one important function of your blood is to supply the cells of your body with oxygen. Where does blood get this oxygen? It gets it from your lungs during pulmonary circulation. **Pulmonary circulation** is the circulation of blood between your heart and lungs.

When oxygen-rich blood returns to the heart from the lungs, it must be pumped to the rest of the body. The circulation of blood between the heart and the rest of the body is called **systemic circulation.** Both types of circulation are diagramed below.

The Flow of Blood Through the Body

The right ventricle pumps oxygen-poor blood into arteries that lead to the lungs. These are the only arteries in the body that carry oxygen-poor blood.

In the capillaries of the lungs, blood absorbs oxygen and releases carbon dioxide. Oxygen-rich blood travels through veins to the left atrium. These are the only veins in the body that carry oxygen-rich blood.

Pulmonary circulation

Oxygen-poor blood travels back to the heart and is delivered into the right atrium by two large veins.

Systemic circulation

The heart pumps oxygen-rich blood from the left ventricle into arteries and then into capillaries.

As blood travels through capillaries, it transports oxygen, nutrients, and water to the cells of the body. At the same time, waste materials and carbon dioxide are carried away.

Blood Flows Under Pressure

When you run water through a hose, you can feel the hose stiffen as the water pushes against the inside of the hose. Blood has the same effect on your blood vessels. The force exerted by blood on the inside walls of a blood vessel is called **blood pressure.**

Like the man shown in **Figure 8,** many people get their blood pressure checked on a regular basis. Blood pressure is reported in millimeters (mm) of mercury, Hg. A blood pressure of 120 mm Hg means the pressure on the vessel walls is great enough to push a narrow column of mercury 120 mm high.

A normal blood pressure is about 120/80. The first number is called the systolic pressure. *Systolic pressure* is the pressure inside large arteries when the ventricles contract. As you read earlier, the surge of blood causes the arteries to bulge and produce a pulse. The second number is called the diastolic pressure. *Diastolic pressure* is the pressure in the arteries when the ventricles relax.

Figure 8 *This nurse is measuring a patient's blood pressure. Consistently high or low blood pressure may suggest a problem with the cardiovascular system.*

Exercise and Blood Flow

When you exercise, your muscles require much more oxygen and nutrients. To solve this problem, the heart beats faster. Physical activity causes as much as 10 times more blood to be sent to the muscles than when your body is at rest.

During exercise, some organs do not need as much blood as the skeletal muscles do. Less blood is sent to the kidneys and the digestive system so that more blood can go to the skeletal muscles, brain, heart, and lungs. This is like turning off certain water faucets in a house to allow more water to flow through other faucets.

REVIEW

1. What is the function of the cardiovascular system?

2. What are the three kinds of blood vessels? Compare their functions.

3. **Identifying Relationships** How is the structure of capillaries related to their function?

Activity

Imagine that you are a scientist that has been chosen to explore the cardiovascular system. After being shrunk down to the size of a red blood cell, you board a miniature submarine and begin your travels. Describe where you go and what you see.

TRY at HOME

What's Your Blood Type?

When a person loses a lot of blood, the person is given blood that has been donated from someone else. The person receiving the blood cannot be given blood from just anyone because people have different blood types. It's safe to mix some blood types, but mixing others causes a person's RBCs to clump together. The clumped cells may form blood clots, which block blood vessels, causing death.

Every person has one of the following blood types: A, B, AB, or O. Your blood type refers to the type of chemicals you have on the surface of your RBCs. These chemicals are called *antigens*. Type A blood has A antigens; type B has B antigens; and type AB has both A and B antigens. Type O blood has neither the A nor B antigen.

To Mix or Not to Mix Different blood types not only have different chemicals on their RBC surfaces but also may have different chemicals in their plasma, the liquid part of blood. These chemicals are *antibodies*. When antibodies bind to RBCs, they cause the RBCs to clump together.

As shown in **Figure 9,** the body makes antibodies against the antigens that are not on its own RBCs. For example, people with type B blood make A antibodies, which attack any blood cell with an A antigen on it. Therefore, people with type B blood can't be given type A or AB blood. Type O blood can be given to anyone because its RBCs don't have any A or B antigens on their surface. A person with type O blood is therefore said to be a *universal donor*. People with type AB blood are *universal recipients*, meaning they can receive any type of blood because they do not make any antibodies against A or B antigens.

Figure 9 *This table shows which antigens and antibodies may be present in each blood type.*

Blood Delivery

A young woman is brought into the emergency room and needs a blood transfusion. Her blood type is AB. You call the blood bank to order AB blood, but you are told the bank is out of that type. What other type or types could the blood bank deliver for her transfusion?

Cardiovascular Problems

When something is wrong with a person's cardiovascular system, the person's health will be affected. Some cardiovascular problems involve the heart and the blood vessels, while other problems affect the blood. Cardiovascular problems can be caused by smoking, high levels of cholesterol in blood, stress, heredity, and other factors.

Atherosclerosis The leading cause of death in the United States is a cardiovascular disease called *atherosclerosis* (ATH uhr OH skluh ROH sis). Atherosclerosis occurs when fatty materials, such as cholesterol, build up on the inside of blood vessels. The fatty buildup causes the blood vessels to become narrower and less elastic. **Figure 10** shows how the pathway through a blood vessel can become clogged. When a major artery that supplies blood to the heart becomes blocked, a person has a heart attack, and part of the heart can die.

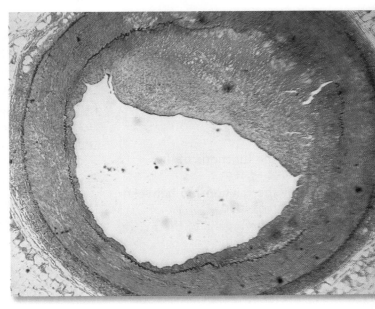

Figure 10 *Atherosclerosis is a common cardiovascular problem. Fatty deposits build up on the inside of blood vessels and block blood flow.*

A Point About Pressure Atherosclerosis also promotes *hypertension,* which is abnormally high blood pressure. Hypertension is dangerous because it overworks the heart and can weaken vessels and make them rupture. If a blood vessel in the brain becomes clogged or ruptures, certain parts of the brain will not receive oxygen and nutrients and may die. This is called a *stroke*.

MATH BREAK

The Beat Goes On

Your heart beats about 100,800 times per day. How many times does it beat per year?

REVIEW

1. Where does blood travel to and from during pulmonary circulation? during systemic circulation?

2. What happens to the oxygen level in blood as it moves through the lungs?

3. **Applying Concepts** Billy has type A blood.
   a. What kind of antigens does he have on his RBCs?
   b. What blood-type antibodies can Billy make?
   c. Which blood types could be given to Billy if he needed a transfusion?

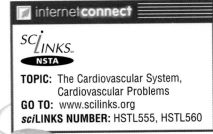

internet**connect**

SciLINKS.
NSTA

TOPIC: The Cardiovascular System, Cardiovascular Problems
GO TO: www.scilinks.org
*sci*LINKS NUMBER: HSTL555, HSTL560

The Lymphatic System

Terms to Learn

lymphatic system   thymus
lymph   spleen
lymph nodes   tonsils

What You'll Do

◆ Discuss the functions of the lymphatic system.
◆ Identify the relationship between lymph and blood.
◆ Describe the organs of the lymphatic system.

Your cardiovascular system is not the only circulatory system in your body. As blood flows through your cardiovascular system, fluid leaks out of the capillaries and mixes with the fluid that bathes your cells. Most of the fluid is reabsorbed by the capillaries, but some is not. To deal with this, your body's **lymphatic system** collects the excess fluid and returns it to your blood.

In addition to collecting the excess fluid surrounding your cells and returning it to your blood, your lymphatic system helps your body fight pathogens. Pathogens are microorganisms and viruses that make you sick.

Vessels of the Lymphatic System

The fluid collected by the lymphatic system is transported through vessels. The smallest vessels of the lymphatic system are *lymph capillaries.* From the spaces between cells, lymph capillaries absorb fluid and any particles too large to enter the blood capillaries. Some of these particles are dead cells or cells that are foreign to the body. The fluid and particles absorbed into lymph capillaries are called **lymph.**

As shown in **Figure 11,** lymph capillaries carry lymph into *lymphatic vessels,* which are larger vessels that have valves. Lymph is not pushed by a pump. Instead, the squeezing of skeletal muscles provides the force to move lymph through vessels, and valves help prevent backflow. Lymph travels through your lymphatic system and then drains into large neck veins of the cardiovascular system.

✓ **Self-Check**

How are the lymphatic system and the cardiovascular system similar? How are they different? *(See page 782 to check your answer.)*

Figure 11 *The white arrows show the movement of lymph into lymph capillaries and through lymphatic vessels.*

Lymphatic Organs

In addition to vessels and capillaries, a variety of other organs are part of the lymphatic system, as shown in **Figure 12.**

Lymph Nodes As lymph travels through lymphatic vessels, it passes through lymph nodes. **Lymph nodes** are small bean-shaped organs where particles, such as pathogens or dead cells, are removed from the lymph.

Lymph nodes contain many white blood cells. Some of these cells engulf pathogens. Other WBCs produce chemicals that become attached to pathogens and mark them for destruction. When the body becomes infected with bacteria or viruses, the WBCs multiply and the nodes sometimes become swollen and painful.

Thymus Your **thymus,** which is located just above your heart, releases WBCs. The WBCs travel to other areas of the lymphatic system.

Spleen The largest lymph organ is your spleen, which is located in the upper left side of your abdomen. The **spleen** filters blood and, like the thymus, releases WBCs. When red blood cells are squeezed through the spleen's capillaries, the older and more fragile cells rupture. The RBCs are broken down, and some of their parts are reused. For this reason, the spleen can be thought of as the red-blood-cell recycling center.

Tonsils **Tonsils** are made up of groups of lymphatic tissue located at the back of your nasal cavity, on the inside of your throat, and at the back of your tongue. WBCs in the tonsils defend the body against infection. Tonsils sometimes become badly infected and must be removed.

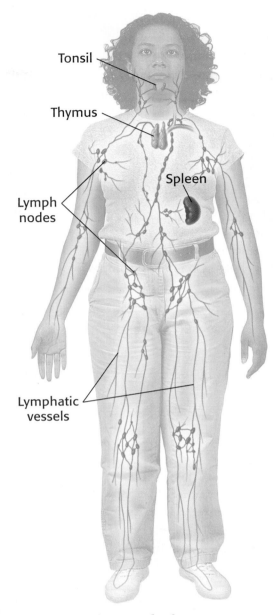

Figure 12 The Lymphatic System

REVIEW

1. What are the main functions of the lymphatic system?

2. Where does lymph go when it leaves the lymphatic system?

3. **Identifying Relationships** How are lymph nodes similar to the spleen?

internet**connect**

SC*i*LINKS
NSTA

TOPIC: The Lymphatic System
GO TO: www.scilinks.org
sciLINKS NUMBER: HSTL565

The Respiratory System

What You'll Do

◆ Describe the flow of air through the respiratory system.
◆ Discuss the relationship between the respiratory system and the cardiovascular system.
◆ Identify respiratory disorders.

Breathing. You do it all the time. You're doing it right now. You hardly ever think about it, though, unless your ability to breathe is suddenly taken away. Then it becomes all too obvious that you must breathe in order to survive. Why is breathing important?

Out with the Bad Air; In with the Good

Your body needs a continuous supply of oxygen in order to obtain energy from the foods you eat. That's where breathing comes in handy. The air you breathe is a mixture of several gases. One of these gases is oxygen. When you breathe, your body takes in air and absorbs the oxygen. Then carbon dioxide from your body is added to the air, and the stale air is exhaled.

The words *breathing* and *respiration* are often thought to mean the same thing. However, breathing is only one part of respiration. **Respiration** is the entire process by which a body obtains and uses oxygen and gets rid of carbon dioxide and water. Respiration is divided into two parts: breathing, which involves inhaling and exhaling, and cellular respiration, which involves the chemical reactions that release energy from food.

Breathing: Brought to You by Your Respiratory System

Breathing is made possible by the respiratory system. The **respiratory system** consists of the lungs, throat, and passageways that lead to the lungs. **Figure 13** shows the parts of the respiratory system.

Nose Your nose is the primary passageway into and out of the respiratory system. Air is inhaled through the nose, where it comes into contact with warm, moist surfaces. Air can also enter and leave through the mouth.

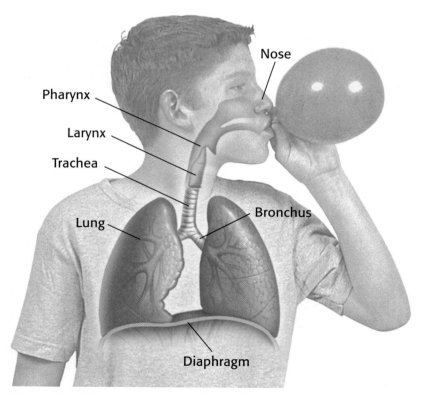

Nose
Pharynx
Larynx
Trachea
Lung
Bronchus
Diaphragm

Figure 13 *Air moves into and out of the body through the respiratory system.*

Pharynx From the nose, air flows into the **pharynx** (FER ingks), or throat. You can use a mirror to see the walls of your pharynx behind your tongue. In addition to air, food and drink also travel through the pharynx on the way to the stomach. The pharynx branches into two tubes. One leads to the stomach and is called the esophagus. The other leads to the lungs and is called the larynx.

Larynx Tilt your head up slightly, and rub a finger up and down the front of your throat. The ridges you feel are the outside of the larynx (LER ingks). The **larynx,** or voice box, contains the vocal cords. The vocal cords are a pair of elastic bands that are stretched across the opening of the larynx. Muscles attached to the larynx control how much the vocal cords are stretched. When air flows between the vocal cords, they vibrate and make sound.

Trachea The larynx guards the entrance to a large tube called the **trachea** (TRAY kee uh), or windpipe. The trachea is the passageway for air traveling from the larynx to the lungs.

Bronchi The trachea splits into two tubes called **bronchi** (BRAHNG kie) (singular, *bronchus*). One bronchus goes to each lung and branches into thousands of tiny tubes called *bronchioles*.

Lungs Your body has two large spongelike lungs. In the lungs, each bronchiole branches to form thousands of tiny sacs called **alveoli** (singular, *alveolus*). Capillaries surround each alveolus. **Figure 14** shows the arrangement of the tubes in the respiratory system.

Chemistry CONNECTION

When people who live at low elevations travel to the mountains, they usually find that they have difficulty exerting themselves. This is because the concentration of oxygen in the air at high elevations is lower than that at low elevations. Until they become used to the change, people have to take more breaths to supply their bodies with the oxygen they need.

Figure 14 *Inside your lungs, the bronchi branch into bronchioles. The bronchioles lead to tiny sacs called alveoli.*

Bronchus

Trachea

Bronchiole

Alveoli

Capillary

How Do You Breathe?

When you breathe, air is sucked in or forced out of your lungs. However, your lungs do not contain muscles that force air in and out. Instead, breathing is done by rib muscles and the *diaphragm,* a dome-shaped muscle underneath the lungs. When the diaphragm contracts and moves down, it increases the chest cavity's volume. At the same time, some of your rib muscles contract and lift your rib cage, causing it to expand. Air is sucked in.

What Happens to the Oxygen? When oxygen has been absorbed by red blood cells, it is transported through the body by the cardiovascular system. Oxygen diffuses inside cells, where it is used in an important chemical reaction known as cellular respiration. During *cellular respiration,* oxygen is used to release energy stored in molecules of carbohydrates, fats, and proteins. When the molecules are broken apart during the reaction, energy is released along with carbon dioxide and water. The carbon dioxide and water leave the cell and return to the bloodstream. The carbon dioxide is carried to the lungs and exhaled. **Figure 15** shows how breathing and blood circulation are related.

LabBook

Would you like to linger longer on lungs? Then look at page 766.

Figure 15 *Blood has an important role in respiration.*

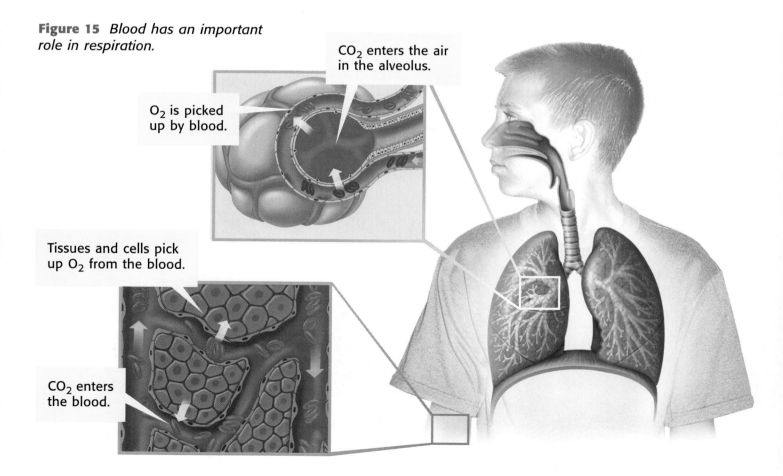

CO$_2$ enters the air in the alveolus.

O$_2$ is picked up by blood.

Tissues and cells pick up O$_2$ from the blood.

CO$_2$ enters the blood.

Respiratory Disorders

Millions of people suffer from respiratory disorders. There are many types of respiratory disorders, including asthma, bronchitis, pneumonia, and emphysema.

In *asthma,* irritants cause tissue around the bronchioles to constrict and secrete large amounts of mucus. As the bronchiole tubes get narrower, the person has difficulty breathing. *Bronchitis* can develop when something irritates the lining of the bronchioles. *Pneumonia* is caused by bacteria or viruses that grow inside the bronchioles and alveoli and cause them to become inflamed and filled with fluid. If the alveoli are filled with too much fluid, the person may suffocate.

The Hazards of Smoking You probably already know that smoking cigarettes is bad for your health. In fact, smoking is the leading cause of cardiovascular diseases and lung diseases, such as *emphysema* and *lung cancer.* People with emphysema have trouble getting the oxygen they need because their lung tissue erodes away, as shown in **Figure 16.**

Why Do People Snore?

Get a **15 cm² sheet of wax paper.** Hum your favorite song. Then take the wax paper, press it against your lips, and hum the song again. Now answer the following questions:

1. How was your humming different when wax paper was pressed to your mouth?

2. Use your observations to guess what might cause snoring.

TRY at HOME

Figure 16 The photo on the left shows healthy lungs. The photo on the right shows the lungs of a person who had emphysema.

REVIEW

1. Describe the path that air travels as it moves through the respiratory system.

2. What is the difference between respiration and cellular respiration?

3. **Identifying Relationships** How is the function of the respiratory system related to that of the cardiovascular system?

internet**connect**

SC*L*INKS
NSTA

TOPIC: The Respiratory System, Respiratory Disorders
GO TO: www.scilinks.org
*sci***LINKS NUMBER:** HSTL570, HSTL575

Chapter Highlights

SECTION 1

Vocabulary

cardiovascular system (*p. 546*)
blood (*p. 546*)
arteries (*p. 549*)
capillaries (*p. 549*)
veins (*p. 549*)
pulmonary circulation (*p. 550*)
systemic circulation (*p. 550*)
blood pressure (*p. 551*)

Section Notes

- The cardiovascular system delivers oxygen and nutrients to the body's cells, takes away the cells' waste products, and helps the body stay healthy. The cardiovascular system is made up of blood, the heart, and blood vessels.

- Blood is a connective tissue made of plasma, red blood cells, white blood cells, and platelets. The heart is a muscular organ that pumps blood through blood vessels.

- Blood moves away from the heart through arteries and then enters capillaries. After leaving capillaries, blood is carried back to the heart through veins.

- In pulmonary circulation, blood vessels carry blood from the heart to the lungs and back to the heart. In systemic circulation, blood flows from the heart to the rest of the body and then back to the heart.

- People have different blood types. Blood type is determined by the presence of certain chemicals on red blood cells.

SECTION 2

Vocabulary

lymphatic system (*p. 554*)
lymph (*p. 554*)
lymph nodes (*p. 555*)
thymus (*p. 555*)
spleen (*p. 555*)
tonsils (*p. 555*)

Section Notes

- The lymphatic system returns excess fluid to the cardiovascular system and helps the body fight infections.

- The lymphatic system includes lymph, lymph capillaries, lymphatic vessels, lymph nodes, the spleen, tonsils, and the thymus.

☑ Skills Check

Math Concepts

A CONTINUOUS BEAT Your heart beats about 100,800 times per day. That means that your heart beats about 4,200 times every hour.

100,800 beats ÷ 24 hours = 4,200 beats

That also means that your heart beats about 70 times every minute.

4,200 beats ÷ 60 minutes = 70 beats

Visual Understanding

AIR PASSAGEWAYS Take another look at Figure 13 on page 556. With your finger, trace the path air takes to reach the lungs. As you do this, reconsider what roles the nose, pharynx, trachea, bronchi, lungs, and diaphragm play in respiration.

Vocabulary

respiration *(p. 556)*

respiratory system *(p. 556)*

pharynx *(p. 557)*

larynx *(p. 557)*

trachea *(p. 557)*

bronchi *(p. 557)*

alveoli *(p. 557)*

Section Notes

- The respiratory system moves air into and out of the body. The respiratory system includes the nose, the mouth, the pharynx, the larynx, the trachea, and the lungs.

- Air enters the lungs through bronchi and travels to the alveoli, which are gas-filled sacs surrounded by capillaries of the cardiovascular system.

- The blood in the capillaries of the lungs absorbs oxygen and releases carbon dioxide. The carbon dioxide is exhaled. The oxygen is carried by the blood to the heart and then on to the cells of the body.

- The body's cells must have oxygen to carry out cellular respiration. Cellular respiration is a chemical process that releases the energy in carbohydrates, fats, and proteins and makes the energy available to the cells.

- Inhaling and exhaling are caused by the contraction and relaxation of the diaphragm and the muscles of the rib cage.

Labs

Build a Lung *(p. 766)*

Carbon Dioxide Breath *(p. 767)*

---

internet connect

GO TO: go.hrw.com

Visit the **HRW** Web site for a variety of learning tools related to this chapter. Just type in the keyword:

KEYWORD: HSTBD2

SCLINKS SM

N S T A

GO TO: www.scilinks.org

Visit the **National Science Teachers Association** on-line Web site for Internet resources related to this chapter. Just type in the *sci*LINKS number for more information about the topic:

TOPIC: The Cardiovascular System	*sci*LINKS NUMBER: HSTL555
TOPIC: Cardiovascular Problems	*sci*LINKS NUMBER: HSTL560
TOPIC: The Lymphatic System	*sci*LINKS NUMBER: HSTL565
TOPIC: The Respiratory System	*sci*LINKS NUMBER: HSTL570
TOPIC: Respiratory Disorders	*sci*LINKS NUMBER: HSTL575

Chapter Review

USING VOCABULARY

To complete the following sentences, choose the correct term from each pair of terms listed below:

1. Oxygen is delivered to the cells of the body by __?__. (*white blood cells* or *red blood cells*)

2. Blood is carried away from the heart in __?__. (*arteries* or *veins*)

3. __?__ carries nutrients to the body's cells. (*Lymph* or *Blood*)

4. The __?__ contains the vocal cords. (*trachea* or *larynx*)

5. The pathway of air through the respiratory system ends at the tiny sacs called __?__. (*alveoli* or *bronchi*)

UNDERSTANDING CONCEPTS

Multiple Choice

6. Blood from the lungs enters the heart at the
   a. left ventricle.
   b. left atrium.
   c. right atrium.
   d. right ventricle.

7. Blood cells are made
   a. in the heart.
   b. from plasma.
   c. from lymph.
   d. in the bones.

8. Which of the following is not part of the lymphatic system?
   a. trachea
   b. lymph node
   c. thymus
   d. spleen

9. Alveoli are surrounded by
   a. veins.
   b. muscles.
   c. capillaries.
   d. lymph nodes.

10. What prevents blood from flowing backward in veins?
    a. platelets
    b. valves
    c. muscles
    d. cartilage

11. Air moves into the lungs when the diaphragm muscle
    a. contracts and moves down.
    b. contracts and moves up.
    c. relaxes and moves down.
    d. relaxes and moves up.

Short Answer

12. What is the difference between pulmonary circulation and systemic circulation in the cardiovascular system?

13. Walton has a blood pressure of 110/65. What do the two numbers mean?

14. What body process produces the carbon dioxide you exhale?

Concept Map

15. Use the following terms to create a concept map: blood, oxygen, alveoli, capillaries, carbon dioxide.

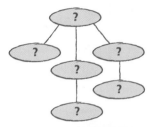

CRITICAL THINKING AND PROBLEM SOLVING

Write one or two sentences to answer the following questions:

16. Why do you think there are hairs in your nose?

17. When a person is not feeling well, sometimes a doctor will examine samples of the person's blood to see how many white blood cells are present. Why would this information be useful?

18. How is the function of the lymphatic system related to the function of the cardiovascular system?

MATH IN SCIENCE

19. After a person donates blood, the blood is stored in one-pint bags until it is needed for a transfusion. A healthy person normally has 5 million RBCs in each cubic millimeter (1 mm^3) of blood.

    a. How many RBCs are there in 1 mL of blood? One milliliter is equal to 1 cm^3 and to 1,000 mm^3.

    b. How many RBCs are there in 1 pt? One pint is equal to 473 mL.

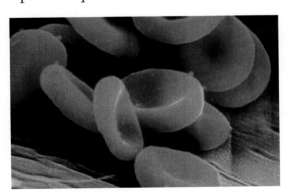

INTERPRETING GRAPHICS

The diagram below shows how the human heart would look in cross section. Examine the diagram, and then answer the questions that follow:

20. Which letter identifies the chamber that receives blood from systemic circulation? What is this chamber's name?

21. Which letter identifies the chamber that receives blood from the lungs? What is this chamber's name?

22. Which letter identifies the chamber that pumps blood to the lungs? What is this chamber's name?

NOW What Do You Think?

Take a minute to review your answers to the ScienceLog questions on page 545. Have your answers changed? If necessary, revise your answers based on what you have learned since you began this chapter.

CATCHING A LIGHT SNEEZE

Do you sneeze when you come out of a dark movie theater into bright sunlight? If not, look around you next time. Chances are several people will sneeze.

Reflex Gone Wrong

For some reason, about one in five people sneeze when they step from a dimly lit area into a brightly lit area. In fact, some may sneeze a dozen times or more! Fortunately, the sneezing usually stops after a few times. This reaction is called a *photic sneeze reflex.* No one knows for certain why it happens.

Normal sneezing is a reflex, which means you do it without thinking about it. Most people sneeze when something tickles the inside of their nose. They sneeze, and moving air pushes the tickling intruder out. For instance, if you get dust in your nose, sneezing pushes the dust out. In the case of people with the photic sneeze, it's a reflex gone wrong.

ACHOO!

A few years ago, some geneticists studied the photic sneeze reflex. They named it the Autosomal Dominant Compelling Helio-ophthalmic Outburst syndrome, or the ACHOO syndrome. Scientists know that the ACHOO syndrome runs in families. So the photic sneeze can be passed from parent to child. Sometimes even the number of times in a row that each person sneezes is the same throughout a family.

Possible Answers

Some scientists have offered a possible explanation for the ACHOO syndrome. First, everyone's pupils contract when they

▲ *Do you sneeze when you see bright light after exiting a dark room?*

encounter bright light. And the nerves from the eyes are right next to the nerves from the nose. Thus, people with the ACHOO syndrome may have their wires slightly crossed: bright light triggers the pupil reflex, and it also triggers the sneeze reflex!

Sneeze Fest

Sunlight is not the only strange trigger for sudden sneezes. Some people sneeze when they rub the inner corner of their eye. Others sneeze when tweezing their eyebrows or brushing their hair. In rare individuals, even eating too much has been known to cause sneezing fits!

Research the Facts

▶ Yawning is also a reflex. Do some research to find out why we yawn.

Health

Goats to the Rescue

They're called transgenic (tranz JEHN ik) goats because their cells contain a human gene. They look just like any other goats, but because of their human gene they produce a chemical that can save lives.

Lifesaving Genes

Heart attacks are the number one cause of death in the United States. Many heart attacks are triggered when large blood clots interfere with the flow of blood to the heart. Human blood cells produce a chemical called *tissue plasminogen activator* (TPA) that dissolves small blood clots. If TPA is given to a person having a heart attack, it can often dissolve the blood clot, stop the attack, and save the person's life. But TPA is difficult to produce in large quantities in the laboratory. This is where the goats come in. Researchers at Tufts University, in Grafton, Massachusetts, have genetically engineered goats to produce this lifesaving drug.

Hybrid Goats

Producing transgenic goats is a complicated process. First, fertilized eggs are surgically removed from normal female goats. The eggs are then injected with hybrid genes that consist of human TPA genes "spliced" into genes from the mammary glands of a goat. Finally, the altered eggs are surgically implanted into female goats, where they develop into young goats, or kids. Some of the kids actually carry the hybrid gene. When the hybrid kids mature, the females' milk contains TPA. Technicians then separate the TPA from the goats' milk for use in heart-attack victims.

The Research Continues

Transgenic research in farm animals such as goats, sheep, cows, and pigs may someday produce drugs faster, cheaper, and in greater quantities than are possible using current methods. The way we view the barnyard may never be the same.

Find Out for Yourself

▶ Using chemicals produced by transgenic animals is just one of many gene therapies. Do some research to find out more about gene therapy, how it is used, and how it may be used in the future.

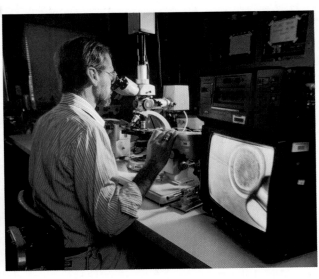

▲ *A scientist at Tufts University injects human TPA genes into fertilized goat eggs.*

24 The Digestive and Urinary Systems

This Really Happened . . .

In 1822, a Canadian fur trader named Alexis St. Martin accidentally shot himself in his left side. An army surgeon named Dr. William Beaumont was able to save St. Martin's life, but the wound never completely healed. A hole approximately 6 cm in diameter remained open in his side, leading through skin and muscle right into his stomach.

Dr. Beaumont seized the opportunity to perform some amazing experiments. To find out what happens to food in the stomach, Dr. Beaumont tied different kinds of food onto strings and inserted them into the opening. He watched the stomach squeeze and relax as it digested the bits of food. When he removed the food, he could see that it had changed. He also found that food changed when he placed it in a test tube with juices from St. Martin's stomach. Beaumont was able to determine that the stomach's juices, not just its squeezing action, were responsible for turning the food to mush.

What began as an unfortunate accident for Alexis St. Martin ended up helping Dr. Beaumont answer many important questions about how food is digested. Read on to find out about the digestive system.

What Do You Think?

In your ScienceLog, try to answer the following questions based on what you already know:

1. What happens to food when it reaches your stomach?

2. What does your urinary system have in common with your skin?

Changing Foods

Dr. William Beaumont watched as Alexis St. Martin's stomach squeezed and relaxed. He saw that the stomach physically changed bits of food. You can see the role this squeezing motion plays in the digestion of food by using a plastic bag to model your stomach.

Procedure

1. Add **200 mL of flour** and **100 mL of water** to a **resealable plastic bag.** Mix **100 mL of vegetable oil** with the flour and water.

2. Seal the plastic bag, and shake it until the flour, water, and oil are well mixed.

3. Remove as much air from the bag as possible, and reseal the bag carefully.

4. Squeeze the bag with your hands for 5 minutes. Record your observations in your ScienceLog. Be careful to keep the bag sealed.

Analysis

5. Describe the mixture before and after you kneaded the bag.

6. How might the changes you saw in the mixture relate to what happens to food you eat?

7. Do you think this is a good model of how your stomach works? Why or why not?

Terms to Learn

digestive system   pancreas
esophagus   liver
stomach   gallbladder
small intestine   large intestine

What You'll Do

◆ Describe the parts and functions of the digestive system.
◆ Compare mechanical digestion with chemical digestion.
◆ Describe some disorders of the digestive system.

The Digestive System

It's your last class before lunch, and you're starving! You are so hungry you can hardly concentrate. Finally the bell rings and you get to eat your peanut butter and jelly sandwich. Yum!

You feel hungry because your brain receives signals that your cells need energy, but eating is only the beginning of the story. Your body must change a meal into substances it can use. Your **digestive system** is a group of organs that work together to digest food so that it can be used by the body.

Digestive System at a Glance

The most obvious part of your digestive system is the *digestive tract,* a series of tubelike organs that are joined end to end. The digestive tract includes your mouth, throat, esophagus, stomach, small intestine, large intestine, rectum, and anus. The human digestive tract may be more than 9 m long! The food you eat is digested as it passes through these organs. The liver, gallbladder, pancreas, and salivary glands are also part of the digestive system because they secrete substances that are used in digestion. The digestive system is shown in **Figure 1.**

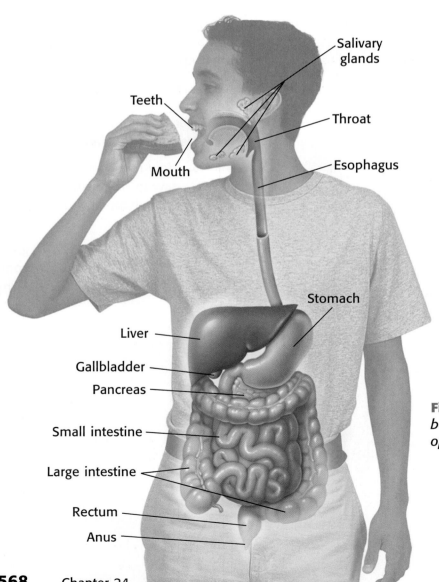

Salivary glands

Teeth

Throat

Mouth

Esophagus

Stomach

Liver

Gallbladder

Pancreas

Small intestine

Large intestine

Rectum

Anus

Figure 1 *The digestive tract is basically a long tube with an opening at each end.*

The Journey of a Sandwich

Digestion is the process of breaking down food, such as a peanut butter and jelly sandwich, into a form that can pass from the digestive tract into the bloodstream. There are two types of digestion—mechanical and chemical. The breaking, crushing, and mashing of food is called *mechanical digestion*. In *chemical digestion*, large molecules are broken down into nutrients. Nutrients are substances in food that the body needs for normal growth, maintenance, and repair.

Three major types of nutrients—carbohydrates, proteins, and fats—make up most of what you eat. In fact, a peanut butter and jelly sandwich contains all three of these nutrients. Special substances called *enzymes* break some nutrients into smaller particles that the body can use. For example, proteins are chains of smaller molecules called amino acids. Proteins are too large to be absorbed into the bloodstream, but enzymes chop up the chain into amino acids. These amino acids are small enough to pass into the bloodstream. This process is illustrated in **Figure 2.**

Break It Up!

1. Drop **one piece of hard candy** into a **clear plastic cup of water.**

2. Wrap an **identical candy** in a **towel,** and crush it with a **hammer.** Drop the crushed candy into a **second clear cup of water.**

3. The next day, examine both cups. What is different about the two candies?

4. What part of digestion is represented by breaking the hard candy?

5. How does chewing your food help the process of digestion?

Figure 2 *Enzymes in the stomach and small intestine break down proteins.*

1 Enzymes act as chemical scissors to cut the long chains of amino acids into small chains.

Enzymes

2 The small chains are then split by other enzymes.

3 Individual amino acids are small enough to enter the bloodstream, where they can be used to make new proteins.

Digestion Begins in the Mouth

Why is chewing so important? There are two reasons. First, chewing creates small, slippery pieces of food that are easier to swallow than big, dry pieces. Second, small pieces of food are easier to digest.

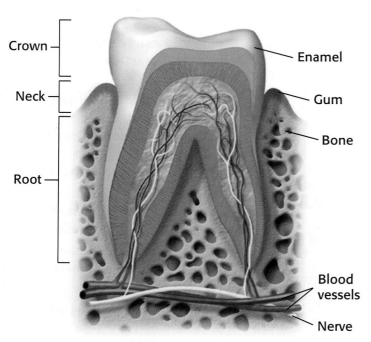

Crown — Enamel

Neck — Gum

— Bone

Root —

Blood vessels

Nerve

Figure 3 *The crown of a tooth, such as this molar, is visible above the gum line. The root is below the gum line.*

Through the Teeth Teeth are very important organs for mechanical digestion. With the help of strong muscles and your jaw bones, teeth are able to break and grind food. The outermost layer of a tooth, the *enamel,* is the hardest material in the body. Enamel protects nerves and softer material inside the tooth. **Figure 3** shows the major parts of the tooth.

Have you ever noticed that your teeth have different shapes? Look at **Figure 4** to locate the different kinds of teeth. The *molars* in the back are well suited for grinding food. The *premolars* are perfect for mashing food. The sharp teeth at the front of your mouth, the *incisors* and *canines,* are for shredding food.

And Over the Gums As you chew, the food gets mixed with a liquid called *saliva.* Saliva is made in salivary glands located in and around the mouth. Saliva contains an enzyme that begins the chemical digestion of carbohydrates. Saliva turns complex carbohydrates into simple sugars.

Look Out Stomach, Here It Comes! Once the food has been reduced to a soft mush, the tongue pushes it into the throat, which leads to a long, straight tube called the **esophagus** (i SAWF uh guhs). The esophagus squeezes the mass of food with rhythmic muscle contractions called *peristalsis* (PER uh STAHL sis). Peristalsis forces the food into the stomach.

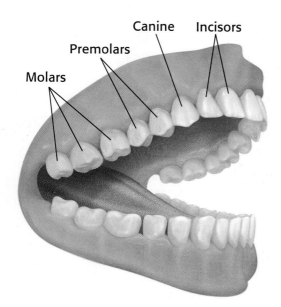

Canine   Incisors

Premolars

Molars

Figure 4 *Most adults have 32 permanent teeth. Each type of permanent tooth has a different function in breaking up food before it is swallowed.*

The Stomach's Harsh Environment

The **stomach** is a muscular, baglike organ attached to the lower end of the esophagus. It is pictured in **Figure 5.** The stomach continues the physical digestion of your meal by squeezing its contents with muscular contractions. While all this squeezing is going on, tiny glands in the stomach produce enzymes and acid. These work together to break food into nutrients. Stomach acid also kills most bacteria that you might swallow with your food. After a few hours of combined physical and chemical action, your peanut butter and jelly sandwich has been reduced to a soupy mixture called *chyme* (kiem).

BRAIN FOOD

A thick substance called mucus covers the stomach's lining and offers some protection from its harsh environment. However, the acids still damage the lining, and the entire lining must be replaced every few days.

Figure 5 *The stomach grinds and mixes food for hours before it releases the mixture into the small intestine.*

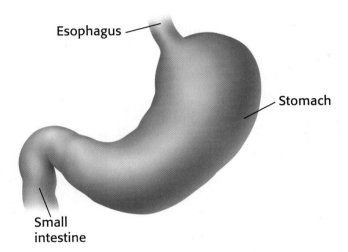

Esophagus

Stomach

Small intestine

Doorway to the Small Intestine The chyme is slowly released into the small intestine through a small ring of muscle that works like a valve. This valve keeps food in the stomach until it has been thoroughly mixed with digestive fluids. Then the valve opens and closes, letting a small amount of chyme squirt into the small intestine each time. Releasing chyme slowly from the stomach gives the intestine more time to mix the chyme with fluids from the liver and pancreas.

REVIEW

1. What is the difference between mechanical digestion and chemical digestion?

2. **Inferring Conclusions** Give two reasons why the following statement is true: Digestion begins in the mouth.

internetconnect

SC/LINKS
NSTA

TOPIC: The Digestive System
GO TO: www.scilinks.org
sciLINKS NUMBER: HSTL580

Still hungry for news about digestion? Enzymes can help you with that steak, you know. Check it out on page 768 of the LabBook.

The Gigantic Small Intestine?

The **small intestine** is a muscular tube that is about 2.5 cm in diameter. Other than its diameter, it's really not that small at all. In fact, if you stretched it out, it would be longer than you are tall—about 6 m!

Villi If you flattened out the surface of the small intestine, it would be larger than a tennis court! How is this possible? The inside wall of the small intestine is covered with fingerlike projections called *villi*, shown in **Figure 6.** The villi are covered with tiny nutrient-absorbing cells. Because the villi extend into the chyme, these cells have greater exposure to nutrients. Once absorbed, the nutrients enter the bloodstream.

Most chemical digestion takes place in the small intestine. Chyme from the stomach moves very slowly through the small intestine by peristalsis. Proteins, carbohydrates, and fats in the chyme are digested with the help of enzymes produced in the small intestine and the pancreas.

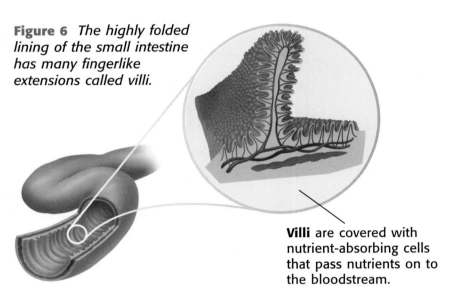

Figure 6 *The highly folded lining of the small intestine has many fingerlike extensions called villi.*

Villi are covered with nutrient-absorbing cells that pass nutrients on to the bloodstream.

The Pancreas

The **pancreas** is a fish-shaped organ located between the stomach and small intestine. It makes pancreatic juice that flows into the small intestine. This juice contains digestive enzymes and bicarbonate that neutralizes the acid in chyme. Without bicarbonate, acids would damage the lining of the intestine and prevent enzymes from doing their work. The pancreas also functions as a part of the endocrine system, making hormones that regulate blood sugar. The pancreas is shown in **Figure 7** on the next page.

The Liver and Gallbladder

The **liver** is a large reddish brown organ that helps with digestion. A human liver can be as large as a football. Your liver is located toward your right side, slightly higher than your stomach, as shown in **Figure 7.** Here are a few of the liver's important jobs:

- Your liver makes a green liquid called *bile* that is used in fat digestion
- Your liver stores nutrients
- Your liver breaks down toxic substances in the blood
- Your liver makes cholesterol for cell membranes

Bile Breaks Up Fat Although bile is made by the liver, it is temporarily stored in a small baglike organ called the **gallbladder,** shown in Figure 7. Bile is squeezed from the gallbladder into the small intestine, where it breaks up large fat droplets into very small droplets. This physical process allows more fat molecules to be exposed to digestive enzymes.

Storing Nutrients and Protecting the Body After nutrients are broken down, they are absorbed into the bloodstream and carried through the body. Nutrients that are not needed right away are stored in the liver. The liver then releases the stored nutrients into the bloodstream as needed. The liver also captures and detoxifies many substances in the body. For instance, it produces enzymes that break down alcohol and many other drugs.

BRAIN FOOD

If three-fourths of the liver were removed, the rest would go on working and would eventually grow to replace the part that was removed.

✔ Self-Check

Is bile used for chemical or mechanical digestion? Explain. *(See page 782 to check your answer.)*

Figure 7 *The liver, gallbladder, and pancreas are linked to the small intestine, but food does not move through them.*

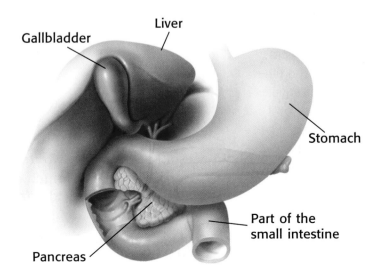

Gallbladder

Liver

Stomach

Part of the small intestine

Pancreas

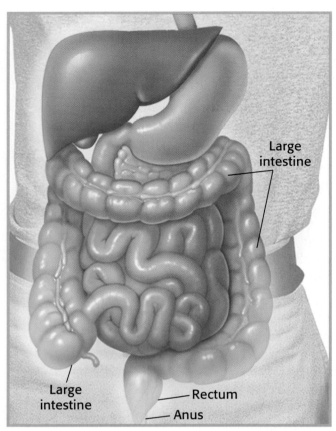

Figure 8 *The large intestine is the final organ of digestion.*

Labels in figure: Large intestine; Large intestine; Rectum; Anus

Environment
CONNECTION

Feces and other human wastes contain microorganisms and other substances that can contaminate drinking water. Every time you flush a toilet, the water and wastes go through the sewer to a sewage treatment plant. Here the disease-causing microorganisms are removed, and the clean water is released back to rivers, lakes, and streams.

The End of the Line

Whatever can't be absorbed into the blood gets pushed into the large intestine. The **large intestine** is the organ of the digestive system that stores, compacts, and then eliminates indigestible material from the body. The large intestine, shown in **Figure 8,** is called "large" because it has a larger diameter than the small intestine. It is about 1.5 m long, and its diameter is about 7.5 cm.

In the Large Intestine Undigested material enters the large intestine as a soupy mixture. The large intestine reabsorbs most of the water in the mixture, changing the liquid into a solid mass called *feces* or *stool.*

Whole grains, fruits, and vegetables contain a carbohydrate, called cellulose, that humans cannot digest. We commonly refer to this material as fiber. Fiber keeps the stool soft and keeps things moving through the large intestine.

A Way Out The *rectum* is the last section of the large intestine. It stores feces until they can be expelled. Feces pass to the outside through an opening called the *anus.* It has taken your sandwich about 24 hours to make this journey.

Problems in the Digestive System

Disorders of the digestive system are frequently related to eating behaviors. However, digestive problems can also be caused by diseases. Some common digestive disorders are described below.

Heartburn The stomach is blocked off at either end by bands of muscle called *sphincters* (SFINGK tuhrz). Occasionally, backflow of chyme from the stomach to the esophagus causes a burning pain in the chest called heartburn. Eating too much, eating right before going to bed, and eating very acidic foods sometimes cause heartburn.

Constipation and Diarrhea When the body does not get enough fiber, water, or exercise, the contents of the large intestine can become dry. Bowel movements become difficult and less frequent. This condition is called *constipation*. When bowel movements are frequent and watery, the condition is called *diarrhea*. Diarrhea occurs when too little water is removed from digested food in the large intestine. Diarrhea may cause dehydration and is especially dangerous for infants and small children, such as the girl in **Figure 9.**

Figure 9 *This child is being given fluids to replace those lost to diarrhea.*

Colon Cancer *Colon cancer* is a serious disease of the digestive tract that can lead to death. The colon is the long tubular portion of the large intestine. When certain colon cells divide uncontrollably, a tumor forms. Tumors interfere with the normal functioning of organs. Cells from a tumor can also break away and start tumors in other areas in the body. Colon cancer can often be treated and cured if detected early.

Gastric Ulcer An open sore in the stomach lining is called a *gastric ulcer*. **Figure 10** shows stomach tissue from a gastric ulcer. Gastric ulcers are often caused by bacteria and can be treated successfully with antibiotics. A high-fat diet, smoking, caffeine, and alcohol may make this condition worse.

Figure 10 *This stomach lining has openings, seen in red, that indicate a gastric ulcer.*

REVIEW

1. What happens to the food that you eat when it gets to the stomach?

2. Describe the roles of the liver, the gallbladder, and the pancreas in digestion.

3. **Analyzing Relationships** How would the inability to make saliva affect digestion?

internet**connect**

SC*LINKS.*
NSTA

TOPIC: Problems in the Digestive System
GO TO: www.scilinks.org
*sci*LINKS NUMBER: HSTL585

Terms to Learn

urinary system   urine
kidney   urinary bladder
nephron

What You'll Do

◆ Describe the parts and functions of the urinary system.
◆ Explain how the kidneys filter blood.
◆ Describe some disorders of the urinary system.

The Urinary System

As your body performs the chemical activities that keep you alive, waste products such as carbon dioxide and nitrogen are produced. Your body has to get rid of these waste products in order to stay healthy. *Excretion* is the process of removing wastes and excess products from the body. Three of your body systems are involved in excretion: your skin releases waste products and water when you sweat, your lungs expel carbon dioxide and water when you exhale, and the **urinary system** removes waste products from your blood. Notice that the digestive system is not involved in excretion. The term *excretion* is used only when substances must pass through a membrane in order to leave the body.

Cleaning the Blood

As blood travels through the tissues, it collects all of the waste products produced by the body's cells. Your blood is like a supply train that comes into a town to drop off supplies and take away garbage. The train has to find a way to get rid of the garbage before it can load up with more supplies. If the garbage is not removed, the townspeople will be in a very unhealthy environment. If the cells in your body cannot get rid of their waste products, they can actually be poisoned! On the next few pages, you will see how the urinary system removes waste materials from your blood so that the blood can transport nutrients again. The urinary system is shown in **Figure 11.**

Kidneys
Ureter
Bladder
Urethra

Figure 11 *The urinary system removes many of the waste products produced by the body.*

Flow-Through Filters

The **kidneys** are a pair of bean-shaped organs that constantly clean the blood. Your kidneys filter about 2,000 L of blood each day. Your body only holds 5.6 L of blood, so your blood cycles through the kidneys about 350 times a day!

Inside each kidney are more than 1 million microscopic filters called **nephrons,** shown below. Nephrons remove a variety of harmful substances from the body. Among the most important of these substances is urea, which contains nitrogen and is formed when cells use protein for energy.

Why does your mouth get so dry when the rest of you is so hot and sweaty? Turn to page 584 to find out.

How the Kidneys Filter Blood

1 A large artery brings blood into each kidney.

2 Tiny blood vessels branch off the main artery and pass through part of each nephron.

3 Water and other small substances, such as glucose, salts, amino acids, and urea, are forced out of the blood vessels and into the nephrons.

4 As these substances flow through the nephrons, most of the water and some nutrients are moved back into blood vessels that wrap around the nephrons. A concentrated mixture of waste materials is left behind in the nephrons.

5 The cleaned blood, now with slightly less water and much less waste material, leaves each kidney in a large vein to recirculate in the body.

6 The yellow fluid that remains in the nephrons is called **urine.** Urine leaves each kidney through a slender tube called the *ureter* and flows into the **urinary bladder,** where it is stored.

7 Urine leaves the body through another tube called the *urethra. Urination* is the process of expelling urine from the body.

Nephron

Artery

Vein

Ureter

Water In, Water Out

Our bodies take in water every day. If we did not excrete an equal amount of water, our bodies would swell up with all the excess. Losing water through sweat and urine is necessary to stay healthy. So how does the body keep the water levels in the proper balance? The balance of fluids is controlled by chemical messengers in the body called *hormones*.

Sweat and Thirst When you get hot, you lose more water in the form of sweat. The evaporation of water from your skin cools you down. As the water content of the blood drops, the salivary glands produce less saliva. This is one of the reasons you feel thirsty.

Antidiuretic Hormone When you get thirsty, other parts of your body react to the water shortage, too. A hormone called *antidiuretic* (AN tie DIE yoo RET ik) *hormone,* or *ADH,* is released. ADH signals the kidneys to take back water from the nephrons and return it to the bloodstream, thereby making less urine. When your blood is too watery, smaller amounts of ADH are released. The kidneys react by allowing more water to stay in the nephron and leave the body as urine.

Diuretics When you are thirsty, your tissues are asking for more water. Some beverages contain caffeine, which is a *diuretic* (DIE yoo RET ik). Diuretics cause the kidneys to make more urine, which decreases the amount of water in the blood. So instead of giving your body more water, caffeinated beverages cause additional water to be lost in urine.

MATH BREAK

How Much Water?

Most adults need to consume about 2,500 mL of water per day. How many 8 oz glasses of drinking water would you need to get enough water? Hint: 1 oz = 29.6 mL

BRAIN FOOD

Fortunately, your kidneys are very efficient. In fact, if you lost one to disease, you could still survive.

APPLY

Beverage Ban

During football season, a football coach insists that all members of the team avoid caffeinated beverages. Many of the players are upset by the news. Pretend that you are the coach. Write a letter to the team explaining why it is better for them to drink water than drinks containing caffeine.

Urinary System Ailments

Since the urinary system regulates body fluids and removes wastes from the blood, any malfunction can become life-threatening. Some common urinary system disorders are described below.

Bacterial Infections Bacteria can get into the bladder and ureters through the urethra and cause painful infections. It is important to treat such an infection early because it could spread to the kidneys and lead to permanent damage to the nephrons.

Kidney Stones Sometimes salts and wastes collect inside the kidneys and form kidney stones, like the one in **Figure 12.** Kidney stones interfere with urine flow and cause pain. Most kidney stones pass naturally from the body, but sometimes a medical procedure is necessary. For example, shockwaves can be used to break the stones into pieces small enough to pass through the urethra.

Kidney Disease Damage to nephrons can prevent normal kidney functioning, leading to kidney disease. If the kidneys do not function properly, a kidney machine can be used to filter waste from the blood. As shown in **Figure 13,** blood is pumped from an artery in the forearm or wrist to a kidney machine, where it is filtered. The cleaned blood is then pumped back into a vein in the arm.

Figure 12 *This kidney stone had to be removed from a patient's urinary system.*

Figure 13 *The kidney machine will filter this man's blood before returning it to his body.*

REVIEW

1. Put the following statements about the urinary system in their proper order:

   a. Water is absorbed back into blood vessels.

   b. Urine leaves the kidney through the ureter.

   c. A large artery brings blood into the kidney.

   d. Water and other small substances, including glucose and urea, leave the blood vessels and enter the nephron.

2. What is the main function of the urinary system?

3. **Applying Concepts** Which contains more water, the blood going into the kidney or the blood leaving the kidney? Explain.

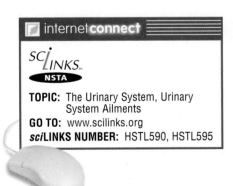

internet**connect**

SC*i*LINKS.
NSTA

TOPIC: The Urinary System, Urinary System Ailments
GO TO: www.scilinks.org
*sci*LINKS NUMBER: HSTL590, HSTL595

Chapter Highlights

SECTION 1

Vocabulary

digestive system *(p. 568)*

esophagus *(p. 570)*

stomach *(p. 571)*

small intestine *(p. 572)*

pancreas *(p. 572)*

liver *(p. 573)*

gallbladder *(p. 573)*

large intestine *(p. 574)*

Section Notes

- Your digestive system is a group of organs that work together to digest food so that it can be used by the body.

- The breaking, crushing, and mashing of food is called mechanical digestion. Chemical digestion is the process in which large molecules are broken down to simpler molecules.

- Chewed food is pushed through the digestive tract by rhythmic contractions called peristalsis.

- The stomach mixes the food with enzymes and acid to break down nutrients. The mixture is called chyme.

- In the small intestine, pancreatic juice and bile are mixed with chyme.

- From the small intestine, nutrients enter the bloodstream and are circulated to the body's cells.

- The large intestine receives undigested material from the small intestine. As water is absorbed back into the body, this material becomes a solid mass called feces.

- Digestive system disorders include heartburn, constipation, diarrhea, colon cancer, and gastric ulcers.

Labs

As the Stomach Churns *(p. 768)*

Enzymes in Action *(p. 770)*

☑ Skills Check

Math Concepts

DRINK UP In the MathBreak on page 578, you determined how many glasses of water you need in order to drink 2,500 mL each day. First you must determine how many ounces are in 2,500 mL:

$$\frac{2{,}500 \text{ mL}}{1 \text{ day}} \times \frac{1 \text{ oz}}{29.6 \text{ mL}} = 84.5 \text{ oz of water}$$

You need to drink 84.5 oz of water each day.

Each glass contains 8 oz, so:

$$\frac{84.5 \text{ oz}}{1 \text{ day}} \times \frac{1 \text{ glass}}{8 \text{ oz}} = 10.6 \text{ glasses}$$

You need to drink 10.6 8-oz glasses of water each day.

Visual Understanding

KIDNEY FUNCTION Look at the illustration on page 577 to review how the kidneys filter the blood.

Vocabulary

urinary system *(p. 576)*

kidney *(p. 577)*

nephron *(p. 577)*

urine *(p. 577)*

urinary bladder *(p. 577)*

Section Notes

- Your skin, lungs, and urinary system are all involved in excretion.

- The urinary system cleans the blood and removes liquid waste as urine. The filtering structures in the kidneys are called nephrons.

- Most of the water and some nutrients that enter nephrons are moved back into the blood vessels.

- When urine leaves the kidneys, it passes into the urinary bladder through a tube called the ureter. The urinary bladder stores the urine until it can be eliminated.

- Urine travels from the urinary bladder to the outside through a tube called the urethra.

- Some disorders of the urinary system include bacterial infections, kidney stones, and kidney disease.

 internetconnect

GO TO: go.hrw.com

Visit the **HRW** Web site for a variety of learning tools related to this chapter. Just type in the keyword:

KEYWORD: HSTBD3

SCiLINKS

N S T A

GO TO: www.scilinks.org

Visit the **National Science Teachers Association** on-line Web site for Internet resources related to this chapter. Just type in the *sci*LINKS number for more information about the topic:

TOPIC: The Digestive System — *sci*LINKS NUMBER: HSTL580

TOPIC: Problems in the Digestive System — *sci*LINKS NUMBER: HSTL585

TOPIC: The Urinary System — *sci*LINKS NUMBER: HSTL590

TOPIC: Urinary System Ailments — *sci*LINKS NUMBER: HSTL595

TOPIC: Tapeworms — *sci*LINKS NUMBER: HSTL600

Chapter Review

To complete the following sentences, choose the correct term from each pair of terms listed below:

1. Urine travels from each kidney to the urinary bladder through the __?__. *(urethra or ureter)*

2. The rhythmic contractions that occur in the digestive tract are called __?__. *(peristalsis or enzymes)*

3. The chemical digestion of carbohydrates begins in the __?__. *(stomach or mouth)*

4. Bile is made in the __?__ and stored in the __?__. *(liver or gallbladder)*

5. __?__ is the process of removing wastes and waste products from the body. This term is only used when substances are passed through a membrane before leaving the body. *(Digestion or Excretion)*

6. Indigestible material is formed into feces in the __?__. *(large intestine or small intestine)*

UNDERSTANDING CONCEPTS

Multiple Choice

7. The hormone that signals the kidneys to make less urine is
   a. urea.
   b. ADH.
   c. cellulase.
   d. ATP.

8. Which of the following aids digestion by producing bile?
   a. stomach
   b. pancreas
   c. gallbladder
   d. liver

9. The part of the kidney that filters the blood is the
   a. artery.
   b. ureter.
   c. nephron.
   d. urethra.

10. The fingerlike projections lining the small intestine are called
    a. emulsifiers.
    b. fats.
    c. amino acids.
    d. villi.

11. Which of the following is not part of the digestive tract?
    a. mouth
    b. pancreas
    c. stomach
    d. rectum

12. The soupy mixture of food, enzymes, and acids in the stomach is called
    a. chyme.
    b. villi.
    c. urea.
    d. vitamins.

Short Answer

13. Give two reasons why it is important that the pancreas releases bicarbonate into the small intestine.

14. How does the structure of the small intestine improve its nutrient absorption?

15. What is a diuretic?

Concept Mapping

16. Use the following terms to create a concept map: teeth, stomach, digestion, bile, saliva, mechanical digestion, gallbladder, chemical digestion.

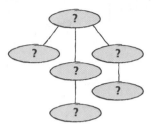

CRITICAL THINKING AND PROBLEM SOLVING

Write one or two sentences to answer the following questions:

17. How would digestion be affected if the liver were damaged?

18. Think about what happens when you put a piece of carbohydrate-dense food, such as bread, potato, or a cracker, in your mouth. If you let a small piece sit near the tip of your tongue, it might begin to taste sweet. What digestive process would explain this change?

MATH IN SCIENCE

19. Mr. Jones has lost all of his molars and two of his premolars. How many teeth does Mr. Jones have?

20. During a one-day water-balance study, a woman drank 1,500 mL of water. The food that she ate contained 750 mL of water, and 250 mL of water was produced internally during normal body processes. She lost 900 mL of water by sweating, 1,500 mL in urine, and 100 mL in feces. Overall, how much water did she gain or lose during the day?

INTERPRETING GRAPHICS

The bar graph below shows how long the average meal spends in each portion of your digestive tract. Use this graph to answer the questions below.

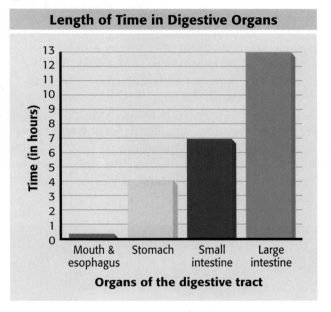

21. Where does the food spend the longest amount of time?

22. On average, how much longer does food stay in the small intestine than in the stomach?

23. Which organ mixes food with special substances to make chyme? Approximately how long does food remain in this organ?

24. Bile breaks up large fat droplets into very small droplets. How long is the food in your body before it comes into contact with bile?

NOW What Do You Think?

Take a minute to review your answers to the ScienceLog questions on page 567. Have your answers changed? If necessary, revise your answers based on what you have learned since you began this chapter.

LIFE SCIENCE • CHEMISTRY

Quench Your Thirst!

Have you ever been really thirsty after a hard workout? Playing sports, riding a bike, and doing other physical activities can make you thirsty—but why? The first reason is sweat. When you are physically active, you lose a lot of water by sweating. This keeps your body from overheating. But what is going on in your body to make your mouth feel so dry? And which is better to quench your thirst, water or a sports drink?

▲ *Activities that make you hot and sweaty make you want to take a drink, but why?*

Thirsty Chemistry

When you lose water, your blood becomes more concentrated. Think about how you make a powdered drink, such as lemonade. If you use the same amount of powder in 1 L of water as you do in 2 L, the drinks will taste different. The lemonade made with 1 L of water will be stronger because it is more concentrated.

Losing water to sweat increases the concentration of sodium and potassium in your blood. The kidneys force the extra potassium out of the blood vessels and into nephrons. From the nephrons, the potassium is eliminated from the body in urine. Nerve cells in your brain react to the high concentration of sodium by sending out two important messages. One message tells the pituitary gland to release antidiuretic hormone. This hormone signals the kidneys to return water to the bloodstream. The second message signals the salivary glands to produce less saliva. With less saliva, your mouth becomes dry, and then you know it's time to get that drink!

With Flavor or Without?

But which is better to drink—water or a sports drink? If you have been exercising, you might think a sports drink is probably better. But studies by Kathy Grunewald, a professor at Kansas State University, indicate that sports drinks may not be necessary unless you have exercised very hard or for more than an hour and a half.

When you drink fluids, you lower the concentration of all the minerals in your blood by adding more water. This is like adding water to the 1 L of strong lemonade. The body also needs to replace the potassium that was lost from the blood. A sports drink can help replace this potassium. But if you drink water, the kidneys will eventually return the potassium concentration to normal. The most important reason for drinking fluids after physical exercise is to get water to your tissues. So whatever physical activity you choose, drink up!

Going Further

▶ If you want to investigate how much you need to drink, weigh yourself before and after your next strenuous activity. Every kilogram that you lose represents about 1 L of water. You should make sure that you drink at least as much water as you lose.

A Voiceless Companion

If you decided to eat the last piece of pizza in the refrigerator, someone just might ask you for a bite, right? But what if you found out that you had a constant mealtime companion who didn't want just a bite but wanted it all? And what if that companion never asked for your permission?

How to Be a Host

This constant mealtime companion might be a tapeworm. Tapeworms are invertebrate flatworms. These flatworms are parasites. A parasite is an organism that obtains its food by living in or on another living organism. The organism in which a parasite makes its home is called a host. People, cows, pigs, fish, cats, dogs, and many insects are the perfect hosts for tapeworms. Without a host, tapeworms can't survive.

Food broken down in the stomach continues to be broken down in the small intestine. Since a tapeworm doesn't have a digestive tract of its own, it borrows its host's. By attaching itself to the inside of its host's small intestine with clamps and suckers, a tapeworm can eat as much as it likes.

Although tapeworms aren't much thicker than a ribbon, they can grow to more than 6 m in length! They do this by adding one postage-stamp-sized segment at a time. Each segment has both male and female reproductive organs and can be filled with thousands of eggs.

Saying "Goodbye" and Avoiding "Hello"

When an egg-filled segment breaks off, it passes through the rest of the host's digestive tract and ends up in the feces. If another animal eats or drinks something contaminated with these feces, the eggs grow into worms in that animal's intestines. The eggs can then spread to muscle tissues (called meat in animals used for food). If humans eat this meat but don't cook it thoroughly enough to kill tapeworm larvae, the cycle begins all over again.

Getting rid of a tapeworm requires removing the head, or scolex. If the scolex is left behind, it simply produces new segments, and the tapeworm regrows itself. Sometimes humans don't realize they have a tapeworm, even though they suffer from symptoms such as weight loss and nausea. And occasionally there are no symptoms at all.

The best way to avoid these parasites is to avoid eating undercooked beef, pork, and fish. If you do this, you won't have any uninvited guests at your next meal!

▲ *What is 10 m long, looks like it's made of postage stamps, and eats your dinner after you do?*

Think About It

▶ Doctors prescribe certain medications to get rid of tapeworms. Research the different ways people got rid of tapeworms before modern medicines were available.

25 Communication and Control

This Really Happened . . .

The arrow shows the path of the tamping rod.

About 150 years ago, a bizarre accident changed the way scientists view the role of the brain. The accident involved a railroad worker named Phineas Gage. One day in 1848, Gage was using a long metal rod to pack explosives into a hole to clear a path for some railroad track. A spark caused an explosion that blew the rod through Gage's head. The rod entered through his left cheek and exited at the top of his skull. You would expect this injury to be fatal, but Gage stood up and was able to speak.

In a little over 2 months, Gage's wounds were healed, but he was not quite the same. The Phineas Gage that people knew before the accident was calm, responsible, and considerate of others. But after the accident he became irresponsible and quick to anger. Scientists who studied Gage's change in behavior learned that the brain is responsible for much more than just movement and senses. In this chapter you will learn more about your brain and the rest of your nervous system. You will also learn how the nervous system and the endocrine system control all of the other systems in your body.

What Do You Think?

In your ScienceLog, try to answer the following questions based on what you already know:

1. What are your senses? How do senses help us survive?

2. Why does your heart beat faster when something frightens you?

3. How do eyeglasses and contact lenses help some people see better?

Investigate!

How Fast Do You React?

When you want to move your hand, your brain must send a message all the way to the muscles in your arms. How long does that take? In this exercise, you will work with a partner to see how quickly you can react.

Procedure

1. Sit in a chair and have a partner stand facing you while holding a **meterstick** in a vertical position, as shown at right. Hold your thumb about 3 cm from your fingers near the bottom end of the stick. The meterstick should be positioned to fall between your thumb and fingers.

2. Tell your partner to let go of the meterstick without warning. When you see this happen, catch the stick by pressing your thumb and fingers together. Your partner should be ready to catch the

top of the meterstick if it begins to tip over. Record the number of centimeters the stick dropped before you caught it. The distance that the meterstick falls before you catch it can be used to evaluate your reaction time.

3. Repeat the procedure several times, and calculate the average number of centimeters. Next try this procedure with your other hand.

4. Exchange places with your partner, and repeat the procedure.

Analysis

5. Compare your results with those of your partner. What factors might influence a person's ability to react quickly?

6. How does your reaction time when using the hand you write with compare with that when using your other hand?

7. Why might each hand have a different reaction time?

The Nervous System

Terms to Learn

central nervous
  system
peripheral
  nervous system
neuron

impulse
receptor
nerve
brain
reflex

What You'll Do

- Explain how neurons in the nervous system work together.
- Compare the central nervous system with the peripheral nervous system.
- Describe the major functions of the brain and the spinal cord.

What do the following events have in common? You hear a knock at the door, you write a book report, you feel your heart pounding after a run, you work a math problem, you are startled by a loud noise, and you enjoy eating a sweet mango. These events are all activities of your nervous system. The nervous system gathers and interprets information about the body's internal and external environments and responds to that information. The nervous system keeps your organs working properly and allows you to speak, smell, taste, hear, see, move, think, and experience emotions.

Two Systems Within a System

Your nervous system controls and coordinates many things that happen in your body. It acts as a central command post, collecting and processing information and making sure appropriate information gets sent to all parts of the body. These tasks are accomplished by two subdivisions of the nervous system, the *central nervous system* and the *peripheral nervous system*. The **central nervous system** (CNS) includes your brain and spinal cord. It processes all incoming and outgoing messages. The **peripheral nervous system** (PNS) consists of communication pathways, or *nerves*, that connect all areas of your body to your CNS. **Figure 1** shows the major divisions of the nervous system.

Figure 1 *The CNS (in orange) acts as the control center for your body. The PNS (in purple) carries information to and from the CNS.*

The Peripheral Nervous System

How long does it take for a light to come on when you flip a light switch? The light seems to come on immediately. In a similar way, specialized cells called **neurons** transfer messages throughout your body in the form of fast-moving electrical energy. A typical neuron is shown in **Figure 2.** The electrical messages that pass along the neurons are called **impulses.** Impulses may travel as fast as 150 m/s or as slow as 1 m/s.

Neuron Structure   A neuron consists of a cell body, dendrites, and axons. The enlarged region called the cell body contains a nucleus and cell organelles. Look again at Figure 2. The neuron generally receives information from other cells through short, branched extensions called *dendrites*. A neuron may have many dendrites, allowing it to receive impulses from thousands of other cells.

From the cell body, information is transmitted to other cells by a fiber called an *axon*. Axons can be very short or quite long. You have some really long axons that extend almost 1 m from your lower back to your toes. The end of an axon often has branches that allow information to pass to yet more cells. The tip of each branch is called an *axon terminal*.

MATH BREAK

Time to Travel

To calculate how long it takes for an impulse to travel a certain distance, you can use the following equation:

$$\text{Time} = \frac{\text{distance}}{\text{speed}}$$

If an impulse travels 100 m/s, about how long would it take for an impulse to travel 10 m?

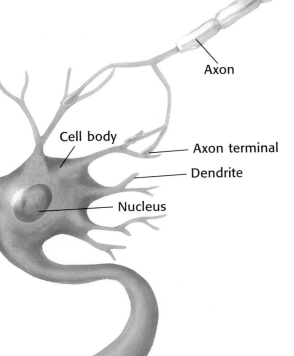

Figure 2 *Neurons are special cells that transfer electrical messages throughout the body.*

Direction of impulse

Axon

Cell body

Axon terminal

Dendrite

Nucleus

Information Collection Special neurons called *sensory neurons* gather information about what is happening in and around your body and send this information on to the central nervous system for processing. Sensory neurons have specialized dendrites called **receptors** that detect changes inside and outside the body. For example, receptors in your eyes detect the light around you. Receptors in your stomach let your brain know when your stomach is full or empty.

Delivering Orders Neurons that send impulses from the brain and spinal cord to other systems are called *motor neurons*. Motor means "to move"; when muscles get impulses from motor neurons, they respond by contracting. For example, motor neurons cause the muscles around your eyes to move when the sensory neurons in your eyes detect bright light. This movement makes you squint, which reduces the amount of light entering the eye. Motor neurons also send messages to your glands, such as sweat glands. These messages tell the sweat glands to release sweat.

Just a Bundle of Axons

The central nervous system is connected to the rest of your body by nerves. **Nerves** are axons bundled together with blood vessels and connective tissue. Nerves extend throughout your body. Most nerves contain the axons of both sensory and motor neurons. **Figure 3** shows the structure of a nerve. The axon in this nerve transmits information from the spinal cord to muscle fibers.

Spinal cord

Nerve

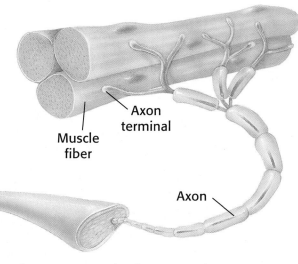

Axon terminal

Muscle fiber

Axon

Figure 3 *In order for a muscle to contract, a message must travel from the spinal cord to the muscle. The message travels along the axon of a motor neuron inside the nerve.*

The Central Nervous System

The central nervous system works closely with the peripheral nervous system. It receives information from the sensory neurons and responds by sending messages to various parts of the body via motor neurons.

Mission Control The **brain,** part of your central nervous system, is the nervous system's largest organ. It has hundreds of different jobs. Many of the processes that the brain controls happen automatically and are referred to as *involuntary.* For example, you couldn't stop digesting the food you have eaten even if you tried. Other activities controlled by your brain are *voluntary.* When you want to move your arm, your brain sends signals along motor neurons to muscles in your arm. This causes the muscles to contract and your arm to move. The brain has three connected parts—the cerebrum, the cerebellum, and the medulla. Each part has its own functions.

Your Thinking Cap The largest part of your brain is called the *cerebrum.* Its shape resembles a mushroom cap over a stalk. This dome-shaped area is where you think and where most memories are stored. It controls voluntary movements and allows you to detect touch, light, sound, odors, taste, pain, heat, and cold.

The cerebrum has two halves called *hemispheres.* The left hemisphere directs the right side of the body, and the right hemisphere directs the left side of the body. This is because axons cross over to the opposite side of the body in the spinal cord. **Figure 4** gives a general model of the activities that each hemisphere controls. However, most brain activity involves both hemispheres.

▼ The **right hemisphere** primarily controls activities that involve imagination, appreciation, and creativity.

Figure 4
The Cerebral Hemispheres

$$x = \frac{-b \pm \sqrt{b^2 - 4ac}}{2a}$$

$$e = mc^2$$

$$\pi = 3.14159625$$

Top of Brain

The **left hemisphere** ▶ primarily controls activities such as speaking, reading, writing, and solving problems.

The Balancing Act The second largest part of your brain is the *cerebellum* (SER uh BEL uhm). It lies underneath the back of your cerebrum and receives sensory impulses from skeletal muscles and joints. This allows the brain to keep track of your body's position. For example, if you begin to lose your balance, like the girl in **Figure 5,** the cerebellum sends impulses to different skeletal muscles to make them contract, keeping you upright.

The Mighty Medulla The part of your brain that connects to your spinal cord is called the *medulla* (mi DOOL uh). The medulla is only about 3 cm long, but you couldn't live without it. The medulla controls your blood pressure, heart rate, involuntary breathing, and some other involuntary activities.

Your medulla constantly receives sensory impulses from receptors in your blood vessels. It uses this information to regulate your blood pressure. If your blood pressure gets too low, the medulla sends out impulses that tell blood vessels to tighten up to increase the blood pressure. The medulla also sends impulses to the heart to make it beat faster or slower as necessary. **Figure 6** shows the location of each part of the brain and some of the functions associated with each part.

Figure 5 *Your cerebellum causes skeletal muscles to make adjustments in order to keep you upright.*

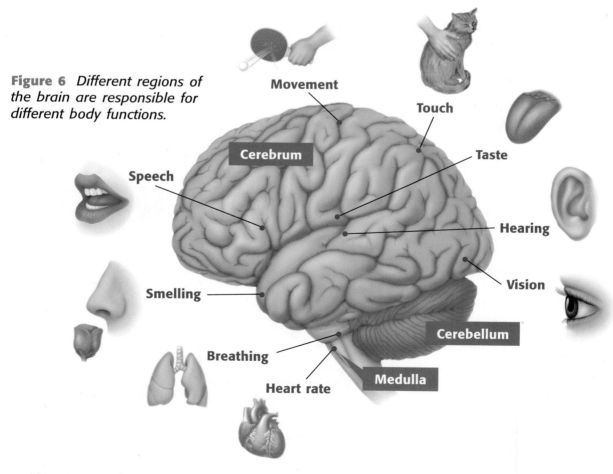

Figure 6 *Different regions of the brain are responsible for different body functions.*

Movement

Touch

Taste

Cerebrum

Speech

Hearing

Smelling

Vision

Cerebellum

Breathing

Medulla

Heart rate

The Spinal Cord

Your spinal cord, part of the central nervous system, is about as big around as your thumb. It contains neurons and bundles of axons that pass impulses to and from the brain. As shown in **Figure 7,** the spinal cord is surrounded by protective bones called *vertebrae* (VUHR tuh BRAY).

The nerve fibers in your spinal cord enable your brain to communicate with your peripheral nervous system. Sensory neurons in your skin and muscles send impulses along their axons to your spinal cord. The spinal cord then conducts impulses to your brain, where they can be interpreted as pain, heat, cold, or other sensations. Impulses moving from the brain down the cord are relayed to motor neurons, which carry the impulses along their axons to muscles and glands all over your body.

Spinal Cord Injury If the spinal cord is injured, any sensory information coming into it below where the damage occurred may be unable to travel to the brain. Likewise, any motor commands the brain sends to an area below the injury may not get through to the peripheral nerves. Thousands of people each year are paralyzed by spinal cord injuries. Many of these injuries occur in automobile accidents. Among young people, spinal cord injuries are often sports related.

Figure 7 *The spinal cord carries information to and from the brain. It is protected by vertebrae.*

Self-Check

1. What part of the brain do you use to do your math homework?
2. What part of the brain helps a gymnast maintain balance on the balance beam?
3. What is the function of the vertebrae?

(See page 782 to check your answers.)

Ouch! That Hurt!

Have you ever stepped on something sharp? You probably pulled your foot up without thinking. This quick, involuntary action is called a **reflex.** Reflexes help protect your body from damage.

When you step on a sharp object, the message "pain" travels to your spinal cord, and a message to move your foot travels back to the muscles in your leg. The muscles in your leg respond before the information ever reaches the brain. By the time your brain finds out what happened, your foot has already moved. If you had to wait for your brain to get the message, your foot might be seriously injured! The man in **Figure 8** lifted his foot before he realized he had stepped on a toy.

Figure 8 *When pain impulses from your foot reach your spine, a message is sent immediately to your leg muscles to lift your foot.*

Quick Lab

Knee Jerks

1. Sit on the edge of a desk or table so your feet don't touch the floor.

2. While your leg is completely relaxed, have a classmate *gently* tap on your knee slightly below the kneecap with the edge of his or her hand. How did your leg respond? Did you have any control over what happened? Explain.

3. Describe the pathway taken by the impulse that started with the tap on the knee.

REVIEW

1. Make a labeled diagram that shows the path of an electrical message from one neuron to another neuron.

2. Explain how the peripheral nervous system connects with the central nervous system.

3. If a spider is crawling up your left arm, which cerebral hemisphere controls the movement that you will use to knock it off?

4. List the three major parts of the brain, and describe their functions.

5. **Applying Concepts** Describe a time when you experienced a reflex.

Section 2

Responding to the Environment

Terms to Learn

retina   iris
rods   lens
cones   cochlea

What You'll Do

◆ List four sensations that are detected by receptors in the skin.
◆ Describe how light relates to vision.
◆ Explain the functions of photoreceptors, taste buds, and olfactory cells.

How do you know when someone taps you on the shoulder or calls your name? How do you feel the touch or hear the sound? Impulses from sensory receptors in your shoulder and in your ears travel to your brain, sending information about your external environment. Your brain depends on this information to make decisions that affect your survival.

Come to Your Senses

Information about your surroundings and the conditions in your body is detected by sensory receptors. This information is converted to electrical signals and sent to your brain for interpretation. Once the signals reach your brain, you become aware of them. This awareness is called a *sensation*. It is in your brain that you have thoughts, feelings, and memories about sensations.

There are many different kinds of sensory receptors in your body. For example, receptors in your eyes detect light. Receptors in your ears detect vibrations called sound waves. The taste buds on your tongue have receptors that detect chemicals in the foods you eat. You have special receptors in your nose that detect tiny particles in the air. Your skin has a variety of receptors as well. Look at **Figure 9** to see some of the different kinds of receptors in the skin.

I've got to hand it to you—you've gotta lotta nerve. See for yourself on page 772 of your LabBook.

Figure 9 *This diagram shows some of the receptors in your skin and what they detect.*

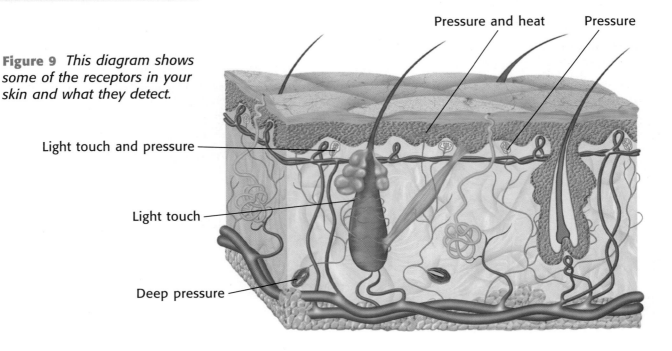

Pressure and heat   Pressure

Light touch and pressure

Light touch

Deep pressure

Something in My Eye

As you read this sentence, you are using one of your most important senses—*vision.* Vision is your awareness of light energy. Your eyes have special receptors that detect visible light, a portion of the sun's energy that reaches the Earth.

An Eyeful The eye is a complex sensory organ. Examine the eye in **Figure 10.** The outer surface of the eye is covered by the cornea, a transparent membrane that protects the eye but allows light to enter. Visible light that is reflected by objects around you enters through an opening at the front of your eye called the *pupil.* Light is detected by cells at the back of your eye in a light-sensitive layer called the **retina.**

The retina is packed with special neurons called *photoreceptors* (*photo* means "light") that convert light into electrical impulses. There are two types of photoreceptors in the retina—rods and cones. **Rods** can detect very dim light. They are important for night vision. Impulses from rods are perceived in tones of gray. In bright light, the **cones** give you a very colorful view of the world.

Light energy produces changes in photoreceptors that trigger nerve impulses. These impulses travel along axons, leaving the back of each eye through an *optic nerve.*

Figure 10 *Carrots look orange because they reflect only orange light. The orange light is detected by cells in your retina.*

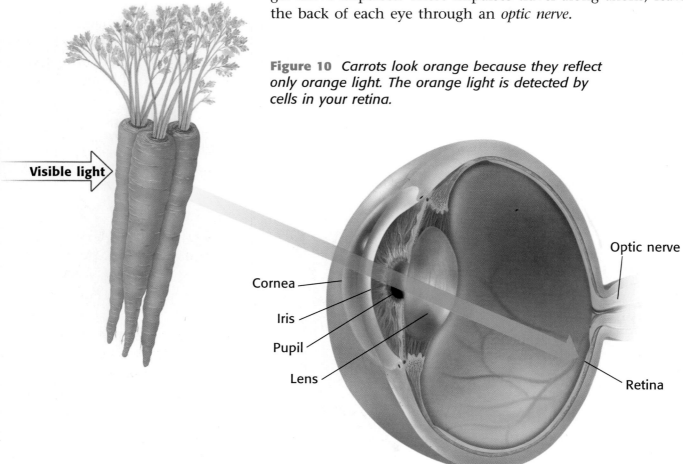

Visible light

Cornea

Iris

Pupil

Lens

Optic nerve

Retina

Seeing the Light Light rays enter the eye through the *pupil*. Your pupil looks like a black dot in the center of your eye, but it is actually an opening. It is surrounded by the **iris,** the part of the eye that gives the eye color. A ring of muscle fibers causes the iris to open and close, making the pupil change size. This regulates the amount of light that passes to the retina. In bright light, your pupil is small, and in dim light, your pupil is large.

Hocus Focus Light travels in straight lines until it passes through the cornea and the *lens*. A **lens** is a piece of curved material behind the pupil that allows light to pass through but changes its direction. The lens focuses the light entering the eye on the retina. The lens of an eye changes shape to adjust focus. When you look at objects close to the eye, the lens becomes more curved. When you look at objects far away, the lens gets flatter.

In some eyes, the lens focuses the light just in front of the retina (resulting in nearsightedness) or just behind the retina (resulting in farsightedness). Glasses or contact lenses can usually correct these vision problems. Focus on **Figure 11** to see how corrective lenses work.

What are some other uses of lenses? Turn to Light on Lenses on page 608 to find out.

Figure 11 *A concave lens bends light rays outward to correct nearsightedness. A convex lens bends light rays inward to correct farsightedness.*

Plane where light is focused

Normal eye

Nearsighted eye

Correction with concave lens

Farsighted eye

Correction with convex lens

Quick Lab

Where's the Dot?

1. Hold this book at arm's length, and close your right eye. Focus your left eye on the solid dot below.

○　　　　●

2. Slowly move the book toward your face. Stay focused on the solid dot.

3. What happens to the white dot?

4. Do some research on the optic nerve to find out why this happens.

TRY at HOME

Physics
C O N N E C T I O N

Sound is produced by vibrating objects. Objects that vibrate more than 20,000 times a second produce sounds too high for humans to hear. Dolphins can detect sounds from objects that vibrate up to 150,000 times per second.

Did You "Ear" That?

When a guitar string is plucked, what enables you to hear the sound? A sound begins when an object, such as the guitar string, begins to vibrate. The vibrations push on surrounding air particles. These air particles push on other air particles, transferring energy in waves away from the source. Hearing is the sensation experienced in response to these sound waves.

Journey of a Sound Wave Your ears are organs specialized for hearing. Each ear has an outer, middle, and inner part. The parts of the ear are shown in **Figure 12.** When sound waves reach the outer ear, they are funneled into the middle ear, where they cause the eardrum to vibrate. The vibrating eardrum makes tiny ear bones vibrate. One of the tiny bones vibrates against the **cochlea** (KAHK lee uh), a tiny snail-shaped organ of the inner ear. Inside the cochlea, the vibrations create waves that are similar to the waves you can make by tapping on a glass of water. Neurons in the cochlea convert these waves to electrical impulses and send them to the area of the brain that interprets sound.

Figure 12 *A sound wave travels into the outer ear. It is converted to bone vibrations in the middle ear, then to liquid vibrations in the inner ear, and finally to nerve impulses.*

Sound waves

Auditory nerve

Cochlea

Eardrum   Ear bones

Does This Suit Your Taste?

When you put food in your mouth, your sense of what the food tastes like comes mostly from your tongue. Taste is the sensation you feel when the brain is made aware of certain dissolved chemicals in your mouth. The receptors for taste are clustered in the *taste buds.* The tongue is covered with tiny bumps called *papillae* (puh PIL ee), and the taste buds are embedded in the sides of these bumps. As shown in **Figure 13,** there are four types of taste buds. Each type responds to one of the four basic tastes: sweet, sour, salty, and bitter.

Your Nose Knows

Have you ever noticed that when you have a congested nose you can't taste food very well? Try eating a piece of peppermint while holding your nose. The mint taste is not very intense until you inhale through your nose. That's because smell and taste are closely related. The brain combines information from your taste buds and nose to give you a sense of flavor. The receptors for smell are located on *olfactory cells* in the upper part of your nasal cavity. They react to chemicals that are inhaled and dissolved in the moist lining of the nasal cavity. The woman in **Figure 14** is using her sense of smell to test the effectiveness of underarm deodorants.

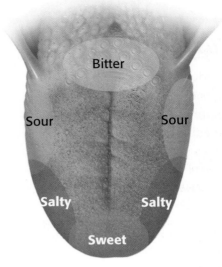

Figure 13 *Taste buds in different parts of the tongue respond to different types of chemicals.*

Figure 14 *This woman's nose is detecting chemicals in the sweat and in the deodorants used by this man. Her brain will generate opinions about the smells that she will then record in her report.*

REVIEW

1. List three sensations that receptors in the skin can detect.

2. Explain why you would have trouble seeing bright colors at a candlelit dinner.

3. How is your sense of taste similar to your sense of smell?

4. **Applying Concepts** If you can focus on objects close to you but things become blurry when they are far away, would a concave or convex lens correct your vision?

internet connect

SC*i*LINKS.
NSTA

TOPIC: The Senses, The Eye
GO TO: www.scilinks.org
*sci*LINKS **NUMBER:** HSTL610, HSTL615

What You'll Do

◆ Explain the function of the endocrine system.
◆ List the glands of the endocrine system and describe some of their functions.
◆ Describe how feedback controls stop and start hormone release.

The Endocrine System

You already know that the job of the nervous system is to communicate with all the other body systems. Its main role is to respond to stimuli. But it is not the only system that has this role. Your **endocrine system** is involved with the control of slower, long-term processes, such as fluid balance, growth, and sexual development. Instead of electrical messages, the endocrine system sends messages via chemicals.

Chemical Messengers

The endocrine system controls body functions with the use of chemicals that are released from endocrine glands. A **gland** is a group of cells that makes special chemicals for your body. Chemicals that are produced by the endocrine glands are called **hormones.** The chemicals made by endocrine glands are released into the bloodstream and carried to other places in the body. Because hormones act as chemical messengers, an endocrine gland near your brain can control the actions of an organ located somewhere else in your body.

Glands at Work Endocrine glands often affect many organs at one time. For example, your adrenal glands prepare your organs to deal with stress. They make the hormone *epinephrine* (ep ih NEF rihn), also known as *adrenalin*. Epinephrine speeds up your heartbeat and breathing rate to prepare your body either to run from danger or to fight for survival. This hormone effect is often referred to as the fight-or-flight response. You may have noticed these effects when you were frightened or angry.

Figure 15 *When you have to move quickly to avoid danger, your adrenal glands help by making more blood glucose available for energy.*

Fight or Flight?

Maria was working late at the library. She was worried about walking home alone. As she started home, she noticed a shadowy figure walking quickly behind her. The figure was gaining on her! She could feel her heart pounding in her chest. She began to run, and then a familiar voice called out her name. It was her father. He had walked to the library to check on her. What a relief!

Maria had a fight-or-flight response. Write a paragraph describing a time when you had a fight-or-flight experience. Include in your story the following terms: *hormones, fight-or-flight*, and *epinephrine.*

Your body has several other endocrine glands, some with many different functions. For example, your pituitary gland stimulates skeletal growth, helps the thyroid function properly, regulates the amount of water in the blood, and stimulates the birth process in pregnant women. The names and some of the functions of this and other endocrine glands are summarized in **Figure 16.**

Figure 16 *Your endocrine glands produce chemicals called hormones that control many of your body functions.*

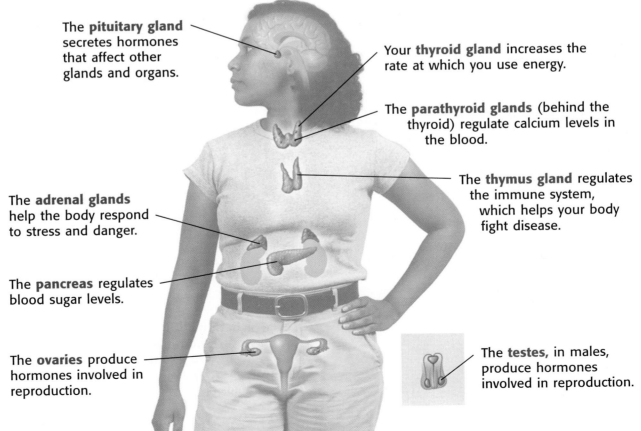

The **pituitary gland** secretes hormones that affect other glands and organs.

Your **thyroid gland** increases the rate at which you use energy.

The **parathyroid glands** (behind the thyroid) regulate calcium levels in the blood.

The **thymus gland** regulates the immune system, which helps your body fight disease.

The **adrenal glands** help the body respond to stress and danger.

The **pancreas** regulates blood sugar levels.

The **ovaries** produce hormones involved in reproduction.

The **testes,** in males, produce hormones involved in reproduction.

Communication and Control   **601**

Controlling the Controls

How do endocrine glands know when to start and stop hormone release? They know because your body has special systems called **feedback controls** that turn endocrine glands on and off. Feedback controls work something like a thermostat on an air conditioner. Once a room reaches the required temperature, the thermostat sends a message to the air conditioner to stop sending in cold air. Much in the same way, a feedback control sends a message to an endocrine gland to stop sending in a particular hormone. **Figure 17** traces the steps of a feedback control that regulates blood sugar.

Figure 17 *In this feedback-control system, the pancreas produces hormones that help your body maintain the correct blood sugar level.*

Glucose Feedback Control

1 After you eat a meal, glucose is absorbed into the bloodstream from the small intestine.

2 When the glucose level in the blood is high, the pancreas releases the hormone insulin into the blood.

3 Insulin signals the liver to take in glucose from the body, convert it to glycogen, and store it for future energy needs.

4 When the blood sugar level returns to normal, the pancreas stops releasing insulin.

5 To keep your blood sugar level from falling below normal, you must eat again.

Pancreas

Pancreas

Liver

Hormone Imbalances

Insulin is a hormone made by the pancreas. When the blood sugar level rises after a person has eaten something, insulin triggers the cells to take in glucose and sends a message to the liver to store glucose. A person whose pancreas cannot make enough insulin has a condition called *diabetes mellitus*. A person with diabetes mellitus may need daily injections of insulin to keep his or her blood glucose levels within safe limits. Some patients, like the woman in **Figure 18,** receive their insulin automatically from a small machine they wear next to their body.

Growth Hormone Sometimes a child may have a pituitary gland that doesn't make enough growth hormone. This causes the child's growth to be stunted. Fortunately, if this problem is detected soon enough, a doctor can prescribe hormone replacement medication and monitor the child's growth. If the pituitary makes too much growth hormone at an early age, the person becomes much taller than expected.

Figure 18 *This young woman has diabetes and must have daily injections of the hormone insulin.*

Thyroxine When a person doesn't get enough iodine in the diet, the thyroid gland cannot make enough of the hormone *thyroxine*. This causes the thyroid to swell up and form a mass called a *goiter*. Because thyroxine increases metabolism, this person's cells are less active than normal, causing fatigue, weight gain, and other problems.

REVIEW

1. What is the function of the endocrine system?

2. Why are feedback controls important?

3. Name four endocrine glands, and tell what each one does in the body.

4. **Applying Concepts** Epinephrine, the fight-or-flight hormone, increases the level of glucose in the blood. Why would this be important in times of stress?

5. **Illustrating Concepts** Look around your house for an example of a feedback control. Draw a diagram explaining how this feedback control works to start and stop an action.

internet**connect**

SC*i*LINKS
NSTA

TOPIC: Hormones
GO TO: www.scilinks.org
*sci*LINKS NUMBER: HSTL620

Chapter Highlights

Vocabulary

central nervous system (p. 588)

peripheral nervous system (p. 588)

neuron (p. 589)

impulse (p. 589)

receptor (p. 590)

nerve (p. 590)

brain (p. 591)

reflex (p. 594)

Section Notes

• The central nervous system includes the brain and spinal cord. The peripheral nervous system includes nerves and sensory receptors.

• A neuron receives information at branched endings called dendrites and passes information to other cells along a fiber called an axon.

• Sensory neurons detect information about the body and its environment. Motor neurons carry messages from the brain and spinal cord to other parts of the body.

• The cerebrum is the largest part of the brain and is involved with thinking, sensations, and voluntary muscle control.

• The cerebellum is the second largest part of the brain. It keeps track of the body's position and helps maintain balance.

• The medulla controls involuntary activities such as heart rate, blood pressure, and breathing.

• Pain signals can trigger a quick, involuntary action, called a reflex, in which a motor neuron sends a message to a muscle without first receiving a signal from the brain.

✓ Skills Check

Math Concepts

THE SPEED OF AN IMPULSE An impulse travels very fast. As shown in the MathBreak on page 589, to calculate the amount of time that it takes for an impulse to travel a certain distance, you must first know the speed it is traveling. Then you can divide the distance by the speed to get the time. For example, if an impulse travels 150 m/s, it would take it 0.02 seconds to travel 3 m.

$$\text{time} = \frac{3 \text{ m (distance)}}{150 \text{ m/s (speed)}} = 0.02 \text{ s}$$

Visual Understanding

PATH OF LIGHT Look back at Figure 10 on page 596 to review the path of light entering the eye. The light first passes through the transparent cornea, then through the opening called the pupil, and then through the lens. At the back of the eye, the light is detected by receptors in the retina.

SECTION 2

Vocabulary

retina *(p. 596)*
rods *(p. 596)*
cones *(p. 596)*
iris *(p. 597)*
lens *(p. 597)*
cochlea *(p. 598)*

Section Notes

- Different kinds of receptors in the skin are responsible for detecting touch, pressure, temperature, and pain.

- The retina of the eye contains photoreceptors that react to light and cause impulses to be sent to the brain.

- The lens of the eye can change shape to adjust the point of focus so that the image is focused on the retina. Improper focus can usually be corrected with glasses or contact lenses.

- Special receptors inside the cochlea of the ear react to sound waves and send impulses to the brain.

- Receptors for taste are located in taste buds on the bumps of the tongue.

- Receptors for smell are on olfactory cells located in the upper part of the nasal cavity.

Labs

You've Gotta Lotta Nerve *(p. 772)*

SECTION 3

Vocabulary

endocrine system *(p. 600)*
gland *(p. 600)*
hormone *(p. 600)*
feedback control *(p. 602)*

Section Notes

- The endocrine system communicates with other systems using chemicals called hormones.

- Hormones are made in endocrine glands.

- The adrenal glands secrete hormones that help the body cope with stress. Epinephrine is the hormone most associated with fight-or-flight situations.

- Feedback control is the body's way of turning glands on and off so that they release hormones only when necessary.

---

internet**connect**

GO TO: go.hrw.com

Visit the **HRW** Web site for a variety of learning tools related to this chapter. Just type in the keyword:

KEYWORD: HSTBD4

SCI**LINKS**sm
NSTA

GO TO: www.scilinks.org

Visit the **National Science Teachers Association** on-line Web site for Internet resources related to this chapter. Just type in the *sci*LINKS number for more information about the topic:

TOPIC: The Nervous System   *sci*LINKS NUMBER: HSTL605
TOPIC: The Senses   *sci*LINKS NUMBER: HSTL610
TOPIC: The Eye   *sci*LINKS NUMBER: HSTL615
TOPIC: Hormones   *sci*LINKS NUMBER: HSTL620

Chapter Review

USING VOCABULARY

To complete the following sentences, choose the correct term from each pair of terms listed below:

1. Your brain and spinal cord make up your __?__. (*central nervous system* or *peripheral nervous system*)

2. Sensory receptors in the __?__ detect vibrations. (*cochlea* or *eardrum*)

3. Epinephrine is produced by the adrenal glands in response to __?__. (*glucose* or *stress*)

4. The part of a neuron that passes an impulse to other cells is the __?__. (*dendrite* or *axon terminal*)

5. The medulla is mostly responsible for activities that are __?__. (*involuntary* or *voluntary*)

6. Receptors that can convert light into impulses are found in the __?__. (*olfactory cells* or *retina*)

UNDERSTANDING CONCEPTS

Multiple Choice

7. Which of the following has receptors for smelling?
   a. cochlea cells   c. olfactory cells
   b. thermoreceptors   d. optic nerve

8. Which of the following gives eyes their color?
   a. iris   c. lens
   b. cornea   d. retina

9. Which of the glands is associated with goiters?
   a. adrenal   c. thyroid
   b. pituitary   d. pancreas

10. Which of the following is not part of the peripheral nervous system?
    a. spinal cord
    b. axons
    c. sensory receptors
    d. motor neurons

11. Which part of the brain regulates blood pressure?
    a. right cerebral hemisphere
    b. left cerebral hemisphere
    c. cerebellum
    d. medulla

12. Which of the following is associated with the endocrine system?
    a. reflex
    b. salivary gland
    c. fight-or-flight response
    d. voluntary response

Short Answer

13. Describe several situations in which your adrenal glands might release epinephrine, causing you to have a fight-or-flight reaction.

14. What causes the size of your pupils to change?

15. What is a reflex? How does a reflex enable you to act quickly?

16. What is the function of the middle-ear bones?

17. Using the terms you learned in this chapter, write down a step-by-step sequence for the path taken by an impulse, beginning at a pain receptor in your left big toe. Be sure to mention each kind of neuron and its parts as well as specific organs in the nervous system.

Concept Map

18. Use the following terms to create a concept map: the nervous system, spinal cord, medulla, peripheral nervous system, brain, cerebrum, central nervous system, cerebellum.

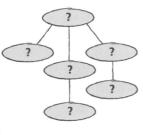

CRITICAL THINKING AND PROBLEM SOLVING

Write one or two sentences to answer the following questions:

19. Why is it important to have a lens that can change shape inside the eye?

20. Why can the nervous system have a faster effect on the body than the endocrine system?

21. Why is it important that reflexes occur without thought?

MATH IN SCIENCE

22. Sound travels about 335 m/s (1 km is equal to 1,000 m). How many kilometers would a sound travel in 1 minute?

23. Some axons can send one impulse every 0.4 milliseconds. One second is equal to 1,000 milliseconds. How many impulses could one of these axons send every second?

INTERPRETING GRAPHICS

Look at the drawing below, and answer the following questions:

24. Which letter identifies the gland that regulates blood sugar?

25. Which letter identifies the gland that releases a hormone that stimulates the birth process in pregnant women?

26. Which letter identifies the gland that helps the body fight disease?

NOW What Do You Think?

Take a minute to review your answers to the ScienceLog questions on page 587. Have your answers changed? If necessary, revise your answers based on what you have learned since you began this chapter.

Science, Technology, and Society

Light on Lenses

Can you see in pitch darkness? No, of course not! You need light to see. But there is something else you need in order to see. You need a lens. A **lens** is a curved transparent object that *refracts,* or bends, light.

Lenses are necessary to focus light in all kinds of applications, including in telescopes, microscopes, binoculars, cameras, contact lenses, eyeglasses, and magnifying lenses.

Light Bounces

To learn how lenses work, you must first know something about how light travels. A ray of light travels in a straight path from its source until it strikes an object. When light strikes an object, much of the light bounces off, or is reflected. The light reflects from the object at the same angle that it struck the object in the first place.

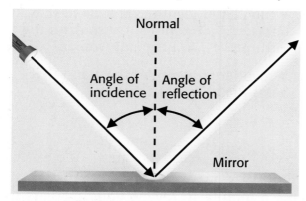

▲ *The angle formed by the incoming light (angle of incidence) always equals the angle of the reflected light (angle of reflection).*

Lenses Bend Light

A lens allows light to travel through it. However, as the light passes through the lens, it is

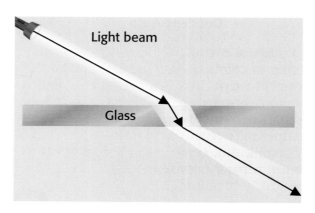

▲ *Light changes speed and direction when it passes from one material into another.*

refracted. **Refraction** is the bending of a light ray as it passes from one transparent material into another, such as when light traveling through air passes through a glass lens.

The type of lens determines how much and in which direction the light is bent. A lens that is thicker in the middle than at its edges is called a **convex lens.** This type of lens bends light toward its center. Convex lenses are used in magnifying glasses, microscopes, and telescopes. The lenses in your eyes are convex lenses.

A lens that is thinner in the middle than at its edges is called a **concave lens.** This type of lens bends light away from its center. Both convex lenses and concave lenses are often used to help correct vision. Convex lenses are also used in combination with concave lenses in cameras to focus light on the film.

Light Your Way

▶ Do some additional research to find out what a photorefractive keratectomy (PRK) is and how it works to correct a person's vision.

Eureka!

Pathway to a Cure

Do you know what would happen if your brain sent out too many impulses to the muscles in your body? First the overload would increase the number of contractions in your muscles, and it would be difficult to carry out simple movements, like scratching your arm or picking up a glass. Even when you wanted to rest, your muscles would continue to tremble. This is what happens to people with Parkinson's disease, and unfortunately, there is still no cure.

The Disease

Parkinson's disease affects the cells in the brain that regulate muscles. These cells require the chemical dopamine, which slows down the activity of nerves so they can function properly. But if the cells that supply the muscle-regulating cells with dopamine are damaged, the brain will send continuous impulses to the muscles. This results in Parkinson's disease.

Parkinson's disease is often diagnosed only after a person has already lost about 80 percent of his or her dopamine-supplying cells. Although there is no known cure for Parkinson's disease, some patients can be treated with chemicals that act like dopamine. Unfortunately, these substitutes are not as good as the real thing. Dopamine itself cannot be given because it cannot pass from the blood into the brain tissue.

Breakthrough

Dr. Bertha Madras studies the effects of drug addiction on the brain. While studying the effects of cocaine addiction, she discovered that a chemical called tropane attaches itself to the same nerves that release dopamine in the brain. This discovery may be used to detect and diagnose Parkinson's disease earlier and at a lower cost to the patient.

A Glow in the Darkness

Madras and her colleagues thought they could use tropane to study the cells that release dopamine. They added a radioactive component to the tropane to make a chemical called altropane. Altropane also attaches to the dopamine-releasing cells. But unlike tropane, altropane glows, so it shows up in a brain scan. Healthy people have large areas where the altropane attaches. Among patients with Parkinson's disease, because of the nerve loss, the altropane attaches to fewer nerves. Therefore, brain scans from these patients do not have as many glowing collections of altropane.

Using this new procedure to diagnose Parkinson's disease could allow doctors to find the disease in people before the neurons are severely damaged or completely lost.

Healthy subject   Parkinson's subject

▲ *Brain scans, such as the ones above, can be used to diagnose Parkinson's disease.*

Activity

▶ Find out what a Single Photon Emission Computed Tomography (SPECT) image is and how it is used to study Parkinson's disease.

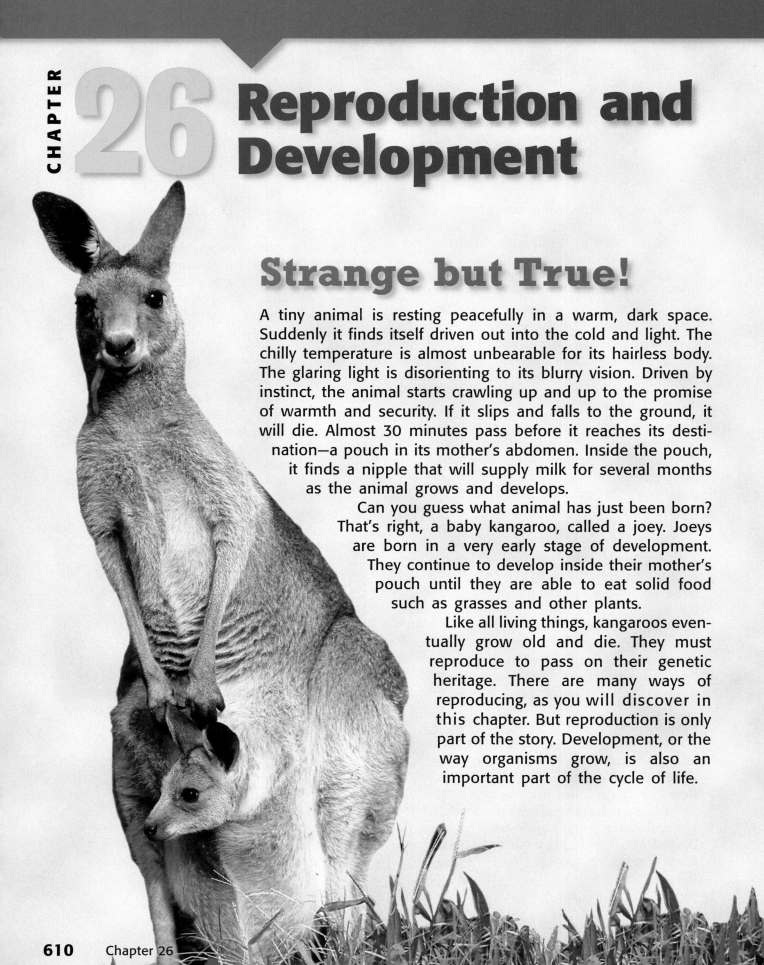

26 Reproduction and Development

Strange but True!

A tiny animal is resting peacefully in a warm, dark space. Suddenly it finds itself driven out into the cold and light. The chilly temperature is almost unbearable for its hairless body. The glaring light is disorienting to its blurry vision. Driven by instinct, the animal starts crawling up and up to the promise of warmth and security. If it slips and falls to the ground, it will die. Almost 30 minutes pass before it reaches its destination—a pouch in its mother's abdomen. Inside the pouch, it finds a nipple that will supply milk for several months as the animal grows and develops.

Can you guess what animal has just been born? That's right, a baby kangaroo, called a joey. Joeys are born in a very early stage of development. They continue to develop inside their mother's pouch until they are able to eat solid food such as grasses and other plants.

Like all living things, kangaroos eventually grow old and die. They must reproduce to pass on their genetic heritage. There are many ways of reproducing, as you will discover in this chapter. But reproduction is only part of the story. Development, or the way organisms grow, is also an important part of the cycle of life.

What Do You Think?

In your ScienceLog, try to answer the following questions based on what you already know:

1. Do all animals have two parents?

2. What makes you physically different from an adult?

3. What percentage of genes do you inherit from your mother? your father?

How Grows It?

As you read this, you are aging. Your body is growing into the body of an adult. Look around at your classmates. Their bodies are also growing. But do you and your classmates' bodies have the same proportions as an adult's body? Do this experiment to find out.

Procedure

1. Pair up with a classmate. Have your partner help you measure your total height, head height, and leg length with a **tape measure** and **meterstick.** Your teacher will tell you how to do these measurements.

2. Calculate your head-to-body proportion and leg-to-body proportion. Use the following equations:

$$\left(\frac{\text{head height}}{\text{body height}}\right) \times 100 = \text{head proportion}$$

$$\left(\frac{\text{leg length}}{\text{body height}}\right) \times 100 = \text{leg proportion}$$

3. Your teacher has written his or her head, body, and leg measurements on the board, along with those of two other adults. Calculate their proportions. Record all the measurements and calculations in your ScienceLog.

Analysis

4. How does your head proportion compare with that of adults? How do the leg proportions compare?

Terms to Learn

asexual reproduction

sexual reproduction

egg

sperm

zygote

external fertilization

internal fertilization

What You'll Do

◆ Distinguish between asexual and sexual reproduction.

◆ Explain the difference between external and internal fertilization.

◆ Describe the three different types of mammalian development.

Animal Reproduction

The life span of some living things is very short compared with ours. For instance, a fruit fly lives only about 80 days. Other organisms live for a long time. A bristlecone pine can live for 2,000 to 6,000 years. But all living things eventually die. If a species is to survive, its members must reproduce.

A Chip off the Old Block

Some animals, particularly simpler ones, reproduce asexually. In **asexual reproduction,** a single parent has offspring that are genetically identical to itself.

One kind of asexual reproduction is called *budding.* This occurs when a small part of the parent's body develops into an independent organism. The hydra shown in **Figure 1** is reproducing asexually by budding. The young hydra is genetically identical to its parent.

Fragmentation is another type of asexual reproduction. In fragmentation, an organism breaks into two or more parts, each of which may grow into a separate individual. Sea stars can reproduce by fragmentation. Because sea stars eat oysters, people used to try to kill sea stars by chopping them into pieces and throwing the pieces back into the water. They didn't know that each arm of a sea star can grow into an entire organism! This can be seen in **Figure 2.**

Figure 1 *The hydra bud will separate from its parent. Buds from other organisms, such as coral, remain attached to the parent.*

Figure 2 *The largest arm on this sea star was a fragment, from which the rest of the sea star has grown. In time, all of the sea star's arms will grow to the same size.*

It Takes Two

Sexual Reproduction produces offspring by combining the genetic material of more than one parent. Most animals, including humans, reproduce sexually. Sexual reproduction most commonly involves two parents, a male and a female. The female parent produces sex cells called **eggs.** The male parent produces sex cells called **sperm.** When an egg's nucleus joins with a sperm's nucleus, a new kind of cell, called a **zygote,** is created. This joining of an egg and sperm is known as *fertilization.*

Review of Meiosis Genes are located in *chromosomes.* All human cells except egg and sperm cells contain 46 chromosomes. Eggs and sperm each contain only 23 chromosomes. Eggs and sperm are formed by a process known as *meiosis.*

In humans, meiosis involves the division of one cell with 46 chromosomes into four sex cells with 23 chromosomes each. When an egg and sperm join to form a zygote, the original number of 46 chromosomes is restored. This combination of genes from the father and mother results in a zygote that will grow into a unique individual. **Figure 3** shows how genes are intermixed through three generations.

MATH BREAK

Chromo-Combos

A cell undergoes meiosis. This cell has 6 chromosomes in 3 pairs. How many chromosomal combinations are possible in the formed sex cells? To find out, use the following formula:

2^x = possible variations where x = the number of pairs.

2^3 (or $2 \times 2 \times 2$) = 8

Therefore, 8 variations are possible.

A typical human cell has 46 chromosomes in 23 pairs. If the cell undergoes meiosis, how many chromosomal combinations are possible in the resulting sex cells?

Figure 3 *Eggs and sperm contain genes. You inherit genes from both of your parents. Your parents each inherited genes from both of their parents.*

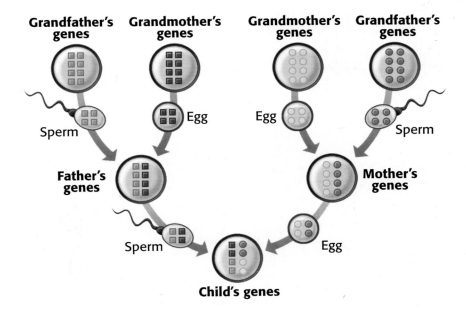

Self-Check

What is the difference between sexual and asexual reproduction? *(See page 782 to check your answer.)*

Internal and External Fertilization

Depending on the animal, fertilization may occur either outside or inside the female's body. Some fishes and amphibians reproduce by **external fertilization,** in which the sperm fertilize the eggs outside the female's body. External fertilization must take place in a moist environment so the delicate zygotes won't dry out.

Many frogs, such as those pictured in **Figure 4,** mate every spring. The female frog releases her eggs first. The male frog then releases sperm over the eggs to fertilize them. The frogs leave the fertilized eggs to develop on their own. In about two weeks, the eggs hatch into tadpoles.

Figure 4 *Frogs fertilize their eggs externally. Some species can produce more than 300 offspring in one season.*

The Inside Story With **internal fertilization,** eggs and sperm join inside the female's body. Reptiles, birds, mammals, and some fishes reproduce by internal fertilization. Many animals that use internal fertilization lay fertilized eggs. The female penguin in **Figure 5,** for example, usually lays one or two eggs after internal fertilization has occurred.

In most mammals, internal fertilization is followed by the development of a fertilized egg inside the mother's body. Many mammals give birth to young that are well developed. Young zebras, like the one in **Figure 6,** can stand up and nurse almost immediately after birth.

Figure 5 *Instead of leaving the eggs to develop on their own, penguin parents take turns crouching over them to keep them warm.*

Figure 6 *This zebra has just been born, but he is already able to stand. Within an hour, he will be able to run.*

Making Mammals

All mammals reproduce sexually and nurture their young with milk. There are some differences in how mammals produce offspring, but every mammal follows one of three types of development.

Monotremes Mammals that lay eggs are *monotremes*. Two families of monotremes live today—the echidna and the platypus. After these animals lay their eggs, there is an incubation period that lasts up to 2 weeks. When the eggs hatch, the babies are very undeveloped. They crawl into a fold of their mother's skin and are nourished by the milk that oozes from her pores.

Marsupials Mammals that give birth to live young that are only partially developed are *marsupials*. There are about 260 species of marsupials. Most of them have pouches where their young develop, but some South American species do not have this feature. Marsupials with pouches have extra bones to help support the weight of their young, as can be seen in **Figure 7.** When a baby marsupial attaches itself to its mother's nipple, the nipple expands in the baby's mouth to prevent the baby from separating from its mother.

Placental Mammals There are almost 4,000 different species of placental mammals. These include whales, elephants, armadillos, bats, horses, and humans. *Placental mammals* nourish their young internally before birth. Newborn placental mammals are highly developed compared with newborn marsupials or monotremes.

Figure 7 *The skeleton of this opposum has two extra bones extending forward from its pelvis to help support the weight of its young.*

REVIEW

1. How many parents are needed to reproduce asexually?

2. What is the difference between monotremes and marsupials?

3. How is a zygote formed?

4. **Applying Concepts** Birds lay eggs, but they are not considered monotremes. Explain why.

internet**connect**

SCI**LINKS**
NSTA

TOPIC: Reproduction
GO TO: www.scilinks.org
*sci***LINKS NUMBER:** HSTL630

Human Reproduction

What You'll Do

◆ Describe the functions of the male and female reproductive systems.
◆ Discuss disorders and diseases that are associated with human reproduction.

When a human sperm and egg combine, a new human begins to grow. About 9 months later, a mother gives birth to her baby. But what happens before that? Where do eggs and sperm come from?

The Male Reproductive System

The male reproductive system, shown in **Figure 8,** produces sperm and delivers it to the female reproductive system. The **testes** (singular, *testis*) make sperm and testosterone. Testosterone is the principal male sex hormone. It regulates the production of sex cells and the development of male characteristics.

Sperm Production The human body is usually around 37°C, but sperm cannot develop properly at such high temperatures. That is why the two testes rest in the *scrotum,* a skin-covered sac that hangs from the body. The scrotum is about 2 degrees cooler than the body. Inside each testis are masses of tightly coiled tubes called *seminiferous* (SEM uh NIF uhr uhs) *tubules* (TOO BYOOLZ), where sperm are produced. A healthy adult male produces several hundred million sperm each day! This massive, continuous sperm production begins at puberty. **Puberty** is the time of life when the sex organs of both males and females become mature.

Before sperm leave a testis, they are stored in a tube called an *epididymis* (EP uh DID i mis). Another tube called a **vas deferens** (vas DEF uh RENZ) passes from each epididymis into the body. As sperm swim through the vas deferens, they mix with fluids from several glands. The mixture of sperm and fluids is called **semen.**

To leave the body, semen passes through the vas deferens into the *urethra,* the tube that runs through the penis. The **penis** transfers semen into the female's body during sexual intercourse.

Figure 8 The Male Reproductive System

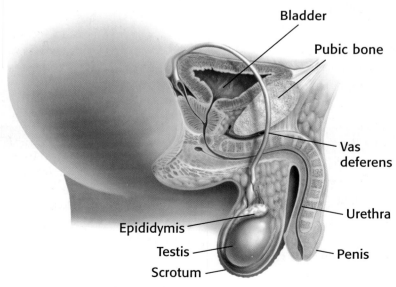

Bladder
Pubic bone
Vas deferens
Urethra
Epididymis
Testis
Scrotum
Penis

The Female Reproductive System

The female reproductive system, shown in **Figure 9,** produces eggs, nurtures fertilized eggs, and gives birth. The **ovaries** produce the eggs. The two ovaries also produce sex hormones, such as estrogen and progesterone, that regulate the release of eggs and direct the development of female characteristics.

The Egg's Journey An ovary contains eggs in various stages of development. As an egg matures, it becomes a huge cell, growing to almost 200,000 times the size of a sperm. During *ovulation,* an egg is ejected through the ovary wall. Then the egg passes into a fallopian (fuh LOH pee uhn) tube. A **fallopian tube** leads from each ovary to the uterus. The **uterus** is the organ where a baby grows and develops.

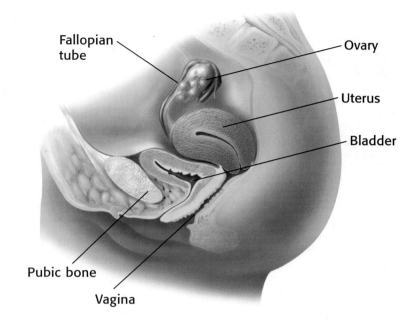

Figure 9 The Female Reproductive System

Fallopian tube

Ovary

Uterus

Bladder

Pubic bone

Vagina

Every month starting at puberty, the lining of the uterus thickens in preparation for pregnancy. If fertilization occurs, the zygote moves down a fallopian tube and embeds in the lining of the uterus. When a baby is born, it passes from the uterus through the vagina. The **vagina** is the same passageway that received the sperm during sexual intercourse.

Menstrual Cycle To prepare for pregnancy, a female's reproductive system goes through several changes. These changes, called the menstrual cycle, usually occur every 28 days. The first day of the cycle is the beginning of *menstruation,* the monthly discharge of blood and tissue from the uterus. Menstruation lasts about 5 days. As soon as menstruation is over, the uterus's lining begins to build up again in preparation for ovulation. Ovulation typically occurs around the 14th day of the cycle. If the egg isn't fertilized by the time it reaches the uterus, it will deteriorate. Menstruation will flush the egg away, starting the cycle over again. A female's menstrual cycle begins at puberty and continues until late middle age.

MATH BREAK

Counting Eggs

1. The average human female ovulates every month from about age 12 to about age 50. How many mature eggs can she produce during that time period?

2. A female's ovaries typically house 2 million immature egg cells. If she ovulates regularly from age 12 to age 50, what percentage of her eggs will mature?

Irregularities and Disorders

In most cases, the human reproductive system completes its functions flawlessly. However, as with any body system, there can sometimes be irregularities or disorders.

Figure 10 *Identical twins have the exact same genes. Many identical twins who are reared apart have similar personalities and interests.*

Multiple Births Have you ever seen a pair of identical twins? Sometimes they are so similar that even their parents can't tell them apart. About one pair of identical twins is born for every 250 births. Another type of twins, called fraternal twins, is also born frequently. Fraternal twins can look very different from each other.

Twins, such as those shown in **Figure 10,** are the most common type of multiple births, but humans can also have triplets (3 babies), quadruplets (4 babies), quintuplets (5 babies), and so on. These types of multiple births are extremely rare. For instance, quadruplets occur only about once in every 705,000 births. Do you know what circumstances result in a multiple birth? To find out, do the Apply exercise at the bottom of this page.

Ectopic Pregnancy In a normal pregnancy, the fertilized egg travels to the uterus and attaches itself to the uterus's wall. In an *ectopic* (ek TAHP ik) *pregnancy,* the fertilized egg attaches itself to a fallopian tube or another area of the reproductive system. Because the zygote cannot develop correctly outside of the uterus, an ectopic pregnancy can be very dangerous for both the mother and child.

Two Types of Twins

Zach and Drew are fraternal twins. They don't look much alike. Emily and Carol are identical twins. They are hard to tell apart. Why are some twins identical and others fraternal? Consider the two possibilities illustrated at right: In *A,* the mass of cells from a single fertilized egg separates into two halves early in development, and in *B* two eggs are released by an ovary and fertilized by two different sperm cells. Record the answers to the following questions in your ScienceLog:

1. Which instance, *A* or *B,* would produce identical twins? Explain your answer.
2. Could fraternal twins be (a) both boys, (b) both girls, (c) one girl and one boy, or (d) all of the above?

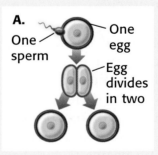

A. One sperm — One egg — Egg divides in two

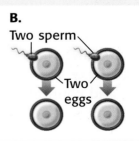

B. Two sperm — Two eggs

Infertility In the United States, about 15 percent of married couples have difficulty producing offspring. Many of these couples are **infertile,** which means they are unable to have children. Men may be infertile because they cannot produce enough healthy sperm. This is called a low sperm count. Women may be infertile because they do not ovulate normally. Sexually transmitted diseases can also cause infertility.

STDs *Sexually transmitted diseases* (STDs) are diseases that can pass from an infected person to an uninfected person during sexual contact. An STD you may have heard about is the acquired immune deficiency syndrome (AIDS). Other common STDs are shown in the table below.

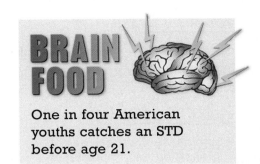

BRAIN FOOD

One in four American youths catches an STD before age 21.

The Spread of STDs in the U.S.	
STD	**Approximate new cases each year**
Chlamydia	3–10 million
Gonorrhea	1–3 million
Genital warts	1 million
AIDS	750,000
Genital herpes	500,000
Syphilis	120,000

Chemistry CONNECTION

Many chemicals in pollutants are similar to female hormones. Studies are beginning to link these chemicals with early menstruation and low sperm counts.

Cancer Cancer, the uncontrolled division of cells, sometimes occurs in the reproductive organs. The testes and the prostate gland, a gland that produces the fluid in semen, are common sites of cancer in men over age 50. In women, the ovaries and breasts are common sites of cancer.

REVIEW

1. What is the difference between sperm and semen?

2. Can a woman become pregnant at any time of the month? Explain.

3. Define *sexually transmitted diseases,* and give three examples.

4. **Applying Concepts** How are the ovaries similar to the testes? How are they different?

internet connect

SCiLINKS

NSTA

TOPIC: Reproductive System Irregularities or Disorders
GO TO: www.scilinks.org
*sci*LINKS **NUMBER:** HSTL640

Growth and Development

What You'll Do

◆ Summarize the processes of fertilization and implantation.
◆ Describe the course of human development.

Every one of us starts out as a single cell that will become a complete person. We are made of millions of cells, each with its own job to do. You, of course, are no exception. You have become a very complex individual, capable of thousands of different thoughts and actions. It is hard to believe that a person as remarkable as you began your life as a single cell, but that is just what happened.

A New Life

The natural process of creating a human baby starts when a man deposits millions of sperm into a woman's vagina during sexual intercourse. Most of the sperm will die because of the vagina's acidic environment, but a few hundred are able to make it through the uterus and into the fallopian tube, as can be seen in **Figure 11.** The surviving sperm cover the egg, releasing enzymes that help dissolve the egg's outer covering. As soon as one sperm gets through, a membrane closes around the fertilized egg. This membrane keeps other sperm cells from entering.

Figure 11 Fertilization and Implantation

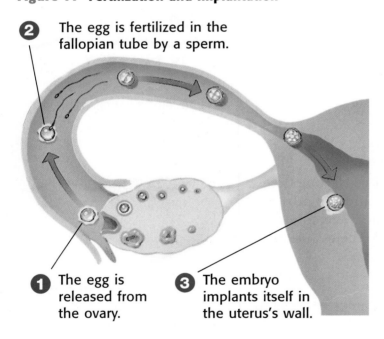

2 The egg is fertilized in the fallopian tube by a sperm.

1 The egg is released from the ovary.

3 The embryo implants itself in the uterus's wall.

Implantation The fertilized egg travels down the woman's fallopian tube toward her uterus. The journey takes about 5 days. The zygote undergoes cell division many times during the trip. By the time it reaches the uterus, it is a tiny ball of cells called an **embryo.** During the next few days, the embryo must embed itself in the thick, nutrient-rich lining of its mother's uterus. This process is called **implantation,** and only about 30 percent of all embryos successfully do it. **Figure 12** shows an implanted embryo.

The embryo's actual size is slightly smaller than the period at the end of this sentence.

Figure 12 *This embryo has implanted in the wall of its mother's uterus.*

Embryo

Before Birth

When the embryo implants itself in a woman's uterus, the woman is officially pregnant. For the embryo to survive, a special two-way exchange organ called a **placenta** begins to grow. The placenta contains a network of blood vessels that provide the embryo with oxygen and nutrients from the mother's blood. Wastes that the embryo produces are removed by the placenta and transported to the mother's blood for her to excrete. Although the embryo's blood and the mother's blood flow very near each other inside the placenta, they never actually mix.

✓ Self-Check

Why is it important that the embryo be implanted in the uterus and not elsewhere? *(See page 782 to check your answer.)*

First Month About 1 week after implantation, the embryo's blood cells and a heart tube form. Then the heart tube begins to twitch, starting the rhythmic beating that will continue for the individual's entire life. By the fourth week, the embryo is almost 2 mm long. Surrounding the embryo is a thin, fluid-filled membrane called the *amnion*, which is formed to protect the growing embryo from shocks. The **umbilical cord** is another new development. It connects the embryo to the placenta. The umbilical cord, amnion, and placenta can be seen in **Figure 13.**

Figure 13 *The placenta, amnion, and umbilical cord are the life support system for the fetus.*

Second Month By the time the embryo is 4 weeks old, it has the beginnings of a brain and spinal cord. It also has tiny limb buds that will eventually develop into arms and legs. Its nostrils, eyelids, hands, and feet then begin to form. Its muscles begin to develop, and for the first time in its life, its brain begins to send signals to other parts of its body. Despite all these transformations, the embryo is still only about the size of a peanut. **Figure 14** shows a 5-week-old embryo.

Figure 14 A 5-Week-Old Embryo

Actual size

Figure 15 **A 12-Week-Old Fetus**

Actual size

Third Month The next stage comes as tiny movements begin to flutter through the embryo's body. The embryo stretches its legs and twitches its arms. It is now 8 weeks old and is developed enough to be called a **fetus.** Three more weeks pass, and it continues to grow at a fast rate, doubling and then tripling its size within a month. The fetus's hands are now the size of teardrops, and its body weighs as much as two pieces of paper. A 12-week-old fetus can be seen in **Figure 15.**

Fourth to Sixth Month The fetus's 13th week of life passes, and suddenly new movement! It can blink its eyes for the first time, swallow, hiccup, make a fist, and curl its toes that now have tiny nails. By the fourth month, the fetus starts to make even bigger movements. The mother now knows when her baby kicks its legs or stretches its arms.

During the fifth month, the fetus is about 20 cm long. Taste buds form on its tongue, and eyebrows form on its face. The fetus begins to hear sounds through the wall of its mother's uterus. Look at the timeline in **Figure 16** to review the changes that take place in the fetus.

Figure 16 **Pregnancy Timeline**

Weeks of the First Three Months	
1 and 2	The egg is fertilized by a sperm. The fertilized egg makes its way to the uterus, where it burrows into the lining. The fertilized egg is now called an embryo.
3 and 4	Most major organ systems have started to form. The heart starts to beat around day 22. The placenta is completely formed by the fourth week.
5 and 6	Facial features begin to take shape. The skeleton begins to form.
7 and 8	Muscle movement begins. The embryo is now called a fetus.
9 and 10	Arms, legs, hands, and feet have formed.
11 and 12	The internal organs have formed.

Weeks of the Second Three Months	
13 and 14	The circulatory system is working.
15 and 16	The mother may start to feel the fetus move.
17 and 18	The fetus responds to sound.
19 and 20	The fetus is now about 20 cm long.
21 and 22	
23 and 24	Eyelashes and eyebrows appear.

Weeks of the Third Three Months	
25 and 26	The eyes open.
27 and 28	The fetus can "practice breathe."
29 and 30	Layers of fat form beneath skin.
31 and 32	
33 and 34	Organs are fully functional.
35 and 36	The fetus responds to light.
Birth	The baby is born.

Seventh to Ninth Month The seventh month is when the fetus's memories begin to form. During this time, its lungs start to "practice breathe," moving up and down continuously as if breathing real air. If the fetus's mother smokes one cigarette during this stage, the fetus's lung movement will stop for up to an hour. The fetus in **Figure 17** is starting its first lung movement.

By the eighth month, the fetus's open eyes can perceive light through its mother's abdominal wall, and its sleeping pattern starts to be influenced by sunlight. When the fetus is asleep, it dreams. Can you imagine what its dreams might be about?

Figure 17 A 21-Week-Old Fetus

Actual size of hand

Birth

After about 9 months, the fetus is ready to live outside of its mother. The mother goes through a series of muscular contractions called *labor*. During labor, the fetus is usually squeezed headfirst through the vagina. There is little room to spare, and the fetus's head is temporarily squashed out of shape as the fetus passes through its mother's pelvis. Suddenly bright lights and cold air surround the newborn baby. It gasps, fills its lungs with air for the first time, and cries.

The baby in **Figure 18** is still connected to the placenta by its umbilical cord. The doctor or midwife assisting the mother ties and cuts the umbilical cord. The baby's navel is all that will remain of the point where the umbilical cord was attached. After the mother expels the placenta from her body, labor is complete.

Figure 18 *This newborn baby is still attached to its umbilical cord. The average mass of a newborn baby is 3.3 kg. The average length is 50 cm.*

From Birth to Death

Of all the animals on this planet, humans have one of the longest life spans. Human infancy lasts 2 years—the same time it takes for most rabbits to be born, grow old, and die. Our childhood extends over a full decade, longer than many cats or dogs live. Humans can live for more than 100 years!

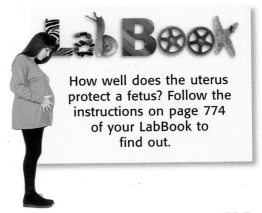

How well does the uterus protect a fetus? Follow the instructions on page 774 of your LabBook to find out.

| Infant | 4 years | 7 years | 11 years | Adult |

Figure 19 *Five different stages of development are shown the same size so you can see how body proportions change as a person develops.*

Infancy What life stages have you gone through since you were born? You have probably gone through most of the stages shown in **Figure 19.** You were an infant from birth to 2 years of age. During this time, you grew rapidly. Your teeth began to appear. You also became more coordinated as your nervous system developed. This enabled you to begin to walk.

Childhood Your childhood extends from 2 years to puberty. This is also a period of rapid growth. Your first set of teeth were slowly shed and replaced by permanent teeth. Your muscles became more coordinated, allowing you to do activities such as riding a bicycle and jumping rope. Your intellectual abilities also developed during this time.

Adolescence You are considered an adolescent from puberty to adulthood. During puberty, the reproductive systems of young males and females become mature. Puberty occurs in most boys sometime between the ages of 11 and 16. The young male body becomes more muscular, the voice becomes deeper, and body and facial hair appear. In most girls, puberty occurs between the ages of 9 and 14. During puberty in females, the amount of fat in the hips and thighs increases, the breasts enlarge, and body hair appears in areas such as the armpits. At this time, the young female also begins to menstruate.

Activity

Create a poster or timeline illustrating the different stages of human growth.

TRY at HOME

Adulthood From about age 20 to age 40, you will be considered a young adult. You will be at the peak of your physical development. Beginning around age 30, certain changes associated with aging begin. The changes will be gradual and slightly different for everyone. Some of the early signs of aging include decreasing muscle flexibility, deteriorating eyesight, increasing body fat, and increasing hair loss.

The aging process will continue in a middle-aged adult (someone between 40 and 65). During this period, hair may become gray, athletic abilities will decline, and skin will wrinkle. Any person over 65 years old is considered an older adult. Although aging persists during this period of an individual's life, older adults can still lead active lives. Some of this country's most productive citizens are older adults, as can be seen in **Figure 20.**

Figure 20 *John Glenn, the first American to orbit Earth, returned to space at the age of 77.*

QuickLab

Life Grows On

Use Figure 19 on the previous page to complete this activity.

1. Use a **ruler** to measure the infant's head height. Then measure the infant's entire body height, including the head.

2. Calculate the percentage of the infant's head height to the infant's total height.

3. Repeat these measurements and calculations for the other stages shown in the figure.

Answer the following question in your ScienceLog:

As a baby grows into an adult, does the head grow faster or slower than the rest of the body? Why do you think this is so?

TRY at HOME

REVIEW

1. What is the difference between an embryo and a fetus?

2. Why does a membrane enclose an egg once a sperm has entered?

3. What developmental changes take place from birth to puberty?

4. **Applying Concepts** When astronauts work in space, they are sometimes attached to the spacecraft by a line called an umbilical. Why do you think the line has been given this name?

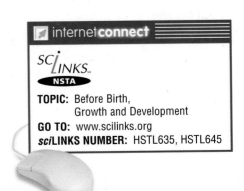

▤ internet**connect**

SC*i*LINKS
NSTA

TOPIC: Before Birth, Growth and Development
GO TO: www.scilinks.org
*sci*LINKS NUMBER: HSTL635, HSTL645

Chapter Highlights

Vocabulary

asexual reproduction *(p. 612)*

sexual reproduction *(p. 613)*

egg *(p. 613)*

sperm *(p. 613)*

zygote *(p. 613)*

external fertilization *(p. 614)*

internal fertilization *(p. 614)*

Section Notes

- During asexual reproduction, a single parent produces off-spring that are genetically identical to the parent. Budding and fragmentation are examples of asexual reproduction.

- During sexual reproduction, there is a union of an egg and a sperm.

- Each egg and sperm is the product of meiosis and con-tains half the usual number of chromosomes. The usual number of chromosomes is restored in the zygote.

- Sperm fertilize eggs outside the female's body in external fertilization. Sperm fertilize eggs inside the female's body in internal fertilization.

- Monotremes are egg-laying mammals. Marsupials are mammals that give birth to partially developed young. Placentals are mammals that give birth to well-developed young.

Vocabulary

testes *(p. 616)*

puberty *(p. 616)*

vas deferens *(p. 616)*

semen *(p. 616)*

penis *(p. 616)*

ovaries *(p. 617)*

fallopian tube *(p. 617)*

uterus *(p. 617)*

vagina *(p. 617)*

infertile *(p. 619)*

☑ Skills Check

Math Concepts

EGGS IN EXILE A woman does not ovulate while she is pregnant. Therefore, if a woman has three children, she will release at least 27 fewer eggs from her ovaries than she would if she never became pregnant.

3 children × 9 months of pregnancy = 27 eggs

Visual Concepts

MALE AND FEMALE REPRODUCTIVE SYSTEMS The diagrams on pp. 616 and 617 show the male and female reproductive systems. Take another look at them, and make sure you recognize all the structures. Also note the similarities between the two systems. For instance, the ovaries have a similar function to the testes, and the fallopian tubes have a similar function to the vas deferens.

SECTION 2

Section Notes

- The male reproductive system produces sperm and delivers it to the female reproductive system. Sperm are produced in the seminiferous tubules and stored in the epididymis. Sperm leave the body through the urethra.

- The female reproductive system produces eggs, nourishes the developing embryo, and gives birth. An egg leaves one of two ovaries each month and travels to the uterus. If the egg is not fertilized, it disintegrates and menstruation occurs.

- Reproductive system disorders include infertility, cancer, and sexually transmitted diseases.

SECTION 3

Vocabulary

embryo *(p. 620)*

implantation *(p. 620)*

placenta *(p. 621)*

umbilical cord *(p. 621)*

fetus *(p. 622)*

Section Notes

- Fertilization occurs in a fallopian tube. From there, the zygote travels to the uterus and implants itself in the uterus's wall.

- After implantation, the placenta develops. The umbilical cord connects the embryo to the placenta. The amnion surrounds and protects the embryo.

- The embryo grows, developing limbs, nostrils, eyelids, and other features. By the eighth week, the embryo is developed enough to be called a fetus.

- Human life stages are infant (birth to 2 years), child (2 years to puberty), adolescent (puberty to 20 years), young adult (20 to 40 years), middle-aged adult (40 to 65 years), and older adult (older than 65 years).

Labs

It's a Comfy, Safe World! *(p. 774)*

My, How You've Grown! *(p. 775)*

 internetconnect

GO TO: go.hrw.com

Visit the **HRW** Web site for a variety of learning tools related to this chapter. Just type in the keyword:

KEYWORD: HSTBD5

 SCILINKSsm

NSTA

GO TO: www.scilinks.org

Visit the **National Science Teachers Association** on-line Web site for Internet resources related to this chapter. Just type in the *sci*LINKS number for more information about the topic:

TOPIC: Reproduction	sciLINKS NUMBER: HSTL630
TOPIC: Before Birth	sciLINKS NUMBER: HSTL635
TOPIC: Reproductive System Irregularities or Disorders	sciLINKS NUMBER: HSTL640
TOPIC: Growth and Development	sciLINKS NUMBER: HSTL645

Chapter Review

USING VOCABULARY

To complete the following sentences, choose the correct term from each pair of terms listed below:

1. Reptiles, birds, and mammals reproduce sexually by __?__. (*internal fertilization* or *external fertilization*)

2. Sperm are produced in the __?__ within the testes. (*epididymis* or *seminiferous tubules*)

3. The sperm-containing fluid that exits the male body is known as __?__. (*semen* or *amniotic fluid*)

4. The release of an egg from the ovary occurs once each month and is called __?__. (*ovulation* or *menstruation*)

5. The organ of exchange between the developing embryo and the mother is the __?__. (*amnion* or *placenta*)

UNDERSTANDING CONCEPTS

Multiple Choice

6. The sea star can reproduce asexually by
   a. fragmentation.
   b. budding.
   c. external fertilization.
   d. internal fertilization.

7. The correct path of sperm through the male reproductive system is
   a. testes → epididymis → urethra → vas deferens.
   b. epididymis → urethra → testes → vas deferens.
   c. testes → vas deferens → epididymis → urethra.
   d. testes → epididymis → vas deferens → urethra.

8. If the first day of the menstrual cycle is the onset of menstruation, on what day does ovulation typically occur?
   a. 2nd day   c. 14th day
   b. 5th day   d. 28th day

9. Monotremes are different from placental mammals because they
   a. are mammals.
   b. have hair.
   c. nurture their young with milk.
   d. lay eggs.

10. All of the following are sexually transmitted diseases *except*
    a. chlamydia.   c. infertility.
    b. AIDS.   d. genital herpes.

11. Fertilization occurs in the __?__, and implantation occurs in the __?__.
    a. uterus, fallopian tube
    b. fallopian tube, vagina
    c. uterus, vagina
    d. fallopian tube, uterus

Short Answer

12. What human reproductive organs produce sperm? egg cells?

13. Through what structure does oxygen from the mother pass into the fetus's body?

14. What are four stages of human life following birth?

15. What two cells combine to make a zygote?

16. What is the difference between budding and fragmentation?

Concept Mapping

17. Use the following terms to create a concept map: asexual reproduction, budding, external fertilization, fragmentation, reproduction, internal fertilization, sexual reproduction.

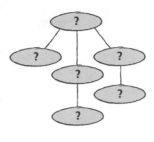

CRITICAL THINKING AND PROBLEM SOLVING

Write one or two sentences to answer the following questions:

18. Explain why the testes are found in the scrotum instead of inside the male body.

19. What is the function of the uterus? How is its function related to the menstrual cycle?

20. How is meiosis important to human reproduction?

MATH IN SCIENCE

21. Hardy Junior High School has 2,750 students. If 1 pair of identical twins is born for every 250 births, about how many pairs of identical twins will be attending the school?

22. Mrs. Schmidt had a baby April 30th. Her baby developed inside her uterus for 9 months. What month was her egg fertilized?

23. In the United States, seven infants die before their first birthday for every 1,000 births. Convert this figure to a percentage. Is your answer greater than or less than 1 percent?

24. In Haiti, a small country in the Caribbean, 74 infants die before their first birthday for every 1,000 births. Convert this figure to a percentage. Is your answer greater or less than 1 percent? Why do you think there is such a difference between the United States and Haiti?

INTERPRETING GRAPHICS

The following graph illustrates the cycles of the male hormone, testosterone, and the female hormone, estrogen. The blue line shows the estrogen level in a female over a period of 28 days. The red line shows the testosterone level in a male over a period of 28 days.

25. What is the major difference between the two hormone levels over the 28-day period?

26. What cycle do you think estrogen affects?

27. Why might the level of testosterone stay the same?

NOW What Do You Think?

Take a minute to review your answers to the ScienceLog questions on page 611. Have your answers changed? If necessary, revise your answers based on what you have learned since you began this chapter.

LIFE SCIENCE • CHEMISTRY

Acne

If you are a teenager, you probably have some firsthand experience with acne. If you don't, you probably will. And contrary to what you may have heard, acne is not caused by greasy foods and candy, though these foods can aggravate the problem. The hormonal fluctuations that occur as young people mature into adults often cause acne.

What Are Pimples?

Skin contains thousands of tiny pores. Each pore contains sebaceous (suh BAY shuhs) glands that produce sebum, the oil you may have noticed on the surface of your skin. This oil is necessary to maintain healthy skin. The production and release of sebum is stimulated by androgens, the male sex hormones, which become active in both girls and boys during puberty.

Sebum usually escapes from the pores without a problem. But sometimes skin cells do not shed properly, and they clog the pores. The sebum that collects in the pores causes lesions, commonly called pimples.

▲ *Acne is caused by the buildup of sebum and dead cells in the pores of the skin.*

Learn Your Lesions

There are two kinds of lesions—noninflamed lesions and inflamed lesions. Noninflamed lesions include blackheads and whiteheads. Some people think blackheads are pores filled with dirt. The dark color of these lesions is actually the result of dark skin pigments or oil trapped in the pores. Whiteheads are white because their contents are hidden under the skin's surface. Inflamed lesions are caused by bacteria and are often red and swollen. Bacteria live in healthy pores, and when pores become clogged, the bacteria are trapped and can cause irritation and infection.

Heredity

Family history appears to be a factor in the development of acne. Unfortunately, if your parents or brothers and sisters had acne, you are likely to have acne too. The causes of hereditary acne remain unclear. Your skin may be genetically programmed to produce more sebum than is produced in other teenagers.

Is There Hope?

Certain over-the-counter products can clean the dead skin cells and sebum out of the pores. Many medications inhibit the production of sebum or encourage the shedding of skin cells. Sometimes doctors prescribe antibiotics, such as tetracycline or erythromycin, to treat severe cases of acne. Most acne clears up as people become adults.

On Your Own

▶ Find out what the active ingredient is in an over-the-counter acne medication. Do some research on this ingredient to find out how it works. Report your findings to the class.

Science, Technology, and Society

Technology in Its Infant Stages

Every year thousands of babies are born with life-threatening diseases or severe birth defects. What if medical treatments were available to these babies before they were born? Doctors at San Francisco, Harvard, and Vanderbilt Universities are performing experimental fetal surgery with encouraging results.

When Is Fetal Surgery an Option?

To date, approximately 100 fetal operations have been performed across the country. Corrective treatments can take place between the 18th and 30th weeks of pregnancy. Many factors determine whether fetal surgery is appropriate. Surgery is considered to be an option only if the condition is life threatening. However, fetuses with several defects or chromosomal abnormalities are not eligible for surgery.

Successful surgeries have been performed on fetal patients with spina bifida, diaphragmatic hernias, malformations of the lungs, and urinary tract obstructions. Spina bifida is a defect that leaves the spine exposed. A diaphragmatic hernia is a hole in the diaphragm. This condition causes severe breathing difficulties.

Surgery on a Small Scale

Fetal surgery can fall into one of three categories. The least traumatic type of treatment uses a laser scalpel or an endoscope. The scalpel is used to remove chest tumors. An *endoscope* is a video-guided tool that combines a camera lens and scissors that are less than 0.2 cm wide. The doctor guides the scissors through a tiny cut in the abdominal and uterine walls. The doctor is unable to see the fetus directly during this surgery because the cut is so small. Therefore, he or she must watch the video images provided by the endoscope during the operation.

A more traumatic option is open fetal surgery. In this treatment, the mother's abdomen and uterus are opened, and the fetus is partially exposed.

The third, and relatively new, option is called fetal stem cell transplant. This treatment is essentially a bone marrow transplant for the fetus. It is used to treat genetic diseases and diseases of the immune system.

▲ *The endoscope shown here is used to perform fetal surgery.*

What the Future Holds

Each fetal surgery results in the improvement of techniques and treatments, as well as in the expansion of the types of defects and diseases that can be treated. As the number of fetal surgeries increases, fetal surgery will become much more routine.

Going Further

▶ The endoscopes used in fetal surgery use a technology called fiber optics. Research what items around your home also use fiber optics.

UNIT 8

Human Health

In many ways, living in the twenty-first century is good for your health. Many deadly diseases that plagued our ancestors now have cures. Some diseases, like smallpox, have been wiped out entirely. And others can be prevented by vaccines and other methods. Many researchers, including the people on this timeline, have worked to understand diseases and to find cures.

But people still get sick, and many diseases have no cure. In this unit you will learn how your body protects itself and fights illness. You will also learn about ways to keep yourself healthy so that your body can operate in top form.

1403

The first quarantine is imposed in Venice, Italy, to stop the spread of the plague, or Black Death.

1717

Lady Mary Wortley Montague introduces a smallpox vaccine in England.

1900

Walter Reed discovers that yellow fever is carried by mosquitoes.

1906

Upton Sinclair writes *The Jungle,* which describes unsanitary conditions in the Chicago stockyards and leads to the creation of the Pure Food and Drug Act.

1921

A tuberculosis vaccine is produced.

1816

R. T. Laennec invents the stethoscope.

1853

Charles Gerhardt synthesizes aspirin for the first time.

1895

X rays are discovered by Wilhelm Roentgen.

1855

Nurse Florence Nightingale introduces hygienic standards to military hospitals during the Crimean War.

1977

Smallpox is eradicated.

1953

Cigarette smoking is linked to lung cancer.

1997

Researchers discover that high doses of alcohol in early pregnancy switch off a gene that controls brain, heart, limb, and skull development.

27 Body Defenses and Disease

Imagine . . .

A doctor arrives at your house with a cow. Your mom isn't surprised at all, and she invites the doctor and the cow right into your living room. The doctor explains that his cow has a disease that he plans to give to you. Your father is thrilled with the idea. This really scares you. Has everyone gone mad? The grown-ups seem to think it's okay to give you a cow disease!

Don't worry, the adults aren't crazy. Around A.D. 700, the Chinese did a similar thing. They realized a dangerous disease called smallpox could be prevented by exposing healthy people to the powdered scabs of infected people. It wasn't until the 1700s that Europeans learned of this technique. In 1796, a British physician named Edward Jenner observed that people who'd had a similar but less serious disease called cowpox did not get smallpox. Jenner started exposing patients to fluid from cowpox blisters. He called his treatment a *vaccine,* from the Latin word *vacca,* meaning "cow."

Read on to find out what causes diseases such as smallpox and how your body responds to them.

What Do You Think?

In your ScienceLog, try to answer the following questions based on what you already know:

1. When you "catch a cold," what is it that infects your body?

2. How does a fever help you get well?

Invisible Invaders

Before the mid-1800s, many people believed that someone got a disease because he or she was being punished. People could not see the disease-causing agents or understand how they were passed from person to person. Here you will use a lab technique that makes seemingly invisible life-forms become visible.

Procedure

1. Obtain **two Petri dishes** containing **nutrient agar.** Label one dish "Washed" and the other "Unwashed."

2. Obtain **two marbles.** Rub both marbles between the palms of your hands. Look at the two marbles. Has their appearance changed?

3. Roll one marble in the Petri dish labeled "Unwashed."

4. Put on a pair of **disposable gloves.** Wash the other marble with **soap** and **warm water** for four minutes. Does the appearance of the marble change after it is washed?

5. Roll the washed marble in the Petri dish labeled "Washed."

6. Secure the lids of the Petri dishes with **transparent tape** and place them on a shelf in a warm, dark place for about a week. **Caution:** Do not open the Petri dishes after they are sealed.

7. Observe the Petri dishes each day. What do you see? Record your observations in your ScienceLog.

Analysis

8. How did the washed marble's appearance compare with that of the unwashed marble?

9. How did the Petri dishes differ after several days?

10. Why do you think it is important to wash your hands before doing things like eating?

Terms to Learn

noninfectious   pathogen
    disease
immunity
infectious disease

What You'll Do

◆ Explain the difference between infectious diseases and non-infectious diseases.
◆ Identify five ways that you might come into contact with a pathogen.
◆ Discuss four methods that have helped reduce the spread of disease.

Disease

You've probably heard it before: "Cover your mouth when you sneeze!" "Wash your hands!" "Don't put that in your mouth!" What is all the fuss about? When people say these things to you, they are concerned about the spread of disease.

What Causes Disease?

When you have a *disease,* your normal body functions are disrupted. Some diseases, such as most cancers and heart disease, are not spread from one person to another. They are called **noninfectious diseases.**

Noninfectious diseases can be caused by a variety of factors. For example, a genetic disorder causes the disease hemophilia, in which a person's blood does not clot properly. The disease scurvy is caused by a lack of vitamin C in the diet. Smoking, lack of physical activity, and a high-fat diet can greatly increase a person's chances of getting certain noninfectious diseases. Avoiding harmful habits may help you avoid noninfectious diseases.

A disease that can be passed from one living thing to another is an **infectious disease.** Infectious diseases are caused by agents called **pathogens.** Viruses and some bacteria, fungi, protists, and worms may all cause diseases. **Figure 1** shows some common pathogens.

Figure 1 *Pathogens, such as these, are often referred to as germs.*

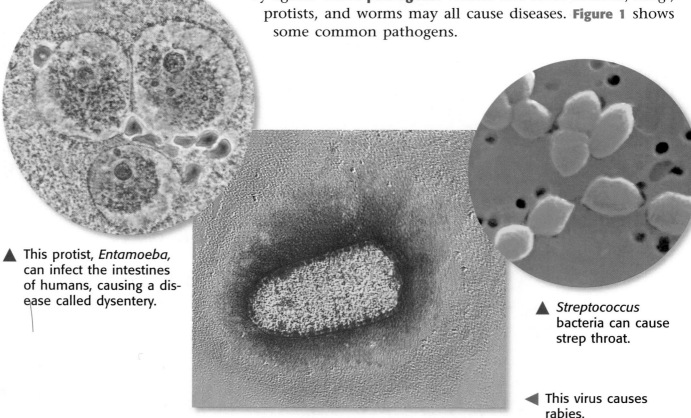

▲ This protist, *Entamoeba,* can infect the intestines of humans, causing a disease called dysentery.

▲ *Streptococcus* bacteria can cause strep throat.

◀ This virus causes rabies.

Pathways to Pathogens

There are many ways pathogens can be passed from one person to another. Being aware of them can help you stay healthy.

Through the Air Some pathogens travel through the air. For example, a single sneeze, like the one shown in **Figure 2,** releases thousands of tiny droplets of moisture that can carry pathogens.

Contaminated Objects A person who is sick may leave bacteria or viruses on objects such as doorknobs, keyboards, drinking glasses, towels, or combs. If you drink from a glass that an infected person has just used, you could become infected with a pathogen.

Person to Person Some pathogens are spread by direct person-to-person contact. You can become infected with some illnesses by kissing, shaking hands, or touching the sores of an infected person.

Animals Some pathogens are carried by animals. For example, humans can get a fungus called ringworm from handling an infected dog or cat. Also, ticks may carry bacteria that cause Lyme disease or Rocky Mountain spotted fever.

Food and Water Drinking water in the United States is generally safe, but water lines can break, or treatment plants can become flooded, allowing microorganisms to enter the public water supply. Bacteria growing in foods and beverages can cause illness too. Refrigerating foods can slow the growth of many of these pathogens, but meat, fish, and eggs that are not cooked enough can still contain dangerous bacteria or parasites. Leaving food out at room temperature can give bacteria such as *Salmonella* time to grow and produce toxins in the food. For these reasons, it is important to wash all used cooking tools.

Figure 2 *A sneeze can force thousands of pathogen-carrying droplets out of your body at up to 160 km per hour.*

In developing countries, 80 percent of diseases are related to contaminated drinking water.

✓ Self-Check

Jackie cut up raw meat on her kitchen counter. If her brother makes a sandwich on the same counter later, how could he come in contact with a pathogen? *(See page 782 to check your answer.)*

Hospitals use a machine called an autoclave to kill bacteria on surgical instruments. An autoclave works by increasing the pressure of steam as its temperature increases. The combined effect of pressure and temperature kills bacteria at a lower temperature than would normally be needed.

Putting Pathogens in Their Place

Until the twentieth century, surgery patients often died of bacterial infections. But as doctors learned more about disease, it became clear that simple cleanliness could help prevent the spread of some diseases. Today, hospitals and clinics use a variety of technologies to prevent the spread of pathogens. For example, ultraviolet radiation, boiling water, and chemicals are used in health facilities to kill pathogens.

Pasteurization During the mid-1800s, Louis Pasteur, a French scientist, discovered that microorganisms caused wine to spoil. The uninvited microorganisms were bacteria. Pasteur devised a method of using heat to kill most of the bacteria in the wine. This method is called *pasteurization,* and it is still used today. The milk that the girl in **Figure 3** is drinking has been pasteurized.

Vaccines and Immunity In the late 1700s, no one knew what a pathogen was. It was during this time that Edward Jenner, the physician discussed on page 634, studied a disease called smallpox. He observed that people who had been infected with cowpox seemed to have protection against smallpox. This protection, or resistance to a disease, is called **immunity.** Jenner's work led to the first modern *vaccine.* A vaccine is a substance that helps your body develop immunity to a disease.

Today vaccines are used all over the world to prevent many serious diseases. Modern vaccines contain pathogens that are killed or specially treated so that they can't make you very sick. The vaccine is enough like the pathogen to allow your body to develop a defense against the disease.

Figure 3 *Today pasteurization is used to kill pathogens in many different types of food, including dairy products, eggs, meats, and juices.*

Antibiotics Bacterial infections can be a serious threat to your health. Fortunately, doctors can usually treat these kinds of infections with antibiotics. An *antibiotic* is a substance that can kill bacteria or slow the growth of bacteria. Antibiotics may also be used to treat infections caused by other microorganisms, like fungi. If you take an antibiotic when you are sick, it is important that you take it according to your doctor's instructions to ensure that all the pathogens are killed.

Viruses, such as those that cause colds, are not affected by antibiotics. The only way to destroy viruses in your body is to locate and kill the cells they have invaded. In the next section, you'll see how a healthy immune system does just that.

Cold Calamity

Frank caught a bad cold just before the opening night of his school play. He visited his doctor and asked her to prescribe antibiotics for his cold. The doctor politely refused and suggested that Frank stay home and get plenty of rest. Why do you think the doctor refused to give Frank antibiotics? Explain your answer.

REVIEW

1. How is an infectious disease different from a noninfectious disease?

2. List five ways that you might come into contact with a pathogen.

3. How does a vaccine work?

4. **Inferring Relationships** Why might the risk of infectious disease be high in a community that has no water-treatment facility?

Terms to Learn

immune system   B cell
macrophage   antibody
T cell   memory B cell

What You'll Do

◆ Describe how your body keeps
out pathogens.
◆ Explain how the immune system
works.
◆ Discuss the purpose of a fever.

Your Body's Defenses

Although you probably don't realize it, your body must constantly protect itself against pathogens that are trying to invade it. But how does your body do that? Luckily, your body has its own built-in defense system.

Your Suit of Armor

For a pathogen to harm you, it must attack a part of your body. Usually, though, only a small percentage of the pathogens around you ever make it past your first lines of defense.

Eyes, Nose, and Mouth Many organisms that try to enter your eyes or mouth are destroyed by special enzymes. Pathogens that enter your nose are washed down the back of your throat by mucus. The mucus carries the pathogens to your stomach, where most are quickly digested.

Skin Your skin is made of many layers of flat cells. The outermost layers are dead. As a result, any pathogen that lands on your skin cannot find a live cell to infect. As **Figure 4** shows, the dead skin cells are constantly dropping off of your body as new skin cells grow from beneath. As the dead skin cells flake off, they carry away viruses, bacteria, and other microorganisms. In addition, glands secrete oil onto your skin's surface. The oil contains chemicals that kill many pathogens.

Figure 4 *Your body loses and replaces approximately 1 million skin cells every 40 minutes. In the process, countless pathogens are sloughed off.*

A Forced Entry

Sometimes skin is burned, cut, or punctured. When this happens, pathogens can enter the body. The body acts quickly to keep out as many pathogens as possible. Blood flow to the injured area increases. Cell parts in the blood called *platelets* help seal the open wound so that no more pathogens can enter.

The increased blood flow also brings cells that belong to the **immune system,** the body system that fights pathogens. The immune system is not localized in any one place in your body, nor is it controlled by any one organ, such as the brain. Instead, it is an army of individual cells, tissues, and organs that work together to combat invading pathogens.

Soldiers of the Immune System

The immune system consists mainly of three kinds of cells. One kind is the **macrophage.** Macrophages engulf, or eat, any microorganisms or viruses floating around. If only a few microorganisms and viruses have entered the wound, the macrophages can easily stop them.

The other two main types of immune-system cells are **T cells** and **B cells.** T cells play an important role in coordinating the immune system. Many B cells make **antibodies,** which are proteins that attach to specific pathogens. Your body is capable of making billions of different antibodies, but each antibody usually attaches to only one type of pathogen, as illustrated in **Figure 5.**

It's Only Skin Deep

Cut an **apple** in half. Place **plastic wrap** over both halves. The plastic wrap will act as skin. Use **scissors** to cut the plastic wrap on one of the apple halves, then use an **eye-dropper** to drip **food coloring** on each apple half. The food coloring represents pathogens coming into contact with your body. Now, answer the following questions:

1. What happened to each apple half?

2. How is the plastic wrap similar to skin?

3. How is the plastic wrap different from skin?

Figure 5 *An antibody's shape is very specialized. It matches a pathogen like a key fits a lock.*

Antibody

Pathogen

B cell

What are antibodies tailored to fit? Find out on page 776 of your LabBook.

1 **Enemy Invasion!** A macrophage displays the pieces of bacteria it has engulfed for other cells to notice. The pieces of bacteria are called *antigens.*

A War Within

Macrophages can take care of a small invasion of pathogens, but what would happen if millions of pathogens invaded your body? Imagine that bacteria have just moved into your throat. A macrophage discovers a bacterium and engulfs it. But the macrophage does not digest the whole pathogen. Instead, the macrophage saves little pieces of the bacterium and sticks them to its surface. This starts the immune system response . . .

Bacterium

2 **The Troops Are Called In** The antigens on the outside of the macrophages activate special T cells called **helper T cells.**

Antigen

Macrophage

Helper T cell

3 **More Commandos** The helper T cells begin dividing as fast as they can to make more helper T cells.

Killer T cell

B cell

Infected cell

4 **Assassins** The helper T cells send word to another kind of T cell called a **killer T cell.** Killer T cells kill any cell infected with pathogens. They recognize an infected cell because the cell places antigens on its surface.

5 **Foot Soldiers** The helper T cells also activate **B cells.** The B cells then make millions of antibodies.

6 The Battle Intensifies The **antibodies** cling to many of the bacteria. The antibodies also act as markers. Once a bacterium has an antibody attached to it, all kinds of immune cells and proteins swarm to attack the bacterium.

Antibody

7 Take No Prisoners Special proteins attach themselves to the antibodies stuck on pathogens. They then punch holes in the sides of the pathogens, destroying them.

Protein

8 Cleanup Crew Macrophages engulf pathogens tagged with antibodies.

Body Defenses and Disease **643**

Heating Things Up

When macrophages activate the helper T cells, they also send a chemical signal that tells your brain to turn up the thermostat. In a few minutes, your body's temperature can rise several degrees. A moderate fever of one or two degrees actually helps you get well faster because it slows the growth of some pathogens. As is shown in **Figure 6,** a fever also helps B cells and T cells multiply faster than usual.

Haven't We Met Somewhere Before?

The immune system responds very quickly if your B cells recognize the invading pathogen and can produce antibodies for it. However, B cells must have had previous contact with a pathogen before they can make the correct antibodies. During the first encounter with a new pathogen, specialized B cells make antibodies that are effective against that particular invader. This process takes about 2 weeks, which is far too long to prevent an infection. Therefore, the first time you are infected, you usually get sick.

A few of the B cells become **memory B cells** that "remember" how to make an antibody for a particular pathogen. If the pathogen shows up again, the memory B cells produce B cells that make enough antibodies to protect you in just 3 or 4 days.

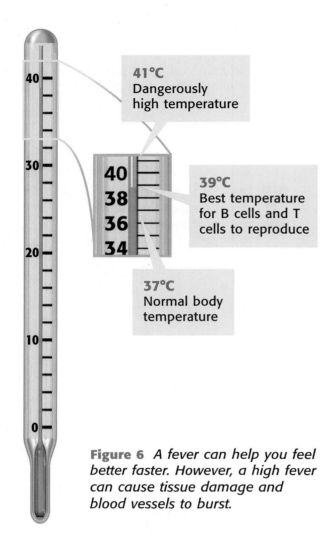

41°C
Dangerously
high temperature

39°C
Best temperature
for B cells and T
cells to reproduce

37°C
Normal body
temperature

Figure 6 *A fever can help you feel better faster. However, a high fever can cause tissue damage and blood vessels to burst.*

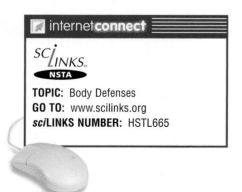

internet**connect**

SC*i*LINKS.
NSTA

TOPIC: Body Defenses
GO TO: www.scilinks.org
*sci*LINKS NUMBER: HSTL665

REVIEW

1. List three ways your body defends itself against pathogens.

2. Name three different cells in the immune system, and describe how they respond to pathogens.

3. Can you make antibodies for diseases you have never come in contact with? Why or why not?

4. **Applying Concepts** If you had chickenpox at age 7, what would be your chances of getting chickenpox again if your memory B cells lived only 2 months?

Terms to Learn

allergy   cancer
autoimmune
  disease

What You'll Do

◆ Explain the difference between allergies and autoimmune diseases.
◆ Discuss what cancer is.
◆ Describe how HIV affects the immune system.

Challenges to the Immune System

The immune system is a very effective body-defense system, but it is not invincible. There are some diseases that the immune system is unable to deal with. There are also conditions in which the immune system does not work properly.

Ragweed pollen

A-a-achoo!

Sometimes the immune system overreacts to antigens that are not dangerous to the body. This inappropriate reaction is called an **allergy.** Allergies may be caused by many things, including certain foods and medicines. Some of the culprits behind allergic reactions are shown in **Figure 7.** Symptoms can range from a runny nose and itchy eyes to more serious conditions, such as asthma.

Doctors are not sure why the immune system overreacts in some people. Scientists think allergies might be useful because the mucus draining from your nose carries away pollen, dust, and microorganisms.

Figure 7 Things That Cause Allergies

Pollen

Dust mite

Animal hair
and dander
(skin flakes)

Cigarette smoke

Figure 8 *In rheumatoid arthritis, immune-system cells cause joint-tissue swelling, which can lead to joint deformities.*

Autoimmune Diseases

An **autoimmune disease** is a disease in which the immune system attacks the body's own cells. This happens when immune-system cells are not able to tell the difference between pathogens and particular body cells. One autoimmune disease is rheumatoid arthritis, in which the immune system attacks the joints. The most common location for rheumatoid arthritis is the joints of the hands, as shown in **Figure 8.** Other autoimmune diseases include type 1 diabetes, Graves' disease, multiple sclerosis, and lupus.

Cancer

Healthy cells divide at a carefully regulated rate. Occasionally, though, a cell doesn't respond to the body's regulation and begins dividing at an uncontrolled rate. As can be seen in **Figure 9,** killer T cells destroy this type of cell. But sometimes division of these cells gets out of the control of the immune system. This causes a condition known as **cancer.**

Many cancers will invade nearby tissues. They can also enter the cardiovascular system or lymphatic system. This way, cancers can be transported to other places in the body. Cancers disrupt the normal activities of organs they have invaded, often leading to death. Today, though, there are many treatments for cancer. Radiation and certain drugs can be used to kill cancer cells or slow their division.

Figure 9 The Destruction of an Unregulated Cell

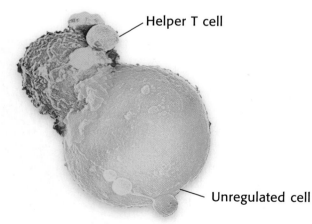

Helper T cell

Unregulated cell

❶ A killer T cell attacks an unregulated cell.

❷ The cell's membrane ruptures as the cell dies.

AIDS

The human immunodeficiency virus (HIV) causes the acquired immune deficiency syndrome (AIDS). Most viruses infect cells in the nose, mouth, lungs, or intestines, but HIV is different. As you can see in **Figure 10,** HIV infects the immune system itself, using helper T cells as factories to produce more viruses. The helper T cells are destroyed in the process. Remember that the helper T cells put the B cells and killer T cells to work.

People with AIDS have very few helper T cells, so nothing activates the B cells and killer T cells. Therefore, the immune system cannot attack HIV or any other pathogen. People with AIDS don't usually die of AIDS itself. They die of other diseases that they are unable to fight off.

Figure 10 *The blue particles on this helper T cell are human immunodeficiency viruses. They were made inside the cell and can now go and infect other cells.*

REVIEW

1. What is the difference between allergies and autoimmune diseases?

2. Why is it important for immune-system cells to be able to recognize all of the body's own cells?

3. What characterizes a cancerous cell?

4. **Interpreting Graphs** Over time, people with AIDS become very sick and are unable to fight off infection. Use the information in the graph below to explain why this occurs.

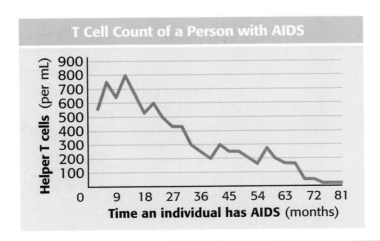

T Cell Count of a Person with AIDS

Helper T cells (per mL) vs. Time an individual has AIDS (months)

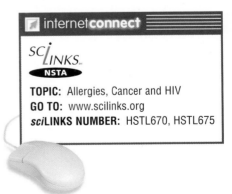

internet connect

SCI LINKS.
NSTA

TOPIC: Allergies, Cancer and HIV
GO TO: www.scilinks.org
*sci*LINKS NUMBER: HSTL670, HSTL675

Chapter Highlights

Vocabulary

noninfectious disease (p. 636)
infectious disease (p. 636)
pathogen (p. 636)
immunity (p. 638)

Section Notes

• A disease disrupts the body's ability to function normally.

• Noninfectious diseases cannot be spread from one person to another.

• Infectious diseases are caused by pathogens that are passed from one living thing to another.

• Pathogens are agents such as viruses or microorganisms that can make us sick.

• Pathogens can travel through the air or can be spread by contact with other people, contaminated objects, animals, or food.

• Cleanliness, pasteurization, vaccines, and antibiotics help control the spread of pathogens.

Labs

Passing the Cold (p. 778)

Vocabulary

immune system (p. 641)
macrophage (p. 641)
T cell (p. 641)
B cell (p. 641)
antibody (p. 641)
memory B cell (p. 644)

Section Notes

• Enzymes in your eyes, nose, and mouth kill most pathogens that try to enter. Other pathogens are washed down the throat and destroyed in the stomach.

• Dead skin cells and oil help to keep germs out of the body.

☑ Skills Check

Math Concepts

SPREAD OF DISEASES It is easy to infect a large group of people with a disease. For instance, suppose a man with the flu gets onto an empty train. The train stops at 10 different towns. If five people get off and five people get on at every stop, how many people could the man expose to his illness?

10 stops × 5 people = 50 people exposed

Visual Understanding

IMMUNE RESPONSE
Look at the immune response illustration on pp. 642–643. Review each step to make sure you understand how your immune system works. Think about how many different cells the immune system uses to destroy pathogens. Also, notice that each cell has a special job.

- When pathogens get into your blood or tissues, the immune system reacts.

- Macrophages engulf pathogens. Macrophages then display parts of the pathogens, called antigens, on their surface.

- Macrophages activate helper T cells. The helper T cells put the killer T cells and B cells to work.

- Killer T cells kill infected cells. B cells make antibodies.

- Antibodies cling to antigens and attract macrophages and other cells. Special proteins kill pathogens with antibodies stuck to them.

- Macrophages cause fever, which speeds the division of T cells and B cells.

- Memory B cells stand ready to produce more B cells that make antibodies if the pathogen appears again.

Labs

Antibodies to the Rescue *(p. 776)*

Vocabulary

allergy *(p. 645)*

autoimmune disease *(p. 646)*

cancer *(p. 646)*

Section Notes

- The immune system can overreact to a harmless antigen. This reaction is called an allergy.

- Autoimmune diseases are diseases in which the immune system attacks the body's healthy tissue.

- Cancer cells can enter the body's circulatory systems and infect other areas of the body.

- HIV attacks helper T cells, preventing the immune system from functioning properly.

---

internet connect

GO TO: go.hrw.com

Visit the **HRW** Web site for a variety of learning tools related to this chapter. Just type in the keyword:

KEYWORD: HSTBD6

GO TO: www.scilinks.org

Visit the **National Science Teachers Association** on-line Web site for Internet resources related to this chapter. Just type in the *sci*LINKS number for more information about the topic:

TOPIC: What Causes Diseases?	*sci*LINKS NUMBER: HSTL655
TOPIC: Pathogens	*sci*LINKS NUMBER: HSTL660
TOPIC: Body Defenses	*sci*LINKS NUMBER: HSTL665
TOPIC: Allergies	*sci*LINKS NUMBER: HSTL670
TOPIC: Cancer and HIV	*sci*LINKS NUMBER: HSTL675

Chapter Review

USING VOCABULARY

To complete the following sentences, choose the correct term from each pair of terms listed below:

1. Diseases caused by pathogens are __?__. (*infectious* or *noninfectious*)

2. Antibiotics can be used to kill some __?__. (*bacteria* or *viruses*)

3. Macrophages attract __?__. (*helper T cells* or *killer T cells*)

4. Certain B cells make __?__. (*antigens* or *antibodies*)

5. An immune system overreaction to a harmless substance is a(n) __?__. (*allergy* or *vaccine*)

6. __?__ attacks helper T cells. (*HIV* or *Cancer*)

UNDERSTANDING CONCEPTS

Multiple Choice

7. Pathogens are
   a. all viruses and microorganisms.
   b. viruses and microorganisms that cause disease.
   c. noninfectious organisms.
   d. all bacteria that live in water.

8. The following is an infectious disease:
   a. allergies
   b. rheumatoid arthritis
   c. asthma
   d. common cold

9. The skin keeps pathogens out by
   a. staying warm enough to kill pathogens.
   b. releasing killer T cells onto the surface.
   c. shedding dead cells and secreting oils.
   d. All of the above

10. Memory B cells
    a. kill pathogens.
    b. activate killer T cells.
    c. activate killer B cells.
    d. produce B cells that make antibodies.

11. A fever
    a. slows pathogen growth.
    b. helps B cells multiply faster.
    c. helps T cells multiply faster.
    d. All of the above

12. Macrophages
    a. make antibodies.
    b. release helper T cells.
    c. live in the gut.
    d. engulf pathogens.

Short Answer

13. Explain how macrophages start an immune response.

14. Describe the role of helper T cells in responding to an infection.

Concept Mapping

15. Use the following terms to create a concept map: macrophages, helper T cells, B cells, antibodies, antigens, killer T cells, memory B cells.

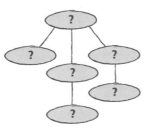

CRITICAL THINKING AND PROBLEM SOLVING

Write one or two sentences to answer the following questions:

16. Why does the disappearance of helper T cells in AIDS patients damage the immune system?

17. Many people take fever-reducing drugs as soon as their temperature exceeds 37°C. Why might it not be a good idea to immediately reduce a fever with drugs? What are the benefits of taking fever-reducing drugs?

18. The risk of dying from a whooping cough vaccine is about one in 1 million. In contrast, the risk of dying from whooping cough itself is about one in 500. Discuss the pros and cons of this vaccination.

MATH IN SCIENCE

19. Suppose you have 50,000 flu viruses on your fingers and you rub your eyes. Only 20,000 viruses make it into your eyes, 10,000 dissolve in chemicals, and 10,000 are washed down into your nose. Of those, you sneeze out 2,000. How many viruses are left to wash down the back of your throat and start an infection?

INTERPRETING GRAPHICS

Immune Response

The graph above compares the concentration of antibodies in the blood the first time you are exposed to a pathogen with the concentration of antibodies the next time you are exposed to the pathogen.

20. Are there more antibodies present during the first week of the first exposure or the first week of the second exposure? Why do you think this is so?

21. What is the difference in recovery time between the first exposure and second exposure? Why?

NOW What Do You Think?

Take a minute to review your answers to the ScienceLog questions on page 635. Have your answers changed? If necessary, revise your answers based on what you have learned since you began this chapter.

CAREERS

NATUROPATHIC PHYSICIAN

Dr. Stacey Kargman of Tucson, Arizona, is a doctor of naturopathic medicine (NMD), commonly referred to as a naturopath. An NMD has similar training to an MD but is less likely than a traditionally trained doctor to use prescription drugs or surgery to treat a patient's symptoms. Naturopaths tend to look for a natural way to treat a patient, using drugs or surgery as a last resort. Dr. Kargman tries to strengthen her patients' immune systems by focusing on things like nutrition.

Dr. Kargman attended the Southwest College of Naturopathic Medicine, where she studied all the sciences a medical doctor would study—like biochemistry, anatomy, pharmacology, and physiology. Beyond the standard medical school sciences, naturopaths spend an additional four years studying subjects like botanical medicines, homeopathy, acupuncture, counseling, and nutrition. "Naturopathy is a way of looking at the person as a whole," says Kargman.

The Keystone to Good Health

Many naturopaths believe that nutrition is the keystone to good health. "Most MDs don't talk to their patients about their diets," Kargman explains. "I'm in a position to talk to them about what they eat and how it may be affecting their health. Food allergies can cause an immune reaction in the body—anything from depression to skin problems to migraine headaches. Even though I can prescribe prescription medications, I usually defer to MDs when it comes to prescription medications."

Dr. Kargman treats many HIV and AIDS patients. She encourages these patients and others who need prescription medications to work with their medical doctor and their naturopath at the same time. That way, patients get the best care.

A Fulfilling Career

Dr. Kargman says the best part of her work is making people feel better. "Someone might come to me and say they have terrible migraines that they can no longer live with and that they've seen every doctor. After examining them, I might be able to tell them something as simple as, 'Stop eating wheat.' The simplest thing can change someone's life . . . It's not like putting a bandage on it. It's fixing the cause of the problem."

On Your Own

▶ Do some research about naturopaths. Find out how an NMD's training and practice differ from the training and practice of an MD.

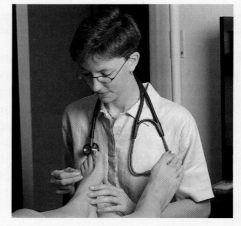

▲ *Stacey Kargman, NMD, tries to treat the patient as a whole.*

Frogs in the Medicine Cabinet?

▲ *African clawed frogs produce a natural antibiotic.*

Frog skin, mouse intestines, cow lungs, and shark stomachs—sounds like the ingredients for a witch's brew, doesn't it? Actually, these animal parts are being tested in an effort to create more effective medicines to combat harmful bacteria.

Leapin' Lily Pads—It's Infection Protection

In 1896, a biologist named Michael Zasloff was studying African clawed frogs. He noticed that cuts in the frogs' skin healed quickly and never became infected. Zasloff decided to investigate further. He found that when a frog was cut, its skin released a liquid antibiotic that killed invading bacteria.

Scientists have found other animals whose bodies contain similar infection fighters. For example, the stomach and tissues of sand sharks (also called dogfish) contain chemicals that kill bacteria and other microorganisms. These useful antibiotics are also in moths, pigs, mice, cows, and even the small intestines of humans!

What's in Dog Spit?

A healthy dog licks cuts, scrapes, and minor wounds to clean them. A mother cat licks her kittens clean. Have you ever wondered why animals do that? Well, dogs, cats, humans, and some other animals have an antibacterial enzyme in their saliva. When animals lick a wound, the enzymes kill the bacteria and help the wound heal.

POW! Punching Holes in Bacteria

Bacteria are becoming resistant to many man-made antibiotics, which means that the drugs no longer affect the bacteria. Scientists now face the challenge of developing new antibiotics that can overcome the resistant strains of bacteria.

Antibiotics from animals pack a different punch than some man-made antibiotics. These substances bore holes through the membranes that surround bacterial cells, causing the cells to disintegrate and die. Bacterial membranes don't mutate often, so they are less likely to become resistant to the animal antibiotics.

Getting Well

▶ When your doctor prescribes antibiotics, you are usually reminded to finish the entire bottle even if you start to feel better. Call or visit a local pharmacy to investigate why this is so important when you are taking antibiotics.

28 Staying Healthy

Imagine . . .

You are part of a nationwide survey of more than 6,000 teenagers. Scientists from the Centers for Disease Control and Prevention are concerned about teen health. They think that certain behaviors put too many teenagers at risk for cancer, heart disease, and other illnesses. The researchers ask you about five health habits: Do you ever smoke cigarettes? Do you exercise regularly? Do you eat plenty of fruits and vegetables? Do you eat a lot of high-fat foods, such as hamburgers, fried foods, and junk foods? Do you sometimes drink alcohol?

This survey of people aged 12 to 17 was actually taken, and 20 percent of those surveyed smoke cigarettes. In addition, 36 percent get little exercise, 85 percent do not eat enough fruits and vegetables, 34 percent eat too many high-fat foods, and 16 percent sometimes drink large amounts of alcohol. Over half of the teenagers (63 percent) engage in two or more of these health-risk behaviors.

Where do you fit into this national survey? Are your habits healthy or risky? This chapter will give you plenty of information about keeping yourself healthy and increasing your chances of having a long, active life.

What Do You Think?

In your ScienceLog, try to answer the following questions based on what you already know:

1. What types of foods do you need to eat daily to have a healthy diet? What foods should you avoid?

2. How are drugs helpful? harmful?

3. What everyday habits can help to keep you healthy?

Investigate!

Conduct a Survey

Like the scientists from the Centers for Disease Control and Prevention, you can conduct your own survey of health habits. How healthy is your class? Collect data and see for yourself.

Procedure

1. Copy the **questionnaire** at right. (Do not write in this book!)

2. Circle *yes* or *no* to answer the questions. Answer honestly, and do not put your name on the survey.

Analysis

3. Record the data from your survey and the surveys of your classmates in a chart. Count the number of students who answered *yes* to each question.

4. For each question, calculate the percentage of your class that answered *yes*. To find the percentage, divide the number that answered *yes* by the total number of students. Then multiply that number by 100.

5. How healthy is your class? What things does your class do well? What health habits can be improved?

6. Questions 1, 3, and 5 are similar to questions on the national survey discussed on page 654. How do the diet and exercise habits of your class compare with those of the teenagers in the national survey?

1. Do you exercise at least three times a week? Yes No

2. Do you wear a seat belt every time you ride in a car? Yes No

3. Do you eat five or more servings of fruits and vegetables every day? Yes No

4. Do you use sunscreen to protect your skin when you are outdoors? Yes No

5. Do you eat a lot of high-fat foods? Yes No

What We Put into Our Bodies

"You are what you eat." Does this familiar saying mean that you are pizza or candy? Of course not! But, the substances in the pizza and candy enter your body. The protein in the cheese may become part of your hair; the carbohydrates in the crust can give you energy to run your next race. The sugar in the candy can give you a quick energy boost but make you tired later when your blood sugar level drops.

Nutrition

Are you more likely to have potato chips or broccoli for a snack? a candy bar or a banana? If you lean toward foods that are high in sugar and fat, such as potato chips and candy, your food choices probably are not as healthy as they could be. Does that mean you have to cut out all of your favorite foods to eat healthy? No! Broccoli *is* a healthier food than potato chips. But eating only broccoli every day, like the person in **Figure 1,** is not much better than eating only potato chips! Either way, you do not get a balanced diet.

Balancing Act In order to stay healthy, you need to take in more than 40 different substances every day. These substances, or **nutrients,** nourish your body and are essential to life. To get them all, you must eat a wide variety of foods. Nutrients are grouped into six categories: *carbohydrates, proteins, fats, vitamins, minerals,* and *water.* Three of these—carbohydrates, proteins, and fats—provide energy for the body. The energy in these nutrients is measured in units called Calories. The other three nutrients—vitamins, minerals, and water—do not provide energy in Calories but help the body use all of the nutrients properly.

Figure 1 *Eating only one food, even a healthy food, will not give you all the substances your body needs.*

Body Fuel A **carbohydrate** is a chemical composed of one or more simple sugars. Carbohydrates are your body's main source of energy. They help digest fats, lubricate joints, and keep skin, bones, and nails healthy. Plant foods are the major source of carbohydrates.

There are two basic types of carbohydrates: simple and complex. *Simple carbohydrates* are sugars. They are easily digested and give your body quick energy. *Complex carbohydrates* are made of many sugar molecules linked together. They are digested more slowly than simple carbohydrates and give your body long-lasting energy.

Body Builders Protein is found in body fluids, muscle, bone, skin, and all other tissues. **Proteins** are nutrients used to build and repair body parts. Your body makes the proteins it needs, but it must have the necessary building blocks, called *amino acids,* to make them. Your digestive system breaks down the protein in food into individual amino acids that are then used to make new proteins. If your body does not get enough carbohydrates, it can also use proteins for energy.

Some foods, such as poultry, fish, milk, and eggs provide all of the essential amino acids. These food sources are called complete proteins. Incomplete proteins contain only some of the essential amino acids. Most plants are incomplete sources of protein, but eating a variety of plant foods each day will provide all of the amino acids your body needs.

Energy Storage Fats are energy-storage nutrients that help the body store some vitamins. Too much fat in the diet has been linked to weight gain, heart disease, and some kinds of cancer. But fats are essential to a balanced diet. They are needed to transport vitamins, produce hormones, keep skin healthy, protect vital organs, and provide insulation. Fats provide more than twice as much energy as proteins and carbohydrates per unit mass.

Simple carbohydrates

Complex carbohydrates

Proteins

Fats

Figure 2 Energy-Producing Nutrients

There are two types of fats, saturated and unsaturated. *Saturated fats* are found in meats, dairy products, coconut oil, and palm oil. Saturated fats are known to raise blood cholesterol levels. *Cholesterol* is a fatlike substance found naturally in the body. Although cholesterol is important to the body, high levels in the blood increase the risk of heart disease. *Unsaturated fats* may help reduce blood cholesterol levels. Your body can make its own saturated fats, but it cannot make certain unsaturated fats. You must get these from your diet. Vegetable oils and fish contain unsaturated fats.

Flushing the System A human cannot survive for more than a few days without water. Your body is about 70 percent water. Water is in every cell and every kind of tissue. Water's three main functions are to transport substances, regulate temperature, and provide lubrication. You should drink 8 to 10 glasses of water daily, as shown in **Figure 3.** You also get water from the other liquids you drink and the foods you eat. Fresh fruits and vegetables, juices, soups, and milk contain large amounts of water.

Small Necessities **Minerals** are elements that are essential for good health. Six minerals are needed in large amounts: calcium, chloride, magnesium, phosphorus, potassium, and sodium. There are at least 12 minerals that are required in very small amounts. These include fluorine, iodine, iron, and zinc. If you eat a balanced diet, you should get all of the minerals you need. Calcium and magnesium are necessary for strong bones and teeth. Magnesium and sodium help the body use proteins. Potassium is needed to regulate your heartbeat and produce muscle movement, and iron is necessary for red blood cell production.

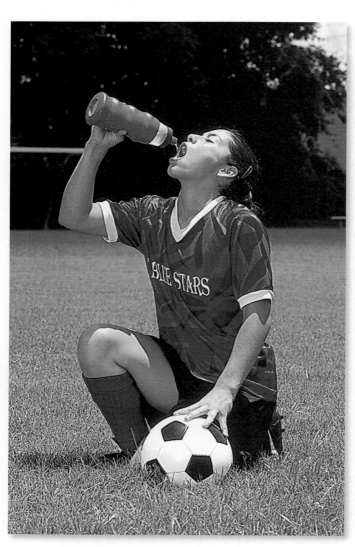

Figure 3 *You need to drink about eight glasses of water a day. When you exercise, you need even more.*

Body Controllers **Vitamins** are organic compounds that control many body functions. Most vitamins cannot be made by the body, so you have to get them from food. The following table provides information about the 13 essential vitamins.

The Essential Vitamins

Vitamin	What it does	Where you get it
A	keeps skin and eyes healthy; builds strong bones and teeth	yellow and orange fruits and vegetables; dark, leafy greens; meat; and milk
B_1 (thiamine)	helps body use carbohydrates; helps nerves and heart function	meats, whole grains, beans, peas, nuts, and seafood
B_2 (riboflavin)	helps cells use carbohydrates and oxygen; keeps skin and eyes healthy	dairy products, fruits, whole grains, eggs, leafy vegetables, and poultry
B_3 (niacin)	helps body use carbohydrates; helps cells use oxygen; helps digestion	meats, peanuts, whole grains, peas, and beans
B_6	helps body use proteins, carbohydrates, and fats	poultry, fish, meat, eggs, potatoes, avocados, and bananas
B_{12}	keeps blood and nerves healthy	meats, poultry, eggs, fish, and milk
Folic acid (a B vitamin)	helps red blood cell formation	leafy greens, peas, beans, nuts, whole grains, liver, and oranges
Pantothenic acid (a B vitamin)	helps body use protein, carbohydrates, and fat; keeps body tissues healthy	meats, fish, whole grains, beans, peas, eggs, and corn
Biotin (a B vitamin)	helps body use protein, carbohydrates, some B vitamins, and fat	eggs, milk, meats, nuts, peas, beans, and whole grains
C	strengthens blood vessels and connective tissue; helps the body absorb iron; helps the body fight disease	citrus fruits; dark, leafy greens; broccoli; peppers; cabbage; tomatoes; potatoes; and strawberries
D	builds strong bones and teeth; helps the body use calcium and phosphorus	sunlight, enriched milk, eggs, and fish
E	protects red blood cells from destruction; needed for some enzymes to work	oils, fats, eggs, whole grains, wheat germ, liver, and leafy greens
K	assists with blood clotting	leafy greens, tomatoes, and potatoes

REVIEW

1. Name the six groups of nutrients, and explain why each is important to the body.

2. If vitamins and minerals do not supply energy, why are they important to a healthy diet?

3. **Applying Concepts** Name some of the nutrients that can be found in a glass of milk.

internetconnect

SCiLINKS
NSTA

TOPIC: Nutrition, Vitamins
GO TO: www.scilinks.org
sciLINKS NUMBER: HSTL680, HSTL685

Eating for Good Health

Now you know what nutrients you need for good health. But how can you be sure to get them all in the right amounts? To begin, keep in mind that most teenage girls need about 2,200 Calories a day and most boys need 2,800 Calories. Since different foods contain different nutrients, *where* you get your Calories is as important as *how many* you get. The food pyramid below can help you make good food choices.

The Food Pyramid

The U.S. Department of Agriculture and the Department of Health and Human Services developed the food pyramid to help Americans make healthy food choices. The food pyramid divides foods into six groups. It shows how many daily servings you need from each group and gives examples of foods for each. This food pyramid also provides sample serving sizes for each group. Within each group, the food choices are up to you. You can eat anything you want. By following the food pyramid, you can achieve a healthy, balanced diet.

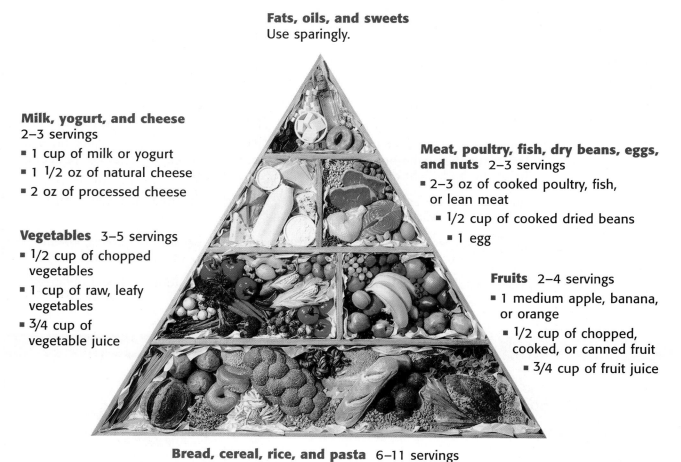

Fats, oils, and sweets
Use sparingly.

Milk, yogurt, and cheese
2–3 servings
- 1 cup of milk or yogurt
- 1 1/2 oz of natural cheese
- 2 oz of processed cheese

Vegetables 3–5 servings
- 1/2 cup of chopped vegetables
- 1 cup of raw, leafy vegetables
- 3/4 cup of vegetable juice

Meat, poultry, fish, dry beans, eggs, and nuts 2–3 servings
- 2–3 oz of cooked poultry, fish, or lean meat
- 1/2 cup of cooked dried beans
- 1 egg

Fruits 2–4 servings
- 1 medium apple, banana, or orange
- 1/2 cup of chopped, cooked, or canned fruit
- 3/4 cup of fruit juice

Bread, cereal, rice, and pasta 6–11 servings
- 1 slice of bread
- 1 oz of ready-to-eat cereal
- 1/2 cup of rice or pasta
- 1/2 cup of cooked cereal

How to Read a Food Label

Packaged foods are required by law to have nutrition information labels. The illustration below shows a nutrition information label for a box of macaroni and cheese. Reading labels will help you make healthy eating choices.

Some of the nutrients found in each serving are listed on the label. The daily values shown are based on a 2,000-Calorie-per-day diet. You will need to calculate your own daily values based on your personal Calorie needs.

The **nutrition facts panel** contains the serving size, the number of servings per container, and the number of Calories per serving. ▶

The **daily value** represents how much of each nutrient you need each day. ▶

The second part of a food label is the **list of ingredients.** It begins with the ingredient used in the greatest amount and ends with the ingredient used in the least amount. ▶

Nutrition Facts

Serving Size 1 cup (59g)
Serving Per Container 2

Amount Per Serving	Prepared
Calories	290
Calories from Fat	90

	% Daily Value
Total Fat 10g	14%
Saturated Fat 3.5g	16%
Cholesterol 10mg	39%
Sodium 30mg	39%
Total Carbohydrate 41g	14%
Dietary Fiber less than 1g	3%
Sugars 4g	
Protein 10g	12%
Vitamin A	8%
Vitamin C	0%
Calcium	15%
Iron	8%
Thiamine	30%
Riboflavin	15%
Niacin	15%
Folic Acid	25%

Ingredients: Enriched Macaroni Product (Wheat Flour, Niacin, Ferrous Sulfate (Iron), Thiamine Mononitrate (Vitamin B1), Riboflavin (Vitamin B2), and Folic Acid), Milk, Cheddar Cheese (Pasteurized Milk, Cheese Culture, Salt, Enzymes), Whey, Margarine (Partially Hydogenated Soybean Oil, Water, Soy Lecithin, Mono- and Diglycerides, Beta Carotene for Color, Vitamin A Palmitate), Salt, Cornstarch, Yeast Extract, Lactic Acid, Sodium Citrate, Spices, Annatto (for color).

MATH BREAK

What Percentage?

Use the nutrition information label on this page to answer the following questions for yourself, based on the Calorie needs of teenagers described on the previous page.

1. What percentage of your daily Calorie needs does one serving of macaroni and cheese provide?

2. The recommended daily value of fat is 72 g for teenage girls and 90 g for teenage boys. What percentage of the daily recommended fat value is provided by one serving of packaged macaroni and cheese?

✓ Self-Check

For breakfast, you eat 1 cup of hot cereal with a banana and 1 cup of milk. What servings from the food pyramid have you eaten? *(See page 782 to check your answer.)*

A Healthy Diet

1. Use the recommended daily Calories for teenagers and the **table** below to estimate how many servings from each group in the food pyramid you should eat daily.

2. Create a menu for 2 days that includes the correct number of servings from each group in the food pyramid.

3. Compare this diet with your normal diet. How different are they? What can you do to improve your diet?

Daily Number of Servings		
Food group	2,200 Calories	2,800 Calories
Bread	9	11
Fruit	3	4
Vegetable	4	5
Dairy	3	3
Meats	6 oz	7 oz

TRY at HOME

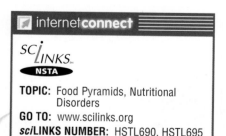

Nutritional Disorders

Unhealthy eating habits can cause nutritional disorders. For example, malnutrition can result from consuming too few Calories or too few of the right nutrients. Eating too many Calories or too many of the wrong nutrients can also cause malnutrition. **Malnutrition** occurs when you do not consume the right combination of nutrients.

Anorexia Nervosa and Bulimia Anorexia nervosa and bulimia can lead to malnutrition. Many of the people who suffer from anorexia nervosa and bulimia are teenage girls. *Anorexia nervosa* is an eating disorder characterized by self-starvation and an intense fear of gaining weight. This can cause weak bones, low blood pressure, and heart problems. *Bulimia* is a disorder characterized by binge eating followed by induced vomiting. Sometimes people suffering from bulimia also use laxatives and diuretics to rid the body of food and water. Bulimia can damage the teeth and digestive system and can also lead to kidney or heart failure. These disorders can both be fatal, but they can be cured with medical help.

Obesity *Obesity* is a condition characterized by an extremely high percentage of body fat. Eating too many foods from the top of the food pyramid and having an inactive lifestyle that involves little exercise can contribute to obesity. Obesity increases the risk of high blood pressure, heart disease, and diabetes.

REVIEW

1. What information is found on a nutrition information label?

2. How do anorexia nervosa and bulimia differ?

3. **Applying Concepts** How can someone who is obese suffer from malnutrition?

Terms to Learn

drug   alcoholism
addiction   narcotics
nicotine

What You'll Do

◆ Distinguish between the positive and negative uses of drugs.
◆ Explain the hazards of tobacco, alcohol, and illegal drugs.

Risks of Alcohol and Other Drugs

You see them in movies and on television. You read about them in magazines. You hear about them in music and in your school. You are exposed to information, and misinformation, about tobacco, alcohol, and other drugs almost every day.

What Is a Drug?

A **drug** is any chemical substance that causes a physical or emotional change in a person. Drugs come in many forms, as shown in **Figure 4.** They can be pills, powders, fumes, liquids, or creams. Some drugs enter the body through the skin, and others are swallowed, inhaled, or injected.

When used safely and correctly, legal drugs can help your body heal a variety of ailments from athlete's foot to pneumonia. They can also provide relief from pain, congestion, and other symptoms. When used illegally or improperly, however, drugs can become killers.

What Effects Do Drugs Have?

Different drugs have different effects. One way to classify drugs is by function. *Analgesics,* like aspirin, are pain-relieving drugs. Drugs that relax muscles and help people sleep are *sedatives.* *Antibiotics* fight bacterial infections, and *antihistamines* help control symptoms of allergies, asthma, and colds.

Another way to classify drugs is by their effect on the central nervous system. *Stimulants* speed up the action of the central nervous system and may cause a person to feel more alert. *Depressants* have the opposite effect. They slow down body functions and may reduce a person's alertness.

Figure 4 *All of these products contain drugs.*

Self-Check

How are tolerance, addiction, and with-drawal symptoms related? (See page 782 to check your answer.)

Dependence and Addiction Regular use of some drugs can cause the body to develop *tolerance*. This means larger and larger doses of the drug are needed to get the same effect. **Addiction** is physical dependence on a drug. When a person is addicted to a drug, the body has a chemical need for the drug. If the body doesn't receive the drug, withdrawal symptoms may occur. These include nausea, vomiting, pain, and other physical symptoms. Once addicted, it is very difficult to stop taking a drug.

Sometimes dependence on a drug is not due to a physical need. Some people form *psychological dependence* on a drug and feel powerful cravings for it.

Types of Drugs

There are many kinds of drugs and many ways to use them. Some drugs are obtained from plants, and some are made synthetically. You can buy some drugs off the shelf, while others must be taken under the supervision of a doctor. Some drugs are illegal to buy, sell, or even possess.

Over-the-Counter and Prescription Drugs An over-the-counter drug can be purchased legally without a doctor's prescription. A prescription is a note written by a doctor to allow a patient to buy a medicine. It specifies the drug, directions for use, and the amount of the drug to be used.

Many over-the-counter and prescription drugs are powerful healing agents. However, some of these drugs also produce unwanted side effects. Side effects are uncomfortable symptoms such as nausea, headaches, drowsiness, or more serious problems caused by a drug.

Whether purchased with or without a prescription, all drugs must be used with care. Each year about 75,000 people in the United States become ill or die from the misuse of drugs. Information on proper use can be found on the label. **Figure 5** shows an example of a prescription drug label. The table below gives some drug safety tips.

Figure 5 *Prescription drug labels provide instructions for use and list possible side effects.*

Drug Safety Tips

- Never take another person's prescription medicine.
- Read the label before each use. Always follow the instructions on the label and those provided by your doctor or pharmacist.
- Do not take more or less medication than prescribed.
- Consult a doctor if you have any side effects.
- Throw away leftover and out-of-date medicines.

Herbal Medicines Information about medicinal herbs has been handed down by word-of-mouth for centuries. Some plants contain chemicals with important healing properties. However, these herbs are drugs and should be used carefully. **Figure 6** shows some medicinal herbs.

Tobacco About 50 million people in the United States—one-third of all adults—smoke. Smoking has serious health risks, and the nicotine in cigarettes is addictive. **Nicotine** is a chemical stimulant in tobacco that increases heart rate and blood pressure. Many smokers also experience a loss of appetite and a decrease in physical endurance. Smoking increases the chances of lung cancer by 10 times, and it has also been linked to other cancers, emphysema, chronic bronchitis, and heart disease. About 400,000 people die from smoking-related illnesses each year. **Figure 7** shows one of the effects of smoking.

Smokeless tobacco is also a health hazard. Nicotine is absorbed through the lining of the mouth, and the amount of nicotine that reaches the blood can be the same as for a smoker. Smokeless tobacco increases the risk of several types of cancer, including mouth and throat cancer. It also causes gum disease and discoloration of the teeth.

Figure 6 *Some herbs can be purchased in health food stores. Medicinal herbs should always be used with care.*

Figure 7 *Cilia in your airways cleanse debris from the air you breathe and prevent debris from entering your lungs. Compare the cilia from the lungs of a nonsmoker, on the left, with those of a smoker, on the right.*

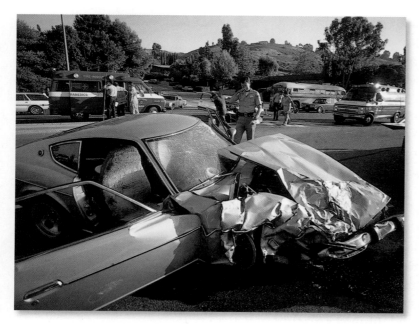

Figure 8 *On average, there is one alcohol-related fatality every 31 minutes.*

Alcohol Alcohol depresses the central nervous system and causes relaxation and memory loss. Excessive use of alcohol can damage the liver, pancreas, brain, nerves, and cardiovascular system. In very large quantities, alcohol can cause respiratory failure and even death. In addition, alcohol is a factor in more than half of all accidental deaths, suicides, and murders. **Figure 8** shows one example of an alcohol-related accident. It is illegal in the United States for people under the age of 21 to use alcohol.

About 10 million alcohol users are alcoholics. They suffer from **alcoholism,** which means that they are physically and psychologically dependent on alcohol. Alcoholism is considered a disease, and genetic factors are thought to influence a person's tendency to become an alcoholic.

Marijuana Marijuana is an illegal drug made from the Indian hemp plant. Marijuana produces a mind-altering effect that varies from user to user. It may cause a relaxed feeling or may increase anxiety. Marijuana slows reaction time, impairs thinking, and causes a loss of coordination.

Cocaine Cocaine and its more purified form, crack, are stimulants made from the South American coca plant. Both drugs are illegal and highly addictive, and users can become dependent on them in a very short time. Cocaine and crack produce feelings of intense excitement followed by anxiety and depression. Both drugs increase heart rate and blood pressure and can cause heart attacks even among first-time users.

Hallucinogens Hallucinogens (huh LOO si nuh juhnz) distort the senses and cause changes in mood and thought processes. Users have hallucinations (huh LOO si NAY shuhnz), which means they see and hear things that are not real. Some hallucinations are extremely frightening and can cause people to respond violently. LSD and PCP, or "angel dust," are two powerful and illegal hallucinogens. Sniffing some glues and solvents also causes hallucinations and can cause serious brain damage.

Deadly Averages

Approximately 2,200 people between the ages of 16 and 20 die in alcohol-related crashes each year. On average, how many die every day?

Narcotics **Narcotics** are drugs made from opium. Some narcotics are used to treat severe pain and are legal when prescribed by a doctor. But many narcotics are illegal.

One illegal narcotic is heroin. Heroin is one of the most addictive drugs known, and large doses can lead to death. Because it is so strongly addictive, users must continue taking the drug in order to prevent painful withdrawal symptoms. Heroin is usually injected, and users often share needles that are contaminated. Therefore, heroin users have a high risk of infecting themselves with diseases like hepatitis and AIDS.

Designer Drugs There are many other illegal drugs. Examples include inhalants, barbiturates (downers), amphetamines (uppers), and "designer" drugs, which are produced by making small changes to existing drugs. Some inhalants, barbiturates, and amphetamines are legal if prescribed by a doctor.

Drug Use and Drug Abuse

A drug user takes a drug to prevent or improve some medical condition. The drug user obtains the drug legally and uses the drug properly. A drug abuser does *not* take a drug to relieve a medical condition. The drug abuser may take drugs for the temporary good feelings they produce, to escape from problems, or to belong to a group. The drug is often obtained illegally, and it is often taken without knowledge of the strength or purity of the drug.

Drug Abuse: How Does It Start? Nicotine, alcohol, and marijuana are called *gateway drugs* because they are usually the first drugs a person tries. The abuse of other more dangerous drugs may follow the abuse of gateway drugs, as illustrated in **Figure 9.** Most teenagers who start smoking cigarettes, drinking alcohol, or using marijuana do not realize that these drugs are addictive or that they can seriously harm their health.

Peer pressure is the reason most young people begin to use drugs. Teenagers may feel the need to drink, smoke, or try marijuana in order to make friends or to avoid being ridiculed or threatened. Many young people feel that "everyone" is using drugs. Because drug abusers often stand out, the fact that many teenagers do not abuse drugs is sometimes hard to see.

Self-Check

1. What is a hallucination?
2. List three dangers of heroin use.

(See page 782 to check your answers.)

Figure 9 *Nicotine, alcohol, and marijuana are called gateway drugs.*

Many people who start using drugs do not recognize the dangers. Misinformation about drugs is everywhere. Several common drug myths are discussed below.

Drug Myths	
Myth	**Reality**
"It's only alcohol, not drugs."	Alcohol is a mood-altering and mind-altering drug. It affects the central nervous system and is addictive.
"I won't get hooked on one or two cigarettes a day."	Addiction is not related to the amount of a drug used. Some people become addicted after using a drug once or twice.
"I can quit any time I want."	Addicts may quit and return to drug usage many times. Their inability to stay drug free shows how powerful the addiction is.

Activity

Write yourself a letter. Tell yourself why you should stay drug free. You may wish to refer to people, goals, activities, or values that are important to you. Put your letter in an envelope, and keep it in a safe place. If you ever find yourself thinking about using drugs, take out your letter and read it.

TRY at HOME

Signs of Use People who begin using drugs generally undergo emotional, physical, and behavioral changes. Teenagers may have problems with school or family. Changes in personality or physical appearance may occur. However, remember that many young people do not take drugs. These changes could be signs of other problems or normal age-related changes.

Getting Off Drugs The first step to quitting drugs is to admit to being a drug abuser and to decide to stop. When quitting drugs, it is important for the addicted person to get proper medical and psychological treatment. Getting off drugs can be extremely difficult. Withdrawal symptoms may be painful, and even after the symptoms are gone, powerful cravings for a drug continue. This is even true of smoking.

internet**connect**

SC*LINKS*
NSTA

TOPIC: Drug and Alcohol Abuse
GO TO: www.scilinks.org
*sci*LINKS NUMBER: HSTL700

REVIEW

1. What is the difference between a prescription drug and an over-the-counter drug?

2. How does addiction occur?

3. **Analyzing Relationships** How are nicotine, alcohol, heroin, and cocaine similar? How are they different?

Terms to Learn

hygiene   stress
aerobic exercise

What You'll Do

- ◆ Describe four important aspects of good hygiene.
- ◆ Explain why exercise and sleep are important to good health.
- ◆ Describe methods of handling stress.
- ◆ List ways to stay safe at home, on the road, and outdoors.

Healthy Habits

Do you like playing sports? acting in plays? going to the movies? swimming in the ocean? No matter what you enjoy, the better your health, the easier it will be to take part in the things you like to do. Keeping yourself healthy is a daily task. If you have healthy habits, you are likely to stay healthy for a long time.

Hygiene and Posture

Hygiene refers to methods of preserving and protecting your health. It sounds simple, but washing your hands is the best way to prevent the spread of disease and infection. You should always wash your hands after using the bathroom and before and after eating or preparing food.

Taking care of your skin, hair, and teeth are other important aspects of good hygiene. Using sunscreens can help prevent sunburn, wrinkles, and skin cancer. Shampoo your hair regularly. To prevent cavities and keep your teeth and gums healthy, eat a healthy diet, brush at least twice a day, and floss at least once daily. Get regular dental exams, and replace your toothbrush about every 3 months.

Posture Posture is also important to health. Good posture helps you look and feel good. Bad posture strains your muscles and ligaments and makes breathing difficult. To have good posture when you stand, imagine a vertical line passing through your ear, shoulder, hip, knee, and ankle, as shown in **Figure 10.** When working at a desk, pull your chair forward and plant your feet firmly on the floor.

Figure 10 *A slumped posture strains your lower back.*

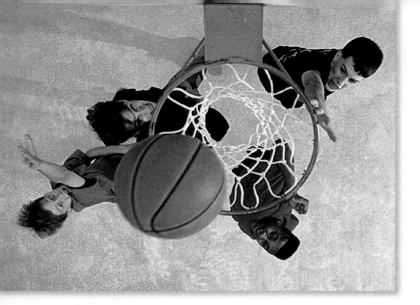

Figure 11 *To stay with aerobic exercise, it is important to choose an activity you enjoy.*

Exercise and Rest

Imagine that school starts at 7:30 A.M. You drag yourself out of bed at 6:00 every morning. You are tired, but somehow you make it through the school day. In the afternoon, you attend play rehearsal. When you get home, you take a break, eat dinner, and start your homework at 8:00 P.M. When you finish, you do not feel ready to sleep, so you watch TV, then read in bed, and finally, at 10:30, you drift off to sleep.

Keeping your body healthy requires giving it plenty of exercise and plenty of rest. If you have a schedule like the one above, you do not get enough of either.

Exercise Regular aerobic exercise at least three times a week is critical to good health. **Aerobic exercise** is vigorous, sustained exercise of the whole body for 20 minutes or more. Walking, running, swimming, and biking are all examples of aerobic exercise. For another example, see **Figure 11.**

Aerobic exercise increases the heart rate. As a result, more oxygen is taken in and distributed throughout the body. Over time, aerobic exercise strengthens the heart, lungs, and bones. It burns Calories, helps your body conserve nutrients, and aids digestion. It also gives you more energy and stamina. In other words, aerobic exercise protects your physical and mental health, and it's free! What a deal!

Sleep Believe it or not, teenagers actually need more sleep than younger children. Do you ever fall asleep in class, like the girl in **Figure 12,** or feel tired in the middle of the afternoon? If so, you may not be getting enough sleep. Scientists say that teenagers need about 9.5 hours of sleep each night.

At night, the body goes through several cycles of progressively deeper sleep, with periods of lighter sleep in between. If you do not sleep long enough, you will not enter the deepest, most restful period of sleep.

Only half of a dolphin's brain sleeps at a time. A full, deep sleep would be a problem because dolphins must come to the surface for air every 20–30 seconds.

Figure 12 *If you fall asleep easily during the day, you are probably not getting enough sleep.*

Coping with Stress

You have a big soccer game tomorrow. Are you excited and ready for action? You got a low grade on your math test. Are you upset or angry? The game and the test are causing you stress. **Stress** is the physical and mental response to pressure.

Some stress is a normal part of life, as shown in **Figure 13.** Stress stimulates your body to prepare for difficult or dangerous situations. However, sometimes you may have no outlet for the stress, and it builds up. Excess stress is harmful to your health and can decrease your ability to carry out your daily activities.

You may not even realize you are stressed until your body reacts. Perhaps you get a headache, have an upset stomach, or lie awake at night. You might feel tired all the time or begin an old nervous habit, such as nail-biting. You may become irritable or resentful. All of these things can be signs of too much stress.

What to Do Different people are stressed by different things. Once you identify the source of the stress, you can find ways to deal with it. Here are some ideas for handling stress.

- Make a list of all the things you would like to get done, and rank them in order of importance. Do the most important things first.

- Exercise regularly, and get enough sleep.

- Pet a friendly animal.

- If you cannot remove a stressor, spend some quiet time alone or practice deep breathing or other relaxation techniques.

- Share your problems. Talk things over with someone you trust.

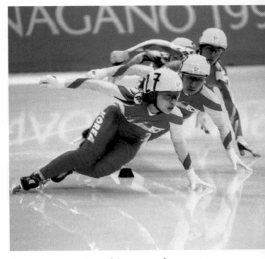

Figure 13 *Working under stress can increase an athlete's ability to perform well.*

Stress SOS

Your mother is out of town helping your grandfather move into a nursing home. Your little brother has been snooping in your room. You have a history project due in two days, an oral report due in English, and quizzes in both math and science! You are ready to scream! What are some healthy ways to handle all the stress you are feeling?

Injury Prevention

Have you ever fallen off your bike or sprained your ankle? Maybe you avoided injury, or maybe you ended up in the emergency room. Accidents happen, and they can cause injury and even death. It is impossible to prevent all accidents, but you can decrease your risk by using your common sense and following basic safety rules.

Safety at Home Many accidents can be avoided. **Figure 14** below shows tips for safety around the house.

Figure 14 Home Safety Tips

- Have your parents install smoke detectors on every floor.

Bathroom
- Never touch electrical switches or appliances while touching water.
- Use nonslip mats in the shower and tub.
- Use a night light.

Living room
- Keep electrical cords out of walkways.
- Do not plug too many electrical devices into one outlet.

Kitchen
- Clean up spills quickly.
- Do not allow pothandles to extend over the edge of the stove.
- Use a stool to reach high shelves.
- Keep grease and drippings away from open flames.

Entrance and stairs
- Use a railing.
- Never leave objects on stairs.

Safety Outdoors Always dress appropriately for the weather and the activity. Never hike or camp alone. Tell someone where you are going and when you expect to return. If you do not bring water from home, be sure to purify any water you drink in the wilderness.

Learn how to swim. It could save your life! Never swim alone, and do not dive into shallow water or water of unknown depth. When in a boat, wear a life jacket. If a storm threatens, get out of the water and seek shelter.

Safety on the Road In the car, always wear a seat belt, even if you are traveling only a short distance. Most car accidents happen close to home, and seat belts save lives. When riding a bicycle, always wear a helmet. Ride with traffic, and obey all traffic rules. Be sure to signal when stopping or turning.

When Accidents Happen

No matter how well we practice safety measures, accidents can still happen. What should you do if a friend chokes on food and cannot breathe? What if he is stung by a bee and has a violent allergic reaction?

Call for Help Once you've checked for other dangers, call for medical help immediately, like the person in **Figure 15.** In most communities you can dial 911. Speak slowly and clearly. Give the complete address and a description of the location. Describe the accident, the number of people injured, and the types of injuries. Ask what to do and listen carefully to the instructions. Let the other person hang up first to be sure they have no more questions or instructions.

Figure 15 *When calling 911, stay calm and listen carefully to what the dispatcher tells you.*

Learn First Aid You may want to learn more about what to do in an emergency by taking a first-aid course or a CPR course, as shown in **Figure 16.** *CPR* is a lifesaving procedure designed to revive a person who is not breathing and has no heartbeat. If you are over 12 years old, you can become certified in both CPR and first aid. Some babysitting courses also provide basics in first aid and are a good idea for anyone who cares for young children. The American Red Cross, community organizations, and local hospitals offer these classes. You should not attempt any lifesaving procedure unless you have been trained.

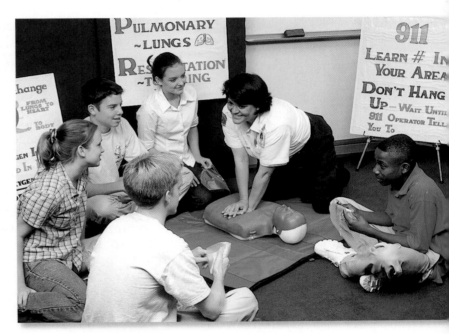

Figure 16 *These teenagers are taking a CPR course to prepare themselves for emergency situations.*

REVIEW

1. What is aerobic exercise? Give three examples.

2. What should you do when calling for help in a medical emergency?

3. What is hygiene, and how does it help you stay healthy?

4. **Applying Concepts** What situations are causing excess stress in your life right now? What can you do to help relieve the stress you are feeling?

Chapter Highlights

Vocabulary

nutrient *(p. 656)*

carbohydrate *(p. 657)*

protein *(p. 657)*

fat *(p. 657)*

mineral *(p. 658)*

vitamin *(p. 659)*

malnutrition *(p. 662)*

Section Notes

• Carbohydrates, proteins, fats, vitamins, minerals, and water are the six types of nutrients that are essential to life.

• Teenage girls need about 2,200 Calories a day. Boys need about 2,800. It is important to obtain Calories from a variety of foods.

• The food pyramid gives information for eating a balanced diet.

• A nutrition information label on a packaged food lists serving size, Calorie and nutrient content, and the ingredients.

• Anorexia nervosa, bulimia, and obesity can lead to malnutrition.

Labs

To Diet or Not to Diet *(p. 780)*

Vocabulary

drug *(p. 663)*

addiction *(p. 664)*

nicotine *(p. 665)*

alcoholism *(p. 666)*

narcotics *(p. 667)*

Section Notes

• A drug is any chemical substance that causes a physical or emotional change in a person.

• Some drugs can cause addiction or psychological dependence.

• Over-the-counter and prescription drugs are legal drugs, many of which are powerful healing agents. Some also have side effects.

• Alcohol and nicotine are legal drugs for adults. Both are addictive and hazardous to your health.

☑ Skills Check

Math Concepts

PERCENTAGE If your recommended daily value of fat is 72 g and you eat a candy bar that has 12 g of fat, what percentage of your daily value of fat have you eaten? To find the percentage, divide the grams of fat in the candy bar by the daily value. Then multiply by 100.

$$12 \text{ g} \div 72 \text{ g} = 0.17 \times 100\% = 17\%$$

The fat in the candy bar is 17 percent of your total daily value.

Visual Understanding

NUTRITION INFORMATION LABELS All packaged foods in the United States are required to have a nutrition label like the one on page 661. On this label you can see that the serving size is 1 cup and that there are two servings in the container. The number of Calories in a serving and the number of Calories from fat are listed. You will also see the percent daily value for a number of nutrients that can be found in one serving. These percentages are based on 2,000 Calories a day.

SECTION 2

- A drug abuser takes a drug, often illegally, for non-medical reasons.

- Drug abuse oftens begins with the use of tobacco, alcohol, or marijuana—the gateway drugs.

- Getting off drugs requires admitting addiction, deciding to stop, going through withdrawal symptoms, and experiencing cravings for the drug.

SECTION 3

Vocabulary

hygiene (*p. 669*)
aerobic exercise (*p. 670*)
stress (*p. 671*)

Section Notes

- Good hygiene is essential to good health.

- Having a healthy body requires getting regular aerobic exercise and getting enough sleep. Posture is also important to good health.

- Some stress is a normal and necessary part of life. Too much stress can result in poor health.

- It is possible to prevent some accidents by using common sense and following basic rules of safety.

- In an emergency, call for help as soon as possible. Do not attempt any lifesaving procedure for which you are not trained.

Labs

Keep It Clean (*p. 781*)

Chapter Review

USING VOCABULARY

To complete the following sentences, choose the correct term from each pair of terms listed below:

1. __?__ are linked to high blood cholesterol levels. *(Saturated fats* or *Unsaturated fats)*

2. Physical dependence on a drug is called __?__. *(addiction* or *tolerance)*

3. The __?__ divides foods into six groups and gives a recommended number of servings for each. *(nutrition information label* or *food pyramid)*

4. One of the characteristics of __?__ is binge eating. *(bulimia* or *anorexia nervosa)*

5. A person who uses drugs for their intended purpose and with the proper dosage is a __?__. *(drug abuser* or *drug user)*

UNDERSTANDING CONCEPTS

Multiple Choice

6. Which of the following is *not* a function of water in the body?
    a. transport substances
    b. regulate temperature
    c. provide Calories
    d. provide lubrication

7. Side effects of over-the-counter and prescription medicines may include
    a. nausea.   c. drowsiness.
    b. headaches.   d. All of the above

8. Which of the following nutrients does *not* provide energy for the body?
    a. carbohydrates   c. fats
    b. vitamins   d. proteins

9. What are the effects of nicotine on the body?
    a. liver damage and decrease in physical endurance
    b. loss of appetite and decrease in physical endurance
    c. loss of appetite and brain damage
    d. liver damage and loss of appetite

10. Which of the following statements about drugs is true?
    a. All drugs are illegal.
    b. Smoking just one or two cigarettes is safe for anyone.
    c. Alcohol is not a drug.
    d. Withdrawal symptoms may be painful.

11. Aerobic exercise does *not*
    a. burn calories.
    b. increase the heart rate.
    c. strengthen the heart, lungs, and bones.
    d. make you weak.

12. When talking to a 911 operator, you should *not*
    a. describe the accident.
    b. ask what to do.
    c. hang up before the dispatcher hangs up.
    d. speak slowly and clearly.

Short Answer

Answer each of the following questions with a few sentences:

13. Are all narcotics illegal? Explain.

14. What are the three types of nutrients that provide energy in Calories? Which three nutrients do not provide energy?

15. If you drink a beer, are you taking a drug? Explain your answer.

Concept Mapping

16. Use the following terms to create a concept map: unsaturated fats, carbohydrates, water, proteins, nutrients, simple sugars, starch, fats, vitamins, minerals, saturated fats.

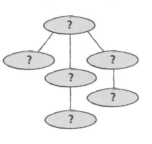

CRITICAL THINKING AND PROBLEM SOLVING

Write one or two sentences to answer the following questions:

17. Many people eat little or no meat. Meat is often the major source of protein in American diets. What other sources of protein can vegetarians choose?

18. You are at a party and a friend offers you a cigarette. He says that one cigarette won't hurt you. Using what you know about tobacco and addiction, explain why his reasoning is false.

MATH IN SCIENCE

19. Assume your diet is 20 percent fat, 30 percent protein, and 50 percent carbohydrates. In order to get 2,000 Calories a day, how many Calories of each nutrient should you be getting?

INTERPRETING GRAPHICS

List the unsafe habits in the following illustrations. For each unsafe habit, tell what the person should be doing instead.

What's wrong here?

20.

21.

NOW What Do You Think?

Take a minute to review your answers to the ScienceLog questions on page 655. Have your answers changed? If necessary, revise your answers based on what you have learned since you began this chapter.

Science, Technology, and Society

Bacteria at Your Service

Wanted: Hard worker to clean up trash. You must have experience curing diseases. The ability to make plastics is a plus. Only microorganisms need apply for this position.

What could possibly be flexible enough to perform so many different activities? Would you believe it's bacteria?

Cleaning Up Our Act

Without bacteria, Earth would be littered with the remains of plants and animals. That's because many bacteria decompose once-living matter. Some bacteria also break down other substances. In fact, they offer solutions to some of our toughest pollution problems.

When an oil spill occurs, it often severely damages the environment. However, scientists have engineered bacteria that actually feed on oil! As the bacteria eat the oil, they break it down into harmless substances. Scientists hope to use the bacteria to clean up large oil spills, but they must first be certain that introducing a large number of these bacteria into the ocean will not harm the environment.

Producing Plastics and Pills

Did you know that some bacteria act like factories? For example, one kind of bacteria makes biodegradable plastic! These amazing bacteria store energy as plastic granules, just as animals store energy as fat and plants store energy as starch. Originally, researchers found that the plastic was stiff and brittle. However, scientists found that when certain substances are added to the bacteria's diet, the plastic they produce is flexible enough to be made into consumer products.

Other bacteria can produce important drugs used to fight disease. In fact, some bacteria even produce antibiotics that can fight infections caused by other bacteria!

Helping Plants Grow

Genetic engineers have designed bacteria that can help make plants pest resistant and cold resistant. Some bacteria even keep foods fresh longer on the grocery store shelves. From the garbage dump to the grocery store to the medicine cabinet, bacteria are at our service!

What Do You Think?

► Many scientists are concerned about the potential side effects of genetic engineering. What could be some consequences of altering the genetic makeup of crops? Do some research to find out for yourself. Write a report or organize a debate with your classmates.

▲ *These bacteria are used to clean up oil spills.*

Health
WATCH WATCH WATCH WATCH WATCH

Meatless Munching

What'll it be today, the hamburger special, chicken surprise, or veggie platter? More and more people are opting for the veggie platter. In fact, research indicates that more than 12 million Americans are now vegetarians, and this number appears to be growing.

It's Not Just Salads

When you think of a vegetarian diet, you might think only of vegetables. Of course, vegetables are important to a vegetarian diet, but not all vegetarian diets are alike. Some vegetarian diets are based solely on plant products, while semivegetarian diets may also include dairy products, eggs, fish, and poultry.

Why the Trend?

There are many different reasons for choosing a vegetarian lifestyle. Some people believe that a vegetarian diet is healthy because a decreased consumption of animal products can lower their intake of saturated fat and cholesterol. Other people have ecological reasons for eating a vegetarian diet. For example, producing a serving of meat requires more land, water, and chemicals than producing a serving of grain. Finally, many vegetarians believe that it is unethical to kill animals for meat when plants are available.

Benefits and Risks

Recent statistics suggest that a vegetarian diet may reduce the risk of heart disease, adult-onset diabetes, and some forms of cancer. However, this type of diet takes careful thought. It is not simply a matter of eliminating meat. People may replace the meat with too

▲ *All of the foods shown here are plant products and are commonly used in vegetarian diets.*

many dairy products and eggs, which are higher in fat than most meats. Others may substitute high carbohydrate foods (such as pasta) and junk food (such as french fries) for their meat choices instead of increasing their fruit and vegetable intake. This could lead to nutritional deficiencies. The key to consuming the recommended amount of calories and nutrients for a healthy diet is to eat a wide variety of nutritious, low-fat foods. This is a good idea whether you want to decrease your meat intake or not.

Prepare a Healthy Menu

▶ Choose one of the nutrients that meats provide, and do some research to find a vegetarian substitute. What difficulties did you encounter in your search? Would you eat the substitute you found?

Contents

SAFETY FIRST!

Exploring, inventing, and investigating are essential to the study of science. However, these activities can also be dangerous. To make sure that your experiments and explorations are safe, you must be aware of a variety of safety guidelines.

You have probably heard of the saying, "It is better to be safe than sorry." This is particularly true in a science classroom where experiments and explorations are being performed. Being uninformed and careless can result in serious injuries. Don't take chances with your own safety or with anyone else's.

Following are important guidelines for staying safe in the science classroom. Your teacher may also have safety guidelines and tips that are specific to your classroom and laboratory. Take the time to be safe.

Safety Rules!

Start Out Right

Always get your teacher's permission before attempting any laboratory exploration. Read the procedures carefully, and pay particular attention to safety information and caution statements. If you are unsure about what a safety symbol means, look it up or ask your teacher. You cannot be too careful when it comes to safety. If an accident does occur, inform your teacher immediately, regardless of how minor you think the accident is.

If you are instructed to note the odor of a substance, wave the fumes toward your nose with your hand. Never put your nose close to the source.

Safety Symbols

All of the experiments and investigations in this book and their related worksheets include important safety symbols to alert you to particular safety concerns. Become familiar with these symbols so that when you see them, you will know what they mean and what to do. It is important that you read this entire safety section to learn about specific dangers in the laboratory.

Eye protection	Clothing protection	Hand safety
Heating safety	Electric safety	Chemical safety
Animal safety	Sharp object	Plant safety

Eye Safety

Wear safety goggles when working around chemicals, acids, bases, or any type of flame or heating device. Wear safety goggles any time there is even the slightest chance that harm could come to your eyes. If any substance gets into your eyes, notify your teacher immediately, and flush your eyes with running water for at least 15 minutes. Treat any unknown chemical as if it were a dangerous chemical. Never look directly into the sun. Doing so could cause permanent blindness.

Avoid wearing contact lenses in a laboratory situation. Even if you are wearing safety goggles, chemicals can get between the contact lenses and your eyes. If your doctor requires that you wear contact lenses instead of glasses, wear eye-cup safety goggles in the lab.

Safety Equipment

Know the locations of the nearest fire alarms and any other safety equipment, such as fire blankets and eyewash fountains, as identified by your teacher, and know the procedures for using them.

Be extra careful when using any glassware. When adding a heavy object to a graduated cylinder, tilt the cylinder so the object slides slowly to the bottom.

Neatness

Keep your work area free of all unnecessary books and papers. Tie back long hair, and secure loose sleeves or other loose articles of clothing, such as ties and bows. Remove dangling jewelry. Don't wear open-toed shoes or sandals in the laboratory. Never eat, drink, or apply cosmetics in a laboratory setting. Food, drink, and cosmetics can easily become contaminated with dangerous materials.

Certain hair products (such as aerosol hair spray) are flammable and should not be worn while working near an open flame. Avoid wearing hair spray or hair gel on lab days.

Sharp/Pointed Objects

Use knives and other sharp instruments with extreme care. Never cut objects while holding them in your hands. Place objects on a suitable work surface for cutting.

Heat

Wear safety goggles when using a heating device or a flame. Whenever possible, use an electric hot plate as a heat source instead of an open flame. When heating materials in a test tube, always angle the test tube away from yourself and others. In order to avoid burns, wear heat-resistant gloves whenever instructed to do so.

Electricity

Be careful with electrical cords. When using a microscope with a lamp, do not place the cord where it could trip someone. Do not let cords hang over a table edge in a way that could cause equipment to fall if the cord is accidentally pulled. Do not use equipment with damaged cords. Be sure your hands are dry and that the electrical equipment is in the "off" position before plugging it in. Turn off and unplug electrical equipment when you are finished.

Chemicals

Wear safety goggles when handling any potentially dangerous chemicals, acids, or bases. If a chemical is unknown, handle it as you would a dangerous chemical. Wear an apron and safety gloves when working with acids or bases or whenever you are told to do so. If a spill gets on your skin or clothing, rinse it off immediately with water for at least 5 minutes while calling to your teacher.

Never mix chemicals unless your teacher tells you to do so. Never taste, touch, or smell chemicals unless you are specifically directed to do so. Before working with a flammable liquid or gas, check for the presence of any source of flame, spark, or heat.

Animal Safety

Always obtain your teacher's permission before bringing any animal into the school building. Handle animals only as your teacher directs. Always treat animals carefully and with respect. Wash your hands thoroughly after handling any animal.

Plant Safety

Do not eat any part of a plant or plant seed used in the laboratory. Wash hands thoroughly after handling any part of a plant. When in nature, do not pick any wild plants unless your teacher instructs you to do so.

Glassware

Examine all glassware before use. Be sure that glassware is clean and free of chips and cracks. Report damaged glassware to your teacher. Glass containers used for heating should be made of heat-resistant glass.

Does It All Add Up?

Your math teacher won't tell you this, but did you know that sometimes 2 + 2 does not equal 4?! (Well, it really does, but sometimes it doesn't *appear* to equal 4.) In this experiment, you will use the scientific method to predict, measure, and observe the mixing of two unknown liquids. You will learn that a scientist does not set out to prove a hypothesis, but rather to test it, and sometimes the results just don't seem to add up!

Materials

- 75 mL of liquid A
- 75 mL of liquid B
- 100 mL graduated cylinders (7)
- glass-labeling marker
- Celsius thermometer
- protective gloves

Make Observations

1. Examine the two mystery liquids in the graduated cylinders given to you by your teacher.
   Caution: Do not taste, touch, or smell the liquids.

2. In your ScienceLog, write down as many observations as you can about each liquid. Are the liquids bubbly? What color are they? What is the exact volume of each liquid? Touch the graduated cylinders. Are they hot or cold?

3. Pour exactly 25 mL of liquid A into each of two graduated cylinders. Combine these samples in one of the graduated cylinders, and record the final volume in your ScienceLog. Repeat this step for liquid B.

Form a Hypothesis

4. Based on your observations and on prior experience, what do you expect the volume to be when you pour these two liquids together?

Make a Prediction

5. Make a prediction based on your hypothesis using an "if-then" format. Explain why you have made your prediction.

Test the Hypothesis

6. In your ScienceLog, make a data table similar to the one below to record your predictions and observations.

	Contents of cylinder A	Contents of cylinder B	Mixing results: predictions	Mixing results: observations
Volume				
Appearance				
Temperature				

DO NOT WRITE IN BOOK

7. Carefully pour exactly 25 mL of Liquid A into a 50 mL graduated cylinder. Mark this cylinder "A." Record its volume, appearance, and temperature in the data table.

8. Carefully pour exactly 25 mL of Liquid B into another 50 mL graduated cylinder. Mark this cylinder "B." Record its volume, appearance, and temperature in the data table.

9. Mark the empty third cylinder "A + B."

10. In the "Mixing results: predictions" column in your table, record the prediction you made earlier. Each classmate may have made a different prediction.

11. Carefully pour the contents of both cylinders into the third graduated cylinder.

12. Observe and record the total volume, appearance, and temperature in the "Mixing results: observations" column of the table.

Analyze the Results

13. Discuss your predictions as a class. How many different predictions were there? Which predictions were supported by testing? Did any of your measurements surprise you?

Draw Conclusions

14. Was your hypothesis supported? Explain why this may have happened.

15. Explain the value of incorrect predictions.

Graphing Data

When performing an experiment it is usually necessary to collect data. To understand the data, it is often good to organize them into a graph. Graphs can show trends and patterns that you might not notice in a table or list. In this exercise, you will practice collecting data and organizing the data into a graph.

Materials

- 200 mL of water
- 400 mL beaker
- ice
- Celsius thermometer with a clip
- hot plate
- clock or watch with a second hand
- graph paper
- heat-resistant gloves

Procedure

1. Pour 200 mL of water into a 400 mL beaker. Add ice to the beaker until the water line is at the 400 mL mark.

2. Place a Celsius thermometer into the beaker. Use a thermometer clip to prevent the thermometer from touching the bottom of the beaker. Record the temperature of the ice water in your ScienceLog.

3. Place the beaker and thermometer on a hot plate. Turn the hot plate on medium heat and record the temperature every minute until the water temperature reaches 100°C.

4. Using heat-resistant gloves, remove the beaker from the hot plate. Continue to record the temperature of the water each minute for 10 more minutes.
   Caution: Don't forget to turn off the hot plate.

5. On a piece of graph paper, create a graph similar to the one below. Label the horizontal axis (the *x*-axis) "Time (min)," and mark the axis in increments of 1 minute as shown. Label the vertical axis (the *y*-axis) "Temperature (°C)," and mark the axis in increments of ten degrees as shown.

6. Find the 1-minute mark on the *x*-axis, and move up the graph to the temperature you recorded at 1 minute. Place a dot on the graph at that point. Plot each temperature in the same way. When you have plotted all of your data, connect the dots with a smooth line.

Analysis

7. Examine your graph. Do you think the water heated faster than it cooled? Explain.

8. Estimate what the temperature of the water was 2.5 minutes after you placed the beaker on the hot plate. Explain how you can make a good estimate of temperature between those you recorded.

9. Explain how a graph may give more information than the same data in a chart.

A Window to a Hidden World

Have you ever noticed that objects underwater appear closer than they really are? That's because light waves change speed when they travel from air into water. Anton van Leeuwenhoek, a pioneer of microscopy in the late seventeenth century, used a drop of water to magnify objects. That drop of water brought a hidden world closer into view. How did Leeuwenhoek's microscope work? In this investigation, you will build a model of it to find out.

Materials

- hole punch
- 3 × 10 cm piece of poster board
- clear plastic wrap
- transparent tape
- eyedropper
- water
- newspaper

Procedure

1. Punch a hole in the center of the poster board with a hole punch, as shown in (a) at right.

2. Tape a small piece of clear plastic wrap over the hole, as shown in (b) at right. Be sure the plastic wrap is large enough so that the tape you use to secure it does not cover the hole.

3. Use an eyedropper to put one drop of water over the hole. Check to be sure your drop of water is dome-shaped (convex), as shown in (c) at right.

4. Hold the microscope close to your eye and look through the drop. Be careful not to disturb the water drop.

5. Hold the microscope over a piece of newspaper and observe the image.

Analysis

6. Describe and draw the image you see. Is the image larger or the same size as it was without the microscope? Is the image clear or blurred? Is the shape of the image distorted?

7. How do you think your model could be improved?

Going Further
Robert Hooke and Zacharias Janssen contributed much to the field of microscopy. Find out who they were, when they lived, and what they did.

a

b

c

Roly-Poly Races

Have you ever watched a bug run? Did you wonder why it was running? The bug you saw running was probably reacting to a stimulus. In other words, something happened that made it run! One characteristic of living things is that they respond to stimuli. In this activity, you will study the movement of roly-polies. Roly-polies are also called pill bugs. They are not really bugs at all; they are land-dwelling crustaceans called isopods. Isopods live in dark, moist areas under rocks or wood. You will provide stimuli to determine how fast your isopod can move and what affects its speed and direction. Remember that isopods are living things and must be treated gently and with respect.

Materials

- small plastic container with lid
- 1 or 2 cm of soil for the container
- metric ruler
- small slice of raw potato
- piece of chalk
- 4 isopods
- watch or clock with a second hand
- protective gloves

Procedure

1. Choose a partner and decide together how you will run your roly-poly race. Discuss some gentle ways you might be able to stimulate your isopods to move. Choose five or six things that might cause movement, such as a gentle nudge or a change in temperature, sound, or light. Check your choices with your teacher.

2. Make a data table similar to the one below. Label your columns with the stimuli you've chosen. Label the rows "Isopod 1," "Isopod 2," "Isopod 3," and "Isopod 4."

Isopod Responses			
	Stimulus 1: _____?_____	**Stimulus 2:** _____?_____	**Stimulus 3:** _____?_____
Isopod 1			
Isopod 2			
Isopod 3			
Isopod 4			

DO NOT WRITE IN BOOK

3. Place 1 or 2 cm of soil in a small plastic container. Add a small slice of potato and a piece of chalk. Your isopods will eat these things.

4. Place four isopods in your container. Observe them for a minute or two before you perform your tests. Record your observations in your ScienceLog.

5. Decide which stimulus you want to test first. Carefully arrange the isopods at the "starting line." The starting line can be an imaginary line at one end of the container.

6. Gently stimulate each isopod at the same time and in the same way. In your data table, record the isopods' responses to the stimulus. Be sure to record the distance each isopod traveled. Don't forget to time the race.

7. Repeat steps 5–6 for each stimulus. Be sure to wait at least two minutes between trials.

Analysis

8. Describe the way isopods move. Do their legs move together?

9. Did your isopods move before or between the trials? Did the movement seem to have a purpose, or were the isopods responding to a stimulus? Explain.

10. Did any of the stimuli you chose make the isopods move faster or go farther? Explain.

Going Further

Isopods may not run for the joy of running like humans do. But humans, like all living things, do react to stimuli. Describe three stimuli that might cause humans to run.

The Best-Bread Bakery Dilemma

The chief baker at the Best-Bread Bakery thinks that the yeast the bakery received may be dead. Yeast is a central ingredient in bread. Yeast is a living organism, a member of the kingdom Fungi, and it undergoes the same life processes as other living organisms. When yeast grows in the presence of oxygen and other nutrients, it produces carbon dioxide. The gas forms bubbles that cause the dough to rise. Thousands of dollars may be lost if the yeast is dead.

The Best-Bread Bakery has requested that you test the yeast. The bakery has furnished samples of live yeast and some samples of the yeast in question.

Procedure

1. Make a data table similar to the one below. Leave plenty of room to write your observations.

2. Examine each yeast sample with a magnifying lens. You may want to sniff the samples to determine the presence of an odor. (Your teacher will demonstrate the appropriate way to detect odors in the laboratory.) Record your observations in the data table.

3. Label three test tubes or plastic cups "Live Yeast," "Sample A Yeast," and "Sample B Yeast."

4. Fill a beaker with 125 mL of water, and place the beaker on a hot plate. Use a thermometer to be sure the water does not get warmer than 32°C. Attach the thermometer to the side of the beaker with a clip so the thermometer doesn't touch the bottom of the beaker. Turn off the hot plate when the temperature reaches 32°C.

Materials

- yeast samples (live, A, and B)
- magnifying lens
- test tubes or clear plastic cups
- test-tube rack
- 250 mL beaker
- 125 mL of water
- hot plate
- Celsius thermometer with clip
- scoopula or small spoon
- sugar
- graduated cylinder
- 3 wooden stirring sticks
- flour
- heat-resistant gloves

	Observations	0 min	5 min	10 min	15 min	20 min	25 min	Dead or alive?
Live yeast								
Sample A yeast								
Sample B yeast								

DO NOT WRITE IN BOOK

5. Add a small scoop (about 1/2 tsp) of each yeast sample to the correctly labeled container. Add a small scoop of sugar to each container.

6. Add 10 mL of the warm water to each container, and stir.

7. Add a small scoop of flour to each container, and stir again. The flour will help make the process more visible but is not necessary as food for the yeast.

8. Observe the samples carefully. Look for bubbles. Make observations at 5-minute intervals. Write your observations in the data table.

9. In the last column of the data table, write "alive" or "dead" based on your observations during the experiment.

Analysis

10. Describe any differences in the yeast samples before the experiment.

11. Describe the appearance of the yeast samples at the conclusion of the experiment.

12. Why was a sample of live yeast included in the experiment?

13. Why was sugar added to the samples?

14. Based on your observations, is either sample alive?

15. Write a letter to the Best-Bread Bakery stating your recommendation to use or not use the yeast samples. Give reasons for your recommendation.

Going Further
Based on your observations of the nutrient requirements of yeast, design an experiment to determine the ideal combination of nutrients. Vary the amount of nutrients or examine different energy sources.

Elephant-Sized Amoebas?

Why can't amoebas grow to be as large as elephants? An amoeba is a single-celled organism. Amoebas, like most cells, are microscopic. If an amoeba could grow to the size of a quarter, it would starve to death. To understand how this can be true, build a model of a cell and see for yourself.

Materials

- cubic cell patterns
- pieces of heavy paper or poster board
- scissors
- transparent tape
- scale or balance
- fine sand

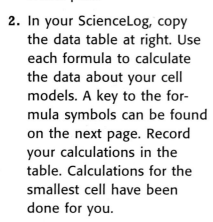

Procedure

1. Use heavy paper to make four cube-shaped cell models from the patterns supplied by your teacher. Cut out each cell model, fold the sides to make a cube, and tape the tabs on the sides. The smallest cell model has sides that are one unit long. The next larger cell has sides of two units. The next cell has sides of three units, and the largest cell has sides of four units. These paper models represent the cell membrane, the part of a cell's exterior through which food and waste pass.

Two-unit cell model

2. In your ScienceLog, copy the data table at right. Use each formula to calculate the data about your cell models. A key to the formula symbols can be found on the next page. Record your calculations in the table. Calculations for the smallest cell have been done for you.

Data Table for Measurements				
Length of side	Area of one side ($A = S \times S$)	Total surface area of cube cell ($TA = S \times S \times 6$)	Volume of cube cell ($V = S \times S \times S$)	Mass of cube cell
1	1 unit^2	6 unit^2	1 unit^3	
2				
3				
4				

DO NOT WRITE IN BOOK

3. Carefully fill each model with fine sand until the sand is level with the top edge. Find the mass of the filled models using a scale or a balance. What does the sand in your model represent?

4. Record the mass of each cell model in the table. (Always remember to use the appropriate mass unit.)

5. In your ScienceLog, make a data table like the one below.

Data Table for Ratios		
Length of side	Ratio of total surface area to volume	Ratio of total surface area to mass
1		
2		
3		
4		

DO NOT WRITE IN BOOK

6. Use the data from your Data Table for Measurements to find the ratios for each of your cell models. Fill in the Data Table for Ratios for each of the cell models.

Analysis

7. As a cell grows larger, does the ratio of total surface area to volume increase, decrease, or stay the same?

8. Which is better able to supply food to all the cytoplasm of the cell—the cell membrane of a small cell or that of a large cell? Explain your answer.

9. As a cell grows larger, does the total surface area to mass ratio increase, decrease, or stay the same?

10. Is the cell membrane of a cell with high mass or the cell membrane of a cell with low mass better able to feed all the cytoplasm of the cell? You may explain your answer in a verbal presentation to the class or you may choose to write a report and illustrate it with drawings of your models.

Key to Formula Symbols
S = the length of one side
A = area
V = volume
TA = total area

Cells Alive!

DISCOVERY LAB

You have probably used a microscope to look at single-celled organisms such as those shown below. They can be found in pond water. In the following exercise, you will look at *Protococcus*—algae that form a greenish stain on tree trunks, wooden fences, flowerpots, and buildings.

Materials

- *Protococcus* (or other algae)
- microscope
- eyedropper
- water
- microscope slide and coverslip

Euglena

Amoeba

Paramecium

Procedure

1. Locate some *Protococcus.* Scrape a small sample into a container. Bring the sample to the classroom, and make a wet mount of it as directed by your teacher. If you can't find *Protococcus* outdoors, look for algae on the glass in an aquarium. Such algae may not be *Protococcus,* but it will be a very good substitute.

2. Set the microscope on low power to examine the algae. In your ScienceLog, draw the cells that you see.

3. Switch to high power to examine a single cell. In your ScienceLog, draw the cell.

4. You will probably notice that each cell contains several chloroplasts. Label a chloroplast on your drawing. What is the function of the chloroplast?

5. Another structure that should be clearly visible in all the algae cells is the nucleus. Find the nucleus in one of your cells, and label it on your drawing. What is the function of the nucleus?

6. What does the cytoplasm look like? Describe any movement you see inside the cells.

Analysis

7. Are *Protococcus* single-celled organisms or multicellular organisms?

8. How are *Protococcus* different from amoebas?

Protococcus

Name That Part!

Plant cells and animal cells have many organelles and other parts in common. For example, both plant and animal cells contain a nucleus and mitochondria. But plant cells and animal cells differ in several ways as well. In this exercise, you will investigate the similarities and differences between animal cells and plant cells.

Materials

- colored pencils or markers
- white, unlined paper

TRY at HOME

Procedure

1. Using colored pencils or markers and white, unlined paper, trace or draw the plant cell and animal cell shown below. Draw each cell on a separate piece of paper. You may color each organelle a different color.

2. Label the parts of each cell.

3. Below each drawing, list all the parts that you labeled and describe their function.

Plant cell

Animal cell

Analysis

4. List at least four structures that plant cells and animal cells have in common.

5. List three structures that plant cells have that animal cells do not have.

The Perfect Taters Mystery

You are the chief food detective at Perfect Taters Food Company. The boss, Mr. Fries, wants you to find a way to keep his potatoes fresh and crisp while they are waiting to be cooked. His workers have tried several methods already, but nothing has worked. Workers in Group A put the potatoes in very salty water, and the potatoes did something unexpected. Workers in Group B put the potatoes in water with no salt, and the potatoes did something else! Workers in Group C didn't put the potatoes in any water, and that didn't work either. Now you must design an experiment to find out what can be done to make the potatoes come out crisp and fresh.

Materials

- potato samples (A, B, and C)
- freshly cut potato pieces
- salt
- 6 small, clear plastic drinking cups
- 4 L of distilled water

1. Before you plan your experiment, review what you know. You know that potatoes are made of cells. Plant cells contain a large amount of water. Cells have membranes that hold water and other materials inside and keep some things out. Water and other materials must travel across cell membranes to get into and out of the cell.

2. Mr. Fries has told you that you can obtain as many samples as you need from the workers in Groups A, B, and C. Your teacher will have these samples ready for you to observe.

3. Make a data table like the one below in your ScienceLog to list your observations. Make as many observations as you can about the potatoes tested by workers in Group A, Group B, and Group C.

Observations	
Group A:	
Group B:	
Group C:	

DO NOT WRITE IN BOOK

Ask a Question

4. Now that you have made your observations, state Mr. Fries's problem in the form of a question that can be answered by your experiment.

Form a Hypothesis

5. Form a hypothesis based on your observations and your questions. The hypothesis should be a statement about what causes the potatoes to shrivel or swell. Based on your hypothesis, make a prediction about the outcome of your experiments. State your prediction in an "if-then" format.

Test the Hypothesis

6. Once you have made a prediction, design your investigation. Check your experimental design with your teacher before you begin. Mr. Fries will give you potato pieces, water, salt, and no more than six containers.

7. Keep very accurate records. Write out your plan and procedure. Make data tables. To be sure of your data, measure all materials carefully and make drawings of the potato pieces before and after the experiment.

Draw Conclusions

8. Explain what happened to the potato cells in Groups A, B, and C in your experiment. Include a discussion of the cell membrane and the process of osmosis.

Communicate Results

9. Write a letter to Mr. Fries that explains your experimental method, your results, and your conclusion. Then make a recommendation about how he should handle the potatoes so they will stay fresh and crisp.

Stayin' Alive!

Every second of your life, your body's trillions of cells take in, use, and store energy. They repair themselves, reproduce, and get rid of waste. Together, these processes are called *metabolism.* Your cells use the food that you eat to provide the energy you need to stay alive.

Your Basal Metabolic Rate (BMR) is a measurement of the energy that your body needs to carry out all the basic life processes while you are at rest. These processes include breathing, keeping your heart beating, and keeping your body's temperature stable. Your BMR is influenced by your gender, your age, and many other things. Your BMR may be different from everyone else's, but it is normal for you. In this activity, you will find the amount of energy, measured in Calories, you need every day in order to stay alive.

Materials

- bathroom scale
- tape measure

TRY at HOME

Procedure

1. Find your weight on a bathroom scale. If the scale measures in pounds, you must convert your weight in pounds to your mass in kilograms. To convert your weight in pounds (lb) to mass in kilograms (kg), multiply the number of pounds by 0.454.

Example: If Carlos weighs 125 lb, his mass in kilograms is:	125 lb $\times$ 0.454 56.75 kg

2. Use a tape measure to find your height. If the tape measures in inches, convert your height in inches to height in centimeters. To convert your height in inches (in.) to your height in centimeters (cm), multiply the number of inches by 2.54.

If Carlos is 62 in. tall, his height in centimeters is:	62 in. $\times$ 2.54 157.48 cm

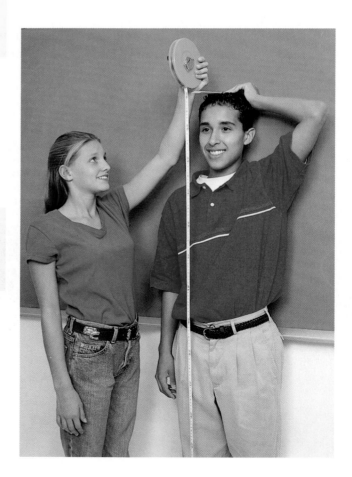

3. Now that you know your height and mass, use the appropriate formula below to get a close estimate of your BMR. Your answer will give you an estimate of the number of Calories your body needs each day just to stay alive.

Calculating Your BMR

Females	Males
65 + (10 × your mass in kilograms)	66 + (13.5 × your mass in kilograms)
+ (1.8 × your height in centimeters)	+ (5 × your height in centimeters)
− (4.7 × your age in years)	− (6.8 × your age in years)

4. Your metabolism is also influenced by how active you are. Talking, walking, and playing games all take more energy than being at rest. To get an idea of how many Calories your body needs each day to stay healthy, select the lifestyle that best describes yours from the table at right. Then multiply your BMR by the activity factor.

Activity Factors

Activity lifestyle	Activity factor
Moderately inactive (normal, everyday activities)	1.3
Moderately active (exercise 3 to 4 times a week)	1.4
Very active (exercise 4 to 6 times a week)	1.6
Extremely active (exercise 6 to 7 times a week)	1.8

Analysis

5. In what way could you compare your whole body to a single cell? Explain.

6. Does an increase in activity increase your BMR? Does an increase in activity increase your need for Calories? Explain your answers.

7. If you are moderately inactive, how many more Calories would you need if you began to exercise every day?

Going Further

The best energy sources are those that supply the correct amount of Calories for your lifestyle and also provide the nutrients you need. Research in the library or on the Internet to find out which kinds of foods are the best energy sources for you. How does your list of best energy sources compare with your diet?

List everything you eat and drink in 1 day. Find out how many Calories are in each item, and find the total number of Calories you have consumed. How does this number of Calories compare with the number of Calories you need each day for all your activities?

Bug Builders, Inc.

Imagine that you are a designer for a toy company that makes toy alien bugs. The president of Bug Builders, Inc., wants new versions of the wildly popular Space Bugs, but he wants to use the bug parts that are already in the warehouse. It's your job to come up with a new bug design. You have studied how traits are passed from one generation to another. You will use this knowledge to come up with new combinations of traits and assemble the bug parts in new ways. Model A and Model B, shown below, will act as the "parent" bugs.

Materials

- 7 allele sacks (supplied by your teacher)
- large marshmallows (head and body segments)
- red and green toothpicks (antennae)
- green and blue pushpins (noses)
- pipe cleaners (tails)
- green and black gumdrops (feet)
- map pins (eyes)
- scissors

Model A ("Mom")
- red antennae
- 3 body segments
- curly tail
- 2 pairs of legs
- green nose
- black feet
- 3 eyes

Model B ("Dad")
- green antennae
- 2 body segments
- straight tail
- 3 pairs of legs
- blue nose
- green feet
- 2 eyes

Make a Prediction

1. If there are two forms of each of the seven characteristics, then there are ___?___ possible combinations.

Collect Data

2. Your teacher will display seven sacks—one for each characteristic. The sacks will contain slips of paper with capital or lowercase letters printed on them. Take two pieces of paper from each sack. (Remember: Capital letters represent dominant alleles, and lowercase letters represent recessive alleles.) One allele is from "Mom" and one allele is from "Dad." After you have recorded the alleles you have drawn, place the slips of paper back into the sack.

3. In your ScienceLog, create a table like the one below. Fill in the first two columns with the alleles that you selected from the sacks. Next fill in the third column with the genotype of the new model ("Baby").

Bug Family Traits				
Trait	Model A "Mom" allele	Model B "Dad" allele	New model "Baby" genotype	New model "Baby" phenotype
Antennae color				
Number of body segments				
Tail shape				
Number of leg pairs				
Nose color				
Foot color				
Number of eyes				

DO NOT WRITE IN BOOK

4. Use the information at right to fill in the last column of the table.

5. Now that you have your table filled out, you are ready to pick the parts you need to assemble your bug. (Toothpicks can be used to hold the head and body segments together and as legs to attach the feet to the body.)

Genotypes and Phenotypes	
RR or *Rr* = red antennae	*rr* = green antennae
SS or *Ss* = 3 body segments	*ss* = 2 body segments
CC or *Cc* = curly tail	*cc* = straight tail
LL or *Ll* = 3 pairs of legs	*ll* = 2 pairs of legs
BB or *Bb* = blue nose	*bb* = green nose
GG or *Gg* = green feet	*gg* = black feet
EE or *Ee* = 2 eyes	*ee* = 3 eyes

Analyze the Results

6. Take a class poll of the traits of the offspring. What are the ratios for each trait?

Draw Conclusions

7. Do any of the new models look exactly like the parents? Explain your findings.

8. What are the possible genotypes of the parents?

9. How many different genotypes are possible in the offspring?

Going Further

Find a mate for your "baby" bug. What are the possible genotypes and phenotypes of the offspring from this match?

Tracing Traits

Have you ever wondered about the traits you inherited from your parents? Do you have a trait that neither of your parents has? In this project, you will develop a family tree, or pedigree, similar to the one shown in the diagram below. You will trace an inherited trait through a family to determine how it has passed from generation to generation.

Procedure *TRY at HOME*

1. The diagram at right shows a family history. On a separate piece of paper, draw a similar diagram of the family you have chosen. Include as many family members as possible, such as grandparents, parents, children, and grandchildren. Use circles to represent females and squares to represent males. You may include other information, such as the family member's name, birthdate, or picture.

2. Draw a chart similar to the one on the next page. Survey each of the family members shown in your family tree. Ask them if they have hair on the middle segment of their fingers. Write each person's name in the appropriate square. Explain to each person that it is normal to have either trait. The presence of hair on the middle segment is the dominant form of this trait.

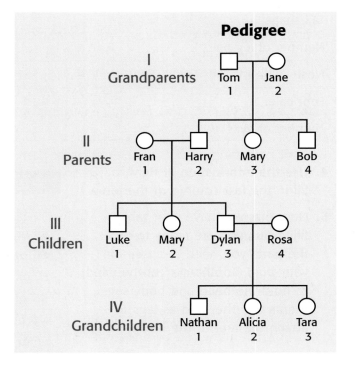

Pedigree

I Grandparents — Tom 1, Jane 2
II Parents — Fran 1, Harry 2, Mary 3, Bob 4
III Children — Luke 1, Mary 2, Dylan 3, Rosa 4
IV Grandchildren — Nathan 1, Alicia 2, Tara 3

Dominant trait	Recessive trait	Family members with the dominant trait	Family members with the recessive trait
Hair present on the middle segment of fingers (H)	Hair absent on the middle segment of fingers (h)	DO NOT WRITE IN BOOK	

3. Trace this trait throughout the family tree you diagrammed in step 1. Shade or color the symbols of the family members who demonstrate the dominant form of this trait.

Analysis

4. What percentage of the family members demonstrate the dominant form of the trait? Calculate this by counting the number of people who have the dominant trait and dividing this number by the total number of people you surveyed. Multiply your answer by 100. An example has been done at right.

Example: Calculating percentage

$$\frac{10 \text{ people with trait}}{20 \text{ people surveyed}} = \frac{1}{2}$$

$$\frac{1}{2} = 0.50 \times 100 = 50\%$$

5. What percentage of the family members demonstrates the recessive form of the trait? Why doesn't every family member have the dominant form of the trait?

6. Choose one of the family members who demonstrates the recessive form of the chosen trait. What is this person's genotype? What are the possible genotypes for the parents of this individual? Does this person have any brothers or sisters? Do they show the dominant or recessive trait?

7. Draw a Punnett square like the one at right. Use this to determine the genotypes of the parents of the person you chose in step 7. Write this person's genotype in the bottom right-hand corner of your Punnett square. **Hint:** There may be more than one possible genotype for the parents. Don't forget to consider the genotypes of the person's brothers and sisters.

Father

?   ?

Mother

?

?

Base-Pair Basics

You have learned that DNA is shaped something like a twisted ladder. The side rails of the ladder are made of sugar molecules and phosphate molecules. The sides are held together by nucleotide bases. These bases join in pairs to form the rungs of the ladder. Each nucleotide base can pair with only one other nucleotide base. Each of these pairs is called a base pair. When DNA replicates, enzymes separate the base pairs. Then each half of the DNA ladder can be used as a template to complete a new half. In this activity, you will make and replicate a model of DNA.

Materials

- white paper or poster board
- colored paper or poster board
- scissors
- large paper bag

Procedure

1. Trace the bases below onto white paper or poster board. Label the pieces A (for adenine), T (for thymine), C (for cytosine), and G (for guanine). Draw the pieces again on colored paper or poster board. Use a different color for each base. Draw the pieces as large as you want, and draw as many of the white pieces and as many of the colored pieces as time will allow.

2. Carefully cut out all of the pieces.

3. Gather all of the colored pieces in the classroom into a large paper bag. Spread all of the white pieces in the classroom onto a large table.

4. Withdraw nine pieces from the bag. Arrange the colored pieces in any order in a straight column so the letters A, T, C, and G are right side up. Be sure to match the sugar and phosphate tabs and notches. Draw this arrangement in your ScienceLog.

Sugar notch

Phosphate tab

5. Find the matching white nucleotide bases for the nine colored bases. Remember the base-pairing rules you have studied, and matching should be easy!

6. Fit the pieces together, matching all tabs and notches. You now have one piece of DNA containing nine base pairs. Draw your results in your ScienceLog.

7. Now separate the base pairs, keeping the sugar and phosphate notches and tabs together. Draw this arrangement in your ScienceLog.

8. Look at each string of bases you drew in step 7. Along each one, write the letters of the bases that should join the string to complete the base pairs.

9. Find all the bases you need to complete your replication. Find white pieces to match the bases on the left, and find colored pieces to match the bases on the right.

Be sure all the tabs and notches fit and the sides are straight. You have now replicated DNA. Are the two models identical? Draw your results in your ScienceLog.

Analysis

10. Name the correct base-pairing rules.

11. What happens when you attempt to pair thymine with guanine? Do they fit together? Are the sides straight? Do all of the tabs and notches fit? Explain.

Going Further

Construct a 3-D model of the DNA molecule, showing its twisted-ladder structure. Use your imagination and creativity to select your materials. You may want to use licorice, gum balls, and toothpicks, or pipe cleaners and paper clips! Display your model in your classroom.

Mystery Footprints

Sometimes scientists find clues preserved in rocks that are evidence of the activities of organisms that lived thousands of years ago. Evidence such as preserved footprints can provide important information about an organism. Imagine that your class has been asked by a group of paleontologists to help analyze some human footprints. These footprints were found embedded in rocks in an area just outside of town.

Materials

- large box of slightly damp sand, at least 1 m² (large enough to contain 3 or 4 footprints)
- metric ruler

Form a Hypothesis

1. Your teacher will provide you with some mystery footprints in sand. Examine the mystery footprints, and brainstorm about the information you might learn about the people who walked on this patch of sand. As a class, make as many hypotheses as possible about the people who left the footprints.

2. Form groups of three people, and choose one hypothesis for your group to investigate.

Test the Hypothesis

3. In your ScienceLog, design a table for recording your data. For example, if your hypothesis is that the footprints were made by two adult males who were walking in a hurry, your table would look similar to the one below.

Mystery Footprints		
	Footprint set 1	Footprint set 2
Length		
Width		
Depth of toe		
Depth of heel		
Length of stride		

DO NOT WRITE IN BOOK

4. With the help of your group, you may first want to analyze your own footprints to help you draw conclusions about the mystery footprints. For example, how long is your stride when you are running? How long is it when you are walking? Does your weight affect the depth of the footprint? What part of your foot touches the ground first when you are running? What part touches the ground first when you are walking? When you are running, which part of your footprint is deeper? Make a list of the kind of footprint each different activity produces. For example, you might write, "A deep impression in the toe area and a long stride are produced by running."

Analyze the Results

5. Compare the data of your footprints with that of the mystery footprints. What similarities are there? What differences are there?

6. Were the mystery footprints made by one person or more than one person? Explain your reasoning.

7. Is there enough evidence to tell if the mystery footprints were made by men, women, children, or a combination? Explain.

8. Based on your observations of your own footprints, were the people who made the mystery footprints standing still, walking, or running?

Draw Conclusions

9. Does your data support your hypothesis? Explain.

10. How could you improve your experiment?

Communicate Results

11. Outline your group's conclusions in a document addressed to the scientists who asked for your help. Begin by stating your hypothesis. Then outline your method of gathering information from the study of your own footprints. Include the comparisons you made between your footprints and the mystery footprints. Before stating your conclusions, offer some suggestions about how you could improve your method of investigation.

12. Create a poster or chart, or use a computer if one is available, to prepare a presentation of your findings for the class.

DISCOVERY LAB

Out-of-Sight Marshmallows

An adaptation is a trait that helps an organism survive in its environment. In nature, camouflage is a form of coloration that enables an organism to blend into its immediate surroundings.

Materials

- 50 white mini-marshmallows
- 50 colored mini-marshmallows (all one color is preferable)
- 50 cm^2 of colored cloth, matching one of the marshmallow colors
- watch or clock with a second hand

Hypothesis

Organisms that are camouflaged have a better chance of escaping from predators and therefore a better chance of survival.

Test the Hypothesis

1. Working in pairs, count out 50 white marshmallows and 50 colored marshmallows. Your marshmallows will represent the prey (food) in this experiment.

2. Place the white and colored marshmallows randomly on the piece of colored cloth.

3. One student per pair should be the hungry hunter (predator). The other student should record the results of each trial. The predator should look at the food for a few seconds, pick up the first marshmallow he or she sees, and then look away.

4. Continue this process without stopping for 2 minutes or until your teacher signals to stop.

Analyze the Results

5. How many white marshmallows did the hungry hunter choose?

6. How many colored marshmallows did the hungry hunter choose?

Draw Conclusions

7. What did the cloth represent in your investigation?

8. Did the color of the cloth affect the color of marshmallows chosen? Explain your answer.

9. Which marshmallow color represented camouflage?

10. Describe an organism that has a camouflage adaptation.

DESIGN YOUR OWN

Survival of the Chocolates

Imagine a world populated with candy, and hold that delicious thought for just a moment. Try to apply the idea of natural selection to a population of candy-coated chocolates. According to the theory of natural selection, individuals who have favorable adaptations are more likely to survive. In the "species" of candy you will study in this experiment, shell strength is an adaptive advantage. Plan an experiment to find out which candy characteristics correspond to shell (candy coating) strength.

Materials

- small candy-coated chocolates in a variety of colors
- other materials as needed, according to the design of your experiment

Form a Hypothesis

1. Form a hypothesis and make a prediction. For example, if you chose to study candy color, your prediction might look like this: If the _____?_____ colored shell is the strongest, then fewer of the candies with this color of shell will _____?_____ when _____?_____.

Test Your Hypothesis

2. Design a procedure to determine which candy is best suited to survive by not "cracking under pressure." In your plan, be sure to include materials and tools you may need to complete this procedure. Check your experimental design with your teacher before you begin. Your teacher will supply the candy and assist you in gathering materials and tools.

3. Record your results in a data table you have designed in your ScienceLog. Be sure to organize your data in a clear and understandable way.

Analyze the Results

4. Write a report that describes your experiment. Explain how your data either support or do not support your hypothesis. Include possible errors and ways to improve your procedure.

Going Further

Can you think of another characteristic of these candies that can be tested to determine which candy is best adapted to survive? Explain your choice.

Dating the Fossil Record

SKILL BUILDER

You have received nine rock samples from a paleontologist in California. Your job is to arrange the samples in order from oldest to youngest according to their fossil content and to determine their relative ages using the process of relative dating. Results from absolute dating methods will not be available from a laboratory for several weeks, and the paleontologist needs the information immediately. You know from previous work that the rocks of Sample 2 are the oldest.

Materials

- set of nine cards representing rock samples
- pencil and paper
- colored markers
- poster board (61 cm²)

Procedure: Part 1

1. Arrange the fossil cards from oldest to youngest. Begin with Sample 2 because you know this sample is the oldest. You may need to try several different arrangements to get the cards in order. **Hint:** After an organism becomes extinct, it does not reappear in younger rocks.

Fossil Key

 Globus slimius

 Circus bozoensis

 Fungus amongius

 Bogus biggus

 Microbius hairiensis

 Bananabana bobana

Sample 1

Sample 2

Sample 3

Sample 4

Sample 5

Sample 6

Sample 7

Sample 8

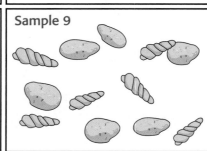

Sample 9

2. Prepare a table similar to the one below. Record the samples in order from bottom to top (oldest to youngest) in the first column. Sample 2 has been done for you.

Name of Fossil Organism						
Order of samples	*Globus slimius*					
Sample 2	X					

3. Identify the fossils with the fossil key, and write their names in order by age from left to right in the top row of the table. **Hint:** Examine your fossil cards carefully to determine where each fossil appears in the rock record. Write an *X* in the appropriate column to indicate which fossil or fossils are present in each sample.

Analysis: Part 1

4. Do the *X*s make a pattern across the table? What would you conclude if there were an *X* outside the pattern?

5. Based on the information in your table, which fossil is the youngest?

6. From the information you have, are you able to tell exactly how old a certain fossil is? Why or why not?

7. What information does relative dating provide to paleontologists?

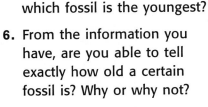

Procedure: Part 2

8. You are planning to prepare a timeline for the paleontologist in California. But when the results, shown at right, come in from the geology lab, you discover that the dates have become separated from the appropriate rock samples. Absolute dating is very expensive, and you can't have it done again. But wait! You have already determined the relative ages of the samples. All you have to do is arrange the dates from oldest to youngest and label your table from bottom to top. Add these dates to your data table.

9. Your table now contains all of the information you need to make a timeline for the paleontologist in California. Use colored markers and poster board to make your timeline. You may want to draw a rock wall showing several layers. To do this, label each layer with a date and the names of the fossils found there. Or you may want to draw a line with the dates labeled on the line and the fossils sketched above the appropriate date. Be creative!

Fossil Ages

The dates provided by the geology lab are as follows: 28.5 mya, 30.2 mya, 18.3 mya, 17.6 mya, 26.3 mya, 14.2 mya, 23.1 mya, 15.5 mya, and 19.5 mya.

Analysis: Part 2

10. Based on absolute dating, which fossil organism lived for the longest period of time? Which fossil organism lived for the shortest period of time? Explain your answers.

11. Based on the information in your timeline, what age range would you assign to the fossil of *Circus bozoensis*? **Hint:** Measure from the year that the fossil first appeared in the rock record to the first year it was absent from the rock record.

12. Determine the age ranges of all of your fossil species.

Going Further

Using the library or the Internet, investigate whether the absolute dating of rock surrounding fossils is the most reliable method of dating. Find out what circumstances prevent absolute dating.

The Half-life of Pennies

Carbon-14 is a special unstable element used in the absolute dating of material that was once alive, such as fossil bones. Every 5,730 years, half of the carbon-14 in a fossil specimen decays or breaks down into a more stable element. In the following experiment you will see how pennies can show the same kind of "decay."

Materials

- 100 pennies
- large container with a cover

 TRY at HOME

Procedure

1. Place 100 pennies in a large, covered container. Shake the container several times, and remove the cover. Carefully empty the container on a flat surface making sure the pennies don't roll away.

2. Remove all the coins that have the "head" side of the coin turned upward. Record the number of pennies removed and the number of pennies remaining in a data table similar to the one at right.

3. Repeat the process until no pennies are left in the container. Remember to remove only the coins showing "heads."

4. In your ScienceLog, draw a graph similar to the one at right. Label the x-axis "Number of shakes," and label the y-axis "Pennies remaining." Using data from your data table, plot the number of coins remaining at each shake on your graph.

Analysis

5. Examine the Half-life of Carbon-14 graph at right. Compare the graph you have made for pennies with the one for carbon-14. Explain any similarities that you see.

6. Recall that the probability of landing "heads" in a coin toss is $\frac{1}{2}$. Use this information to explain why the remaining number of pennies is reduced by about half each time they are shaken and tossed.

Shake number	Number of coins remaining	Number of coins removed
1		
2		
3		

DO NOT WRITE IN BOOK

Half-life of Pennies

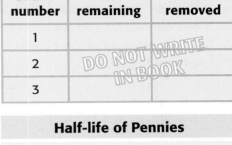

DO NOT WRITE IN BOOK

Half-life of Carbon-14

Shape Island

You are a biologist exploring uncharted parts of the world looking for new animal species. You sailed for days across the ocean and finally found Shape Island, hundreds of miles south of Hawaii. This island has some very unusual organisms. Each of them has some variation of a geometric shape. You have spent more than a year collecting specimens and classifying them according to Linnaeus's system. You have been able to assign a two-part scientific name to most species you have collected. You must assign all the names to the final 12 specimens before you begin your journey home.

1
2

Procedure TRY at HOME

1. In your ScienceLog, draw each of the organisms pictured on this page. Beside each organism, draw a line for its name, as shown on the following page. The first one has been named for you, but you have 12 more to name. Use the glossary of Greek and Latin prefixes, suffixes, and root words below to help you name the organisms.

3
4

Greek and Latin roots, prefixes, and suffixes	Meaning
ankylos	angle
antennae	external sense organs
tri-	three
bi-	two
cyclo-	circle
macro-	large
micro-	small
mono-	one
peri-	all around
-plast	body
-pod	foot
quad-	four
stoma	mouth
uro-	tail

5
6

7
8

9

10

11

12

13

1. _Cycloplast quadantennae_
   (cyclo + plast   quad + antennae)

2. _____
   DO NOT WRITE
   IN BOOK

3. _____

2. One more organism exists on Shape Island, but you have not been able to capture it. However, your supplies are running out, and you must start sailing for home. You have had a good look at the unusual animal and can draw it in detail. In your ScienceLog, draw an animal that is different from all the others, and give it a two-part scientific name.

Analysis

3. If you gave species 1 a common name, such as round-face-no-nose, would any other scientist know which of the newly discovered organisms you were referring to? Explain. How many others have a round face and no nose?

4. Describe two characteristics shared by all your newly discovered specimens.

Going Further

Look up the scientific names listed below. You can use the library, the Internet, a taxonomy index, or field guides.

- _Mertensia virginica_
- _Porcellio scaber_

For each organism answer the following questions: Is the organism a plant or an animal? How many common names does it have? How many scientific names does it have?

Think of the name of your favorite fruit or vegetable. Find out if it has other common names, and find out its two-part scientific name.

Voyage of the USS *Adventure*

You are a crew member on the USS *Adventure.* The *Adventure* has been on a 5-year mission to collect life-forms from outside the solar system. On the voyage back to Earth, your ship went through a meteor shower, which ruined several of the compartments containing the extraterrestrial life-forms. Now it is necessary to put more than one life-form in the same compartment.

    You have only three undamaged compartments in your starship. You and your crewmates must stay in one compartment, and that compartment should be used for extraterrestrial life-forms only if absolutely necessary. You and your crewmates must decide which of the life-forms could be placed together. It is thought that similar life-forms will have similar needs. You can use only observable characteristics to group the life-forms.

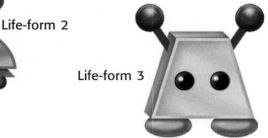

Life-form 1

Life-form 2

Life-form 3

Life-form 4

Procedure TRY at HOME

1. Make a data table similar to the one below. Label each column with as many characteristics of the various life-forms as possible. Leave enough space in each square to write your observations. The life-forms are pictured on this page.

Life-form Characteristics				
	Color	**Shape**	**Legs**	**Eyes**
Life-form 1				
Life-form 2				
Life-form 3				
Life-form 4				

DO NOT WRITE IN BOOK

Life-form 5

2. Describe each characteristic as completely as you can. Based on your observations, determine which of the life-forms are most alike.

Life-form 7

Life-form 6

3. Make a data table like the one below. Fill in the table according to the decisions you made in step 2. State your reasons for the way you have grouped your life-forms.

Life-form Room Assignments		
Compartment	Life-forms	Reasons
1		
2		
3		

DO NOT WRITE IN BOOK

4. The USS *Adventure* has to make one more stop before returning home. On planet X437 you discover the most interesting life-form ever found outside of Earth—the CC9, shown at right. Make a decision, based on your previous grouping of life-forms, about whether you can safely include CC9 in one of the compartments for the trip to Earth.

CC9

Analysis

5. Describe the life-forms in compartment 1. How are they similar? How are they different?

6. Describe the life-forms in compartment 2. How are they similar? How do they differ from the life-forms in compartment 1?

7. Are there any life-forms in compartment 3? If so, describe their similarities. In which compartment will you and your crewmates remain for the journey home?

8. Are you able to safely transport life-form CC9 back to Earth? Why or why not? If you are able to include CC9, in which compartment will it be placed? How did you decide?

Going Further

In 1831, Charles Darwin sailed from England on a ship called the HMS *Beagle.* You have studied the finches that Darwin observed on the Galápagos Islands. What were some of the other unusual organisms he found there? For example, find out about the Galápagos tortoise.

Aunt Flossie and the Intruder

Aunt Flossie is a *really* bad housekeeper! She *never* cleans the refrigerator, and things get really gross in there. Last week she pulled out a plastic resealable bag that looked like it was going to explode! The bag was full of gas that she did not put there! Aunt Flossie remembered from her school days that gases are released from living things as waste products. Something had to be alive in the bag! Aunt Flossie became very upset that there was an intruder in her refrigerator. She said she would not bake another cookie until you determine the nature of the intruder.

Materials

- items to be determined by the students and approved by teacher as needed for each experiment such as resealable plastic bags, food samples, a scale, or a thermometer.

- protective gloves

Procedure

1. Design an investigation to determine how gas got into Aunt Flossie's bag. In your ScienceLog, make a list of the materials you will need, and prepare all the data tables you will need for recording your observations.

2. As you design your investigation, be sure to include each of the steps listed at right.

3. Get your teacher's approval of your experimental design and your list of materials before you begin.

4. Dispose of your materials according to your teacher's instructions at the end of your experiment.
   Caution: Do not open any bags of spoiled food or allow any of the contents to escape.

- Ask a question
- Form a hypothesis
- Test the hypothesis
- Analyze the data
- Draw conclusions
- Communicate your results

Analysis

5. Write a letter to Aunt Flossie describing your experiment. Explain what produced the gas in the bag and your recommendations for preventing these intruders in her refrigerator in the future. Invite her to bake cookies for your class!

Going Further

Research in the library or on the Internet to find out how people kept food fresh before refrigeration. Find out what advances have been made in food preservation as a result of the space program.

Viral Decorations

Although viruses are made of only protein and nucleic acids, their structures have many different shapes that help them attach to and invade living cells. One viral shape can be constructed from the template provided by your teacher. In this activity you will construct and modify a model of a virus.

Materials

- virus model template
- construction paper
- colored markers
- scissors
- glue or tape
- pipe cleaners, twist-ties, buttons, string, plastic wrap, and other scrap materials for making variations of the virus

Procedure

1. Obtain a virus model template from your teacher. Carefully copy the template on a piece of construction paper. You may make the virus model as large as your teacher allows.

2. Plan how you will modify your virus. For example, you might want to add the tail and tail fibers of a bacteriophage or wrap the model in plastic to represent the envelope that surrounds the protein coat in HIV.

3. Color your virus model, and cut it out by cutting on the solid black lines. Then fold the virus model along the dotted lines.

4. Glue or tape each lettered tab under the corresponding lettered triangle. For example, glue or tape the large Z tab under the Z-shaded triangle. When you are finished, you should have a closed box with 20 sides.

5. Apply the modifications that you planned. Give your virus a name, and write it on the model. Decorate your classroom with your virus and those of your classmates.

Analysis

6. Describe the modifications you made to your virus model, and explain how the virus might use them.

7. If your virus causes disease, explain what disease it causes, how it reproduces, and how the virus is spread.

Going Further

Research in the library or on the Internet an unusual virus that causes an illness, such as the influenza virus, HIV, or Ebola virus. Explain what is unusual about the virus, what illness it causes, and how it might be avoided.

Making a Protist Mobile

You have studied many of the diverse species of organisms within the kingdom Protista. This may be the first time you have ever seen many of these single-celled eukaryotes. In this activity you will have an opportunity to express a bit of creativity using what you have learned about these interesting organisms.

Materials

- heavyweight paper (construction paper or poster board)
- recycled material of your choice
- scissors
- transparent tape or glue
- colored markers
- string, yarn, lightweight wire, or fishing line
- wire coat hanger

Procedure

1. Research the different kinds of protists you have studied. You may cut out pictures of them from magazines, or you may find examples of protists on the Internet. You may want to investigate *Plasmodium, Euglena,* amoebas, slime molds, *Radiolaria, Paramecium, Foraminifera,* various other protozoans, or even algae.

2. Using the paper and recycled materials, make a model of each protist you want to include on your mobile. Be sure to include the special features of each protist, such as vacuoles, pseudopods, shells, cilia, or flagella.

3. Use tape or glue to attach special features to give your protists a three-dimensional look.

4. Provide labels for your protist models. For each protist, provide its name, classification, method of movement (if any), method for obtaining food, and any other interesting facts you have learned about it.

5. Attach your protist models to the wire hanger with wire or string. Use tape or glue to attach your labels to each model.

Analysis

6. Explain what you have learned about the diversity of protists. Include at least three habitats where protists may be found.

Going Further

Choose a disease-causing protist. Write a report describing the disease, its effect on people or the environment, and the efforts being made to control it.

There's a Fungus Among Us!

Fungi share many characteristics with plants. For example, most fungi live on land. But fungi have several unique features that suggest that they are not closely related to any other kingdom of organisms. In this activity you will observe some of the unique structures of a mushroom, a member of the kingdom Fungi.

Materials

- mushroom
- tweezers
- 2 sheets of white paper
- masking tape
- fruit-juice agar plate
- incubator
- microscope or magnifying lens
- transparent tape

Procedure

1. Obtain a mushroom from your teacher. Carefully pull the cap of the mushroom from the stem. Place the stem to the side for later use. Using tweezers, remove one of the gills from the underside of the cap. Place the gill on a sheet of white paper.

2. Place the mushroom cap gill-side down on the other sheet of paper and tape it in place with masking tape. Label this sheet of paper with your name, and place the paper aside for at least 24 hours.

3. Use tweezers to take several 1 cm pieces from the stem and place them in your agar plate. Record the appearance of the plate in your ScienceLog. Cover the agar plate, and label it with your name. Incubate your agar plate overnight.

4. Use tweezers to gently pull the remaining mushroom stem apart lengthwise. The individual fibers or strings you see are the hyphae that form the structure of the fungus. Place a thin strand on the same piece of paper with the gill you removed from the cap.

5. Observe the gill and the stem hyphae with a magnifying lens or microscope. Record your observations in your ScienceLog. **Caution:** Never direct sunlight through your magnifying lens or microscope.

6. After at least 24 hours, record any changes that occurred on the agar plate in your ScienceLog. Carefully remove the mushroom cap from the paper. Place a piece of

transparent tape over the print left behind on the paper. Record your observations in your ScienceLog.

Analysis

7. Describe the structures you saw on the gill and hyphae.

8. What is the print on the white paper?

9. Describe the structure at the bottom edge of the mushroom gill. Explain how this structure is connected to the print.

10. Explain how the changes that occurred in your agar plate are related to methods of fungal reproduction.

Leaf Me Alone!

Imagine you are a naturalist all alone on an expedition in a rain forest. You have found several plants that you think have never been seen before. You must contact a botanist, a scientist who studies plants, to confirm your suspicion. Because there is no mail service in the rain forest, you must describe these species completely and accurately by radio. The botanist must be able to draw the leaves of the plants from your description.

In this activity, you will carefully describe five plant specimens using the examples and vocabulary lists in this lab.

Materials

- 5 different leaf specimens
- plant guidebook (optional)
- protective gloves

Procedure

1. Examine the leaf characteristics illustrated in this lab. These examples can be found on the following page. You will notice that more than one term is needed to completely describe a leaf. The leaf shown at right has been labeled for you using the examples and vocabulary lists found in this lab.

2. In your ScienceLog, draw a diagram of a leaf from each plant specimen.

3. Next to each drawing, carefully describe the leaf. Include general characteristics, such as relative size and color. For each plant, identify the following: leaf shape, stem type, leaf arrangement, leaf edge, vein arrangement, and leaf-base shape. Use the terms and vocabulary lists provided to describe each leaf as accurately as possible and to label your drawings.

Compound Leaf

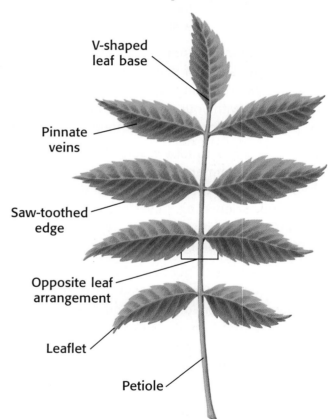

V-shaped leaf base

Pinnate veins

Saw-toothed edge

Opposite leaf arrangement

Leaflet

Petiole

Analysis

4. What is the difference between a simple leaf and a compound leaf?

5. Describe two different vein arrangements in leaves.

6. Based on what you know about adaptation, explain why there are so many different leaf variations.

Going Further

Choose a partner. Using the keys and vocabulary in this lab, describe a leaf, and see if your partner can draw the leaf from your description. Switch roles, and see if you can draw a leaf from your partner's description.

Leaf Shapes Vocabulary List

cordate—heart shaped

lanceolate—sword shaped

lobate—lobed

oblong—leaves rounded at the tip

orbicular—disk shaped

ovate—oval shaped, widest at base of leaf

peltate—shield shaped

reniform—kidney shaped

sagittate—arrow shaped

Stems Vocabulary List

woody—bark or barklike covering on stem

herbaceous—green, nonwoody stems

Leaf Arrangements Vocabulary List

alternate—alternating leaves or leaflets along stem or petiole

compound—leaf divided into segments or several leaflets on a petiole

opposite—compound leaf with several leaflets arranged oppositely along a petiole

palmate—single leaf with veins arranged around a center point

palmate compound—several leaflets arranged around a center point

petiole—leaf stalk

pinnate—single leaf with veins arranged along a center vein

pinnate compound—several leaflets on either side of a petiole

simple—single leaf attached to stem by a petiole

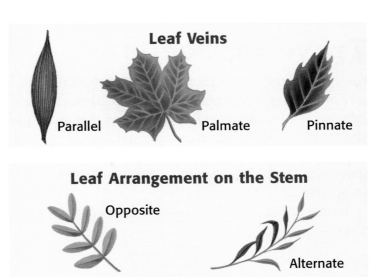

Leaf Veins

Parallel　　Palmate　　Pinnate

Leaf Arrangement on the Stem

Opposite

Alternate

Leaf Division

Pinnate compound

Simple

Palmate compound

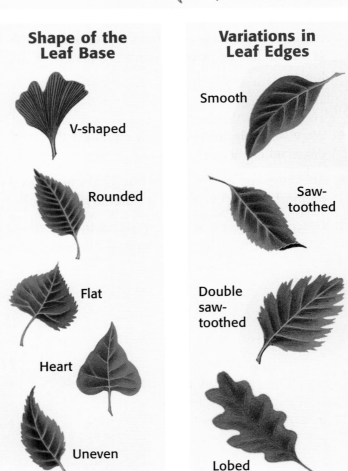

Shape of the Leaf Base

V-shaped

Rounded

Flat

Heart

Uneven

Variations in Leaf Edges

Smooth

Saw-toothed

Double saw-toothed

Lobed

Travelin' Seeds

You have learned from your study of plants that there are some very interesting and unusual plant adaptations. Some of the most interesting adaptations are modifications that allow plant seeds and fruits to be dispersed, or scattered, away from the parent plant. This dispersal enables the young seedlings to obtain the space, sun, and other resources they need without directly competing with the parent plant.

In this activity, you will use your own creativity to disperse a seed.

Materials

- bean seed
- seed-dispersal challenge card
- various household or recycled materials (examples: glue, tape, paper, paper clips, rubber bands, cloth, paper cups and plates, paper towels, cardboard)

Procedure

1. Obtain a seed and a dispersal challenge card from your teacher. In your ScienceLog, record the type of challenge card you have been given.

2. Create a plan for using the available materials to disperse your seed as described on the challenge card. Record your plan in your ScienceLog. Get your teacher's approval before proceeding.

3. With your teacher's permission, test your seed-dispersal method. Perform several trials. Make a data table in your ScienceLog, and record the results of your trials.

Analysis

4. Were you able to successfully complete the seed-dispersal challenge? Explain.

5. Are there any modifications you could make to your method to improve the dispersal of your seed?

6. Describe some plants that disperse their seeds in a way similar to your seed-dispersal method.

◀ Mangrove seed

◀ Cottonwood

Wild berry ▶

Grass bur ▶

Build a Flower

Scientists often make models in the laboratory to help them understand processes or structures. In this activity, you will use your creativity and your understanding of the structure of a flower to make a model from recycled materials and art supplies.

Materials

- recycled items (examples: paper plates and cups, yogurt containers, wire, string, beads, buttons, cardboard, bottles)
- art materials (examples: glue, tape, scissors, colored paper, pipe cleaners, yarn)
- index card

Procedure

1. In your ScienceLog, draw a flower similar to the one shown below. Label each of the structures on your drawing. The flower shown has both male and female parts. Not all flowers have this arrangement.

2. Examine the available materials. Decide which materials are appropriate for each flower part, and build a three-dimensional model of a flower. The flower you create should contain each of the parts listed below.

Parts of a Flower

- Petals
- Sepals
- Stem
- Pistil (stigma, style, ovary)
- Stamen (anther, filament)

3. Draw a key for your flower model on an index card. Label each of the structures represented on your flower.

Analysis

4. List the structures of a flower, and explain the function of each part.

5. Explain how your model flower might attract pollinators. What modifications could you make to increase the number of pollinators?

6. Describe how self-pollination could take place in your model flower.

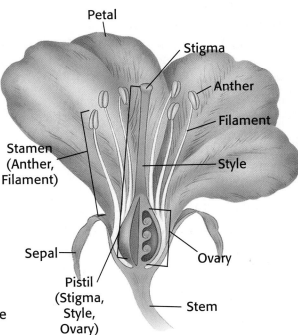

Petal

Stigma

Anther

Filament

Style

Ovary

Stem

Stamen (Anther, Filament)

Sepal

Pistil (Stigma, Style, Ovary)

Food Factory Waste

Plants use photosynthesis to produce food. We cannot live without the waste products from this process. In this activity, you will observe the process of photosynthesis and determine the rate of photosynthesis for *Elodea*.

Procedure

1. Add 450 mL of baking-soda-and-water solution to a beaker.

2. Put two or three sprigs of *Elodea* in the beaker. The baking soda will provide the *Elodea* with the carbon dioxide it needs for photosynthesis.

3. Place the wide end of the funnel over the *Elodea*. The end of the funnel with the small opening should be pointing up. The *Elodea* and the funnel should be completely under the solution, as shown at right.

4. Fill a test tube with the remaining baking-soda-and-water solution. Place your thumb over the end of the test tube. Turn the test tube upside down, taking care that no air enters. Hold the opening of the test tube under the solution and place the test tube over the small end of the funnel. Try not to let any solution out of the test tube as you do this.

5. Place the beaker setup in a well-lit area near a lamp or in direct sunlight.

6. In your ScienceLog, prepare a data table similar to the one below.

Materials

- 500 mL of 5% baking-soda-and-water solution
- 600 mL beaker
- 20 cm long *Elodea* sprigs (2–3)
- glass funnel
- test tube
- metric ruler
- protective gloves

Amount of Gas Present in the Test Tube		
Days of exposure to light	**Total amount of gas present (mm)**	**Amount of gas produced per day (mm)**
0		
1		
2		
3		
4		
5		

DO NOT WRITE IN BOOK

7. Record that there was 0 gas in the test tube on day 0. (If you were unable to place the test tube without getting air in the tube, measure the height of the column of air in the test tube in millimeters. Record this value for day 0.) Measure the gas in the test tube from the middle of the curve on the bottom of the upside-down test tube to the level of the solution.

8. For days 1 through 5, measure the amount of gas in the test tube. Record the measurements in your data table under the heading "Total amount of gas present (mm)."

9. Calculate the amount of gas produced each day by subtracting the amount of gas present on the previous day from the amount of gas present today. Record these amounts under the heading "Amount of gas produced per day (mm)."

10. Construct a graph similar to the one at right. Plot the data from your table on the graph.

Amount of Gas Produced by Photosynthesis

Total amount of gas produced (mm) — DO NOT WRITE IN BOOK — *Day*

Analysis

11. Using information from your graph, describe what happened to the amount of gas in the test tube.

12. How much gas was produced in the test tube after day 5?

13. Write the equation for photosynthesis in your ScienceLog. Explain each part of the equation. For example, what "ingredients" are necessary for photosynthesis to take place? What substances are produced by photosynthesis? What gas is produced that we need in order to live?

14. Write a report describing your experiment, your results, and your conclusions.

Going Further

Hydroponics is the growing of plants in nutrient-rich water, without soil. Research hydroponic techniques, and try to grow a plant without soil.

Weepy Weeds

You are trying to find a way to drain an area that is flooded with water polluted with fertilizer. You know that a plant releases water through the stomata in its leaves. As water evaporates from the leaves, more water is pulled up from the roots through the stem and into the leaves. By this process, called transpiration, water and nutrients are pulled into the plant from the soil. About 90 percent of the water a plant takes up through its roots is released into the atmosphere as water vapor through transpiration. Your idea is to add plants to the flooded area that will transpire the water and take up the fertilizer in their roots.

How much water can a plant take up and release in a certain period of time? In this activity, you will observe transpiration and determine one stem's rate of transpiration.

Materials

- 2 test tubes
- test-tube rack
- water
- coleus or other plant stem cutting
- glass-marking pen
- metric ruler
- clock
- graph paper

Procedure

1. In your ScienceLog, make a data table similar to the one below for recording your measurements.

Height of Water in Test Tubes		
Time	**Test tube with plant**	**Test tube without plant**
Initial		
After 10 min		
After 20 min		
After 30 min		
After 40 min		
Overnight		

DO NOT WRITE IN BOOK

2. Fill each test tube approximately three-fourths full of water. Place both test tubes in a test-tube rack.

3. Place the plant stem so that it stands upright in one of the test tubes. Your test tubes should look like the ones in the photograph at right.

4. Use the glass-marking pen to mark the water level in each of the test tubes. Be sure you have the plant stem in place in its test tube before you mark the water level. Why is this necessary?

5. Measure the height of the water in each test tube. Be sure to hold the test tube level, and measure from the waterline to the bottom of the curve at the bottom of the test tube. Record these measurements on the row labeled "Initial."

6. Wait 10 minutes, and measure the height of the water in each test tube again. Record these measurements in your data table.

7. Repeat step 6 three more times. Record your measurements each time.

8. Wait 24 hours, and measure the height of the water in each test tube. Record these measurements in your data table.

9. Construct a graph similar to the one below. Plot the data from your data table. Draw a line for each test tube. Use a different color for each line, and make a key below your graph.

10. Calculate the rate of transpiration for your plant by using the following operations:

Test tube with plant:
Initial height
− Overnight height
Difference in height of water **(A)**

Test tube without plant:
Initial height
− Overnight height
Difference in height of water **(B)**

Water height difference due to transpiration:
Difference **A**
− Difference **B**
Water lost due to transpiration (in millimeters) in 24 hours

Analysis

11. What was the purpose of the test tube that held only water?

12. What caused the water to go down in the test tube containing the plant stem? Did the same thing happen in the test tube with water only? Explain your answer.

13. What was the calculated rate of transpiration per day?

14. Using your graph, compare the rate of transpiration with the rate of evaporation alone.

15. Prepare a presentation of your experiment for your class. Use your data tables, graphs, and calculations as visual aids.

Going Further

How many leaves did your plant sprigs have? Use this number to estimate what the rate of transpiration might be for a plant with 200 leaves. When you have your answer in millimeters of height in a test tube, pour this amount into a graduated cylinder to measure it in milliliters.

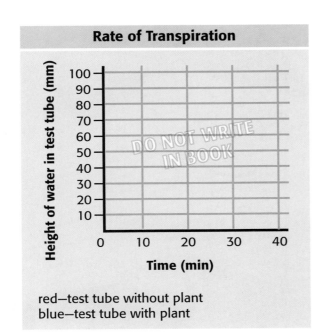

Rate of Transpiration

Height of water in test tube (mm)

100
90
80
70
60
50
40
30
20
10

DO NOT WRITE IN BOOK

0   10   20   30   40

Time (min)

red—test tube without plant
blue—test tube with plant

Wet, Wiggly Worms!

Earthworms have been digging in the Earth for more than 100 million years! Earthworms fertilize the soil with their waste and loosen the soil when they tunnel through the moist dirt of a garden or lawn. Worms are food for many animals, such as birds, frogs, snakes, rodents, and fish. Some say they are good food for people, too!

In this activity, you will observe the behavior of a live earthworm. Remember that earthworms are living animals that deserve to be handled gently. Be sure to keep your earthworm moist during this activity. The skin of the earthworm must stay moist so that the worm can get oxygen. If the earthworm's skin dries out, the worm will suffocate and die. Use a spray bottle to moisten the earthworm with water.

Materials

- spray bottle
- dissecting pan
- paper towels
- water
- live earthworm
- probe
- celery leaves
- flashlight
- shoe box with lid
- clock
- soil
- metric ruler

Procedure

1. Place a wet paper towel in the bottom of a dissecting pan. Put a live earthworm on the paper towel, and observe how the earthworm moves. Record your observations in your ScienceLog.

2. Use the probe to carefully touch the anterior end (head) of the worm. Gently touch other areas of the worm's body with the probe. Record the kinds of responses you observe.

3. Place celery leaves at one end of the pan. Record how the earthworm responds to the presence of food.

4. Shine a flashlight on the anterior end of the earthworm. Record the earthworm's reaction to the light.

5. Line the bottom of the shoe box with a damp paper towel. Cover half of the shoe box with the box top.

6. Place the worm on the uncovered side of the shoe box in the light. Record your observations of the worm's behavior for 3 minutes.

7. Place the worm in the covered side of the box. Record your observations for 3 minutes.

8. Repeat steps 6–7 three times.

9. Spread some loose soil evenly in the bottom of the shoe box so that it is about 4 cm deep. Place the earthworm on top of the soil. Observe and record the earthworm's behavior for 3 minutes.

10. Dampen the soil on one side of the box, and leave the other side dry. Place the earthworm in the center of the box between the wet and dry soil. Cover the box, and wait 3 minutes. Uncover the box, and record your observations. Repeat this procedure 3 times. (You may need to search for the worm!)

Analysis

11. How did the earthworm respond to being touched? Were some areas more sensitive than others?

12. How is the earthworm's behavior influenced by light? Based on your observations, describe how an animal's response to a stimulus might provide protection for the animal.

13. How did the earthworm respond to the presence of food?

14. When the worm was given a choice of wet or dry soil, which did it choose? Explain this result.

Going Further

Based on your observations of an earthworm's behavior, prepare a poster showing where you might expect to find earthworms. Draw a picture with colored markers, or cut out pictures from magazines. Include all the variables that you used in your experiment, such as soil or no soil, wet or dry soil, light or dark, and food. Write a caption at the bottom of your poster describing where earthworms might be found in nature.

Aunt Flossie and the Bumblebee

Materials

- to be determined by each experimental design and approved by the teacher

Last week Aunt Flossie came to watch the soccer game, and she was chased by a big yellow-and-black bumblebee. Everyone tried not to laugh, but Aunt Flossie did look pretty funny. She was running and screaming, all perfumed and dressed in a bright floral dress, shiny jewelry, and a huge hat with a big purple bow. No one could understand why the bumblebee tormented Aunt Flossie and left everyone else alone. She said that she would not come to another game until you determine why the bee chased her.

Your job is to design an experiment that will determine why the bee was attracted to Aunt Flossie. You may simulate the situation by using objects that contain the same sensory clues that Aunt Flossie wore that day—bright, shiny colors and strong scents.

Ask a Question

1. Use the information in the story above to help you form questions. Make a list of Aunt Flossie's characteristics on the day of the soccer game. What was Aunt Flossie wearing? What do you think she looked like to a bumblebee? What scent was she wearing? Which of those characteristics may have affected the bee's behavior? What was it about Aunt Flossie that affected the bee's behavior?

Form a Hypothesis

2. Write a hypothesis about insect behavior based on your observations of Aunt Flossie and the bumblebee at the soccer game. A possible hypothesis is, "Insects are attracted to strong floral scents." Write your own hypothesis.

Test the Hypothesis

3. Outline a procedure for your experiment. Be sure to follow the steps in the scientific method. Design your procedure to answer specific questions. For example, if you want to know if insects are attracted to different colors, you might want to display cutouts of several colors of paper.

4. Make a list of materials for your experiment. You may want to include colored paper, pictures from magazines, or strong perfumes as bait. You may not use living things as bait in your experiment. Your teacher must approve your experimental design before you begin.

5. Determine a place to conduct your experiment. For example, you may want to place your materials in a box on the ground, or you may want to hang items from a tree branch. **Caution:** Be sure to remain at a safe distance from your experimental setup. Do not touch any insects. Have an adult help you release any insects that are trapped or collected.

6. Develop data tables for recording the results of your trials. For example, a data table similar to the one at right may be used to record the results of testing different colors to see which insects are attracted to them. Design your data tables to fit your investigation.

Analyze the Results

7. Describe your experimental procedure. Did your results support your hypothesis? Explain.

8. Compare your results with those of your classmates. Which hypotheses were supported? What conclusions can you draw from the class results?

Communicate Results

9. Write a letter to Aunt Flossie telling her what you have learned. Tell her what caused the bee attack. Invite her to attend another soccer game, and advise her about what she should or should not wear!

Effects of Color

Color	Number of bees	Number of ants	Number of wasps
Red			
Blue			
Yellow			

DO NOT WRITE IN BOOK

Porifora's Porosity

Sponges are aquatic invertebrate animals that make up the phylum Porifera. Sponges pump water through many tiny pores into their interior. Food for the sponge is filtered out of the water, and then the water leaves through an opening at the top of the sponge.

Early biologists thought sponges were plants because they resemble plants in many ways. For example, the adults attach to a surface and do not move. They cannot chase their food. Sponges absorb and filter a lot of water to get food. In this activity, you will determine how much water sponges can absorb.

Materials

- natural sponges
- balance
- water
- beaker
- bowl (large enough for sponge and water)
- calculator (optional)

Procedure

1. Estimate how much water your sponge can hold. Write your predictions in your ScienceLog.

2. Make data tables for recording your observations.

3. Measure the mass of your sponge before you add water. Record the result. Why do you think this is a necessary step?

4. Pour 500 mL of water into the bowl. Soak the sponge in the bowl. If you are unable to completely soak the sponge, add 100 mL of water to the bowl.

5. Measure how much water is left in the bowl when you remove the sponge. How much water did the sponge absorb?

Analysis

6. How many milliliters of water does your sponge hold per gram of sponge tissue? For example, if your sponge has a dry mass of 12 g and it holds 59.1 mL of water, then your sponge holds 4.9 mL of water per gram. (59.1 mL ÷ 12 g)

7. What feeding advantage does a sponge have because of its ability to hold an enormous amount of water?

Going Further

Repeat this experiment using another kind of absorbent material, such as a paper towel or an artificial sponge. How many milliliters of water does it hold per gram? How does it compare with a natural sponge?

The Cricket Caper

Insects are a special class of invertebrates with more than 750,000 known species. Insects may be the most successful group of animals on Earth. In this activity you will observe a cricket's structure and the simple adaptive behaviors that help make it so successful. Remember, you will be handling a living animal that deserves to be treated with care.

Materials

- 2 crickets
- 600 mL beakers (2)
- plastic wrap
- apple
- hand lens (optional)
- masking tape
- aluminum foil
- lamp
- 2 sealable plastic bags
- crushed ice
- hot tap water

Procedure

1. Place a cricket in a clean 600 mL beaker, and quickly cover the beaker with plastic wrap. The supply of oxygen in the container is enough for the cricket to breathe while you complete your work.

2. While the cricket is getting used to the container, make a data table in your ScienceLog similar to the one below. Be sure to allow enough space to write your descriptions.

Cricket Body Structures	
Number	**Description**
Body segments	
Antennae	DO NOT WRITE IN BOOK
Eyes	
Wings	

3. Without making much movement, begin to examine the cricket. Fill in your data table with your observations of the cricket's structure.

4. Place a small piece of apple in the beaker. Set the beaker on a table. Sit quietly for several minutes and observe the cricket. Any movement may cause the cricket to stop what it is doing. Record your observations in your ScienceLog.

5. Remove the plastic wrap from the beaker, remove the apple, and quickly attach a second beaker. Join the two beakers together at the mouths with masking tape. Handle the beakers carefully. Remember, there is a living animal inside.

6. Wrap one of the joined beakers with aluminum foil.

7. If the cricket is hiding under the aluminum foil, gently tap the sides of the beaker until the cricket is exposed. Lay the joined beakers on their sides, and shine a lamp on the uncovered side. Record the cricket's location.

8. Record the cricket's location after 5 minutes. Without disturbing the cricket, carefully move the aluminum foil to the other beaker. After 5 minutes, record the cricket's location. Repeat this process one more time to see if you get the same result.

9. Fill a sealable plastic bag halfway with crushed ice. Fill another bag halfway with hot tap water. Seal each bag, and arrange them side by side on the table.

10. Remove the aluminum foil from the beakers. Gently rock the joined beakers from side to side until the cricket is in the center. Place the beakers on the plastic bags, as shown below.

11. Observe the cricket's behavior for 5 minutes. Record your observations in your ScienceLog.

12. Set the beakers on one end for several minutes to allow them to return to room temperature. Repeat steps 10–12 three times. (Why do you think it is necessary to allow the beakers to return to room temperature each time?)

13. Set the beakers on one end. Carefully remove the masking tape, and separate the beakers. Quickly replace the plastic wrap over the beaker containing the cricket. Allow your cricket to rest while you make two data tables in your ScienceLog similar to those at right.

14. Observe the cricket's movement in the beaker every 15 seconds for 3 minutes. Fill in the Cricket (alone) data table using the following codes: 0 = no movement, 1 = slight movement, and 2 = rapid movement.

15. Obtain a second cricket from your teacher, and place this cricket in the container with the first cricket. Every 15 seconds, record the movement of each cricket in the Cricket A and Cricket B data table using the codes given in step 14.

Analysis

16. Describe crickets' feeding behavior. Are they lappers, suckers, or chewers?

17. Do crickets prefer light or darkness? Explain.

18. From your observations, what can you infer about a cricket's temperature preferences?

19. Based on your observations of Cricket A and Cricket B, what general statements can you make about the social behavior of crickets?

Going Further

Make a third data table titled "Cricket and Another Species of Insect." Introduce another insect, such as a grasshopper, into the beaker. Record your observations for 3 minutes. Write a short summary of the cricket's reaction to another species.

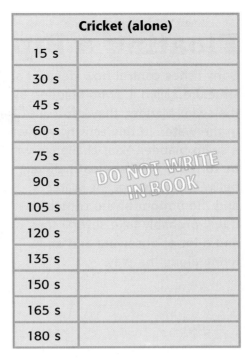

Cricket (alone)	
15 s	
30 s	
45 s	
60 s	
75 s	
90 s	DO NOT WRITE IN BOOK
105 s	
120 s	
135 s	
150 s	
165 s	
180 s	

Cricket A and Cricket B		
	A	B
15 s		
30 s		
45 s		
60 s		
75 s		
90 s	DO NOT WRITE IN BOOK	
105 s		
120 s		
135 s		
150 s		
165 s		
180 s		

Floating a Pipe Fish

Bony fishes control how deep or shallow they swim with a special structure called a swim bladder. By adding or taking away gases in the swim bladder, they can control how their body rises or sinks in the water. In this activity, you will make a model of a fish with a swim bladder. Your challenge will be to make the fish float halfway between the top of the water and the bottom of the container. It will probably take several tries and a lot of observing and analyzing along the way.

Materials

- water
- container for water at least 15 cm deep
- slender balloon
- small cork
- 12 cm length of PVC pipe, 3/4 in. diameter
- rubber band

Procedure

1. Estimate how much air you will need in the balloon so that your pipe fish will float halfway between the top of the water and the bottom of the container. Will you need to inflate the balloon halfway, just a small amount, or all the way? It will have to fit inside the pipe, but there will need to be enough air to make the pipe float.

2. Inflate your balloon. Hold the neck of the balloon so that no air escapes, and push the cork into the end of the balloon. If the cork is properly placed, no air should leak out when the balloon is held underwater.

3. Place your swim bladder inside the pipe, and place a rubber band along the pipe as shown. The rubber band will keep the swim bladder from coming out of either end.

4. Place your pipe fish in the water, and note where the fish floats. Record your observations in your ScienceLog.

5. If the pipe fish does not float where you want, take it out of the water, adjust the amount of air in the balloon, and try again.

6. You can release small amounts of air from the bladder by carefully lifting the neck of the balloon away from the cork. You can add more air by removing the cork and blowing more air into the balloon. Keep adjusting and testing until your fish floats halfway between the bottom of the container and the top of the water.

Cork with balloon attached

Pipe   Rubber band

Analysis

7. Was the estimate you made in step 1 the correct amount of air your balloon needed to float halfway? Explain your answer.

8. In relation to the length and volume of the entire pipe fish, how much air was needed to make the fish float? State your answer in a proportion or percentage.

9. Based on the amount of space the balloon took up inside the pipe in your model, how much space do you estimate is taken up by a swim bladder inside a living fish? Explain.

Going Further
Some fast-swimming fishes, such as sharks, and marine mammals, such as whales and dolphins, do not have a swim bladder. Find out from the library or the Internet how these animals keep from sinking to the bottom of the ocean. Create a poster, and explain your results on index cards. Include drawings of the fish or marine mammals you have researched.

A Prince of a Frog

Imagine that you are a scientist interested in amphibians. You have heard in the news about amphibians disappearing all over the world. What a great loss it will be to the environment if all amphibians become extinct! Your job is to learn as much as possible about how frogs normally behave so that you can act as a resource for other scientists who are studying the problem.

In this activity, you will observe a normal frog in a dry container and in water.

Materials

- live frog in a dry container
- live crickets
- 600 mL beaker
- container half-filled with dechlorinated water
- large rock (optional)
- protective gloves

Procedure

1. In your ScienceLog, make a table similar to the one below to note all of your observations of the frog in this investigation.

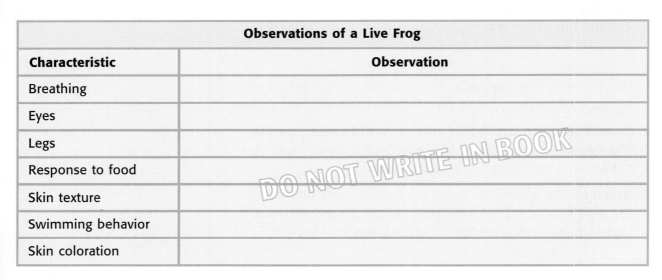

Observations of a Live Frog	
Characteristic	**Observation**
Breathing	
Eyes	
Legs	
Response to food	
Skin texture	
Swimming behavior	
Skin coloration	

DO NOT WRITE IN BOOK

2. Observe a live frog in a dry container. Draw the frog in your ScienceLog. Label the eyes, nostrils, front legs, and hind legs.

3. Watch the frog's movements as it breathes air with its lungs. Write a description of the frog's breathing in your ScienceLog.

4. Look closely at the frog's eyes, and note their location. Examine the upper and lower eyelids as well as the transparent third eyelid. Which of these three eyelids actually moves over the eye?

5. Study the frog's legs. Note in your data table the difference between the front and hind legs.

6. Place a live insect, such as a cricket, in the container. Observe and record how the frog reacts.

7. Carefully pick up the frog, and examine its skin. How does it feel?
Caution: Remember that a frog is a living thing and deserves to be handled gently and with respect.

8. Place a 600 mL beaker in the container. Place the frog in the beaker. Cover the beaker with your hand, and carry it to a container of dechlorinated water. Tilt the beaker and gently submerge it in the water until the frog swims out of the beaker.

9. Watch the frog float and swim in the water. How does the frog use its legs to swim? Notice the position of the frog's head.

10. As the frog swims, bend down and look up into the water so that you can see the underside of the frog. Then look down on the frog from above. Compare the color on the top and the underneath sides of the frog. Record your observations in your data table.

Analysis

11. From the position of the frog's eyes, what can you infer about the frog's field of vision? How might the position of the frog's eyes benefit the frog while it is swimming?

12. How can a frog "breathe" while it is swimming in water?

13. How are the hind legs of a frog adapted for life on land and in water?

14. What differences did you notice in coloration on the frog's top side and its underneath side? What advantage might these color differences provide?

15. How does the frog eat? What senses are involved in helping the frog catch its prey?

Going Further

Observe another type of amphibian, such as a salamander. How do the adaptations of other types of amphibians compare with those of the frog you observed in this investigation?

What? No Dentist Bills?

When you and I eat food, we must chew it well. Our teeth are made for chewing because breaking food down into small bits is the first step in the digestive process. But birds don't have teeth. How do birds make big chunks of food small enough to begin digestion? In this activity, you will design and build a model of a bird's digestive system to find an answer to that question.

Materials

- several sealable plastic bags of various sizes
- birdseed
- aquarium gravel
- water
- string
- drinking straw
- transparent tape
- scissors or other materials as needed

Procedure

1. Examine the diagram below of a bird's digestive system. Design a model of a bird's digestive system that you can build using the materials provided by your teacher. Include in your model as many of the following parts as possible: esophagus, crop, gizzard, intestine, cloaca.

2. Obtain a plastic bag and the materials you need from your teacher, and build your model.

3. Test your model using the birdseed provided by your teacher.

Analysis

4. How can a bird break down food particles without teeth?

5. Did your bird gizzard grind the food?

6. What are gizzard stones, and what do they do?

7. Does the amount of material added to your model gizzard change its ability to work effectively?

8. Describe how you could improve your model.

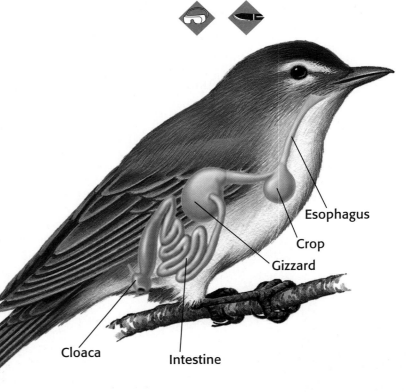

Esophagus

Crop

Gizzard

Cloaca

Intestine

Going Further

Did you know that "gizzard stones" have been found at the sites of fossilized dinosaur skeletons? Look in the library or on the Internet for information about the evolutionary relationship between dinosaurs and birds. List the similarities and differences you find.

Wanted: Mammals on Mars

The year is 2256. There have been colonies on Mars for almost 50 years. Martian water is scarce but available, and temperatures are still extreme but livable. The Martian planet has slowly developed an atmosphere that humans can breathe due to the efforts of many scientists during the last 200 years. The Interplanetary Commission has decreed that mammals from several different habitats on Earth should be sent to Mars. There they will be housed in a zoo so they can become accustomed to the climate before they are released in the wild.

Your job is to prepare a presentation for the Interplanetary Commission that describes at least three mammals that you think might be able to survive in a zoo on Mars. Select one mammal from a water environment, one mammal from a land environment, and one mammal that lives in the air part of the time.

Materials

- colored markers, crayons, pens, or similar drawing equipment
- poster paper, rolls of newsprint, or other drawing paper
- other materials as needed

TRY at HOME

Procedure

1. Research in the library or on the Internet to obtain information about the Martian environment as it is today. How might an atmosphere change the environment?

2. Research in the library or on the Internet to learn about different species of mammals and their environments on Earth. Use this information to select mammals that you think might be able to live on Mars.

3. Prepare your presentation for the Interplanetary Commission. Your presentation can be a poster, a mural, a diorama, a computer presentation, or any other format that you choose. Make sure your format is approved by your teacher.

Analysis

4. Name and describe the mammals you chose. Explain why you think your choice of mammals would be the right one for a zoo on Mars.

5. Describe what additions or changes should be made at the zoo to accommodate each of your mammals.

Adaptation: It's a Way of Life

Since the beginning of life on Earth, species have had special characteristics called adaptations that have helped them survive changes in environmental conditions. Changes in a species' environment include climate changes, habitat destruction, or the extinction of prey. These things can cause a species to die out unless the species has a characteristic that helps it survive. For example, a species of bird may have an adaptation for eating sunflower seeds and ants. If the ant population dies out, the bird can still eat seeds and can therefore survive.

In this activity, you will explore several adaptations and design an organism with adaptations you choose. Then you will describe how these adaptations help the organism survive.

Materials

- poster board
- colored markers
- magazines for cutouts
- other arts-and-crafts materials
- scissors

Procedure

1. Study the chart below. Choose one adaptation from each column. For example, an organism might be a scavenger that burrows underground and has spikes on its tail!

Adaptations		
Diet	**Type of transportation**	**Special adaptation**
carnivore	flies	uses sensors to detect heat
herbivore	glides through the air	is active only at night and has excellent night vision
omnivore	burrows underground	changes colors to match its surroundings
scavenger	runs fast	has armor
decomposer	swims	has horns
	hops	can withstand extreme temperature changes
	walks	secretes a terrible and sickening scent
	climbs	has poison glands
	floats	has specialized front teeth
	slithers	has tail spikes
		stores oxygen in its cells so it does not have to breathe continuously
		one of your own invention

2. Design an organism that has the three adaptations you have chosen. Use poster board, colored markers, picture cutouts, or craft materials of your choosing to create your organism.

3. Write a caption on your poster describing your organism. Describe its appearance, its habitat, its niche, and how its adaptations help it survive. Give your animal a two-part "scientific" name based on its characteristics.

4. Display your creation in your classroom. Share with classmates how you chose the adaptations for your organism.

Analysis

5. What does your imaginary organism eat?

6. In what environment or habitat would your organism be most likely to survive—in the desert, tropical rain forest, plains, ice-caps, mountains, or ocean? Explain your answer.

7. Is your creature a mammal, a reptile, an amphibian, a bird, or a fish? What modern organism (on Earth today) or ancient organism (extinct) is your imaginary organism most like? Explain the similarities between the two organisms. Do some research outside of the lab, if necessary, to find out about a real organism that your imaginary organism may be similar to.

8. If a sudden climate change occurred, such as daily downpours of rain in a desert, would your imaginary organism survive? What adaptations for surviving such a change does it have?

Going Further

Call or write to an agency such as the U.S. Fish and Wildlife Service to get a list of endangered species in your area. Choose an organism on that list. Describe the organism's niche and any special adaptations it has that help it survive. Find out why it is endangered and what is being done to protect it.

Examine the illustration of the animal at right. Based on its physical characteristics, describe its habitat and niche. Is this a real animal?

Capturing the Wild Bean

When wildlife biologists study a group of organisms in an area, they need to know how many organisms live there. Occasionally, biologists worry that a certain organism is outgrowing the environment's carrying capacity. Other times, scientists need to know if an organism is becoming rare so steps can be taken to protect it. However, animals can be difficult to count because they can move around and hide. Because of this, biologists have developed methods to estimate the number of animals in a specific area. One of these counting methods is called the mark-recapture method.

In this activity, you will enter the territory of the wild pinto bean to get an estimation of the number of beans that live in their paper-bag habitat.

Materials

- small paper lunch bag
- pinto beans
- permanent marker
- calculator (optional)

Procedure

1. Prepare a data table in your ScienceLog like the one below.

Mark-Recapture Data Table				
Number of animals in first capture	Total number of animals in recapture	Number of marked animals in recapture	Calculated estimate of population	Actual total population
	DO NOT WRITE IN BOOK			

2. Your teacher will provide you with a paper bag containing an unknown number of beans. Carefully reach into the bag and remove a handful of beans.

3. Count the number of beans you have "captured," and record this number in your data table under "Number of animals in first capture."

4. Use the permanent marker to carefully mark each bean that you have just counted. Allow the marks to dry completely. When you are certain that all the marks are dry, place the marked beans back into the bag.

5. Gently mix the beans in the bag so the marks won't rub off. Once again, reach into the bag, "capture," and remove a handful of beans.

6. Count the number of beans in your "recapture." Record this number in your data table under "Total number of animals in recapture."

7. Count the beans in your recapture with marks from the first capture. Record this number in your data table under "Number of marked animals in recapture."

8. Calculate your estimation of the total number of beans in the bag using the following equation:

$$\frac{\text{total number of beans in recapture} \times \text{total number of beans marked}}{\text{number of marked beans in recapture}} = \begin{array}{c}\text{calculated estimate of} \\ \text{population}\end{array}$$

Enter this number in your data table under "Calculated estimate of population."

9. Replace all the beans in the bag. Then empty the bag on your work table. Be careful that no beans escape! Count each bean as you place them one at a time back into the bag. Record the number in your data table under "Actual total population."

Analysis

10. How close was your estimate to the actual number of beans?

11. If your estimate was not close to the actual number of beans, how might you change your mark-recapture procedure? If you did not recapture any marked beans, what might be the cause?

Going Further
How could you use the mark-recapture method to estimate the population of turtles in a small pond? Explain your procedure.

Nitrogen Needs

The nitrogen cycle is one of several cycles that are vital to living organisms. Without nitrogen, living organisms cannot make amino acids, the building blocks of proteins. Animals obtain nitrogen by eating plants that contain nitrogen and by eating animals that eat those plants. When animals die, decomposers return the nitrogen to the soil in the form of a chemical called ammonia.

In this activity, you will be investigating the nitrogen cycle inside a closed system to discover how decomposers return nitrogen to the soil.

Materials

- 2 pieces of filter paper
- funnel
- 50 mL beaker
- balance
- commercially prepared potting soil without fertilizer
- 25 mL graduated cylinder
- 60 mL of distilled water
- pH paper
- 1 pt (or 500 mL) jar with lid
- 5 large, dead insects from home or schoolyard
- protective gloves

Procedure

1. Fit a piece of filter paper into a funnel. Place the funnel inside a 50 mL beaker, and pour 5 g of soil into the funnel. Add 25 mL of distilled water to the soil.

2. Test the filtered water with pH paper, and record your observations in your ScienceLog.

3. Place some soil in a jar to cover the bottom about 5 cm deep. Add 10 mL of distilled water to the soil.

4. Place the dead insects in the jar, and seal the jar with the lid.

5. Check the jar each day for 5 days for an ammonia odor. (If you do not know what ammonia smells like, ask your teacher.) Record your observations in your ScienceLog. **Caution:** Your teacher will demonstrate how to check for a chemical odor by wafting. Do not put your nose in the jar and inhale!

6. On the fifth day, place a second piece of filter paper into the funnel, and place the funnel inside a 50 mL beaker. Remove about 5 g of soil from the jar, and place it in the funnel. Add 25 mL of distilled water to the soil.

7. Once again, test the filtered water with pH paper, and record your observations in your ScienceLog.

Analysis

8. What was the pH of the water in the beaker in the first trial? A pH of 7 indicates that the water is neutral. A pH below 7 indicates that the water is acidic, and a pH above 7 indicates that the water is basic.

9. What was the pH of the water in the beaker in the second trial? Explain the difference, if any, between the results of the first trial and the results of the second trial.

10. Based on the results of your pH tests, do you think ammonia is acidic or basic?

11. On which days in your investigation were you able to detect an ammonia odor? Explain what caused the odor.

12. Describe the importance of decomposers in the nitrogen cycle.

Going Further

Test ammonia's importance to plants. Fill two 12 cm flowerpots with commercially prepared potting soil and water. Be sure to use soil that has had no fertilizer added. Plant six radish seeds in each pot. Water your seeds so that the soil is constantly damp but not soaked. Keep your pots in a sunny window. You may plant other seeds of your choice, but do not use legume (bean) seeds. Research to find out why!

   Use a plant fertilizer mixed according to the directions on the container to fertilize one of the pots once a week. Water the other pot once a week with tap water.

   After the seedlings appear, use a metric ruler to measure the growth of the plants in both pots. Measure the plants once a week, and record your results in your ScienceLog.

A Passel o' Pioneers

MAKING MODELS

Succession is the natural process of the introduction and development of living things in an area. The area could be one that has never supported life before and has no soil, such as a recently cooled lava flow from a volcano. In an area where there is no soil, the process is called primary succession. In an area where soil already exists, such as an abandoned field or a forest after a fire, the process is called secondary succession.

In this investigation, you will build a model of secondary succession using natural soil.

Materials

- 500 g of soil from home or schoolyard
- balance
- large fishbowl
- 250 mL of water
- 250 mL graduated cylinder
- plastic wrap
- protective gloves

Procedure

1. Place the natural soil you brought from home or the schoolyard into the fishbowl, and dampen the soil with 250 mL of water. Cover the top of the fishbowl with plastic wrap, and place the fishbowl in a sunny window. **Caution:** Do not touch your face, eyes, or mouth during this activity. Wash your hands thoroughly when you are finished.

2. For 2 weeks, observe the fishbowl for any new growth. Describe and draw any new organisms you observe. Record these and all other observations in your ScienceLog.

3. Identify and record the names of as many of these new organisms as you can.

Analysis

4. What kinds of plants sprouted in your model of secondary succession? Were they tree seedlings, grasses, or weeds?

5. Were the plants that sprouted in the fishbowl unusual or common for your area?

6. Explain how the plants that grew in your model of secondary succession can be called pioneer species.

Going Further

Examine each of the photographs on this page. Determine whether each area, if abandoned forever, would undergo primary or secondary succession. You may decide that an area will not undergo succession at all. Explain your reasoning.

Bulldozed land

Eutrophic pond

Shipping port parking lot

Mount St. Helens volcano

Life in the Desert

Organisms that live in the desert have some very unusual methods for conserving water. Conserving water is an important function for all organisms that live on land, but it is a special challenge for animals that live in the desert. In this activity you will invent an "adaptation" for a desert animal, represented by a piece of sponge, to find out how much water the animal can conserve over a 24-hour period. You will protect your wet desert sponge so it will dry out as little as possible.

Materials

- 2 pieces of dry sponge (8 × 8 × 2 cm)
- water
- balance
- other materials as needed

Procedure

1. Plan a method for keeping your "desert animal" from drying out. Your "animal" must be in the open for at least 4 hours during the 24-hour period. Real desert animals often expose themselves to the dry desert heat in order to search for food. Write your plan in your ScienceLog. Write down your predictions about the outcome of your experiment.

2. Design data tables, if necessary, and draw them in your ScienceLog. Have your teacher approve your plan before you begin.

3. Soak two pieces of sponge in water until they begin to drip. Place each piece on a balance, and record its mass in your ScienceLog.

4. Immediately begin to protect one piece of sponge according to your plan. Place both of the pieces together in an area where they will not be disturbed. You may take your protected "animal" out for feeding as often as you want, for a total of at least 4 hours.

5. At the end of 24 hours, place each piece of sponge on the balance again, and record its mass in your ScienceLog.

Analysis

6. Describe the adaptation you used to help your "animal" survive. Was it effective? Explain.

7. What was the purpose of leaving one of the sponges unprotected? How did the water loss in each of your sponges compare?

Going Further

Conduct a class discussion about other adaptations and results. How can you relate these invented adaptations to adaptations for desert survival among real organisms?

Discovering Mini-Ecosystems

In your study of ecosystems you learned that a biome is a very large ecosystem that includes a set of smaller, related ecosystems. For example, a coniferous forest biome may include a river ecosystem, a wetland ecosystem, and a lake ecosystem. Each of those ecosystems may include several other smaller, related ecosystems. Even cities have mini-ecosystems! You may find a mini-ecosystem on a patch of sidewalk, in a puddle of rainwater, under a leaky faucet, in a shady area, or under a rock. In this activity, you will design a method for comparing two different mini-ecosystems found near your school.

Materials

- materials as needed for each investigation

Procedure

1. Examine the grounds around your school, and select two different areas you wish to investigate. Be sure to get your teacher's approval before you begin.

2. Decide what you want to learn about your mini-ecosystems. For example, you may want to know what kind of living things each area contains. You may want to list the abiotic factors of each mini-ecosystem.

3. For each mini-ecosystem, make data tables for recording your observations. You may choose to observe the mini-ecosystems for an hour. You may choose to observe the mini-ecosystems for a short period of time at several different times during the day or at the same time for several days. Get your plan approved by your teacher, and make the appropriate data tables.

Analysis

4. What factors determine the differences between your mini-ecosystems? Identify the factors that set each mini-ecosystem apart from its surrounding area.

5. How do the populations of your mini-ecosystems compare?

6. Identify some of the adaptations that the organisms living in your two mini-ecosystems have. Describe how the adaptations help the organisms survive in their environment.

7. Write a report describing and comparing your mini-ecosystems with those of your classmates.

Too Much of a Good Thing?

Plants require nutrients, such as phosphates and nitrates. Phosphates are often found in detergents. Nitrates are often found in animal wastes and fertilizers. When large amounts of these nutrients are released into rivers and lakes, algae and plant life grow rapidly and then die off. Microorganisms that decompose the dead matter use up oxygen in the water, causing the death of fish and other animals that depend on oxygen. This process often results in a pond or lake filling unnaturally.

In this activity, you will observe the effect of fertilizers on organisms that live in pond water.

Materials

- wax pencil
- 1 qt (or 1 L) jars (3)
- 2.25 L of distilled water
- fertilizer
- graduated cylinder
- stirring rod
- 300 mL of pond water containing living organisms
- eyedropper
- microscope
- microscope slides with coverslips
- plastic wrap
- protective gloves

Procedure

1. Use a wax pencil to label one jar "Control," the second jar "Fertilizer," and the third jar "Excess fertilizer."

2. Pour 750 mL of distilled water in each of the jars. Read the label on the fertilizer container to determine the recommended amount of fertilizer. To the "Fertilizer" jar, add the amount of fertilizer recommended for 750 mL of water. To the "Excess fertilizer" jar, add 10 times this amount. Stir the contents of each jar to dissolve the fertilizer.

3. Obtain a sample of pond water. Stir it gently but thoroughly to make sure that the organisms in it are evenly distributed. Pour 100 mL of pond water into each of the three jars.

4. Observe a drop of pond water from each jar under the microscope. Draw at least four of the organisms. Determine whether the organisms you see are algae, which are usually green, or consumers, which are usually able to move. Describe the number and type of organisms in the pond water.

5. Cover each jar loosely with plastic wrap. Place them near a sunny window, but do not place them in direct sunlight.

Common Pond-Water Organisms

Volvox
(producer)

Spirogyra
(producer)

Vorticella
(consumer)

Daphnia
(consumer)

6. Based on your understanding of how ponds and lakes eventually fill to become dry land, make a prediction about how the pond organisms will grow in each of the three jars.

7. Make three data tables in your ScienceLog. Be sure to allow enough space to record your observations. Title one table "Control," as shown below. Title another table "Fertilizer," and title the third table "Excess fertilizer."

Control			
Date	**Color**	**Odor**	**Other observations**

DO NOT WRITE IN BOOK

8. Observe the jars when you first set them up and at least once every 3 days for the next 3 weeks. Note the color, odor, and any visible presence of organisms. Record your observations.

9. When organisms begin to be visible in the jars, use an eyedropper to remove a sample from each jar, and observe the sample under the microscope. How have the number and type of organisms changed since you first looked at the pond water? Record your observations.

10. At the end of the 3-week period, remove a sample from each jar and observe each sample under the microscope. Draw at least four of the most abundant organisms and describe how the number and type of organisms have changed since your last microscopic observation.

Analysis

11. After 3 weeks, which jar shows the most abundant growth of algae? What may have caused this growth?

12. Did you observe any effects on organisms (other than the algae) in the jar with the most abundant algal growth? Explain.

13. Did your observations match your prediction? Explain.

14. How might the rapid filling of natural ponds and lakes be prevented or slowed?

Using Scientific Methods

Biodiversity—What a Disturbing Thought!

Biodiversity is important for the survival of each organism in a community. Producers, consumers, and decomposers all play a cooperative role in an ecosystem.

In this activity you will investigate areas outside your school to determine which areas contain the greatest biodiversity. You will use the information you gather to determine whether a forest or an area planted with crops is more diverse.

Materials

- materials and tools necessary to carry out your investigation with your teacher's approval. Possible materials include a meterstick, binoculars, magnifying lens, twine, and forceps.

Form a Hypothesis

1. Based on your understanding of biodiversity, do you expect a forest or an area planted with crops to be more diverse?

Make a Prediction

2. Select an area that is highly disturbed (such as a mowed yard) and one that is relatively undisturbed (such as an abandoned flower bed or a vacant lot). Make a prediction about which area contains the greater biodiversity. Get your teacher's approval of your selected locations.

Conduct an Experiment

3. Design a procedure to determine which area contains the greatest biodiversity, and have your plan approved by your teacher before you begin.

4. To discover smaller organisms, measure off a square meter, set stakes at the corners, and mark the area with twine. Use a magnifying lens to observe tiny organisms. Don't worry about the scientific names. When you record your observations, refer to organisms in the following way: Ant A, Ant B, and so on. Observe each area quietly, and make note of any visits by birds or other larger organisms.

5. In your ScienceLog, create any data tables that you might need for recording your data. If you observe your areas on more than one occasion, be sure to make data tables for each observation period. Organize your data into categories that are clear and understandable.

Analyze the Results

6. Did your data support your hypothesis? Explain.

7. What factors did you consider before deciding which habitats were disturbed or undisturbed? Explain why those factors were important.

8. What problems did you find in making observations and recording data for each habitat? Describe how you solved them.

9. Describe possible errors in your investigation method. Suggest ways to improve your procedure to eliminate those errors.

Draw Conclusions

10. Do you think the biodiversity outside your school has decreased since the school was built? Why or why not?

11. Both areas shown in the photographs at right are beautiful to observe. One of them, however, is very low in biodiversity. Describe each photograph, and account for the difference in biodiversity.

Going Further
Research rain-forest biodiversity in the library or on the Internet. Find out what factors exist in the rain forest that make that biome so diverse. How might the biodiversity of a rain forest compare with that of a forest community near your school?

Prairie grasses and wildflowers

Wheat field

Deciding About Environmental Issues

You make hundreds of decisions every day. Some of them are complicated, but many of them are very simple, such as what to wear or what to eat for lunch. Deciding what to do about an environmental issue can be very difficult. There are many different factors that must be considered. How will a certain solution affect people's lives? How much will it cost? Is it ethically right?

In this activity you will analyze an issue in four steps to help you make a decision about it. Find out about environmental issues that are being discussed in your area. Examine newspapers, magazines, and other publications to find out what the issues are. Choose one local issue to evaluate. For example, you could evaluate whether the city should spend the money to provide recycling bins and special trucks for picking up recyclable trash.

Materials

- newspapers, magazines, and other publications containing information about environmental issues

TRY at HOME

A Four-Step Decision-Making Model

Gather Information

↓

Consider Values

↓

Explore Consequences

↓

Make a Decision

Procedure

1. In your ScienceLog, write a statement about an environmental issue.

2. **Gather Information** Read about your issue in several publications. Summarize important facts in your ScienceLog.

3. **Consider Values** The values of an issue are the things that you consider important. Examine the diagram below. Several values are given. Which values do you think apply most to the environmental issue you are considering? Are there other values that you believe will help you make a decision about the issue? Consider at least four values in making your decision.

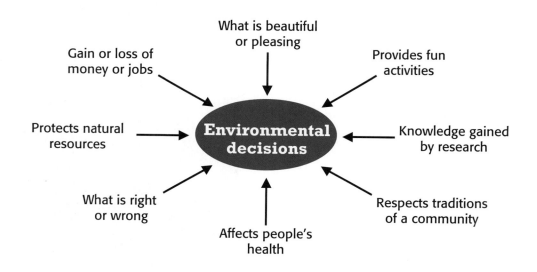

What is beautiful or pleasing

Gain or loss of money or jobs

Provides fun activities

Protects natural resources

Environmental decisions

Knowledge gained by research

What is right or wrong

Affects people's health

Respects traditions of a community

4. **Explore Consequences** Consequences are the things that result from a certain course of action. In your ScienceLog, create a table similar to the one below. Use your table to organize your thoughts about consequences related to your environmental issue. List your values at the top. Fill in each space with the consequences for each value.

Consequences Table				
Consequences	**Values**			
Positive short-term consequences				
Negative short-term consequences				
Positive long-term consequences				
Negative long-term consequences				

DO NOT WRITE IN BOOK

5. **Make a Decision** Thoroughly consider all of the consequences you have recorded in your table. Evaluate how important each consequence is. Make a decision about what course of action you would choose on the issue.

Analysis

6. In your evaluation, did you consider short-term consequences or long-term consequences to be more important? Why?

7. Which value or values had the greatest influence on your final decision? Explain your reasoning.

Going Further

Compare your table with your classmates' tables. Did you all make the same decision about a similar issue? If not, form teams, and organize a formal classroom debate of a specific environmental issue.

Muscles at Work

Have you ever exercised outside on a cold fall day wearing only a thin warm-up suit or shorts? How did you stay warm? The answer is that your muscle cells contracted, and when contraction takes place, some energy is used to do work and the rest is converted to thermal energy. This helps your body maintain a constant temperature in cold conditions. When you exercise strenuously on a hot summer day, your muscles can cause your body to become overheated.

In this activity, it is your job to find out how the release of energy can cause a change in your body temperature.

Materials

- clock or watch with a second hand
- small hand-held thermometer
- other materials as approved by your teacher

Procedure

1. Form a group of four students. In your group, discuss several exercises that can produce a change in body temperature. Form a hypothesis, and write your hypothesis in your ScienceLog.

2. Develop an experimental procedure that includes the steps necessary to test your hypothesis. Be sure to get your teacher's approval before you begin.

3. Assign tasks to individuals in the group, such as note taking, data recording, and timing. What observations and data will you be recording? Design your data tables in your ScienceLog accordingly.

4. Perform your experiment as planned by your group. Be sure to record all observations made during the experiment in your data tables.

Analysis

5. How did you determine if muscle contractions cause the release of thermal energy? Was your hypothesis supported by your data? Explain your results in a written report. Describe how you could improve your experimental method.

Going Further

Why do humans shiver in the cold? Do all animals shiver? Find out why shivering is one of the first signs that your body is becoming too cold.

Seeing Is Believing

Fingernails are part of your body's integumentary system, which includes the skin that covers your entire body. Nails are a modification of the outer layer of the skin, and they grow continuously throughout your life. In this activity, you will measure the rate at which fingernails grow.

Materials

- permanent marker
- metric ruler
- graph paper (optional)

Procedure

1. Trace around each of your hands. Then fill in some of the details, such as the fingernails, as shown below. Choose one of the fingers you have drawn, and label the parts of the fingernail, as shown at right. Notice that the nail bed is the area where the nail is attached to the finger. The illustration at right shows how far inside your finger your fingernail begins.

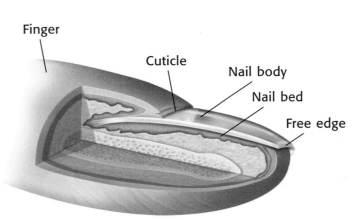

Finger · Cuticle · Nail body · Nail bed · Free edge

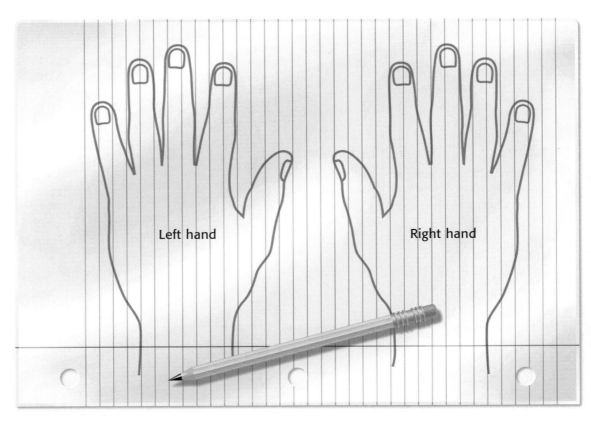

Left hand · Right hand

2. Find the center of the nail bed on your right index finger (the finger next to your thumb). Make a mark with the permanent marker on the center of your nail bed, as shown at right. **Caution:** Do not get the permanent marker ink on your clothing.

Base of nail

Mark

3. Measure from the mark to the base of your nail. Record this measurement on your hand drawing. Label this measurement "Day 1."

4. Repeat steps 2–3 for your left index finger. Then switch roles with your lab partner.

5. Let your fingernails grow for 2 days. Normal, daily activity will not wash away the stain completely, but you may need to freshen the mark periodically throughout this lab.

6. Measure the distance from the mark on your nail to the base of your nail. Record this distance on your hand drawing. Label this measurement "Day 3."

7. Continue measuring and recording the growth of your nails every other day for 2 weeks. Refresh the mark as necessary. You may continue to file or trim your nails as usual throughout this lab.

8. After you have completed your measurements and recorded them on your hand drawings, prepare a graph similar to the one below to display your findings.

Fingernail Growth

Distance of growth (mm) — vertical axis: 0, 4, 4, 6, 8, 10

Time allowed for growth (days) — horizontal axis: Day 1, Day 3, Day 5, Day 7, Day 9, Day 11

——— Left index finger

——— Right index finger

Analysis

9. Did one hand have a faster-growing nail? Write two possible explanations for why one fingernail might grow faster than another.

10. Who has the fastest-growing nails among your classmates? Who has the slowest-growing nails? What is the difference in the total nail growth between these two students?

11. Among your classmates, is there a difference between nail-growth rates for males and nail-growth rates for females? Is there a relationship between nail growth and other physical characteristics, such as height?

Going Further
Do some research in the library or on the Internet to find answers to the following questions:

• How are nails important to you? What do they help you do? Give at least three examples to support your answers.

• Are your fingernails an indication of your health or state of nutrition?

Build a Lung

You have learned that when you breathe, you actually pull air into your lungs because your diaphragm muscle causes your chest to expand. You can see this is true by placing your hands on your ribs and inhaling slowly. Did you feel your chest expand?

In this activity, you will build a model of a lung using some common materials. You will see how the diaphragm muscle works to inflate your lungs. Refer to the diagrams at right as you construct your model.

Materials

- small balloon
- plastic drinking straw
- 2 rubber bands
- golf-ball-sized piece of clay
- metric ruler
- top half of a 2 L bottle
- small plastic trash bag
- transparent tape

Procedure

1. Attach the balloon to the end of the straw with a rubber band. Make a hole through the clay, and insert the other end of the straw through the hole. Be sure at least 8 cm of the straw extends beyond the clay. Squeeze the ball of clay gently to seal the clay around the straw.

2. Insert the balloon end of the straw into the neck of the bottle. Use the ball of clay to seal the straw and balloon into the bottle.

3. Turn the bottle gently on its side. Place the trash bag over the cut end of the bottle. Expand a rubber band around the bottom of the bottle to secure the bag. You may wish to reinforce the seal with tape. Before the plastic is completely sealed, gather the excess material of the bag into your hand, and press toward the inside of the bottle slightly. (You may need to tie a knot about halfway up from the bottom of the bag to take up excess material.) Use tape to finish sealing the bag to the bottle with the bag in this position. This will push the excess air out of the bottle.

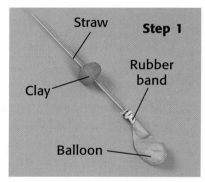

Straw — Step 1
Rubber band
Clay —
Balloon —

Step 2
Bottle neck —

Analysis

4. What can you do with your model to make the "lung" inflate?

5. What do the balloon, the plastic wrap, and the straw represent in your model?

6. Using your model, demonstrate to the class how air enters the lung and how air exits the lung.

Step 3

Going Further

Do some research to find out what an "iron lung" is and why it was used in the past. Find out what is used today to help people who have difficulty breathing.

Carbon Dioxide Breath

Plants take in carbon dioxide and give off oxygen as a byproduct of photosynthesis. Animals, including you, use this oxygen and release carbon dioxide as a byproduct of respiration.

In this activity, you will explore your own carbon dioxide exhalation. Phenol red turns yellow in the presence of carbon dioxide. You will use it to detect carbon dioxide in your breath.

Materials

- 150 mL graduated cylinder
- 100 mL of water
- 150 mL Erlenmeyer flask
- eyedropper
- phenol red indicator solution
- plastic drinking straw
- paper towel
- clock with a second hand or a stopwatch
- protective gloves

Procedure

1. Place 100 mL of water into a 150 mL flask. Using an eye-dropper, carefully place four drops of phenol red indicator solution into the water. The water should turn orange.

2. Place a plastic drinking straw into the solution of phenol red and water. Drape a paper towel over the beaker to prevent splashing. Carefully blow through the straw into the solution. **Caution:** Do not inhale through the straw. Do not drink the solution, and do not share a straw with anyone.

3. Have your lab partner time how long it takes for the solution to change color. Begin timing when you start blowing. Record the time in your ScienceLog. What color does the solution become?

Analysis

4. Compare your data with those of your classmates. What was the longest length of time it took to see a color change? the shortest? How do you account for the difference?

5. Is there a relationship between the length of time it takes to change the solution from orange to yellow and the person's physical characteristics, such as gender or whether the tester has an athletic build?

Going Further

Do jumping jacks or sit-ups for 3 minutes, and then repeat the experiment. Did the timing change? Describe and explain any change.

As the Stomach Churns

The stomach, as you know, performs not only mechanical digestion but also chemical digestion. As the stomach churns, it moves the food particles around while the digestive juices—acid and enzymes—are added to begin protein digestion.

Commercially prepared meat tenderizers contain enzymes from plants that break down, or digest, proteins. Two types of meat tenderizer are commonly available at grocery stores. One type contains an enzyme called papain, from papaya. Another type contains an enzyme called bromelain, from pineapple. In this lab, you will test the effects of these two different types of meat tenderizers on beef stew meat.

Ask a Question

1. Which meat tenderizer will work faster? Which will make the meat more tender? Will there be a color change in the meat or in the water? What might these changes, if any, indicate? Determine what you will look for as you plan your experiment.

Form a Hypothesis

2. Examine the list of ingredients on the labels of each of the meat tenderizers. Form a hypothesis about which tenderizer will make the beef more tender.
   Caution: Do not taste any of the materials in this activity.

Materials

- 4 test tubes
- test-tube rack
- test-tube marker
- masking tape
- 25 mL graduated cylinder
- water
- eyedropper
- 1/4 tsp measuring spoon
- very dilute (0.1 M) hydrochloric acid
- commercially prepared meat tenderizer containing bromelain
- commercially prepared meat tenderizer containing papain
- 1 cm cubes of beef stew meat (3)
- protective gloves

Conduct an Experiment

3. Identify any variables and controls present in your experiment. Make a data table in your ScienceLog to record your observations and results.

4. Label two of the test tubes with the name of the tenderizer being investigated. Label the third test tube "Control." What will be the contents of this tube?

5. Pour 20 mL of water into each test tube.

6. With the eyedropper, add four drops of very dilute hydrochloric acid to each test tube. **Caution:** Hydrochloric acid can burn your skin. If any touches your skin, rinse the area with running water and tell your teacher immediately.

7. Using the measuring spoon, add ¼ tsp of a meat tenderizer to each correspondingly labeled test tube.

8. Add 1 cube of beef to each test tube.

9. Record your observations of each test tube immediately, after 5 minutes, after 15 minutes, after 30 minutes, and again after 24 hours.

Analyze the Results

10. Did you notice any differences in the beef in the three test tubes immediately? At what time interval did you notice a significant difference in the appearance of the beef in the test tubes?

11. Did one meat tenderizer perform better than the other? Explain how you determined which tenderizer was most efficient.

Draw Conclusions

12. Was your hypothesis supported? Explain.

13. Many animals that sting have venom composed of proteins. Explain how applying meat tenderizer to the wound helps relieve the pain of such a sting.

Enzymes in Action

DISCOVERY LAB

You know how important enzymes are in the process of digestion. This lab will help you see enzymes at work. Hydrogen peroxide is continuously produced by your cells. If it is not quickly broken down, hydrogen peroxide will kill your cells. Luckily, your cells contain an enzyme that converts hydrogen peroxide into two non-poisonous substances. This enzyme is also present in the cells of beef liver. In this lab, you will observe the action of this enzyme on hydrogen peroxide.

Materials

- 1 cm cubes of beef liver (3)
- tweezers
- small plate
- 10 mL graduated cylinder
- water
- 3 test tubes
- test-tube rack
- 4 mL of fresh hydrogen peroxide
- mortar and pestle (or fork and watch glass)
- spatula
- protective gloves

Procedure

1. In your ScienceLog, draw a data table similar to the one below. Be sure to leave enough space to write your observations.

Data Table

Size and condition of liver	Experimental liquid	Observations
1 cm cube beef liver	2 mL water	
1 cm cube beef liver	2 mL hydrogen peroxide	
1 cm cube beef liver (mashed)	2 mL hydrogen peroxide	

DO NOT WRITE IN BOOK

2. Get three equal-sized pieces of beef liver from your teacher, and use your forceps to place them on your plate.

3. Pour 2 mL of water into a test tube labeled "Water and liver."

4. Using the tweezers, carefully place one piece of liver in the test tube. Record your observations in your data table.

5. Pour 2 mL of hydrogen peroxide into a second test tube labeled "Liver and hydrogen peroxide."
Caution: Do not splash hydrogen peroxide on your skin. If you do get hydrogen peroxide on your skin, rinse the affected area with running water immediately, and tell your teacher.

6. Using the tweezers, carefully place one piece of liver in the test tube. Record your observations of the second test tube in your data table.

7. Pour another 2 mL of hydrogen peroxide into a third test tube labeled "Ground liver and hydrogen peroxide."

8. Using a mortar and pestle (or fork and watch glass), carefully grind the third piece of liver.

9. Using the spatula, scrape the ground liver into the third test tube. Record your observations of the third test tube in your data table.

Analysis

10. What was the purpose of putting the first piece of liver in water? Why was this a necessary step?

11. Describe the difference you observed between the liver and the ground liver when each was placed in the hydrogen peroxide. How can you account for this difference?

Going Further

Do plant cells contain enzymes that break down hydrogen peroxide? Try this experiment using potato cubes instead of liver to find out.

You've Gotta Lotta Nerve

Your skin has thousands of nerve receptors that detect sensations, such as heat, cold, and pressure. Your brain is designed to filter out or ignore most of the input it receives from these skin receptors. If that were not the case, simply wearing clothes would trigger so many responses that we couldn't function.

Some areas of the skin, such as the back of your hand, are more sensitive than others. In this activity, you will map the receptors for heat, cold, and pressure on the back of your hand.

Procedure

1. Form groups of three. One of you will volunteer the back of your hand to be tested, one will do the testing, and the third will record the results. Check with your teacher to see if you may switch roles so each of you may play each part.

2. Use a fine-point washable marker or pen and a metric ruler to mark off a 3 × 3 cm square on the back of your partner's hand. Draw a grid within the area, spacing the lines approximately 0.5 cm apart. You will have 36 squares in the grid when you are finished. Examine the photograph below to make sure you have drawn the grid correctly.

3. Mark off three 3 × 3 cm areas on the graph paper. Make a grid in each area exactly as you did on the back of your partner's hand. Label one grid "Cold," another grid "Hot," and the third grid "Pressure."

Materials

- fine-point washable pens or markers
- metric ruler
- graph paper
- eyedropper
- very cold water
- hot tap water
- dissecting pin with a small piece of cork or a small rubber stopper stuck on the sharp end

4. Begin locating receptors on your partner's hand. Your partner should not look while his or her hand is being tested! How do you think your partner's looking might influence your results? Use the eyedropper to apply one small droplet of cold water on each square in the grid. On your graph paper, mark an X on the *Cold* grid in the square that corresponds to where the sensation of cold was felt on the hand. You will need to carefully blot the water off your partner's hand after several drops.

5. Repeat the test using hot-water droplets. The water will cool enough as it drops from the eyedropper so that it will not hurt you. Mark an X on the *Hot* grid to indicate where the sensation of heat was felt on the hand.

6. Repeat the test using the head—not the point!—of the pin. Touch the skin to detect pressure receptors. Use a very light touch. Mark an X on the *Pressure* grid to indicate where pressure was felt on the hand.

Analysis

7. Count the number of Xs in each grid. How many heat receptors are there per 3 cm²? cold receptors? pressure receptors?

8. Do you have areas on the back of your hand where the receptors overlap? Why or why not?

9. How do you think the results of this experiment would be similar or different if you mapped an area of your forearm? the back of your neck? the palm of your hand?

10. Prepare a written report that includes a description of your investigation and a discussion of questions 7–9.

Going Further

In the library or on the Internet research what happens if a receptor is continuously stimulated. Does the kind of receptor make a difference? Does it make a difference how intense the stimulation is? Explain.

It's a Comfy, Safe World!

Before human babies are born, they lead a comfy life. By the seventh month, they just lie around, sucking their thumb, blinking their eyes, and perhaps even dreaming. Baby birds live inside a hard, protective shell until the baby has used up all the food supply. Most mammal babies develop within their mother's uterus, surrounded by fluid and a placenta before they are born. Is the internal environment in a placental mammal safer than a baby bird's environment? In this activity you will create a model of a placental mammal's uterus to see how well it protects a fetus.

Materials

- sealable plastic bags
- water
- mineral oil, cooking oil, syrup, or other thick liquid to represent fluid surrounding the fetus
- cotton, soft fabric, or other soft materials
- 3–5 soft-boiled eggs
- protective gloves

Procedure

1. Brainstorm several ideas about how you will construct and test your model. A peeled, soft-boiled egg will represent the fetus in your mammalian model. Build your model.

2. Make a data table in your ScienceLog similar to the First Model Test table at right. Test your model, examine the egg for damage, and record your results.

3. Modify your design as necessary, repeat step 2, and record your results.

4. When you are satisfied with the design of your model, obtain another peeled, soft-boiled egg and an egg in the shell.

5. Make another data table in your ScienceLog similar to the Final Model Test table at right. Repeat step 2 with your new eggs. Record your results in your data table.

First Model Test	
Original model	**Modified model**
DO NOT WRITE IN BOOK	

Final Model Test	
	Test Results
Model	
Egg in shell	DO NOT WRITE IN BOOK

Analysis

6. Explain any differences in the test results for the model and the egg in a shell.

7. What modification to your model was the most effective in protecting your fetus?

Going Further

Compare the development of placental mammals with that of marsupial mammals and monotremes.

My, How You've Grown!

In humans, the process of development that takes place between fertilization and birth lasts about 266 days. In 4 weeks, the new individual grows from a single fertilized cell to an embryo whose heart is beating and pumping blood. All of the organ systems and body parts are completely formed by the end of the seventh month. During the last 2 months before birth, the baby grows and its organ systems mature. At birth, the average mass of a baby is about 33,000 times as much as that of an embryo at 2 weeks of development! In this activity you will discover just how fast a fetus grows.

Materials

- graph paper
- colored pencils

 TRY at HOME

Procedure

1. Using graph paper, make two graphs— one titled "Length" and one titled "Mass"—in your ScienceLog. On the length graph, use intervals of 25 mm on the *y*-axis. Extend the *y*-axis to 500 mm. On the mass graph, use intervals of 100 g on the *y*-axis. Extend this *y*-axis to 3,300 g. Use 2-week intervals for time on the *x*-axes for both graphs. Both *x*-axes should extend to 40 weeks.

2. Examine the data table at right. Plot the data in the table on your graphs. Use a colored pencil to draw the curved line that joins the points on each graph.

Analysis

3. Describe the change in mass of a developing fetus. How can you explain this change?

4. Describe the change in length of a developing fetus. How does the change in mass compare to the change in length?

Increase of Mass and Length of Average Human Fetus		
Time (wks)	Mass (g)	Length (mm)
2	0.1	1.5
3	0.3	2.3
4	0.5	5.0
5	0.6	10.0
6	0.8	15.0
8	1.0	30.0
13	15.0	90.0
17	115.0	140.0
21	300.0	250.0
26	950.0	320.0
30	1,500.0	400.0
35	2,300.0	450.0
40	3,300.0	500.0

Going Further

Using the information in your graphs, estimate how tall a child would be at age 3 if he or she continued to grow at the same average rate a fetus grows.

Antibodies to the Rescue

Some cells of the immune system, called B cells, make antibodies that attack and kill invading viruses and microorganisms. These antibodies help make you immune to disease. Have you ever had chickenpox? If you have, your body has built up antibodies that can recognize that particular virus. Antibodies will attach themselves to the virus, tagging it for destruction. If you are exposed to the same disease again, the antibodies remember that virus. They will attack the virus even quicker and in greater number than they did the first time. That is why you will probably never have chicken-pox more than once.

In this activity, you will construct simple models of viruses and their antibodies. You will see how antibodies are specific for a particular virus.

Materials

- craft materials, such as buttons, fabric scraps, pipecleaners, and recycled materials
- scissors
- tape or glue
- colored paper

Procedure

1. Draw the virus patterns shown on this page on a separate piece of paper, or design your own virus models from the craft supplies. Remember to design different receptors on each of your virus models.

2. In your ScienceLog, write a few sentences describing how your viruses are different.

3. Cut out the viruses, and attach them to a piece of colored paper with tape or glue.

A

Virus

Receptor

Viruses

Receptor

B

Virus

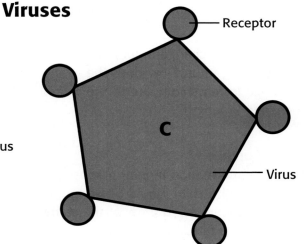

Receptor

C

Virus

4. Select the antibodies drawn below or design your own antibodies that will exactly fit on the receptors on your virus models. Draw or create each antibody enough times to attach one to each receptor site on the virus.

Antibodies

5. Cut out the antibodies you have drawn. Arrange the antibodies so that they bind to the virus at the appropriate receptor. Attach them to the virus with tape or glue.

Analysis

6. Explain how an antibody "recognizes" a particular virus.

7. After the attachment of antibodies to the receptors, what would be the next step in the immune response?

8. Many vaccines use weakened copies of the virus to protect the body. Use the model of a virus and its specific antibody to explain how vaccines work.

9. Use your model of a virus to demonstrate to the class how a receptor might change or mutate so that a vaccine would no longer be effective.

Going Further

Research in the library or on the Internet to find information about the discovery of the Salk vaccine for polio. Include information on how polio affects people today.

Research in the library or on the Internet to find information about filoviruses. What do they look like? What diseases do they cause? Why are they especially dangerous? Is there an effective vaccine against any filovirus? Explain.

Passing the Cold

There are more than 100 viruses that cause the symptoms of the common cold. Any of the viruses can be passed from person to person—through the air or through direct contact. In this activity you will track the progress of an outbreak in your class.

Materials

- 200 mL beaker or a cup of similar size
- eyedropper
- 50 mL of an unknown solution
- protective gloves

Ask a Question

1. How are cold viruses passed from person to person? How can the progress of an outbreak be modeled?

Conduct an Experiment

2. Obtain an empty cup or beaker, an eyedropper, and 50 mL of one of the solutions from your teacher. Only one of you will have the "cold virus" solution. You will see a change in your solution when you have become infected.

3. Your teacher will divide the class into two equal groups. If there is an extra student, that person will record data on the chalkboard. Otherwise, the teacher will act as the recorder.

4. Each group will form a straight line and face each other.

5. Each time your teacher says "Mix," fill your eyedropper with your solution, and place 10 drops of your solution in the beaker of the person in the line opposite you without touching your eyedropper to the liquid.

6. Gently stir the liquid in your cup with your eyedropper. Do not put your eyedropper in anyone else's solution.

7. If your solution changes color, raise your hand so that the recorder can record the number of students who have been "infected."

8. Your teacher will instruct one line to move one person to the right. The person at the end of the line without a partner should go to the other end of the line.

9. Repeat steps 5–8 nine more times for a total of 10 trials.

Collect Data

10. Return to your desk, and create a data table in your ScienceLog similar to the one below. The column with the title "Total number of people" will remain the same in every row. Enter the data on the board into your data table.

11. Find the percentage of infected people for the last column by dividing the number of infected people by the total number of people and multiplying by 100 in each line.

Results			
Trial	Number of infected people	Total number of people	Percentage of infected people
1			
2			
3			
4			
5			
6			
7			
8			
9			
10			

Analyze the Results

12. Did you become infected? If so, during which trial did you become infected?

13. Did everyone eventually become infected? If so, how many trials were necessary to infect everyone?

14. Explain at least one reason why this simulation may underestimate the number of people who might have been infected in real life.

15. Use your results to create a line graph showing the change in the infection percentage per trial.

Going Further

Research in the library or on the Internet to find out some of the factors that contribute to the spread of a cold virus. What is the best and easiest way to reduce your chances of catching a cold? Explain your answer.

To Diet or Not to Diet

DISCOVERY LAB

There are six main classes of foods that we need in order to keep our bodies functioning properly: water, vitamins, minerals, carbohydrates, fats, and proteins. In this activity you will investigate the importance of a well-balanced diet in maintaining a healthy body. Then you will create a poster or picture that illustrates the importance of one of the three energy-producing nutrients—carbohydrates, fats, and proteins.

Materials

- nutrition reference books
- diet books
- white unlined paper
- crayons or colored markers
- fast-food menus (optional)

Procedure

1. In your ScienceLog, create a table like the one below. Research in the library, on nutrition labels, in nutrition or diet books, or on the Internet to find the information you need to fill out the chart.

Nutrition Data Table			
	Fats	**Carbohydrates**	**Proteins**
Found in which foods			
Functions in the body			
Consequences of deficiency			

DO NOT WRITE IN BOOK

2. Choose one of the foods you have learned about in your research, and create a poster or picture that describes its importance in a well-balanced diet.

Analysis

3. Based on what you have learned in this lab, how might you change your eating habits to have a well-balanced diet? Does the nutritional value of foods concern you? Why or why not? Write your answers in your ScienceLog, and explain your reasoning.

Going Further

- Write a paragraph explaining why water is a nutrient.
- Analyze a typical fast-food meal, and determine its overall nutritional value.

Keep It Clean

One of the best ways of preventing the spread of bacterial and viral infections is to wash your hands with soap and water frequently. Many companies advertise that their soap ingredients will destroy bacteria normally found on the body. In this activity you will investigate how effective antibacterial soaps are at killing bacteria.

Materials

- wax pencil
- new scrub brush
- 4 agar plates (Petri dishes filled with sterile nutrient agar)
- liquid antibacterial soap
- incubator
- transparent tape

Procedure

1. Use the wax pencil to label the bottoms of four agar plates with: "control," "unwashed," "no soap," and "soap." Open the control dish for 1 minute. Cover the dish, and leave it closed for the rest of the experiment.

2. Without washing your hands, carefully press different surfaces of your hands on the agar plate marked "unwashed." Replace the cover of the plate immediately.

3. Hold your right hand under running water for two minutes. During this time, ask your partner to scrub all surfaces of your hand with the scrub brush. Be sure to scrub under your fingernails. When you are finished, your partner should turn off the water and open the plate marked "no soap." Without touching anything first, carefully press the same surfaces of your right hand on the plate, as you did in step 2.

4. Repeat step 3 using liquid antibacterial soap on your left hand. Make sure that you do not touch anything before pressing your left hand on the plate marked "soap."

5. Secure the lid of each plate to its bottom half with transparent tape. Place the dishes upside down. Incubate all three plates overnight at 37°C.

6. Remove the plates from the incubator and turn them right side up. Check each plate for the presence of bacterial colonies, and count the number of colonies present on each plate. Record this information in your ScienceLog.
Caution: Do not remove the lids on any of the plates.

Analysis

7. Compare the bacterial growth on the dishes. Which dish contained the most growth? Which contained the least?

8. Does water alone effectively kill bacteria? Explain.

Going Further

Try this experiment again. This time scrub your hands for 2 minutes with regular liquid soap. Account for any differences you observe.

Self-Check Answers

Chapter 1—The World of Life Science

Page 12: 2. Insecticides caused the frog deformities.

Page 15: Jar C is the control group.

Chapter 2—It's Alive!! Or, Is It?

Page 37: Your alarm clock is a stimulus. It rings, and you respond by shutting it off and getting out of bed.

Chapter 3—Cells: The Basic Units of Life

Page 63: Cells need DNA to control cell processes and to make new cells.

Page 66: 1. The surface-to-volume ratio decreases as the cell size increases. 2. A eukaryotic cell has a nucleus and membrane-covered organelles.

Page 70: Cell walls surround the cell membranes of some cells. All cells have cell membranes, but not all cells have cell walls. Cell walls give structure to some cells.

Chapter 4—The Cell in Action

Page 85: In pure water, the grape would absorb water and swell up. In water mixed with a large amount of sugar, the grape would lose water and shrink.

Page 93: After duplication, there are four chromatids—two from each of the homologous chromosomes.

Chapter 5—Heredity

Page 117: 1. four 2. two 3. They make copies of themselves once. They divide twice. 4. Two, or half the number of chromosomes in the parent, are present at the end of meiosis. After mitosis, there would be four chromosomes, the same number as in the parent cell.

Chapter 6—Genes and Gene Technology

Page 131: TGGATCAAC

Page 137: 1. 1000 amino acids 2. DNA codes for proteins. Your flesh is composed of proteins, and the way those proteins are constructed and combined influences much about the way you look.

Chapter 7—The Evolution of Living Things

Page 165: The population of light-colored moths would increase.

Chapter 8—The History of Life on Earth

Page 179: 5 g, 2.5 g

Page 185: b, c, d, a

Chapter 9—Classification

Page 210: 1. The two kingdoms of bacteria are different from all other kingdoms because bacteria are prokaryotes—single-celled organisms that have no nucleus. 2. The organisms in the kingdom Protista are all eukaryotes.

Chapter 10—Bacteria and Viruses

Page 227: Cyanobacteria were once classified as plants because they use photosynthesis to make food.

Chapter 11—Protists and Fungi

Page 246: No, some funguslike protists are parasites or consumers.

Page 252: 1. Cilia are used to move a ciliate through the water and to sweep food toward the organism. 2. Ciliates are classified as animal-like protists because they are consumers and they move.

Chapter 12—Introduction to Plants

Page 272: Plants need a cuticle to keep the leaves from drying out. Algae grow in a wet environment, so they do not need a cuticle.

Page 288: Stems hold up the leaves so that the leaves can get adequate sunshine for photosynthesis.

Chapter 13—Plant Processes

Page 301: Fruit develops from the ovary, so the flower can have only one fruit. Seeds develop from the ovules, so there should be six seeds.

Page 305: The sun is the source of the energy in sugar.

Page 308: 1. (See concept map below.)
2. During negative phototropism, the plant would grow away from the stimulus (light), so it would be bending to the left.

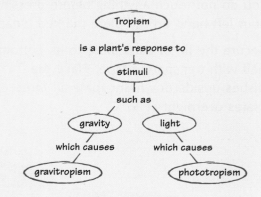

Chapter 14—Animals and Behavior

Page 324: Like other vertebrates, humans have a skull and a backbone.

Chapter 15—Invertebrates

Page 349: Because medusas swim through the water by contracting their bodies, they must have a nervous system that can control these actions. Polyps move very little, so they don't need as complex a nervous system.

Page 359: Segmented worms belong to the phylum Annelida. Centipedes are arthropods. Centipedes have jointed legs, antennae, and mandibles. Segmented worms have none of these characteristics.

Chapter 16—Fishes, Amphibians, and Reptiles

Page 383: Amphibians use their skin to absorb oxygen from the air. Their skin is thin, moist, and full of blood vessels, just like a lung.

Page 389: 1. Thick, dry skin and amniotic eggs help reptiles live on dry land. 2. The hard shell prevents fertilization, so the egg must be fertilized before the shell is added.

Chapter 17—Birds and Mammals

Page 402: 1. Down feathers are not stiff and smooth and could not give structure to the wings. They are adapted to keep the bird warm. 2. Birds need tremendous amounts of food for fuel because it takes a lot of energy to fly.

Page 416: Monotremes are mammals that lay eggs. Marsupials bear live young but carry them in pouches or skin folds before they are able to live independently. Placentals develop inside the mother's body and are nourished through a placenta before birth.

Page 421: 1. Bats bear live young, have fur, and do not have feathers. 2. Rodents and lagomorphs both are small mammals with long sensitive whiskers and gnawing teeth. Unlike rodents, lagomorphs have two sets of incisors and a short tail.

Chapter 18—Interactions of Living Things

Page 439: Humans are omnivores. An omnivore eats both plants and animals. Humans can eat meat and vegetables as well as animal products, such as milk and eggs, and plant products such as grains and fruit.

Page 440: A food chain shows how energy moves in one direction from one organism to the next. A food web shows that there are many energy pathways between organisms.

Page 445: 1. If an area has enough water to support 10 organisms, any additional organisms will cause some to go without water and move away, or die. 2. Weather favorable for growing the food that deer eat will allow the forest to support more deer.

Chapter 19—Cycles in Nature

Page 464: The main difference between primary and secondary succession is that primary succession begins with the formation of soil. Secondary succession begins on preexisting soil, such as when an existing community is disrupted by a natural disaster or by farming. Pioneer species in primary succession are usually lichens, which begin the formation of soil. Pioneer species in secondary succession are usually seed plants, which germinate and take root in the soil.

Chapter 20—The Earth's Ecosystems

Page 479: Deciduous forests tend to exist in mid-latitude or temperate regions, while coniferous forests tend to exist in higher, colder latitudes, closer to the poles.

Page 484: Answers include: the amount of sunlight penetrating the water, its distance from land, the depth of the water, the salinity of the water, and the water's temperature. 2. There are several possible answers. Some organisms are adapted for catching prey at great depths; some feed on dead plankton and larger organisms that filter down from above; and some, such as the bacteria around thermal vents, make food from chemicals in the water.

Chapter 21—Environmental Problems and Solutions

Page 501: 1. We use nonrenewable resources when we burn fossil fuels when driving or riding in a car or burning coal for heat. When we use minerals that are mined, we are using a nonrenewable resource. Pumping ground water is another use of a non-renewable resource, if the water is used faster than it is replenished. 2. If a nonrenewable resource is used up, we can no longer rely on that resource. Certain oil and coal deposits have been building since life began on the planet. It may take hundreds of years to replace a mature forest that can be cut in a day.

Page 507: 1. Turn off lights, CD players, radios, and computers when leaving a room. Set thermostats a little lower in the winter (wear sweaters). Don't leave the refrigerator door open while deciding what you want. 2. plastic bags, rechargeable batteries, water, clothing, toys; The difference between a reused and a recycled object is that a reused article may be cleaned but is basically unchanged. A recycled article has been broken down and re-formed into another usable product.

Chapter 22—Body Organization and Structure

Page 532: Curl-ups use flexor muscles; push-ups use extensor muscles.

Page 535: Blood vessels belong to the cardio-vascular system.

Chapter 23—Circulation and Respiration

Page 550: The hollow tube shape of arteries and veins allows blood to reach all parts of the body. Valves in the veins prevent blood from flowing backward.

Page 554: Like blood vessels, lymph capillaries receive fluid from the spaces surrounding cells. The fluid absorbed by lymph capillaries flows into lymph vessels. These vessels drain into large neck veins instead of into an organ, such as the heart. Lymph does not deliver oxygen and nutrients.

Chapter 24—The Digestive and Urinary Systems

Page 573: Bile is involved in the physical digestion because emulsification does not change the chemical composition of the fat molecules; it only increases the surface area of each fat droplet.

Chapter 25—Communication and Control

Page 593: 1. cerebrum 2. cerebellum 3. to protect the spinal cord

Chapter 26—Reproduction and Development

Page 613: In asexual reproduction, one animal produces offspring that are genetically identical to itself. In sexual reproduction, the genes of two individuals are mixed when sex cells join to form a zygote. This zygote develops into a unique individual.

Page 621: The uterus provides the nutrients and protection that the embryo needs to continue growing. The uterus is also the only place the placenta will form.

Chapter 27—Body Defenses and Disease

Page 637: If Jackie did not wash the counter after cutting up the meat, bacteria could grow on the counter where the meat was. This bacteria could contaminate her brother's sandwich.

Chapter 28—Staying Healthy

Page 661: You have eaten two servings from the bread, cereal, rice, pasta group; one serving from the fruit group, and one from the milk, yogurt and cheese group.

Page 664: Regular use of some drugs may cause tolerance or addiction. Withdrawal symptoms occur when the body does not receive a drug that it is addicted to.

Page 667: 1. A hallucination is a vision or sound that is not real. 2. Heroin is highly addictive and potentially deadly. If shared needles are used to inject it, users risk getting diseases like hepatitis or AIDS.

CONTENTS

Concept Mapping: A Way to Bring Ideas Together

What Is a Concept Map?

Have you ever tried to tell someone about a book or a chapter you've just read and found that you can remember only a few isolated words and ideas? Or maybe you've memorized facts for a test and then weeks later discovered you're not even sure what topics those facts covered.

In both cases, you may have understood the ideas or concepts by themselves but not in relation to one another. If you could somehow link the ideas together, you would probably understand them better and remember them longer. This is something a concept map can help you do. A concept map is a way to see how ideas or concepts fit together. It can help you see the "big picture."

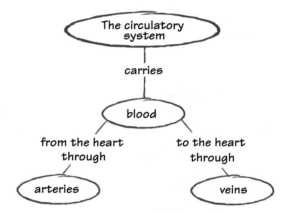

How to Make a Concept Map

1 Make a list of the main ideas or concepts.

It might help to write each concept on its own slip of paper. This will make it easier to rearrange the concepts as many times as necessary to make sense of how the concepts are connected. After you've made a few concept maps this way, you can go directly from writing your list to actually making the map.

2 Arrange the concepts in order from the most general to the most specific.

Put the most general concept at the top and circle it. Ask yourself, "How does this concept relate to the remaining concepts?" As you see the relationships, arrange the concepts in order from general to specific.

3 Connect the related concepts with lines.

4 On each line, write an action word or short phrase that shows how the concepts are related.

Look at the concept maps on this page, and then see if you can make one for the following terms:

plants, water, photosynthesis, carbon dioxide, sun's energy

One possible answer is provided at right, but don't look at it until you try the concept map yourself.

SI Measurement

The International System of Units, or SI, is the standard system of measurement used by many scientists. Using the same standards of measurement makes it easier for scientists to communicate with one another.

SI works by combining prefixes and base units. Each base unit can be used with different prefixes to define smaller and larger quantities. The table below lists common SI prefixes.

SI Prefixes			
Prefix	**Abbreviation**	**Factor**	**Example**
kilo-	k	1,000	kilogram, 1 kg = 1,000 g
hecto-	h	100	hectoliter, 1 hL = 100 L
deka-	da	10	dekameter, 1 dam = 10 m
		1	meter, liter
deci-	d	0.1	decigram, 1 dg = 0.1 g
centi-	c	0.01	centimeter, 1 cm = 0.01 m
milli-	m	0.001	milliliter, 1 mL = 0.001 L
micro-	μ	0.000 001	micrometer, 1 μm = 0.000 001 m

SI Conversion Table		
SI units	**From SI to English**	**From English to SI**
Length		
kilometer (km) = 1,000 m	1 km = 0.621 mi	1 mi = 1.609 km
meter (m) = 100 cm	1 m = 3.281 ft	1 ft = 0.305 m
centimeter (cm) = 0.01 m	1 cm = 0.394 in.	1 in. = 2.540 cm
millimeter (mm) = 0.001 m	1 mm = 0.039 in.	
micrometer (μm) = 0.000 001 m		
nanometer (nm) = 0.000 000 001 m		
Area		
square kilometer (km^2) = 100 hectares	1 km^2 = 0.386 mi^2	1 mi^2 = 2.590 km^2
hectare (ha) = 10,000 m^2	1 ha = 2.471 acres	1 acre = 0.405 ha
square meter (m^2) = 10,000 cm^2	1 m^2 = 10.765 ft^2	1 ft^2 = 0.093 m^2
square centimeter (cm^2) = 100 mm^2	1 cm^2 = 0.155 $in.^2$	1 $in.^2$ = 6.452 cm^2
Volume		
liter (L) = 1,000 mL = 1 dm^3	1 L = 1.057 fl qt	1 fl qt = 0.946 L
milliliter (mL) = 0.001 L = 1 cm^3	1 mL = 0.034 fl oz	1 fl oz = 29.575 mL
microliter (μL) = 0.000 001 L		
Mass		
kilogram (kg) = 1,000 g	1 kg = 2.205 lb	1 lb = 0.454 kg
gram (g) = 1,000 mg	1 g = 0.035 oz	1 oz = 28.349 g
milligram (mg) = 0.001 g		
microgram (μg) = 0.000 001 g		

Temperature Scales

Temperature can be expressed using three different scales: Fahrenheit, Celsius, and Kelvin. The SI unit for temperature is the kelvin (K).

Although 0 K is much colder than 0°C, a change of 1 K is equal to a change of 1°C.

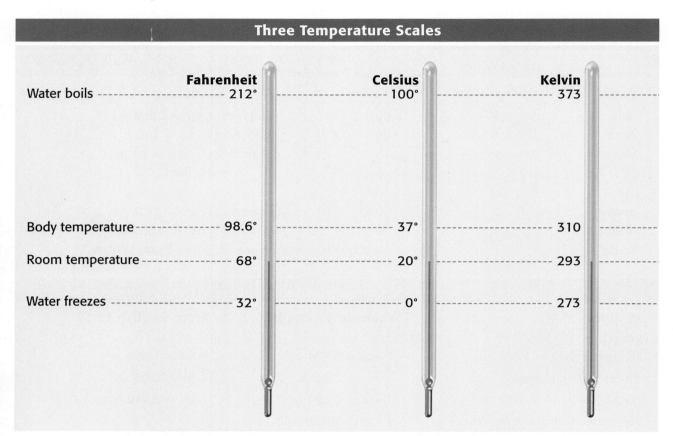

Three Temperature Scales

	Fahrenheit	Celsius	Kelvin
Water boils	212°	100°	373
Body temperature	98.6°	37°	310
Room temperature	68°	20°	293
Water freezes	32°	0°	273

Temperature Conversions Table

To convert	Use this equation:	Example
Celsius to Fahrenheit $°C \longrightarrow °F$	$°F = \left(\dfrac{9}{5} \times °C\right) + 32$	Convert 45°C to °F. $°F = \left(\dfrac{9}{5} \times 45°C\right) + 32 = 113°F$
Fahrenheit to Celsius $°F \longrightarrow °C$	$°C = \dfrac{5}{9} \times (°F - 32)$	Convert 68°F to °C. $°C = \dfrac{5}{9} \times (68°F - 32) = 20°C$
Celsius to Kelvin $°C \longrightarrow K$	$K = °C + 273$	Convert 45°C to K. $K = 45°C + 273 = 318\ K$
Kelvin to Celsius $K \longrightarrow °C$	$°C = K - 273$	Convert 32 K to °C. $°C = 32\ K - 273 = -241°C$

Measuring Skills

Using a Graduated Cylinder

When using a graduated cylinder to measure volume, keep the following procedures in mind:

❶ Make sure the cylinder is on a flat, level surface.

❷ Move your head so that your eye is level with the surface of the liquid.

❸ Read the mark closest to the liquid level. On glass graduated cylinders, read the mark closest to the center of the curve in the liquid's surface.

Using a Meterstick or Metric Ruler

When using a meterstick or metric ruler to measure length, keep the following procedures in mind:

❶ Place the ruler firmly against the object you are measuring.

❷ Align one edge of the object exactly with the zero end of the ruler.

❸ Look at the other edge of the object to see which of the marks on the ruler is closest to that edge. **Note:** Each small slash between the centimeters represents a millimeter, which is one-tenth of a centimeter.

Using a Triple-Beam Balance

When using a triple-beam balance to measure mass, keep the following procedures in mind:

❶ Make sure the balance is on a level surface.

❷ Place all of the countermasses at zero. Adjust the balancing knob until the pointer rests at zero.

❸ Place the object you wish to measure on the pan. **Caution:** Do not place hot objects or chemicals directly on the balance pan.

❹ Move the largest countermass along the beam to the right until it is at the last notch that does not tip the balance. Follow the same procedure with the next-largest countermass. Then move the smallest countermass until the pointer rests at zero.

❺ Add the readings from the three beams together to determine the mass of the object.

❻ When determining the mass of crystals or powders, use a piece of filter paper. First find the mass of the paper. Then add the crystals or powder to the paper and re-measure. The actual mass of the crystals or powder is the total mass minus the mass of the paper. When finding the mass of liquids, first find the mass of the empty container. Then find the mass of the liquid and container together. The mass of the liquid is the total mass minus the mass of the container.

Scientific Method

The series of steps that scientists use to answer questions and solve problems is often called the **scientific method.** The scientific method is not a rigid procedure. Scientists may use all of the steps or just some of the steps of the scientific method. They may even repeat some of the steps. The goal of the scientific method is to come up with reliable answers and solutions.

Six Steps of the Scientific Method

1 **Ask a Question** Good questions come from careful **observations.** You make observations by using your senses to gather information. Sometimes you may use instruments, such as microscopes and telescopes, to extend the range of your senses. As you observe the natural world, you will discover that you have many more questions than answers. These questions drive the scientific method.

Questions beginning with *what, why, how,* and *when* are very important in focusing an investigation, and they often lead to a hypothesis. (You will learn what a hypothesis is in the next step.) Here is an example of a question that could lead to further investigation.

Question: How does acid rain affect plant growth?

2 **Form a Hypothesis** After you come up with a question, you need to turn the question into a **hypothesis.** A hypothesis is a clear statement of what you expect the answer to your question to be. Your hypothesis will represent your best "educated guess" based on your observations and what you already know. A good hypothesis is testable. If observations and information cannot be gathered or if an experiment cannot be designed to test your hypothesis, it is untestable, and the investigation can go no further.

Here is a hypothesis that could be formed from the question, "How does acid rain affect plant growth?"

Hypothesis: Acid rain causes plants to grow more slowly.

Notice that the hypothesis provides some specifics that lead to methods of testing. The hypothesis can also lead to predictions. A **prediction** is what you think will be the outcome of your experiment or data collection. Predictions are usually stated in an "if . . . then" format. For example, **if** meat is kept at room temperature, **then** it will spoil faster than meat kept in the refrigerator. More than one prediction can be made for a single hypothesis. Here is a sample prediction for the hypothesis that acid rain causes plants to grow more slowly.

Prediction: If a plant is watered with only acid rain (which has a pH of 4), then the plant will grow at half its normal rate.

3 **Test the Hypothesis** After you have formed a hypothesis and made a prediction, you should test your hypothesis. There are different ways to do this. Perhaps the most familiar way is to conduct a **controlled experiment.** A controlled experiment tests only one factor at a time. A controlled experiment has a **control group** and one or more **experimental groups.** All the factors for the control and experimental groups are the same except for one factor, which is called the **variable.** By changing only one factor, you can see the results of just that one change.

Sometimes, the nature of an investigation makes a controlled experiment impossible. For example, dinosaurs have been extinct for millions of years, and the Earth's core is surrounded by thousands of meters of rock. It would be difficult, if not impossible, to conduct controlled experiments on such things. Under such circumstances, a hypothesis may be tested by making detailed observations. Taking measurements is one way of making observations.

Test the Hypothesis

4 **Analyze the Results** After you have completed your experiments, made your observations, and collected your data, you must analyze all the information you have gathered. Tables and graphs are often used in this step to organize the data.

Analyze the Results

5 **Draw Conclusions** Based on the analysis of your data, you should conclude whether or not your results support your hypothesis. If your hypothesis is supported, you (or others) might want to repeat the observations or experiments to verify your results. If your hypothesis is not supported by the data, you may have to check your procedure for errors. You may even have to reject your hypothesis and make a new one. If you cannot draw a conclusion from your results, you may have to try the investigation again or carry out further observations or experiments.

Draw Conclusions

Do they support your hypothesis?

No

Yes

6 **Communicate Results** After any scientific investigation, you should report your results. By doing a written or oral report, you let others know what you have learned. They may want to repeat your investigation to see if they get the same results. Your report may even lead to another question, which in turn may lead to another investigation.

Communicate Results

Scientific Method in Action

The scientific method is not a "straight line" of steps. It contains loops in which several steps may be repeated over and over again, while others may not be necessary. For example, sometimes scientists will find that testing one hypothesis raises new questions and new hypotheses to be tested. And sometimes, testing the hypothesis leads directly to a conclusion. Furthermore, the steps in the scientific method are not always used in the same order. Follow the steps in the diagram below, and see how many different directions the scientific method can take you.

Ask a question

START

Form a hypothesis

Make observations

Test the hypothesis

Perform experiments

Analyze the results

YES

NO

Do Observations and Experiments Support Hypothesis?

YES

NO

Was process faulty?

Draw conclusions

Communicate results

Making Charts and Graphs

Circle Graphs

A circle graph, or pie chart, shows how each group of data relates to all of the data. Each part of the circle represents a category of the data. The entire circle represents all of the data. For example, a biologist studying a hardwood forest in Wisconsin found that there were five different types of trees. The data table at right summarizes the biologist's findings.

Wisconsin Hardwood Trees	
Type of tree	**Number found**
Oak	600
Maple	750
Beech	300
Birch	1,200
Hickory	150
Total	3,000

How to Make a Circle Graph

1 In order to make a circle graph of this data, first find the percentage of each type of tree. To do this, divide the number of individual trees by the total number of trees and multiply by 100.

$$\frac{600 \text{ oak}}{3,000 \text{ trees}} \times 100 = 20\%$$

$$\frac{750 \text{ maple}}{3,000 \text{ trees}} \times 100 = 25\%$$

$$\frac{300 \text{ beech}}{3,000 \text{ trees}} \times 100 = 10\%$$

$$\frac{1,200 \text{ birch}}{3,000 \text{ trees}} \times 100 = 40\%$$

$$\frac{150 \text{ hickory}}{3,000 \text{ trees}} \times 100 = 5\%$$

2 Now determine the size of the pie shapes that make up the chart. Do this by multiplying each percentage by 360°. Remember that a circle contains 360°.

$20\% \times 360° = 72°$ $25\% \times 360° = 90°$
$10\% \times 360° = 36°$ $40\% \times 360° = 144°$
$5\% \times 360° = 18°$

3 Then check that the sum of the percentages is 100 and the sum of the degrees is 360.

$20\% + 25\% + 10\% + 40\% + 5\% = 100\%$
$72° + 90° + 36° + 144° + 18° = 360°$

4 Use a compass to draw a circle and mark its center.

5 Then use a protractor to draw angles of 72°, 90°, 36°, 144°, and 18° in the circle.

6 Finally, label each part of the graph, and choose an appropriate title.

A Community of Wisconsin Hardwood Trees

Population of Appleton, 1900–2000	
Year	Population
1900	1,800
1920	2,500
1940	3,200
1960	3,900
1980	4,600
2000	5,300

Line Graphs

Line graphs are most often used to demonstrate continuous change. For example, Mr. Smith's science class analyzed the population records for their hometown, Appleton, between 1900 and 2000. Examine the data at left.

Because the year and the population change, they are the *variables*. The population is determined by, or dependent on, the year. Therefore, the population is called the **dependent variable**, and the year is called the **independent variable**. Each set of data is called a **data pair.** To prepare a line graph, data pairs must first be organized in a table like the one at left.

How to Make a Line Graph

❶ Place the independent variable along the horizontal (*x*) axis. Place the dependent variable along the vertical (*y*) axis.

❷ Label the *x*-axis "Year" and the *y*-axis "Population." Look at your largest and smallest values for the population. Determine a scale for the *y*-axis that will provide enough space to show these values. You must use the same scale for the entire length of the axis. Find an appropriate scale for the *x*-axis too.

❸ Choose reasonable starting points for each axis.

❹ Plot the data pairs as accurately as possible.

❺ Choose a title that accurately represents the data.

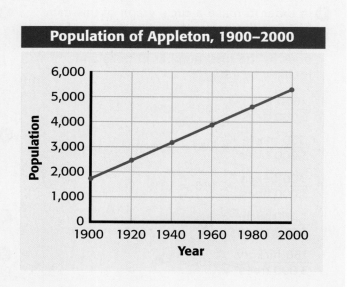

Population of Appleton, 1900–2000

How to Determine Slope

Slope is the ratio of the change in the *y*-axis to the change in the *x*-axis, or "rise over run."

❶ Choose two points on the line graph. For example, the population of Appleton in 2000 was 5,300 people. Therefore, you can define point *a* as (2000, 5,300). In 1900, the population was 1,800 people. Define point *b* as (1900, 1,800).

❷ Find the change in the *y*-axis.
(*y* at point *a*) − (*y* at point *b*)
5,300 people − 1,800 people = 3,500 people

❸ Find the change in the *x*-axis.
(*x* at point *a*) − (*x* at point *b*)
2000 − 1900 = 100 years

❹ Calculate the slope of the graph by dividing the change in *y* by the change in *x*.

$$slope = \frac{change\ in\ y}{change\ in\ x}$$

$$slope = \frac{3,500\ people}{100\ years}$$

slope = 35 people per year

In this example, the population in Appleton increased by a fixed amount each year. The graph of this data is a straight line. Therefore, the relationship is **linear.** When the graph of a set of data is not a straight line, the relationship is **nonlinear.**

Using Algebra to Determine Slope

The equation in step 4 may also be arranged to be:

$$y = kx$$

where y represents the change in the y-axis, k represents the slope, and x represents the change in the x-axis.

$$\text{slope} = \frac{\text{change in } y}{\text{change in } x}$$

$$k = \frac{y}{x}$$

$$k \times x = \frac{y \times x}{x}$$

$$kx = y$$

Bar Graphs

Bar graphs are used to demonstrate change that is not continuous. These graphs can be used to indicate trends when the data are taken over a long period of time. A meteorologist gathered the precipitation records at right for Hartford, Connecticut, for April 1–15, 1996, and used a bar graph to represent the data.

Precipitation in Hartford, Connecticut April 1–15, 1996			
Date	Precipitation (cm)	Date	Precipitation (cm)
April 1	0.5	April 9	0.25
April 2	1.25	April 10	0.0
April 3	0.0	April 11	1.0
April 4	0.0	April 12	0.0
April 5	0.0	April 13	0.25
April 6	0.0	April 14	0.0
April 7	0.0	April 15	6.50
April 8	1.75		

How to Make a Bar Graph

1 Use an appropriate scale and a reasonable starting point for each axis.

2 Label the axes, and plot the data.

3 Choose a title that accurately represents the data.

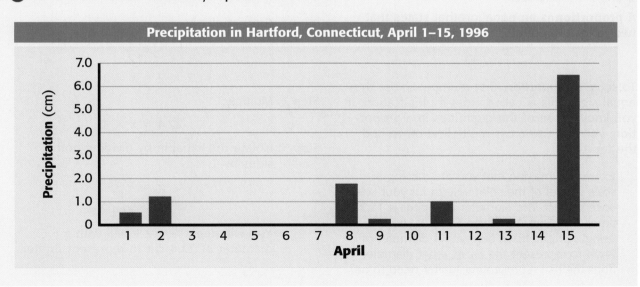

Math Refresher

Science requires an understanding of many math concepts. The following pages will help you review some important math skills.

Averages

An **average,** or **mean,** simplifies a list of numbers into a single number that *approximates* their value.

> **Example:** Find the average of the following set of numbers: 5, 4, 7, and 8.

Step 1: Find the sum.

$$5 + 4 + 7 + 8 = 24$$

Step 2: Divide the sum by the amount of numbers in your set. Because there are four numbers in this example, divide the sum by 4.

$$\frac{24}{4} = 6$$

The average, or mean, is **6.**

Ratios

A **ratio** is a comparison between numbers, and it is usually written as a fraction.

> **Example:** Find the ratio of thermometers to students if you have 36 thermometers and 48 students in your class.

Step 1: Make the ratio.

$$\frac{36 \text{ thermometers}}{48 \text{ students}}$$

Step 2: Reduce the fraction to its simplest form.

$$\frac{36}{48} = \frac{36 \div 12}{48 \div 12} = \frac{3}{4}$$

The ratio of thermometers to students is **3 to 4,** or $\frac{3}{4}$. The ratio may also be written in the form 3:4.

Proportions

A **proportion** is an equation that states that two ratios are equal.

$$\frac{3}{1} = \frac{12}{4}$$

To solve a proportion, first multiply across the equal sign. This is called cross-multiplication. If you know three of the quantities in a proportion, you can use cross-multiplication to find the fourth.

> **Example:** Imagine that you are making a scale model of the solar system for your science project. The diameter of Jupiter is 11.2 times the diameter of the Earth. If you are using a plastic-foam ball with a diameter of 2 cm to represent the Earth, what diameter does the ball representing Jupiter need to be?
>
> $$\frac{11.2}{1} = \frac{x}{2 \text{ cm}}$$

Step 1: Cross-multiply.

$$\frac{11.2}{1} \diagup\!\!\!\!\diagdown \frac{x}{2}$$

$$11.2 \times 2 = x \times 1$$

Step 2: Multiply.

$$22.4 = x \times 1$$

Step 3: Isolate the variable by dividing both sides by 1.

$$x = \frac{22.4}{1}$$

$$x = 22.4 \text{ cm}$$

You will need to use a ball with a diameter of **22.4 cm** to represent Jupiter.

Percentages

A **percentage** is a ratio of a given number to 100.

> **Example:** What is 85 percent of 40?

Step 1: Rewrite the percentage by moving the decimal point two places to the left.

$$\underset{\curvearrowleft}{.85}$$

Step 2: Multiply the decimal by the number you are calculating the percentage of.

$$0.85 \times 40 = 34$$

85 percent of 40 is **34.**

Decimals

To **add** or **subtract decimals,** line up the digits vertically so that the decimal points line up. Then add or subtract the columns from right to left, carrying or borrowing numbers as necessary.

> **Example:** Add the following numbers: 3.1415 and 2.96.

Step 1: Line up the digits vertically so that the decimal points line up.

$$\begin{array}{r} 3.1415 \\ + \ 2.96 \\ \hline \end{array}$$

Step 2: Add the columns from right to left, carrying when necessary.

$$\begin{array}{r} {}^{1\ 1} \\ 3.1415 \\ + \ 2.96 \\ \hline 6.1015 \end{array}$$

The sum is **6.1015.**

Fractions

Numbers tell you how many; **fractions** tell you *how much of a whole.*

> **Example:** Your class has 24 plants. Your teacher instructs you to put 5 in a shady spot. What fraction does this represent?

Step 1: Write a fraction with the total number of parts in the whole as the denominator.

$$\frac{?}{24}$$

Step 2: Write the number of parts of the whole being represented as the numerator.

$$\frac{5}{24}$$

$\frac{5}{24}$ of the plants will be in the shade.

Reducing Fractions

It is usually best to express a fraction in simplest form. This is called *reducing* a fraction.

> **Example:** Reduce the fraction $\frac{30}{45}$ to its simplest form.

Step 1: Find the largest whole number that will divide evenly into both the numerator and denominator. This number is called the greatest common factor (GCF).

factors of the numerator 30: 1, 2, 3, 5, 6, 10, **15,** 30

factors of the denominator 45: 1, 3, 5, 9, **15,** 45

Step 2: Divide both the numerator and the denominator by the GCF, which in this case is 15.

$$\frac{30}{45} = \frac{30 \div 15}{45 \div 15} = \frac{2}{3}$$

$\frac{30}{45}$ reduced to its simplest form is $\frac{2}{3}$.

Adding and Subtracting Fractions

To **add** or **subtract fractions** that have the **same denominator,** simply add or subtract the numerators.

Examples:

$$\frac{3}{5} + \frac{1}{5} = ? \quad \text{and} \quad \frac{3}{4} - \frac{1}{4} = ?$$

Step 1: Add or subtract the numerators.

$$\frac{3}{5} + \frac{1}{5} = \frac{4}{} \quad \text{and} \quad \frac{3}{4} - \frac{1}{4} = \frac{2}{}$$

Step 2: Write the sum or difference over the denominator.

$$\frac{3}{5} + \frac{1}{5} = \frac{4}{5} \quad \text{and} \quad \frac{3}{4} - \frac{1}{4} = \frac{2}{4}$$

Step 3: If necessary, reduce the fraction to its simplest form.

$$\frac{4}{5} \text{ cannot be reduced, and } \frac{2}{4} = \frac{1}{2}.$$

To **add** or **subtract fractions** that have **different denominators,** first find the least common denominator (LCD).

Examples:

$$\frac{1}{2} + \frac{1}{6} = ? \quad \text{and} \quad \frac{3}{4} - \frac{2}{3} = ?$$

Step 1: Write the equivalent fractions with a common demominator.

$$\frac{3}{6} + \frac{1}{6} = ? \quad \text{and} \quad \frac{9}{12} - \frac{8}{12} = ?$$

Step 2: Add or subtract.

$$\frac{3}{6} + \frac{1}{6} = \frac{4}{6} \quad \text{and} \quad \frac{9}{12} - \frac{8}{12} = \frac{1}{12}$$

Step 3: If necessary, reduce the fraction to its simplest form.

$$\frac{4}{6} = \frac{2}{3}, \text{ and } \frac{1}{12} \text{ cannot be reduced.}$$

Multiplying Fractions

To **multiply fractions,** multiply the numerators and the denominators together, and then reduce the fraction to its simplest form.

Example:

$$\frac{5}{9} \times \frac{7}{10} = ?$$

Step 1: Multiply the numerators and denominators.

$$\frac{5}{9} \times \frac{7}{10} = \frac{5 \times 7}{9 \times 10} = \frac{35}{90}$$

Step 2: Reduce.

$$\frac{35}{90} = \frac{35 \div 5}{90 \div 5} = \frac{7}{18}$$

Dividing Fractions

To **divide fractions**, first rewrite the divisor (the number you divide *by*) upside down. This is called the reciprocal of the divisor. Then you can multiply and reduce if necessary.

Example:

$$\frac{5}{8} \div \frac{3}{2} = ?$$

Step 1: Rewrite the divisor as its reciprocal.

$$\frac{3}{2} \rightarrow \frac{2}{3}$$

Step 2: Multiply.

$$\frac{5}{8} \times \frac{2}{3} = \frac{5 \times 2}{8 \times 3} = \frac{10}{24}$$

Step 3: Reduce.

$$\frac{10}{24} = \frac{10 \div 2}{24 \div 2} = \frac{5}{12}$$

Scientific Notation

Scientific notation is a short way of representing very large and very small numbers without writing all of the place-holding zeros.

> **Example:** Write 653,000,000 in scientific notation.

Step 1: Write the number without the place-holding zeros.

$$653$$

Step 2: Place the decimal point after the first digit.

$$6.53$$

Step 3: Find the exponent by counting the number of places that you moved the decimal point.

$$6.53000000$$

The decimal point was moved eight places to the left. Therefore, the exponent of 10 is positive 8. Remember, if the decimal point had moved to the right, the exponent would be negative.

Step 4: Write the number in scientific notation.

$$\textbf{6.53} \times \textbf{10}^\textbf{8}$$

Area

Area is the number of square units needed to cover the surface of an object.

> **Formulas:**
> Area of a square = side × side
> Area of a rectangle = length × width
> Area of a triangle = $\frac{1}{2}$ × base × height
>
> **Examples:** Find the areas.

Triangle
Area = $\frac{1}{2}$ × base × height
Area = $\frac{1}{2}$ × 3 cm × 4 cm
Area = **6 cm²**

Rectangle
Area = length × width
Area = 6 cm × 3 cm
Area = **18 cm²**

Square
Area = side × side
Area = 3 cm × 3 cm
Area = **9 cm²**

Volume

Volume is the amount of space something occupies.

> **Formulas:**
> Volume of a cube = side × side × side
>
> Volume of a prism = area of base × height
>
> **Examples:**
> Find the volume of the solids.

Cube
Volume = side × side × side
Volume = 4 cm × 4 cm × 4 cm
Volume = **64 cm³**

Prism
Volume = area of base × height
Volume = (area of triangle) × height
Volume = $\left(\frac{1}{2} \times 3 \text{ cm} \times 4 \text{ cm} \right) \times 5$ cm
Volume = 6 cm² × 5 cm
Volume = **30 cm³**

Periodic Table of the Elements

Each square on the table includes an element's name, chemical symbol, atomic number, and atomic mass.

Atomic number ——— 6
Chemical symbol ——— **C**
Element name ——— Carbon
Atomic mass ——— 12.0

The background color indicates the type of element. Carbon is a nonmetal.

The color of the chemical symbol indicates the physical state at room temperature. Carbon is a solid.

Background
- Metals
- Metalloids
- Nonmetals

Chemical symbol
- Solid
- Liquid
- Gas

Period 1

1
H
Hydrogen
1.0

	Group 1	Group 2
Period 2	3 **Li** Lithium 6.9	4 **Be** Beryllium 9.0
Period 3	11 **Na** Sodium 23.0	12 **Mg** Magnesium 24.3

			Group 3	Group 4	Group 5	Group 6	Group 7	Group 8	Group 9
Period 4	19 **K** Potassium 39.1	20 **Ca** Calcium 40.1	21 **Sc** Scandium 45.0	22 **Ti** Titanium 47.9	23 **V** Vanadium 50.9	24 **Cr** Chromium 52.0	25 **Mn** Manganese 54.9	26 **Fe** Iron 55.8	27 **Co** Cobalt 58.9
Period 5	37 **Rb** Rubidium 85.5	38 **Sr** Strontium 87.6	39 **Y** Yttrium 88.9	40 **Zr** Zirconium 91.2	41 **Nb** Niobium 92.9	42 **Mo** Molybdenum 95.9	43 **Tc** Technetium (97.9)	44 **Ru** Ruthenium 101.1	45 **Rh** Rhodium 102.9
Period 6	55 **Cs** Cesium 132.9	56 **Ba** Barium 137.3	57 **La** Lanthanum 138.9	72 **Hf** Hafnium 178.5	73 **Ta** Tantalum 180.9	74 **W** Tungsten 183.8	75 **Re** Rhenium 186.2	76 **Os** Osmium 190.2	77 **Ir** Iridium 192.2
Period 7	87 **Fr** Francium (223.0)	88 **Ra** Radium (226.0)	89 **Ac** Actinium (227.0)	104 **Rf** Rutherfordium (261.1)	105 **Db** Dubnium (262.1)	106 **Sg** Seaborgium (263.1)	107 **Bh** Bohrium (262.1)	108 **Hs** Hassium (265)	109 **Mt** Meitnerium (266)

A row of elements is called a period.

A column of elements is called a group or family.

Lanthanides	58 **Ce** Cerium 140.1	59 **Pr** Praseodymium 140.9	60 **Nd** Neodymium 144.2	61 **Pm** Promethium (144.9)	62 **Sm** Samarium 150.4
Actinides	90 **Th** Thorium 232.0	91 **Pa** Protactinium 231.0	92 **U** Uranium 238.0	93 **Np** Neptunium (237.0)	94 **Pu** Plutonium 244.1

These elements are placed below the table to allow the table to be narrower.

This zigzag line reminds you where the metals, nonmetals, and metalloids are.

Group 18

Group 13	Group 14	Group 15	Group 16	Group 17	2 **He** Helium 4.0
5 **B** Boron 10.8	6 **C** Carbon 12.0	7 **N** Nitrogen 14.0	8 **O** Oxygen 16.0	9 **F** Fluorine 19.0	10 **Ne** Neon 20.2

			13 **Al** Aluminum 27.0	14 **Si** Silicon 28.1	15 **P** Phosphorus 31.0	16 **S** Sulfur 32.1	17 **Cl** Chlorine 35.5	18 **Ar** Argon 39.9

Group 10	Group 11	Group 12						
28 **Ni** Nickel 58.7	29 **Cu** Copper 63.5	30 **Zn** Zinc 65.4	31 **Ga** Gallium 69.7	32 **Ge** Germanium 72.6	33 **As** Arsenic 74.9	34 **Se** Selenium 79.0	35 **Br** Bromine 79.9	36 **Kr** Krypton 83.8
46 **Pd** Palladium 106.4	47 **Ag** Silver 107.9	48 **Cd** Cadmium 112.4	49 **In** Indium 114.8	50 **Sn** Tin 118.7	51 **Sb** Antimony 121.8	52 **Te** Tellurium 127.6	53 **I** Iodine 126.9	54 **Xe** Xenon 131.3
78 **Pt** Platinum 195.1	79 **Au** Gold 197.0	80 **Hg** Mercury 200.6	81 **Tl** Thallium 204.4	82 **Pb** Lead 207.2	83 **Bi** Bismuth 209.0	84 **Po** Polonium (209.0)	85 **At** Astatine (210.0)	86 **Rn** Radon (222.0)
110 **Uun** Ununnilium (271)	111 **Uuu** Unununium (272)	112 **Uub** Ununbium (277)						

The names and symbols of elements 110–112 are temporary. They are based on the atomic number of the element. The official name and symbol will be approved by an international committee of scientists.

63 **Eu** Europium 152.0	64 **Gd** Gadolinium 157.3	65 **Tb** Terbium 158.9	66 **Dy** Dysprosium 162.5	67 **Ho** Holmium 164.9	68 **Er** Erbium 167.3	69 **Tm** Thulium 168.9	70 **Yb** Ytterbium 173.0	71 **Lu** Lutetium 175.0
95 **Am** Americium (243.1)	96 **Cm** Curium (247.1)	97 **Bk** Berkelium (247.1)	98 **Cf** Californium (251.1)	99 **Es** Einsteinium (252.1)	100 **Fm** Fermium (257.1)	101 **Md** Mendelevium (258.1)	102 **No** Nobelium (259.1)	103 **Lr** Lawrencium (262.1)

A number in parentheses is the mass number of the most stable isotope of that element.

Physical Science Refresher

Atoms and Elements

Every object in the universe is made up of particles of some kind of matter. **Matter** is anything that takes up space and has mass. All matter is made up of elements. An **element** is a substance that cannot be separated into simpler components by ordinary chemical means. This is because each element consists of only one kind of atom. An **atom** is the smallest unit of an element that has all of the properties of that element.

Atomic Structure

Atoms are made up of small particles called subatomic particles. The three major types of subatomic particles are **electrons, protons,** and **neutrons.** Electrons have a negative electric charge, protons have a positive charge, and neutrons have no electric charge. The protons and neutrons are packed close to one another to form the **nucleus.** The protons give the nucleus a positive charge. Electrons are most likely to be found in regions around the nucleus called **electron clouds.** The negatively charged electrons are attracted to the positively charged nucleus. An atom may have several energy levels in which electrons are located.

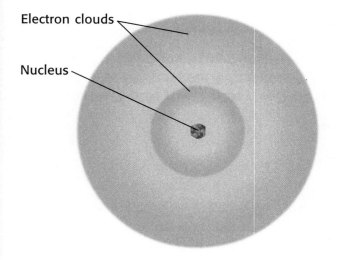

Electron clouds

Nucleus

Atomic Number

To help in the identification of elements, scientists have assigned an **atomic number** to each kind of atom. The atomic number is the number of protons in the atom. Atoms with the same number of protons are all the same kind of element. In an uncharged, or electrically neutral, atom there are an equal number of protons and electrons. Therefore, the atomic number equals the number of electrons in an uncharged atom. The number of neutrons, however, can vary for a given element. Atoms of the same element that have different numbers of neutrons are called **isotopes.**

Periodic Table of the Elements

In the periodic table, the elements are arranged from left to right in order of increasing atomic number. Each element in the table is in a separate box. An atom of each element has one more electron and one more proton than an atom of the element to its left. Each horizontal row of the table is called a **period.** Changes in chemical properties of elements across a period correspond to changes in the electron arrangements of their atoms. Each vertical column of the table, known as a **group,** lists elements with similar properties. The elements in a group have similar chemical properties because their atoms have the same number of electrons in their outer energy level. For example, the elements helium, neon, argon, krypton, xenon, and radon all have similar properties and are known as the noble gases.

Molecules and Compounds

When two or more elements are joined chemically, the resulting substance is called a **compound.** A compound is a new substance with properties different from those of the elements that compose it. For example, water, H_2O, is a compound formed when hydrogen (H) and oxygen (O) combine. The smallest complete unit of a compound that has the properties of that compound is called a **molecule.** A chemical formula indicates the elements in a compound. It also indicates the relative number of atoms of each element present. The chemical formula for water is H_2O, which indicates that each water molecule consists of two atoms of hydrogen and one atom of oxygen. The subscript number is used after the symbol for an element to indicate how many atoms of that element are in a single molecule of the compound.

Acids, Bases, and pH

An ion is an atom or group of atoms that has an electric charge because it has lost or gained one or more electrons. When an acid, such as hydrochloric acid, HCl, is mixed with water, it separates into ions. An **acid** is a compound that produces hydrogen ions, H^+, in water. The hydrogen ions then combine with a water molecule to form a hydronium ion, H_3O^+. A **base,** on the other hand, is a substance that produces hydroxide ions, OH^-, in water.

To determine whether a solution is acidic or basic, scientists use pH. The **pH** is a measure of the hydronium ion concentration in a solution. The pH scale ranges from 0 to 14. The middle point, pH = 7, is neutral, neither acidic nor basic. Acids have a pH less than 7; bases have a pH greater than 7. The lower the number is, the more acidic the solution. The higher the number is, the more basic the solution.

Chemical Equations

A chemical reaction occurs when a chemical change takes place. (In a chemical change, new substances with new properties are formed.) A chemical equation is a useful way of describing a chemical reaction by means of chemical formulas. The equation indicates what substances react and what the products are. For example, when carbon and oxygen combine, they can form carbon dioxide. The equation for the reaction is as follows: $C + O_2 \rightarrow CO_2$.

The Six Kingdoms

Kingdom Archaebacteria

The organisms in this kingdom are single-celled prokaryotes.

Archaebacteria		
Group	**Examples**	**Characteristics**
Methanogens	*Methanococcus*	found in soil, swamps, the digestive tract of mammals; produce methane gas; can't live in oxygen
Thermophiles	*Sulpholobus*	found in extremely hot environments; require sulphur, can't live in oxygen
Halophiles	*Halococcus*	found in environments with very high salt content, such as the Dead Sea; nearly all can live in oxygen

Kingdom Eubacteria

There are more than 4,000 named species in this kingdom of single-celled prokaryotes.

Eubacteria		
Group	**Examples**	**Characteristics**
Bacilli	*Escherichia coli*	rod-shaped; free-living, symbiotic, or parasitic; some can fix nitrogen; some cause disease
Cocci	*Streptococcus*	spherical-shaped, disease-causing; can form spores to resist unfavorable environments
Spirilla	*Treponema*	spiral-shaped; responsible for several serious illnesses, such as syphilis and Lyme disease

Kingdom Protista

The organisms in this kingdom are eukaryotes. There are single-celled and multicellular representatives.

Protists		
Group	**Examples**	**Characteristics**
Sacodines	*Amoeba*	radiolarians; single-celled consumers
Ciliates	*Paramecium*	single-celled consumers
Flagellates	*Trypanosoma*	single-celled parasites
Sporozoans	*Plasmodium*	single-celled parasites
Euglenas	*Euglena*	single-celled; photosynthesize
Diatoms	*Pinnularia*	most are single-celled; photosynthesize
Dinoflagellates	*Gymnodinium*	single-celled; some photosynthesize
Algae	*Volvox*, coral algae	4 phyla; single- or many-celled; photosynthesize
Slime molds	*Physarum*	single- or many-celled; consumers or decomposers
Water molds	powdery mildew	single- or many-celled, parasites or decomposers

Kingdom Fungi

There are single-celled and multicellular eukaryotes in this kingdom. There are four major groups of fungi.

Fungi		
Group	**Examples**	**Characteristics**
Threadlike fungi	bread mold	spherical; decomposers
Sac fungi	yeast, morels	saclike; parasites and decomposers
Club fungi	mushrooms, rusts, smuts	club-shaped; parasites and decomposers
Lichens	British soldier	symbiotic with algae

Kingdom Plantae

The organisms in this kingdom are multicellular eukaryotes. They have specialized organ systems for different life processes. They are classified in divisions instead of phyla.

Plants		
Group	**Examples**	**Characteristics**
Bryophytes	mosses, liverworts	reproduce by spores
Club mosses	*Lycopodium*, ground pine	reproduce by spores
Horsetails	rushes	reproduce by spores
Ferns	spleenworts, sensitive fern	reproduce by spores
Conifers	pines, spruces, firs	reproduce by seeds; cones
Cycads	*Zamia*	reproduce by seeds
Gnetophytes	*Welwitschia*	reproduce by seeds
Ginkgoes	*Ginkgo*	reproduce by seeds
Angiosperms	all flowering plants	reproduce by seeds; flowers

Kingdom Animalia

This kingdom contains multicellular eukaryotes. They have specialized tissues and complex organ systems.

Animals		
Group	**Examples**	**Characteristics**
Sponges	glass sponges	no symmetry or segmentation; aquatic
Cnidarians	jellyfish, coral	radial symmetry; aquatic
Flatworms	planaria, tapeworms, flukes	bilateral symmetry; organ systems
Roundworms	*Trichina*, hookworms	bilateral symmetry; organ systems
Annelids	earthworms, leeches	bilateral symmetry; organ systems
Mollusks	snails, octopuses	bilateral symmetry; organ systems
Echinoderms	sea stars, sand dollars	radial symmetry; organ systems
Arthropods	insects, spiders, lobsters	bilateral symmetry; organ systems
Chordates	fish, amphibians, reptiles, birds, mammals	bilateral symmetry; complex organ systems

Using the Microscope

Parts of the Compound Light Microscope

- The **ocular lens** magnifies the image 10×.

- The **low-power objective** magnifies the image 10×.

- The **high-power objective** magnifies the image either 40× or 43×.

- The **revolving nosepiece** holds the objectives and can be turned to change from one magnification to the other.

- The **body tube** maintains the correct distance between the ocular lens and objectives.

- The **coarse-adjustment knob** moves the body tube up and down to allow focusing of the image.

- The **fine-adjustment knob** moves the body tube slightly to bring the image into sharper focus.

- The **stage** supports a slide.

- **Stage clips** hold the slide in place for viewing.

- The **diaphragm** controls the amount of light coming through the stage.

- The light source provides a **light** for viewing the slide.

- The **arm** supports the body tube.

- The **base** supports the microscope.

Ocular lens

Fine-adjustment knob

Body tube

Coarse-adjustment knob

Revolving nosepiece

Objective lens

Arm

Stage clip

Stage

Diaphragm

Light

Base

Proper Use of the Compound Light Microscope

1. Carry the microscope to your lab table using both hands. Place one hand beneath the base, and use the other hand to hold the arm of the microscope. Hold the microscope close to your body while moving it to your lab table.

2. Place the microscope on the lab table at least 5 cm from the edge of the table.

3. Check to see what type of light source is used by your microscope. If the microscope has a lamp, plug it in, making sure that the cord is out of the way. If the microscope has a mirror, adjust it to reflect light through the hole in the stage.
   Caution: If your microscope has a mirror, do not use direct sunlight as a light source. Direct sunlight can damage your eyes.

4. Always begin work with the low-power objective in line with the body tube. Adjust the revolving nosepiece.

5. Place a prepared slide over the hole in the stage. Secure the slide with the stage clips.

6. Look through the ocular lens. Move the diaphragm to adjust the amount of light coming through the stage.

7. Look at the stage from eye level. Slowly turn the coarse adjustment to lower the objective until it almost touches the slide. Do not allow the objective to touch the slide.

8. Look through the ocular lens. Turn the coarse adjustment to raise the low-power objective until the image is in focus. Always focus by raising the objective away from the slide. *Never focus the objective downward.* Use the fine adjustment to sharpen the focus. Keep both eyes open while viewing a slide.

9. Make sure that the image is exactly in the center of your field of vision. Then switch to the high-power objective. Focus the image, using only the fine adjustment. *Never use the coarse adjustment at high power.*

10. When you are finished using the microscope, remove the slide. Clean the ocular lens and objective lenses with lens paper. Return the microscope to its storage area. Remember, you should use both hands to carry the microscope.

Making a Wet Mount

1. Use lens paper to clean a glass slide and a coverslip.

2. Place the specimen you wish to observe in the center of the slide.

3. Using a medicine dropper, place one drop of water on the specimen.

4. Hold the coverslip at the edge of the water and at a 45° angle to the slide. Make sure that the water runs along the edge of the coverslip.

5. Lower the coverslip slowly to avoid trapping air bubbles.

6. Water might evaporate from the slide as you work. Add more water to keep the specimen fresh. Place the tip of the medicine dropper next to the edge of the coverslip. Add a drop of water. (You can also use this method to add stain or solutions to a wet mount.) Remove excess water from the slide by using the corner of a paper towel as a blotter. Do not lift the coverslip to add or remove water.

Glossary

abdomen the body part of an animal that usually contains the gut and other digestive organs (357)

abiotic describes nonliving factors in the environment (434, 474)

absolute dating determining the age of an object or event in years, usually by measuring the amount of unstable atoms in the sample (177)

active transport the movement of particles through proteins in the cell membrane against the direction of diffusion; requires cells to use energy (86)

adaptation a characteristic that helps an organism survive in its environment (150)

addiction a physical dependence on a drug (664)

adenine (AD uh NEEN) one of the four bases that combine with sugar and phospate to form a nucleotide subunit of DNA; adenine pairs with thymine (128)

aerobic exercise vigorous, sustained exercise of the whole body for 20 minutes or more (670)

alcoholism a disorder in which a person is physically and psychologically dependent on alcohol (666)

algae (AL JEE) protists that convert the sun's energy into food through photosynthesis (246)

alien an organism that makes a home for itself in a new place (502)

alleles different forms of a single gene (111)

allergy an inappropriate immune-system reaction to a harmless antigen (645)

altricial chick (al TRISH uhl) a chick that hatches weak, naked, and helpless (406)

alveoli (al VEE uh LIE) tiny sacs that form the bronchiole branches of the lungs (557)

amnion a thin, fluid-filled membrane surrounding a placental mammal's fetus (621)

amniotic egg (AM nee AH tik) an egg containing amniotic fluid to protect the developing embryo; usually surrounded by a hard shell (400)

amphibian a type of vertebrate ectotherm that usually begins life in the water with gills and later develops lungs (382)

anaerobic describes an organism that does not need oxygen (183)

angiosperm (AN jee oh SPUHRM) a plant that produces seeds in flowers (273)

Animalia the classification kingdom containing complex, multicellular organisms that lack cell walls, are usually able to move around, and possess nervous systems that help them be aware of and react to their surroundings (213)

anorexia nervosa a disorder characterized by self-starvation and an intense fear of gaining weight (662)

antennae feelers on an arthropod's head that respond to touch, taste, or smell (358)

antibiotic a substance used to kill or slow the growth of bacteria or other microorganisms (230, 639)

antibody a special protein that can recognize specific pathogens (641)

antigen pieces of a pathogen that generate an immune response from immune-system cells (642)

anus the opening at the end of the digestive tract through which feces pass to the outside (574)

Archaebacteria (AHR kee bak TIR ee uh) a classification kingdom containing bacteria that thrive in extreme environments (209)

area the measure of how much surface an object has (24)

arteries blood vessels that carry blood away from the heart (549)

asexual reproduction reproduction in which a single parent produces offspring that are genetically identical to the parent (38, 612)

asymmetrical without symmetry (344)

ATP adenosine triphosphate; the molecule that provides energy for a cell's activities (45)

atrium an upper chamber of the heart (548)

australopithecine (ah STRA loh PITH uh seen) an early hominid that evolved more than 3.6 million years ago (190)

autoimmune disease a disease in which the immune system attacks the cells of the body it is meant to protect (646)

axon a long cell fiber in the nervous system that transfers intercellular messages (589)

B

B cell an immune-system cell that matures in bones and makes antibodies (641)

bacteria extremely small, single-celled organisms without a nucleus; prokaryotic cells (66, 209)

bilateral symmetry a body plan in which two halves of an organism's body are mirror images of each other (344)

bile a green liquid made by the liver and stored in the gallbladder; used in fat digestion (573)

binary fission the simple cell division in which one cell splits into two; used by bacteria (92, 225)

biodegradable capable of being broken down by the environment (504)

biodiversity the number and variety of living things (503)

biological clock an internal control of natural cycles (330)

biome a large region characterized by a specific type of climate and certain types of plant and animal communities (474)

bioremediation (BIE oh ri MEE dee AY shun) the use of bacteria and other microorganisms to change pollutants in soil and water into harmless chemicals (230)

biosphere the part of the Earth where life exists (437)

biotic describes living factors in the environment (434)

blood a connective tissue made up of platelets, white blood cells, red blood cells, and plasma (546)

blood pressure the amount of force exerted by blood on the inside walls of a blood vessel (551)

brain the mass of nerve tissue that is the main organ of the nervous system (591)

bronchi (BRAHNG kie) the two tubes that connect the lungs with the trachea (557)

brooding when a bird sits on its eggs until they hatch (405)

budding a type of asexual reproduction in which a small part of the parent's body develops into an independent organism (258, 612)

bulimia a disorder characterized by binge eating followed by induced vomiting to rid the body of food (662)

C

Calorie a unit that expresses the amount of energy found in food (656)

camouflage the coloration and/or texture that enables an animal to blend in with its environment (327)

cancer a condition in which certain body cells begin dividing at an uncontrolled rate (646)

capillaries the smallest blood vessels (549)

carbohydrate a biochemical composed of one or more simple sugars bonded together that is used to provide and store energy (43, 657)

carbon cycle the movement of carbon from the nonliving environment into living things and then back into the nonliving environment (459)

cardiac muscle the type of muscle found in the heart (530)

cardiovascular system a collection of organs that transport blood to and from your body's cells; the organs in this system include the heart, the arteries, and the veins (546)

carnivore a consumer that eats animals (419, 439)

carrying capacity the largest population that a given environment can support over a long period of time (445)

cartilage a flexible tissue that gives support and protection but is not rigid like bone (528)

cell a membrane-covered structure that contains all of the materials necessary for life (36)

cell cycle the life cycle of a cell; in eukaryotes it consists of chromosome duplication, mitosis, and cytokinesis (92)

cell membrane a phospholipid layer that covers a cell's surface and acts as a barrier between the inside of a cell and the cell's environment (44, 63)

cell theory the three-part theory about cells that states: (1) All organisms are composed of one or more cells, (2) the cell is the basic unit of life in all living things, and (3) all cells come from existing cells (62)

cell wall a structure that surrounds the cell membrane of some cells and provides strength and support to the cell membrane (69)

cellular respiration the process of producing ATP in the cell from oxygen and glucose; releases carbon dioxide and water (89, 305, 558)

Cenozoic era the period in the geologic time scale beginning about 65 million years ago and continuing until the present day (187)

central nervous system a collection of organs that processes all incoming and outgoing messages from the nerves; the organs in this system include the brain and the spinal cord (588)

centromere the region that holds chromatids together when a chromosome is duplicated (93)

cephalothorax (SEF uh loh THOR aks) the body part of arachnids that consists of both a head and a thorax and that usually has four pairs of legs attached (359)

cerebellum (SER uh BEL uhm) the part of the brain that keeps track of the body's position (592)

cerebrum the part of the brain that detects touch, sight, sound, odor, taste, pain, heat, and cold and controls all voluntary acts, including thought (591)

chemical digestion the process in which large molecules are broken down into simpler molecules or chemical building blocks (569)

chlorophyll a green pigment in chloroplasts that absorbs light energy for photosynthesis (270, 304)

chloroplast an organelle found in plant and algae cells where photosynthesis occurs (71)

chromatids identical chromosome copies (93)

chromosome a coiled structure of DNA and protein that forms in the cell nucleus during cell division (92)

circadian rhythm a natural, daily cycle (330)

class the level of classification after phylum; the organisms in all phyla are sorted into classes (203)

classification the arrangement of organisms into orderly groups based on their similarities and presumed evolutionary relationships (202)

closed circulatory system a circulatory system in which a heart circulates blood through a network of vessels that forms a closed loop (354)

club fungus a type of fungus characterized by umbrella-shaped mushrooms (259)

cochlea (KAHK lee uh) an ear organ that converts sound waves into electrical impulses (598)

coelom (SEE luhm) a cavity in the body of some animals where the gut and organs are located (345)

coevolution (KOH ev uh LOO shuhn) the long-term changes that take place in two species because of their close interactions with one another (448)

combustion the process of burning; includes the burning of fossil fuels (460)

commensalism (kuh MEN suhl iz uhm) a symbiotic relationship in which one organism benefits and the other is unaffected (447)

communication a transfer of a signal from one animal to another that results in some type of response (332)

community all of the populations of different species that live and interact in an area (60, 436)

compact bone the type of bone tissue that does not have open spaces (527)

competition two or more species or individuals trying to use the same limited resource (445)

compound eye an eye that is made of many identical, light-sensitive cells that work together (358)

compound light microscope a microscope that consists of a tube with lenses, a stage, and a light source (19)

cones photoreceptors that can detect bright light and help you see colors (596)

conifer a tree that produces seeds in cones (476)

connective tissue one of the four main types of tissue in the body; functions include support, protection, insulation, and nourishment (523)

conservation the wise use of and preservation of natural resources (505)

consumer an organism that eats producers or other organisms for energy (40, 227, 325, 439)

contour feather a feather made of a stiff, central shaft with many side branches called barbs (401)

controlled experiment an experiment that tests only one factor at a time (14)

cotyledon (KAHT uh LEED uhn) a seed leaf inside a seed (283)

cuticle a waxy layer that coats the surface of stems, leaves, and other plant parts exposed to air (270)

cytokinesis (SIET oh ki NEE sis) the process in which cytoplasm divides after mitosis (95)

cytoplasm cellular fluid surrounding a cell's organelles (63)

cytosine (SIET oh SEEN) one of the four bases that combine with sugar and phosphate to form a nucleotide subunit of DNA; cytosine pairs with guanine (128)

D

deciduous describes trees with leaves that change color in autumn and fall off in winter (310, 475)

decomposer an organism that gets energy by breaking down the remains of dead organisms or animal wastes and consuming or absorbing the nutrients (40, 439)

decomposition the breakdown of dead materials into carbon dioxide and water (460)

deep-water zone the zone of a lake or pond below the open-water zone where no light reaches (487)

deforestation the clearing of forest lands (503)

dendrite a short, branched extension of a neuron where the neuron receives impulses from other cells (589)

denticles small, sharp, toothlike structures on the skin of cartilaginous fishes (380)

depressant a drug that slows the actions of the central nervous system (663)

dermis the layer of skin below the epidermis (535)

desert a hot, dry biome inhabited by organisms adapted to survive high daytime temperatures and long periods without rain (479)

diaphragm (DIE uh FRAM) the sheet of muscle underneath the lungs of mammals that helps draw air into the lungs (413, 558)

dichotomous key (die KAWT uh muhs) an aid to identifying unknown organisms that consists of several pairs of descriptive statements; of each pair of statements, only one will apply to the unknown organism, and that statement will lead to another set of statements, and so on, until the unknown organism can be identified (206)

diffusion the movement of particles from an area where their concentration is high to an area where their concentration is low (84)

digestive system a collection of organs that break down food so that it can be used by the body; the organs in this system include the stomach, the pancreas, the liver, the gallbladder, the small intestine, and the large intestine (568)

diversity a measure of the number of species an area contains (477)

DNA deoxyribonucleic (dee AHKS ee RIE boh noo KLEE ik) acid; hereditary material that controls all the activities of a cell, contains the information to make new cells, and provides instructions for making proteins (38, 69, 128)

dominant trait the trait observed when at least one dominant allele for a characteristic is inherited (109)

dormant describes an inactive state of a seed (302)

down feather a fluffy, insulating feather that lies next to a bird's body (401)

drug any chemical substance that causes a physical or emotional change in a person (663)

drug abuser a person who takes drugs for a purpose other than to relieve a medical condition (667)

E

ecology the study of the interactions between organisms and their environment (434)

ecosystem a community of organisms and their nonliving environment (60, 436)

ectotherm an animal whose body temperature fluctuates with the environment's temperature (376)

egg a sex cell produced by a female (613)

electron microscope a microscope that uses tiny particles of matter to produce magnified images (20)

embryo an organism in the earliest stage of development (324, 620)

enamel the outermost layer of a tooth; the hardest material in the body (570)

endocrine system a collection of glands that control body-fluid balance, growth, and sexual development (600)

endocytosis (EN doh sie TOH sis) the process in which a cell membrane surrounds a particle and encloses it in a vesicle to bring it into the cell (87)

endoplasmic reticulum (EN doh PLAZ mik ri TIK yuh luhm) a membrane-covered cell organelle that produces lipids, breaks down drugs and other substances, and packages proteins for delivery out of the cell (70)

endoskeleton an internal skeleton (363)

endospore a bacterium surrounded by a thick, protective membrane (225)

endotherm an animal that maintains a constant body temperature despite temperature changes in its environment (376)

energy pyramid a diagram shaped like a triangle that shows the loss of energy at each level of the food chain (441)

enzyme a protein that makes it possible for certain chemical reactions to occur quickly (42, 569)

epidermis the outermost layer of the skin (535); *also* the outermost layer of cells covering roots, stems, leaves, and flower parts (285)

epididymis (EP uh DID i mis) the area of the testes where sperm are stored before they enter the vas deferens (616)

epithelial tissue one of the four main types of tissue in the body; the tissue that covers and protects underlying tissue (522)

esophagus (i SAWF uh guhs) a long, straight tube that connects the throat to the stomach (570)

estivation a period of reduced activity that some animals experience in the summer (329)

estuary an area where fresh water from streams and rivers spills into the ocean (485)

Eubacteria (YOO bak TIR ee uh) a classification kingdom containing mostly free-living bacteria found in many varied environments (209)

eukaryotic cell (eukaryote) (yoo KER ee OHT) a cell that contains a central nucleus and a complicated internal structure (67, 184)

evaporation the change of state from liquid to vapor (458)

evergreen describes trees that keep their leaves year-round (310)

evolution the process by which populations accumulate inherited changes over time (151)

excretion the process of removing wastes from the body; term used only when substances must pass through a membrane in order to leave the body (576)

exocytosis (EK soh sie TOH sis) the process used to remove large particles from a cell; during exocytosis, a vesicle containing the particles fuses with the cell membrane (87)

exoskeleton an external skeleton made of protein and chitin; found on arthropods (358)

extensor a muscle that straightens part of the body (531)

external fertilization the fertilization of eggs by sperm that occurs outside the body of the female (378, 614)

extinct describes a species of organism that has died out completely (179)

F

factor anything in an experiment that can influence the experiment's outcome (14)

fallopian tube the tube that leads from an ovary to the uterus (617)

family the level of classification after order; the organisms in all orders are sorted into families (203)

farsighted describes someone who has better vision for distant objects than for near ones (597)

fat energy-storing nutrients that help the body store some vitamins (657)

Glossary **811**

feedback controls a system that turns endocrine glands on or off (602)

fermentation the breakdown of sugars to make ATP in the absence of oxygen (89)

fetus an embryo during the later stages of development within the uterus (622)

fibrous root a type of root in which there are several roots of the same size that spread out from the base of the stem (285)

fins fanlike structures that help fish move, turn, stop, and balance (378)

flexor a muscle that bends part of the body (531)

food chain a diagram that represents how the energy in food molecules flows from one organism to the next (440)

food web a complex diagram representing the many energy pathways in a real ecosystem (440)

fossil the solidified remains or imprints of a once-living organism (152, 176)

fossil record a historical sequence of life indicated by fossils found in layers of the Earth's crust (152)

fragmentation a type of reproduction in which an organism breaks into two or more parts, each of which may grow into a separate individual (612)

Fungi a kingdom of complex organisms that obtain food by breaking down other substances in their surroundings and absorbing the nutrients (212)

fungus an organism in the kingdom Fungi (255)

funguslike protist a protist that obtains its food from dead organic matter or from the body of another organism (245)

G

gallbladder a small, baglike organ that stores bile (573)

gametophyte (guh MEET oh FIET) a stage in a plant life cycle during which eggs and sperm are produced (271)

ganglia groups of nerve cells (345)

generation time the period between the birth of one generation and the birth of the next generation (164)

genes segments of DNA that carry hereditary instructions and are passed from parent to offspring; located on chromosomes (111)

genetic engineering the manipulation of genes that allows scientists to put genes from one organism into another organism (141)

genotype the inherited combination of alleles (111)

genus the level of classification after family; the organisms in all families are sorted into genera (203)

geologic time scale the division of Earth's history into distinct intervals of time (178)

gestation period (jeh STAY shuhn) the time during which an embryo develops within the mother (416)

gills organs that remove oxygen from the water and carbon dioxide from the blood (378)

gland a group of cells that make special chemicals for the body (600)

Golgi complex the cell organelle that modifies, packages, and transports materials out of the cell (72)

gravitropism (GRAV i TROH PIZ uhm) a change in the growth of a plant in response to gravity (308)

ground water water stored in underground caverns or porous rock (459)

guanine (GWAH NEEN) one of the four bases that combine with sugar and phosphate to form a nucleotide subunit of DNA; guanine pairs with cytosine (128)

gut the pouch where food is digested in animals (345)

gymnosperm (JIM noh SPUHRM) a plant that produces seeds but not flowers (273)

H

habitat the environment where an organism lives (442)

hair follicle a small organ in the dermis layer of the skin that produces hair (536)

half-life for a particular radioactive sample, the time it takes for one-half of the sample to decay (177)

hallucinogen (huh LOO si nuh juhn) a drug that distorts the senses, causes changes in mood and thought processes, and causes hallucinations (666)

head the body part of animals where the brain is located (357)

helper T cell an immune-system cell that activates killer T cells and B cells (642)

hemoglobin (HEE moh GLOH bin) the protein in red blood cells that attaches to oxygen so that oxygen can be carried through the body (42, 546)

herbivore a consumer that eats plants (439)

heredity the passing of traits from parent to offspring (38, 106)

hibernation a period of inactivity that some animals experience in winter that allows them to survive on stored body fat (329)

homeostasis (HOH mee OH STAY sis) the maintenance of a stable internal environment (37, 522)

hominid the family referring specifically to humans and several extinct, humanlike species, some of which were human ancestors (189)

homologous chromosomes chromosomes with matching information (93)

hormone a chemical messenger that carries information from one part of an organism to the other; in mammals, hormones are made by the endocrine glands (600)

host an organism on which a parasite lives (233, 246, 350, 448)

hygiene methods of preserving and protecting your health (669)

hyphae (HIE fee) chains of cells that make up multicellular fungi (256)

hypothesis a possible explanation or answer to a question (12)

I

immune system a collection of cells, tissues, and organs that fight disease-causing agents (641)

immunity resistance to a disease (638)

imperfect fungus a fungus that does not fit into other standard groups of fungi (260)

implantation the process in which an embryo imbeds itself in the lining of the uterus (620)

impulse an electrical message that passes along a neuron (589)

infectious disease a disease caused by a pathogen (636)

infertile the state of being unable to have children (619)

innate behavior a behavior that is influenced by genes and does not depend on learning (328)

integumentary system (in TEG yoo MEN tuhr ee) a collection of organs that helps the body maintain a stable and healthy internal environment; the organs in this system include skin, hair, and nails (534)

internal fertilization the fertilization of an egg by sperm that occurs inside the body of a female (378, 614)

invertebrate an animal without a backbone (323, 344)

iris the colored part of the eye (597)

J

joint the place where two or more bones connect (528)

K

kidney a bean-shaped organ that removes many harmful substances from the blood (577)

killer T cell an immune-system cell that kills body cells infected with pathogens (642)

kingdom the most general of the seven levels of classification (203)

L

lactic-acid bacteria bacteria that digest the milk sugar lactose and convert it into lactic acid (231)

landmark a fixed object used to determine location during navigation (331)

large intestine a large organ that reabsorbs water from the digestive tract and stores, compacts, and eliminates indigestible material from the body (574)

larynx (LER ingks) the area of the throat that contains the vocal cords (557)

lateral line system a row or rows of tiny sense organs along the sides of a fish's body (378)

learned behavior a behavior that has been learned from experience or observation (328)

lens a curved, transparent object that forms an image by refracting light (597)

lichen the combination of a fungus and an alga that grows intertwined and exists in a symbiotic relationship (261)

life science the study of living things (6)

lift an upward force on an object caused by differences in pressure above and below the object; lift opposes the downward pull of gravity (404)

ligament a strong band of tissue that connects bones to bones (529)

limiting factor a needed resource that is in limited supply (444)

lipid a type of biochemical, including fats and oils, that does not dissolve in water; lipids store energy and make up cell membranes (44)

littoral zone the zone of a lake or pond closest to the edge of the land (487)

liver a large, reddish brown organ that produces bile and stores nutrients; the liver has more than 200 functions in the body (573)

lung a saclike organ that takes oxygen from the air and delivers it to the blood (382)

lymph the fluid and particles absorbed into lymph capillaries (554)

lymph nodes small, bean-shaped organs that contain small fibers that work like nets to remove particles from the lymph (555)

lymphatic system a collection of organs that collect extracellular fluid and return it to the blood; the organs in this system include the lymph nodes and the lymphatic vessels (554)

lysosome a special vesicle in a cell that digests food particles, wastes, and foreign invaders (74)

M

macrophage an immune-system cell that engulfs pathogens (641)

malnutrition   a disorder resulting from not consuming the right combination of nutrients (662)

mammary glands   glands that secrete a nutritious fluid called milk (411)

mandible   a jaw found on some arthropods (359)

marine   describes an ecosystem based on salty water (481)

marsh   a treeless wetland ecosystem where such plants as cattails and rushes grow (488)

marsupial   a mammal that gives birth to live, partially developed young that continue to develop inside the mother's pouch or skin fold (415, 615)

mass   the amount of matter that something is made of; its value does not change with the object's location (26)

mass extinction   a period when a large number of species die out at the same time (179)

matter   anything that occupies space and has mass (458)

mechanical digestion   the breaking, crushing, and mashing of food (569)

medulla   (mi DOOL uh) the part of the brain that connects to the spinal cord and controls many involuntary processes in the body (592)

medusa   a body form of some cnidarians; resembles a mushroom with tentacles (348)

meiosis   cell division that produces sex cells (115, 613)

melanin   a darkening chemical in the skin that determines skin color (534)

memory B cell   an immune-system cell that "remembers" how to make a specialized antibody for a particular pathogen (644)

menstruation   the monthly discharge of blood and tissue from the uterus (617)

Mesozoic era   the period in the geologic time scale beginning about 248 million years ago and ending about 65 million years ago (186)

metabolism   (muh TAB uh LIZ uhm) the combined chemical processes that occur in a cell or living organism (38)

metamorphosis   the process in which an insect or other animal changes form as it develops from an embryo or larva to an adult (361, 384)

meter   the basic unit of length in the SI system (23)

migrate   to travel from one place to another in response to the seasons or environmental conditions (329)

mineral   an element that is essential for good health (658)

mitochondria   (MIET oh KAHN dree uh) cell organelles surrounded by two membranes that break down food molecules to make ATP (71)

mitosis   nuclear division in eukaryotic cells in which each cell receives a copy of the original chromosomes (93)

mold   shapeless, fuzzy fungi (257)

monotreme   a mammal that lays eggs (414, 615)

motor neuron   a neuron that sends impulses from the brain and spinal cord to other systems (590)

multicellular   made of many cells (59, 323)

muscle tissue   one of the four main types of tissue in the body; contains cells that contract and relax to produce movement (523)

muscular system   a collection of organs whose primary function is movement; organs in this system include the muscles and the connective tissue that attaches them to bones (530)

mutagen   anything that can damage or cause changes in DNA (138)

mutation   a change in the order of the bases in an organism's DNA; deletion, insertion, or substitution (138, 163)

mutualism   (MYOO choo uhl IZ uhm) a symbiotic relationship in which both organisms benefit (447)

mycelium   (mie SEE lee uhm) a twisted mass of fungal hyphae that have grown together (256)

N

narcotics   drugs made from opium (667)

natural selection   the process by which organisms with favorable traits survive and reproduce at a higher rate than organisms without the favorable trait (162)

Neanderthal   a species of hominid that lived in Europe and western Asia from 230,000 years ago to about 30,000 years ago (192)

nearsighted   describes someone who has better vision for near objects than for distant ones (597)

nephron   a microscopic filter in the kidney that removes a variety of harmful substances from the blood (577)

nerve   an axon bundled together with blood vessels and connective tissue (590)

nervous system   a collection of organs that gather and interpret information about the body's internal and external environment and respond to that information; the organs in this system include the brain, nerves, and spinal cord (588)

nervous tissue   one of the four main types of tissue in the body; the tissue that sends electrical signals through the body (522)

neuron   a specialized cell that transfers messages throughout the body in the form of fast-moving electrical energy (589)

niche   an organism's way of life and its relationships with its abiotic and biotic environments (442)

nicotine a chemical stimulant found in tobacco that increases heart rate and blood pressure (665)

nitrogen cycle the movement of nitrogen from the nonliving environment into living organisms and back again (460)

nitrogen fixation the process of changing nitrogen gas into forms that plants can use (461)

noninfectious disease a disease that cannot spread from one person to another (636)

nonrenewable resource a natural resource that cannot be replaced or that can be replaced only over thousands or millions of years (501)

nonvascular plant a plant that depends on the processes of diffusion and osmosis to move materials from one part of the plant to another (272)

nucleic acid a biochemical that stores information needed to build proteins and other nucleic acids; made up of subunits called nucleotides (45)

nucleotide a subunit of DNA consisting of a sugar, a phosphate, and one of four nitrogenous bases (45, 128)

nucleus the membrane-covered organelle found in eukaryotic cells; contains the cell's DNA and serves as a control center for the cell (66)

nutrient a substance that must be consumed or taken in by an organism to promote normal growth, maintenance, and repair (569, 656)

O

obesity a disorder characterized by an extremely high percentage of body fat (662)

omnivore a consumer that eats a variety of organisms (439)

open circulatory system a circulatory system consisting of a heart that pumps blood through spaces called sinuses (354)

open-water zone the zone of a lake or pond that extends from the littoral zone out across the top of the water and that is only as deep as light can reach through the water (487)

optic nerve a nerve that transfers electrical impulses from the eye to the brain (596)

order the level of classification after class; the organisms in all the classes are sorted into orders (203)

organ a combination of two or more tissues that work together to perform a specific function in the body (57, 324, 523)

organ system a group of organs that works together to perform body functions (58, 523)

organelle (OHR guh NEL) a structure within a cell, sometimes surrounded by a membrane (63)

organism anything that can independently carry out life processes (59)

osmosis the diffusion of water across a cell membrane (85)

ovary in animals, an organ in the female reproductive system producing eggs (617); in flowers, the structure containing ovules that will develop into fruit following fertilization (291)

overpopulation a condition that occurs when the number of individuals within an environment becomes so large that there are not enough resources to support them all (502)

ovulation the process in which an egg is ejected through the ovary wall (617)

ozone a gas molecule that is made up of three oxygen atoms; absorbs ultraviolet radiation from the sun (184)

P

Paleozoic era the period in the geologic time scale beginning about 570 million years ago and ending about 248 million years ago (185)

pancreas a fish-shaped organ between the stomach and small intestine that produces enzymes for chemical digestion (572)

Pangaea the single landmass that contained all the present-day continents 200 million years ago (180)

parasite an organism that feeds on another living creature, usually without killing it (246, 350, 448)

parasitism (PAR uh SIET IZ uhm) a symbiotic association in which one organism benefits while the other is harmed (448)

passive transport the diffusion of particles through proteins in the cell membrane from areas where the concentration of particles is high to areas where the concentration of particles is low (86)

pasteurization a method of heating food and beverages to kill bacteria (638)

pathogen an agent that causes a disease (636)

pathogenic bacteria bacteria that invade a host organism and obtain the nutrients they need from the host's cells (232)

pedigree a diagram of family history used for tracing a trait through several generations (140)

penis the male reproductive organ that transfers semen into the female's body during sexual intercourse (616)

peripheral nervous system the collection of communication pathways, or nerves, whose primary function is to transfer information from all areas of the body and the outside environment to the central nervous system and from the central nervous system to the rest of the body (588)

peristalsis (PER uh STAHL sis) a rhythmic muscle contraction in the digestive tract (570)

permafrost the permanently frozen ground below the soil surface in the arctic tundra (480)

petals   the often colorful structures on a flower that are usually involved in attracting pollinators (290)

pharynx   (FER ingks) the upper portion of the throat (557)

phenotype   an organism's inherited appearance (111)

pheromone   a chemical produced by animals for communication (333)

phloem   (FLOH EM) a specialized plant tissue that transports sugar molecules from one part of the plant to another (284)

phospholipid   a type of lipid molecule that forms much of a cell's membrane (44)

photoreceptors   specialized neurons in the retina that detect light (596)

photosynthesis   (FOHT oh SIN thuh sis) the process by which plants capture light energy from the sun and convert it into sugar (88, 184, 270)

phototropism   a change in the growth of a plant in response to light (307)

phylum   the level of classification after kingdom; the organisms from all the kingdoms are sorted into several phyla (203)

phytoplankton   (FITE oh PLANK tuhn) a microscopic photosynthetic organism that floats near the surface of the ocean (481)

pioneer species   the first organisms to grow in an area undergoing ecological succession; usually lichens in primary succession and fast-growing, weedy plants in secondary succession (463)

pistils   the female reproductive structures in a flower that consist of a stigma, a style, and an ovary (291)

placenta   a special organ of exchange that provides a developing fetus with nutrients and oxygen (416, 621)

placental mammal   a mammal that nourishes its unborn offspring with a placenta inside the uterus and gives birth to well-developed young (416, 615)

plankton   very small organisms floating at or near the ocean's surface that form the base of the ocean's food web (481)

Plantae   the kingdom that contains plants—complex, multicellular organisms that are usually green and use the sun's energy to make sugar by photosynthesis (211)

plasma   the fluid part of blood (546)

plate tectonics   the study of the forces that drive the movement of pieces of Earth's crust around the surface of the planet (181)

platelet   a cell fragment that helps clot blood (547)

pollen   the dustlike particles that carry the male gametophyte of seed plants (278)

pollination   the transfer of pollen to the female cone in conifers or to the stigma in angiosperms (281)

pollutant   a harmful substance in an environment (498)

pollution   the presence of harmful substances in an environment (498)

polyp   a body form of some cnidarians; resembles a vase (348)

population   a group of individuals of the same species that live together in the same area at the same time (59, 436)

Precambrian time   the period in the geologic time scale beginning when Earth originated, 4.6 billion years ago, and ending when complex organisms appeared, about 540 million years ago (182)

precipitation   water that moves from the atmosphere to the land and ocean, including rain, snow, sleet, and hail (458)

precocial chick   (pree KOH shuhl) a chick that leaves the nest immediately after hatching and is fully active (406)

predator   an organism that eats other organisms (326, 446)

preening   the activity in which a bird uses its beak to spread oil on its feathers (401)

prescription   a note written by a doctor to allow a patient to buy a medicine (664)

prey   an organism that is eaten by another organism (326, 446)

primate   a type of mammal that includes humans, apes, and monkeys; typically distinguished by opposable thumbs and binocular vision (188, 423)

probability   the mathematical chance that an event will occur (112)

producer   organisms that make their own food, usually by using the energy from sunlight to make sugar (40, 227, 438)

prokaryotic cell (prokaryote)   (proh KER ee OHT) a cell that does not have a nucleus or any other membrane-covered organelles; also called a bacterium (66, 183, 224)

prosimian   the first primate ancestors; *also* a group of living primates that includes lorises and lemurs (190)

protein   a biochemical that is composed of amino acids; its functions include regulating chemical reactions, transporting and storing materials, and providing support (42, 657)

protist   an organism that belongs to the kingdom Protista (244)

Protista   a kingdom of eukaryotic single-celled or simple, multicellular organisms; kingdom Protista contains all eukaryotes that are not plants, animals, or fungi (210)

protozoa animal-like protists that are single-celled consumers (250)

pseudopodia (soo doh POH dee uh) structures that amoebas use to move around (250)

puberty the time of life when the sex organs become mature (616)

pulmonary circulation the circulation of blood between the heart and lungs (550)

Punnett square a tool used to visualize all the possible combinations of alleles from parents (111)

pupil the opening to the inside of the eye (597)

R

radial symmetry a body plan in which the parts of the body are arranged in a circle around a central point (344)

receptor a specialized cell, sometimes a dendrite, that detects changes inside or outside the body (590)

recessive trait a trait that is apparent only when two recessive alleles for the same characteristic are inherited (109)

rectum the last section of the large intestine; where fecal material is stored until it can be expelled from the body (574)

recycling the process of making new products from reprocessed used products (507)

red blood cell a cell that carries oxygen from the lungs to all cells of the body and carries carbon dioxide back to the lungs to be exhaled (546)

reflex a quick, involuntary response to a stimulus (594)

relative dating determining whether an event or object, such as a fossil, is older or younger than other events or objects (177)

renewable resource a natural resource that can be used and replaced over a relatively short time period (501)

resource recovery the process of transforming into usable products things normally thrown away (508)

respiration the exchange of gases between living cells and their environment; includes breathing and cellular respiration (556); *see* cellular respiration

respiratory system a collection of organs whose primary function is to take in oxygen and expel carbon dioxide; the organs of this system include the lungs, the throat, and the passageways that lead to the lungs (556)

retina a layer of light-sensitive cells in the back of the eye (596)

rhizoids small, hairlike threads of cells that help hold nonvascular plants in place (274)

rhizome the underground stem of a fern (276)

ribosome a small organelle in cells where proteins are made from amino acids (70, 137)

rods photoreceptors that detect very dim light (596)

S

sac fungus a type of fungus that reproduces using spores, which develop in a sac called an ascus (250)

salivary glands organs located around the mouth that produce a liquid that begins chemical digestion (570)

saturated fat a type of fat found in meats, dairy products, coconut oil, and palm oil; known to raise blood cholesterol levels (658)

savanna a tropical grassland biome with scattered clumps of trees (478)

scales bony structures that cover the skin of bony fishes (380)

scavenger an animal that feeds on the bodies of dead animals (439)

scientific method a series of steps that scientists use to answer questions and solve problems (10)

scrotum a skin-covered sac that hangs from the male body and contains the testes (616)

sediment fine particles of sand, dust, or mud that are deposited over time by wind or water (176)

segment one of many identical or almost identical repeating body parts (355)

selective breeding the breeding of organisms that have a certain desired trait (160)

self-pollinating plant a plant that contains both male and female reproductive structures (107)

semen a mixture of sperm and fluids (616)

seminiferous tubules (SEM uh NIF uhr uhs TOO BYOOLZ) the coiled tubes inside the testes where sperm cells are produced (616)

sensory neuron a special neuron that gathers information about what is happening in and around the body and sends this information on to the central nervous system (590)

sepals the leaflike structures that cover and protect an immature flower (290)

sex cell an egg or sperm; a sex cell carries half the number of chromosomes found in other body cells (114)

sex chromosomes the chromosomes that carry genes that determine the sex of offspring (119)

sexual reproduction reproduction in which two sex cells join to form a zygote; sexual reproduction produces offspring that share characteristics of both parents (38, 613)

sexually transmitted disease a disease that can pass from an infected person to an uninfected person during sexual contact (619)

skeletal muscle the type of muscle that moves bones and helps protect inner organs (530)

skeletal system a collection of organs whose primary function is to support and protect the body; the organs in this system include bones, cartilage, ligaments, and tendons (526)

small intestine a muscular tube about 2.5 cm in diameter and up to 6 m long; the site of most chemical digestion (572)

smooth muscle the type of muscle found in the blood vessels and the digestive tract (530)

social behavior the interaction between animals of the same species (332)

speciation the process by which two populations of the same species become so different that they can no longer interbreed (166)

species the most specific of the seven levels of classification; characterized by a group of organisms that can mate with one another to produce fertile offspring (150, 203)

sperm a sex cell produced by a male (613)

spleen an organ that filters blood and produces lymphocytes (555)

spongy bone a type of bone tissue that has many open spaces and contains marrow (527)

spore a small reproductive cell protected by a thick wall (256)

sporophyte (SPOH roh FIET) a stage in a plant life cycle during which spores are produced (271)

stamen the male reproductive structure in a flower that consists of a filament topped by a pollen-producing anther (291)

stigma the flower part that is located at the tip of the pistil (291)

stimulant a drug that speeds up the action of the central nervous system (663)

stimulus anything that affects the activity of an organism, organ, or tissue (37, 307)

stomach a muscular, baglike organ of the digestive tract that is attached to the lower end of the esophagus (571)

stomata openings in the epidermis and cuticle of a leaf that allow carbon dioxide to enter the leaf (289, 306)

stress a physical and mental response to situations that create pressure (671)

succession the gradual regrowth or development of a community of organisms over time (462)

surface-to-volume ratio the amount of a cell's outer surface in relationship to its volume (64)

swamp a wetland ecosystem in which trees and vines grow (489)

sweat glands small organs in the dermis layer of the skin that release sweat (534)

swim bladder a balloonlike organ that is filled with oxygen and other gases; gives bony fish their buoyancy (380)

symbiosis (SIM bie OH sis) a close, long-term association between two or more species (251, 447)

systemic circulation the circulation of blood between the heart and the body (excluding the lungs) (550)

T

T cell an immune-system cell that matures in the thymus (641)

tadpole the aquatic larvae of an amphibian (384)

taproot a type of root that consists of one main root that grows downward, with many smaller branch roots coming out of it (285)

taxonomy the science of identifying, classifying, and naming living things (204)

technology the application of knowledge, tools, and materials to solve problems and accomplish tasks; technology can also refer to the objects used to accomplish tasks (18)

temperature a measure of how hot or cold something is (26)

tendon a tough connective tissue that connects skeletal muscles to bones (531)

territory an area occupied by one animal or a group of animals from which other members of the species are excluded (332)

testes the organs in the male reproductive system that make sperm and testosterone (616)

theory a unifying explanation for a broad range of hypotheses and observations that have been supported by experimentation (18)

therapsid (thuh RAP sid) a prehistoric reptile ancestor of mammals (387, 410)

thorax the central body part of an arthropod or other animal; where the heart and lungs are located (357)

threadlike fungus a fungus that develops from a spore called a zygospore (257)

thymine one of the four bases that combine with sugar and phosphate to form a nucleotide subunit of DNA; thymine pairs with adenine (128)

thymus a lymph organ that produces lymphocytes (555)

tissue a group of similar cells that work together to perform a specific job in the body (57, 324, 522)

tonsils small masses of soft tissue located at the back of the nasal cavity, on the inside of the throat, and at the back of the tongue (555)

toxic poisonous (499)

trachea (TRAY kee uh) the air passageway from the larynx to the lungs (557)

trait a distinguishing quality that can be passed from one generation to another (160)

transpiration the loss of water from plant leaves through openings called stomata (306)

tributary a small stream or river that flows into a larger one (486)

tropism a change in the growth of a plant in response to a stimulus (307)

true-breeding plant a plant that always produces offspring with the same traits as the parent(s) (108)

tundra a far-northern biome characterized by long, cold winters, permafrost, and few trees (480)

U

umbilical cord the cord that connects an embryo to a placenta (621)

unicellular made of a single cell (59)

unsaturated fat a type of fat that usually comes from plant sources and helps reduce blood cholesterol levels (658)

ureter a slender tube that carries urine from each kidney to the urinary bladder (577)

urethra in males, a slender tube that carries urine and semen through the penis to the outside; in females, a slender tube that carries urine to the outside (577, 616)

urinary bladder a baglike organ that stores urine until it can be eliminated through the urethra (577)

urinary system a collection of organs that remove waste from the blood; this system includes the kidneys, ureters, urethra, and the urinary bladder (576)

urine a concentrated mixture of waste materials that forms in the nephrons of the kidney (577)

uterus the organ in the female reproductive system where a zygote grows and develops (617)

V

vaccine a substance that helps the body develop an immunity to a pathogen (638)

vacuole (VAK yoo OHL) a large membrane-covered structure found in plant cells that serves as a storage container for water and other liquids (73)

vagina the passageway in the female reproductive system that receives sperm during sexual intercourse (617)

variable a factor in a controlled experiment that changes (14)

vas deferens (vas DEF uh RENZ) a tube in males where sperm is mixed with fluids to make semen (616)

vascular plant a plant that has specialized tissues called xylem and phloem, which move materials from one part of the plant to another (273)

veins blood vessels that direct blood to the heart (549)

ventricle a lower chamber of the heart (548)

vertebrae (VUHR tuh BRAY) segments of bone or cartilage that interlock to form a backbone (375)

vertebrate an animal with a skull and a backbone; includes mammals, birds, reptiles, amphibians, and fish (322, 374)

vesicle a membrane-covered compartment in a eukaryotic cell that forms when part of the cell membrane surrounds an object and pinches off (73)

vestigial structure (ves TIJ ee uhl) the remnant of a once-useful anatomical structure (153)

villi fingerlike projections on the inside wall of the small intestine (572)

virus a microscopic particle that invades a cell and often destroys it (233)

vitamin an organic compound that controls many body functions, including cell growth and hormone production (659)

volume the amount of space that something occupies or the amount of space that something contains (24)

W

water cycle the movement of water between the ocean, atmosphere, land, and living things (458)

water vascular system a system of water pumps and canals found in all echinoderms that allows them to move, eat, and breathe (364)

wetland an area of land where the water level is near or above the surface of the ground for most of the year (488)

white blood cell a blood cell that protects the body against pathogens (547)

X

xylem (ZIE luhm) a specialized plant tissue that transports water and minerals from one part of the plant to another (284)

Z

zooplankton (ZOH oh PLANGK tuhn) protozoa that, along with the phytoplankton they consume, form the base of the ocean's food web (481)

zygote a fertilized egg (613)

Boldface numbers refer to an illustration on that page.

resource
    depletion, 501, **501**
    nonrenewable, 501, 506
    recovery, 508, **508**
    recycling of, 508, **508**
    renewable, 501
respiration, 556. *See also* cellular
    respiration
    in carbon cycle, **459,** 460
respiratory system, **524,** 556–559,
    556–558
    air flow through, 556–558, **556,**
        558
    cilia in, **665**
    disorders of, 559, **559**
    parts of, 556–557, **556–557**
retina, 596, **596**
rheumatoid arthritis, 646, **646**
rhinoceros, **410,** 420
rhizoids, 274–275
rhizome, 276
rib cage, **526,** 558
ribosomes, 66, **66,** 70, **70, 74,** 75,
    137, **137**
ring canal, **364**
ringworm, 637
river, 60, 486, **486**
rodents, 417, **417**
rods (photoreceptors), 596
root cap, 285, **285**
root hair, 285
roots, 284–285, **284–285**
    functions of, 284
    fungi growing on, 255
    gravitropism of, 308, **308**
    structure of, 285, **285**
    types of, 285, **285**
rose, 278, 282–283
roundworms, 351, **351**
runner (plant), **303**
rusts, 260

S

sac fungi, 258, **258**
safety
    drug safety tips, 664
    at home, 672, **672**
    outdoors, 672
    on road, 672
safety rules, 27, 682–685
safety symbols, **27,** 682–685,
    682–685
salamanders, **40,** 382–385,
    382–383, 385, 487
saliva, 570, 578, 584, 653
salivary glands, 568, **568,** 570
Salmonella, 637
salt-loving bacteria, 228, **228**
salt marsh, 436–437, **436–437**
sand dollar, 363, 365, **365**
sandy beach, 482, 485
Sargasso Sea, 484, **484**
Sargassum, 484

saturated fats, 658, 679
savanna, **474,** 478, **478**
scarlet tanager, 409, **409**
scavenger, 439, **439**
Schleiden, Matthias, 62
school (fish), 446
Schwann, Theodor, 62
scientific method, 10–17, **10, 17,**
    790–792
    analyzing results of an
        experiment, 16, **16**
    communicating results of an
        experiment, 17, **17**
    data collection, 11, **11**
    drawing conclusions, 16
    hypothesis, 12–16, **12**
    observations, 11
    predictions, 13
    testing the hypothesis, 14–15,
        15
scientific name, 205–206
scientific notation, 799
scolex, 585
scrambled egg slime mold, 245
scrotum, 616, **616**
sea anemone, 325, 344, **345, 348,**
    349, **482**
sea croaker, **436**
sea cucumber, 363, 365, **365**
seals, 411, 419
seaside sparrow, 436, **437**
seasonal
    behavior of animals, 329, **329**
    responses in plants, 309–311,
        309–311
seasons
    causes of, 309, **309**
sea star, 324, 363–364, **363–364,**
    482, 484, 485, 612, **612**
seat belts, 672
sea turtle, 390, **390, 482**
sea urchin, 363, **363,** 365, **483,**
    484
seaweed, 246–247, **246, 444**
secondary succession, 464
sedatives, 663
sediment, 176, **176**
seed, 279, **279,** 291
    characteristics in garden pea,
        108–110, **108–110,** 118, **118**
    development of, 301, **301**
    dormant, 302
    germination of, 279, 302, **302**
    structure of, 279, **279**
seed coat, 279, **279**
seedless plants, 274–277, **274–277**
seed plants, 278–287, **278–287**
segments
    in annelids, 355, **355**
    in arthropods, 357
selective breeding, 104, 141, 160
self-pollinating plant, 107, **107**
semen, 616, **616**
seminiferous tubules, 616, **616**
semivegetarian diet, 679

senses, 595–599
sensory lobes
    of flatworms, 350, **350**
sensory neuron, 590, 593
sensory receptors, 595, **595**
sepal, 290, **290**
sewage treatment plant, 574
sex cells, 114–115, 271, **271,** 613,
    613
sex chromosomes, 119, **119**
sexually transmitted disease, 619
sexual reproduction, 38, **38,** 114,
    254, **254,** 256, 324, **324,** 613,
    613
shark, **324,** 379–380, **379**
    denticles of, 380, **380**
    relationship with remoras, 447,
        447
shell
    of amniotic egg, 373, **373,**
        388–389, **389**
    of mollusks, **353**
    of protozoa, 251, **251**
    of turtle, 390
shrew, 417, 480
shrimp, **344,** 359, **436**
Siberian tiger, 9, **9,** 419
sickle cell anemia, 139, **139**
sieve plate, **364**
Silurian period, **178**
simple carbohydrates, 657
sinuses, 354
sirenia, 422
SI units, 22, **22,** 787
    conversion chart, 22, 787
    prefixes, 787
skeletal muscle, 526, 530–531,
    530–531, 554
skeletal system, 524, 526–529,
    526–529
    comparing structures from differ-
        ent species, 156, **156**
    differences between hominids
        and other primates, 189, **190**
    storage function, 526
    support function, 526
skin, 57, **57**
    of amphibians, 383, **383**
    of cartilaginous fishes, 380, **380**
    color of, 534, **534**
    follicle mites on, 454
    functions of, 534
    infections on, 537
    layers of, 535, **535**
    as a protective barrier, 537, 640,
        640
    receptors in, 595, **595**
    of reptiles, 388, **388**
    wound healing, 537, **537**
skin cancer, 138, 184, 500, 534,
    537, **537**
skunk, 200, **200,** 206, 327, 329
sleep, 670, **670**
sliding joint, **528**
slime mold, 210, **210, 244–245,** 245

INDEX

Credits

Abbreviations used: (t) top, (c) center, (b) bottom, (l) left, (r) right, (bkgd) background

ILLUSTRATIONS

All illustrations, unless otherwise noted below by Holt, Rinehart and Winston.

Huxtable/Black Creative; 529, John Huxtable/Black Creative; 531 (br), Christy Krames; 535 (br), Morgan-Cain & Associates; 535 (cr), Marty Roper/Planet Rep; 537 (t), Morgan-Cain & Associates; 538 (br), John Huxtable/Black Creative 540 (br), Christy Krames; 541 (tr), Morgan-Cain & Associates.

Chapter Twenty Three Page 546 (tr), Christy Krames; 547 (b), Keith Kasnot; 548, Kip Carter; 549 (c), Kip Carter; 550 (b), Kip Carter; 552 (tl), Jared Schneidman Design; 552 (br), Marty Roper/Planet Rep; 554 (br), Kip Carter; 555 (tr), Christy Krames; 556 (bl), Christy Krames; 557 (b), Christy Krames; 558 (br), Christy Krames; 558 (bc,bl), Kip Carter; 560 (br), Christy Krames; 562 (tl), Kip Carter; 563 (cr), Kip Carter.

Chapter Twenty Four Page 568 (bc), Christy Krames; 569 (b), Brian Evans; 570 (tl,bl), Keith Kasnot; 571 (cl), Christy Krames; 571 (cr), Brian Evans; 572 (tl), Marty Roper/Planet Rep; 572 (cl), Christy Krames; 572 (c), Brian Evans; 573, Christy Krames; 574 (br), Christy Krames; 576 (cl), Christy Krames; 577 (br), Keith Kasnot; 580 (cr), Brian Evans; 580 (tr), Keith Kasnot; 581 (tr), Christy Krames; 582 (br), Keith Kasnot; 582 (tr), Brian Evans.

Chapter Twenty Five Page 588 (bl), Christy Krames; 589 (b), Scott Thorn Barrows/The Neis Group; 590 (b), Scott Thorn Barrows/The Neis Group; 591 (bc), Brian Evans; 592 (b), Brian Evans; 593 (tr), Christy Krames; 595 (b), Morgan-Cain & Associates; 596 (bc), Keith Kasnot; 596 (br), Carlyn Iverson; 597 (bl), Keith Kasnot; 598 (b), Christy Krames; 599 (tr), Keith Kasnot; 600 (b), Dan McGeehan/Koralick Associates; 601 (b), Christy Krames; 602, Christy Krames; 604 (br), Keith Kasnot; 605 (cl), Dan McGeehan/Koralick Associates; 606 (tr), Christy Krames; 607 (tr), Christy Krames.

Chapter Twenty Six Page 613 (bl), Rob Schuster/Hankins and Tegenborg; 616 (bl), Keith Kasnot; 617 (tr), Keith Kasnot; 618 (br), Rob Schuster/Hankins and Tegenborg; 620 (cl), David Fischer; 621 (cr), Christy Krames; 629 (cr), Sidney Jablonski; 630 (bl), Morgan-Cain & Associates.

Chapter Twenty Seven Page 640 (br), Scott Thorn Barrows/The Neis Group; 641 (bl), Scott Thorn Barrows/The Neis Group; 642-643, Blake Thornton/Rita Marie; 644 (l), Stephen Durke/Washington Artists; 648 (br), Blake Thornton/Rita Marie; 650 (bc), Scott Thorn Barrows/The Neis Group; 651 (tr), Sidney Jablonski.

Chapter Twenty Eight Page 667 (br), Marty Roper/Planet Rep; 672 (c), Uhl Studios, Inc.; 675 (tl), Marty Roper/Planet Rep.

LabBook Page 691 (cr), Keith Locke; 693 (br), Blake Thornton/Rita Marie; 694 (tl), David Merrell/Suzanne Craig Represents Inc.; 694 (cr), Rob Schuster/Hankins and Tegenborg; 697 (cr), Morgan-Cain & Associates; 704 (br), Kip Carter; 706 (b), Rob Schuster/Hankins and Tegenborg; 708 (r), Frank Ordaz/Dimension; 709 (tr,br), John White/The Neis Group; 710 (br), Keith Locke; 711 (cr), Keith Locke; 715 (br,cr), Rob Schuster/Hankins and Tegenborg; 716 (b,r), Rob Schuster/Hankins and Tegenborg; 717 (r), Keith Locke; 718, Rob Schuster/Hankins and Tegenborg; 719 (cr), Rob Schuster/Hankins and Tegenborg; 720 (br), Keith Locke; 723 (cr), Will Nelson/Sweet Reps; 724 (cr), Will Nelson/Sweet Reps; 725 (tr), Cori Zeller; 725 (br), Will Nelson/Sweet Reps; 727 (cr), Sarah Woodward/Morgan-Cain & Associates; 729 (br), John White/The Neis Group; 733 (br), Carlyn Iverson; 734 (br), Keith Locke/Suzanne Craig Represents Inc.; 735 (tr), John White/The Neis Group; 737 (br), Marty Roper/Planet Rep; 739 (bc), Keith Locke; 741 (br), David Merrell/Suzanne Craig Represents Inc.; 741 (tr), John Huxtable/Black Creative; 744 (br), Will Nelson/Sweet Reps; 745 (b), Blake Thornton/Rita Marie; 747 (tr), Blake Thornton/Rita Marie; 747 (br) Lori Anzalone/Jeff Lavaty Artist Agent; 754 (r), John White/The Neis Group; 756 (br), Carlyn Iverson; 763 (cr), Morgan-Cain & Associates; 763 (b), Annie Bissett; 764 (tr), Kip Carter; 765 (t), Rob Schuster/Hankins and Tegenborg; 776 (b, c), Rob Schuster/Hankins and Tegenborg; 777 (tc), Rob Schuster/Hankins and Tegenborg; 781, Dan McGeehan/Koralick Associates.

Appendix Page 785 (cl), Blake Thornton/Rita Marie; 788 (t), Terry Guyer; 792 (b), Mark Mille/Sharon Langley; 800-801, Kristy Sprott; 802 (bl), Stephen Durke/Washington Artists; 803 (tl,c) Stephen Durke/Washington Artists; 803 (b), Bruce Burdick; 803 (cl), Stephen Durke/Washington Artists.

PHOTOGRAPHY

Cover: (tl, spine, back cover), Kim Taylor/Bruce Coleman, Inc.; (cl), Frans Lanting/Minden Pictures; (c), Peter Peterson/Tony Stone Images; (cr), Chris Jaffe; (bl), Carr Clifton; (br), ©Gerry Ellis/GerryEllis.com

Title page: (cr), Frans Lanting/Minden Pictures; (tc), Kim Taylor/Bruce Coleman, Inc.

Feature Borders: Unless otherwise noted below, all images copyright ©2001 PhotoDisc/HRW. Across the Sciences, all images by HRW; Careers, (sand bkgd and Saturn), Corbis Images; (DNA), Morgan Cain & Associates; (scuba gear), ©1997 Radlund & Associates for Artville; Eureka!, copyright ©2001 PhotoDisc/HRW; Eye on the Environment:, (clouds and sea in bkgd), HRW; (bkgd grass, red eyed frog), Corbis Images; (hawks, pelican), Animals Animals/Earth Scenes; (rat), Visuals Unlimited/John Grelach; (endangered flower), Dan Suzio/Photo Researchers, Inc.; Health Watch:, (dumbell), Sam Dudgeon/HRW Photo; (aloe vera, EKG), Victoria Smith/HRW Photo; (basketball), ©1997 Radlund & Associates for Artville; (shoes, bubbles), Greg Geisler; Scientific Debate:, Sam Dudgeon/HRW Photo; Science Fiction:, (saucers), Ian Christopher/Greg Geisler; (book), HRW; (bkgd telescope), Dave Cutler Studio, Inc./SIS; Science Technology and Society, (robot), Greg Geisler;Weird Science:,(mite), David Burder/Tony Stone Images; (atom balls), J/B Woolsey Associates; (walking stick, turtle), EclectiCollection.

Table of Contents: v(br), Uniphoto; vi(tl), Leonard Lessin/Photo Researchers, Inc.; vii(bl), Visuals Unlimited/R. Calentine; vii(tr), Robert Brons/BPS/Tony Stone Images; viii(tr), Frans Lanting/Minden Pictures; viii(br), Biophoto Associates/Photo Researchers, Inc.; ix Centre National de Prehistoire, Perigueux, France; x(tl), G. Randall/FPG; x(bl), Fran Heyl Associates; xi(bl), SuperStock; xi(br), Phil Degginger; xii(bl), Richard R. Hansen/Photo Researchers, Inc.; xiii(tl), Daniel Schaefer/HRW Photo; xiii(bl), Visuals Unlimited/James Beveridge; xiii(bl), Brian Parker/Tom Stack; xiii(tr), Carl Roessler/FPG; xiv(cr), Edwin & Peggy Bauer/Bruce Coleman; xiv(tl), Tui De Roy/Minden Pictures; xv(tl), Stuart Westmorland/Tony Stone Images; xvii(tc), Dr. Dennis Kunkel/Phototake, Inc. xvii(br), Image Bank; xviii(bl), Lennart Nilsson/Albert Bonniers Forlag AB, A CHILD IS BORN

Unit One: 2(t), O.S.F./Animals Animals; 2(cr), University of Pennsylvania/Hulton Getty; 3(cl), Hulton Getty; 3(bl), Peter Veit/DRK Photo; 3(c), National Portrait Gallery, Smithsonian Institution/Art Resource; 3(br), O. Louis Mazzatenta/National Geographic Society Image Collection; **Chapter One:** 4(c), Minnesota Pollution Control Agency; 7(tl), NASA; 7(tc), Gerry Gropp; 7(tr), Chip Simmons/Discover Channel; 7(cr), Charles C. Place/Image Bank; 8(tl), Hank Morgan/Photo Researchers, Inc.; 8(bl), Mark Lennihan/AP/Wide World Photos; 9(b), George Holton/Photo Researchers, Inc.; 9(cr), Dale Miquelle/National Geographic Society Image Collection; 12(tl), Fernando Bueno/Image Bank; 13 Mark E. Gibson; 14(tl, bc), John Mitchell/Photo Researchers, Inc.; 18(tl), John Reader/Science Photo Library/Photo Researchers, Inc.; 18(cl), Greg Greico/PENN State; 19(bl), CENCO; 19(bc), Robert Brons/Tony Stone Images; 20(cl), Sinclair Stammers/Science Photo Library/Photo Researchers, Inc.; 20(cr), RJ Lee Instruments Limited; 20(bl), Microworks/Phototake; 20(bl), Visuals Unlimited/Karl Aufderheide; 21(tr), Scott Camazine/Photo Researchers, Inc.; 21(cr), Alfred Pasieka/Photo Researchers, Inc.; 21(b), Howard Sochurek/The Stock Market; 23(tr), David Austen/Publishers Network, Inc.; 25(tr), Science Kit & Boreal Laboratories; 27 Dr. Jeremy Burgess/Science Photo Library/Photo Reseachers, Inc.; 29(cr), CENCO; 30 Charles C. Place/Image Bank; 32(tl), Eric Pianka/University of Texas; 32(br), Charles C. Place/Image Bank;

Chapter Two: 34(tr), Patrick Landmann/Gamma-Liaison; 34(cl, br), Chris Landmann/Gamma-Liaison; 35(bl), Steve Dunwell/Image Bank; 36(tr), Visuals Unlimited/Cabisco; 36(bl), Visuals Unlimited/Science Visuals Unlimited; 36(br), Wolfgang Kaehler/Liaison International; 37(cl, cr), David M. Dennis/Tom Stack and Associates; 37(br), Visuals Unlimited/Fred Rohde; 38(tl), Visuals Unlimited/Stanley Flegler; 38(c), James M. McCann/Photo Researchers, Inc.; 38(bl), Lawrence Migdale/Photo Researchers, Inc.; 40 Robert Dunne/Photo Researchers, Inc.; 41(tr), Wolfgang Bayer; 41(cr), Visuals Unlimited/Rob Simpson ; 42(bl), Photo Researchers, Inc.; 42(bc), Hans Reinhard/Bruce Coleman, Inc.; 46 Visuals Unlimited/Stanley Flegler; 47 Wolfgang Bayer; 49(bl), Dede Gilman/Unicorn Stock Photos; 50(tc, c), NASA

Unit Two: 52(tr), Visuals Unlimited/Kevin Collins; 52(c), Ed Reschke/Peter Arnold, Inc.; 52(br), Cold Spring Harbor Laboratory; 52(cl), Glen Allison/Tony Stone Images; 53(tc), Ed Reschke/Peter Arnold; 53(cr), Keith Porter/Photo Researchers, Inc.; 53(br), Dr. Ian Wilmut/Liaison; 53(cl), The National Archives/Corbis; 53(bc), Dan McCoy/Rainbow; **Chapter Three:** 54 Biology Media/Photo Researchers, Inc.; 56(cl), Image Copyright ©2001 Photodisc, Inc.; 56(bl, bcl, bcr), Dr. Yorgos Nikas/Science Photo Library/Photo Researchers, Inc.; 56(br), Lennart Nilsson; 57(tc), Visuals Unlimited/Fred Hossler; 57(tl), National Cancer Institute/Science Photo Library/Photo Researchers, Inc.; 57(tr), GW Willis/BPS/Tony Stone Images; 57(cr), Visuals Unlimited/G. Shih and R. Kessel; 59(tc), Visuals Unlimited/Michael Abbey; 59(tr), Robert Brons/BPS/Tony Stone Images; 59(tl), David M. Phillips/Photo Researchers, Inc.; 59(b), E.S. Ross; 60(t), Joe McDonald/DRK Photo; 61(cl, c), C.C. Lockwood/DRK Photo; 61(b), Visuals Unlimited/Kevin Collins; 61(br), Leonard Lessin/Peter Arnold; 62(tl), Visuals Unlimited/Doug Sokell; 62(tr), Visuals Unlimited/K. G. Murti; 62(cl), Visuals Unlimited/D. M. Phillips; 63(br), Biophoto Associates/Science Source/Photo Reserachers, Inc.; 63(tr), Dr. Petit/Rapho/Liaison International; 65 AP/Wide World Photos; 73(tr), Biology Media/Photo Researchers, Inc.; 76(tr), Robert Brons/BPS/Tony Stone Images; 76(c), Joe McDonald/DRK Photo; 78 Biophoto Associates/Science Source/Photo Reserachers, Inc.; 80(l), Hans Reinhard/Bruce Coleman; 80(tr), Andrew Syred/Tony Stone Images; 81 Dr. Smith/University of Akron

Chapter Four: 85(cr), Visuals Unlimited/Stanley Flegler; 85(br), Visuals Unlimited/David M. Philips ; 87(cr), Birgit H. Satir; 88 Runk/Schoenberger/Grant Heilman; 92 CNRI/Science Photo Library/Photo Researchers, Inc.; 93(tr), L. Willatt, East Anglian Regional Genetics Service/Science Photo Library/Photo Researchers, Inc.; 93(br), Biophoto Associates/Photo Researchers, Inc.; 94(all), Ed Reschke/Peter Arnold, 95(cr), Visuals Unlimited/R. Calentine; 95(tr, cr), Biology Media/Photo Researchers, Inc.; 96(tl), Visuals Unlimited/Stanley Flegler; 97 Ed Reschke/Peter Arnold; 98 CNRI/Science Photo Library/Photo Researchers, Inc.; 99(cl, c), Biophoto Associates/Science Source/Photo Researchers, Inc.; 100 Lee D. Simons/Science Souce/Photo Researchers, Inc.

Unit Three: 102(t), Library of Congress/Corbis; 102(bl), John Reader/Science Photo Library/Photo Researchers, Inc.; 102(br), NASA; 102(c), Kenneth Eward/Science Source/Photo Researchers, Inc.; 103(bc), Biophoto Associates/Science Source/Photo Researchers, Inc.; 103(c), Marine Biological Laboratory Archives; 103(cl), John Reader/Science Photo Library/Photo Researchers, Inc.; 103(cr), Ted Thai/Time Magzine; **Chapter Five:** 104(tr), Dr. Paul A. Zahl/Photo Researchers, Inc.; 104(tl), Gerard Lacz/Peter Arnold; 104(bl), Runk/Schoenberger/Grant Heilman; 104(br), SuperStock; 106(c), Frans Lanting/Minden Pictures; 106(br), Corbis; 107 Runk/Schoenberger/Grant Heilman Photography; 113(br), Image Copyright ©2001 Photodisc, Inc.; 113(tr), Gerard Lacz/Animals Animals; 114(cl), Phototake/CNRI/ Phototake NYC; 114(bc), Biophoto Associates/Photo Researchers, Inc.; 119 Phototake/CNRI/Phototake NYC; 120 Frans Lanting/Minden Pictures; 124 Hank Morgan/Rainbow; 125(t, c), Dr. F. R. Turner, Biology Dept., Indiana University

Chapter Six: 127(cr, whorl), Leonard Lessin/Peter Arnold; 127(cr, arch), Federal Bureau of Investigation; 127(br), Archive Photos; 129(tr), Science Photo Library/Photo Researchers, Inc.; 129(br), Archive Photos; 131 Dr. Gopal Murti/Science Photo Library/Photo Researchers, Inc.; 132(cl), Phil Jude/Science Photo Library/Photo Researcher, Inc.; 133(cl), Biophoto Associates/Photo Researchers, Inc.; 133(tl), J.R. Paulson & U.K. Laemmli/University of Geneva; 133(bl), Dan McCoy/Rainbow; 134(br), Lawrence Migdale/Photo Researchers, Inc.; 139(br, cr), Jackie Lewin/Royal Free Hospital/Science Photo Library/Photo Researchers, Inc.; 141(cl), Remi Benali

**Acknowledgements
continued from page iv.**

Terry J. Rakes
Science Teacher
Elmwood Junior High School
Rogers, Arkansas

Elizabeth Rustad
Science Teacher
Crane Middle School
Yuma, Arizona

Debra A. Sampson
Science Teacher
Booker T. Washington Middle School
Elgin, Texas

Charles Schindler
Curriculum Advisor
San Bernadino City Unified Schools
San Bernadino, California

Bert J. Sherwood
Science Teacher
Socorro Middle School
El Paso, Texas

Patricia McFarlane Soto
Science Teacher and Dept. Chair
G. W. Carver Middle School
Miami, Florida

David M. Sparks
Science Teacher
Redwater Junior High School
Redwater, Texas

Elizabeth Truax
Science Teacher
Lewiston-Porter Central School
Lewiston, New York

Ivora Washington
Science Teacher and Dept. Chair
Hyattsville Middle School
Washington, D.C.

Elsie N. Waynes
Science Teacher and Dept. Chair
R. H. Terrell Junior High School
Washington, D.C.

Nancy Wesorick
Science and Math Teacher
Sunset Middle School
Longmont, Colorado

Alexis S. Wright
Middle School Science Coordinator
Rye Country Day School
Rye, New York

John Zambo
Science Teacher
E. Ustach Middle School
Modesto, California

Gordon Zibelman
Science Teacher
Drexel Hill Middle School
Drexell Hill, Pennsylvania

CREDITS